Recreation Lakes of California
12th Edition

ANNIVERSARY 25Th

California ALLAKES

by **Diane Dirksen**
James Dirksen
John McKinney

ACTIVE MEMBER
OUTDOOR WRITERS
O W A
ASSOCIATION OF AMERICA

Recreation Sales Publishing
Post Office Box 1028
Aptos, CA 95001
(800) 668-0076

ISBN 0-943798-20-5

INFORMATION IS PRESENTED AS IT APPEARS WHEN LAKES ARE AT FULL CAPACITY.

WEATHER CONDITIONS MUST BE CONSIDERED.

ALL FEES AND INFORMATION ARE SUBJECT TO CHANGE.

MAPS ARE NOT TO SCALE AND SHOULD BE USED

IN CONJUNCTION WITH STANDARD ROAD MAPS

TELEPHONE AREA CODES ARE
CONSTANTLY CHANGING
WE ARE SORRY FOR THE
INCONVENIENCE THIS CAUSES

Credits

Cover Design & Cartoons: Greg Dirksen

Back Cover Photograph: Jean Vandevort

Printing by Bertelsmann Industries, Valencia
Binding by PEL, Santa Fe Springs

Copyright © 1999

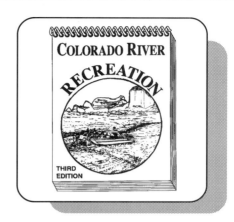

INTRODUCTION

We are celebrating our 25th year in business with

The New 12th Edition of
RECREATION LAKES of CALIFORNIA.

The cover photograph was used in 1978 and pictures Jim Dirksen and our young sons Greg, Trevor and Jake Dirksen. These boys are now grown men with blossoming families of their own. We have always considered this publication as a 4th child and it now has grown to its 25th year. We take great pride in self-publishing this book.

The support of the US Forest Service, the Bureau of Land Management, Army Corps of Engineers, the California State Park System, the Department of Fish and Game is invaluable. Chambers of Commerce, Visitor's Bureaus and the many private owners and managers of facilities are equally supportive. We give our special appreciation to you, the reader. Your use of *RECREATION LAKES of CALIFORNIA* has made it a bestseller.

Thank you!

Each Lake is described according to location, elevation, size and facilities. The book is divided into three sections which are marked by black bleedoffs at the bottom of the page; the left is the North Section, the middle is Central and the right is the South Section of California. Campgrounds for tents and R.V.s, picnic areas, launch ramps, marinas and other facilities are located on each map. Also hiking, bicycle and equestrian trails are shown. While boating, fishing and camping are basic to most Lakes, we have also included swimming, hiking, backpacking and equestrian information. Waterslides, boat tours, golf courses, airports and other specific attractions are mentioned. The maps show major recreation areas near each Lake, such as State and National Parks, Wilderness Areas, the Pacific Crest Trail and the Califorma Aqueduct Bikeway.

Information is as accurate and current as possible at the time of publication although area codes and fees are constantly changing. *RECREATION LAKES OF CALIFORNIA* will help you enjoy the many outdoor pleasures this wonderful State has to offer.

TABLE OF CONTENTS

Lakes correspond to page numbers, divided into three sections: *North, Central* and *South*—areas of California. Each section begins with a Map illustrating that region, with an approximate location of each Lake in that area, referenced by a page number. Several maps include supplementary pages with information on campgrounds, resorts, marine facilities, etc. *See Index at back of book for a complete alphabetical listing of Lakes.*

Numbers around highways represent lakes in numerical order in this book. *See Index for complete listing.*

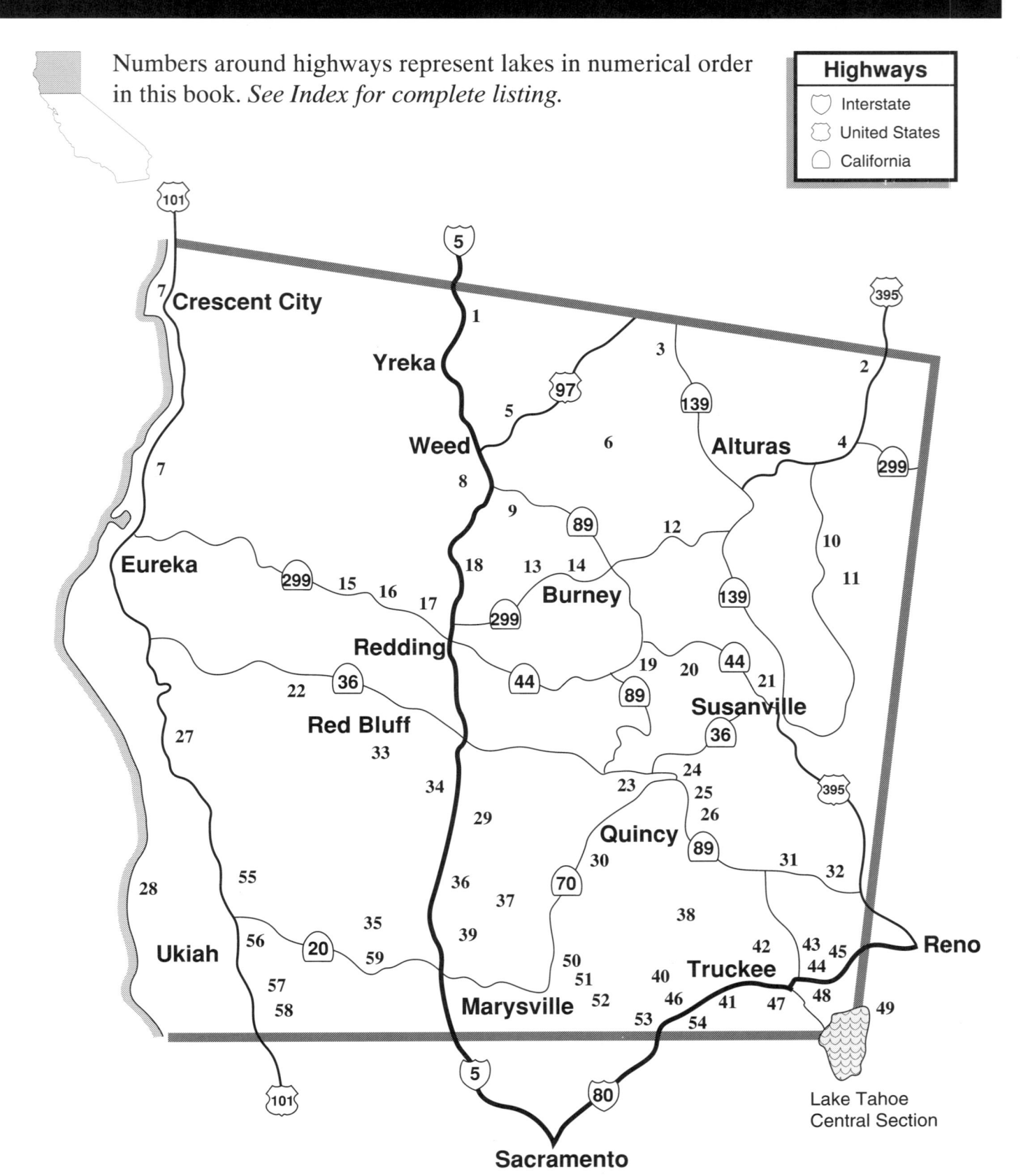

Highways	
◯	Interstate
◯	United States
◯	California

Crescent City

Yreka

Weed

Alturas

Eureka

Burney

Redding

Red Bluff

Susanville

Quincy

Ukiah

Truckee

Reno

Marysville

Sacramento

Lake Tahoe
Central Section

IRON GATE RESERVOIR and COPCO LAKE

Iron Gate Reservoir and Copco Lake are located east of Interstate 5 near the Oregon border. Copco Lake, elevation 2,613 feet, has a surface area of 1,000 acres and is 5 miles long. The Wild Upper Klamath River above Copco Lake has native rainbow trout. Six fishing access areas with parking are available. From May through October, this is a popular part of the River for experienced white water rafters. You can put in at John Boyle Dam, go 17 miles and take out at Copco Lake. Iron Gate, elevation 2,343 feet, is almost 7 miles long and covers a surface area of 825 acres. Each Lake has an abundant yellow perch fishery as well as rainbow trout and largemouth bass. The Klamath River provides a good salmon and steelhead crop. River guides are available from September through March.

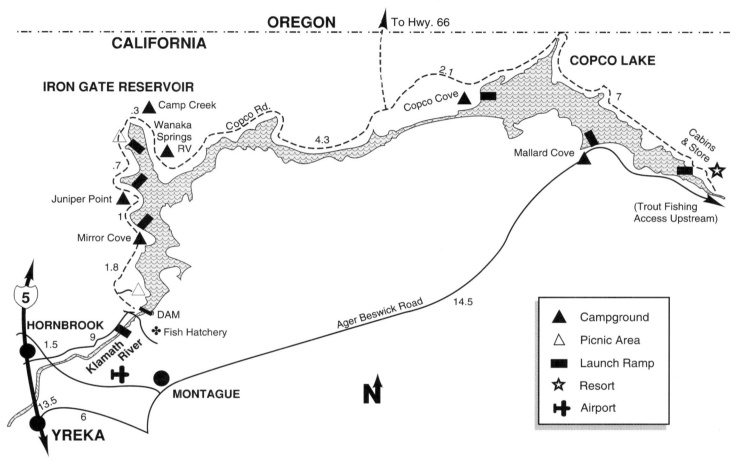

INFORMATION: Pacific Power, 300 S. Main, Yreka 96097—Ph: (530) 842-3521

CAMPING	BOATING	RECREATION	OTHER

Iron Gate Reservoir:
   Camp Creek - 22 Sites,
     with Water
   Juniper Point - 9 Sites,
     No Water
   Mirror Cove - 10 Sites,
     No Water
Copco Lake:
   BLM Campgrounds
   No Hookups
	Power, Row, Canoe, Sail
	   & Inflatable
	10 MPH Speed Limit in
	   Designated Areas
	Copco Lake - Upper 1/3
	   Set Aside for Fishing
	   (No Wake)
	Launch Ramps
	Rentals: Fishing Boats
	   with Motors - Copco
	   Lake Store Only
	Docks
		Fishing:
		   Trout, Catfish, Crappie,
		   Largemouth Bass,
		   Yellow Perch, Salmon
		   & Steelhead-Klamath
		   River
		Swimming
		Picnicking
		Hiking & Riding Trails
		Rafting
		Hunting:
		   Deer, Quail, Dove,
		   Waterfowl, Wild Turkey
			Copco Only:
			   Cabins - Reserve
			
			Copco Lake Store
			27734 Copco Rd.
			Montague 96064
			Ph: (530) 459-3655
			Groceries, Bait & Tackle
			
			Full Facilities at Hornbrook
			
			River Flow & Reservoir
			Levels: Ph: (800) 547-1501

GOOSE, CAVE and LILY LAKES and FEE RESERVOIR

Goose Lake rests on the California-Oregon border at an elevation of 4,800 feet. This shallow 108,800 surface acre Lake is used primarily for waterfowl hunting and boating. Cave and Lily Lakes offer excellent fishing for brook and rainbow trout but boating is limited. These two small mountain Lakes are neighbors at 6,000 feet in the Modoc National Forest. Poor access roads limit use of trailers. Fee Reservoir, at 4,000 feet, can produce large rainbow trout.

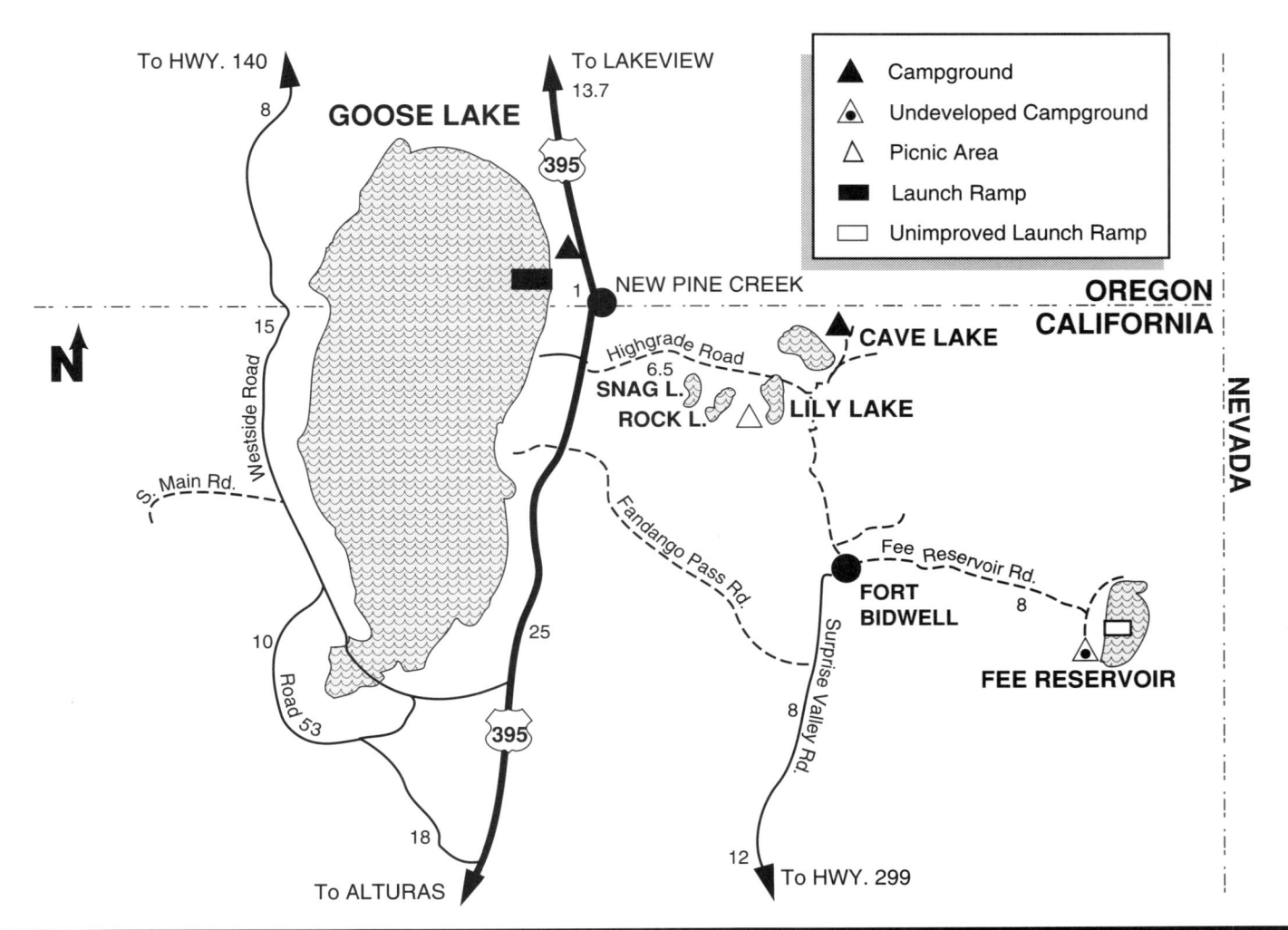

INFORMATION: Warner Mountain Ranger District, P.O. Box 220, Cedarville 96104—Ph: (530) 279-6116			
CAMPING	**BOATING**	**RECREATION**	**OTHER**

Cave Lake:
  6 Tent/RV Sites to
    30 People
  Drinking Water
 	
Goose Lake:
  Oregon State Parks
  48 Tent/RV Sites
  Water & Electric
  Hookups - Fee
  Disposal Station
	Lily & Cave Lakes:
	  No Motors
	  Hand Launch
	Goose Lake:
	  Open to all Boating
	  Paved Launch Ramp
	Fee Reservoir:
	  Unimproved Launch
	    Ramp
	  Shallow Draft Boats
	    Advised
		Fishing: Brook &
		  Rainbow Trout
		Picnicking - Lily Lake
		  6 Sites
		  No Drinking Water
		Hiking & Riding Trails
		Backpacking & Nature
		  Study
		Swimming
		Hunting: Upland Game,
		  Waterfowl, Deer
		Birdwatching
			Oregon State Parks
			  Region 4
			  P.O. Box 5309
			  Bend, Oregon 97708
			  Ph: (503) 388-6211
			
			Facilities Limited to Nearby
			  Towns

LOWER KLAMATH, TULE and CLEAR LAKES—KLAMATH BASIN NATIONAL WILDLIFE REFUGES

This is waterfowl country! These Lakes are within the Klamath Basin National Wildlife Refuges which has one of the greatest concentrations of migratory waterfowl in the world. Photography and wildlife observation (over 270 species of birds have been identified) are popular activities. This is a hunter's paradise. Since rules and boundaries are strictly enforced, it is essential you contact the Fish and Wildlife Service for detailed information. Except for canoeing at Tulelake, boating is auxiliary to hunting. There is no fishing. Accommodations can be a problem, especially during hunting season, so plan ahead by contacting the facilities listed below or the *Tulelake Chamber of Commerce, P.O. Box 592, Tulelake 96134, Ph: (530) 667-5178.*

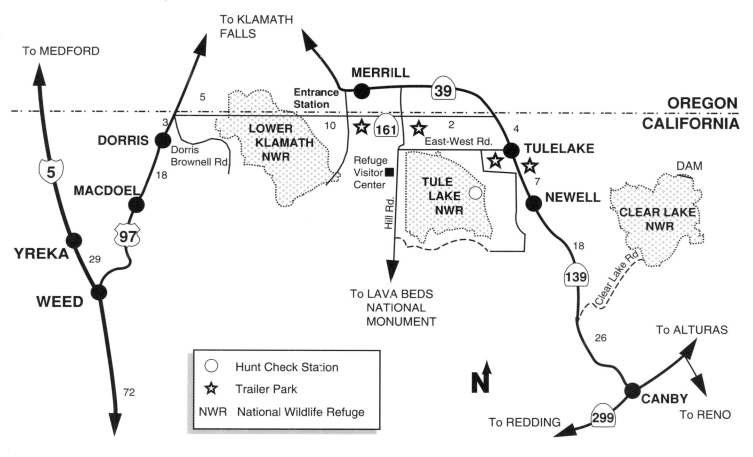

	Hunt Check Station
☆	Trailer Park
NWR	National Wildlife Refuge

INFORMATION: Klamath Basin NWR, Route 1, Box 74, Tulelake 96134—Ph: (530) 667-2231

CAMPING	BOATING	RECREATION	OTHER
Shady Lanes Trailer Park: 　P.O. Box 297 　Tulelake 96134 　Ph: (530) 667-2617 　58 RV Sites 　Full Hookups Stateline R.V. Park: 　Rt. 1, Box 45-A 　Tulelake 96134 　Ph: (530) 667-4849 　60 Tent/RV Sites 　Full Hookups: $16	Boats are Allowed only 　During Hunting Season 　Except for Canoe Area 　at Tulelake NWR - Open July 　through September Air Thrust & Water 　Thrust Boats are 　Prohibited	Hunting: Geese, Ducks, 　Coots, Snipe & 　Pheasants *Steel Shot is Required for 　Waterfowl Hunting* Birdwatching Nature Study Photography	Lava Beds Nat. Monument: 　40 Tent/RV Sites 　Ph: (530) 667-2282 Refuge Visitor Center: Open Monday-Friday 　8:00 am - 4:30 pm Open Saturday & Sunday 　10:00 am - 4:00 pm: 　Tulelake Fish & 　Wildlife Hdqtrs. 　Hill Road 　Tulelake 96134 　Ph: (530) 667-2231

BIG SAGE, "C", "F", DUNCAN, GRAVEN, BAYLEY and DORRIS RESERVOIRS—DELTA LAKE

Although facilities are limited, there are recreational opportunities at these Lakes in the Modoc National Forest and Modoc County. Big Sage Reservoir rests at an elevation of 4,900 feet on a sage and juniper covered plateau. This 5,400 acre Reservoir is open to all boating and provides a warm water fishery. Nearby Reservoirs "C", and "F" and Duncan provide a good opportunity to catch the large Eagle Lake trout. Dorris Reservoir is in the Modoc National Wildlife Refuge. It is closed during waterfowl hunting season. The angler will find trout and a warm water fishery. Graven, Bayley and Delta are under the jurisdiction of Modoc County. They are shallow and muddy and primarily known for their good catfishing. Bayley also has excellent trout fishing. The roads into these Reservoirs are very rough.

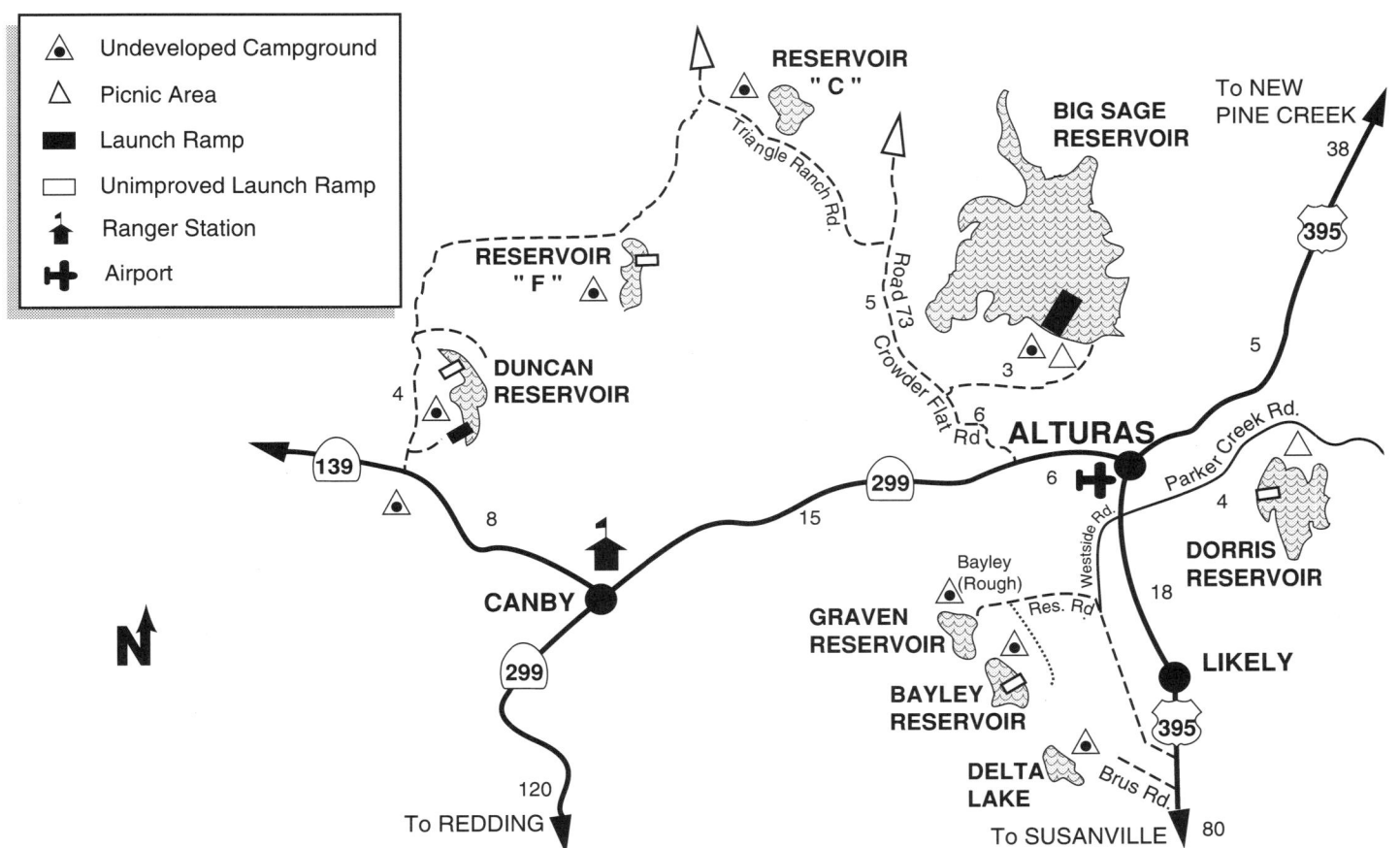

⊙	Undeveloped Campground
△	Picnic Area
■	Launch Ramp
▭	Unimproved Launch Ramp
⌂	Ranger Station
✈	Airport

INFORMATION: Devil's Garden Ranger District, 800 West 12th St., Alturas 96101—Ph: (530) 233-5811				
CAMPING	**BOATING**	**RECREATION**	**OTHER**

Undeveloped Campsites as Shown on Map
No Drinking Water
Limited Trailer Access
 	
Dorris Reservoir:
  Walk-In Public
  Access
  Mid-January to
  March 31 and
  Early October
  Before Waterfowl
  Season
	Big Sage: Open to All
	  Boating
	  Paved Launch Ramp
	Dorris:
	  Boating: Apr. 1-Sept. 30
	  Waterskiing: June 1 -
	  Sept. 30
	  Unimproved Ramp
	  Underwater Hazards
	
	Other Lakes Open to
	  Small Hand Launched
	  Boats
		Fishing: Trout, Bass,
		  Catfish & Panfish,
		  Eagle Lake Trout at
		  Res. "C", Res."F" &
		  Duncan
		Hiking & Riding Trails
		Nature & Bird Study
		Hunting: Waterfowl,
		  Upland Game, Deer &
		  Antelope
		No Hunting at Dorris
			Dorris Reservoir:
			  Modoc National
			  Wildlife Refuge
			  P.O. Box 1610
			  Alturas 96101
			  Ph: (530) 233-3572
			
			Graven, Bailey & Delta:
			  Modoc County
			  202 W. 4th St.
			  Alturas 96101
			  Ph: (530) 233-3939

These Lakes along Highway 97 from Weed to the Oregon Border provide a variety of recreational experiences. The alkaline waters in Indian Tom support a unique Cutthroat fishery. Meiss Lake is within the Butte Valley Wildlife Area. Waterfowl hunting and wildlife observation are the primary activities. Juanita is a pretty mountain Lake resting at an elevation of 5,100 feet. There is a nice campground which provides facilities for the physically disabled. The trout fishing is good. Orr is a USFS Lake open to the public for boating, fishing and wildlife viewing. Lake Shastina is a popular private facility providing good fishing and all boating. Contact the Chamber of Commerce at P.O. Box 366, Weed 96094 or phone (530) 938-4624 for information.

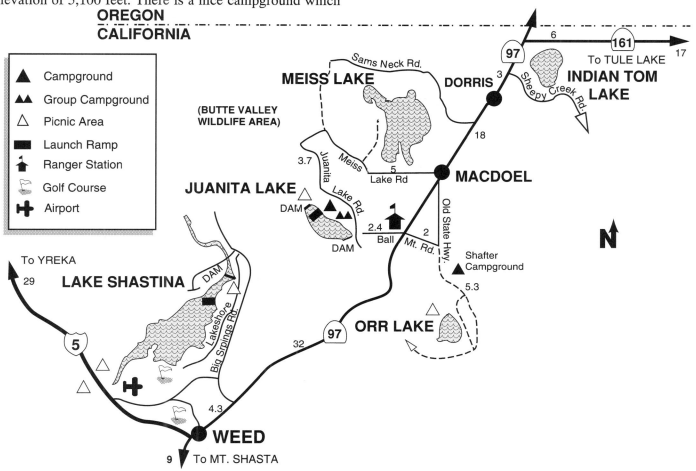

INFORMATION: Goosenest Ranger Station, 37805 Hwy. 97, Macdoel 96058—Ph: (530) 398-4391

CAMPING	BOATING	RECREATION	OTHER

Juanita Lake:
  23 Dev. Sites
  2 Handicap Sites
    Fee: $8
  1 Multiple Unit Site
    Fee: $10
Group Camp - 50 People
  Maximum Fee: $15
  Reservations Required
No Firearms Discharged in
  Campground
Shafter Campground:
  10 Sites - $8
	Juanita:
	  Open to All
	  Non-Powered Boating
	  Launch Ramp
	Shastina:
	  Open to All
	  Boating
	Orr & Indian Tom:
	  Small Hand Launch
	  Craft - Max. 10 HP
	Meiss (State Fish & Game):
	  Shallow Draft
	  Non-Powered Boating
		Fishing:
		Juanita: Brown &
		  Rainbow Trout,
		  Largemouth Bass &
		  Brown Bullhead Catfish
		Shastina: Trout, Silver
		  Salmon, Bass,
		  Catfish & Crappie
		Indian Tom: Cutthroat
		Hunting: Waterfowl, Deer,
		  Quail
		Swimming & Picnicking
		Hiking & Backpacking
			Full Facilities in Weed &
			  Tule Lake & Dorris
			Gas & Grocery Store at
			  Macdoel
			Butte Valley
			  Wildlife Area
			  P.O. Box 249
			  Macdoel 96058
			  Ph: (530) 398-4627
			Juanita Lake:
			  1-1/2 Mile Barrier Free
			  Trail Around Lake

MEDICINE LAKE

Medicine Lake is in the Modoc National Forest at an elevation of 6,700 feet. Once the center of a volcano, this 640-acre Lake has no known outlets and is 150 feet deep in places. The lodgepole pine-covered campgrounds are maintained by the U.S. Forest Service. Points of interest include Lava Beds National Monument, Glass Mountain, Burnt Lava Flow, Medicine Lake Glass Flow and Undertakers Crater. Although remote, this is a popular Lake for boating, waterskiing and sailing. The fishing is good from shore or boat. The small 5-acre Bullseye Lake has a Rainbow and Brook trout fishery.

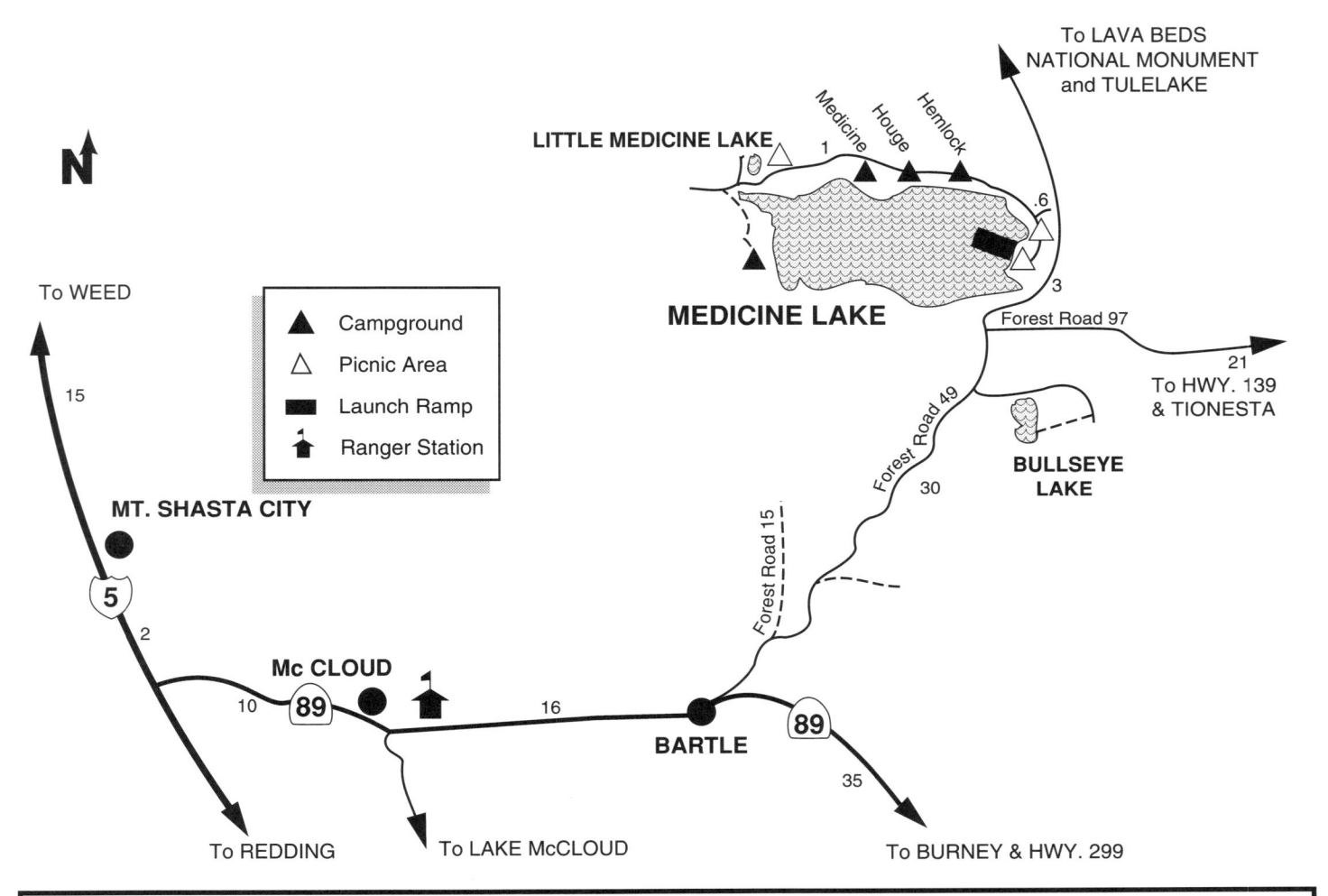

CAMPING	BOATING	RECREATION	OTHER
73 Dev. Sites for Tents & R.V.s Fee: $9 per Vehicle per Night No Hook-ups No Reservations	Power, Row, Canoe, Sail, Inflatable, Waterski, Jets Launch Ramp - Paved Courtesy Dock Bullseye Lake: No Motors Hand Launch	Fishing: Rainbow & Brook Trout Swimming Picnicking Hiking Horseback Riding Hunting: Deer, Bear, Grouse Accessible Disabled Facilities	Other Facilities: 14 Miles at Lava Beds National Monument & 35 miles at Tulelake Full Facilities: 33 miles at Bartle & 25 miles at Tionesta

INFORMATION: Doublehead Ranger District, P.O. Box 369, Tulelake 96134—Ph: (530) 667-2246

LAKE EARL, FISH LAKE, FRESHWATER LAGOON, STONE LAGOON and BIG LAGOON

Big Lagoon and its smaller neighbors, Stone and Freshwater Lagoons are three of California's most unusual Lakes. Separated from the Pacific Ocean by a narrow strip of sand, these Lakes offer the angler a unique opportunity to fish for trout in fresh water and a few feet away cast for surf perch in salt water. Lakes Earl and Talawa are part of the Lake Earl Wildlife Area. These shallow water Lakes offer a variety of game fish as well as an abundance of waterfowl and animal life. Fish Lake, at an elevation of 1,800 feet, is a popular freshwater fishing spot. No motors are allowed on this small 22-acre Lake. The Forest Service maintains a nice campground amid fir and huckleberries. There are a variety of trails leading to Red Mountain Lake and on to Blue Lake.

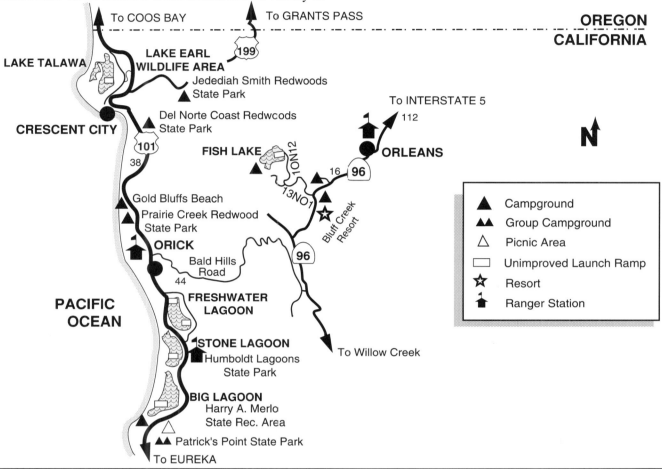

INFORMATION: Calif. State Parks, North Coast Redwoods, 3431 Fort Ave., Eureka 95501—Ph: (707) 445-6547

CAMPING	BOATING	RECREATION	OTHER

Redwood State Parks:
  Jedediah Smith
  Del Norte Coast
  Prairie Creek
  Gold Bluffs Beach
State Parks:
  Patrick's Point
Reserve:
  Ph: (800) 444-7275
	Lake Earl: Fishing Boats
	  Beach Launch
	Stone Lagoon: Canoes &
	  Fishing Boats
	  Speed Limit
	Big Lagoon: Fishing &
	  Small Sailboats
	Fish Lake: Non-Power
	  Boats Only
	  Unimproved Ramp
		Fishing: Rainbow, Brown
		  & Cutthroat Trout
		Stone Lagoon: Special
		  Fishing Regulations
		Picnicking
		Swimming at Lagoons
		Hiking & Nature Trails
		Beach Combing
		Tidal Pools
		Redwood Groves
		Birdwatching
		Hunting: Waterfowl
			Fish Lake:
			  Ukonom Ranger Station
			  P. O. Drawer 410
			  Orleans 95556
			  Ph: (530) 627-3291
			
			Trailer Park at Bluff
			Creek Resort

LAKE SISKIYOU and CASTLE LAKE

Lake Siskiyou is a man-made Reservoir, at an elevation of 3,181 feet, located in the shadows of Mount Shasta. At the headwaters of the Sacramento River, the Lake has 437 surface acres with 5-1/4 shoreline miles surrounded by pine trees. There are 1,000 feet of sandy swimming beach, a complete marina and store. The Pacific Crest Trail is located nearby and the fishing is good. Crystal clear Castle Lake is located just south of Lake Siskiyou. Although primarily for fishing, this pretty little Lake also allows swimming. There is a small picnic area near Castle Lake and 5 campsites for tents.

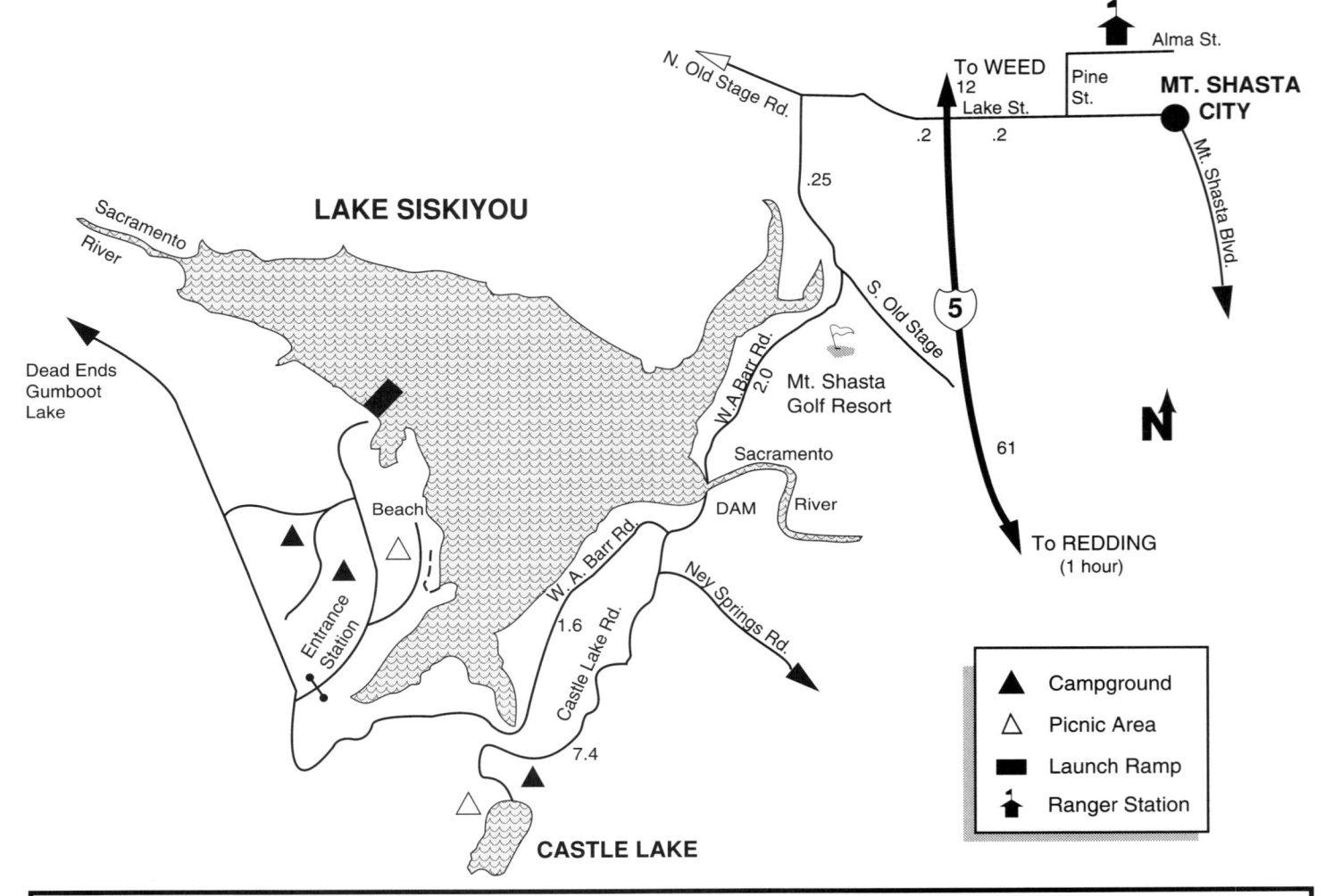

INFORMATION: Lake Siskiyou, P.O. Box 276, Mount Shasta 96067—Ph: (530) 926-2618

CAMPING	BOATING	RECREATION	OTHER
363 Dev. Sites for Tents & RVs Full Hook-ups with TV Fee: $10.50 - $22.50 Group Camps Disposal Station Day Use: $1 per person	Power, Row, Canoe, Windsurfing, Sail & Inflatables 10 MPH Speed Limit Marina - Bait & Tackle Shop Launch Ramp - Free Rentals: Fishing, Canoe, Pedalboats, Pontoons, Kayaks and Misc. Watertoys Berths, Docks, Moorings, Dry Storage	Fishing: Rainbow, Kamloop, Brown, & Brook Trout, Large & Smallmouth Bass Fishing Dock & Cleaning Station Swimming Picnicking & Hiking Backpacking [Parking] 2 Children's Playgrounds Volleyball Court Free Family Movies Arcade	Rental R.V.s Groceries, Deli, Gift Shop Laundromat Propane Community-Sized BBQ Handicap Fishing Dock Geodesic Dome Complex: Group Indoor Dining Banquet Room Rec. Hall with Large User Kitchen
Castle Lake: Mount Shasta Ranger District 5 Tent Sites			

The dam on the McCloud River was constructed by P.G. & E. in 1965. At an elevation of 3,000 feet, the surface area of this 520-acre Lake belongs to P.G. & E., and the surrounding land belongs to the Hearst Corporation. The U.S. Forest Service was deeded a narrow strip of land between the road and high watermark from the boat ramp to Star City Creek. The steep shoreline provides a beautiful setting for the Lake with pine trees towering above the rocky terrain. This is a popular Lake for fishing. There are no developed campsites on the Lake, but there is a small unimproved campground at Star City Creek. A Forest Service campground is located on the McCloud River at Ah-Di-Na. The Pacific Crest Trail passes through this area.

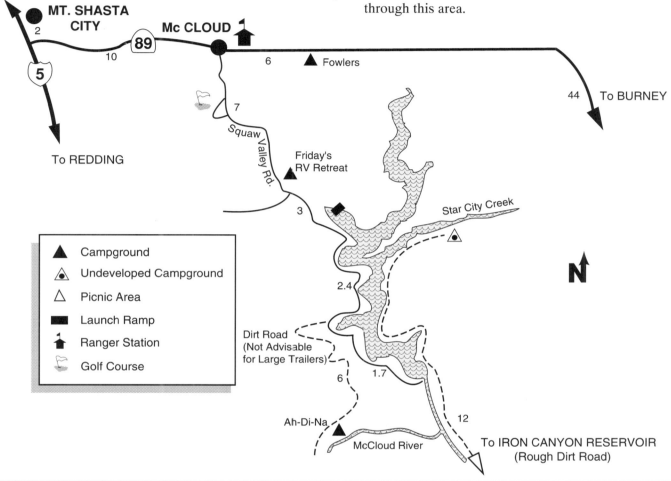

▲	Campground
⊙	Undeveloped Campground
△	Picnic Area
■	Launch Ramp
⚑	Ranger Station
⚐	Golf Course

INFORMATION: McCloud Ranger District, P. O. Box 1620, McCloud 96057—Ph: (530) 964-2184

CAMPING	BOATING	RECREATION	OTHER
Star City Creek: Small Unimproved Campground	Power, Row, Canoe Launch Ramp	Fishing: Rainbow & Brown Trout (All Dolly Varden Trout must be released)	Full Facilities in McCloud
Ah-Di-Na: 16 Camp Sites Narrow Dirt Road Not Advised for Large Trailers		Fly Fishing School and Ponds at Fridays RV Retreat	Fridays RV Retreat P. O. Box 68 Squaw Valley Rd. McCloud 96057 Ph: (530) 964-2878 30 Sites for Tents & R.V.s Full Hook-Ups
Fowlers: 40 Units Water		Picnicking Hiking Nature Study	Fees: $12 - $17 Hot Showers, Laundromat

WEST VALLEY RESERVOIR

West Valley Reservoir, 970 surface acres, is located in the northeastern corner of California, off Highway 395 just east of Likely. Resting at an elevation of 4,770 feet, the 7 miles of shoreline is relatively sparse with only a few clusters of small trees. All types of boating are permitted including boat camping. Waterskiing is popular. Eagle Lake trout are the primary game fish and they are often "big ones." There are also catfish and Sacramento perch. Support facilities are limited to a single-lane paved ramp and primitive campsites. This is a relatively remote Reservoir, but if you are a dedicated angler, give it a try. The Lake is usually frozen over from December to early March.

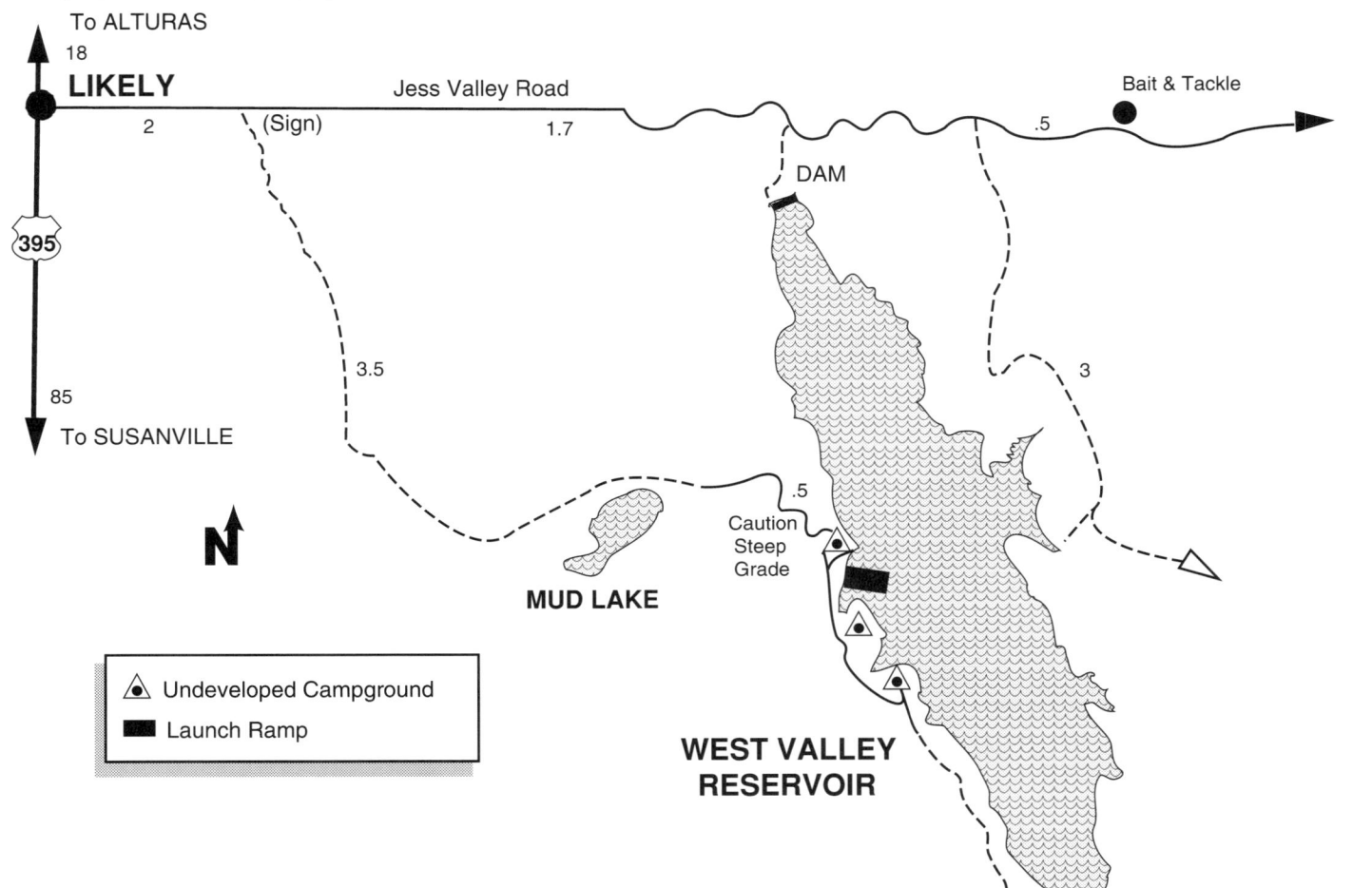

INFORMATION: Modoc County, 202 W. 4th Street, Alturas 96101—Ph: (530) 233-3939			
CAMPING	**BOATING**	**RECREATION**	**OTHER**
Primitive Camping Water & Toilets	Power, Row, Canoe, Sail, Waterski, Jets, Windsurfing & Inflatable Overnight Camping In Boat Permitted Anywhere *High Winds Can Be Hazardous*	Fishing: Eagle Lake Trout, Catfish, Sacramento Perch Swimming Picnicking Hiking Backpacking [Parking] Hunting: Deer & Rabbit	Full Facilities - 6 miles at Likely

Blue Lake, 28 miles southeast of Alturas, is in the Modoc National Forest. This pretty mountain Lake of 160 surface acres is surrounded by Ponderosa Pine, White Fir and meadows at an elevation of 6,000 feet. This is a popular, well-used facility near the South Warner Wilderness area. The Lake fishing is good for rainbow and brown trout. There are no boating facilities other than a paved launch ramp, but all boating is permitted. For the hiker, backpacker, horseback rider or energetic fisherman, the South Warner Wilderness offers good trails. A Wilderness Permit is not required for the South Warner Wilderness. Fishing from shore can be good at Clear Lake.

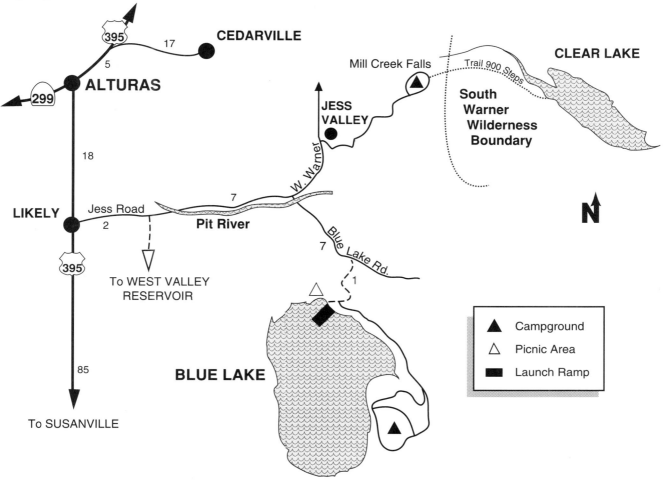

INFORMATION: Warner Mountain Ranger District, Box 220, Cedarville 96104—Ph: (530) 279-6116

CAMPING	BOATING	RECREATION	OTHER
Blue Lake Camp: 48 Dev. Sites for Tents/RVs Under 22 Feet Fee: $7 Mill Creek Falls: 19 Dev. Sites for Tents/RVs Under 22 Feet Fee: $6	Power, Row, Canoe, Sail, & Inflatable 15 MPH Speed Limit *No Waterskiing or Jets* Paved Launch Ramp Handicap Accessible Facilities	Fishing: Rainbow & Brown Trout Handicap Accessible Fishing Platform Picnicking Hiking Swimming Hunting: Deer in Vicinity	Likely: Grocery Store Restaurant Gas Station Full Facilities - 28 miles at Alturas

EASTMAN, TULE, BIG, FALL RIVER, CRYSTAL and BAUM LAKES

The Fall River Valley is an angler's paradise. Nestled between the Sierra and Cascade mountain ranges, these Lakes are fed by Hat Creek, Pit and Fall Rivers. Baum has 89 surface acres and Crystal has 60 acres. Each of these Lakes are connected and support trophy sized brown trout as well as rainbow and eastern brook. The warm water fisheries of Big,

Tule, Eastman and Fall River Lakes are all contiguous. This area also has rainbow trout up to 4 pounds. The streams and rivers offer prime fishing. Hat Creek and Fall River are designated "Wild Trout" Streams which provide trophy trout. Artificial lures must be used and other special rules apply.

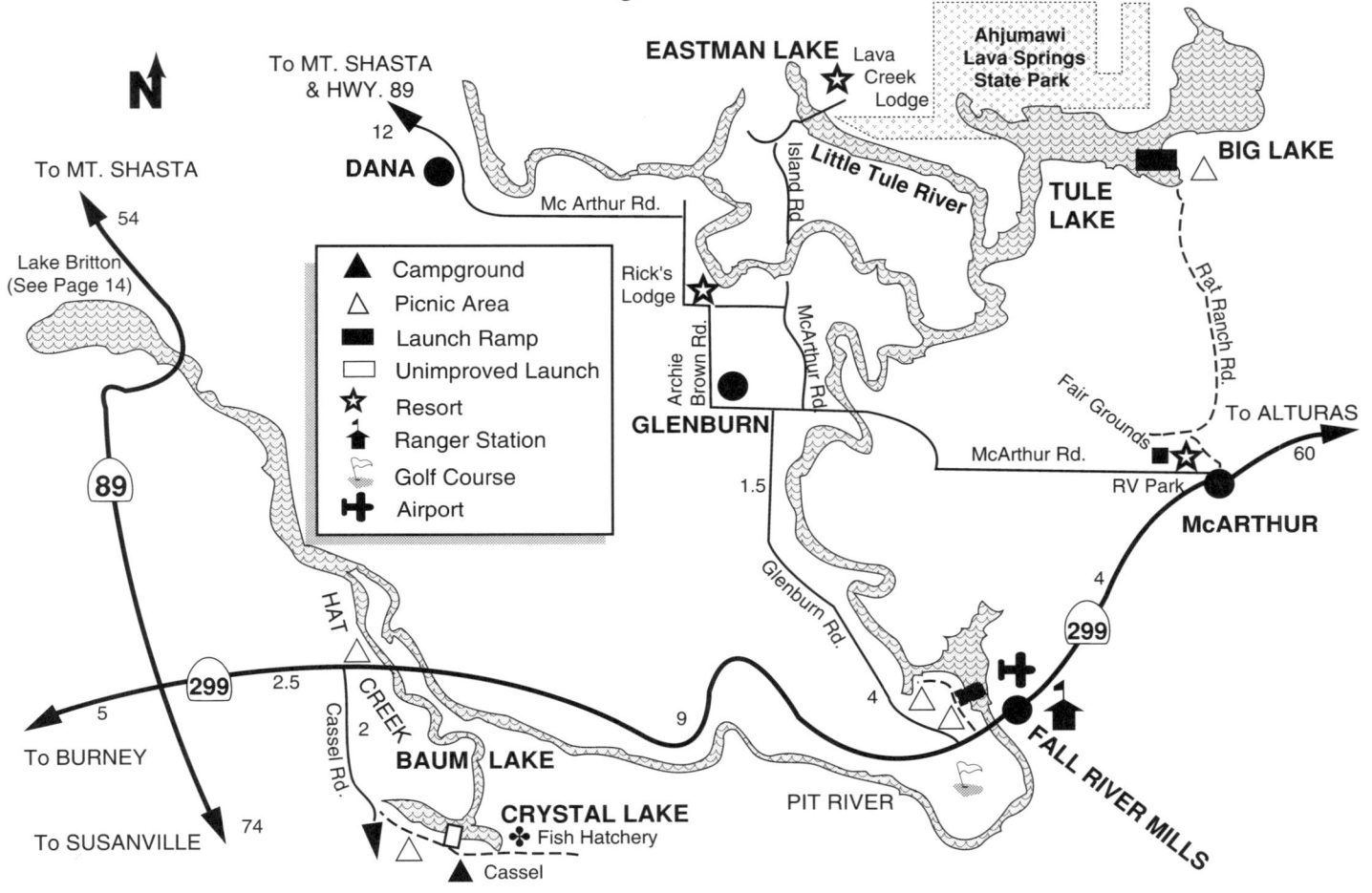

▲	Campground
△	Picnic Area
■	Launch Ramp
☐	Unimproved Launch
☆	Resort
🏠	Ranger Station
⛳	Golf Course
✈	Airport

INFORMATION: Chamber of Commerce, P.O. Box 475, Fall River Mills, 96028—Ph: (530) 336-5840

CAMPING	BOATING	RECREATION	OTHER

See Lake Britton
 	
P.G. & E.:
  Ph: (916) 386-5164
  Cassel - 1 mile
  South of Baum
  Lake - 27 Sites
  Fee: $10
Ahjumawi State Park
  Ph: (530) 335-2777
  Above Big Lake
  9 Primitive Sites
  Boat-in Only
	Baum & Crystal:
	  No Power Boating
	Other Lakes:
	  10 MPH
	Lava Creek Lodge
	  Boat Rentals, Guides &
	  Boat Launch
	Rick's Lodge
	  Guest Boat Rentals
	  Guides Available
	  $75 Includes Pickup &
	  Return Plus 12 Hours of
	  Fishing
		Fishing: Largemouth
		  Bass, Catfish, Green
		  Sunfish, Brown,
		  Rainbow & Eastern
		  Brook Trout
		Hiking: Pacific Crest Trail
		Hunting: Ducks, Geese
		  Quail, Dove, Pheasant
		  & Bear
		Swimming: Fall River
		  Lake & Big Lake
			Lava Creek Lodge:
			  Glenburn Star Route
			  Island Road
			  Fall River Mills 96028
			  Ph: (530) 336-6288
			  Rooms & Cabins
			  with Full Service Menu
			Rick's Lodge:
			  Glenburn Star Route
			  Fall River Mills 96028
			  Ph: (530) 336-5300
			Full Facilities at
			  Fall River Mills

IRON CANYON RESERVOIR

Iron Canyon Reservoir is at an elevation of 2,700 feet in the Shasta-Trinity National Forest. This beautiful 500-surface acre Lake has 15 miles of forested shoreline. Larger boats with deep draft are not recommended due to shallow Lake levels, but owners of smaller, low-speed boats find Iron Canyon ideal. The Lake level varies greatly during the year depending on weather and P.G. & E. power needs. There are some big trout and the fishing can be good. The U.S. Forest Service has a self-service campground providing a quiet atmosphere amid pine and fir trees. P.G. & E., in co-operation with U.S.F.S., has a campground and paved launch ramp at Hawkins Landing. This Lake is perfect for those seeking solitude.

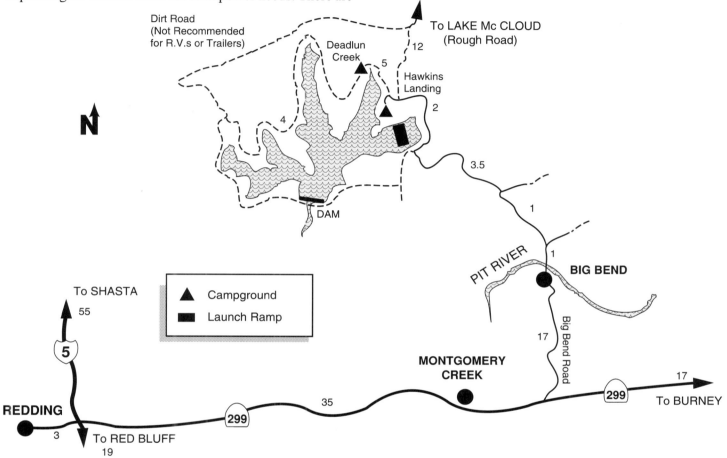

INFORMATION: Shasta Lake Ranger District, 14225 Holiday Drive, Redding 96003—Ph: (530) 275-1587

CAMPING	BOATING	RECREATION	OTHER

U.S.F.S. Deadlun Creek: 30 Dev. Sites for Tents/RVs to 24 feet - Fee
 	
P.G. & E.
  Ph: (916) 386-5164
Hawkins Landing: 10 Dev. Sites for Tents/RVs Fee: $15
	Power, Row, Canoe, & Inflatables
	Launch Ramp at Hawkins Landing
	  Campground
		Fishing: Rainbow & Brown Trout
		Swimming
		Picnicking
		Hiking
		Bird Watching
		Hunting: Deer
			At Big Bend:
			  Grocery Store
			  Bait & Tackle
			  Gas Station
			  (Hours of Operation are Limited)
			U.S.F.S. Guard Station and Fire Station
			
			Caution: Heavy Logging Truck Traffic at Times

LAKE BRITTON

Lake Britton, located in the Shasta-Trinity National Forest, is at an elevation of 2,760 feet. This 1,600 surface acre Lake has 18 shoreline miles and is nestled amid evergreen forests on the Pit River. The McArthur-Burney Falls Memorial State Park has 900 acres stretching from Burney Falls along Burney Creek to the shoreline of Lake Britton. Burney Creek is planted with trout weekly in season. This park, established in 1920, is not only one of the oldest in the State Park System, but one of the best facilities in Northern California. There are also U.S. Forest Service and P.G. & E. campgrounds in the area. Called by Teddy Roosevelt "the eighth wonder of the world," Burney Falls is the popular attraction of the area. This is a good boating Lake although *caution should be used as there can be floating debris and fluctuating water levels.*

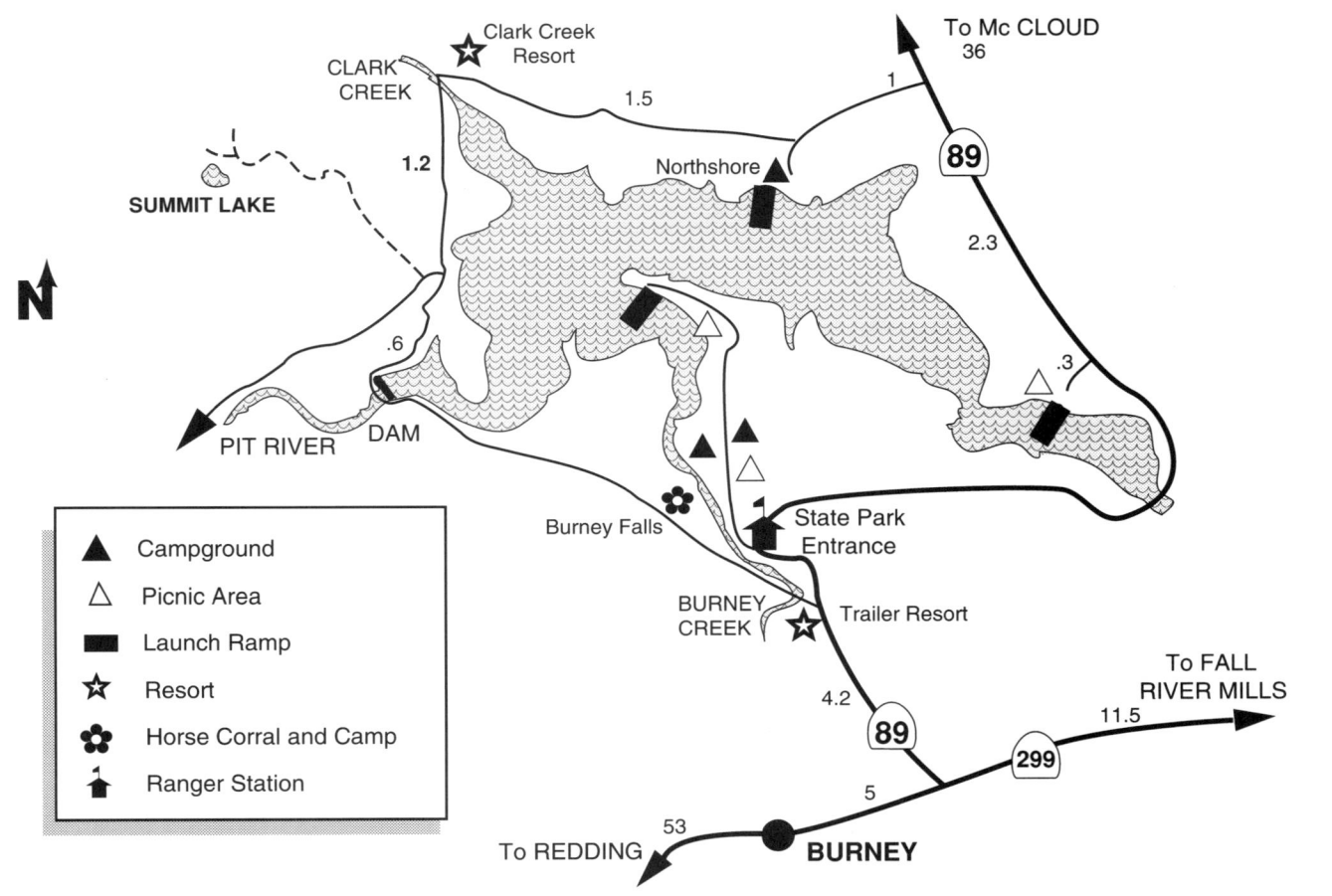

INFORMATION: State Park, Route 1, Box 1260, Burney 96013—Ph: (530) 335-2777

CAMPING	BOATING	RECREATION	OTHER

State Park Camps:
    128 Dev. Sites for
    Tents/R.V.s to 35 Feet
Fee: $16
Reserve:
    Ph: (800) 444-7275
P.G.&E.:
Ph: (916) 386-5164
Northshore:
Dev. Sites for
    Tents/R.V.s
Fee: $15
Plus Group Sites
	Power, Row, Canoe, Sail,
	    Waterskiing, Jets,
	    Windsurf & Inflatables
	Launch Ramps - Fee
	Rentals: Fishing Boats &
	    Canoes
	Moorings
	Boat Storage
		Fishing: Trout, Crappie,
		    Bass
		Swimming
		Picnicking
		Backpacking
		Nature Trails
		Horseback Riding Trails &
		    Corral
		Bird Watching
		Campfire Program
			Snack Bar
			Grocery Store
			Bait & Tackle
			Gas Station - 1 mile
			
			Full Facilities - 11 miles at
			    Burney
			
			Clark Creek Resort:
			    Cabins
			    Restaurant

Trinity Lake, is one of California's finest recreation spots. A part of the Whiskeytown-Shasta-Trinity National Recreation Area, this 16,400 surface acre Lake offers prime outdoor opportunities. Houseboaters find the often uncrowded 145 miles of pine, cedar and oak-covered shoreline ideal for "getting away from it all." There are hundreds of quiet coves for the angler to tie up and catch a meal or better yet, catch a world record smallmouth bass. While water level fluctuation in late season can create hazards, boaters will always find plenty of water to ski, cruise or sail. Trinity Lake rests at an elevation of 2,370 feet just below the rugged, granite peaks of the Trinity Alps Wilderness.

...Continued...

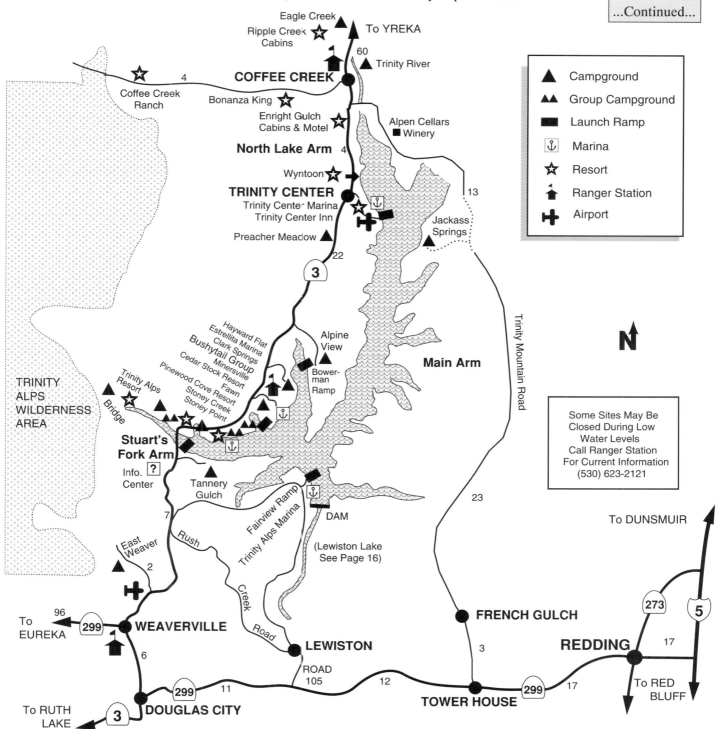

Legend:
- ▲ Campground
- ▲▲ Group Campground
- ■ Launch Ramp
- ⚓ Marina
- ★ Resort
- 🏠 Ranger Station
- ✈ Airport

Some Sites May Be Closed During Low Water Levels Call Ranger Station For Current Information (530) 623-2121

TRINITY LAKE...............Continued

<u>U.S.F.S. CAMPGROUNDS</u>

Phone Ranger Station to check lake conditions - some sites will close during low water levels
All sites have paved parking, drinking water and flush toilets unless otherwise noted.
Fees Subject to Change

<u>STUART FORK ARM:</u>

TANNERY - 87 Sites, R.V.s to 40 ft., Launch Ramp for Campers Only, Beach, Amphitheater,
$12 - Single Family Sites, $5 Extra Vehicle
$18 - Multiple Family Sites, $5 Extra Vehicle
HAYWARD FLAT - 98 Sites, R.V.s to 40 ft., Beach, Fee: $12 - Single, $18 - Multiple, $5 Extra Vehicle
(The Two Above Campgrounds: Reserve: Ph: (800) 280-CAMP
STONEY POINT - 22 Walk-In Sites, Tents Only, Fee: $10
MINERSVILLE - 21 Sites, R.V.s to 18 ft., Fee: $10 to $17
ALPINE VIEW - 66 Sites, R.V.s to 32 ft., Fee: $12 to $18, $5 Extra Vehicle, Wheel Chair Access
RIDGEVILLE - 21 Boat-In Sites
RIDGEVILLE ISLAND - 3 Boat-In Sites
MARINER'S ROOST - 7 Boat-In Sites
CLARK SPRINGS - 21 Sites, R.V.s to 20 ft., Fee $8 (Next to Clark Springs Day Area)

<u>MAIN ARM:</u>

JACKASS SPRINGS - 21 Sites, R.V.s to 32 ft., Dirt Access and Interior Road, No Water, No Fee
CAPTAIN'S POINT - 3 Boat-In Sites
Boat-In Sites Offer Vault Toilets, No Water, No Fee

<u>NORTH SHORE:</u>

TRINITY RIVER - 7 Sites, R.V.s to 32 ft., Fee: $12
EAGLE CREEK - 17 Sites, R.V.s to 27 ft., Fee: $12

<u>GROUP CAMPGROUNDS</u> - **Reserve: Ph: (800) 280-CAMP**

STONEY CREEK - 50 People Maximum, Fee: $50
FAWN - 3 Loops, 100 People Per Loop, Fee: $60 Per Loop
BUSHYTAIL - 200 People Maximum, Fee: $60

<u>U.S.F.S. DAY USE AREAS</u>

CLARK SPRINGS - Picnic Area, Swim Beach, Bath House, Boat Ramp, Flush Toilets
STONEY CREEK - Swim Beach, Bath House, Flush Toilets

...Continued...

INFORMATION: Weaverville Ranger Station, Box 1190, Weaverville 96093—Ph: (530) 623-2121

CAMPING	BOATING	RECREATION	OTHER
U.S.F.S. 　Dev. Tent/RV Sites 　No Hookups 　Boat-In Sites 　3 Group Campgrounds See Following Pages for 　Private Facilities	Open to All Boating 　4 Full Service Marinas 　7 Public Launch Ramps 　Launch Fee: $5 Rentals: 　Houseboats, Fishing, 　Pontoon & Ski Boats	Fishing: 　Large & Smallmouth 　Bass, 　Bluegill, Catfish 　Kokanee, Brown & 　Rainbow Trout Swim Beaches Picnic Areas Hiking & Riding Trails Back & Horse Packing Hunting: Deer, Bear	Complete Destination 　Facilities at Some 　Resorts and Trinity 　Center Airports - Trinity Center, 　Weaverville

PRIVATE MARINAS

TRINITY ALPS MARINA - Trinity Center 96091 - (530) 286-2282 - Launch Ramp, Mooring, Fuel Dock, OMC Dealership, Houseboats, Ski Boats, Fishing Boats, Jets, Ski Equipment, Tubes & Canoe Rentals, Grocery & Souvenir Store.

ESTRELLITA MARINA - 49160 State Hwy. 3, Trinity Center 96091 - (530) 286-2215 or (800) 747-2215 - Houseboat Rentals, Day Boats, Personal Watercraft, Fishing Boats, Ski Boats, Grocery Store, Fuel Dock, Propane, Mooring, OMC Service Dealer.

CEDAR STOCK RESORT - 45810 State Hwy. 3, Trinity Center 96091 - (530) 286-2225 - Restaurant & Lounge, Cabins, Full Service Marina, Paved Launch Ramp, OMC Dealershp, Repairs, Fuel Dock, Propane, Mooring, Dry Storage, Houseboats, Deck, Ski and Fishing Boat Rentals, Grocery Store.

TRINITY CENTER MARINA - Trinity Center 96091 - (530) 286-2225 - Paved Launch Ramp, Store, Fuel Dock, Slips, Moorage, Ski, Fishing, Deck and Houseboat Rentals.

PRIVATE RESORTS
(Prices Vary - Call Resort for Current Information)

RIPPLE CREEK CABINS - Box 4020, Star Rte. 2, Trinity Center 96091 - (530) 266-3505 - Housekeeping Cabins for 2 - 4 People, Secluded Area, Decks, Wood Stoves, Swimming, Hiking, Handicapped Cabin and Group Facilities, Panoramic Views, Pets Welcome, High and Low Season Rates - Open All Year.

COFFEE CREEK GUEST RANCH - HC2, Box 4940, Trinity Center 96091 - (800) 624-4480 - Northern California's Only 3-Star Diamond Dude Ranch, Secluded Cabins, Pool/Spa, Horseback Riding, Hayrides, Wilderness Pack Trips and Hunting, Stocked Fishing Pond, Gold Panning, Hiking, Summer Youth Programs, Square/Line Dancing, Reunions, Retreats, Small Meeting Planners, Complimentary Conference Room, Handicap Accessible, Spring/Fall/Senior Discounts, Open All Year, on Coffee Creek in the Trinity Alps.

TRINITY ALPS RESORT - 1750 Trinity Alps Rd., Trinity Center 96091 - (530) 286-2205 - Rustic Housekeeping Cabins, Bar, Restaurant, General Store, Snack Bar, Horse Rides, Hiking Trails, Volleyball, Basketball, Horseshoes, Bingo, Bonfires, Movies and Talent Shows, Tennis Court, River Swim Beach, Square Dancing, High and Low Season Rates.

PINEWOOD COVE RESORT - 45110 State Highway 3, Trinity Center 96091 - (530) 286-2201 or (800) 988-LAKE (5253) 84 Tent/R.V. Sites, 43 Full Hookups, Disposal Station, Grocery Store, Ramp, Dock, Slips, Fishing Boat Rentals, Propane, Game Room, Recreation Hall, Cabin and Trailer Rentals, Laundromat, Swimming Pool, Organized Recreation Activities.

WYNTOON RESORT - Box 70, Trinity Center 96091 - (530) 266-3337 - Complete 90 Acre Destination Resort, 136 R.V. Sites, Full Hookups, 80 Tent Sites, Cabins, Grocery Store, Gas Station, Propane, Snack Bar, Rental Boats, Private Dock, Laundromat., Swimming Pool.

ENRIGHT GULCH CABINS and MOTEL - 3500 Highway 3, Box 244, Trinity Center 96091 - (530) 266-3600 or (888)) 383-5583 - Housekeeping Cabins and Motel Units, Quiet Private Road Surrounded by National Forest, Hiking Trails, Full Facilities Within 5 Miles.

This is only a partial list of the excellent private facilities around Trinity Lake. For further information contact:

TRINITY CHAMBER OF COMMERCE
P.O. BOX 517
WEAVERVILLE, CA 96093
(530) 623-6101 OR (800) 421-7259

LEWISTON LAKE

Lewiston Lake is at an elevation of 1,902 feet in the Shasta Trinity National Forest. This beautiful Lake is 5 miles long and has a surface area of 610 acres with 15 miles of shoreline. It is open to all boating but subject to a 10 MPH speed limit. The very cold, constantly moving water flows into Lewiston Lake from the bottom waters of Trinity Lake providing an ideal habitat for large trout. Just below Lewiston Dam, the Trinity River, Rush Creek and other streams offer prize salmon and steelhead as well as trout. The Lewiston Fish Hatchery is the world's most automated salmon and steelhead hatchery.

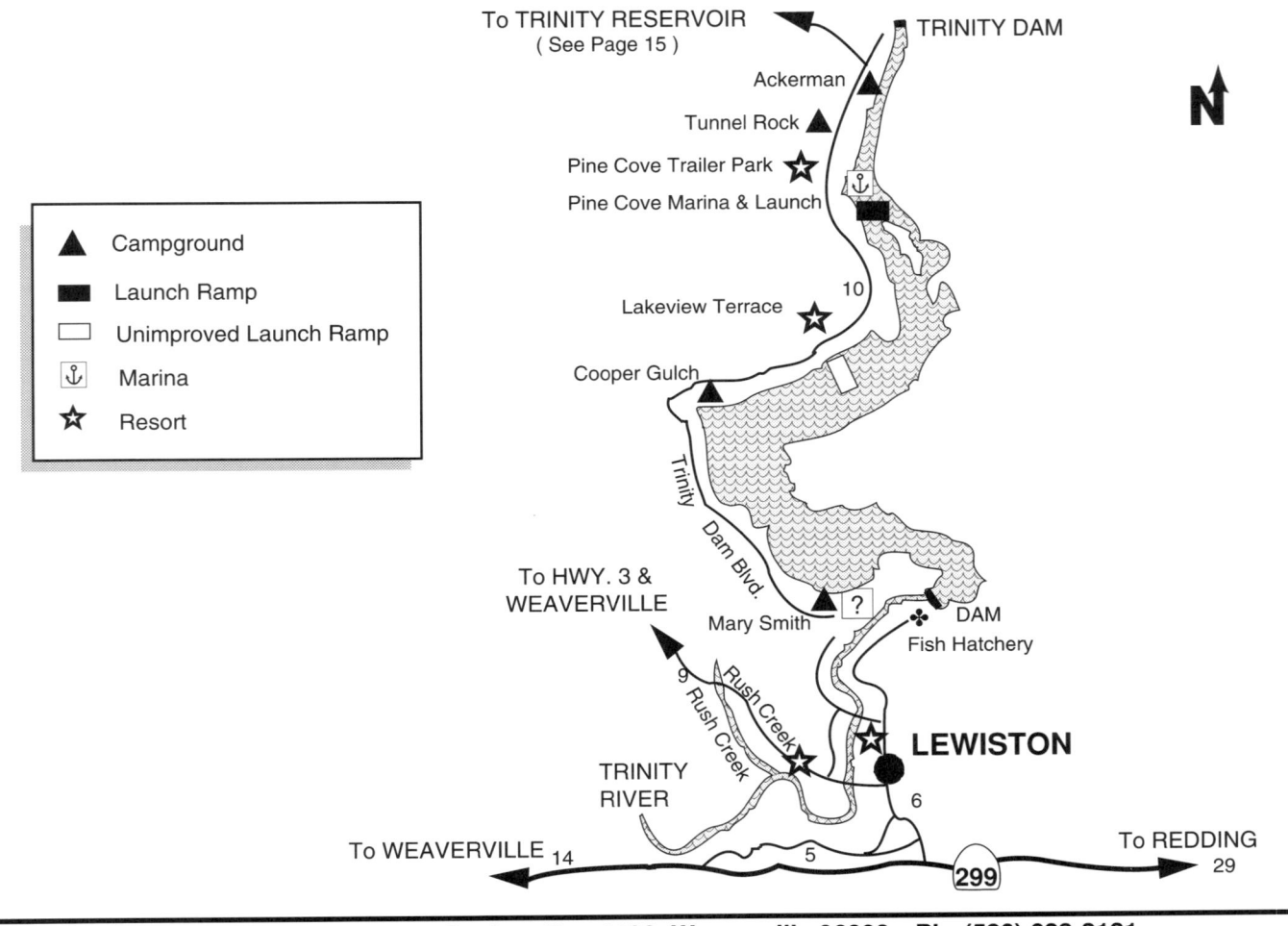

▲	Campground
■	Launch Ramp
▢	Unimproved Launch Ramp
⚓	Marina
☆	Resort

INFORMATION: Weaverville Ranger Station, Box 1190, Weaverville 96093—Ph: (530) 623-2121			
CAMPING	**BOATING**	**RECREATION**	**OTHER**
Ackerman: 66 Dev. Sites RVs to 40 ft. Disposal Station Fee: $10 Tunnel Rock: 6 Sites - RVs to 15 ft. No Water Fee: $5 Cooper Gulch: 5 Dev. Sites RVs to 16 ft. - Fee: $10 Mary Smith: 18 Sites Tents Only - Fee: $9 Additional Campsites at Private Resorts	Power, Row, Canoe, Sail & Inflatable Speed Limit - 10 MPH Launch Ramps Rentals: Fishing Boats Docks, Gas Dry Storage	Fishing: Rainbow, Brook & Brown Trout, Kokanee Salmon Picnicking 5 Wildlife Viewing Areas Hunting: Deer, Bear, Fowl & Squirrel	Resorts: Contact: Trinity County Chamber of Commerce Box 517 Weaverville 96093 (530) 623-6101 or (800) 421-7259 Snack Bars Restaurants Grocery Stores Bait & Tackle

Whiskeytown Lake, at an elevation of 1,209 feet, has 36 miles of coniferous shoreline although the water may drop as much as 10 to 30 feet in winter months. Tree-shaded islands, numerous coves and 3,200 surface acres of clear blue water invite the watersport enthusiast. The boater will find complete marina facilities and over 5 square miles of open water. The water is reasonably warm and there are some nice swimming beaches. Fishing is good from bank or shore for trout, kokanee salmon, bass and pan fish. The National Park Service maintains the facilities which include picnic areas and campgrounds. Approximately 50 miles of dirt roads and 40,000 acres of backcountry are open for visitor use. Keswick Reservoir is at an elevation of 587 feet and has a surface area of 630 acres. Fed by cold water released from Shasta Dam, Keswick provides the angler with large rainbows. Shore fishing at Keswick is poor because of steep banks and heavy brush in most areas.

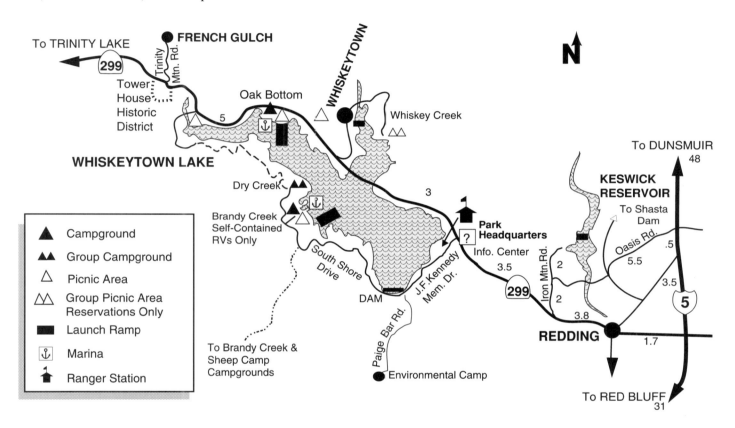

INFORMATION: Whiskeytown National Rec. Area, P.O. Box 188, Whiskeytown 96095—Ph: (530) 241-6584

CAMPING	BOATING	RECREATION	OTHER
National Park - Oak Bottom: 100 Dev. Walk-in Tent Sites & 22 R.V. Sites to 36 Ft. Fees: $8 - $16 Disposal Station Reserve: (800) 365-CAMP Brandy Creek: 37 Self-Cont. R.V. Sites Fees: $7 - $14 Disposal Station Dry Creek: Group Camp to 160 People - Reserve @ NRA	Whiskeytown : Open to All Boats Full Service Marina Rentals: Fishing, Ski, Sail, Canoe & Pontoon Boats Sailing Regattas Keswick: Open to All Boats Paved Launch Ramp	Fishing: Kokanee Salmon, Brown & Rainbow Trout, Spotted, Large & Smallmouth Bass, Bluegill, Crappie & Catfish Swimming Scuba Diving Picnicking - Groups Reserve (800) 365-CAMP Hiking & Riding Trails Ranger Guided Tours	Whiskeytown NRA Day Use $5 per Vehicle Campground Programs Gold Panning Grocery Store Snack Bar Bait & Tackle Keswick Reservoir: Bureau of Reclamation Shasta Dam Redding 96003 Ph: (530) 275-1554

SHASTA LAKE

Shasta Lake is one of California's prime recreation lakes. It is located on the northern tip of the Sacramento Valley just off Interstate 5 at an elevation of 1,067 feet. The four main arms of this huge Lake, 30,000 surface acres, converge at the junction of the Cascade and Klamath Mountain Ranges and are fed by the Sacramento, McCloud and Pit Rivers and Squaw Creek. When at full water capacity, there are 370 miles of wooded and sometimes steep shoreline around the Lake. This is more shoreline by a third than San Francisco Bay. Not only is it the State's largest man-made Lake, it is also one of its most popular. Boaters will find a variety of opportunities from quiet sheltered coves for houseboaters to warm open water for waterskiers. In addition to the many private marinas, there are 6 conveniently located public launch ramps. The angler will find over 16 species of fish from several varieties of bass to trout or sturgeon. Shasta is operated under the jurisdiction of the U. S. Forest Service which provides many developed and boat-in campsites. In addition, shoreline camping is permitted. *Call regarding possible low water levels as with all Lakes.*

....Continued....

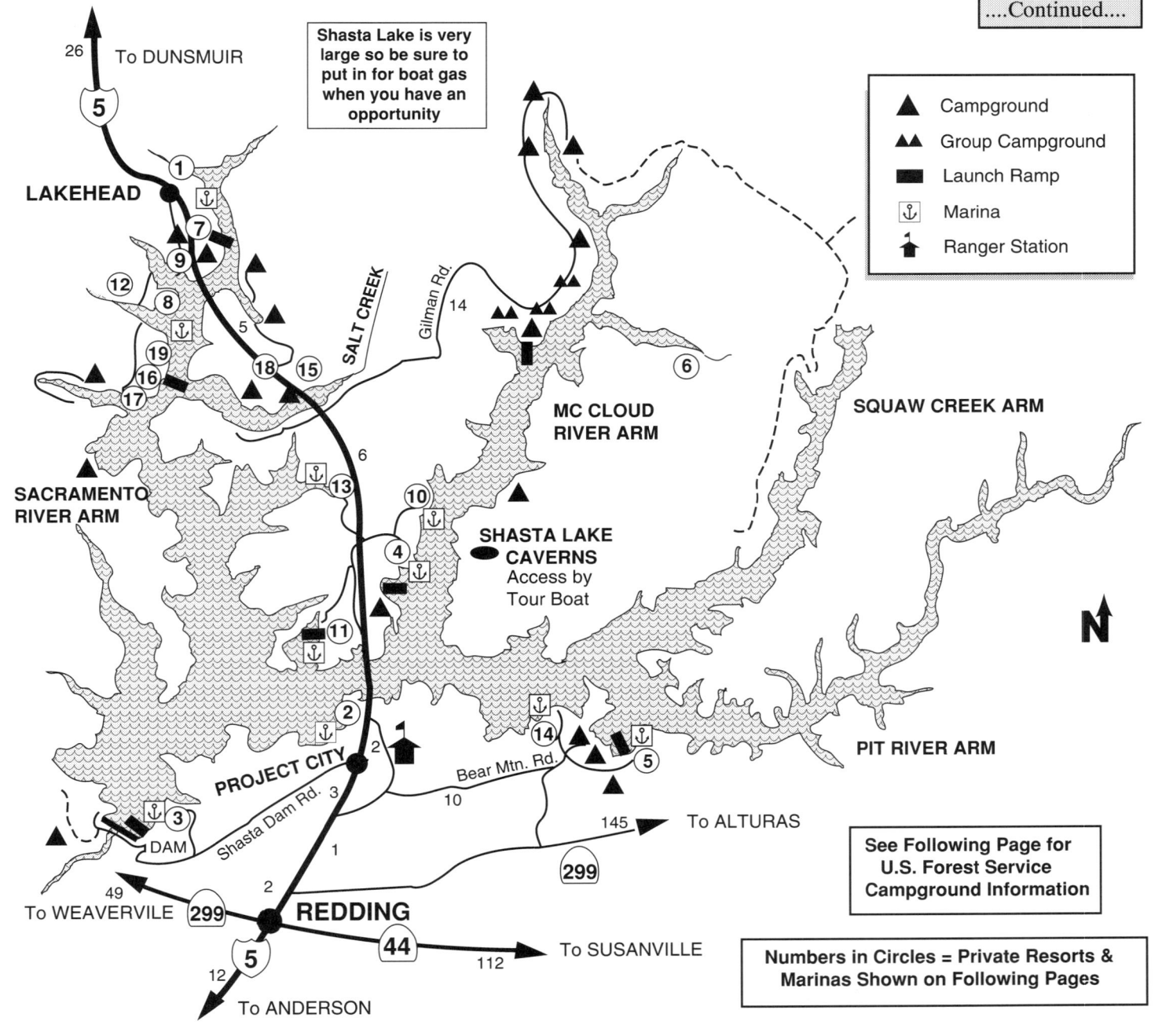

Shasta Lake is very large so be sure to put in for boat gas when you have an opportunity

To DUNSMUIR

LAKEHEAD

SALT CREEK

Gilman Rd.

▲ Campground
▲▲ Group Campground
■ Launch Ramp
⚓ Marina
⛴ Ranger Station

MC CLOUD RIVER ARM

SQUAW CREEK ARM

SACRAMENTO RIVER ARM

SHASTA LAKE CAVERNS
Access by Tour Boat

N

PIT RIVER ARM

PROJECT CITY

Shasta Dam Rd.

DAM

Bear Mtn. Rd.

To ALTURAS

299

To WEAVERVILLE 299

REDDING

44 To SUSANVILLE

To ANDERSON

See Following Page for U.S. Forest Service Campground Information

Numbers in Circles = Private Resorts & Marinas Shown on Following Pages

U.S.F.S. CAMPGROUNDS

Reservations at Sites Shown Below:
Ph: (800) 280-CAMP
Fees are Charged at all Campgrounds
and Boat Ramps

FEES VARY WITH SEASON.
Check Lake Level - Some Sites May Be Closed Because Of Low Water

PIT RIVER ARM:

From Interstate 5:
> 11 Miles NE - Jones Valley - 27 Tent/R.V. Sites to 30 feet, Boat Access
> 11 Miles NE - Jones Inlet - Primitive Shoreline Camp Sites for Tent/R.V.s to 30 feet
> Campfire Permit Required.

McCLOUD ARM:

At O'Brien: 1 Mile E
> Bailey Cove - 5 Single & 2 Double Tent/R.V. Sites - Launch Ramp - Reservations Accepted

At Gilman Rd.:
> 9 Miles E - Hirz Bay - 38 Single & 10 Double Tent/R.V. Sites to 40 feet - Reservations Accepted
> Launch Ramp
> 10 Miles E - Dekkas Rock Group Camp - Reservations Required
> 11 Miles E - Moore Creek - 12 Tent/R.V. Sites to 30 feet
> 15 Miles E - Ellery Creek - 19 Tent/R.V. Sites to 30 feet - Reservations Accepted
> 16 Miles E - Pine Point - 14 Tent/R.V. Sites to 30 feet
> 17 Miles E - McCloud Bridge - 20 Tent/R.V. Sites to 35 feet
> 9 Miles E - Hirz Bay Group Camp
>> Camp #1 - Max. Capacity - 120 People
>> Camp #2 - Max. Capacity - 80 People
>> Reservations Required

...Continued....

INFORMATION: Shasta Recreation Company, P.O. Box 378, Lakehead 96051—Ph: (530) 238-2824

CAMPING	BOATING	RECREATION	OTHER
Dev. Sites for Tents & R.V.s	Power, Row, Canoe, Sail, Waterski,	Fishing: Trout, Bass, Catfish, Bluegill,	Motels & Cabins
Walk-In Sites	Jets, Windsurf	Perch, Crappie &	Snack Bars
Boat-In Sites	& Inflatable	Kokanee Salmon	Restaurants
Group Camps	Full Service Marinas	Swimming - Lake & Pools	Grocery Stores
	Launch Ramps	Picnicking	Bait & Tackle
See Following Pages	Rentals: Houseboats,	Hiking	Laundromats
	Fishing & Ski Boats	Shasta Caverns	Gas Stations
	Docks, Berths, Gas,	Hunting: Deer, Elk,	Trailer Parks
	Moorings, Storage	Bear, Turkey	Disposal Stations
	Overnight in Boat	Spelunking	Floating Toilets
	Permitted Anywhere		on Lake

SHASTA LAKE...............Continued

U.S.F.S. CAMPGROUNDS.....Continued

SACRAMENTO RIVER ARM

At Salt Creek:
  1/2 Mile W - Nelson Point - 9 Primitive Tent/R.V. Sites to 40 feet
  3 Miles NE - Gregory Creek - 18 Tent/RV Sites to 30 feet
      Gregory Beach - Primitive Shoreline Camp Sites for Tent/R.V.s to 40 feet
At Lakehead:
  1.7 Miles S - Antlers - 41 Single & 18 Double Tent/R.V. Sites to 40 feet - Reservations Accepted
      Launch Ramp, Adjacent to Resort with Full Facilities
  2.5 Miles S - Lakeshore - 20 Single & 6 Double Tent/R.V. Sites to 35 feet - Reservations Accepted
      Adjacent to Resort with Full Facilities
  4.6 Miles S - Beehive - Primitive Shoreline Camp Sites for Tent/R.V.s to 40 feet
----

BOAT ACCESS ONLY CAMPING
Pit River Arm: Arbuckle Flat - 11 Sites & Ski Island - 29 Sites with Water
McCloud River Arm: Green Creek - 11 Sites
Sacramento River Arm: Gooseneck Cove - 10 Sites
Boat Launch Area Fees: $5 per Vehicle with Vessels up to 29 ft. - $15 per Vessel 30 ft. or more

DISPERSED CAMPING:
Jones Valley Inlet, Mariner's Point, Gregory Beach, Beehive - $6 - $8 Parking Fee per Night per Vehicle
Contact Shasta Recreation Company for Further Information - Ph: (530) 238-2824

SOME PRIVATE FACILITIES: See Map for Number Symbols - in Circles
(Prices Vary - Call for Current Information)

1 **ANTLER'S RV PARK N CAMPGROUND** - P.O. Box 127, Lakehead 96051, (530) 238-2322 or (800) 642-6849
Campsites, Hookups, Showers, Laundry, Store, Snack Bar, Bait & Tackle, Swimming Pool.

1 **ANTLER MARINA RESORT** - P.O. Box 140, Lakehead 96051, (530) 238-2553 or (800) 238-3924 - Full Service Marina, Bait & Tackle, Fuel, Moorage, Ice, Conference Room for Rent, Cabins, Swimming Pool for Cabin Guests, Houseboat, Sea Doo, Ski Boat & Competition Ski Boat Rentals.

2 **BRIDGE BAY RESORT** - 10300 Bridge Bay Road, Redding 96003, (530) 275-3021 or (800) 752-9669 - Full Service Marina, Ramp, Boat & Jet Rentals, Motel, Restaurant, Lounge, General Store, Bait & Tackle, Swimming Pool.

3 **DIGGER BAY MARINA** - P.O. Box 1516, Central Valley 96019, (530) 275-3072 or (800) 752-9669 - Full Service Marina, Ramp, Boat & Jet Rentals, General Store, Bait & Tackle, Gas, Private Moorage.

4 **HOLIDAY HARBOR RESORT** - P.O. Box 112, O'Brien 96070, (530) 238-2383 or (800) 776-BOAT- Full Service Marina, Ramp, Restaurant, Campsites, Hookups, Showers, General Store, Gas, All Types of Boat Rentals Including Houseboats, Jets, Parasailing.

5 **JONES VALLEY RESORT** - 22300 Jones Valley Marina Dr., Redding 96003, (800) 223-7950 - Full Service Marina, General Store, Bait & Tackle, Boat Rentals from Luxury Houseboats to Jet Skis, Gas.

6 **KAMPLOOPS CAMP** - Via Boat from Hirz Bay, P. O. Box 90133, Redding 96099, (530) 357-2951 - Campsites, Showers, Flush Toilets, Group Camps Available with Cook Shack, Equipment Included, Docks, Seasonal.

7 **LAKEHEAD CAMPGROUND and R.V. PARK** - 20999 Antlers Rd., P.O. Box 647, Lakehead 96051, (530) 238-2671, Campsites, Hookups, Laundry, Dump Station, Showers, General Store, Swimming Pool, Trailer Rentals, Basketball, Ping-pong, Horseshoes, Volleyball, Pavilion for Groups.

....Continued....

8   **LAKESHORE RESORT & MARINA - 20479 Lakeshore Dr., Lakehead 96051, Ph: (530) 238-2301** - Full Service Marina, Cabins, Restaurant & Lounge, Campsites, Hookups, Showers, General Store, Bait & Tackle, Swimming Pool, Gas, Camp Supplies, Houseboat, Patio, Fishing & Ski Boat Rentals, Jets....May Be Closed - Call for Current Information.

9   **LAKE SHORE VILLA R. V. PARK - 20672 Lakeshore Dr., Lakehead 96051, Ph: (800) 238-8688** - 92 R.V. Sites, Full Hookups, 15 Pull Throughs over 70 Feet Plus, Laundry, Dump Station, Showers, Docks, Cable T.V., Putting Green.

10   **LAKEVIEW MARINA RESORT - P.O. Box 992272, Redding 96099, Ph: (530) 223-3003** - Full Service Marina, Private Boat Ramp, Cabins, General Store, Ice, Bait & Tackle.

11   **PACKER'S BAY MARINA - 16814 Packers Bay Rd., Lakehead 96051, Ph: (800) 331-3137 or (530) 275-5570** - Houseboat Rentals, Boat Gas, Ice.

12   **SHASTA LAKE R.V. RESORT & CAMPGROUND - P.O. Box 450, 20433 Lakeshore Dr., Lakehead 96051, Ph: (800) 3-SHASTA or (530) 238-2370** - 53 Full Hookup RV Sites, Secluded Tent Sites, On-Site Trailer Rentals, Store, Hot Showers, Laundry, Swimming Pool, Private Boat Dock.

13   **SHASTA MARINA RESORT - 18390 O'Brien Inlet Rd., Lakehead 96051, Ph: (530) 238-2284** - Full Service Marina, Boat Ramp, Campsites, Hookups, Showers, Laundry, Gas, General Store, Bait & Tackle, Houseboat, Patio, Ski & Fishing Boat Rentals, Moorage, Open All Year.

14   **SILVERTHORN RESORT - P.O. Box 4205, Redding 96099, Ph: (530) 275-1571** - Full Service Marina, Boat Ramp, Cabins, Lounge, General Store, Bait & Tackle, Houseboats, Patio, Ski and Fishing Boat and Personal Watercraft Rentals.

15   **SALT CREEK RV PARK & CAMPGROUND - 19663 SOLUS CAMPGROUND RD., Lakehead 96051, Ph: (800) 954-1824 or (530) 238-8500** - 50 Campsites, 27 Full Hookups, Pull Thru's, Laundry, Showers, Pool, Playground, Store, Cabin, Video Game Room, Storage, Monthly's Available.

16   **SUGARLOAF COTTAGES - 19667 Lakeshore Dr., P.O. Box 768, Lakehead 96051, Ph: (530) 238-2448** - Lakeside Cabins, Free Moorage on Private Dock, Pool, Playground, Basketball, Volleyball.

17   **SUGARLOAF MARINA & RESORT, 19671 Lakeshore Dr., Lakehead 96051, Ph: (530) 238-2711** - Full Service Marina, General Store, Bait & Tackle, Fuel, Boat Rentals from Luxury Houseboats to Jets.

18   **TRAIL IN Campground and Store, 19765 Gregory Creek Rd., Lakehead 96051, Ph: (530) 238-8533** - Pull Through Campsites, Hookups, Pool, Laundry, Showers, Mini-Market, Playground, Bait & Tackle, R.V. Supplies.

19   **TSASDI RESORT - 19990 Lakeshore Dr., Lakehead 96051, Ph: (800) 995-0291 or (530) 238-2575** - Cabins, Cable TV, General Store, Bait, Heated Swimming Pool, Free Boat Slip on Private Dock, Playground..

(*Full Service Marina = Boat Rentals, Moorage, & Boat Gas)

For Further Information on Private Facilities Contact:

Shasta Lake Business Owners Association
P.O. Box 709
Lakehead, CA 96051

For Regional Information and Free Brochure
(800) 8-SHASTA

MANZANITA, BUTTE, SUMMIT and JUNIPER LAKES and McCUMBER RESERVOIR

Manzanita, Butte , Summit and Juniper are within the 106,000 acres expanse of the beautiful Lassen Volcanic National Park. There are over 150 miles of trails including a part of the Pacific Crest Trail for the hiker, backpacker and equestrian. Pets and vehicles are not allowed on trails. Pack and saddle stock must overnight in corrals by prior reservation. Grazing is not permittted so you must pack in feed. The Lakes listed outside the Park boundaries are good fishing spots. McCumber Reservoir, Grace and Nora are P.G. & E. Lakes off Highway 44 while Diamond and Pear Lakes are reached by primitive roads south of Mineral.

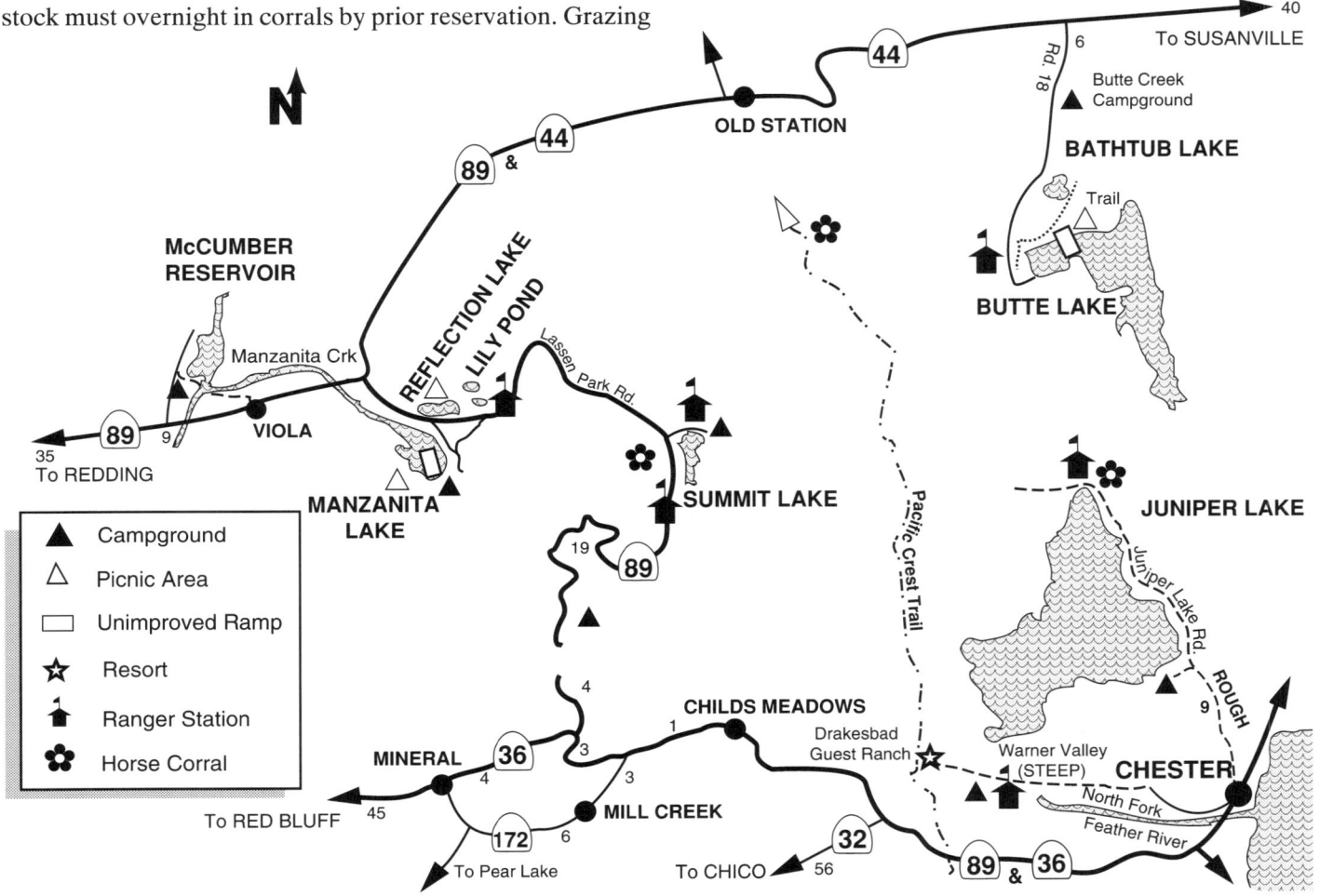

Legend	
▲	Campground
△	Picnic Area
▭	Unimproved Ramp
☆	Resort
⚑	Ranger Station
❁	Horse Corral

INFORMATION: Lassen Volcanic National Park, P.O. Box 100, Mineral 96063—Ph: (530) 595-4444

CAMPING	BOATING	RECREATION	OTHER

Manzanita: 179 Sites
  Tents & R.V.s: $14
Summit: 94 Sites
  Tents & R.V.s: $12 - $14
Juniper: 18 Sites
  Tents Only: $10
  No Running Water
	No Power Motors
	Row, Sail, Windsurf
	  & Inflatables Only
	Unimproved
	  Launch Ramps:
	  Manzanita & Butte Only
		Fishing: Rainbow, Brook
		  & Brown Trout
		Manzanita:
		  Catch & Release
		  With Barbless Hooks Only
		Juniper: *No Fishing*
		
		Swimming - Picnicking
		Hiking
		Backpacking [*Parking*]
		Horseback Riding
		  Trails & Corrals
		Campfire Programs
			For Lodging Contact:
			  Lassen Volcanic
			  National Park
			
			P.G. & E.
			  Ph: (916) 386-5164
			McCumber Reservoir
			  7 Tent Sites
			  5 Walk-In Sites
			  Fee: $15
			
			No ORV's

CRATER, CARIBOU and SILVER LAKES

In the Lassen National Forest, these Lakes provide a bounty of natural recreational opportunities. Crater Lake, at 6,800 feet elevation, has a surface area of 27 acres. This volcanic crater offers excellent fishing for trout. The Lakes near Silver Lake border the Caribou Wilderness, a gently rolling, forested plateau which can easily be explored by the hiker, backpacker or horseman. Silver Lake and its neighbor, Caribou Lake, provide a quiet remote area for the small boater, camper and fisherman. The roads are dirt and rough, especially into Crater Lake so large trailers are not advised.

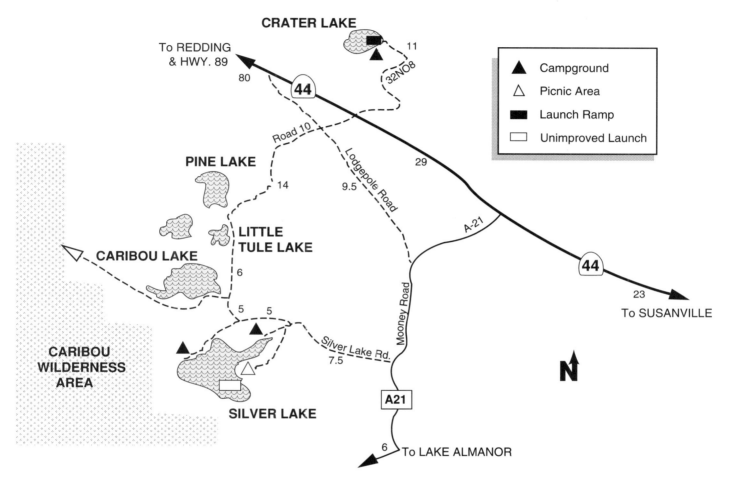

INFORMATION: Almanor Ranger District, P.O. Box 767, Chester 90620—(530) 258-2141

CAMPING	BOATING	RECREATION	OTHER

Silver Lake:
  Rocky Knoll:
    7 Tent Sites
    11 Tent/R.V. Sites
    Fee: $10
  Silver Bowl:
    18 Tent/R.V. Sites
    Fee: $10
Crater Lake:
  17 Tent/R.V. Sites
  Fee: $12
  R.V.s Under 16 Feet
	Silver & Caribou Lakes:
	  Cartop Boats
	  Hand Launch Only
	
	Crater Lake:
	  No Gas Motors
	    Allowed
	  Launch Ramp
		Fishing: Rainbow
		  Trout
		Picnicking
		Swimming
		Hiking & Riding Trails
		Backpacking
		Hunting: Antelope, Deer,
		  Rabbit, Quail & Grouse
			Crater Lake Campground:
			Eagle Lake Ranger District
			477-050 Eagle
			  Lake Rd.
			Susanville 96130
			(530) 257-2151

EAGLE LAKE

Eagle Lake is at an elevation of 5,100 feet in the Lassen National Forest. With a surface area of 27,000 acres and over 100 miles of timbered shoreline, it is the second largest natural Lake in California. The slightly alkaline water is the natural habitat for the famous Eagle Lake trout, a favorite of the fisherman for its size of 3 pounds or better. The water is warm and clear. There are 4 Forest Service campgrounds and 2 group campgrounds amid tall pines. Full hook-ups for R.V.s are located at Eagle Lake Park. McCoy Flat is a small Reservoir for fishing with brown and rainbow trout. *Contact USFS to check condition of McCoy as it may be dry.*

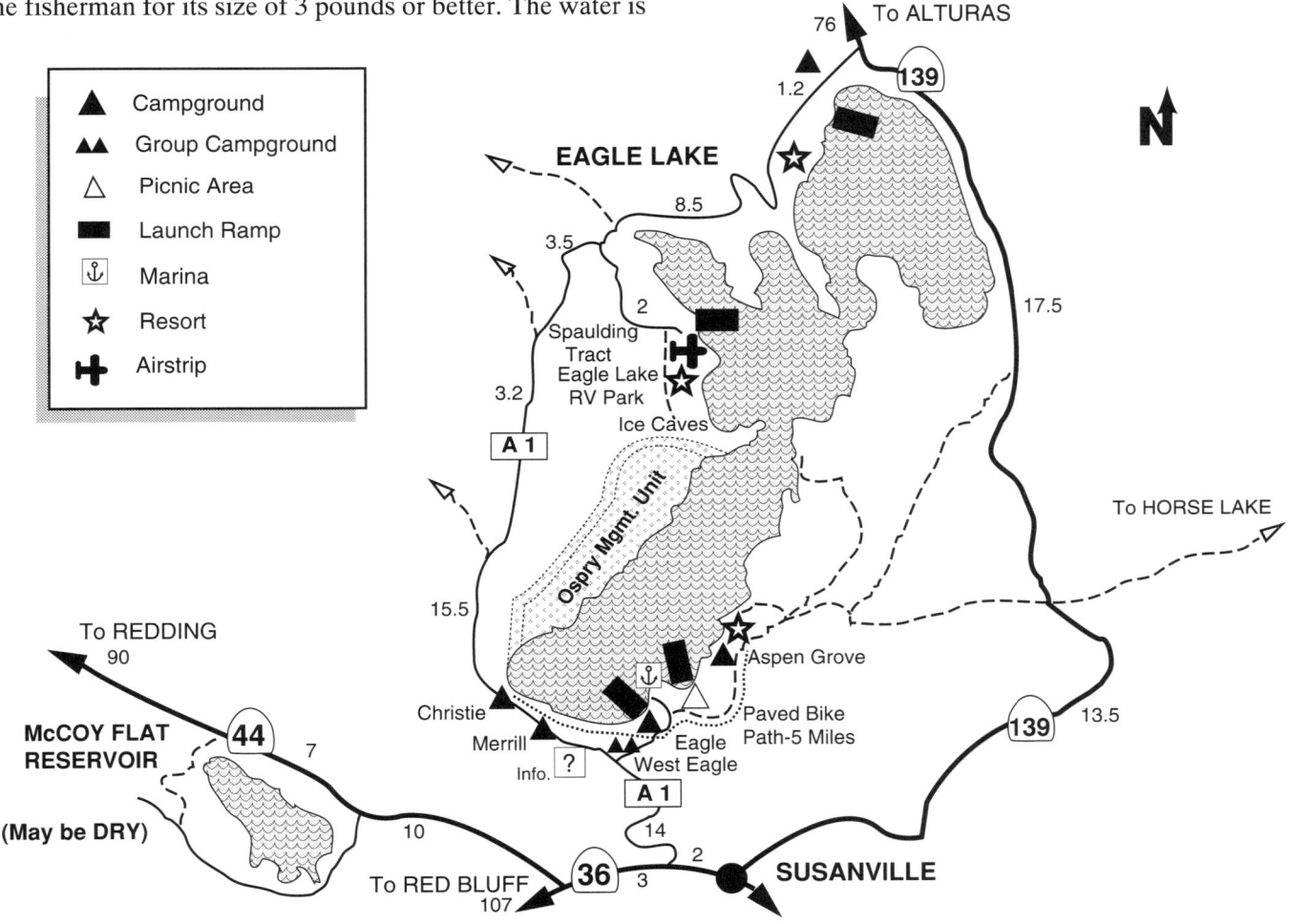

Legend	
▲	Campground
▲▲	Group Campground
△	Picnic Area
◼	Launch Ramp
⚓	Marina
☆	Resort
✠	Airstrip

INFORMATION: Eagle Lake Ranger District, 477-050 Eagle Lake Rd., Susanville 96130—Ph: (530) 257-4188

CAMPING	BOATING	RECREATION	OTHER
300 Dev. Sites for Tents & R.V.s 11 Multiple Sites Reserve: Ph: (800) 280-CAMP 2 Group Camps #1 - 100 People #2 - 75 People Aspen Grove: 25 Dev. Sites for Tents Bur. of Land Management: 17 Dev. Sites	Power, Row, Canoe, Sail, Waterski, Jets, Windsurfing, Inflatables Full Service Marinas Launch Ramps Rentals: Fishing Boats & Motors Docks, Moorings, Berths	Fishing: Eagle Lake, Rainbow & Brown Trout Swimming Picnicking Hiking Nature Walks 5 Mile Paved Bicycle Path Campfire Programs Hunting: Deer & Waterfowl Birdwatching: Bald Eagles, Osprey, Grebes, Pelicans	Eagle Lake R.V. Park 687-125 Palmetto Way Susanvile 96130 (530) 825-3133 46 Full Hook-ups Cabins & Grocery Store Laundromat - Showers Disposal Station Gas & Propane Lake View Inn Motel & Restaurant (530) 825-3223 Airstrip

Ruth Lake is half way between Eureka and Red Bluff on Highway 36 within the boundaries of the Six Rivers National Forest. This is quite a drive on a narrow road at times but well worth the trip if you plan to stay awhile in this beautiful country. The Lake rests at an elevation of 2,654 feet and has a surface area of 1,200 acres. It was formed by damming the Mad River in 1962. This is now a popular recreation facility offering boating of all kinds, fishing and camping. The Mad River flows into and out of Ruth Lake and can provide good steelhead fishing. Call Ruth Lake Community Services for additional information.

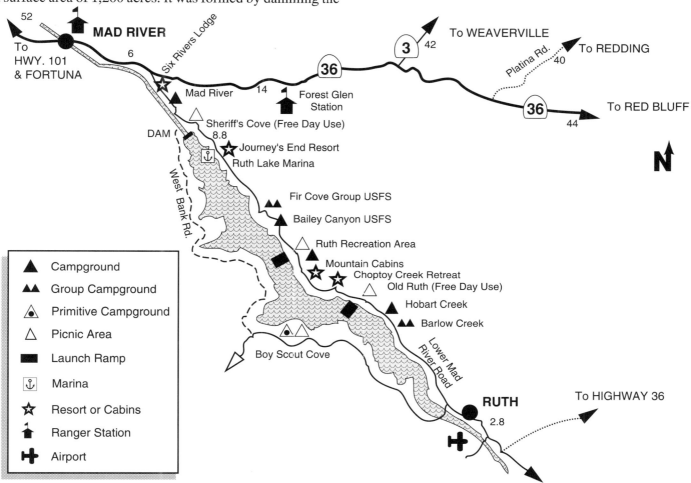

INFORMATION: Ruth Lake Community Services, P.O. Box 31, Mad River 95552—(707) 574-6332

CAMPING	BOATING	RECREATION	OTHER
U.S.F.S. 81 Dev. Sites for Tents & R.V.s Fee: $6 1 Group Site - Reserve: (707) 574-6233 Ruth Lake Community 85 Dev. Sites for Tents & R.V.s Fee: $11 per car Barlow Group Camp & Picnic Area Reserve: (800) 500-0285	Power, Row, Canoe, Sail, Waterski, Jets, Windsurf & Inflatables Full Service Marina Ph: (707) 574-6524 Launch Ramps - Free Rentals: Fishing Boats & Motors, Waterski Boats & Pontoon Docks, Moorings, Slips Boat Storage	Fishing: Rainbow Trout, Kokanee Salmon, Large & Smallmouth Bass, Catfish Waterplay Picnicking Hiking Horseback Riding Hunting: Deer, Boar, Bear Quail, Grouse, Wild Turkey	Choptoy Retreat Mobile Home Rental (707) 574-6375

ROUND VALLEY RESERVOIR

Round Valley Reservoir is at an elevation of 4,600 feet in the Plumas National Forest. Located 2 miles south of Greenville, this small secluded Lake is the water supply for Greenville so water sports are limited to fishing and boating. Swimming or body contact with the water is not permitted. Famous for black bass, Round Valley is an excellent warm water Lake. The area offers nice hiking and nature study trails. Campsites are available at the Resort and also at the Greenville Campground.

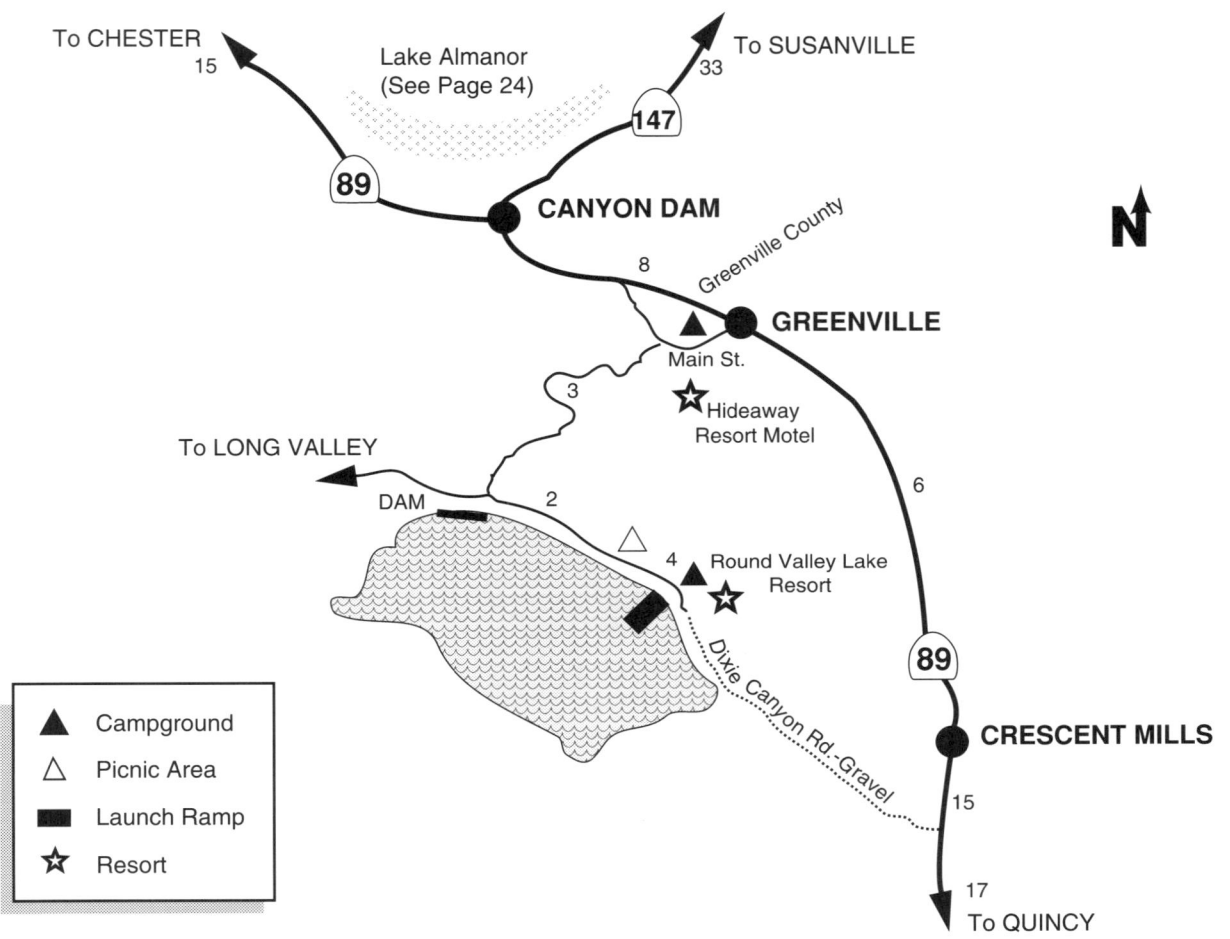

Map legend:
- ▲ Campground
- △ Picnic Area
- ■ Launch Ramp
- ☆ Resort

INFORMATION: Round Valley Lake Resort, P.O. Box 959, Greenville 95947—Ph: (530) 258-7751

CAMPING	BOATING	RECREATION	OTHER
50 Dev. Sites for Tents & R.V.s Fee: $16 - 2 People $5.50 Each Additional Adult & $2.25 Each School Age Child Hot Showers Plumas County: Greenville Campground 23 Dev. Sites	Fishing Boats Only Rocked Launch Ramp Rentals: Rowboats - $20 Motorboats - $30 2 Boat/Fishing Docks	Fishing: Black Bass, Catfish & Bluegill Picnicking Hiking No Swimming Horse Trails 1 Mile Self-Guided Nature Walk at Dam Bird Watching: Bald Eagle & Osprey	Hideaway Resort Motel Ph: (530) 284-7915 Spring Meadow Motel Ph: (530) 284-6768 Oak Grove Motor Lodge Ph: (530) 284-6671 Plumas County Visitor's Bureau Ph: (800) 326-2247 Indian Valley Chamber of Commerce Ph: (530) 284-6633

Lake Almanor rests at an elevation of 4,500 feet in the Lassen National Forest. There is an abundance of pine-sheltered campgrounds operated by P.G. & E., the Forest Service and private resorts. The Lake is 13 miles long and 6 miles wide with a surface area of 28,000 acres. It is one of the largest man-made Lakes in California. Almanor's clear, blue waters offer complete boating facilities. Caution is advised because small islands are exposed during low water levels. Gusty winds can also make boating hazardous. Fishing can be excellent for a variety of species in the Lake. Nearby streams are also productive. Mountain Meadow Reservoir is a small fishing Lake in a scenic area near Westwood. There are no facilities but it is surrounded by numerous hiking and equestrian trails.

...Continued...

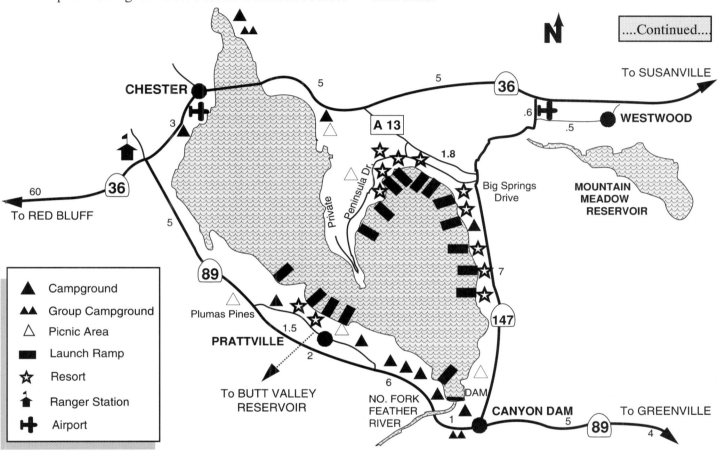

Legend:

- ▲ Campground
- ▲▲ Group Campground
- △ Picnic Area
- ▬ Launch Ramp
- ☆ Resort
- ⬆ Ranger Station
- ✈ Airport

INFORMATION: P. G. & E. Land Projects, P.O. Box 277444, Sacramento 95827–Ph: (916) 386-5164

CAMPING	BOATING	RECREATION	OTHER
P.G. & E.: 112 Dev. Sites for Tents & R.V.s Fee - $15 Group Camp to 40 People Maximum U. S. F. S.: 101 Dev. Sites for Tents & R.V.s Fee: $9 *Private Campgrounds See Following Page*	Power, Row, Canoe, Sail, Waterski, Jets, Inflatables Full Service Marinas Launch Ramps Rentals: Fishing, Canoe, Patio & Ski Boats, Parasailing Docks, Berths, Gas	Fishing: Rainbow & Brown Trout, Smallmouth Bass, Catfish & King Salmon Fishing Guides Swimming Picnicking Hiking Horseback Riding Golf Hunting: Deer, Waterfowl	Cabins & Motels Snack Bars Restaurants Grocery Stores Bait & Tackle Laundromats Disposal Stations Gas Stations Plumas County Visitors Bureau Ph: (800) 326-2247

P.G.&E. CAMPGROUNDS - (916) 386-5164

Lake Almanor Campground - Off Highway 89 Westshore.
100 Tent/R.V. Sites, Disposal Station
Yellow Creek Campground - Off Highway 89 Westshore.
10 Tent/RV Sites near Soda Springs Historic Site.
Camp Conery Group Camp - Off Highway 89 East of Dam.
40 People Maximum, Multi-purpose Utility Building with Cook area, Grill, Refrigeration, Showers
and 5 Bunk Houses, Swimming Beach and Picnic Area - Reservations Only.
Last Chance Creek Campground - 4 miles northeast of Chester on Juniper Lake Road.
13 Tent/R.V. Group Sites - Reservation Only & 12 Tent/R.V. Family Sites, Horse Camping.

U. S. FOREST SERVICE - ALMANOR RANGER DISTRICT
P. O. Box 767, Chester 96020, Ph: (530) 258-2141
Reserve: 800-280-CAMP
Almanor Campground - Off Highway 89 West Shore.
15 Tent Only Sites, 86 Tent/R.V. Sites to 22 Feet, Handicapped Facilities.
Almanor Group Camp - Off Highway 89 West Shore.
Groups to 100 People by Reservation Only.

SOME PRIVATE RESORTS - Call for Current Prices

Plumas Pines Resort, 3000 Almanor Dr. West, Canyon Dam 95923, Ph: (530) 259-4343 - R.V. Sites with Full Hookups, No Tent Camping, Motel, Housekeeping Cottages, Laundromat, Fox's Lakeside Cafe, Marina, Boat Launch, Parasailing, Home of all Sailboat Regattas.

Lichti's Lakeside Resort - 300 Peninsula Dr., Lake Almanor 96137, Ph: (530) 596-3959 - 9 Housekeeping Units with Kitchens, Marina for Guests, Picnic & BBQ, Restaurant & Groceries Nearby - NO pets.

Northshore Campground - P.O. Box 1102, Chester 96020, Ph: (530) 258-3376 - 36 Tent Sites, 89 R.V. Sites, Full Hookups, Dump Station, Hot Showers, Laundromat, General Store, Library, Boat Rentals, Propane, Launch & Dock Facilities.

Lake Almanor Resort - 2706 Big Springs Rd., Lake Almanor 96137, Ph: (530) 596-3337 - 13 R.V. Sites, Full Hookups with Cable TV, 5 Cabins, Lodge with 8 Housekeeping Units, Showers, Laundry, Launch Ramp, Docks, Limited Boat Rentals, Grass Lawns with Group Barbercues, General Store, Bait & Tackle, .

Lake Cove Resort and Marina - 3584 Highway 147, Lake Almanor 96137, Ph: (530) 284-7697 or (800) 605-6595 - 55 R.V. Sites, Full & Partial Hookups, Cable TV, Disposal Station, Showers, Laundry, Ramp, Slips, Rental Boats, General Store, Bait & Tackle, Gas Station, Propane.

Lassen View Resort - 7457 Hwy. 147, Lake Almanor 96137, Ph: (530) 596-3437 - 45 R.V. Sites, 14 Tent Sites, Showers, Cabins, Snack Bar, General Store, Marina, Fuel Dock, Boat Rentals.

Little Norway Resort - 432 Peninsula Dr., Lake Almanor 96137, Ph: (530) 596-3225 - Cabins, Full Service Marina, Fishing, Ski, Pontoon and Wave Runner Rentals, Parasailing.

Wilson's Camp Prattville - 2932 Lake Almanor Dr. West, Canyondam 95923, Ph: (530) 259-2464
32 R.V. Sites, Showers, Flush Toilets, Housekeeping Units, Marina, Ramp, Docks, Restaurant, General Store, Bait & Tackle.

The above are a random selection of facilities around the Lake. For additional information contact:

Chester - Lake Almanor Chamber of Commerce - (530)-258-2426 ..... or
Plumas Visitors Bureau - (800)-326-2247

Butt Valley Reservoir rests at an elevation of 4,150 feet in the Lassen National Forest. This picturesque mountain Lake is five miles long and three-quarters of a mile at its widest point. It is connected to Lake Almanor by a tunnel. Butt Valley Reservoir is the second level of P.G. & E.'s "stairway of power" which flows down the Feather River into Lake Oroville. This is a nice boating Lake although marina facilities are limited to a launch ramp. There is a good fishery for planted rainbows as well as native brown and rainbow trout. The well-kept campground and picnic areas are under the jurisdiction of P.G. & E.

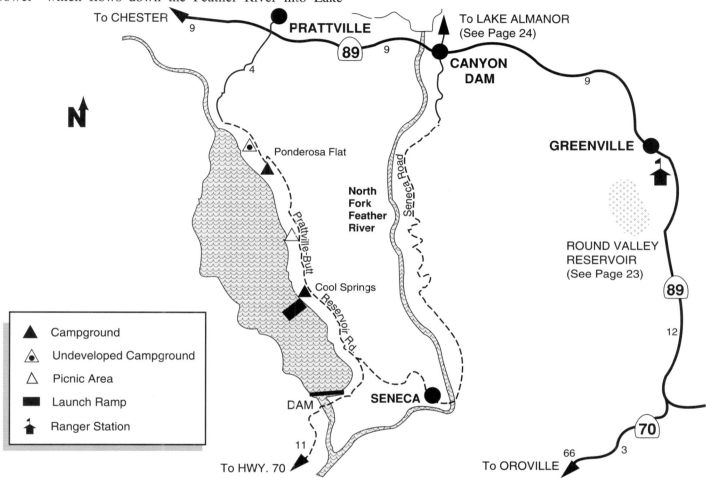

CAMPING	BOATING	RECREATION	OTHER

Cool Springs:
  22 Sites for Tents
  & R.V.s
  Fee: $15
Ponderosa Flat:
  50 Sites for Tents
  & R.V.s
  Fee: $15
Butt Overflow:
  20 Sites
  Fee: $15
	Open to All Boating
	Launch Ramp
	No Waterskiing
		Fishing: Rainbow &
		  Brown Trout, Catfish
		Picnicking
		Swimming
		Hiking
		Nature Study
		Hunting: Waterfowl & Deer
		Horseback Riding
			Full Facilities in Chester
			  9 Miles
			
			Plumas County
			  Visitors Bureau
			  Ph: (800) 326-2247

INFORMATION: P.G. & E. Land Projects, P.O. Box 277444, Sacramento 95827–Ph: (916) 386-5164

ANTELOPE LAKE

The Antelope Lake Recreation Area rests at an elevation of 5,000 feet in the Plumas National Forest. The Lake has 15 miles of timbered shoreline and a surface area of 930 acres. The sheltered coves and islands make this beautiful Lake a pleasant boating haven. The well maintained Forest Service campgrounds provide the camper with nice sites amid pine and fir trees. Good-sized Rainbow and Eagle Lake trout await the fisherman. Indian Creek, below the dam, has some large German Brown trout as well as Rainbows.

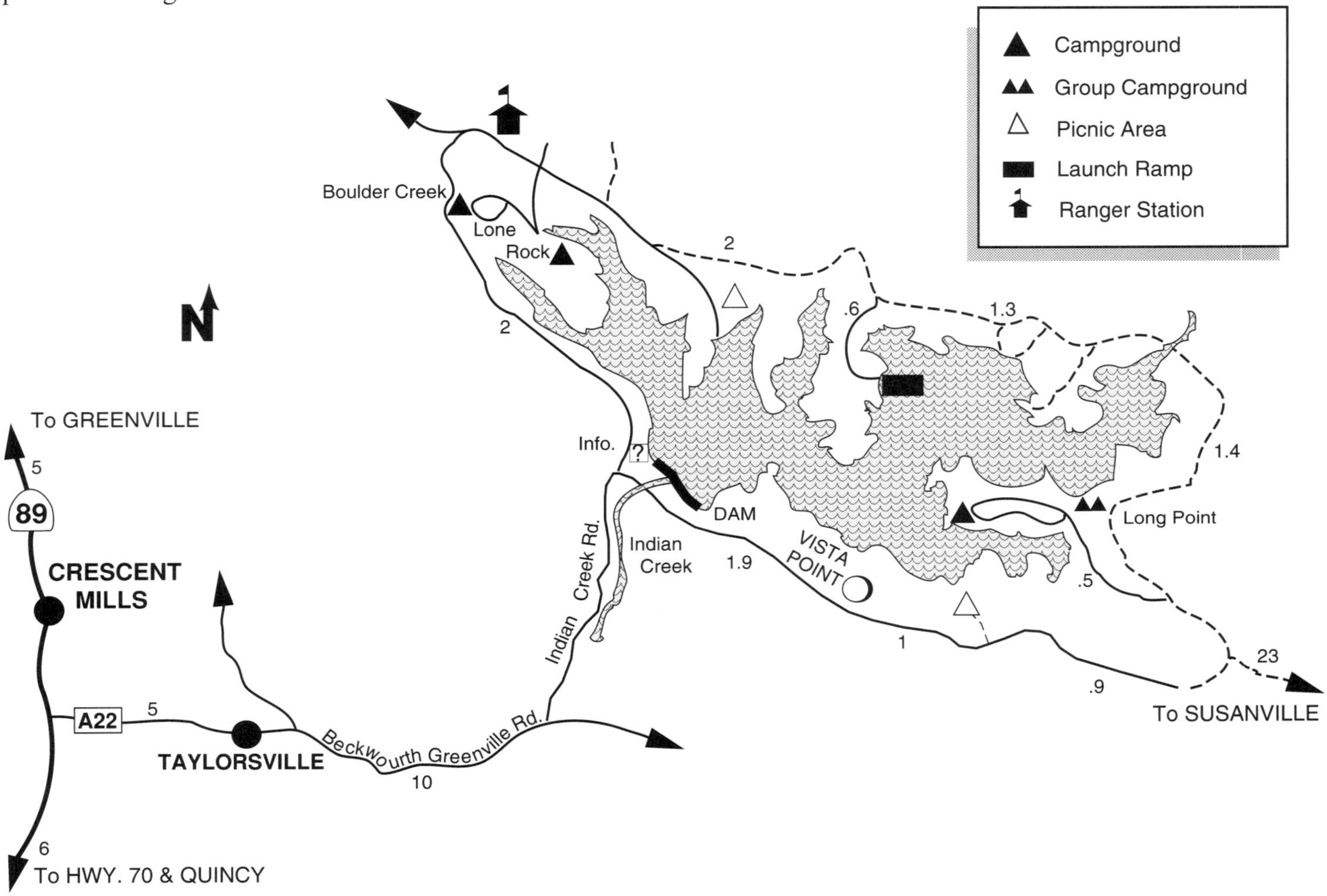

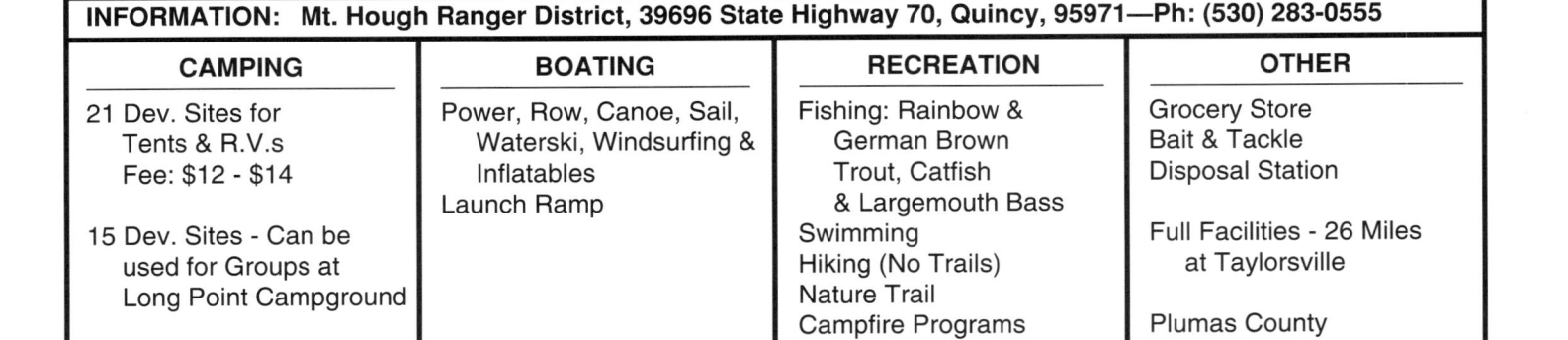

Legend	
▲	Campground
▲▲	Group Campground
△	Picnic Area
■	Launch Ramp
⚑	Ranger Station

INFORMATION: Mt. Hough Ranger District, 39696 State Highway 70, Quincy, 95971—Ph: (530) 283-0555

CAMPING	BOATING	RECREATION	OTHER
21 Dev. Sites for Tents & R.V.s Fee: $12 - $14	Power, Row, Canoe, Sail, Waterski, Windsurfing & Inflatables Launch Ramp	Fishing: Rainbow & German Brown Trout, Catfish & Largemouth Bass	Grocery Store Bait & Tackle Disposal Station
15 Dev. Sites - Can be used for Groups at Long Point Campground		Swimming Hiking (No Trails) Nature Trail Campfire Programs Hunting: Deer	Full Facilities - 26 Miles at Taylorsville
Reserve: (800) 280-CAMP			Plumas County Visitors Bureau Ph: (800) 326-2247

Benbow Lake State Recreation Area is at an elevation of 364 feet off Highway 101 in the Redwood Empire. This 230 acre Lake is created every summer by damming the South Fork of the Eel River. Boating is limited to small non-powered craft so this is a nice Lake for sailing and rowing. The California Department of Parks and Recreation maintains a 1,200 acre park with picnic areas, campground and a swimming beach. The Benbow Inn, adjacent to the Lake, is a lovely old hotel and restaurant. The Benbow Valley R.V. Resort offers 112 campsites with full hook-ups, cable T.V., swimming pool, jacuzzi and playgrounds. A 9-hole golf course is adjacent to the R.V. Park.

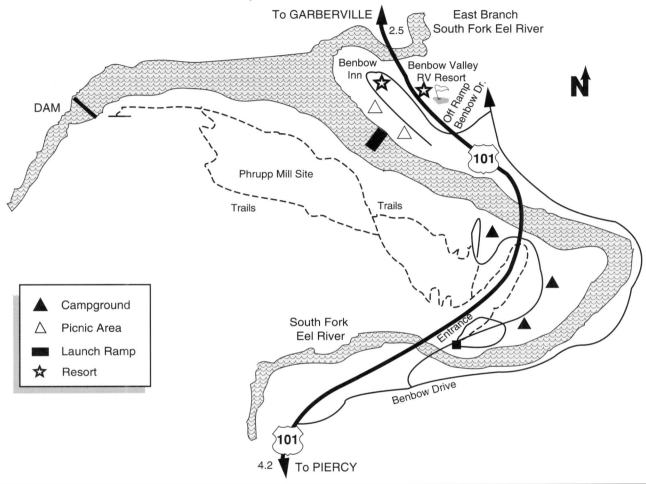

INFORMATION: Benbow Lake State Recreation Area, 1600 Hwy. 101, Garberville 95542—Ph: (707) 247-3318

CAMPING	BOATING	RECREATION	OTHER
State Park 75 Dev. Sites for Tents & Self-Contained Units No Hook-ups Cold Showers Disposal Station Fee: $16 Reservations in Season Day Use - Fee	Row, Sail, Canoe, Windsurfing & Inflatables No Motors Rentals: Canoes, Yak Boards Launch Ramp *Summer Only*	Fishing: Not Recommended in Summer due to Young Steelhead & Salmon Swimming Picnicking Hiking Nature Study Campfire Programs 9 Hole Golf Course	Benbow Valley R.V. Resort & Golf Course 7000 Benbow Dr. Garberville 95442 Ph: (707) 923-2777 112 R.V. Sites Full Hook-ups Fee: $33 Benbow Inn and Restaurant Ph: (707) 923-2125 Full Facilities in Garberville

LAKE CLEONE

Lake Cleone is at elevation of 20 feet within the MacKerricher State Park. This nice park along the scenic Mendocino Coast provides a variety of natural habitats from forest and wetlands to sand dunes and a 6-mile beach. Although swimming is not advised due to cold, turbulent waters, the 500 yard black sandy beach is a popular attraction. Lake Cleone, 40 surface acres, is open to shallow draft non-powered boating. The angler may fish for trout and an occasional bass at the Lake. Steelhead and salmon are in nearby rivers. Surf fish, rock fish and Ling cod can be caught in the ocean. Skin divers enjoy the nearby coves. Hikers and naturalists will find trails around the Lake and along the beach.

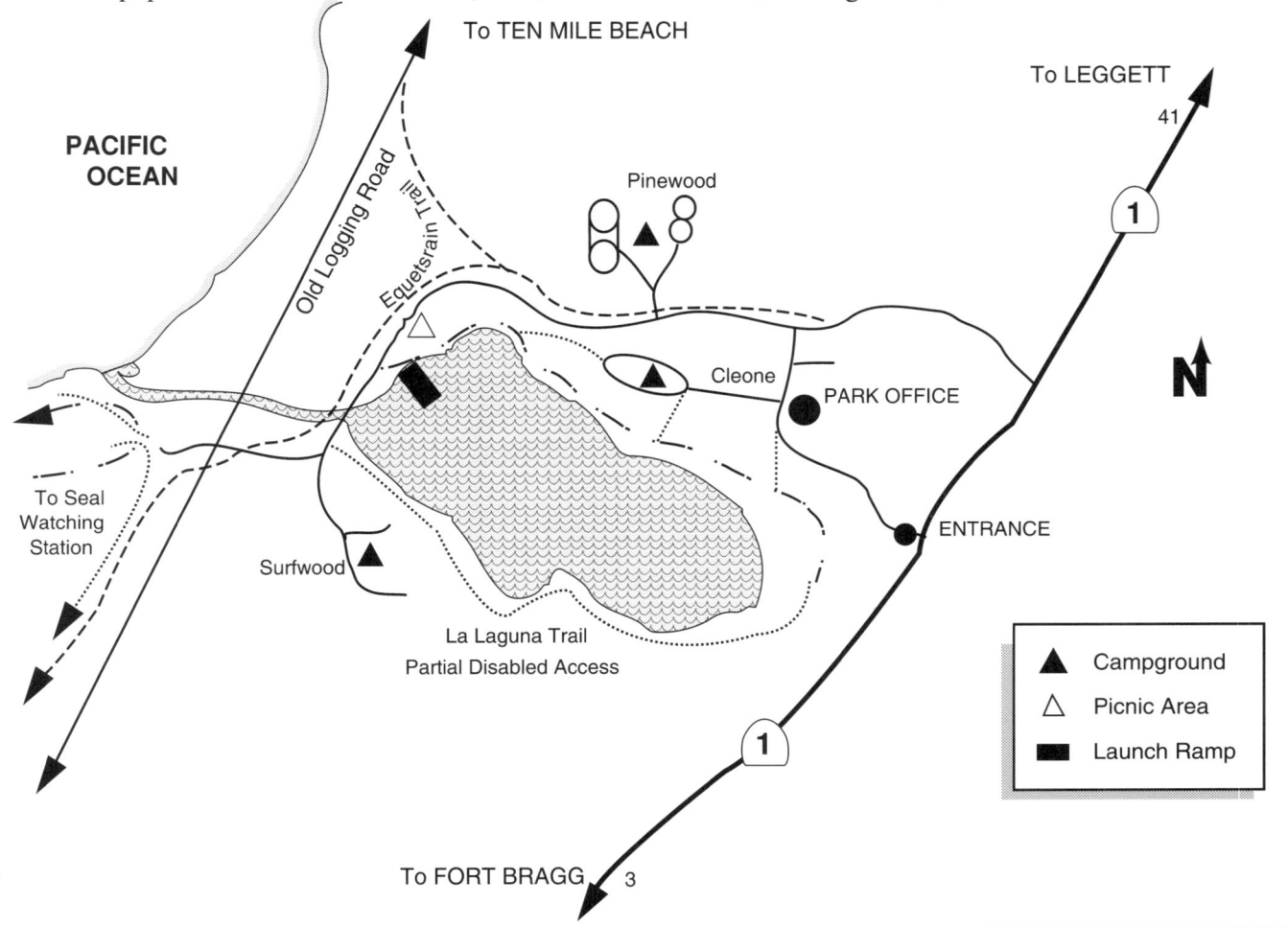

INFORMATION: MacKerricher State Park, P. O. Box 440, Mendocino 95460—Ph: (707) 937-5804

CAMPING	BOATING	RECREATION	OTHER
140 Dev. Sites for Tents & R.V.s to 35 Feet Hot Showers Disposal Station Reserve: Ph: (800) 444-7275 10 Walk-In Camps	Open to Small, Shallow Draft Non-Powered Boats Paved Launch Ramp	Fishing: Trout Picnicking Hiking & Nature Study Trails Disabled Access Trails Horseback Riding Trails Campfire Programs Birding Beach Combing Skin Diving Seal Watching Station	Grocery Store Near Park Entrance Full Facilities at Fort Bragg

These Lakes range in elevation from 3,000 feet at Paradise Lake to 5,000 feet at Philbrook Lake. Snag Lake does not have game fish but Philbrook is a good fishing Lake. Trailers, however, are not advised on this road. These two Lakes are part of the Lassen National Forest. P.G. & E. maintains a resort for its employees only at De Sabla Reservoir but the public may fish for Rainbow and some Browns on the south and east sides of the Lake nearest Skyway Boulevard. A group picnic site is also available. Paradise Lake is a popular for day use fishing. The angler will find planted rainbows, some brown trout, bass, and channel catfish. *Snag Lake is usually drained in mid-summer.*

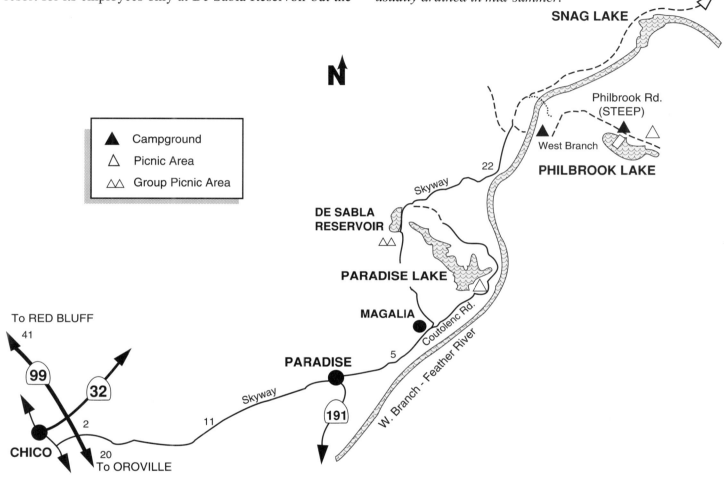

INFORMATION: Almanor Ranger District, P.O. Box 767, Chester 96020—Ph: (530) 258-2141

CAMPING	BOATING	RECREATION	OTHER
U.S.F.S. West Branch 15 Campsites P.G. & E.: Ph: (916) 386-5164 Philbrook Lake 20 Campsites Fee: $15	Philbrook: Cartop Launch Area Fishing Access Paradise Lake: Rowboats, Canoes & Electric Motors Minimal Facilities *Snag Lake is usually Drained Mid-Summer*	Fishing: Rainbow, Brown & Eastern Brook Trout, Small & Largemouth Bass, Channel Catfish Picnicking De Salba Reservoir: Group Picnic Area Reservations - PG&E: Ph: (916) 386-5164 Hiking & Backpacking Swimming - Philbrook Lake Only	Recreation Permits and Fees are Required at Paradise Lake

BUCKS, SILVER and SNAKE LAKES

The Bucks Lake Recreation Area in the Plumas National Forest is rich in wildlife and offers an abundance of outdoor recreation. Bucks Lake, at 5,153 feet elevation, has a surface area of 1,827 acres. There are facilities for all types of boating. Silver Lake, at 5,800 feet, offers excellent trout fishing. There is also good stream fishing. The Bucks Lake Wilderness Area of 24,000 acres and the Pacific Crest Trail welcome the hiker, horseback rider and backpacker to this area of gently rolling terrain, glaciated granite, forested meadows and perennial streams. Snake Lake can be closed to boating and fishing during summer months.

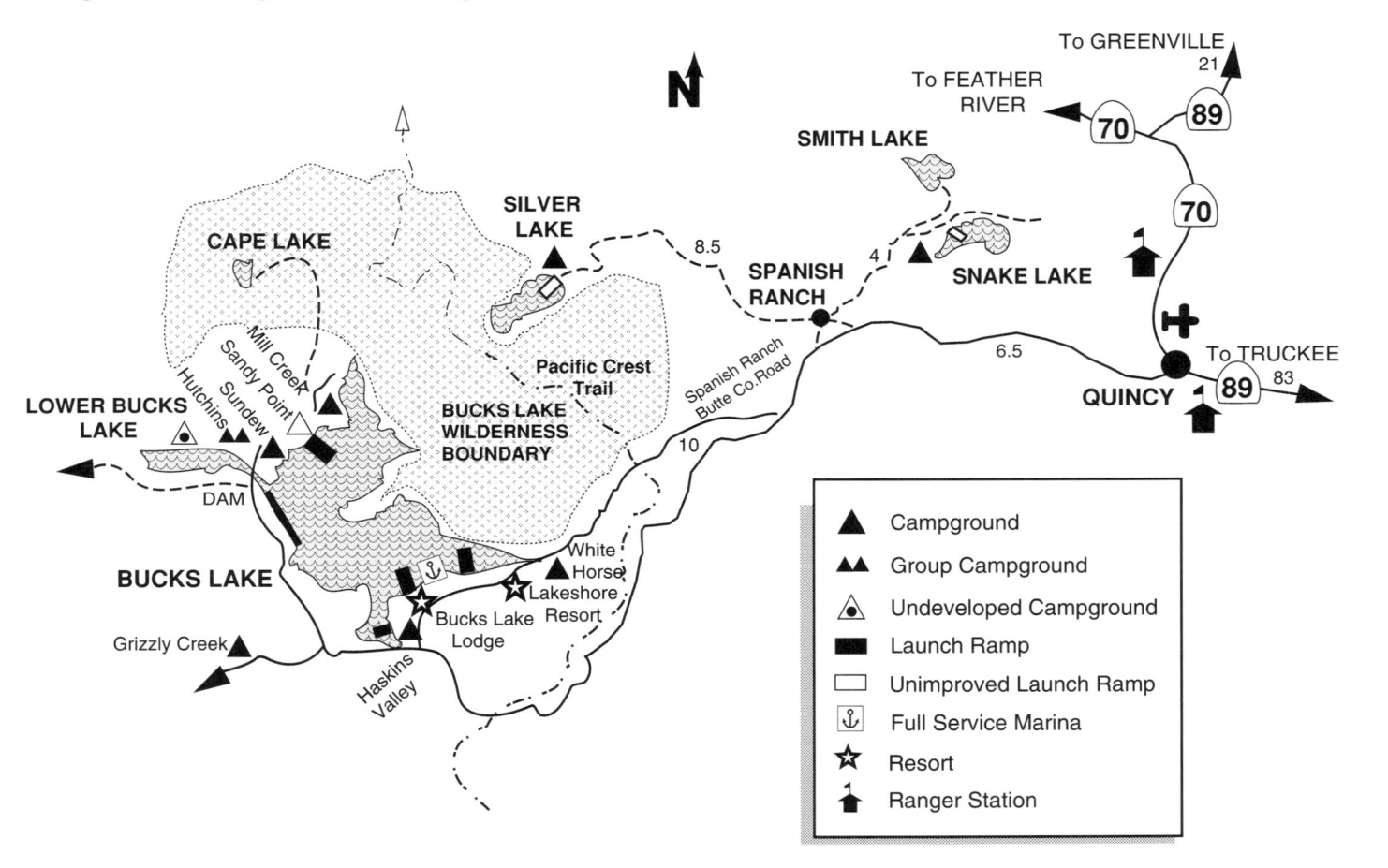

▲	Campground
▲▲	Group Campground
⬙	Undeveloped Campground
▬	Launch Ramp
▭	Unimproved Launch Ramp
⚓	Full Service Marina
☆	Resort
⬆	Ranger Station

INFORMATION: Mt. Hough Ranger District, 39696 Highway 70, Quincy 95971—Ph: (530) 283-0555

CAMPING	BOATING	RECREATION	OTHER

U.S.F.S.
  62 Dev. Sites for
  Tents & R.V.s to 22 feet
  Plus Walk-in Sites
  Hutchins Meadow:
  Reserve 3 Group Camps
P. G. & E.
  Ph: (916) 386-5164
Haskins Valley: 65 Dev.
  Sites for Tents & R.V.s
City of Santa Clara:
Grizzly Forebay: 7 Walk-Ins
	Bucks Lake:
	  Open to All Boats
	  Full Service Marina
	  Rental Fishing Boats
	Snake & Silver Lakes:
	  Rowboats & Canoes
	    Only
	  No Motors
	  Hand Launch
		Fishing: Rainbow,
		  German Brown &
		  Brook Trout,
		  Kokanee Salmon
		Swimming & Ski Beaches
		Hiking & Picnicking
		Backpacking [*Parking*]
		Horseback Riding
		  Trails & Rentals
		Hunting: Deer, Bear,
		  Rabbits, Waterfowl
			Lakeshore Resort
			  P.O. Box 338
			  Meadow Valley 95956
			  (530) 283-6900
			Tent & R.V. Sites-Hookups
			  $12-$24 & Cabins on Lake
			  Restaurant & Bar, Marina
			Bucks Lake Lodge
			  P.O. Box 236
			  Quincy 95971
			  (530) 283-2262
			Cabins, Store, Restaurant,
			Bait & Tackle, Gas Station

The Lake Davis Recreation Area is located in the Plumas National Forest, 7 miles north of Portola. The Lake is at an elevation of 5,775 feet and has a total surface area of 4,026 acres. A concessionaire, under permit from the Forest Service, maintains three nice campgrounds on the eastern shore of the Lake as well as launch ramps around the 32 miles of tree-covered shoreline. Steady winds make this an ideal Lake for sailing although afternoon winds can be a hazard for small craft. Lake Davis is open to all types of boating but water skiing is not permitted. There is a good warm water fishery along with an abundant population of both native and stocked trout. A major threat to native trout and salmon are Northern pike. These fish have been eliminated at Lake Davis due to the efforts of the Department of Fish and Game.

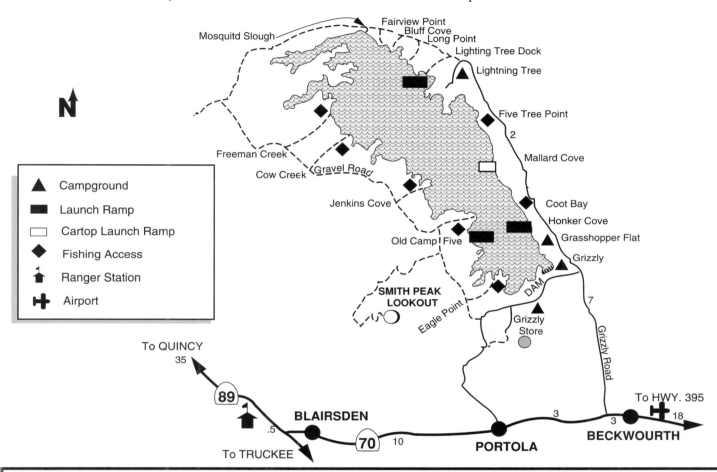

INFORMATION: Beckwourth Ranger District, Box 7, 23 Mohawk Rd., Blairsden 96103—Ph: (530) 836-2575

CAMPING	BOATING	RECREATION	OTHER
125 Dev. Sites for Tents & R.V.s Fee: $13 40 Sites for Self-Contained R.V.s Only Disposal Station - Fee: $5 Reserve Above Sites: (800) 280-CAMP Grizzly Camp: Ph:(530) 832-0270 34 Dev. Sites for Tents & R.V.s - Hookups Seasonal Rates	Power, Row, Canoe, Sail, Windsurf & Inflatables *No Waterskiing* Launch Ramps Floating Boat Docks Cartop Boat Launch Areas Rentals: Fishing Boats at Grizzly Store	Fishing: Rainbow, Brown, Eagle Lake, Kamloop Trout, Bass & Catfish Numerous Fishing Access Sites Swimming Picnicking Hiking Hunting: Deer, Waterfowl, Upland Game Birds	Grizzly Store & Camp P.O. Box 1498 Portola 96122 Ph: (530) 832-0270 Store, Bait & Tackle Propane & Firewood Boat Rentals R.V. & Boat Storage Airport & Full Facilities at Beckwourth

FRENCHMAN LAKE RECREATION AREA

The Frenchman Recreation Area offers a variety of recreational opportunities from waterskiing to ice fishing in the winter. Frenchman Lake at an elevation of 5,588 feet, is within the Plumas National Forest. The 1,580 surface acres are surrounded by 21 miles of open sage and pine dotted shoreline. There are five campgrounds managed by concession permit from the Forest Service. There are also 15 picnic sites and 5 fishing access points around the lake. All types of boating are permitted. Fishing is very good for rainbow and brook trout. This is a prime hunting area for the Rocky Mountain Mule Deer, but it must be done beyond the boundaries of the Recreation Area and the Game Refuge.

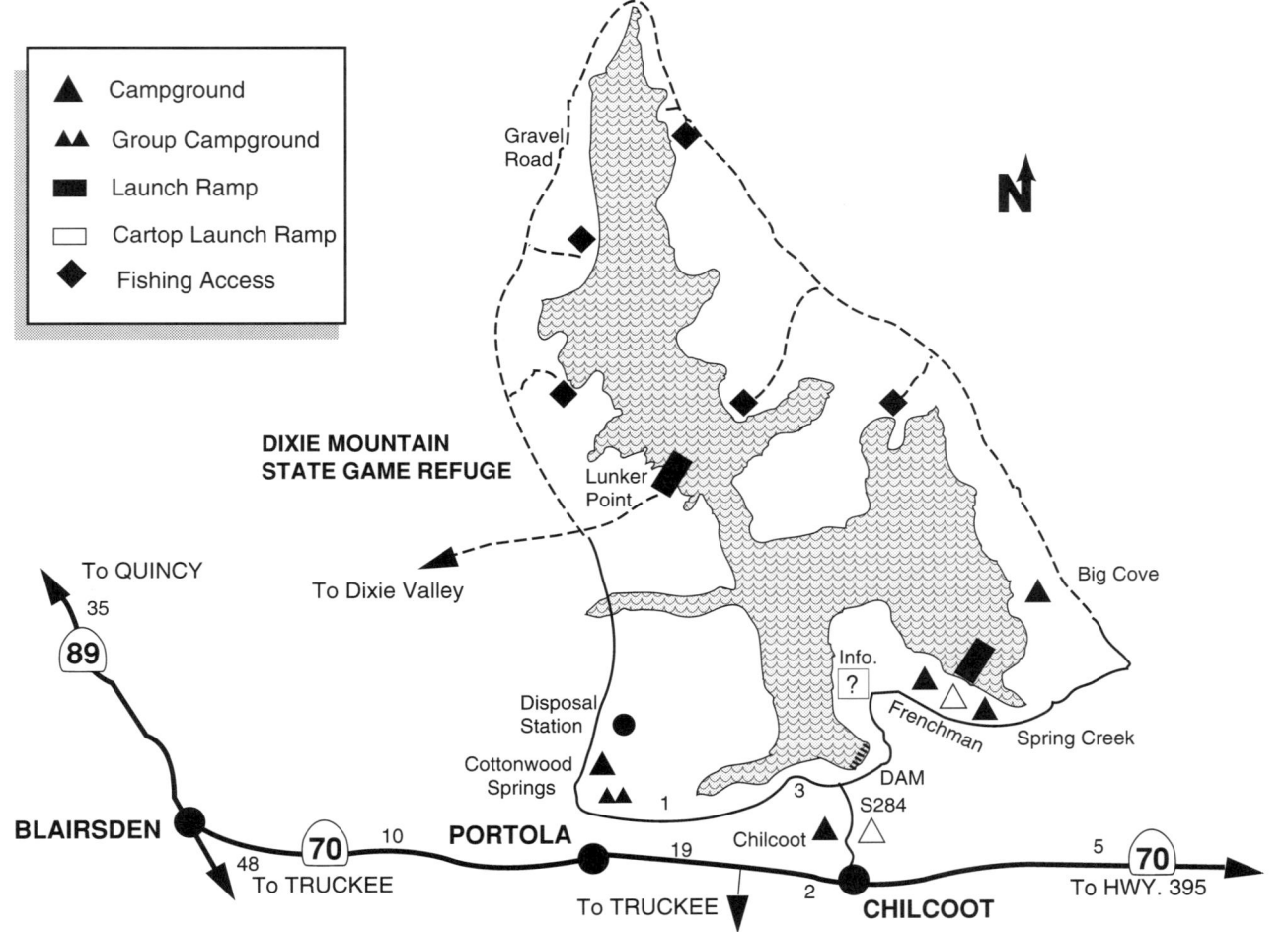

INFORMATION: Beckwourth Ranger Dist. P.O. Box 7, 23 Mohawk Rd., Blairsden 96103—Ph: (530) 836-2575

CAMPING	BOATING	RECREATION	OTHER

Cottonwood Springs:
    20 Single Sites-Fee: $12
    2 Group Sites
        25 & 50 People Max.
        Fees: $44 & $87
Chilcot: 5 Walk-in &
    35 Single Sites-Fee: $12
Spring Creek: 35 Sites - $12
Frenchman: 38 Sites - $12
Big Cove: 19 Singles - $12
    & 19 Double Sites - $24
Reserve:
    (800) 280-CAMP
	Power, Row, Canoe,
	    Sail, Waterski,
	    Jets, Windsurf,
	    Inflatables
	Launch Ramps
	
	*Check Current Water
	Levels*
		Fishing: Brown &
		    Rainbow Trout
		Swimming
		Picnicking: 15 Sites
		Hiking
		Backpacking [Parking]
		Hunting: Deer, Waterfowl,
		    Upland Game
		No Hunting on West Side
		of Lake in Game Refuge
			Supplies at Wiggens Store
			    7 Miles at Chilcoot
			
			Handicapped Facilities
			    Available at Lake
			
			*Off Road Vehicle Travel is
			Prohibited in Recreation
			Area*
			
			Plumas County
			    Visitors Bureau
			    Ph: (800) 326-2247

East Park Reservoir is operated by the Bureau of Reclamation. This warm water fishery is known for good bass fishing. All boating is allowed and there is open primitive camping around most of the Lake. Plaskett Lake, elevation 6,000 feet and Letts Lake at 4,500 feet, are within the boundaries of the Mendocino National Forest. These remote Lakes are good for trout fishing. Gas or electric powered boats are *not* allowed. Letts Lake is popular with hikers and backpackers who can enjoy the Snow Mountain Wilderness with Summit Springs Trailhead nearby. Trailers over 16 feet are not advised at Plaskett or Letts Lakes due to poor access roads.

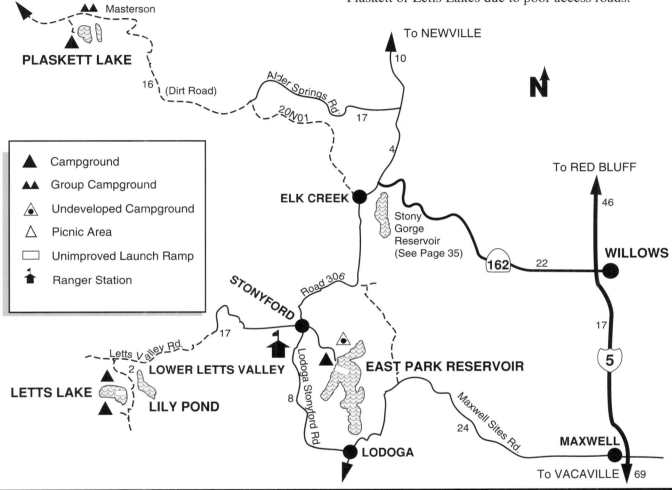

▲	Campground
▲▲	Group Campground
⌂	Undeveloped Campground
△	Picnic Area
▭	Unimproved Launch Ramp
♦	Ranger Station

INFORMATION: East Park Reservoir, Bureau of Reclamation, P.O. Box 988, Willows 95988--Ph: (530) 275-1554

CAMPING	BOATING	RECREATION	OTHER
East Park Reservoir: Open Primitive Camping Around Most of the Lake	East Park Reservoir: Open to All Boats *Subject to Low Water Hazards* Unimproved Ramp Boating Laws Strictly Enforced Ordinance Against Parasailing at East Park	Fishing: East Park: Black & Spotted Bass, Bluegill, Crappie, Catfish, Perch Plaskett: Trout Letts: Bass Swimming Hiking/Nature Trails *East Park: No Hunting, No Firearms No ORV's*	Plaskett & Letts Lakes USFS-Stonyford RD P.O. Box 160 Stonyford 95979 Ph: (530) 963-3128 Camping (Dogs on Leash): Letts - 42 Sites - Fee: $8 Plaskett - 32 Sites - Fee: $8 Masterson Group Site by Reservation - Fee: $35 No Gas or Electric Boats

BLACK BUTTE LAKE

Black Butte is surrounded by rolling hills with basalt buttes and open grassland spotted with oak trees. It rests at an elevation of 470 feet. This 4,500 surface-acre Lake has a shoreline of 40 miles. The U.S. Army Corps of Engineers administers the well-maintained campgrounds and facilities at the Lake. Water level can change rapidly. Boaters are cautioned against possible hazards, such as sand bars, exposed during low water. This is a good warm water fishery especially in the spring when the crappie are hungry. There is abundant wildlife, and the birdwatcher will find a wide variety of avian life.

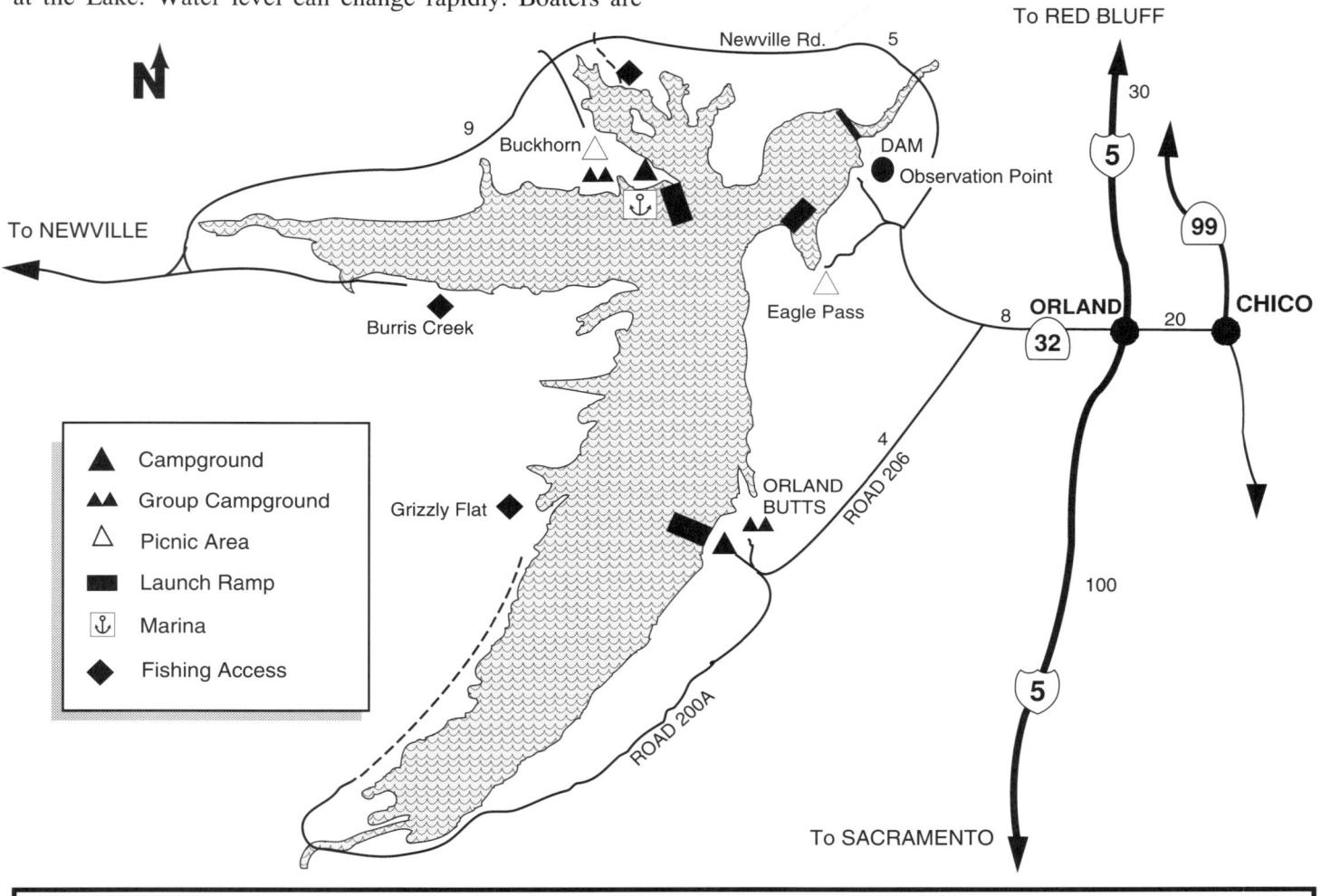

Legend:
- ▲ Campground
- ▲▲ Group Campground
- △ Picnic Area
- ■ Launch Ramp
- ⚓ Marina
- ◆ Fishing Access

INFORMATION: Park Manager, 19225 Newville Rd., Orland 95963—Ph: (530) 865-4781

CAMPING	BOATING	RECREATION	OTHER
Buckhorn: 65 Dev.Sites Tents & R.V.s-Fee: $10-$12 20 Undev. Sites - $8 Group Camp to 200 People - Fee: $50 Open Year Round Orland Buttes: 35 Dev. Sites Tents & R.V.s-Fee: $10-$12 Group Camp to 100 People - Fee: $50 Open Late April-July Reserve for Groups Only 14-Day Camping Limit	Power, Row, Canoe, Sail, Waterski, Jets, Windsurf, Inflatables Launch Ramps - Fee: $2 Black Butte Marina 500 Buckhorn Rd. Orland 95963 Ph: (530) 865-2665 Rentals: Fishing Boats & Paddle Boats Docks, Berths, Storage, Gas	Fishing: Large & Smallmouth Bass, Blue, White & Channel Catfish, Crappie, Bluegill & Green Sunfish Swimming & Hiking Picnicking & Playground Campfire Programs Hunting: Deer, Dove, Quail, Waterfowl *(Shotgun & Archery Only)*	Camping Information: Ph: (530) 865-4781 Limited Supplies at Grocery Store Bait & Tackle Hot Showers Disposal Station 75-Acre ATV Park Open May 20 through February Full Facilities - 8 Miles at Orland

Stony Gorge Reservoir is at an elevation of 800 feet in the foothills west of Willows in the upper Sacramento Valley. The Lake has a surface area of 1,275 acres and is under the administration of the U. S. Bureau of Reclamation. The rolling hills surrounding the 25 miles of shoreline are dotted with oak, digger pine and brush. Although there are a number of campsites, they are relatively primitive. Boating facilities are limited to a paved launch ramp which is unusable during late summer and fall . The fishing is good for warm water species in this pretty Lake.

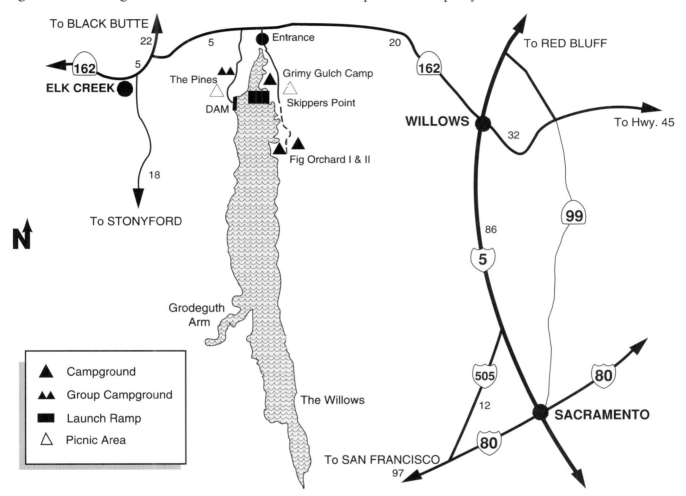

INFORMATION: Bureau of Reclamation, P.O. Box 988, Willows 95988—Ph: (530) 275-1554			
CAMPING	**BOATING**	**RECREATION**	**OTHER**
150 Primitive Sites for Tents & R.V.s Group Camp or Day Use - 200 People Max. Reservations No Fees No Drinking Water Figs Campground Closed Sept. 30 thru Mid April	Power, Row, Canoe, Sail, Waterski, Windsurf & Inflatables No Houseboats Permitted Launch Ramp *Underwater Hazards Due to Fluctuation in Lake Level*	Fishing: Catfish, Bluegill, Crappie, Bass & Perch Swimming Picnicking - 200 People Group Site No ORV's and No Hunting	Elk Creek: Country Store Gas Station Full Facilities in Elk Creek or Willows

Oroville Dam is the highest dam in the United States towering 770 feet above the City of Oroville. The Park encompasses 28,450 acres. Lake Oroville, at 900 feet elevation, has 15,500 surface acres with a shoreline of 167 miles. Although water levels drop late in the summer, the Lake offers unlimited recreation the year around. This is an excellent boating Lake with good marina facilities. There are numerous boat-in campsites and houseboat moorings for those who wish to spend the night on the Lake. The angler will find an extensive variety of game fish from smallmouth bass to king salmon. Thermalito Forebay has 300 surface acres for boating, fishing and swimming.

....Continued...

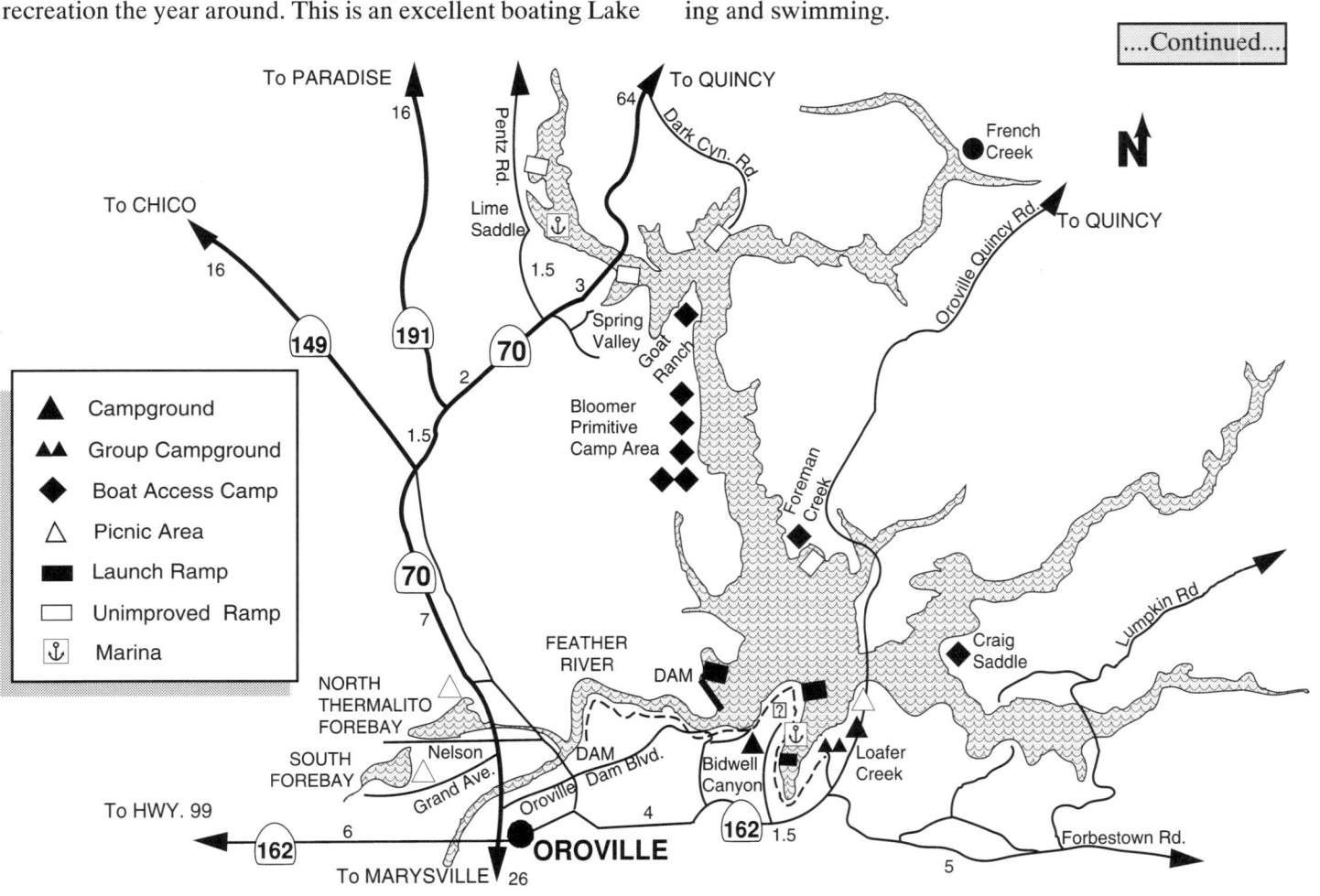

INFORMATION: State Recreation Area, 400 Glen Dr., Oroville 95966—Ph: (530) 538-2200

CAMPING	BOATING	RECREATION	OTHER

Family Campsites
R.V. Hookup Sites
Boat-In Campsites
Group Campsites
Floating Campsites:
   2-Story Houseboats
   Moored in a Cove
Horse Camp
Some Campsites:
   Reserve:
   Ph: (800) 444-7275
See Following Page
	All Boating Allowed
	Full Service Marinas
	Paved Launch Ramps
	Hand Launch Ramps
	Docks, Berths &
	   Moorings
	Rentals: Fishing,
	   Waterskiing &
	   Houseboats
		Fishing: Rainbow &
		   Brown Trout, Large
		   & Smallmouth Bass,
		   Coho & King Salmon
		Picnicking
		Hiking & Riding
		   Trails
		Hunting: Upland Game,
		   Dove, Pheasant
		Swimming (No Diving)
		Visitor Center
		Fish Hatchery
			Full Facilities in
			   Oroville & Paradise
			Grocery Stores & Motels
			   7 Miles from
			   Lime Saddle

CAMPGROUNDS:

LOAFER CREEK:

137 Sites for Tents & R.V.s to 31 feet. - Fee: $14.
Water, Flush Toilets, Showers, Laundry Tubs, Disposal Station, 100 Picnic Sites, Swim Beach, Launch Ramp.
Campground Ph: (530) 538-2217.

Group Camps: 6 Well-Developed Group Camps Each Accommodating 25 People. Fee: $40.
Campground Ph: (530) 538-2217.

BIDWELL CANYON:

75 R.V. Sites to 40 Feet (Include Boat Trailer in Total RV length) - Full Hookups - Fee: $20
Launch Ramp, Boat Rentals, Full Service Marina - Ph: (530) 589-3165)
Grocery Store, Laundry Tubs, Snack Bar. Campground Ph: (530) 538-2218.
Reserve: Ph: (800) 444-7275

BOAT-IN CAMPS: *NO Drinking Water*

109 sites at: Craig Saddle, Foreman Point, Goat Ranch, Bloomer,
Primitive Area - North Point, Knoll, South Cove, Bloomer. Fee: $10.

Group Camp for 75 People Located at South Bloomer : Fees: $30 - $45
Tables, Toilets,
Reserve: Ph: (800) 444-7275

LIME SADDLE MARINA, P.O. Box 1088, Paradise 95969—Ph: (530) 877-2414 or (800) 834-7517
Convenient location 1-1/2 miles of Hwy. 70 on Pentz Rd.
Full Service Marina, 5-Lane Launch Ramp, Gas, Boat Shop, OMC-Johnson Sales/Service.
Rentals: Houseboats, Ski Boats, Fishing & Patio Boats, Sea Doos
Overnight Moorings, Docks, Covered & Open Slips, Water Ski Sales and Rentals, Marine Supplies
Grocery Store, Bait & Tackle, Ice, Propane & Pumpout Station.

BIDWELL CANYON MARINA, 801 Bidwell Canyon Road, Oroville 95966—Ph: (530) 589-3165 or (800) 637-1767
Full Service Marina, Gas.
Rentals: Fishing, Patio, Houseboats, Water Ski Sales and Rentals, Overnight Moorings,
Docks, Covered & Open Slips, Dry Storage,
Gift Shop, Grocery Store, Bait & Tackle Shop, Pumpout Station and Ice.

PAVED LAUNCH RAMPS ALSO LOCATED AT:

SPILLWAY: 3-Lane Launch Ramp, Parking, Toilets, Overnight Camping for Self-Contained R.V.s.
ENTERPRISE: Free 2-Lane Launch Ramp, Cartop Launch During Low Water.

THERMALITO FOREBAY

The North End of the Forebay is for Day Use. There are 300 Surface Acres. Facilities include a 2-lane launch ramp, sandy swim beach , picnic tables, shade ramadas, potable water and many lovely trees. This area is for sailboats and other non-power boats only. *The Group Area is by Reservation at Park Headquarters.*
The South End of the Forebay has a 4-1ane launch ramp. There is no shade or potable water. Chemical toilets.

LITTLE GRASS VALLEY, SLY CREEK and LOST CREEK RESERVOIRS

Little Grass Valley, at 5,040 feet elevation, and Sly Creek, at 3,560 feet elevation, are pretty Lakes in the Plumas National Forest. Little Grass Valley which has a surface area of 1,615 acres is a good boating lake. There is an abundance of developed campsites in this forested area. Sly Creek Reser-

voir has 562 surface acres with facilities for boating and camping. Its neighbor, Lost Creek Reservoir, is surrounded by private land except for a small portion of Forest Service land on the north side which is relatively unusable due to the steep slopes.

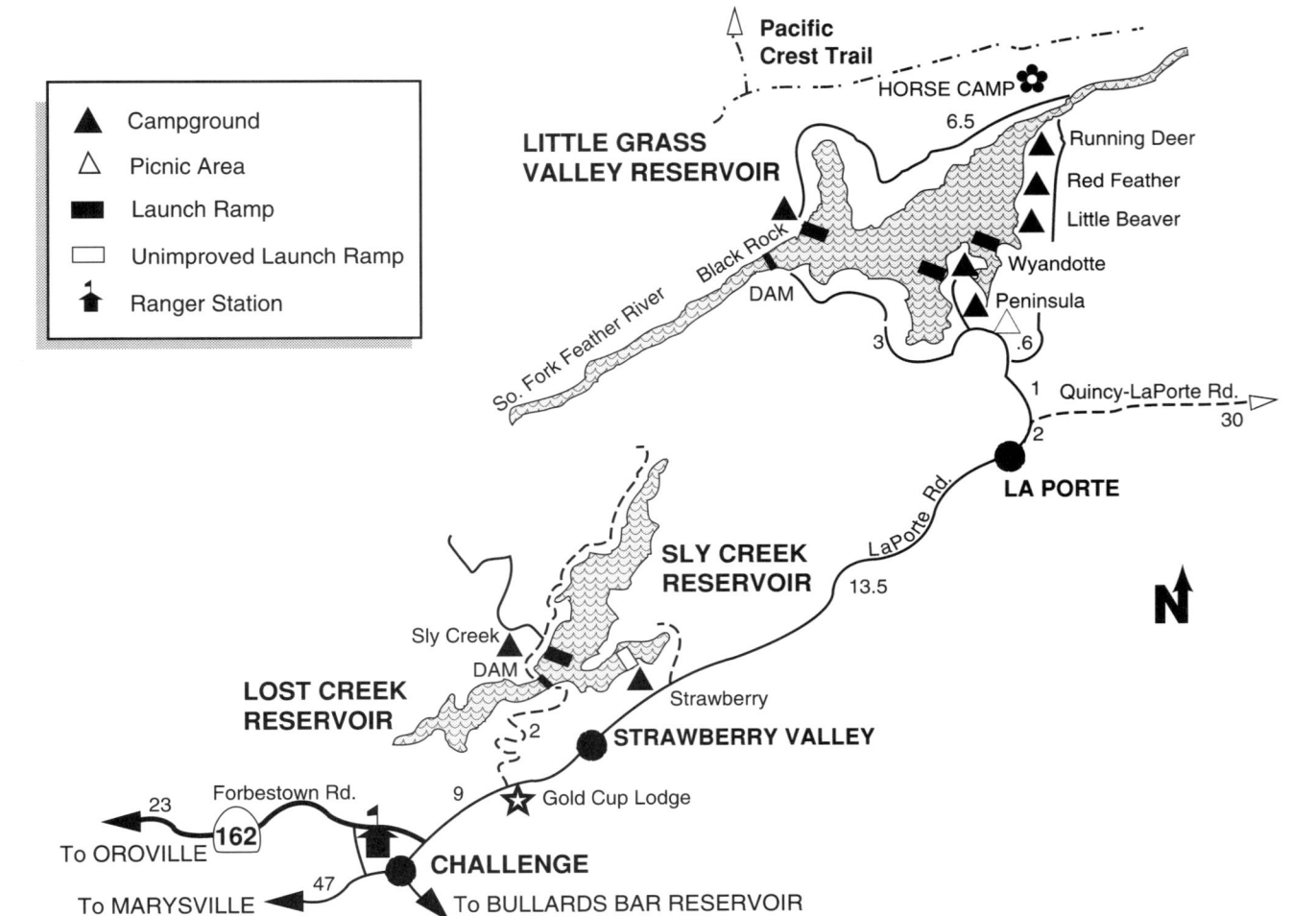

CAMPING	BOATING	RECREATION	OTHER
Little Grass Valley: 320 Dev. Sites Tents/ R.V.s Plus Horse Camp 40 Ft. Max. Length Fee: $8 - $12 Reservations for Red Feather Reservations: (800) 280-CAMP 2 Disposal Stations Sly Creek: 34 Dev. Sites for Tents & R.V.s Fee: $12	Little Grass Valley: Open to Small Boats 3 Paved Launch Ramps Sly Creek: Open to Small Boats 1 Paved Launch Ramp 1 Cartop Launch Ramp	Fishing: Rainbow, Brook & Brown Trout Swimming Picnicking Hiking & Riding Backpacking Nature Study Hunting: Waterfowl Upland Game & Deer	Facilities: 3-1/2 Miles at La Porte Abandoned Mining Towns Nearby Access to: Pacific Crest Trail

INFORMATION: Feather River Ranger District, 875 Mitchell Ave., Oroville 95965—Ph: (530) 534-6500 or 675-1146

GOLD LAKE and THE LAKES BASIN RECREATION AREA

More than 50 small glacial lakes and numerous streams filled with trout are located in this scenic area. Gold Lake is the largest. Elevations range from 5,000 to 6,000 feet. Several of the Lakes can be reached by car but many can only be reached by trail. This is a popular fly fishing area especially along the Middle Fork of the Feather River which has been designated a natural Wild and Scenic River. The Lakes Basin is in both the Plumas and Tahoe National Forests. The hiker and packer will find trails leading to the Pacific Crest Trail. Although this area remains relatively unspoiled, there are a number of resorts and facilities that complement the natural setting of this beautiful country.

...Continued....

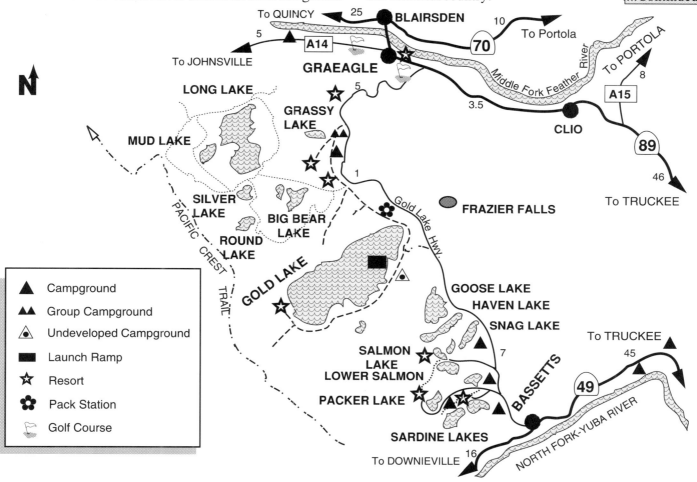

INFORMATION: Beckwourth Ranger Station, P.O. Box 7, 23 Mohawk Rd., Blairsden 96103—Ph: (530) 836-2575

CAMPING	BOATING	RECREATION	OTHER
US Forest Service Campgrounds in Area Fee: $12	Gold Lake: Power, Row, Sail, Windsurfing & Waterskiing Launch Ramp	Fishing: Rainbow, Brown & Brook Trout Mackinaw	Numerous Facilities & Resorts in this Area
Lakes in North Area: Beckwourth Ranger Sta. Ph: (530) 836-2575 Group Camp to 25 People - Fee: $45 Reserve: Ph: (800) 280-CAMP		Picnicking Hiking & Riding Trails Backpacking Gold Lake Pack Station Ph: (530) 836-0940 Swimming	*See Following Page* Plumas County Visitors Bureau Ph: 800-326-2247
Lakes in South Area: North Yuba Ranger Dist. Ph: (530) 288-3231		Hunting: Deer Golf Courses: 9-Hole & 18-Hole	Sierra County Chamber of Commerce Ph: 800-200-4949

GOLD LAKE and THE LAKES BASIN RECREATION AREA............Continued

The following is a list of some accommodations in the Lakes Basin Recreation Area, in alphabetical order. Many of the lodges and resorts are fully booked one year in advance in season so reservations are imperative.

CHALET VIEW LODGE - Box 20575, Highway 70, Graeagle 96103—Ph: (530) 832-0335
6 Housekeeping Cabins, Playground, Putting Green, BBQ, Pets OK, Open mid-April to mid-October.

CLIO'S RIVER'S EDGE R V PARK - Box 111, 3754 Highway 89, Clio 96106—Ph: (530) 836-2375
R.V.s to 40 feet, Hookups, Showers, Cable TV, Open May 1 to October 31.

ELWELL LAKES LODGE - Box 68, Gold Lake Rd., Blairsden 96103—Ph: (530) 836-2347
10 Housekeeping Cabins, B&B Rooms, Main Lodge with Recreation Room, Complimentary Boats for Guests, Creek-filled Swimming Pool, Picnic Area, BBQ, No Pets, Open June-September.

FEATHER RIVER INN - Box 67, Blairsden 96103—Ph: (530) 836-2623 OR (888) 324-6400
3/4 mile west of Blairsden, 50 Units, Conference Facilities, Catering, Golf Course, Golf Package Available, No Pets.

FEATHER RIVER PARK RESORT, Box 37, Highway 89, Blairsden 96103—Ph: (530) 836-2328
35 Housekeeping Log Cabins, Weekly Rental Only from mid-June to Labor Day, 3 Swimming Pools, 9-Hole Golf Course, Tennis Court, Playground, Bicycle Rental, Lodge with Games & Snacks, Pets OK, Open May to mid-October.

GOLD LAKE BEACH RESORT, 5920 Butler Rd., Penryn 95663--Ph: (530) 836-2491
On Gold Lake's Edge, Pick-up at Dock, Cabins, Complete Meal Service, 3-Night Minimun, Open June-September.
GOLD LAKE PACK STATION & STABLES, 1540 Chandler Rd., Quincy 95971—Ph: (530) 836-0940

GOLD LAKE LODGE, Box 25, Graeagle 96103—Ph: (530) 836-2350
11 Cabins, Breakfast & Dinner Included, Maid Service, Family Discounts, Daily/Weekly Rates, Lodge, Restaurant, No Pets, Open mid-June to Early October.

GRAY EAGLE LODGE, Box 38, Gold Lake Rd., Graeagle 96103—Ph: (530) 836-2511
18 Cabins, Breakfast & Dinner Included, 3-Night Min., Lodge, Restaurant, Game Room, Pets OK, Open May-October.

HIGH COUNTRY INN, Highway 49 & Gold Lake Rd., Sierra City 96125—Ph: (530) 862-1530 or (800) 862-1530
4 Rooms, Views of Sierra Buttes & River, Deck, No Pets, Open All Year.

LAYMAN RESORT, Box 8, Highway 70, Blairsden 96103—Ph: (530) 836-2356
13 Housekeeping Cabins, Picnic & BBQ Area, Off-Season Rates, Open April to early November.

LITTLE BEAR R.V. PARK, Box 103, Blairsden 96103—Ph: (530) 836-2774
R.V.s to 40 ft., Hookups, Satellite TV, Showers, Store, Open May 1 to October 31.

MOVIN' WEST TRAILER RANCH, Box 1010, 305 Johnsville Rd., Graeagle 96103—Ph: (530) 836-2614
R.V.s to 40 Feet, Hookups, Showers, Cable TV, Open May 1 to October 31.

PACKER LAKE LODGE, Box 237, 3901 Packer Lake Rd., Sierra City 96125—Ph: (530) 862-1221
14 Cabins, 8 with Kitchens, Complimentary Boat Included, Store, Restaurant, Bar, Pets OK, Open May-October.

RIVER PINES RESORT, Box 249, Highway 89, Clio 96106—Ph: (530) 836-2552 or in California (800) 696-2551
1/4 Mile North of Graeagle, 62 Units, Motel Rooms, Some with Kitchens, Housekeeping Cottages, Pool, Jacuzzi, Playground, Recreation Room, BBQ Area, Restaurant, Lounge, Golf Packages, Open All Year.

SALMON LAKE LODGE, Box 121, Sierra City 96125—Write for Information
Cabins, Central Utility House with Refrigerator & Showers, Bring Own Sleeping Bags, Pans & Groceries, Parking at East End of Lake, Barge Transports Guest & Baggage Across Lake, Fishing Boats, Sailboats and Canoes for Guests.

SARDINE LAKES RESORT—Ph: (530) 862-1196 - Cabins, Lunch & Dinner by Reservations, Rental Boats

Bullards Bar Reservoir is at an elevation of 2,000 feet in the Tahoe and Plumas National Forests surrounded by rugged countryside. This beautiful large Lake of 4,700 surface acres has 56 shoreline miles. The area is heavily wooded so all campsites are shaded by trees. All boating is allowed and the waterskiing is some of the best in California. Fishing is open year around for both warm and cold water fish. This is a prime

Lake for Kokanee salmon. The Yuba County Water Agency and the U.S. Forest Service maintain 30 boat access camps and lakeside camping. The Emerald Cove Marina is a full service facility offering houseboat and fishing boat rentals and private houseboat moorings. The Emerald Cove Resort & Marina make Bullards Bar Reservoir a good place to visit for a variety of outdoor recreation.

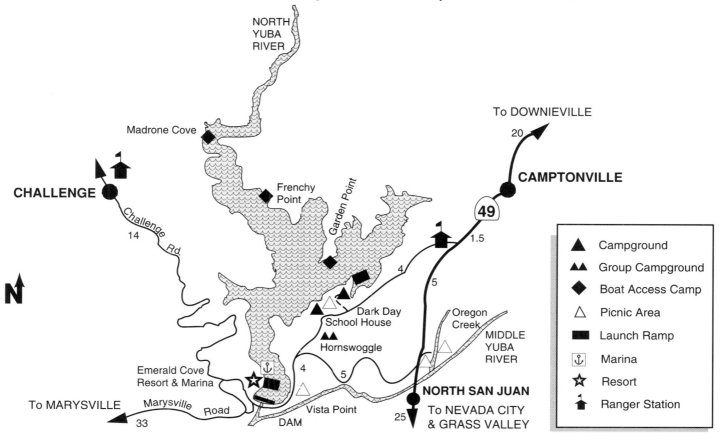

INFORMATION: Emerald Cove Resort & Marina, P.O. Box 1954, Nevada City 95959—Ph: (530) 692-3200

CAMPING	BOATING	RECREATION	OTHER

Emerald Cove Resort:
   Accepts Reservations
   Dev. Sites for Tents
     & RVs
   Boat Access Camps
   Shoreline Camping
   Fee: $14 up to 6 People
Hornswoggle Group Camps
   4 Sites - 15-25 People
     Fee: $50
   1 Site - 35-50 People
     Fee: $100
Plus $5 Reservation Fee
	Open to All Boating
	Waterskiing
	Launch Ramps - No Fee
	Full Service Marina
	Gas and Propane
	Rentals: Fishing, Ski,
	   Patio, Paddle &
	   Houseboats
	Private Houseboat
	   Moorings
	Overnight Slips &
	   Dry Storage
		Fishing: Rainbow &
		   Brown Trout,
		   Bluegill, Catfish,
		   Crappie, Large &
		   Smallmouth Bass,
		   Kokanee Salmon
		Swimming
		Picnicking
		Hiking Trails
			Snack Bar
			Groceries
			Beer, Wine, Ice
			Bait & Tackle
			
			USFS-N. Yuba Ranger
			   Station
			   Ph: (530) 288-3231

BOWMAN LAKE

Bowman Lake is the largest of several small Lakes in the scenic Bowman Road Area of the Tahoe National Forest. Bowman is 6 miles south of Jackson Meadows Reservoir and 16 miles north of Highway 20. These are often steep and rocky roads; 4-wheel drive vehicles are advised. The Lakes range in altitude from 5,600 feet to 7,000 feet in this beautiful high Sierra country. The Forest Service maintains a number of campsites in this area but be sure to bring your own drinking water. Stream and lake fishing can be excellent in this rugged and remote but scenic environment.

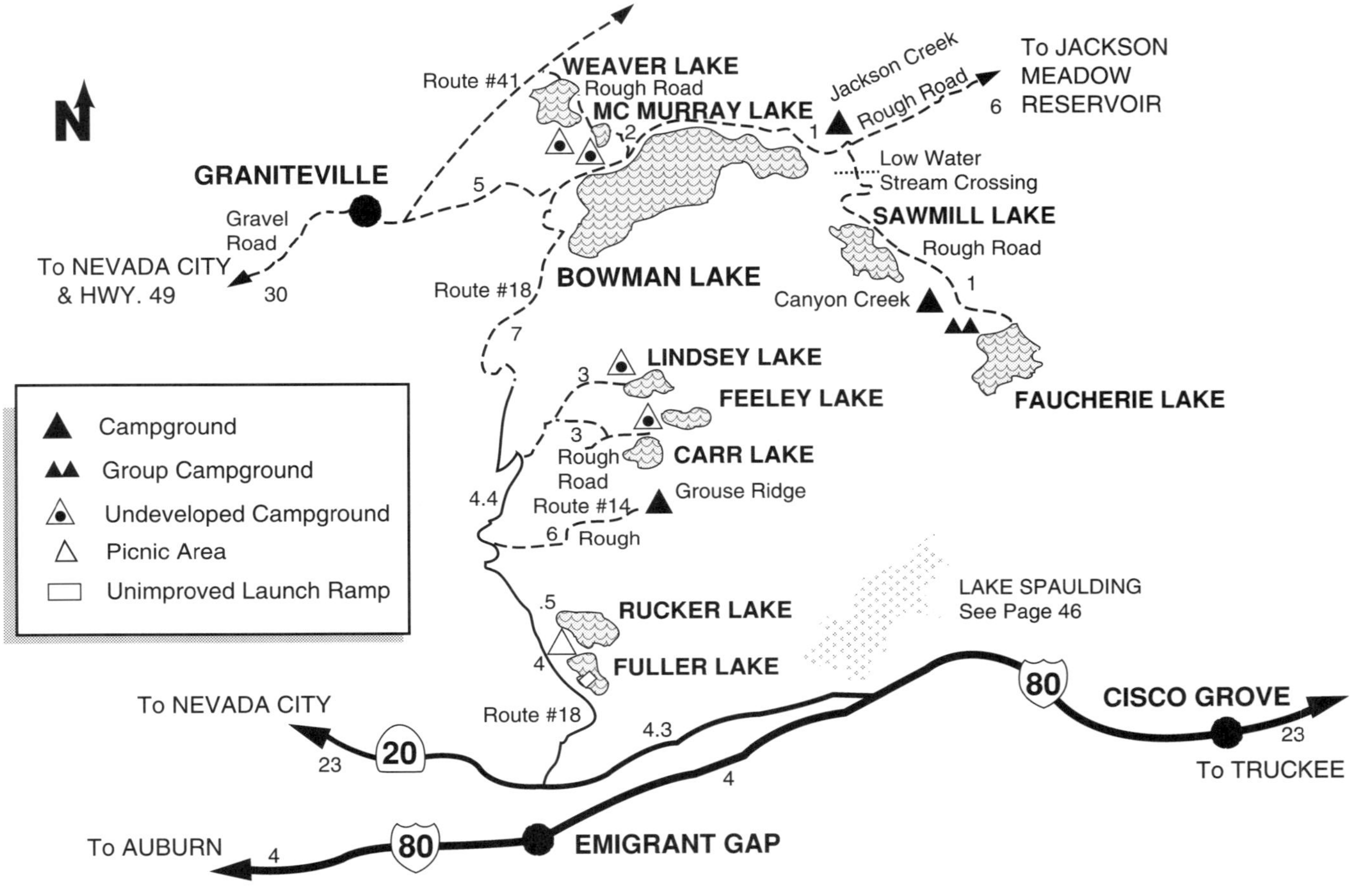

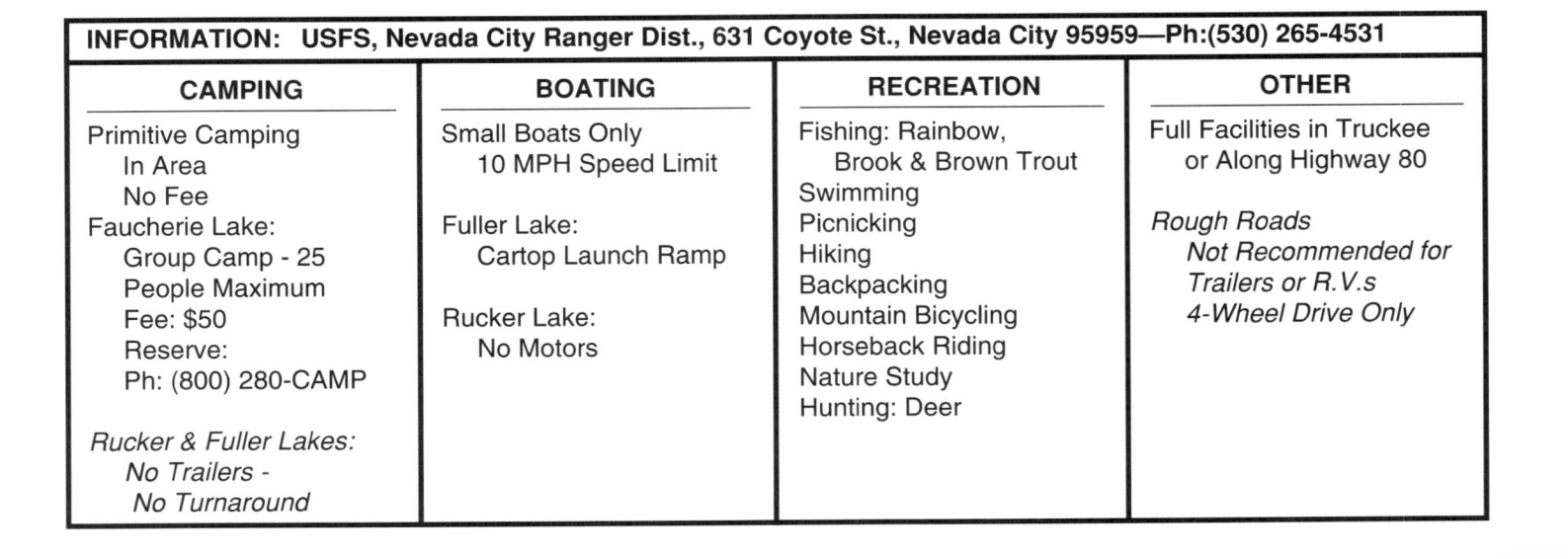

INFORMATION: USFS, Nevada City Ranger Dist., 631 Coyote St., Nevada City 95959—Ph:(530) 265-4531			
CAMPING	**BOATING**	**RECREATION**	**OTHER**
Primitive Camping In Area No Fee Faucherie Lake: Group Camp - 25 People Maximum Fee: $50 Reserve: Ph: (800) 280-CAMP *Rucker & Fuller Lakes: No Trailers - No Turnaround*	Small Boats Only 10 MPH Speed Limit Fuller Lake: Cartop Launch Ramp Rucker Lake: No Motors	Fishing: Rainbow, Brook & Brown Trout Swimming Picnicking Hiking Backpacking Mountain Bicycling Horseback Riding Nature Study Hunting: Deer	Full Facilities in Truckee or Along Highway 80 *Rough Roads Not Recommended for Trailers or R.V.s 4-Wheel Drive Only*

FORDYCE, STERLING, EAGLE, KIDD, CASCADE, LONG and SERENE LAKES

These Lakes, off Interstate Highway 80 near Soda Springs, rest at elevations of about 7,000 feet in the Tahoe National Forest. This beautiful high Sierra country offers a variety of recreational opportunities. Boating is limited to non-powered craft with limited facilities, but you will find rentals at Serene Lakes. The angler will find trout and catfish. Numerous trails invite the hiker, backpacker and equestrian to get away from it all in this natural paradise. The roads into Eagle, Fordyce, and Sterling are not advised for any vehicles but 4-wheelers.

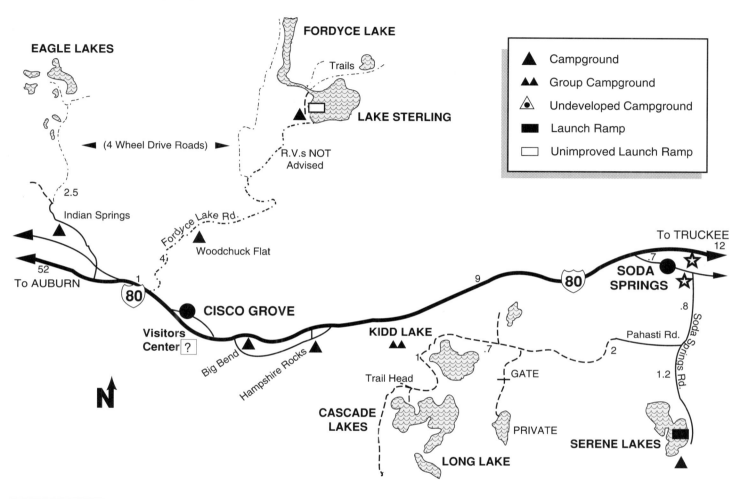

▲	Campground
▲▲	Group Campground
⚠	Undeveloped Campground
■	Launch Ramp
▭	Unimproved Launch Ramp

INFORMATION: Chamber of Commerce 10065 Donner Pass Rd., Truckee 96161—Ph: (530) 587-2757

CAMPING	BOATING	RECREATION	OTHER
U.S.F.S. Nevada City Ranger District Sites for Tents & R.V.s - Call for Fees Ph: (530) 265-4531 P.G.&E. Kidd Lake: Group Campground to 100 People Maximum 10 People per Site Fee Reserve: Ph: (916) 386-5164	Electric Motors Allowed at Sterling Lake No Motors at Other Lakes Rentals at Serene Lakes	Fishing: Trout & Catfish Swimming Picnicking Numerous Hiking & Riding Trails Mountain Bicycling Horseback Riding Backpacking Nature Study Photography	Facilities at Cisco Grove & Soda Springs

JACKSON MEADOW RECREATION AREA

The Jackson Meadow Recreation Area is at an elevation of 6,200 feet in the Tahoe National Forest. This area of forested slopes, alpine meadows, lakes and streams provides an abundance of recreational opportunities. Jackson Meadows Reservoir is the hub with well maintained camping and recreational facilities dotting its 11 miles of shoreline. Nearby Milton Reservoir and the Middle Fork of the Yuba River between Jackson Meadow and Milton are subject to specific artificial lure, species and size limitations. Refer to the California Sport Fishing Regulations for details. The hiker, backpacker and equestrian will find a trailhead to the Pacific Crest Trail nearby.

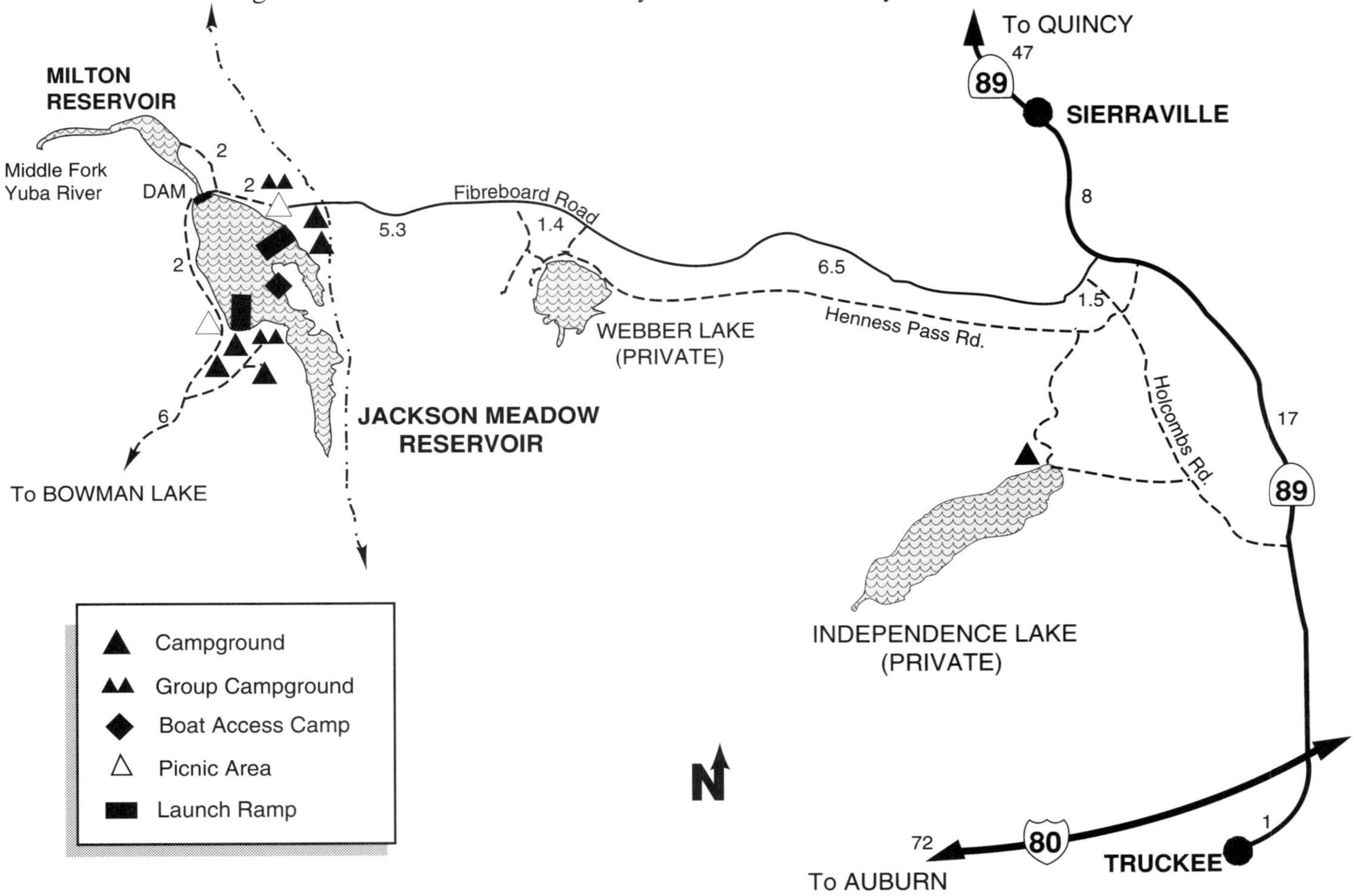

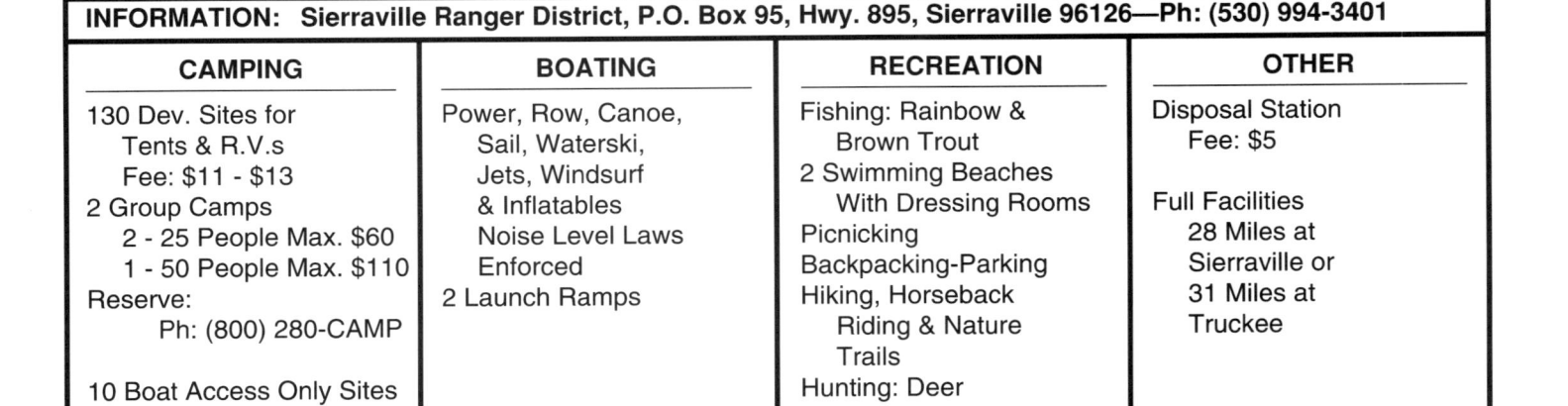

INFORMATION:	Sierraville Ranger District, P.O. Box 95, Hwy. 895, Sierraville 96126—Ph: (530) 994-3401		
CAMPING	**BOATING**	**RECREATION**	**OTHER**
130 Dev. Sites for Tents & R.V.s Fee: $11 - $13 2 Group Camps 2 - 25 People Max. $60 1 - 50 People Max. $110 Reserve: Ph: (800) 280-CAMP 10 Boat Access Only Sites	Power, Row, Canoe, Sail, Waterski, Jets, Windsurf & Inflatables Noise Level Laws Enforced 2 Launch Ramps	Fishing: Rainbow & Brown Trout 2 Swimming Beaches With Dressing Rooms Picnicking Backpacking-Parking Hiking, Horseback Riding & Nature Trails Hunting: Deer Only in Season Outside Recreation Area	Disposal Station Fee: $5 Full Facilities 28 Miles at Sierraville or 31 Miles at Truckee

STAMPEDE RESERVOIR

Stampede Reservoir is at an elevation of 5,949 feet in the Tahoe National Forest northeast of Truckee. Stampede has a surface area of 3,440 acres with 25 miles of sage and coniferous covered shoreline. This large open Lake offers westerly winds for the sailor, and its vast open waters are enjoyed by the waterskier. Fishing is very popular and anglers will find rainbow and brown trout. While the campground at Davies Creek has limited facilities, a concessionaire, under permit from the Forest Service, maintains nicely developed campsites near the Lake at Logger Campground. The Reservoir is lower during the end of the season and in drought years.

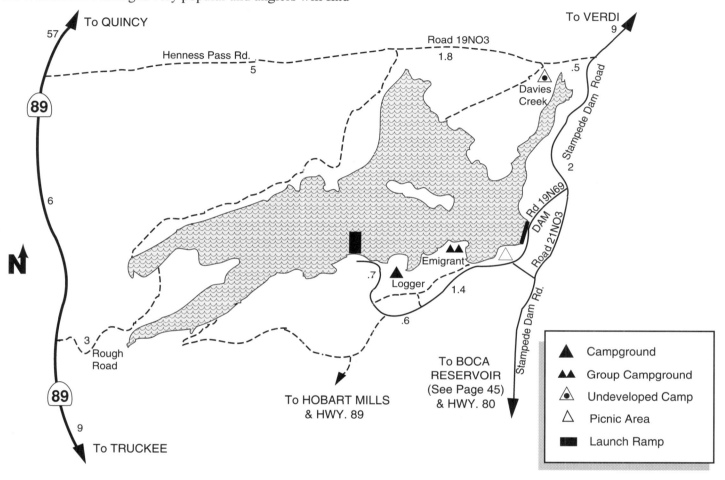

▲	Campground
▲▲	Group Campground
⊙	Undeveloped Camp
△	Picnic Area
▬	Launch Ramp

INFORMATION: Truckee Ranger District, 10342 Highway 89 North, Truckee 96161—Ph: (530) 478-6257

CAMPING	BOATING	RECREATION	OTHER

U.S.F.S. - Logger:
  252 Dev. Sites for
Tents & R.V.s - Fee: $13
  Disposal Station
Emigrant Group Camps:
2-25 People - Fee: $50
2-150 People - Fee: $100
Reserve Both:
  Ph: (800) 280-CAMP
Davies Creek:
  7 Primitive Sites
  No Water - No Fee
  Horses Allowed
	Power, Row, Canoe
	  Sail, Waterski,
	  Jets, Windsurf
	  & Inflatables
	
	Water Low In Fall
	
	Launch Ramp Extended
	  for Low Water
	  Launching
		Fishing: Rainbow
		  Brown Trout,
		  Kokanee Salmon
		Swimming
		Picnicking
		Mountain Bicycling
		Hunting: Deer - By Special
		  Draw Only
			Full Facilities
			  14 Miles at Truckee

PROSSER CREEK RESERVOIR

Prosser Creek Reservoir is at an elevation of 5,711 located in the scenic Tahoe National Forest. This 740 surface acre Lake rests in an open canyon surrounded by 11 miles of sage and coniferous-covered hills. The Donner Camp picnic area was the site of the Donner Party tragedy of the winter of 1846-47.

Boating is limited to 10 MPH. Waterskiing, power boating and jets are not allowed at this facility. Launching is hampered in the fall by low water conditions. You can fish for trout and the scenery is beautiful with grassy open meadows at this high elevation Reservoir.

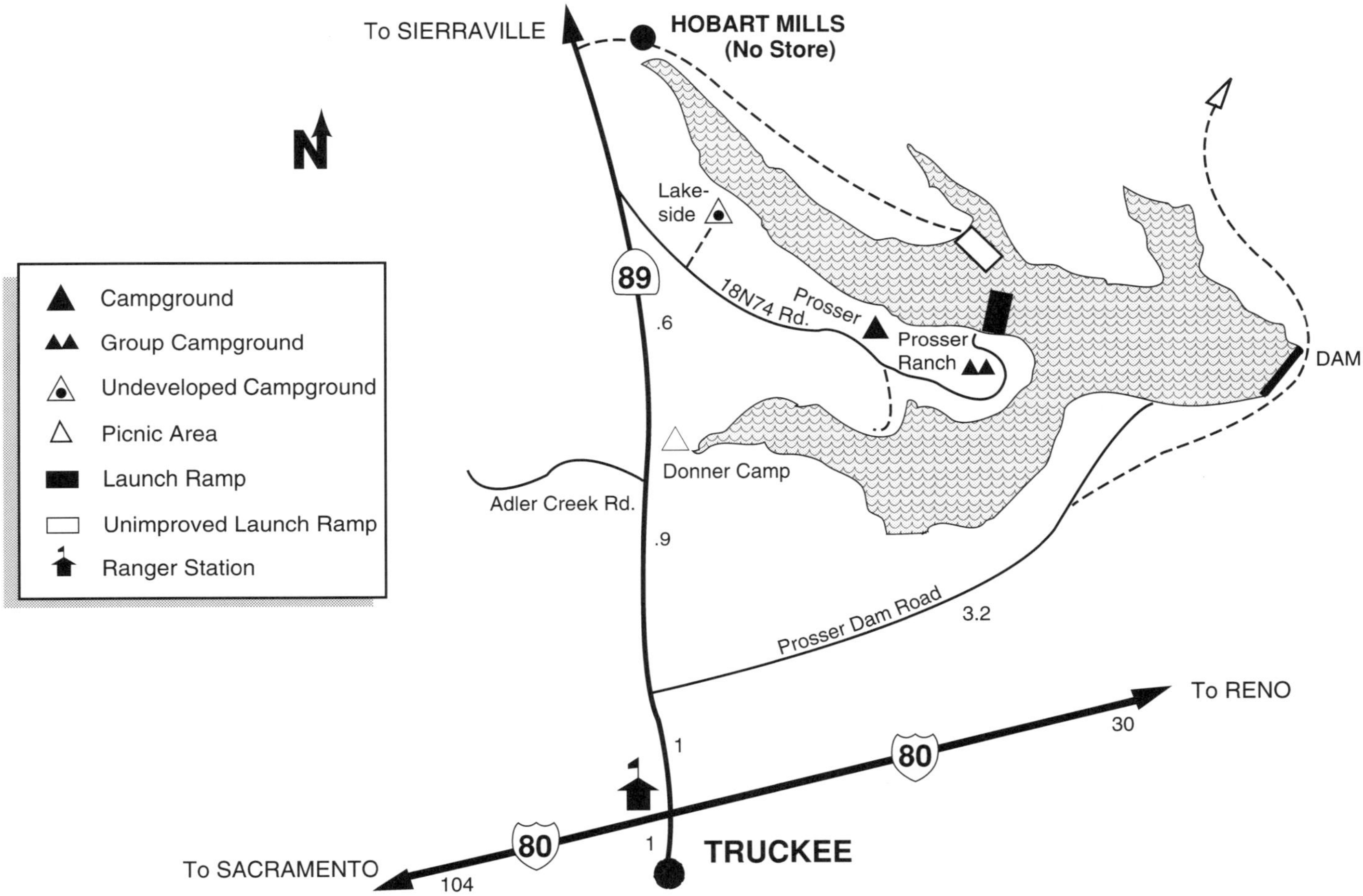

To SIERRAVILLE

HOBART MILLS (No Store)

N

Lake-side

89

.6

18N74 Rd.

Prosser

Prosser Ranch

Prosser Ranch

DAM

Donner Camp

Adler Creek Rd.

.9

Prosser Dam Road   3.2

To RENO

30

80

1

To SACRAMENTO

80

104

1

TRUCKEE

Legend

- ▲ Campground
- ▲▲ Group Campground
- ⊙ Undeveloped Campground
- △ Picnic Area
- ◼ Launch Ramp
- ▢ Unimproved Launch Ramp
- ⌂ Ranger Station

INFORMATION: Truckee Ranger District, 10342 Highway 89 North, Truckee 96161—Ph: (530) 478-6257

CAMPING	BOATING	RECREATION	OTHER

Prosser Family:
    29 Dev. Sites for
    Tents & R.V.s to 24 Feet
    Fee: $10
Prosser Ranch Group
    Camp - Fee: $75
Reserve Both:
    Ph: (800) 280-CAMP
Lakeside:
    24 Primitive Sites
    for Tents & R.V.s
        Water
    Fee: $8
	Power, Row, Canoe,
	    Sail, Windsurf, &
	    Inflatables
	Speed Limit- 10 MPH
	Launch Ramps
		Fishing: Rainbow Trout
		Swimming
		Picnicking at
		    Donner Camp
		Hiking
		Interpretive Trail at
		    Donner Camp
		Hunting: Deer
			Full Facilities - 5
			    Miles at Truckee

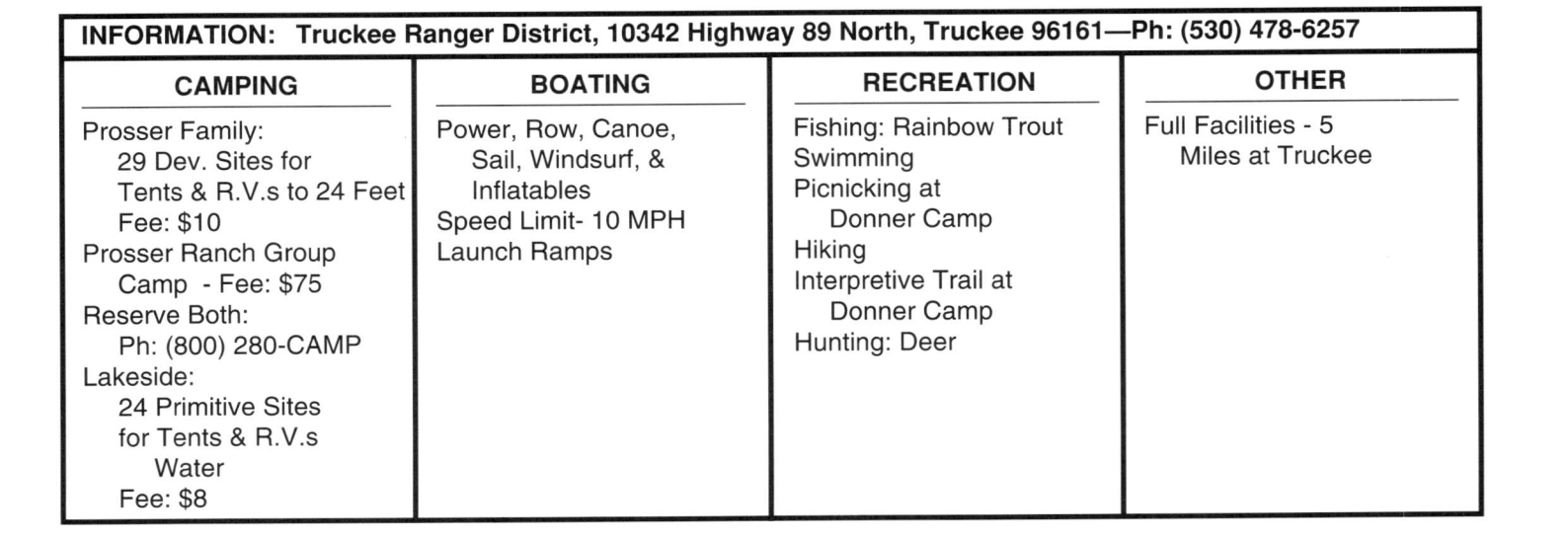

Boca Reservoir is in the Tahoe National Forest at an elevation of 5,700 feet. The Lake has a surface area of 980 acres and 14 miles of shoreline which is a lovely combination of steep bluffs and low grassy areas amid tall pine trees. Campgrounds include U.S. Forest Service sites which all charge fees. The many inlets and prevailing winds create an excel-lent atmosphere for sailing and boating. *The speed limit in all inlets is 5 mph.* The water level lowers at the end of the season. Boca is fed by Stampede Reservoir, 5 miles above. *During drought conditions boat ramp can be completely out of the water. Always check before you leave home.*

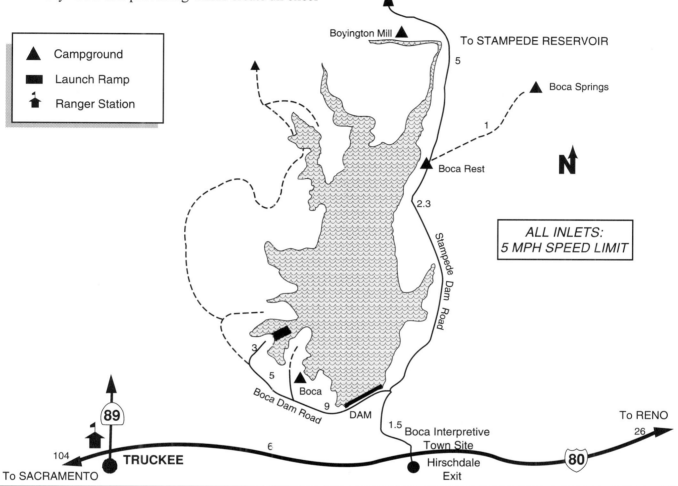

Boyington Mill

To STAMPEDE RESERVOIR

5

Boca Springs

1

Boca Rest

2.3

Stampede Dam Road

N

ALL INLETS:
5 MPH SPEED LIMIT

Campground
Launch Ramp
Ranger Station

3

5

Boca

9

DAM

Boca Dam Road

6

89

104

To SACRAMENTO

TRUCKEE

1.5 Boca Interpretive
Town Site

Hirschdale
Exit

80

To RENO

26

INFORMATION: Truckee Ranger District, 10342 Highway 89 North, Truckee 96161—Ph: (530) 478-6257

CAMPING	BOATING	RECREATION	OTHER
Boca: 20 Sites Fee: $10 - No Water Boca Rest: 25 Sites Fee: $8 - Water Boca Springs: 17 Sites Fee: $10 - Water Horses Permitted Boyington Mill: 12 Sites Fee: $10 - No Water Call USFS for R.V. and Trailer Access Information	Power, Row, Canoe, Sail, Waterski, Jets, Windsurf & Inflatables Launch Ramp	Fishing: Rainbow Trout Swimming Picnicking Hiking Horseback Riding Hunting: Deer	Full Facilities - 7 Miles in Truckee Limited Facilities at Hirschdale Exit

LAKE SPAULDING

Lake Spaulding rests at an elevation of 5,014 feet in a glacier carved bowl of granite. The Lake has a surface area of 698 acres surrounded by giant rocks and conifers. Now a part of Pacific Gas and Electric Company's Drum-Spaulding Project, the dam was originally built in 1912 for hydraulic mining. P.G. & E. operates the facilities at this pretty Lake which includes a campground and launch ramp. The Lake is open to all types of boating although launching large boats can be difficult. Fishing from the bank or boat is often rewarding. This is a fine Lake for a family outing with a spectacular setting of granite boulders dipping into the clear, blue waters.

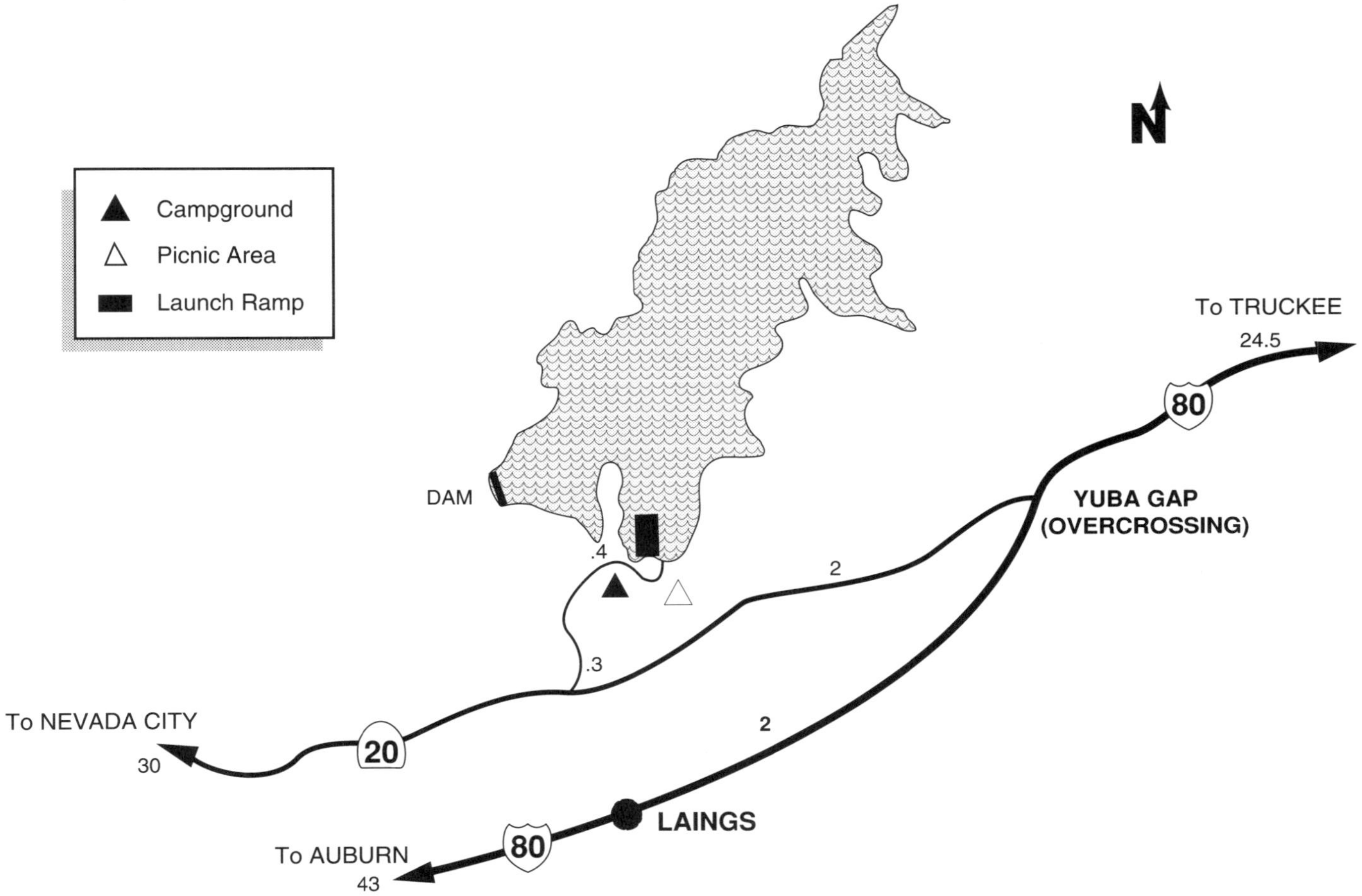

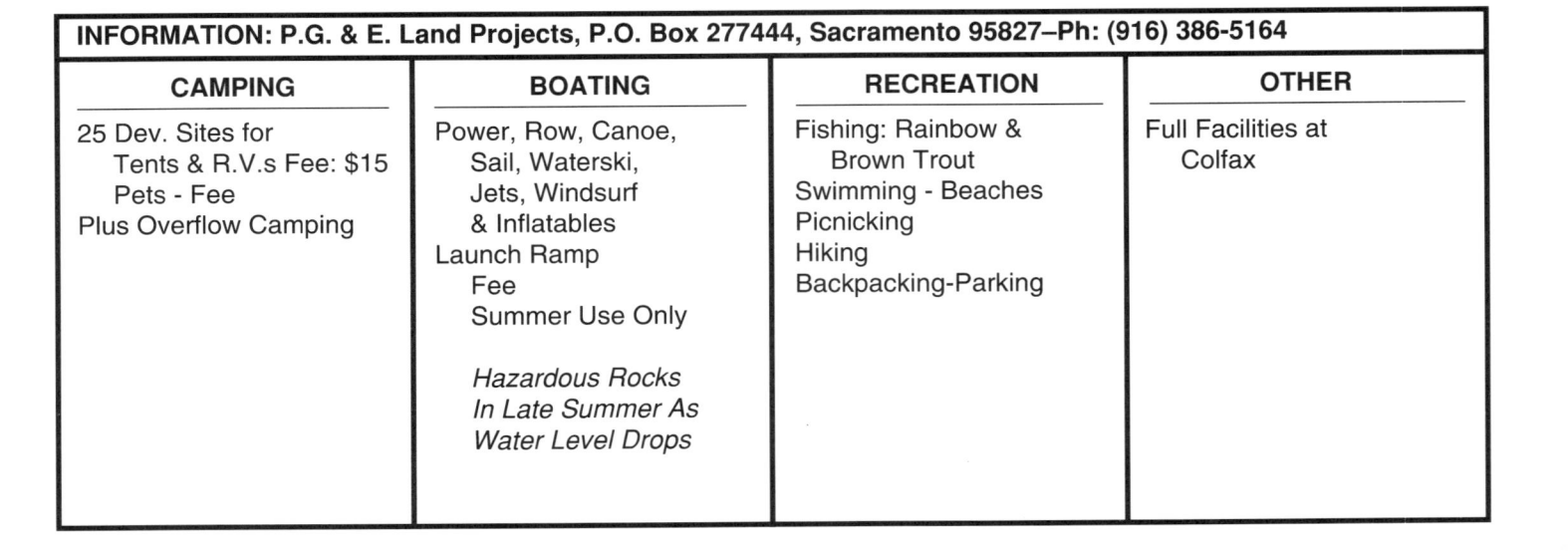

▲	Campground
△	Picnic Area
■	Launch Ramp

To TRUCKEE 24.5
80
YUBA GAP (OVERCROSSING)
DAM
.4
2
.3
To NEVADA CITY 30
20
2
To AUBURN 43
80
LAINGS

INFORMATION: P.G. & E. Land Projects, P.O. Box 277444, Sacramento 95827–Ph: (916) 386-5164			
CAMPING	**BOATING**	**RECREATION**	**OTHER**
25 Dev. Sites for Tents & R.V.s Fee: $15 Pets - Fee Plus Overflow Camping	Power, Row, Canoe, Sail, Waterski, Jets, Windsurf & Inflatables Launch Ramp Fee Summer Use Only *Hazardous Rocks In Late Summer As Water Level Drops*	Fishing: Rainbow & Brown Trout Swimming - Beaches Picnicking Hiking Backpacking-Parking	Full Facilities at Colfax

Donner Lake is at an elevation of 5,963 feet in the Tahoe National Forest next to Interstate 80 west of Truckee. The Lake is 3 miles long and 3/4 mile wide with a shoreline of 7-1/2 miles of high alpine woods. Donner has numerous private homes (no access) on the south shore and portions of the north shore. The Donner State Memorial Park, on the east shore, was named after the tragic Donner Party whose fate in the winter of 1846 attests to the hardships encountered by California's early settlers. This well-maintained park has 154 developed campsites with campfire programs and nature trails. The Emigrant Trail Museum is open daily from 10 a.m. to 4 p.m. The water in the Lake is clear and cold. A popular sailing Lake, Donner has its own local Sailing Club. *Beware of periodic afternoon winds that can be hazardous.*

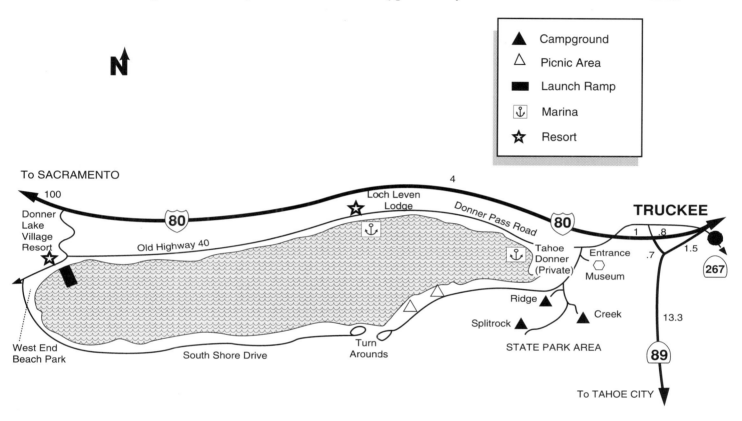

▲	Campground
△	Picnic Area
■	Launch Ramp
⚓	Marina
★	Resort

INFORMATION: Donner Memorial State Park, 12593 Donner Pass Rd., Truckee 96161--Ph: (530) 582-7892

CAMPING	BOATING	RECREATION	OTHER
Donner Memorial State Park 150 Dev. Sites for Tents & R.V.s Fee: $16 Ph: (530) 582-7892 or Reserve: Ph: (800) 444-7275 (On First Come Basis at Times) Day Use - Fee	Power, Row, Canoe, Sail, Waterski, Jets, Windsurf & Inflatables No Launching From State Park Public Launch Ramp At West End Rentals: Fishing, Sail, Pontoon & Paddleboats	Fishing: Rainbow Trout, Mackinaw, Kokanee Salmon Swimming - Beaches Picnicking Hiking Bicycle Trails Horseback Riding Trails & Rentals Campfire Programs Nature Study Playgrounds	Motels, Cabins Snack Bar Restaurant Cocktail Lounge Grocery Store Bait & Tackle Laundromat Gas Station Airport With Auto Rentals - 5 Miles Tennis, Golf, Movies Museum

MARTIS CREEK LAKE

Martis Creek Lake was California's first "Wild Trout Lake" and probably one of its most unique. Originally built in 1972 by the U. S. Army Corps of Engineers for flood control and a water supply for Reno, this 70 acre minimum pool lake was selected by the California Department of Fish and Game as an exclusive naturally producing trophy trout fishery for the endangered Lahontan Cutthroat Trout. Martis Creek is a trophy German Brown fishery in the catch and release program. The facilities and nearby 1,000 acre wildlife area are administered by the Corps of Engineers.

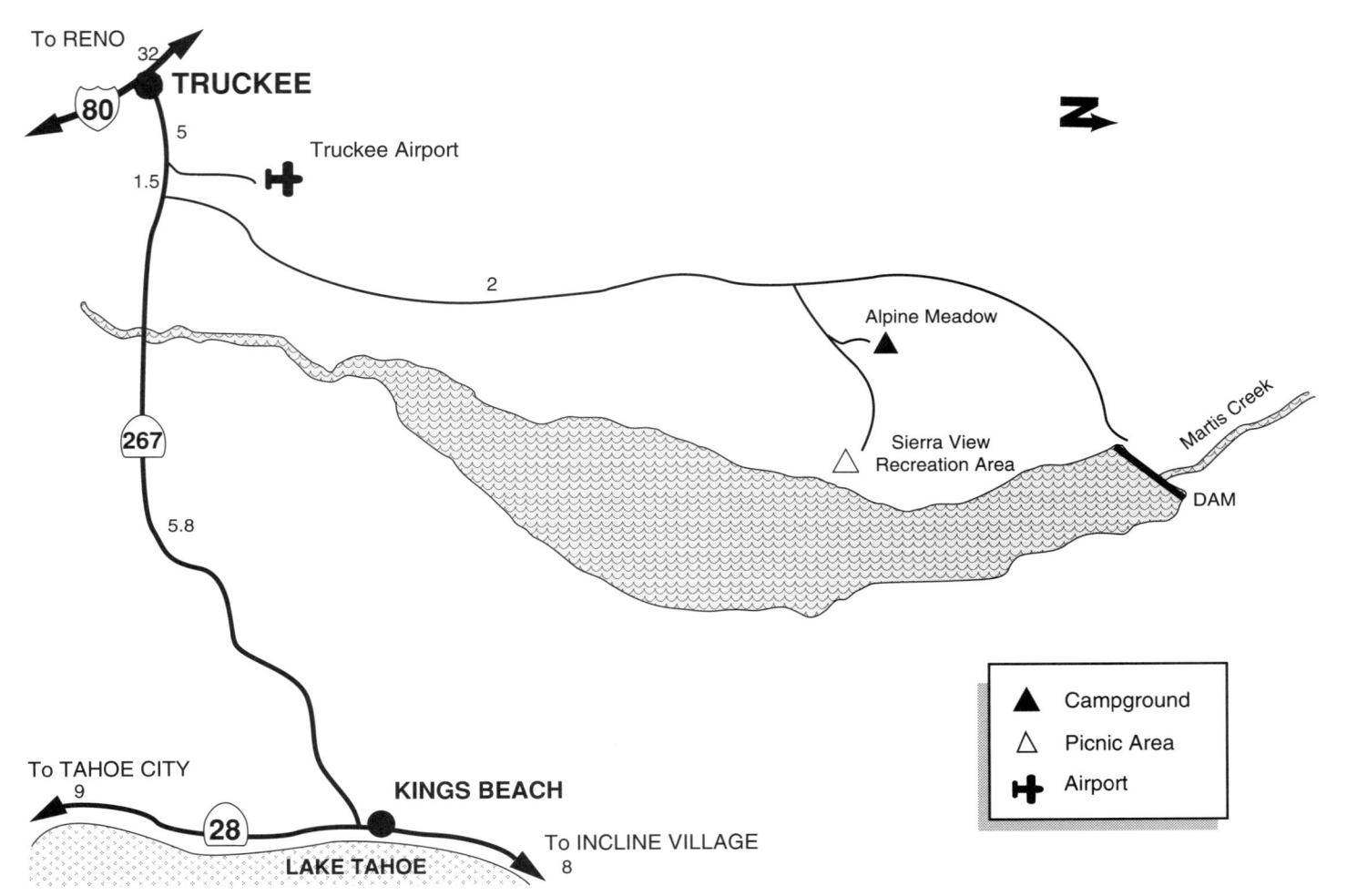

INFORMATION: Park Manager, P.O. Box 6, Smartville 95977—Ph: (530) 639-2342

CAMPING	BOATING	RECREATION	OTHER
19 Dev. Sites for R.V.s	No Power Boats	Fishing: Brown & Rainbow Trout	Full Facilities 6 Miles at Truckee
6 Dev. Sites for Tents	Sail, Row, Canoe, Inflatables & Windsurf Only	*Artificial Lures and Flies Only*	Airport Within 3 Miles
Fee: $10		*Barbless Hooks*	
		Catch & Release	
2 Handicap Sites May Be Reserved	Hand Launch Only	Picnicking Hiking	
		Nature Trails	
Campground Closed in Winter		Campfire Programs	

The Lake Tahoe Nevada State Park has jurisdiction over these Lakes and the surrounding backcountry spanning over 13,000 acres. Marlette Lake is one of the most beautiful in the Sierras. No fishing is permitted as it is a fish hatchery for rainbow trout. Fishing is allowed at Hobart Reservoir. Check for fishing conditions at Spooner Lake. This Lake is a trailhead for equestrians, hikers and mountain bikers including connections to the spectacular Tahoe Rim Trail - 150 miles and growing. Numerous trails are throughout this entire area. For details contact the State Park. Wildlife and wildflower viewing can be spectacular.

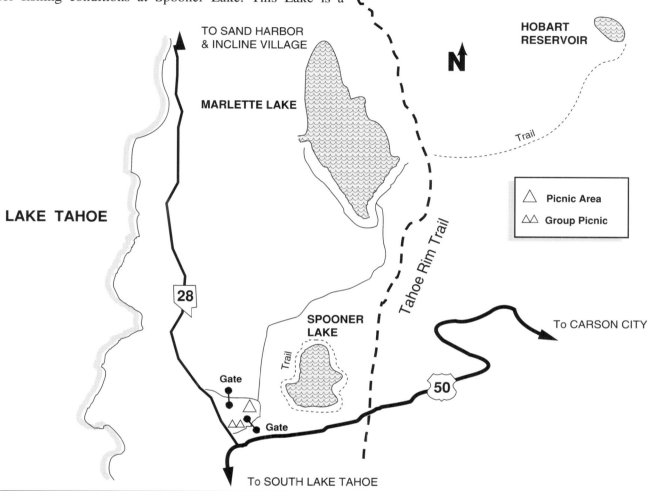

INFORMATION: Lake Tahoe Nevada State Parks, P.O. Box 8867, Incline, NV 89452—Ph: (775) 831-0494

CAMPING	BOATING	RECREATION	OTHER

Backcountry:
   In Designated Areas
	Lake Tahoe Boating
	   Facilities
	   See Page 65
		Fishing: Trout
		   Spooner Lake:
		   Catch & Release
		   Barbless Artificial
		     Lures Only
		   Fishing Clinics
		Hiking & Equestrian Trails
		Mountain Bike Trails
		   15 mph Max.
		Picnicking
		   Spooner Lake:
		   Group Use Pavilion
			Tahoe Rim Trail
			P.O. Box 4647
			Stateline, NV 89449
			   Ph: (775) 588-0686
			Information for
			   Volunteers
			   Memberships
			   Trail Maps

COLLINS LAKE

The Collins Lake Recreation Area is at an elevation of 1,200 feet in the delightful Mother Lode Country. The Lake has a surface area of over 1,000 acres with 12-1/2 miles of shoreline. The modern campground and R.V. Park provide well separated sites under oak and pine trees. There is a broad, sandy beach and many family and group picnic sites. All boating is allowed. Loud unmuffled boats and small personal watercraft such as jets are *not permitted*. Waterskiing is permitted from May 15 to September 30. One of the finest fishing Lakes in California, Collins is famous for trophy trout along with a variety of warm water species. There are zones for the exclusive use of fishermen throughout the year.

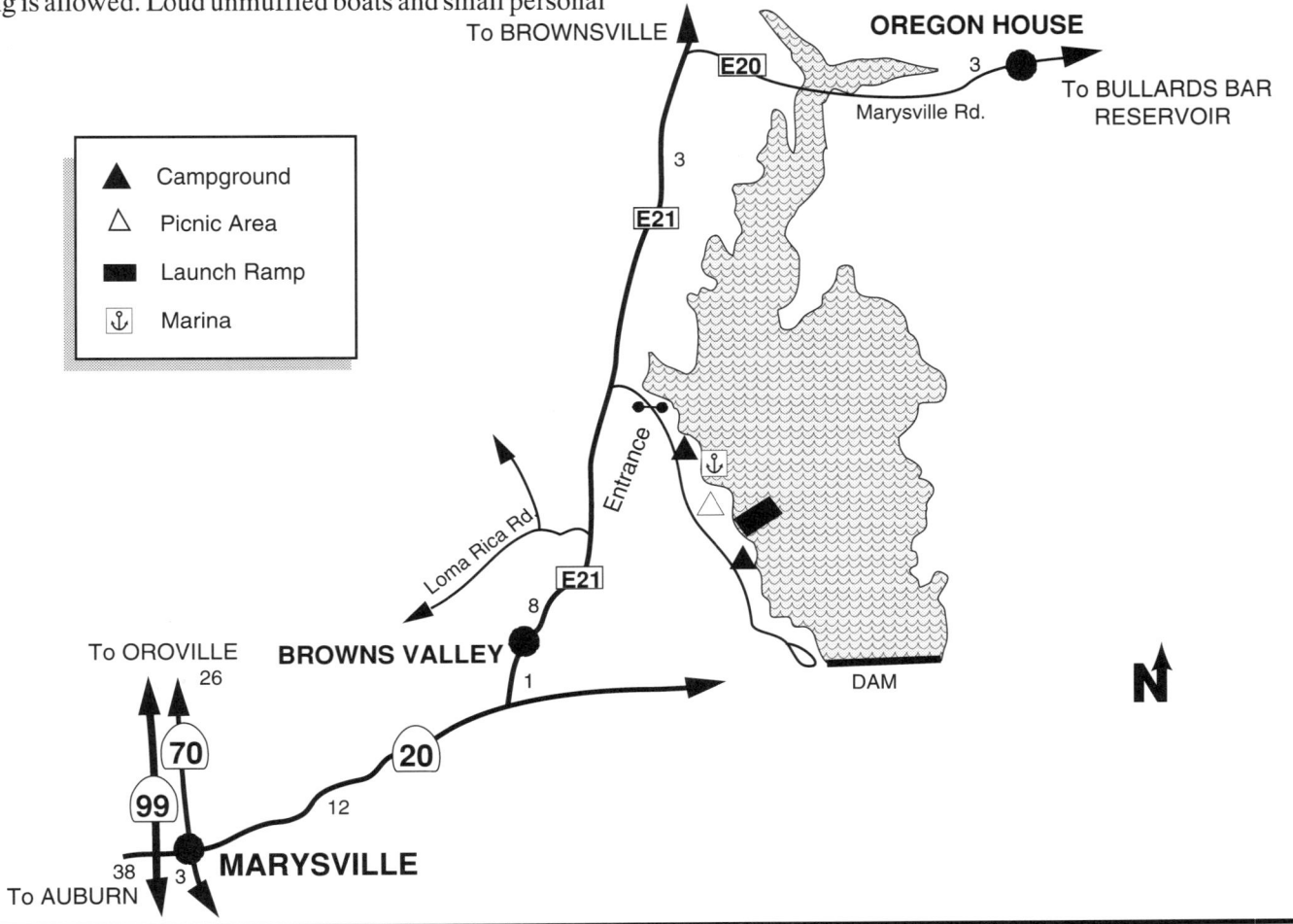

INFORMATION: Collins Lake Recreation Area, P.O. Box 300, Oregon House 95962—Ph: 1 (800) 286-0576

CAMPING	BOATING	RECREATION	OTHER

158 Dev. Sites for Tents & R.V.s
Fee: $18 - $25
  Electric, Water, & Sewer Hookups Available
Reservations Recommended
 	
Open Camp Areas Along Shoreline
  Fee: $15
	Power, Row, Canoe, Sail, Waterski, Windsurf & Inflatables
	Launch Ramp or Boat Use Fee: $5
	Rentals :
	  Outboard Fishing, Row, Paddle & Patio Boats
	Docks, Berths, Moorings, Dry Storage
		Fishing: Trout, Catfish, Bluegill, Crappie, Bass
		Swimming - Sand Beach
		Picnicking -
		  Families & Groups
			Snack Bar
			Grocery Store
			Bait & Tackle
			Hot Showers
			Disposal Station
			Gas Station
			Propane
			
			Full Facilities Within 6 Miles

ENGLEBRIGHT RESERVOIR

Englebright Reservoir is at an elevation of 527 feet northeast of Marysville. The Lake has a surface area of 815 acres with a shoreline of 24 miles that reaches 9 miles above the dam. Englebright is a boat camper's bonanza. Boats can be launched near the dam or at Joe Miller. They can also be rented at Skippers Cove. You can then proceed by boat up the Lake to a campsite. The shoreline is steep and rocky except at the campgrounds where there are some sandy beaches with pine and oak trees above the high water line. Fishing is good in the quiet, narrow coves. *Waterskiing is not allowed above Upper Boston. Be aware when you use boat-in camps that water levels can fluctuate.*

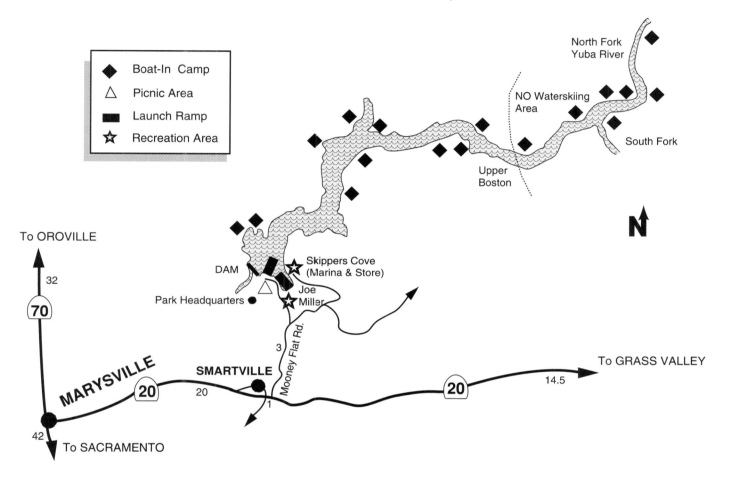

INFORMATION: U.S. Army Corps of Engineers, P. O. Box 6, Smartville 95977—Ph: (530) 639-2342

CAMPING	BOATING	RECREATION	OTHER
100 Developed Boat-In Sites Fee: $6 *Water levels may fluctuate Use caution when you boat camp as low water levels may occur overnight*	Power, Row, Canoe, Sail, Waterski, Jets, Windsurf & Inflatables Full Service Marina Launch Ramps Fee: $2 May-Sept Rentals: Fishing, Canoe & Waterski Boats, Houseboats & Patio Boats Docks, Berths, Moorings, Gas	Fishing: Trout, Bass, Catfish, Bluegill, Bass & Kokanee Swimming Picnicking Hiking	Skippers Cove Marina 13104 Marina Smartville 95977 Ph: (530) 639-2272 Grocery Store Hot Sandwiches Beer & Wine Gas - Propane Bait & Tackle

SCOTTS FLAT LAKE

Scotts Flat Lake is at an elevation of 3,100 feet at the gateway to the Tahoe National Forest. The Lake has a surface area of 850 acres with 7-1/2 miles of coniferous shoreline. This is a nice boating Lake with two launch ramps and marina facilities. Fishing is good for trout and warm water fish. The Scotts Flat Campground is family oriented with modern campsites, a picnic area, sandy beaches and a store. This is a quiet, relaxing facility where nature provides a beautifully forested environment. Don't forget a camera.

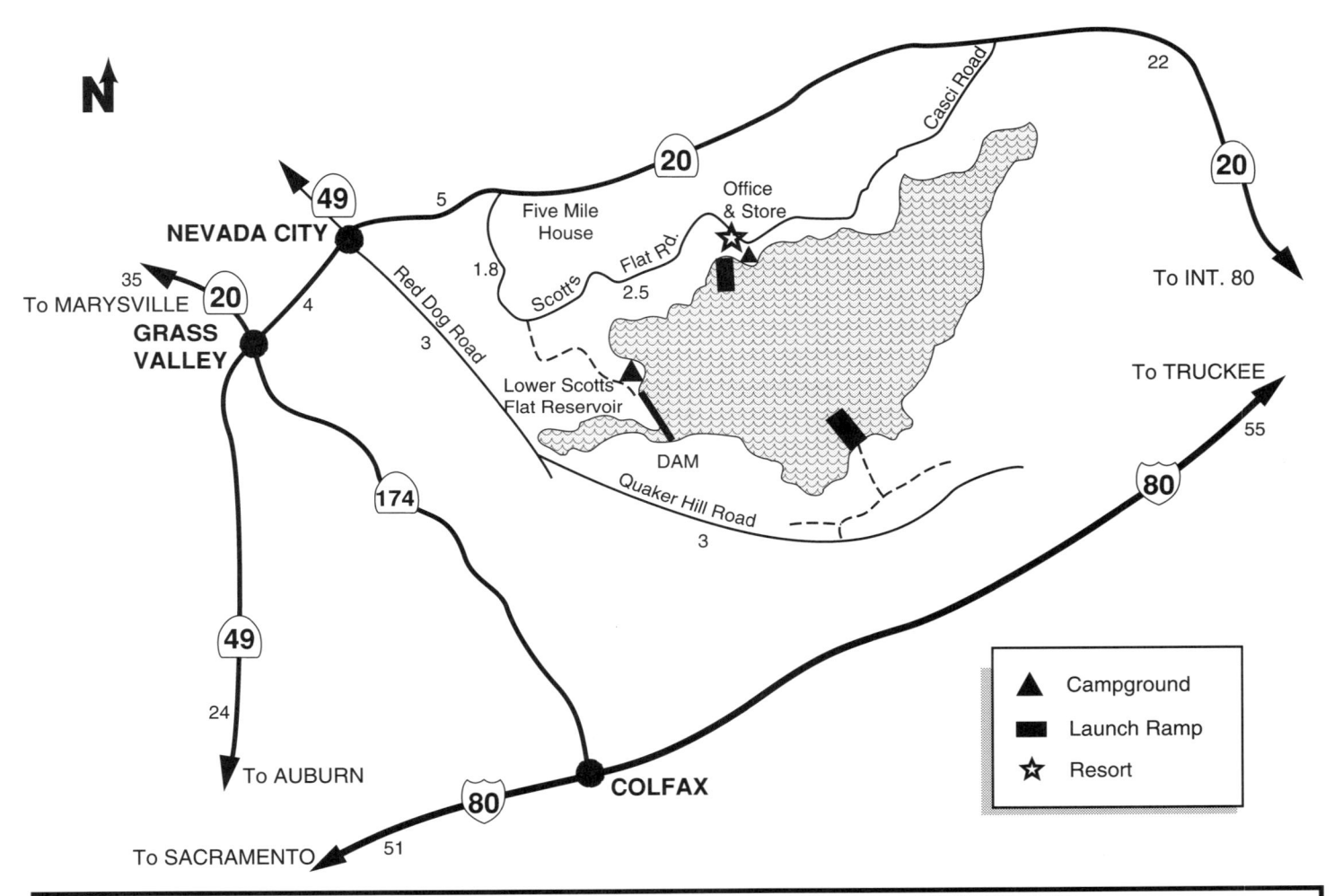

	Campground
	Launch Ramp
☆	Resort

INFORMATION: Scotts Flat, 23333 Scotts Flat Rd., Nevada City 95959—Ph: (530) 265-5302

CAMPING	BOATING	RECREATION	OTHER
20 Dev. Sites for Tents 165 Dev. Sites for R.V.s Fees: Sept. 15 to May 15 　All Sites - $14-$16 May 15 to Sept. 15 　Water Sites - $23 　Inland Sites - $17 Reservations Accepted	Power, Row, Canoe, 　Sail, Waterski & 　Inflatables Full Service Marina Launch Ramps Rentals: Fishing 　& Pedal Boats Moorings & Dry 　Storage *No Jets - PWC's*	Fishing: Rainbow & 　German Brown 　Trout, Large & 　Smallmouth Bass, 　Kokanee Barrier Free Fishing 　Platform Swimming Picnicking Hiking Volleyball Goldpanning Horseshoes	Grocery Store Bait & Tackle Hot Showers Disposal Station Children's Playground *No Motorbikes, 　Motorcyles or 　Horses*

Rollins Lake, situated in the heart of the Gold Country at an elevation of 2,100 feet, is right off Interstate 80 near Colfax and Grass Valley. The Lake has approximately 825 surface acres of water and a shoreline of 26 miles. Rollins Lake boasts 4 individual family-owned and operated campgrounds. Each has their own convenience store, boat ramp, sandy beach and roped off swim area. Flush toilets and hot showers are at each site. The individual campgrounds take their own reservations. This is a great Lake for boating and waterskiing with many coves and long stretches of open water. Fishing is good from both boat and shore for a wide variety of trout and warm water species.

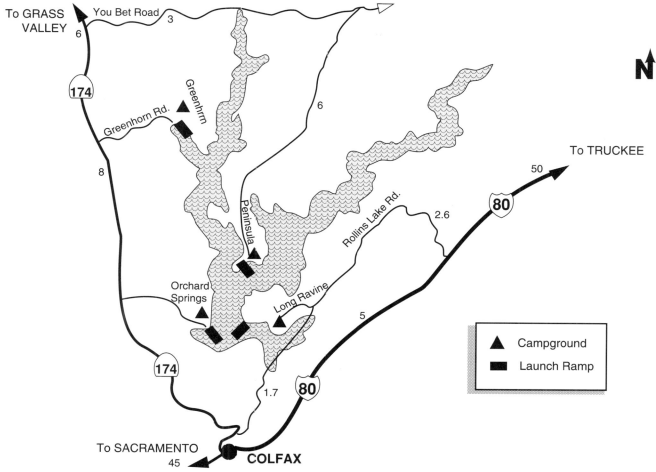

CAMPING	BOATING	RECREATION	OTHER
250 Dev. Sites for Tents & R.V.s Fee: $18 - $25 Some Full Hookups	Power, Row, Canoe, Sail, Waterski, Jets, Windsurfers, Gas Dock	Fishing: Rainbow & Brown Trout, Small & Largemouth Bass, Crappie,	Snack Bar & Grill Restaurant & Lounge Bait & Tackle Fishing Licenses
Group Camping R.V. & Trailer Storage Disposal Station	4 Launch Ramps Rentals: Fishing Boats, Canoes, Paddle Boats & Kayaks	Catfish & Sunfish Picnicking Swimming Bicycling	Volleyball Court Reservations: Greenhorn: (530) 272-6100
Additional Fees for Watercraft, Pets and Extra Vehicles	Boat Docks Dry Storage	Hiking Trails	Peninsula: (530) 477-9413 Orchard Springs: (530) 346-2212 Long Ravine:(530) 346-6166

INFORMATION: Each Campground has its own Phone Number - See Below

LAKE VALLEY RESERVOIR and KELLY LAKE

Lake Valley Reservoir is at 5,800 feet elevation. The shoreline is surrounded by tall trees and granite boulders. The campsites are very pretty, situated under the trees near the Lake. Waterskiing is not allowed. The steep shoreline combined with the steady west wind allows for good sailing.

Coming out from Lake Valley to Highway 80, the second right turn goes into Kelly Lake. This is a small, lovely Lake well worth a day's outing, with 5 picnic sites, tables and firepits. Trout fishing can be excellent at both these High Sierra Lakes.

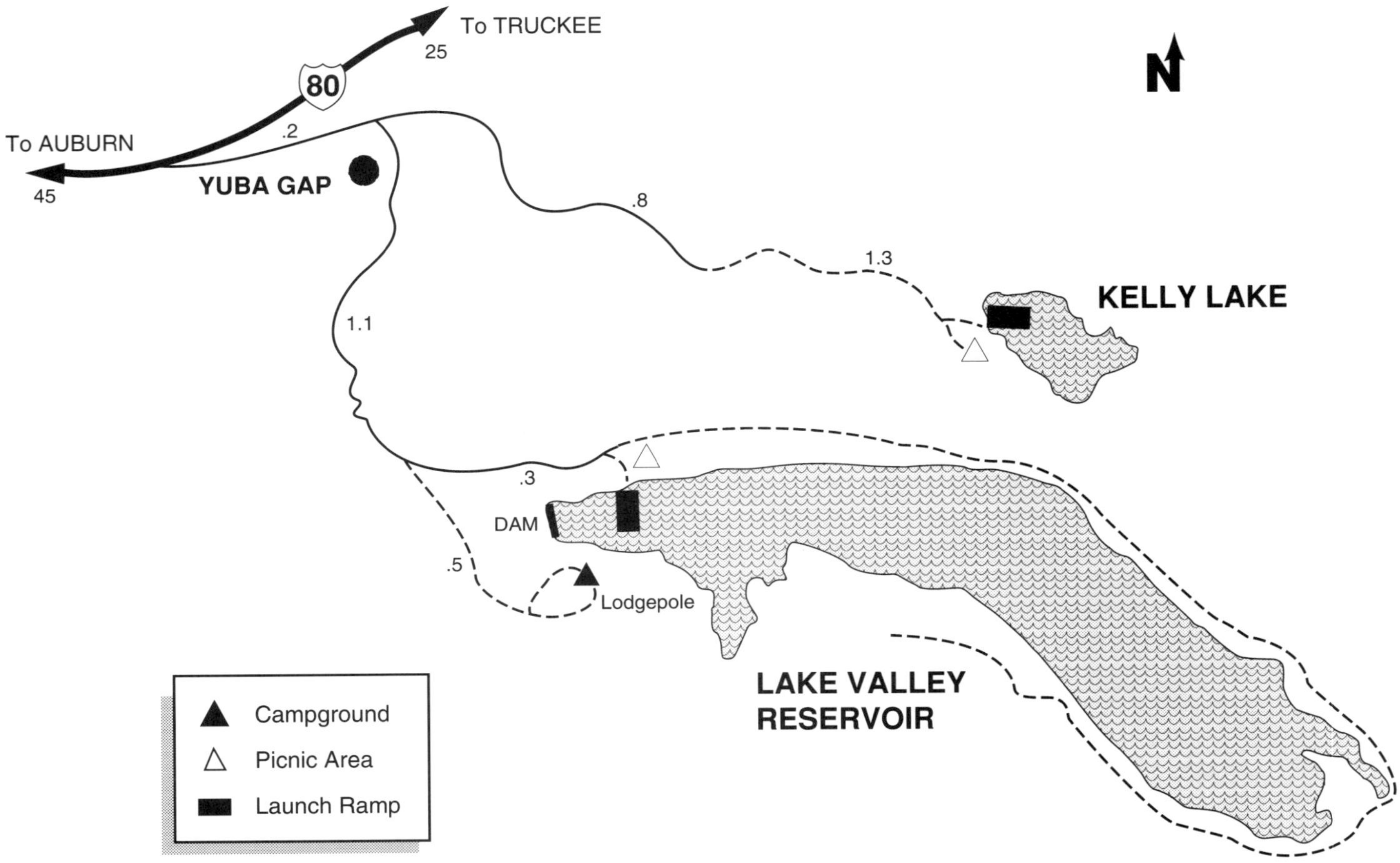

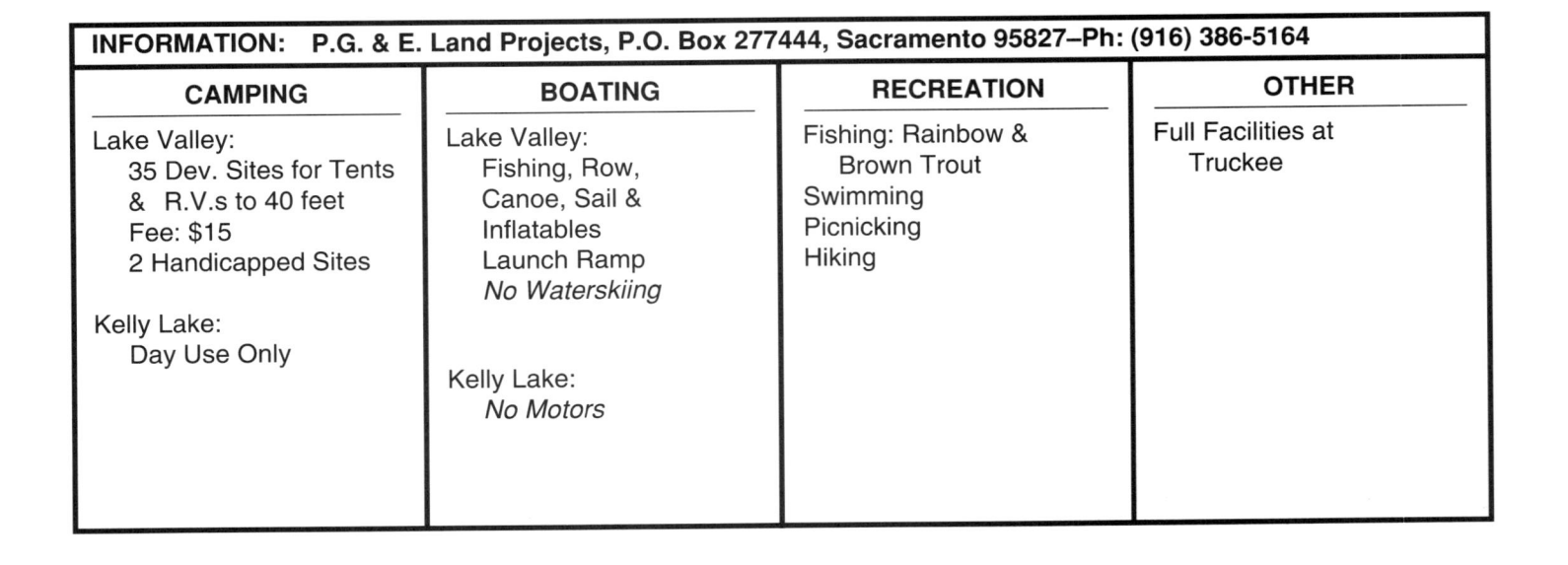

INFORMATION:	P.G. & E. Land Projects, P.O. Box 277444, Sacramento 95827–Ph: (916) 386-5164		
CAMPING	**BOATING**	**RECREATION**	**OTHER**

Lake Valley:
    35 Dev. Sites for Tents
    & R.V.s to 40 feet
    Fee: $15
    2 Handicapped Sites
 	
Kelly Lake:
    Day Use Only
	Lake Valley:
	    Fishing, Row,
	    Canoe, Sail &
	    Inflatables
	    Launch Ramp
	    No Waterskiing
	
	Kelly Lake:
	    No Motors
		Fishing: Rainbow &
		    Brown Trout
		Swimming
		Picnicking
		Hiking
			Full Facilities at
			    Truckee

LAKE PILLSBURY

The Lake Pillsbury Recreation Area provides a wide range of outdoor opportunities. Located in a mountainous setting at an elevation of 1,818 feet in the Mendocino National Forest, this 2,003 maximum surface acre Lake has 65 miles of varied shoreline. It is open to all types of boating including boat camping in designated areas. Anglers will also find trout, steelhead and salmon in season in the nearby Eel River and its tributaries. The Bloody Rock Area is popular with equestrians. Hang gliding at Hull Mountain (elevation 6,873 feet) offers spectacular views of the surrounding country. *For further information: Lake County Visitor Center, 875 Lakeport Blvd., Lakeport 95453, Ph: (800) LAKESIDE.*

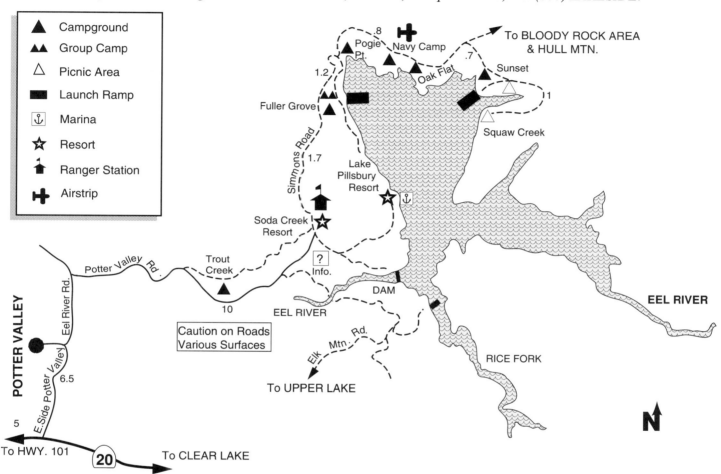

INFORMATION: Upper Lake Ranger District, 10025 Elk Mountain Rd., Upper Lake 95485—Ph: (707) 275-2361

CAMPING	BOATING	RECREATION	OTHER
U.S.F.S.: 141 Tent/RV Sites Fee: $10	Open to All Boating Overnight in Designated Areas	Fishing: Black Bass, Rainbow Trout, Sunfish, Salmon & Steelhead	Snack Bars, Groceries Restaurant-Cocktails Bait & Tackle
P.G. & E.: Ph: (916) 386-5164 Navy Camp-20 Dev. Sites Trout Creek-14 Dev. Sites Fee: $15 Fuller Grove Group to 50 People Max. - Reserve	Launch Ramps Rentals: Fishing Boats & Canoes Marina: Fuel, Slips & Supplies	Swimming Picnicking Hiking & Riding Trails Backpacking Hang Gliding	Gas Station Lake Pillsbury Resort P.O. Box 37 Potter Valley 95469 Ph: (707) 743-1581 30 Tent Sites Soda Creek Resort Lake Pillsbury Potter Valley 95469 Ph: (707) 743-1593

Lake Mendocino is at an elevation of 748 feet above Coyote Dam on the East Fork of the Russian River. This is wine country with many small valleys of vineyards and pear trees. The Lake has a surface area of 1,740 acres with 15 miles of oak-wooded shoreline. The U.S. Army Corps of Engineers maintain the quality facilities which include numerous camp-sites, picnic sites and 7 group picnic shelters each with a massive stone barbecue pit. There is a large protected swim beach and a 5-kilometer hiking trail. Equestrians will find a staging area and riding trails. The fishing is good with Channel catfish going to 30 pounds and Stripers to 40 pounds. A seasonal Fish Hatchery is open to the public from November to March.

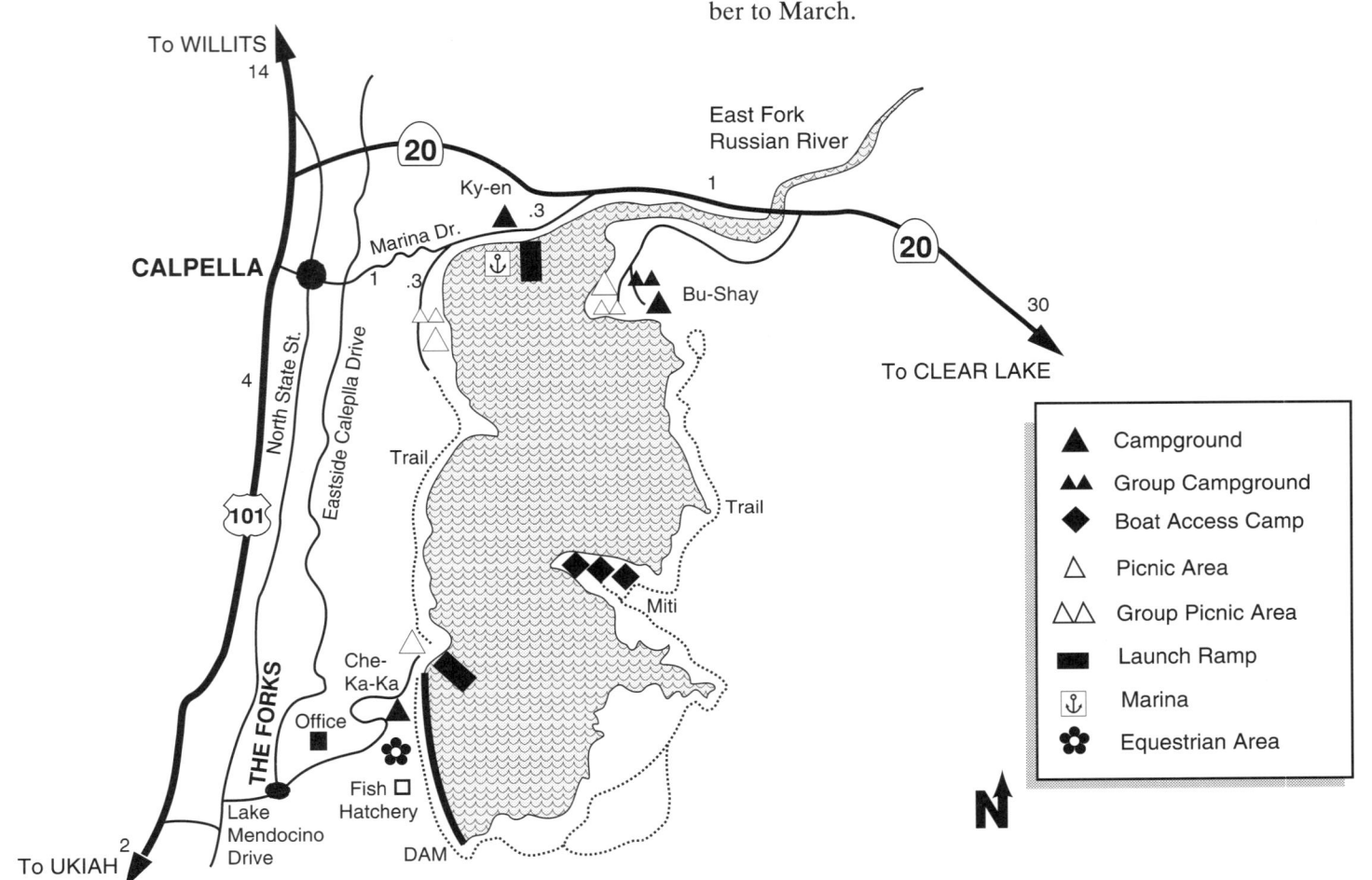

INFORMATION: Park Manager, 1160 Lake Mendocino Dr., Ukiah 95482—Ph: (707) 462-7581

CAMPING	BOATING	RECREATION	OTHER
319 Dev. Sites for Tents & R.V.s Fee: $14 to $16 No Reservations 22 R.V.s Only Sites Reservations Accepted Ph: (707) 485-8644 for Information 3 Group Camps By Reservation 165 People Maximum 18 Boat Access Only Sites	Power, Row, Canoe, Sail, Waterski & Inflatables, Jets, Wind Surfers Full Service Marina Launch Ramps Rentals: Fishing, Power, Canoe, Waterski & Pontoon Docks, Berths Dry Storage, Gas	Fishing: Catfish Bluegill, Crappie, Large, Smallmouth & Striped Bass Swimming Picnicking Hiking Junior Ranger & Interpretive Programs Hunting: Waterfowl Special Seasonal Turkey Hunts	Lake Mendocino Marina: P.O. Box 13 Calpella 95418 Ph: (707) 485-8644 (Off Highway 20 at North End) Snack Bar Mini-Market Beer, Wine, Ice Boat & Slip Rentals Gasoline for Boats

The Blue Lakes are at an elevation of 1,400 feet off Highway 20 between Clear Lake and Lake Mendocino. These popular Lakes are nestled in a beautiful setting of dense groves of madrones, oak, and evergreen. They are spring fed and have been in existence for over 10,000 years. The clear blue waters make this a delightful retreat for fishing, swimming, boating or just plain relaxing. The private resorts surrounding the Lakes provide complete vacation facilities including shaded campsites, cabins, restaurants, boat rentals, swim beaches and picnic areas.

...Continued...

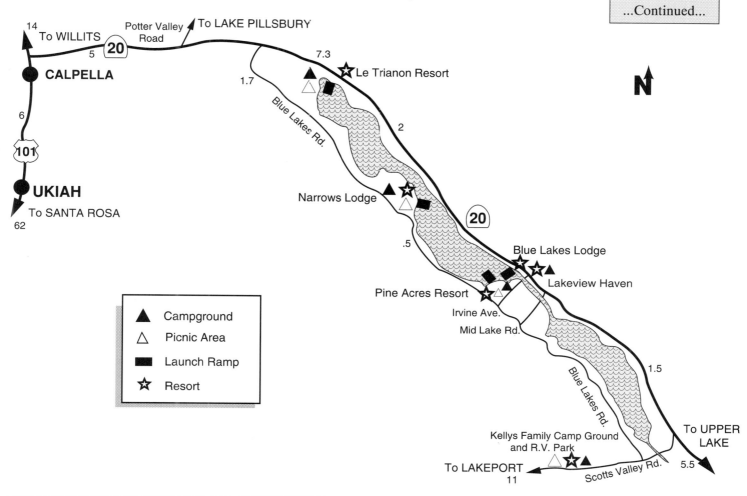

	Campground
▲	Campground
△	Picnic Area
■	Launch Ramp
☆	Resort

INFORMATION: Lake County Visitor Info. Center, 875 Lakeport Blvd., Lakeport 95485—Ph: (800) 525-3743			
CAMPING	**BOATING**	**RECREATION**	**OTHER**
Private Resorts: Sites for Tents & R.V.s *See Following Page*	Power, Row, Canoe, Sail, Windsurf & Inflatables 5 MPH Speed Limit Launch Ramps Rentals: Rowboats, Motorboats, Canoes & Paddleboats (Check following page) Docks	Fishing: Trout, Catfish, Bluegill & Largemouth Bass Swimming - Beaches Picnicking	*See Following Page*

BLUE LAKES - LAKE COUNTY..............Continued

LE TRIANON RESORT: 5845 E. Hwy. 20, Ukiah 95482—Ph: (707) 275-2262

Le Trianon Resort offers housekeeping cabins as well as 200 sites for tent camping, R.V.s or trailers. There are electricity and water hookups, disposal station, laundry, toilets and showers. Also available are a launch ramp, dock, swim area and boat rentals.

NARROWS LODGE: 5690 Blue Lakes Road, Upper Lake 95485—Ph: (707) 275-2718

The Narrows Lodge Resort provides all the comforts of modern conveniences in a lovely tree-studded setting. There are fully equipped housekeeping cabins and motel units with coffee service. The R.V. Park has 20 sites with complete hookups. 10 sites have water and electric hookups. Tent sites are also available. The Resort has a launch ramp, fishing dock, swim area, BBQ's, picnic tables, disposal station, bait and tackle shop and game room. Rowboats, motorboats, kayaks, canoes and paddleboats can be rented. Open year round.

PINE ACRES RESORT: 5328 Blue Lakes Road, Upper Lake 95485—Ph: (707) 275-2811 or FAX (707) 275-9549

Pine Acres Resort offers a motel and fully equipped cabins. 30 R.V. sites are available, 26 with water and electric hookups and 4 with full hookups. There are shaded lawns, BBQs, picnic tables, horseshoe court, swimming beach with float, fishing pier, launch ramp, boat rentals, bait and tackle shop, disposal station and satellite T.V.. A gazebo has been built for pot lucks, square dancing, conferences, family reunions and other uses for R.V. groups.

BLUE LAKES LODGE: 5315 W. Highway 20, Upper Lake 95485—Ph: (707) 275-2178

This Resort has a motel with housekeeping units with T.V.s including free HBO, complimentary coffee and air conditioning. A restaurant and cocktail bar are open year round with live entertainment and dancing on weekends. There is a launch ramp along with fishing docks, swim area and boat rentals including a patio boat rental for parties. Picnic tables, barbecues, horseshoes and a large parking area for R.V. (no hookups) are also available. There are facilities for banquets, weddings and seminars. A swimming pool and exercise room complete this full facility Resort.

KELLY'S KAMP: 8220 Scotts Valley Road, Upper Lake 95485—Ph: (707) 263-5754

Kelly's Family Kamp Ground and R.V. Park offers quiet family camping on spacious sites with frontage on Scotts Creek. There are 30 tent sites and 48 R.V. sites with water and electric hookups. Also available are the Kamp Store, modern restrooms, laundromat, disposal station, hot showers, firewood, picnic tables, fire pits and BBQ grills. Recreational facilities include swimming, 2-acre Lake with floats, fishing, volleyball, basketball, horseshoes and hiking. A horseback riding trail is nearby. R.V. storage is available and a pavilion area with a built-in barbecue for large groups.

LAKEVIEW HAVEN RESORT: 5135 West Highway 20, Upper Lake 95485—Ph: (707) 275-2178

Lakeview Haven has a 46 site R.V. park with full hookups. There is a restaurant, cocktail lounge and game room nearby. Also available are a launch ramp and a swimming pool.

Call Resort for Current Prices

Clear Lake is at an elevation of 1,320 feet with a surface area of 43,000 acres. The Lake's shoreline of over 100 miles offers a huge variety of recreational activities. This was once the home of the Pomo and Lile'ek tribes who were drawn here by the abundant fish and game. Often called "Bass Capital of the West," Clear Lake provides the angler with a productive warm water fishery. Miles of open water, many coves and inlets entice the boater and waterskiier. This Lake is also known for excellent sailing conditions. Numerous launch ramps, marinas, beaches, campgrounds and resorts dot the shoreline. Nearby Highland Springs Reservoir offers warm water fishing and non-powered boating.

...Continued.....

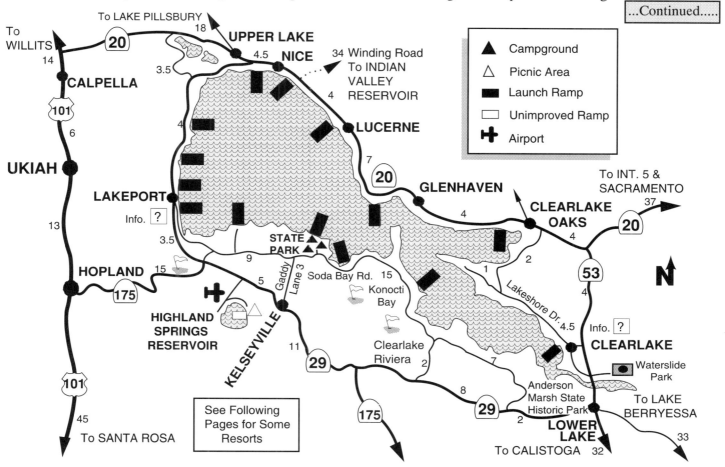

INFORMATION: Visitor Information Center, 875 Lakeport Blvd., Lakeport 95453—Ph: (707) 263-9544

CAMPING	BOATING	RECREATION	OTHER
Clear Lake State Park 5300 Soda Bay Rd. Kelseyville 95451 Ph: (707) 279-4293 147 Dev. Tent/R.V. Sites to 35 Feet Fee: $19 Reserve: Ph: (800) 444-7275 *For Additional Resorts & Campgrounds, See Following Pages*	Open to All Boating Full Service Marinas 11 Public Launch Ramps Boat Rentals: Fishing, Waterski Boats & Pontoons (*Water can get rough when windy in afternoon*) Clear Lake Queen Cruise Boat	Fishing: Florida & Northern Bass, Yellow & Blue Channel Catfish, Trout, Crappie & Bluegill Swimming: Beaches & Pools Picnicking at State Parks Hiking & Nature Trails Rock Hounding Hunting Nearby: Deer, Dove, Quail, & Waterfowl, Turkey	Winery Tours Waterslide Park Glider Flights Golf Courses Complete Facilities in Nearby Towns Anderson Marsh State Historical Park Archeological Sites of Indian Villages and Sanctuary for Water Birds and Fish Gambling Casinos

CLEAR LAKE.............Continued

**THERE ARE OVER 100 PRIVATE CAMPGROUNDS AND RESORTS AROUND CLEAR LAKE.
THE FOLLOWING ARE RANDOMLY SELECTED FACILITIES, MANY WITH LAUNCH RAMPS
CALL FOR CURRENT PRICES:**

NORTHSHORE, NICE, LUCERNE

HOLIDAY HARBOR
P.O. Box 26, 3605 Lakeshore Blvd., Nice 95464—Ph: (707) 274-1136
33 Sites, Hookups, Disposal Station, Hot Showers, Laundry, Concrete Ramp, Marine Gas, 130 Boat Slips.

NORTHSHORE RESORT & MARINA
P.O. Box 493, 2345 Lakeshore Blvd., Nice 95464—Ph: (707) 274-7771
31 Sites, Hookups, Showers, Laundry.

ARROW TRAILER PARK
P.O. Box 1735, E. Hwy. 20, Lucerne 95458—Ph: (707) 274-7715
24 Sites, Full Hookups, 2 Pull-Thrus, Disposal Station, Hot Showers, Laundry, BBQ Area, Ramp, Pier, Mooring, Storage, Bait & Tackle, Guest Suite for 2.

TALLEY'S FAMILY RESORT
P.O. Box 538, 3827 Hwy. 20, Nice 95464—Ph: (707) 274-1177
10 Cottages with T.V., 7 R.V. Sites, Hookups, Showers, Laundry, Fish Room, Snack Bar, BBQ, Beach, Pier, Mooring, Launch, Boat Rentals.

GLENHAVEN - CLEARLAKE OAKS

GLENHAVEN BEACH CAMPGROUND & MARINA
P.O. Box 406, 9625 E. Hwy. 20, Glenhaven 95423—Ph: (707) 998-3406
44 RV Sites, Hookups, Hot Showers, Laundry, Paved Ramp, Mooring, Slips, Fuel Dock, Rental Boats, Groceries.

ISLAND PARK
P.O. Box 126, 12840 Island Dr., Clearlake Oaks 95423—Ph: (707) 998-3940
19 R.V. Sites, Hookups, Tent Sites Available, Showers, Laundry, Boat Launch, Docks with Electric Hookups.

BLUE FISH COVE
P. O. Box 1252, 10573 E. Hwy. 20, Clearlake Oaks 95423—Ph: (707) 998-1769
Housekeeping Units on the Lake, Pier, Beach, Game Room, Rental Fishing Boats.

HARBOR MOTEL
P. O. Box 1192, 130 Short St., Clearlake Oaks 95423—Ph: (707) 998-3587
8 Units with Kitchenettes, 2 RV Spaces, Pier, Boat Mooring.

INDIAN BEACH RESORT
P. O. Box 648, 9945 E. Hwy. 20, Glenhaven 95443—Ph: (707) 998-3760
Housekeeping Cabins with Full Equipped Kitchenettes, Beach Setting, Large Oak Trees, Pier, Launch Ramp, BBQ Areas, Mini-Store, Bait, Boat Slips.

LAKE MARINA MOTEL
10215 E. Hwy. 20, Clearlake Oaks 95423—Ph: (707) 998-3787
13 Units with Kitchenettes, Boat Launching, Pier, Beach, Catfishing Area, Boat Rentals.

SEA BREEZE RESORT
P. O. Box 653, Glenhaven 95443—Ph: (707) 998-3327
Small Resort with Kitchenette Units, Well Landscaped, Lighted Pier, Boat Docks.

....Continued....

CLEARLAKE - SOUTH SHORE

GARNER'S RESORT
P.O. Box 509, 6235 Old Hwy. 53, Clearlake 95422—Ph: (707) 994-6267
92 Tent/RV Sites, Hookups, Disposal Station, Groceries, Bait & Tackle, Pool, Ramp, Rental Boats, Fuel Dock, Slips.
ALBATROSS ACRES
P. O. Box 4415, 5545 Old Hwy. 53, Clearlake 95422—Ph: (707) 994-1194
R.V. Sites, Hookups, Boat Launch, Docks, Fishing Area.

KELSEYVILLE - SODA BAY - KONOCTI BAY

EDGEWATER RESORT
1 Mile West of Clear Lake State Park
6420 Soda Bay Rd., Soda Bay, Kelseyville 95451—Ph: (707) 279-0208
Reserve: (800) 396-6224
61 R.V./Tent Sites, Full Hookups with Water, Sites to 40 ft. with Slide Outs, Hot Showers,
8 Cabins for 2-12 People, Full Kitchens, Bath, AC & Cable TV,
230 ft. Lighted Fishing Pier, Boat Dock, Launch and Rentals, 300 ft. Swim Beach, Swimming Pool,
Clubhouse, General Store, Bait and Tackle, Laundry, Game Room, Volleyball Court,
Ping-Pong & Horseshoe Pits, Group Camping, Pets on Leash Welcome, Special Events.
RICHMOND PARK
9435 Konocti Bay Rd., Kelseyville 95451—Ph: (707) 277-7535
10 Tent Sites, 8 R.V. Sites, Hookups, Ramp, Rental Boats, Snack Bar, Lounge.
FERNDALE RESORT
6190 Soda Bay Rd., Kelseyville 95451—Ph: (707) 279-4866
18 Rooms w/Kitchens, 2 Cottages, Pets OK, T.V., Paved Ramp, Slips, Pier, Large Rental Fleet,
Tackle Shop, Fuel Dock, Marine Parts, Repair Shop, Snack Bar.
Home of the Clear Lake Queen Paddle Wheel Cruise Boat.
KONOCTI HARBOR INN
8727 Soda Bay Rd., Kelseyville 95451—Ph: (707) 279-4281
250 Rooms, Restaurant & Lounge, 4 Swimming Pools, Tennis, Ramps, Piers, Slips,
Boat Rentals, Full Service Marina.

LAKEPORT

ANCHORAGE INN
950 N. Main St., Lakeport 95453—Ph: (707) 263-5417
34 Units, T.V., Laundry, Pool, Sauna, Jacuzzi, Ramp, Berthing, Dock.
CLEAR LAKE INN
1010 N. Main St., Lakeport 95453—Ph: (707) 263-3551
40 Units, TV, Pool, Dock, Fishing Pier.
SKYLARK SHORES RESORT/MOTEL
1120 N. Main St., Lakeport 95453—Ph: (707) 263-6151
45 Units, T.V., Swimming Pool, Dock, Playground.

In addition to the above and other resorts not mentioned, there are 11 public launch ramps as shown on our map. The State Park is shown on the graph. For information on additional resorts and other attractions, contact:

Lake County Visitor Information Center
875 Lakeport Blvd., Lakeport 95453
Ph: (707) 263-9544 (California) 800-LAKESIDE

Lakeport Chamber of Commerce
P.O. Box 295 (290 S. Main St.), Lakeport 95453
Ph: (707) 263-5092

Clear Lake Chamber of Commerce
Austin Park - P.O. Box 629, Clearlake 95422
Ph: (707) 994-3600

INDIAN VALLEY RESERVOIR

Indian Valley Reservoir is under the jurisdiction of the Yolo County Flood Control District. Resting at an elevation of 1,476 feet, this very remote 3,800 acre Lake has 39 shoreline miles. Access is by a 10 mile dirt road. The Lake is an excellent Rainbow trout fishery and a developing warm water fishery. Since there is a 10 MPH speed limit, this is a quiet place for sailing, canoeing and fishing. High winds, however, can occur particularly in the afternoon. The concession at Indian Valley Store operates a developed campground. The area surrounding the Reservoir is an important wintering area for both bald and golden eagles and waterfowl.

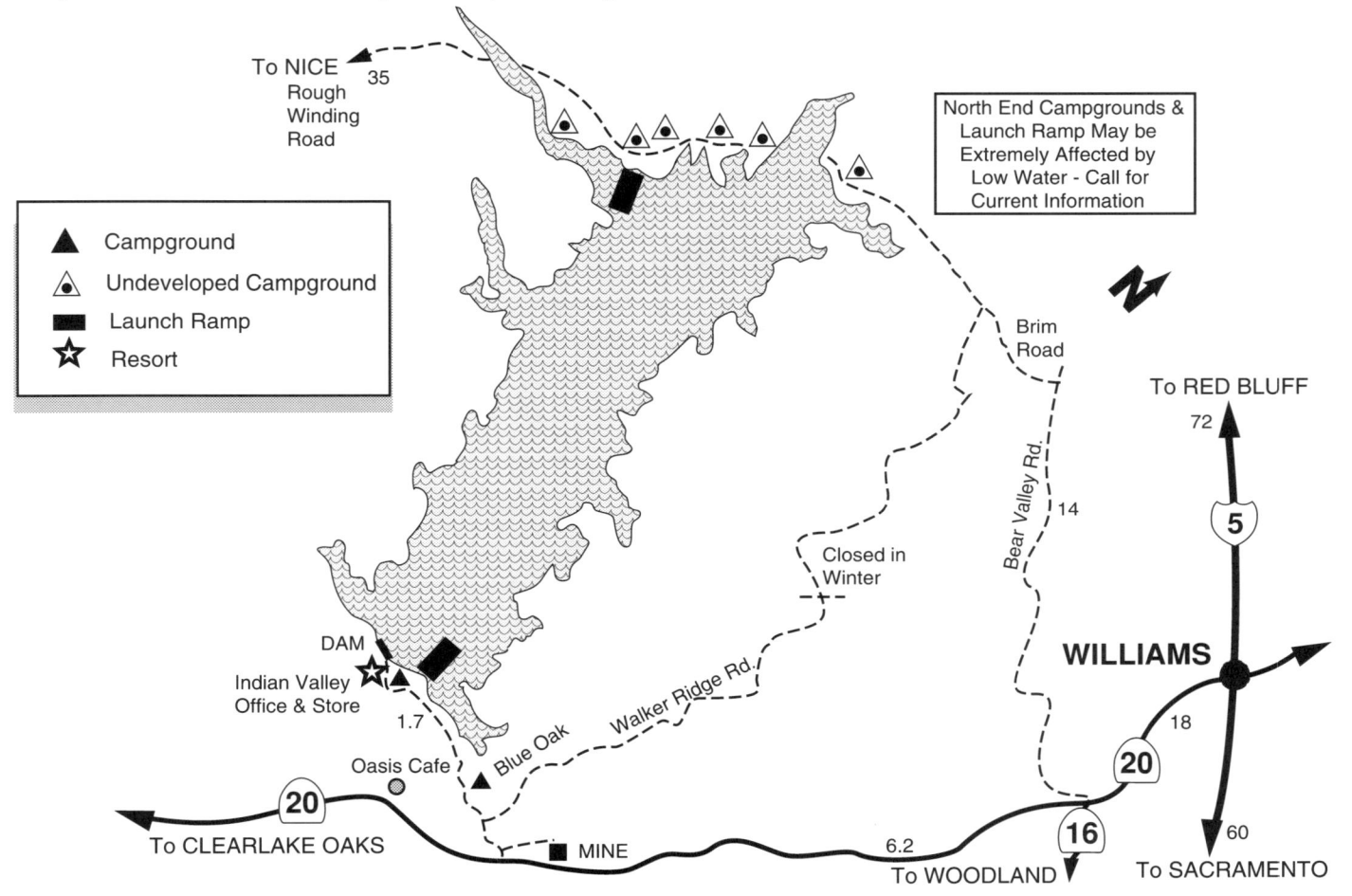

To NICE
Rough Winding Road   35

North End Campgrounds & Launch Ramp May be Extremely Affected by Low Water - Call for Current Information

▲ Campground
⊿ Undeveloped Campground
■ Launch Ramp
★ Resort

Brim Road

To RED BLUFF   72

Bear Valley Rd.   14

Closed in Winter

DAM

Indian Valley Office & Store

1.7

Oasis Cafe

Blue Oak

Walker Ridge Rd.

WILLIAMS

5

20   18

20

To CLEARLAKE OAKS

■ MINE

6.2

16

To WOODLAND

60

To SACRAMENTO

INFORMATION: Indian Valley Store—Recorded Information Only Ph: (530) 662-0607			
CAMPING	**BOATING**	**RECREATION**	**OTHER**
15 Dev. Sites for Tents 20 Dev. Sites for R.V.s Fee: $8 - Plus $1 Extra Per Person Disposal Station Day Use Fee: $5 2 People per Vehicle Plus $1 Extra Per Person	Open to All Boating 10 MPH Speed Limit Paved Launch Ramp *Beware of Underwater Hazards and Afternoon Winds*	Fishing: Eagle Lake & Rainbow Trout, Large & Smallmouth Bass, Catfish, Blue Gill, Red Ear Perch & Crappie Picnicking Swimming Hiking Birdwatching & Nature Study Hunting on Adjacent BLM Land: Waterfowl, Quail, Dove, Turkey, Pigs & Bear	Grocery Store Bait & Tackle Propane On Hwy. 20: Oasis Cafe Access: 10 Mile Dirt Road

Numbers around highways represent lakes in numerical order in this book.
See Index for complete listing.

Highways
Interstate
United States
California

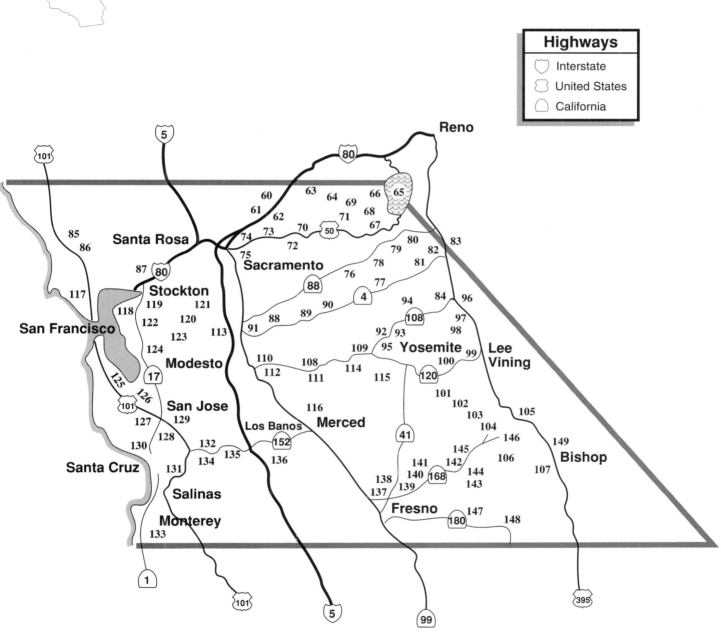

SUGAR PINE and BIG RESERVOIRS—LAKE CLEMENTINE

Sugar Pine Reservoir, at an elevation of 3,618 feet, is a 160 surface acre Reservoir in the Tahoe National Forest. The modern recreation complex offers handicapped facilities and will accommodate R.V.s and trailers up to 40 feet. Its neighbor, Big or sometimes called Morning Star Lake, rests at 4,092 feet in a heavily forested area. The facilities at this 70 acre Lake are under concession to Morning Star Resort. Down the road in the foothill canyons of the American River, Lake Clementine is a part of the Auburn State Recreation Area. The lake is a 3-1/2 mile long stretch of the North Fork of the American River. Campgrounds are primitive although there is a launch ramp and the Lake is open to all boating.

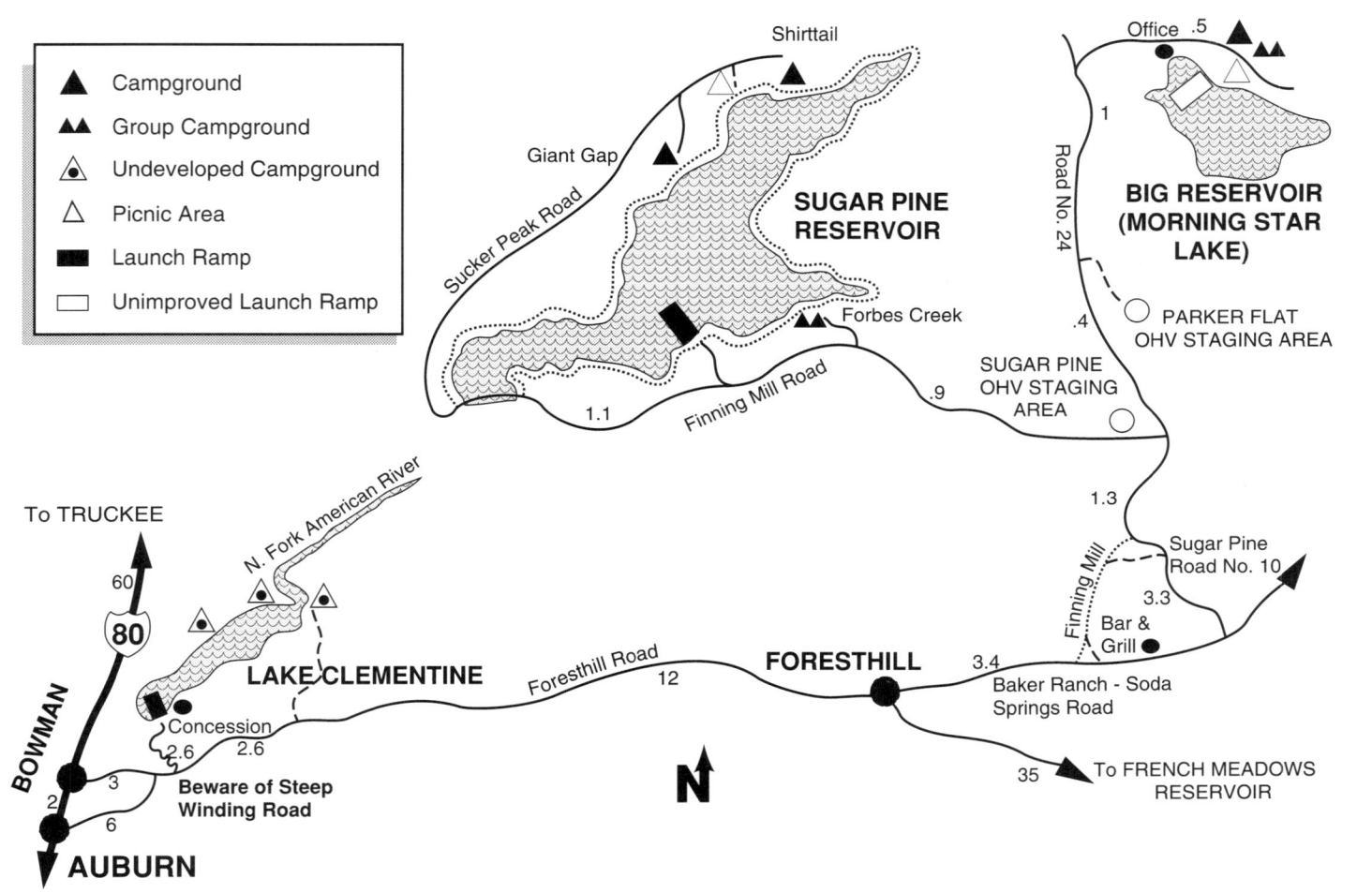

INFORMATION: Foresthill Ranger Station, 22830 Foresthill Rd., Foresthill 95631—Ph: (530) 367-2224 or 478-6254

CAMPING	BOATING	RECREATION	OTHER
Sugar Pine: 　60 Dev. Sites for Tents & R.V.s & Group Sites 　Fees: $10, $18, $27 Reserve:Ph:(800) 280-CAMP Big Reservoir: 　120 Dev. Sites for Tents & 　R.V.s - Fee: $15-$25 　2 Group Sites for Tents Lake Clementine: 　Unimproved Campground 　Fees: $9 & $11 Reserve: (800) 444-7275	Sugar Pine: 　Open to All Boating 　10 MPH Speed Limit 　Launch Ramp Big Reservoir: 　Open to Non- 　　Powered Boating 　Electric Motors 　　Permitted 　Car Top Launch 　Fishing by Permit Lake Clementine: 　25 MPH Speed Limit	Fishing: Rainbow & 　Brown Trout, Black 　Bass, Bluegill & 　Perch Picnicking Paved & Unpaved Trails Swimming Hiking & Backpacking OHV Trails Nearby Hunting: Deer & Bear	Morning Star Lake Resort P.O. Box 119 Foresthill 95631 Reservations: Ph: (530) 367-2129 Lake Clementine 　Auburn State Rec. Area 　P.O. Box 3266 　Auburn 95604 　Ph: (530) 885-4527 Facilities at Foresthill

Camp Far West Lake is at an elevation of 320 feet in the Sierra foothills northeast of Roseville. The Lake has a surface area of 2,000 acres, 29 miles of shoreline and 800 acres of open camping, hiking, bicycle and horse trails. The water temperature rises up to 85 degrees in the summer when the climate can be quite hot although there are many oak trees providing ample shade. The Lake is open year around but the south entrance is closed at the end of summer. This is a good Lake for all types of boating and waterskiing. The boater should be aware of the rocky area as noted on the map. The water level of the Lake can fluctuate. There is a warm water fishery for landlocked smallmouth and black bass at the Bear River and Rock Creek Arms. A horse camp is also available.

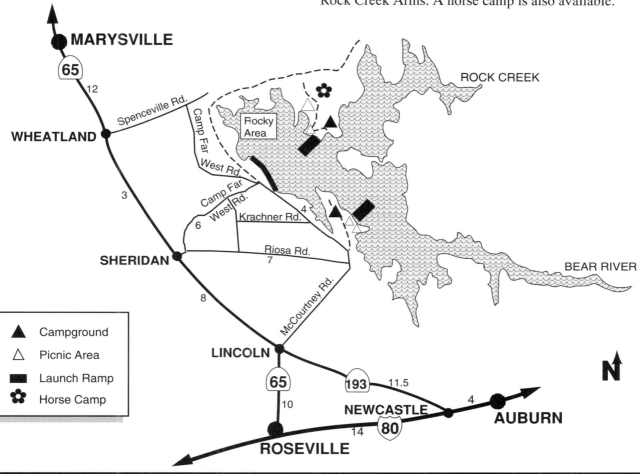

INFORMATION: Camp Far West, Box 929, Wheatland 95692—South Ph:(916) 645-0484, North Ph:(530) 633-0803

CAMPING	BOATING	RECREATION	OTHER
143 Dev. Sites for Tents & R.V.s 10 with Full Hookups Fees: $12 - $18 Overflow Area Horse Camp Disposal Stations 3 Group Camps - to 250 People Reservations Accepted Day Use: $5 $10 with Boat	Power, Row, Canoe, Sail, Waterski, Jets, Windsurf & Inflatables 2 Launch Ramps Gas, Dry Storage Water Toys & Equipment Rentals at North Shore	Fishing: Florida Largemouth, Black, Striped & Smallmouth Bass, Crappie & Catfish Swimming Picnicking Bicycling Hiking Horseback Riding Trails	Grocery Stores Bait & Tackle

FRENCH MEADOWS RESERVOIR

French Meadows Reservoir rests at an elevation of 5,200 feet on the western slope of the Sierra Nevada. This manmade reservoir of 1,920 surface acres is often subject to low water levels late in the season. Although open to all types of boating, these low water conditions along with underwater hazards, including tree stumps, make waterskiing and speed boating extremely dangerous. If the angler can suffer through the loss of tackle from these hazards, you are sometimes rewarded with a beautiful German brown or rainbow trout up to 7 pounds. The U.S. Forest Service maintains numerous campsites around the lake along with picnic areas and two launch ramps. There are several natural swimming beaches. This is a nice family camping area though remote so plan on staying awhile.

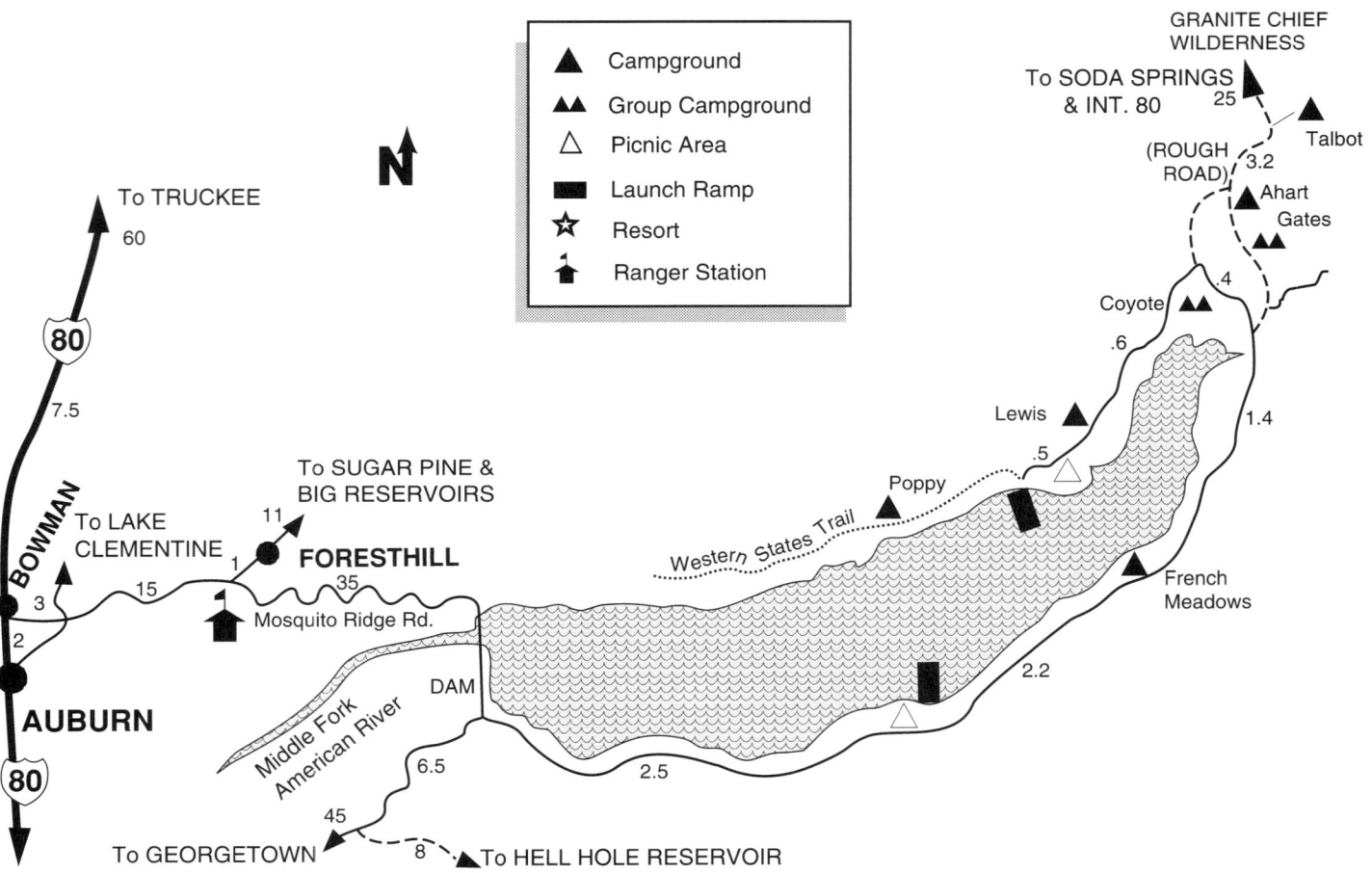

INFORMATION: Fotesthill Ranger District, 22830 Foresthill Rd., Foresthill 95631—Ph: (530) 478-6254			
CAMPING	**BOATING**	**RECREATION**	**OTHER**

115 Dev. Sites
    Fee: $10
  12 Boat or Walk-In
    Sites
  7 Group Sites
    Fees: $40 - $55
 	
Reservations:
    Ph: (800) 280-CAMP
	French Meadows:
	    Open to All Boats
	
	*Speed Boats &
	Waterskiing Not
	Advised Due to
	Submerged Hazards*
		Fishing: Rainbow &
		    Brown Trout
		Picnicking
		Swimming
		Hiking
		Backpacking [Parking]
		
		Granite Chief Wilderness
		    7 Miles East
			Nearest Supplies and
			    Facilities 39 Miles
			    in Foresthill

HELL HOLE RESERVOIR and RALSTON AFTERBAY

Hell Hole Reservoir is in the Eldorado National Forest at an elevation of 4,700 feet. The facilities are operated and maintained by the U.S. Forest Service. Hell Hole is 15 miles south of French Meadows Reservoir in a rugged, rocky area on the Rubicon River. The Lake of 1,300 surface acres is in a deep gorge surrounded by granite boulders with cold, clear water, creating a beautiful setting. It is especially scenic where the water leaves the power house and drops into the Lake. Be sure to bring a camera. Extreme water fluctuation can occur seasonally. There are no facilities other than the launch ramp and campgrounds so come well supplied. Ralston Afterbay is on the Middle Fork of the American River with a nice picnic area and gravel launch ramps. *Campers should be prepared for Bears.*

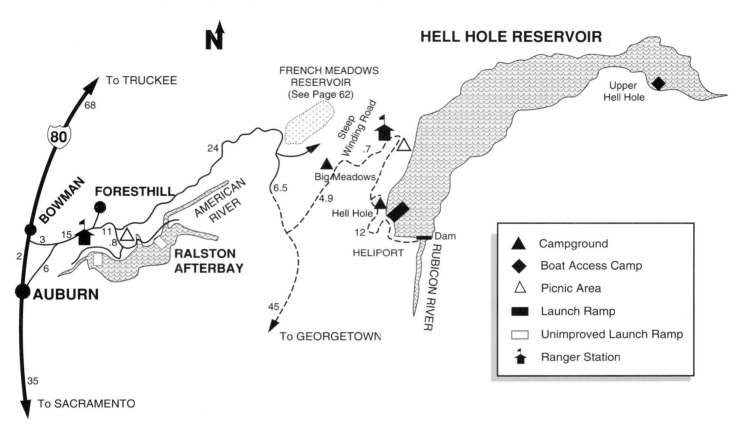

INFORMATION: Georgetown Ranger Dist., 7600 Wentworth Springs Rd., Georgetown 95634—Ph: (530) 333-4312

CAMPING	BOATING	RECREATION	OTHER

Hell Hole:
   10 Tent Sites
   No Reservations
Upper Hell Hole:
   15 Boat Access Sites
   No Fee - No Water
Big Meadows:
   55 Tent/RV Sites
No Reservations
 	
Ralston Afterbay:
   No Campgrounds
	Hell Hole:
	   Power, Row, Canoe,
	   Sail, Waterski &
	   Inflatable
	Launch Ramp
	Caution - Afternoon
	* Winds Can Be*
	* Hazardous*
	
	Ralston Afterbay:
	   Small Craft Only
	   Hand Launch
		Fishing: Rainbow,
		   Brown, Cutthroat
		   & Kamloop Trout,
		   Kokanee Salmon
		Picnicking
		Hiking
		Backpacking
		Horseback Riding
		   Trails
		Hunting: Deer, Bear
			Nearest Facilities
			   From Hell Hole
			   Reservoir: 55 Miles at
			   Georgetown

STUMPY MEADOWS RESERVOIR and FINNON LAKE

Stumpy Meadows is at an elevation of 4,260 feet in the Eldorado National Forest. This pretty Lake of 320 acres is surrounded by conifers and the water is clear and cold. Boating is restricted to 5 MPH so waterskiing is not allowed. The angler will often find German Brown and Rainbow Trout. Finnon Lake, at 2,420 feet, is a small Lake adminis-tered by the Mosquito Volunteer Fire Department. Boating is limited to rowboats. Fishing, swimming, hiking and horse-back riding are the primary activities. *Small trailers only are advised at these Lakes.* Lake levels can fluctuate so call for current information.

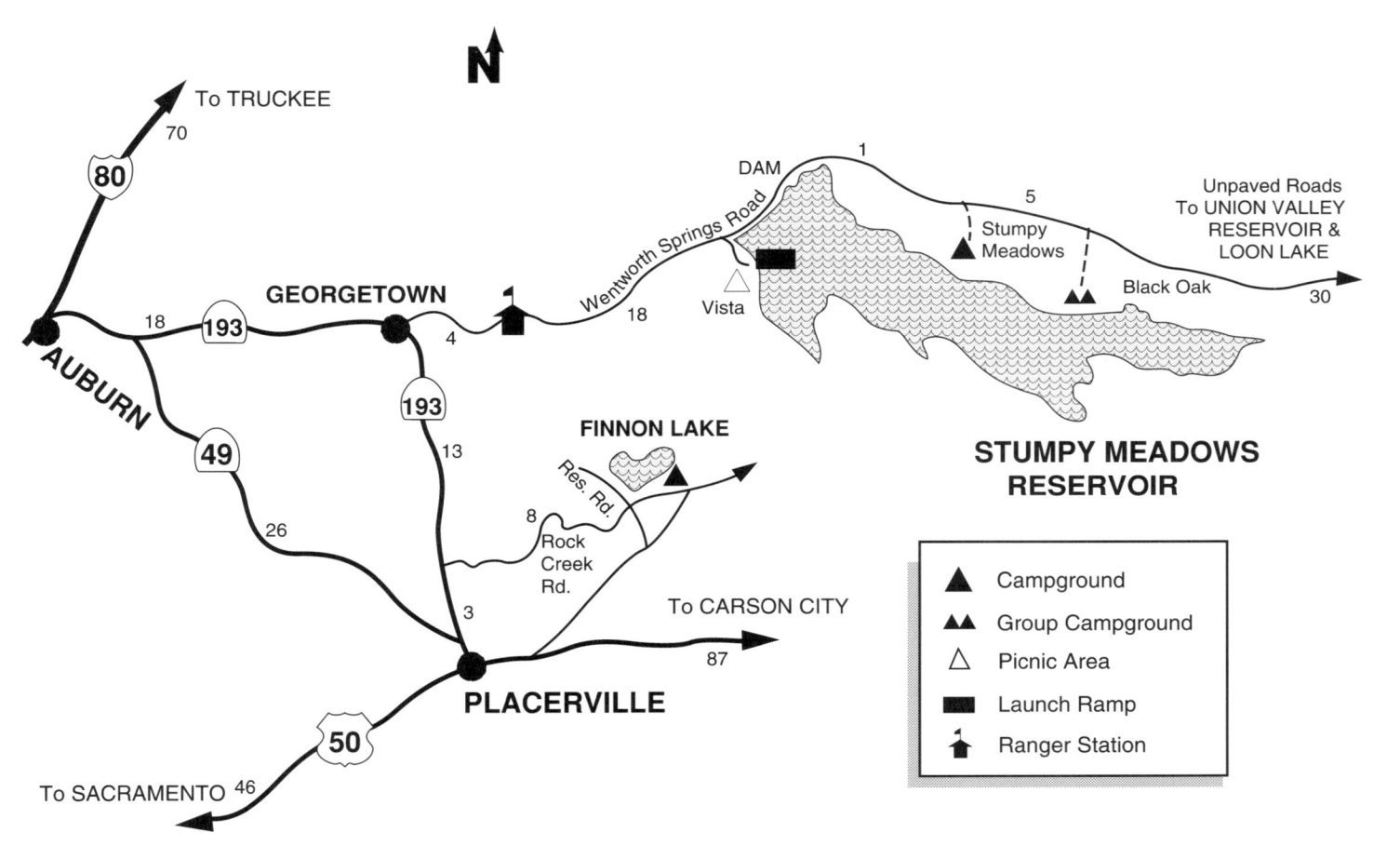

▲	Campground
▲▲	Group Campground
△	Picnic Area
■	Launch Ramp
⚑	Ranger Station

INFORMATION: Georgetown Ranger Dist., 7600 Wentworth Springs Rd., Georgetown 95634—Ph: (530) 333-4312

CAMPING	BOATING	RECREATION	OTHER

Stumpy Meadows:
  40 Dev. Sites for
  Tents & R.V.s to
   22 Feet
  4 Group Sites to
   200 People
  Reserve:
   Ph: (800) 280-CAMP
 	
Finnon Lake:
  28 Dev. Sites
  Small Trailers
	Stumpy Meadows:
	  Open to All Boats
	  5 MPH Speed Limit
	
	Improved Launch Ramp
	
	Finnon Lake:
	  Rowboats Only
		Fishing: Rainbow &
		  Brown Trout
		Finnon Lake: Bass,
		  Perch & Catfish
		Picnicking
		Swimming
			Finnon Lake Resort:
			  9100 Rock Creek Rd.
			  Placerville 95667
			  Ph: (530) 622-9314
			
			Finnon Lake:
			  Store
			  Snack Bar
			  Restaurant

At 6,225 feet elevation, Tahoe is one of America's largest and most beautiful mountain Lakes. It is 22 miles long, 12 miles wide and 72 miles around. Tahoe is a prime recreation lake with a variety of opportunities and facilities. Boaters, skiers and sailors make great use of the vast expanse of clear open water. The varied trout fishery ranges from planted rainbows to the huge lake trout or mackinaw and salmon. Hikers, backpackers and equestrians can enjoy the numerous trails within the surrounding mountains and nearby Desolation Wilderness. Add to these outdoor activities, the excitement and luxury of Nevada's casinos, the "Lake" has it all.

....Continued.....

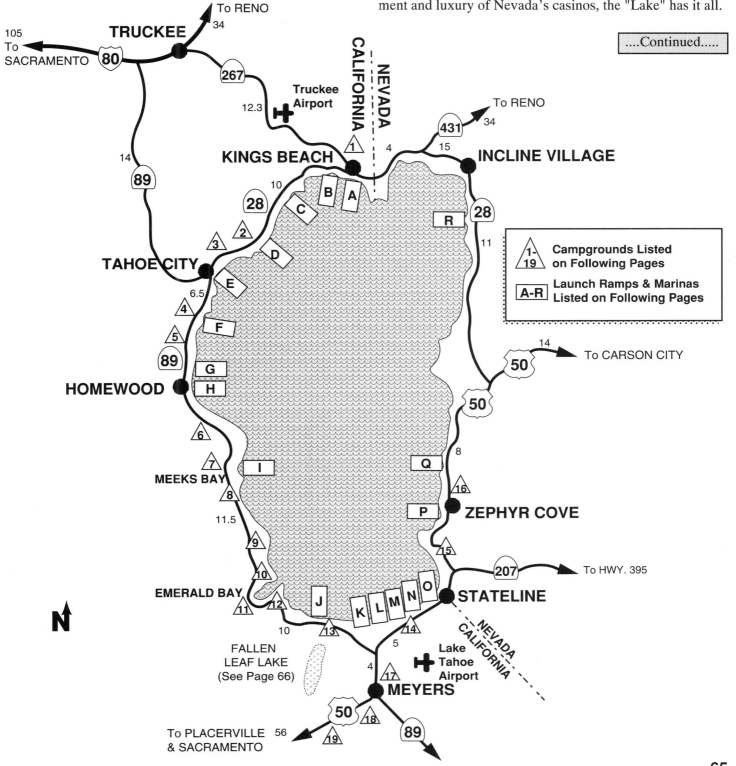

N

FALLEN
LEAF LAKE
(See Page 66)

Campgrounds Listed
1-19 on Following Pages

A-R Launch Ramps & Marinas
Listed on Following Pages

LAKE TAHOE.............Continued

Managed by California Land Management by Special Use Permit of the USDA Forest Service, Lake Tahoe Basin Management Unit Information Ph: (530) 544-5994
Reserve the following Sites Except for Bayview through **Ph: (800) 280-CAMP**

4. WILLIAM KENT - 2 Miles South of Tahoe City on Hwy. 89, - *Fee: $12* - 95 Tent/RV Sites to 24 Feet, Disposal Station, Swim Beach.

5. KASPIAN - 1 Miles North of Tahoe Pines on Hwy. 89 - *Fee: $10* - 10 Tent/RV Sites to 20 Feet, Picnic Area.

8. MEEKS BAY - 2 Miles South of Tahoma on Hwy. 89, - *Fee: $14* - 40 Tent/RV Sites to 20 Feet, Handicapped Access, Swim Beach.

15. NEVADA BEACH - 2 Miles North of Stateline off Hwy. 50, -*Fee: $14-16* - 54 Tent/RV Sites to 24 Ft, Handicapped Access, Boat-In Picnic Area, Group Picnic Area to 100 People.

11. BAYVIEW - On Hwy. 89 at Emerald Bay - *Fee: $5* - 10 Tent Sites, No Water, 2-Days Stay Limit.
(Pets okay on Leash at Above Sites)

Operated by California State Park Campgrounds
Reserve Ph: (800) 444-7275
Reservation Fee: $7.50 - Family Sites - 7 Months in Advance
Group Sites - 7 Months in Advance.

3. TAHOE STATE RECREATION AREA - 1/4 Mile East of Tahoe City - *Fee: $16* - 31 Tent/RV Sites to 24 Feet, Pets $1 a Day, Picnic Sites, Showers, Groceries, Laundromat, Fishing Pier - Information: (530) 583-3074.

6. GENERAL CREEK - SUGAR PINE POINT - One Mile South of Tahoma off Hwy. 89 - *Fee: $16* - 175 Tent/RV Sites to 30 Feet, Pets $1 a Day, Showers
Group Camps (Limit 6 R.V.s Over 15 Feet per Camp) - Fee: $75 - Open All Year.
All Camps can Accommodate up to 400 People - Information: (530) 525-7982.

9. D. L. BLISS STATE PARK - 3 Miles North of Emerald Bay, off Hwy. 89 - *Fee: $16 - $20* - 168 Tent/RV Sites to 15 Feet, Group Camp, Pets $1 a Day, Showers, Information: (530) 525-7277.

10. EMERALD BAY STATE PARK - 8 Miles North of South Lake Tahoe off Hwy. 89 - *Fee: $10* - 20 Tent Sites Information: (530) 525-7277.

12. EAGLE POINT - Off Hwy. 89 at Emerald Bay-*Fee: $16* -100 Tent/RV Sites to 21 Feet, Pets $1 a Day, Showers, Information: (530) 525-7277

Operated by the City of South Lake Tahoe
1180 Rufus Allen, South Lake Tahoe, CA 96150
Information: (530) 542-6096
Open April 1 to October 31

14. CAMPGROUND BY THE LAKE
2.3 Miles West of Stateline on
Hwy. 50 & Rufus Allen Blvd.

Fee: $17 per Vehicle & 4 People per Night
$2 for Extra Person, $1 a Day for Pets
157 Tent/RV Sites, No Hookups, Group Sites,
Disposal Station, Showers
Free Casino Shuttles
Reservations by Phone or Mail
Adjacent to Complex with Swimming Pool,
Horseshoes, Volleyball
Gym Ph: (530) 542-6056
Bijou 9-Hole Golf Course Ph: (530) 542-6097

Operated by Tahoe City Parks and Recreation
380 North Lake Blvd., Tahoe City 96145
Information: (530) 583-5544

2. LAKE FOREST CAMPGROUND
2 Miles East of Tahoe City
Fee: $10
21 Tent/RV Sites to 23 Feet
Boat Ramp, Swim Beach
Pets Okay on Leash.

....Continued....

PRIVATELY OPERATED CAMPGROUNDS: SEE NUMBER IN TRIANGLE ON MAP

1. SANDY BEACH - at Kings Beach on Hwy. 28 - *Fee: From $15 - Ph: (530) 546-7682* - 44 Tent/RV Sites to 35 Feet, Hookups, Pets $1.50 a Day, Showers, Boat Ramp.

7. MEEKS BAY RESORT, P.O. Box 787, Tahoma 96142 - 10 Miles South of Tahoe City - *Fee :From $18 - Ph: (530) 525-6946 or Toll Free (877) 326-3357* - 10 RV Sites, Full Hookups, 18 Tent Sites, No Pets, Disposal Station, Cabins, Launch Ramp, Full Service Marina. (Under USFS Permit)

13. CAMP RICHARDSON RESORT, P. O. Box 9028, South Lake Tahoe 96158 - 3 Miles West of the "Y" - *Fee: From $19 - Ph: (530) 541-1801 or (800) 544-1801* - 333 Tent/RV Sites, Group Sites, Hookups, No Pets, Showers, Disposal Station, Lodge Units, Beach Motel, Groceries, Propane, Supplies, Boat Ramp, Horse Stables, Bicycle Rentals, Open All Year. (Under USFS Permit)

16. ZEPHYR COVE RESORT - 4 Miles North of Stateline - *Fee: From $17 - Ph: (775) 588-6644* - 170 Tent/RV Sites to 40 Feet, Group Sites, Pets $2 a Day, Showers, Cabins, Lodge, Marina, Groceries, Propane, Restaurant, MS Dixie II Paddlewheeler, Open All Year. (Under USFS Permit)

17. TAHOE VALLEY CAMPGROUND, P. O. Box 9026, South Lake Tahoe 96155 - 1/4 Mile South of Highway 89 - *Fee: From $22 - Ph: (530) 541-2222* - 413 Tent/RV Sites, Full Hookups, Group Sites, Pets $2 a Day, Disposal Station, Showers, Playground, Laundromat, Groceries, Propane, Recreation Room, Cable T.V., Swimming Pool in Season.

18. TAHOE PINES CAMPGROUND AND RV PARK, Box 11918, South Lake Tahoe 96155 - Off Hwy. 50, West of Meyers *Fee: From $22 - Ph: (530) 577-1653* - 50 Tent Sites, 21 RV Sites with Full Hookups to 40 Feet, Pets $3.50 a Day, Disposal Station, Showers, Laundromat, Groceries, Playground, Private Wooded River & Creek Sites.

19. KOA KAMPGROUND, Box 11552, South Lake Tahoe 96155 - Off Hwy. 50 West of Meyers - *Fee: From $23 - Ph: (530) 577-3693* or (800) 562-3477 - 16 Tent Sites, 52 RV Sites to 40 Feet, Full Hookups, Pets $3.50 a Day, Disposal Station, Showers, Laundry, Mini-Market, Propane, Swimming Pool, Recreation Room, Playground, Picnic Tables, Campfire Rings and BBQ Grills at Every Site, Wooded Area.

LAUNCH RAMPS AND MARINA FACILITIES: SEE LETTER IN RECTANGLE ON MAP

A. KINGS BEACH STATE RECREATIONAL AREA - North Tahoe Parks & Recreation, P.O. Box 139, Tahoe Vista 96148 Ph: (530) 546-7248 - *Launch & Parking Fee: $5* - Launch Ramp Open for Small Boats - Experienced Boaters Only - Use at Own Risk, Rentals: 12 & 14 Feet Sailboats & Jets.

B. NORTH TAHOE MARINA - 7360 N. Lake Blvd., Tahoe Vista 96148—Ph: (530) 546-8248 - *Launch Fees: To 20 Feet $22; Over 20 Feet $1.50 per Foot* - Paved Ramp - *Power Boats Only,* Full Service Marina, Buoys, Fuel and Repairs, Accessory Sales, Power Boat & Ski Equipment Rentals.

C. SIERRA BOAT CO. - 5146 North Lake Blvd., Carnelian Bay 96146—Ph: (530) 546-2552 - *Fees: Sailboats $3 per Foot; Boats to 24 Feet $25; Over 24 Feet $30-$35* - Hoist, Buoys, Slips, Fuel and Repairs, Supplies, Dry Storage.

D. LAKE FOREST BOAT RAMP - Hwy. 28 at end of Lake Forest Rd. near U. S. Coast Guard Station - Ph: (530) 583-3796 - May be closed - Call for Information.

....Continued....

LAUNCH RAMPS AND MARINA FACILITIES: SEE NUMBER IN RECTANGLE ON MAP

E. TAHOE BOAT COMPANY - 700 No. Lake Blvd., Box 6651, Tahoe City 96145—Ph: (530) 583-5567, Hoist (No Ramp), Full Service Marina, Fuel, Repairs, Marine Accessories, Ski Boat Rentals, Winter Storage, Boat Sales.

F. SUNNYSIDE RESORT - P.O. Box 5969, Tahoe City 95730—Ph: (530) 583-7200, Hoist, Slips, Buoys, Pump Station, Fuel, Repairs, Restaurant, Ski & Sail Boat Rentals & Sales, Ski School, Store & Supplies.

G. HIGH & DRY HOMEWOOD MARINA - HIGH & DRY, P.O. Box 1735, Tahoe City 96145 @ 5190 Hwy. 89, Homewood —Ph: (530) 525-5966, Hoist (No Ramp), Fuel, Power Boat Rentals, Complete Service and Chandlery.

H. OBEXERS, 5355 West Lake Blvd., Homewood 96141—Ph: (530) 525-7962, Paved Ramp and Travel Lift, Fork Lift, Fuel, Marine Accessories, Boat Service, Groceries.

I. MEEKS BAY RESORT AND MARINA - 7941 Emerald Bay Rd., Meeks Bay 96142—Ph: (530) 525-6946 or (Toll Free (877) 326-3357, Paved Ramp, Slips, Row, Power & Sail Boat Rentals, Groceries, Bait & Tackle, Snack Bar, Cabins, RV Park.

J. RICHARDSON'S RESORT, ANCHORAGE MARINA - Off Hwy. 89, 2 Miles Northwest of "Y" - Ph: (530) 542-6570 - *Fees: Call for Information* - Launch Ramp, Gas, Supplies, Repairs, Rentals, Moorings.

K. TAHOE KEYS MARINA - 2435 Venice Dr. East, South Lake Tahoe 96150—Ph: (530) 541-2155 - *Fees: $25 Round Trip* Double Paved Ramp, 45 Ton Capacity Travel Lift, Paved Full Service Marina, Sail and Power Boat Rentals, Fuel, Repairs, Chandlery, Mini-Mart, 300 Slips, Largest Marina on Lake, Overnight Parking, Restaurant.

L. EL DORADO BEACH PUBLIC BOAT RAMP - US 50 & Lakeview Ave., South Lake Tahoe 96150—Ph: (530) 542-6056, *Launch Fee: $10*, Public Use Facility, Paved Ramp, Swim Beach, Picnic Area with BBQ's, Campground across Street on Rufus Allen Blvd.

M. TIMBER COVE MARINA - 3411 Lake Tahoe Blvd., South Lake Tahoe 96150—Ph: (530) 544-2942 - *Fees: Call for Information* - Unpaved Ramp, Hoist, Mooring, Fuel, Repairs, Power, Sail Boat and Jet Rentals, Snack Bar, Gift Shop, Boat Charters.

N. SKI RUN MARINA - 900 Ski Run Blvd. P.O. Box 14272, South Lake Tahoe 96150—Ph: (530) 544-0200 - *Fees: Call for Information* - Moorings, Slips, Power & Sail Boat Rentals, Fuel, Repairs, Cafe, Beer Garden, On the Water Restaurant, Shops, Home to the 500 Passenger *Tahoe Queen* Paddle Wheeler Cruises.

O. LAKESIDE MARINA - Hwy. 50 at end of Park Ave., South Lake Tahoe - Ph: (530) 541-6626 - *Fees: $10 In - $10- Out* - Ramp Access - All Boats Under 27 Feet, Slips, Gas, Supplies, Slips, Moorings, Dry Storage.

P. ZEPHYR COVE MARINA - 760 US 50, Zephyr Cove, NV 89448—Ph: (775) 588-3833, *Fees: Call for Information* - Moorings, Fuel, Power & Sail Boat Rentals, Full Resort Facilities, Picnic Area, Cabins, Campground, Restaurant.

Q. CAVE ROCK PUBLIC LAUNCH FACILITY - Off Hwy. 50, North of Zephyr Cove - Ph: (775) 831-0494 - *Fees: Launch $10 - Day Use $5* - Paved Ramp, Swim Beach, Fishing Area, Restrooms.

R. SAND HARBOR - 4 Miles South of Incline Village - Ph: (775) 831-0494 - *Fees: Launch $12 - Day Use $6* - Paved Launch Ramp, Swim Beach, Picnic Areas, Group Use Picnic Area, Nature Hike, Restrooms.

....Continued....

GENERAL INFORMATION

Lodging and accommodations are extensive throughout the Lake Tahoe Basin. The casinos offer luxurious hotel rooms with complete facilities. Condominiums, bed & breakfasts, cabins and houses are available for rent. In addition to the enormous variety of lodging available, there is an abundance of recreational and service facilities.

For Full Information and Reservations Contact:

Lake Tahoe Basin Management Unit
USDA, Forest Service
870 Emerald Bay Road, Suite 1
South Lake Tahoe, CA 96150
Ph: (530) 573-2600

Eldorado National Forest
Information Center
3070 Camino Heights Drive
Camino, CA 97509
Ph: (530) 644-6048

Toiyabe National Forest
Carson Ranger Station
1536 S. Carson Street
Carson City, NV 89701
Ph: (775) 882-2766

California State Parks
Sierra District
P. O. Drawer D
Tahoma, CA 96142
Ph: (530) 525-7232

Nevada State Parks
Sand Harbor
P. O. Box 8867
2005 Highway 28
Incline Village, NV 89450
Ph: (775) 831-0494

Chambers of Commerce:

South Lake Tahoe
3066 Lake Tahoe Blvd.
South Lake Tahoe, CA 96150
Ph: (530) 541-5255

North Lake Tahoe
P.O. Box 884
Tahoe City, CA 96145
Ph: (530) 583-3494

Tahoe - Douglas
P. O. Box 401
Zephyr Cove, NV 89448
Ph: (775) 588-4591

Lake Tahoe Incline Village
Crystal Bay Visitors &
Convention Bureau
969 Tahoe Blvd.
Incline Village, NV 89451
*Ph: (775) 832-1606 or
(800) GO TAHOE*

Lake Tahoe Visitors Authority
South Shore
1156 Ski Run Blvd.
South Lake Tahoe, CA 96150
*Ph: (800) AT TAHOE (288-2463)
Reservations*
Ph: (530) 544-5050 - Information

North Lake Tahoe
Resort Association
P.O. Box 5459
Tahoe City, CA 96145
Ph: (530) 583-3494 - Reservations
Ph: (800) 824-6348 - Information

FALLEN LEAF LAKE

Fallen Leaf Lake is at an elevation of 6,400 feet in the Lake Tahoe Basin Management Unit. The lovely property around this Lake is partially private and partially National Forest land. The shoreline is heavily forested with pine trees to the water's edge. It is within easy access to the Desolation Wilderness and near the numerous attractions at South Lake Tahoe and the casinos at Stateline. The Forest Service maintains a campground on the north end of the Lake.

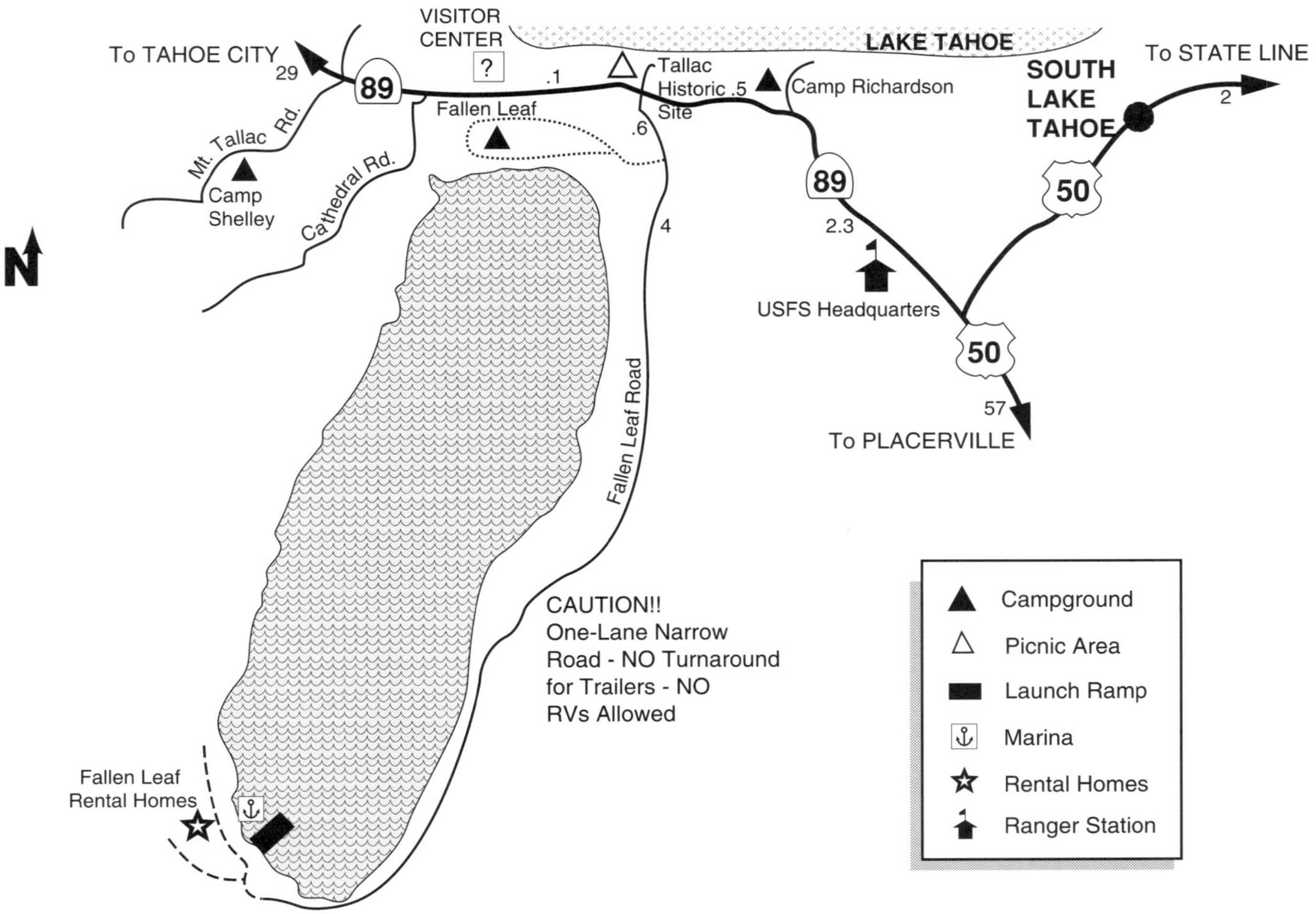

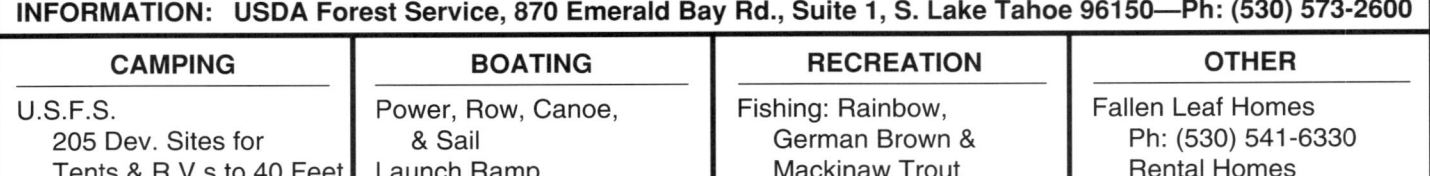

To TAHOE CITY — 89 — VISITOR CENTER — LAKE TAHOE — To STATE LINE — SOUTH LAKE TAHOE — Tallac Historic Site — Camp Richardson — 89 — 50 — USFS Headquarters — To PLACERVILLE — Fallen Leaf — Camp Shelley — Fallen Leaf Road — CAUTION!! One-Lane Narrow Road - NO Turnaround for Trailers - NO RVs Allowed — Fallen Leaf Rental Homes

▲ Campground
△ Picnic Area
■ Launch Ramp
⚓ Marina
☆ Rental Homes
⚑ Ranger Station

INFORMATION: USDA Forest Service, 870 Emerald Bay Rd., Suite 1, S. Lake Tahoe 96150—Ph: (530) 573-2600

CAMPING	BOATING	RECREATION	OTHER

U.S.F.S.
    205 Dev. Sites for
Tents & R.V.s to 40 Feet
Fee: $16
Reserve:
    Ph: (800) 280-CAMP
Camp Shelly:
1-1/2 Miles on Mt. Tallac Rd
Ph: (530) 541-6985
    26 Tent/RV Sites to
22 Feet - Fee: $17
	Power, Row, Canoe,
	    & Sail
	Launch Ramp
	Rentals: Rowboats, Fishing
	    Boats with Motors
	    & Ski Boats
	
	*NO R.V.s on Road
	to Marina & Launch
	Ramp*
		Fishing: Rainbow,
		    German Brown &
		    Mackinaw Trout
		Swimming
		Picnicking
		Hiking
		Backpacking
		Horseback Riding
		    Trails
		Nature Study
		Mountain Biking
			Fallen Leaf Homes
			    Ph: (530) 541-6330
			    Rental Homes
			    Fully Furnished
			
			Marina
			Grocery Store
			Bait & Tackle

Echo Lake is nestled at 7,414 feet in between high mountains near Echo Summit off Highway 50. This is one of the most beautiful natural Lakes to be found in the High Sierra. All types of boating are allowed, but waterskiing is not permitted on Upper Echo Lake. The bordering Desolation Wilderness has 63,475 acres of trails, lakes and streams easily accessible for the backpacker or horseman. Echo Chalet, the only facility on the Lake, provides a taxi service to the Upper Lake which shortens the hike into the Wilderness Area by 3-1/2 miles. The Rubicon and American Rivers along with over 50 Lakes and streams welcome expectant anglers to the un-crowded waters of this area.

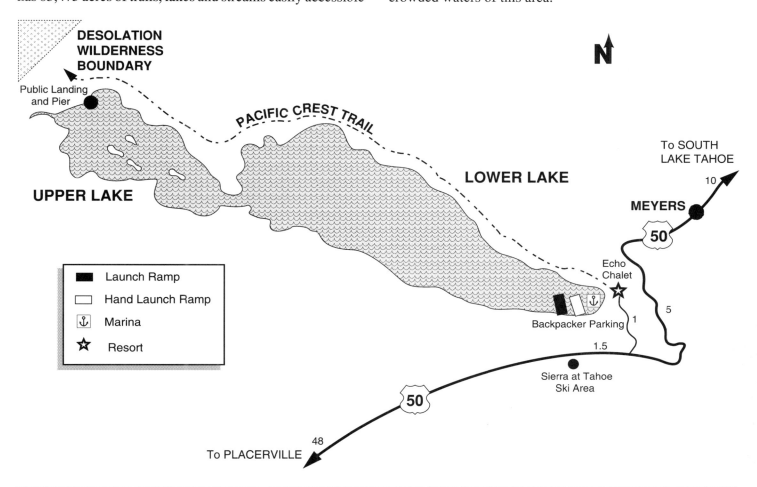

DESOLATION WILDERNESS BOUNDARY

Public Landing and Pier

PACIFIC CREST TRAIL

LOWER LAKE

N

UPPER LAKE

To SOUTH LAKE TAHOE

10

MEYERS

50

Echo Chalet

5

Backpacker Parking

1

1.5

Sierra at Tahoe Ski Area

50

48

To PLACERVILLE

Launch Ramp
Hand Launch Ramp
Marina
Resort

INFORMATION: Echo Chalet, Echo Lake 95721—Ph: (530) 659-7207

CAMPING	BOATING	RECREATION	OTHER
No Overnight Camping or Trailers Allowed in Echo Lake Basin Camping Allowed in Desolation Wilderness Area with Permit from U.S.F.S.	Power, Row, Canoe, Sail, Waterski, Windsurf & Inflatable Full Service Marina Launch Ramp - $10 Cartops and Inflatables - $6 Rentals: Fishing Boats, Canoes & Kayaks Docks, Berths, Gas, Storage	Fishing: Rainbow, Brook & Cutthroat Trout, Kokanee Salmon Swimming Picnicking Hiking Backpacking [Parking] Horseback Riding Trails Hunting: Deer, Quail	Housekeeping Cabins Snack Bar Grocery Store Hardware & Sporting Goods Bait & Tackle Fishing Licenses Gas Station Day Hike Permits to Wilderness Area

WRIGHTS LAKE

Wrights Lake has a surface area of 65 acres. It is at an elevation of 7,000 feet in the Eldorado National Forest, one of many Lakes in this area. The high Sierra setting provides a unique retreat for the outdoorsman. Two Trailheads for Desolation Wilderness Area border the Lake, making it popular for the equestrian, hiker and backpacker. Wrights Lake offers good fishing, and the other Lakes and streams in this vicinity are equally inviting to the angler. Boating is restricted to hand launching. Motors are not allowed. Wilderness permits are required for entry into the Desolation Wilderness Area. They are available at the U.S.F.S. Information Center on Highway 50.

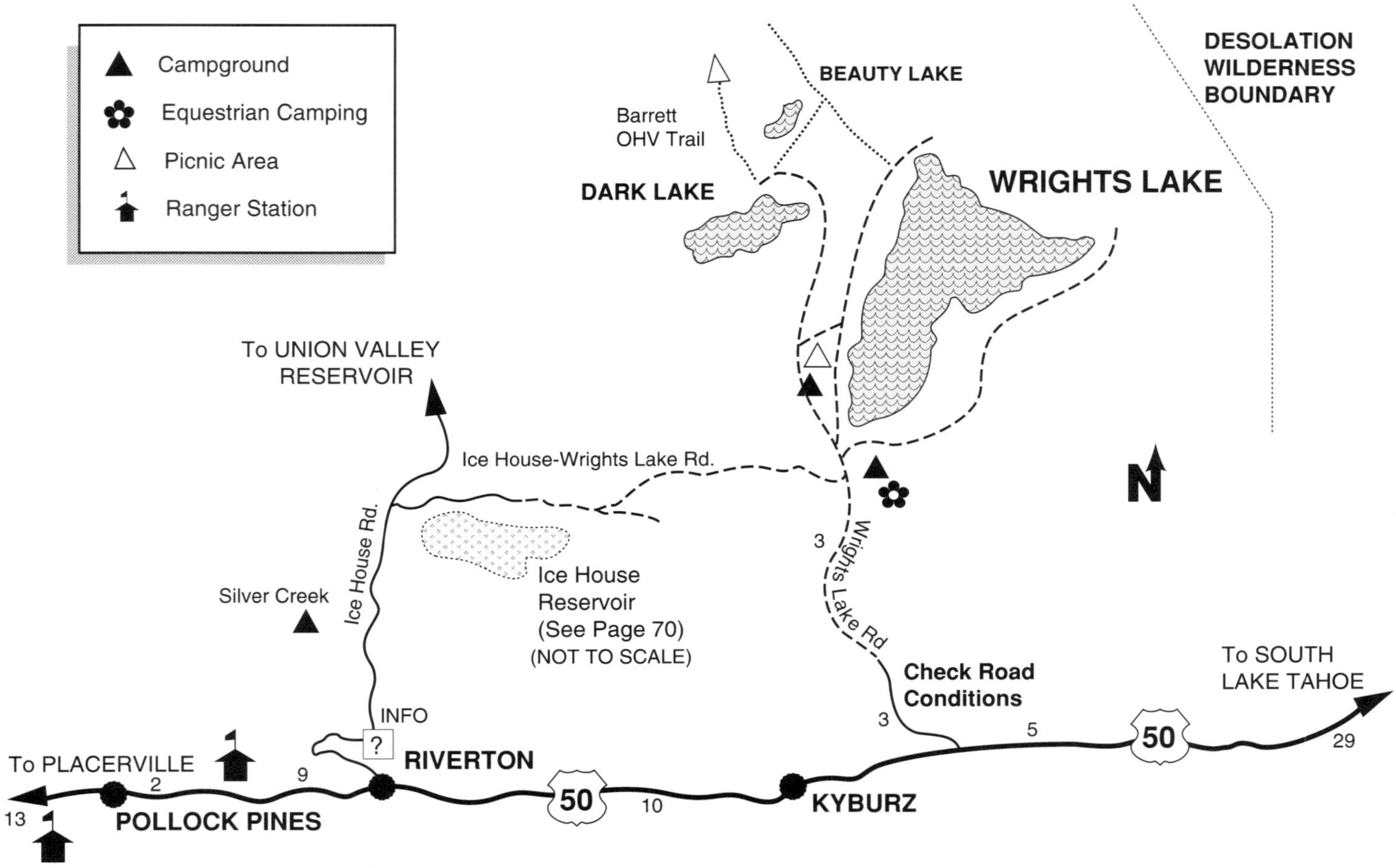

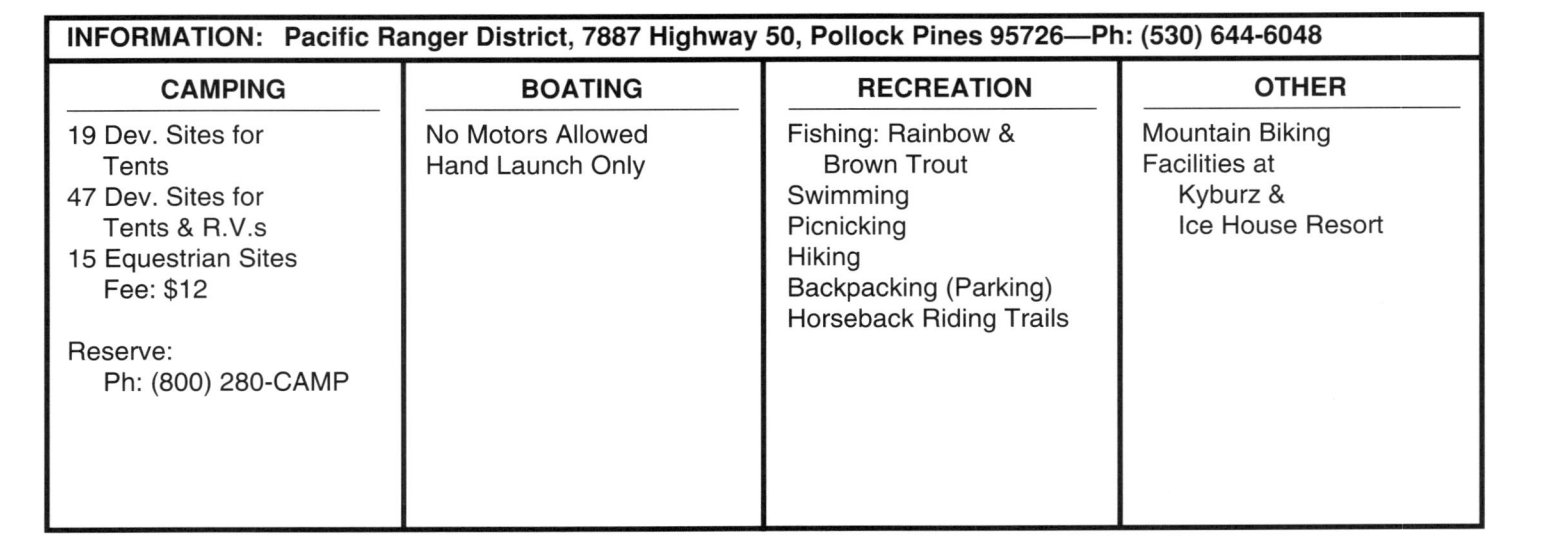

▲	Campground	△	Picnic Area
✿	Equestrian Camping	♟	Ranger Station

INFORMATION: Pacific Ranger District, 7887 Highway 50, Pollock Pines 95726—Ph: (530) 644-6048

CAMPING	BOATING	RECREATION	OTHER
19 Dev. Sites for Tents 47 Dev. Sites for Tents & R.V.s 15 Equestrian Sites Fee: $12 Reserve: Ph: (800) 280-CAMP	No Motors Allowed Hand Launch Only	Fishing: Rainbow & Brown Trout Swimming Picnicking Hiking Backpacking (Parking) Horseback Riding Trails	Mountain Biking Facilities at Kyburz & Ice House Resort

Loon Lake is at an elevation of 6,500 feet in the Crystal Basin Recreation Area of the Eldorado National Forest. This beautiful high mountain Lake, with crystal clear water, appears carved out of granite. The Forest Service maintains the campgrounds, picnic areas, paved launch ramp, and a walk-in or boat-in campground. This is a good Lake for sailing and boating in general, but waterskiing is not advised due to extremely cold water. Fishing can be excellent for Rainbow and German Brown trout. There is trailhead parking for the Desolation Wilderness, and trail conditions are good for hikers and horses. Gerle Creek Reservoir has a 50-site campground and picnic area with a handicap fishing pier. Boats with motors are not allowed at this facility.

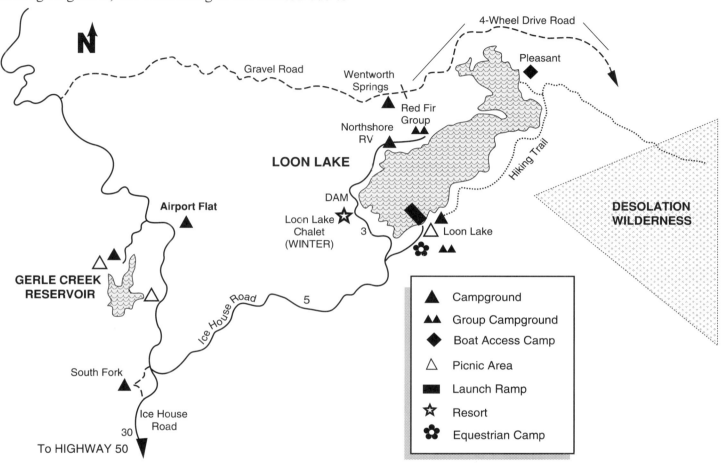

INFORMATION: Pacific Ranger Station, 7887 Highway 50, Pollock Pines 95726—Ph: (530) 644-6048

CAMPING	BOATING	RECREATION	OTHER
Loon Lake Complex: 53 Dev. Sites for Tents & R.V.s - Fee: $13 3 Group Camps: 25, 35 & 50 People Fee: $50-$75 9 Equestrian Units: $13 Northshore: 15 RV Sites Fee: $5 - No Water Red Fir Group: 25 People No Trailers - Fee: $35	Power, Row, Canoe & Sail Launch Ramp *Waterskiing is NOT Recommended* Gerle Creek Reservoir: No Motorboats	Fishing: Rainbow & German Brown Trout Picnicking Hiking Backpacking [Parking] Entrance to Desolation Wilderness Horseback Riding Trails OHV Trails Mountain Biking	Gerle Creek: 50 Dev. Sites for Tents & R.V.s - Fee: $13 Airport Flat: 16 Units No Fee, No Water OHVs Allowed Wentworth Springs: 8 Sites 4WD - No Fee, No Water South Fork: 17 Sites No Fee, No Water Reserve: Ph: (800) 280-CAMP Full Facilities: 23 Miles

ICE HOUSE RESERVOIR

Ice House Reservoir is at an elevation of 5,500 feet in the Crystal Basin Recreation Area of the Eldorado National Forest. The surface area of the Lake is 678 acres of clear, cold water. The surrounding shoreline is covered with conifers. The Ice House campground, launch ramp and picnic facilities are run by a concessionaire. The Forest Service operates Northwind and Strawberry Point campgrounds. There are nice swimming areas. The roads are paved and well maintained, but beware of logging trucks. This is an excellent boating Lake especially for sailing. The Reservoir is stocked during the summer months and the angler will find good fishing for trout and Kokanee.

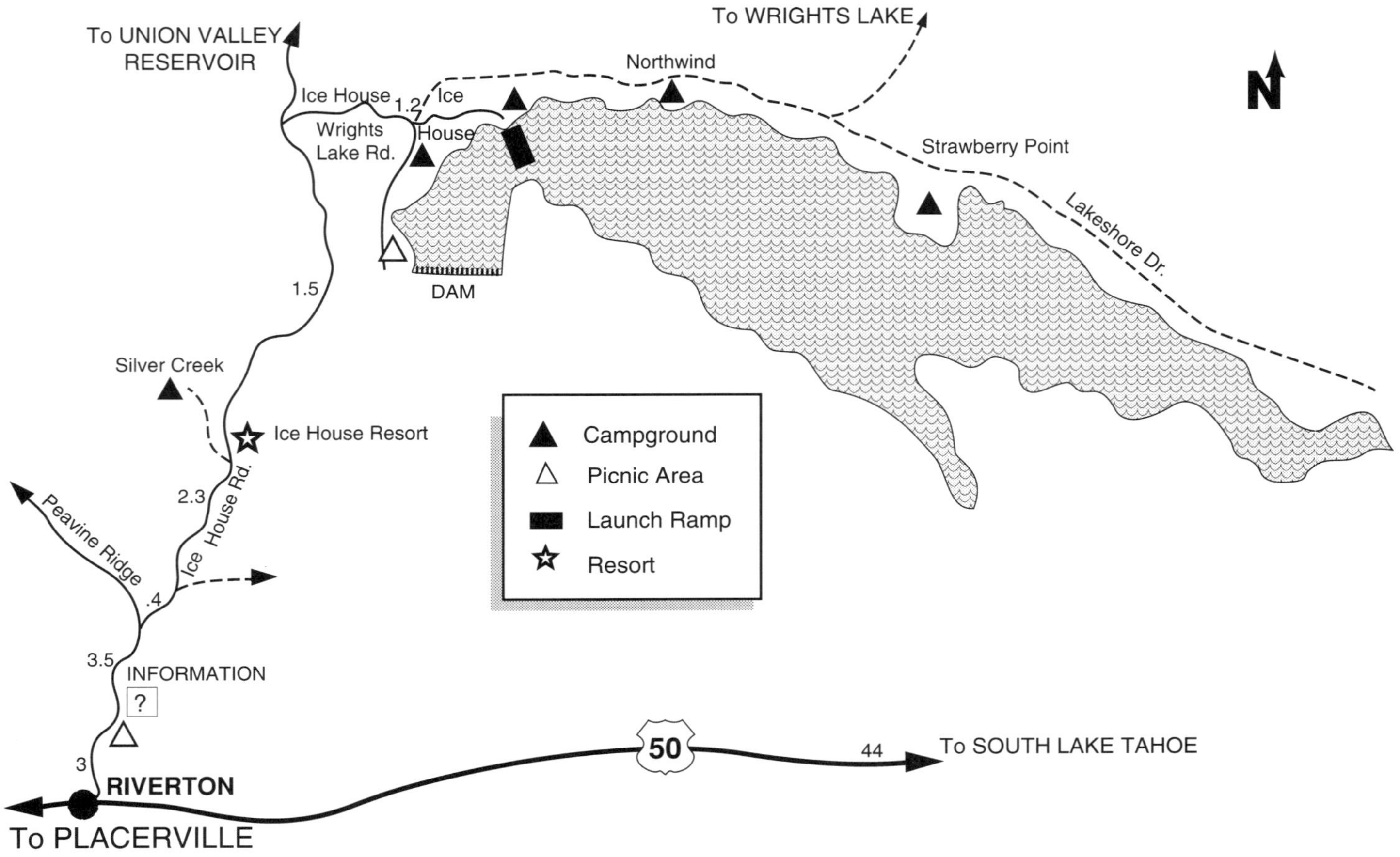

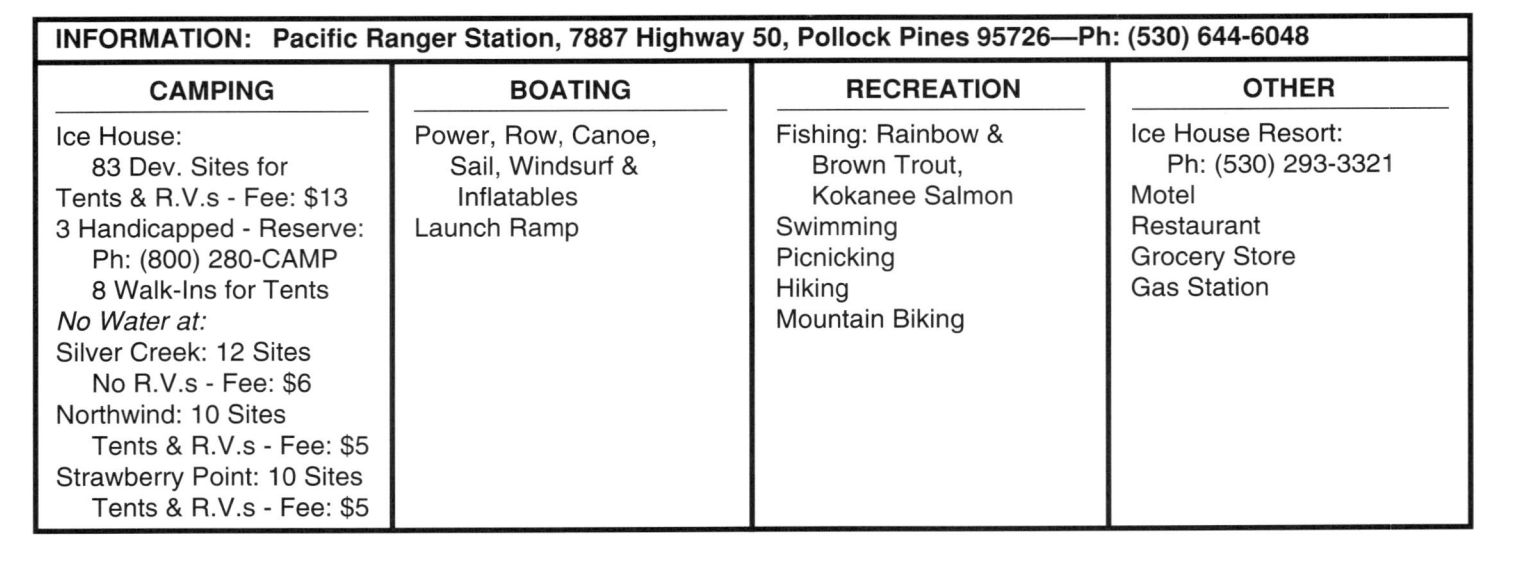

INFORMATION: Pacific Ranger Station, 7887 Highway 50, Pollock Pines 95726—Ph: (530) 644-6048

CAMPING	BOATING	RECREATION	OTHER

Ice House:
  83 Dev. Sites for
Tents & R.V.s - Fee: $13
3 Handicapped - Reserve:
  Ph: (800) 280-CAMP
  8 Walk-Ins for Tents
No Water at:
Silver Creek: 12 Sites
  No R.V.s - Fee: $6
Northwind: 10 Sites
  Tents & R.V.s - Fee: $5
Strawberry Point: 10 Sites
  Tents & R.V.s - Fee: $5
	Power, Row, Canoe,
	  Sail, Windsurf &
	  Inflatables
	Launch Ramp
		Fishing: Rainbow &
		  Brown Trout,
		  Kokanee Salmon
		Swimming
		Picnicking
		Hiking
		Mountain Biking
			Ice House Resort:
			  Ph: (530) 293-3321
			Motel
			Restaurant
			Grocery Store
			Gas Station

Union Valley Reservoir is located at an elevation of 4,900 feet in the Crystal Basin Recreation Area of the Eldorado National Forest. This area is in the pine and fir forests of the western Sierra and is dominated by the high granite peaks of the Crystal Range. The Reservoir has a surface area of 2,860 acres. The Forest Service maintains 3 launch ramps at the Lake, as well as a picnic area and campgrounds. Union Valley is an excellent Lake for sailing, and many clubs use this facility during the summer. Fishing can be excellent from your boat or along the shoreline.

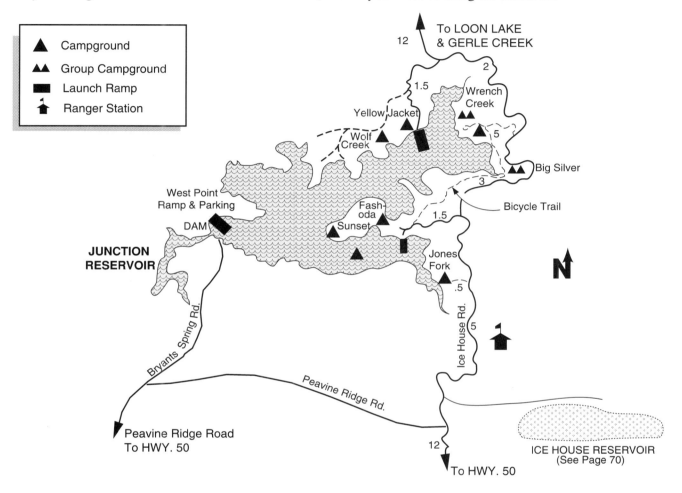

CAMPING	BOATING	RECREATION	OTHER

Sites for Tents & R.V.s:
Yellowjacket-40 Sites - $13
Wolf Creek-42 Sites - $13
Sunset - $13
Jonesfork-10 Sites - $5
   No Water at this Site
Wench & Big Silver Group
   Sites for Tents & R.V.s
   Group - Fee:$60
Fashoda - 30 Tents *Only*
   Walk-In Sites &
   1 Handicapped Site
   First Come Basis
	Canoes, Power,
	   Rowboats,
	   Sail, Windsurf,
	   Inflatables
	Launch Ramps
		Fishing: Rainbow &
		   Brown Trout
		Swimming
		Picnicking
		Hiking
		Bicycling
		   Trails
		
		Boat-In & Bike-In
		   Campgrounds
		   Scheduled to
		   Open - Phone for
		   Details
			Disposal Station
			
			Facilities - 7 Miles
			   at Ice House Resort
			
			Yellowjacket, Sunset &
			   Wench Campgrounds:
			   Reserve:
			   Ph: (800) 280-CAMP

INFORMATION: Pacific Ranger Station, 7887 Highway 50, Pollock Pines 95726—Ph: (530) 644-6048

JENKINSON LAKE - SLY PARK RECREATION AREA

Jenkinson Lake is at an elevation of 3,478 feet in the Sly Park Recreation Area south of Pollock Pines. The Lake has a surface area of 640 acres with 8 miles of coniferous tree-covered shoreline. The Eldorado Irrigation District has jurisdiction over the modern facilities at this pretty Lake. Facilities include 2 launch ramps with floats. There are a variety of individual and group campsites offering equestrian, handicapped and youth facilities. The water is clear, and fishing can be good along the coves. Winds are usually favorable for sailing. Waterskiing is in a counterclockwise direction in the central section of the Lake.

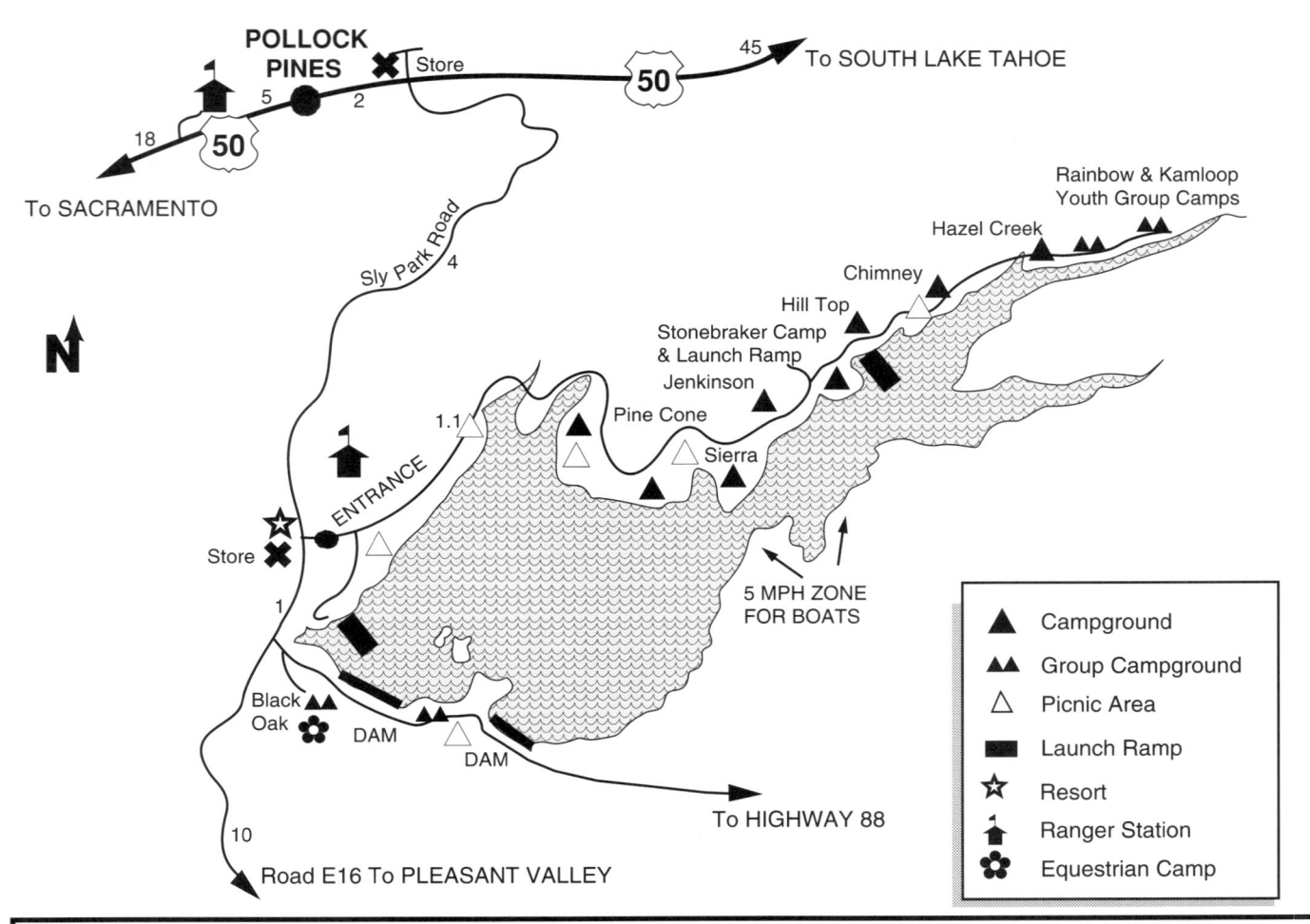

CAMPING	BOATING	RECREATION	OTHER
159 Dev. Sites for Tents & R.V.s Fee: $15 - 1st Vehicle	Power, Row, Canoe, Sail, Waterski, Windsurf & Inflatables *No Jets*	Fishing: Rainbow, Brown & Mackinaw Trout, Smallmouth Bass & Bluegill	Sly Park Store 4782 Sly Park Road Pollock Pines 95726 Ph: (530) 644-1113
Handicapped & Equestrian Facilities	2 Launch Ramps Fee: $5	Swimming	Bar & Grill Grocery Store
Group & Youth Camp Areas	Courtesy Docks	Picnicking	Bait & Tackle
Day Use: $5 or With a Boat $10	Rentals - May-September: Pedal Boats, Kayaks, Canoes - $8 Hour	Hiking & Bike Trails Equestrian Trails	Gas Station Disposal Station
Reservations Recommended for All Campsites Ph: (530) 644-2792		Nature Trails Small Museum	Additional Facilities in Pollock Pines - 5 Miles

INFORMATION: Sly Park Recreation Area, P.O. Box 577, Pollock Pines 95726—Ph: (530) 644-2545

The Folsom Lake State Recreation Area is one of the most complete recreation parks in California. This 18,000 acre Recreation Area offers an abundance of campsites, picnic areas, swimming beaches and marina facilities. With excellent waters for sailing and other types of boating, Folsom Lake has 11,930 surface acres with 75 shoreline miles. You can camp aboard your self-contained boat after registering at the Marina off Green Valley Road or at Granite Bay. This is a popular equestrian area with 80 miles of riding and hiking trails. There is a bicycle trail that links Beals Point via the American River Bike Trail to downtown Sacramento.

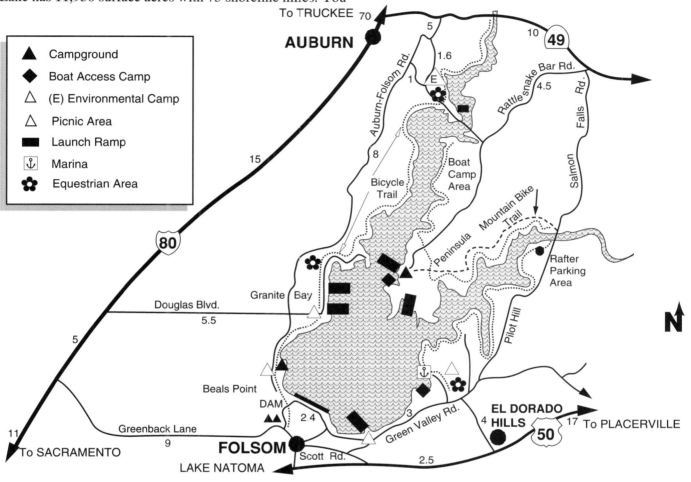

Legend:
- ▲ Campground
- ◆ Boat Access Camp
- △ (E) Environmental Camp
- △ Picnic Area
- ■ Launch Ramp
- ⚓ Marina
- ❀ Equestrian Area

INFORMATION: Folsom Lake, 7806 Folsom-Auburn Rd., Folsom 95630—Ph: (916) 988-0205

CAMPING	BOATING	RECREATION	OTHER

149 Dev. Sites
    Tents & R.V.s to 31 Feet
    Fee: $15
    Reserve:
    Ph: (800) 444-7275
Environmental Camp
    Reached by Foot
    or Horseback
Equestrian Area up to 50
    Riders & Horses
    Contact Park Hdqtrs.
Boat Camping
	Open to All Boating
	Full Service Marina
	Launch Ramps - Fees
	Rentals: Fishing,
	    Canoe, Sail &
	    Windsurfing
	Docks, Berths, Dry
	    Storage & Gas
	Windsurfing Lessons
	Low Water Hazards
	Fishing: Rainbow
		Trout, Coho Salmon,
		    Catfish, Bluegill,
		    Crappie, Bass,
		    Perch & Sturgeon
		Picnicking
		Swimming Beaches
		Bicycle, Hiking &
		    Riding Trails
		Horse Rentals
		Campfire Programs
			Snack Bar
			Bait & Tackle
			
			Day Use Fee
			
			Full Facilities in
			    Folsom

LAKE NATOMA

Lake Natoma is a part of the Folsom Lake Recreation Area. Resting at an elevation of 126 feet just below Folsom Dam, Natoma is the regulating Reservoir for Folsom Lake. The water is very cold and levels can fluctuate 3 or 4 feet in a day. This small Lake of 500 surface acres flows over dredger piles.

While the piles can create a good fish habitat, they are a boating hazard. Fishing can be difficult, but for those who know the Lake, it can be rewarding. Good trails are available for the equestrian, bicyclist and hiker.

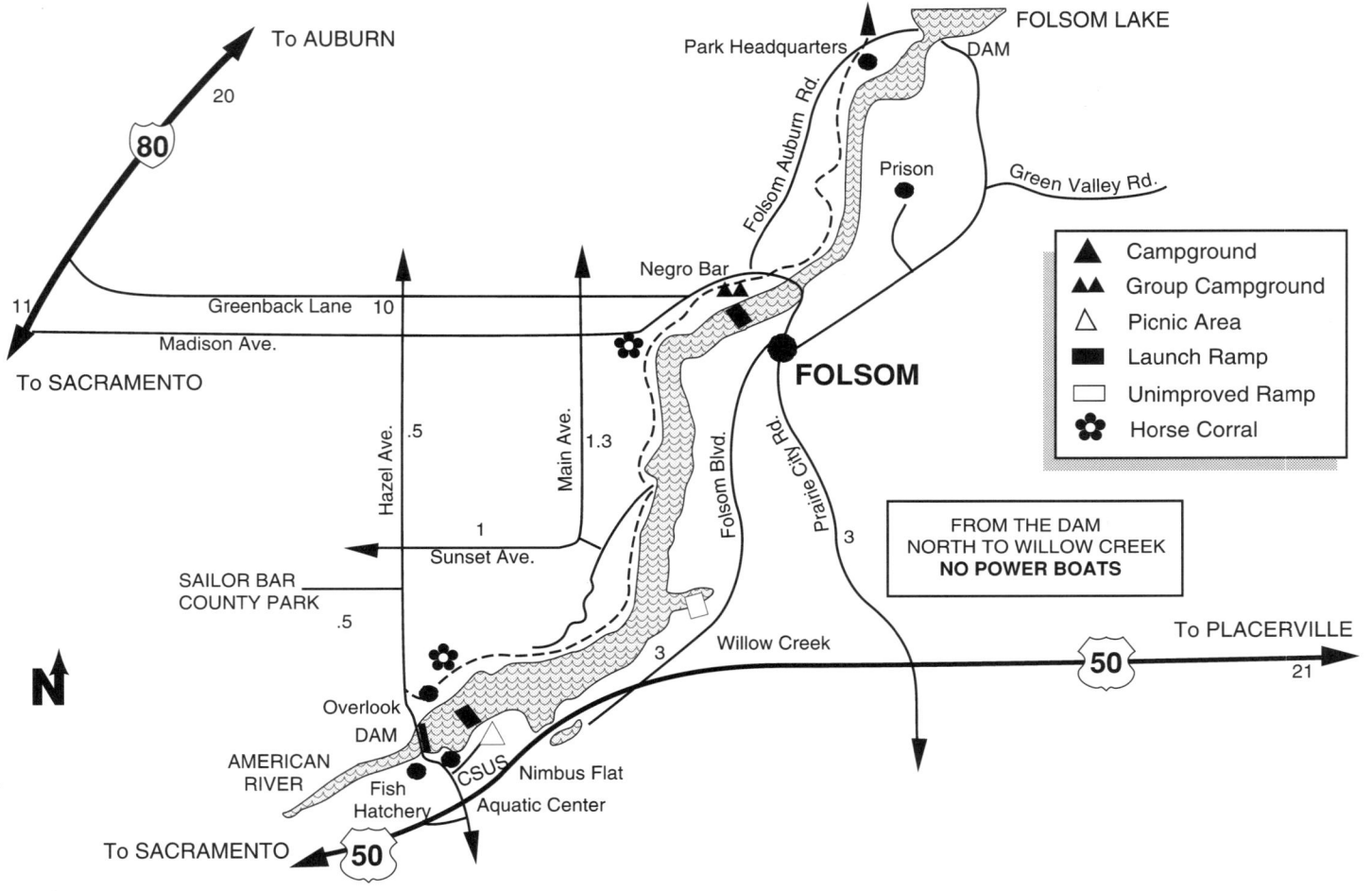

INFORMATION: Folsom Lake, 7806 Folsom-Auburn Rd., Folsom 95630—Ph: (916) 988-0205

CAMPING	BOATING	RECREATION	OTHER
3 Group Camps at Negro Bar A & B to 50 People $75.00 C to 25 People $37.50 Reserve: Ph: (800) 444-7275	Power, Row, Canoe, Sail, Windsurf & Inflatables Speed Limit - 5 MPH Launch Ramps - Fee CSUS Aquatic Center: Ph: (916) 985-7239 Rowing, Waterski, Sail, Canoe, Kayak & Windsurfing Lessons	Fishing: Rainbow Trout, Bluegill, Catfish, Crappie, Large & Smallmouth Bass Swimming - Beaches Picnicking Hiking Horseback Riding Bicycle Trails Home of the Pacific Coast Rowing Championships	Day Use Fee Entrance Fees Enforced Year Round When Park-Ur-Self Machines are in Use Correct Change is Necessary Full Facilities - 1 Mile at Folsom

With all the qualities of a working ranch, Gibson Ranch Regional Park, 325 acres, is an unique facility. A fishing lake, swimming hole and numerous equestrian activities and trails make it an ideal day use area for families. It offers 5 large picnic sites for groups. Elk Grove Regional Park, 125 acres, includes a 3 acre fishing lake, a swimming pool and numerous ball diamonds and picnic areas. Both these Parks are maintained by the County of Sacramento.

Under the jurisdiction of the Sacramento Municipal Utility District, the 400-acre Rancho Seco Recreational Area surrounds a 160-acre, warm-water lake fed by the Folsom South Canal. The water is recirculated daily and maintained at a constant level year round, providing ideal conditions for swimming, fishing, windsurfing and boating. No gas-powered motorboats are permitted. The camping facilities include a group campsite and reservations are available. There is a good swim area with sandy beach and lifeguards on duty Memorial Day through Labor Day.

▲	Campground
△△	Group Picnic Area
△	Picnic Area
■	Launch Ramp
◆	Fishing Dock
❀	Equestrian Center
⚑	Golf Course

INFORMATION: County Regional Parks, 3711 Branch Center Rd., Sacramento 95827-Ph: (916) 875-6336

CAMPING	BOATING	RECREATION	OTHER
Gibson Ranch & Elk Grove - Day Use	Gibson Ranch & Elk Grove - No Boating	Swimming Hole - Gibson Pool - Elk Grove	Horseshoe Pit Ball Diamonds
Rancho Seco Park: R.V./Tent Sites Some Hookups Group Camping Area Disposal Station Reservations: Ph: (916) 452-3211 Ext. 4408	Ranch Seco: Electric Motorboats, Sailboats & Rowboats 2 Launch Ramps Fishing Docks	Rancho Seco: Windsurfiing Rentals & Lessons Kayak-Paddleboat Rentals Fishing: Rainbow Trout, Florida Bass Bluegill, Sunfish, Catfish & Crappie Family & Group Picnic Areas - Reserve Swimming Area	General Store Fish Cleaning Station Coin-Operated Solar Showers Sacramento Unitility Dist. P.O. Box 15830 Sacramento 95852 Ph: (916) 452-3211 Full Facilities Nearby

SALT SPRINGS RESERVOIR

Salt Springs Reservoir rests at an elevation of 3,900 feet in the spectacular Mokelumne River Canyon of the Eldorado National Forest. This P.G. & E. Reservoir has a surface area of 961 acres. Hazardous afternoon winds can create problems for small boats. Fishing is often productive in both the Lake and the Mokelumne River as well as other nearby streams.

The Forest Service maintains three campgrounds along the river just below the dam. A trailhead into the beautiful 105,000 acre Mokelumne Wilderness is located just above the dam. *This is a high fire hazard area - NO campfires allowed - use portable stoves.*

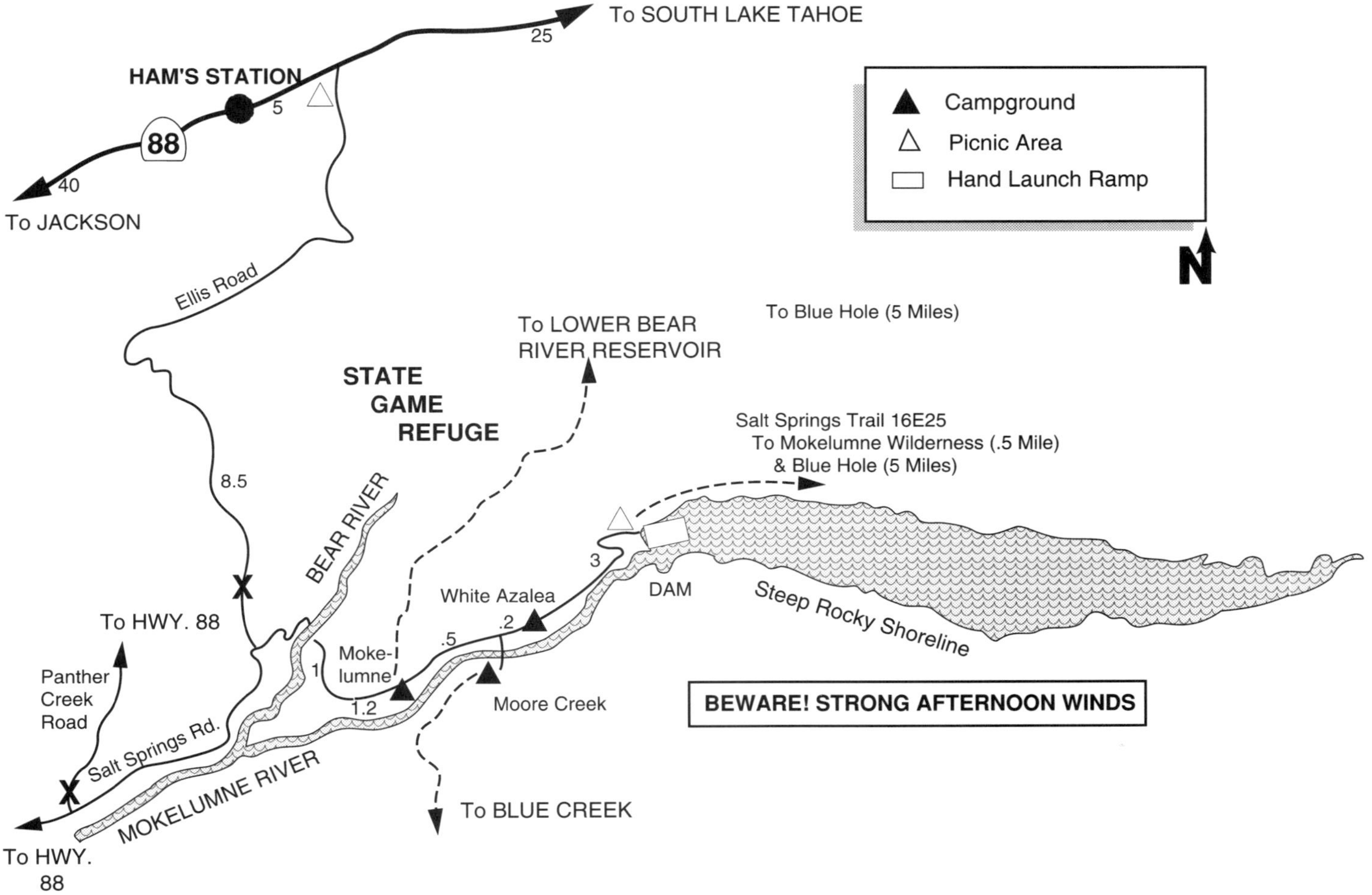

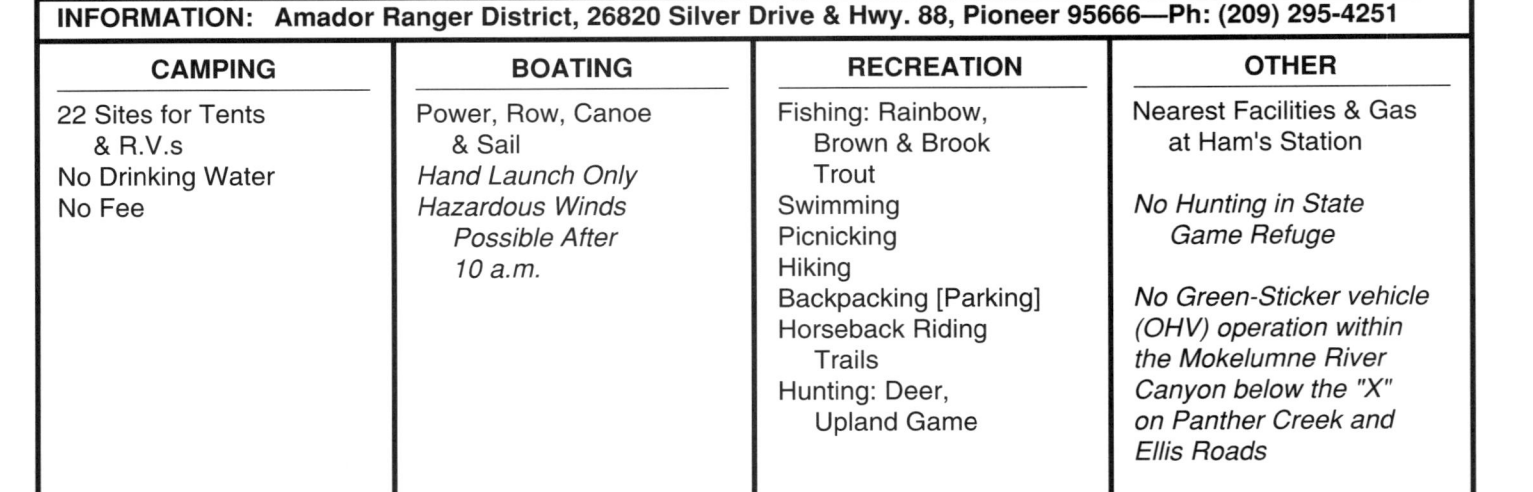

BEWARE! STRONG AFTERNOON WINDS

INFORMATION: Amador Ranger District, 26820 Silver Drive & Hwy. 88, Pioneer 95666—Ph: (209) 295-4251			
CAMPING	**BOATING**	**RECREATION**	**OTHER**
22 Sites for Tents & R.V.s No Drinking Water No Fee	Power, Row, Canoe & Sail *Hand Launch Only* *Hazardous Winds Possible After 10 a.m.*	Fishing: Rainbow, Brown & Brook Trout Swimming Picnicking Hiking Backpacking [Parking] Horseback Riding Trails Hunting: Deer, Upland Game	Nearest Facilities & Gas at Ham's Station *No Hunting in State Game Refuge* *No Green-Sticker vehicle (OHV) operation within the Mokelumne River Canyon below the "X" on Panther Creek and Ellis Roads*

Lower Bear River Reservoir rests at an elevation of 5,849 feet in the Eldorado National Forest. This pretty Lake of 727 acres is surrounded by a coniferous forest reaching to water's edge. There are good vacation and boating facilities. Afternoon breezes make sailing a delight. The Lake is regularly stocked, and fishing is usually productive. The Forest Service campgrounds are operated by a concessionaire. Overnight camping is limited to designated sites only. The Bear River Resort has complete camping and marina facilities with hot showers, groceries, bait and tackle, snack bar, trailer rentals and storage.

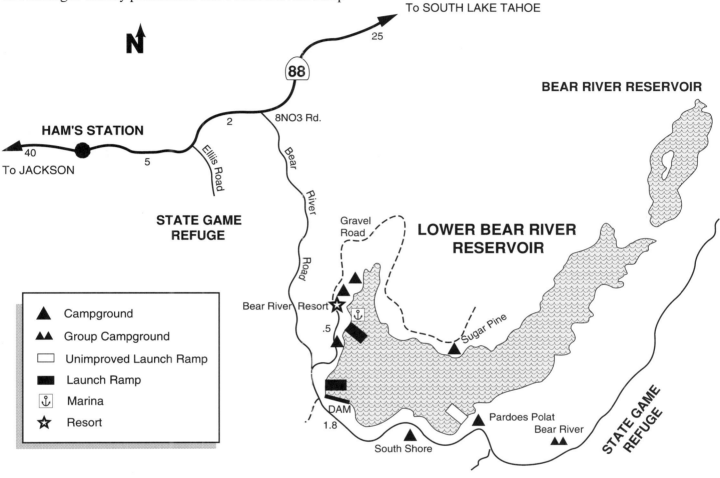

INFORMATION: Amador Ranger Station, 26820 Silver Drive & Hwy. 88, Pioneer 95666—Ph: (209) 295-4251

CAMPING	BOATING	RECREATION	OTHER
South Shore: 22 Dev. Sites for Tents & R.V.s Fee: $11 (Extra Veh. $5) Pardoes Pt. & Sugar Pine: 10 Sites for Tents & R.V.s - No Water Fee: $8 (Extra Veh. $4) Bear River Group Camps: 2 Sites - 25 People - $50 1 Site - 50 People - $100 Group Reservations: Ph: (209) 295-4512	Open to All Boating Full Service Marina Paved Launch Ramp Rentals: Fishing Boats *Low Water Hazards Late in Season*	Fishing: Rainbow, Macinaw & Brown Trout Picnicking Swimming - No Lifeguards Hiking - Backpacking Hunting: Deer	Lower Bear River Resort 40800 Hwy. 88 Pioneer 95666 Ph: (209) 295-4868 125 Dev. Sites with Hookups Fee: $20 Group Camp to 60 People Disposal Station Laundromat

SILVER LAKE

Silver Lake rests at an elevation of 7,200 feet in a large granite basin just west of the Sierra Summit in the Eldorado National Forest. This exceptionally beautiful Lake was once a resting place on the Emigrant Trail leading to the gold fields. You can still see the trail markers carved in trees. The descendants of Raymond Peter Plasse, who established a trading post in 1853, operate a good resort at the Lake from June through September. They offer campsites, horse camping and several recreational acitivties including horse rentals. A dining room and bar is also available. Silver Lake has been a popular recreation area for over a century offering a variety of natural resources and facilities for the camper, angler, boater, hiker and equestrian.

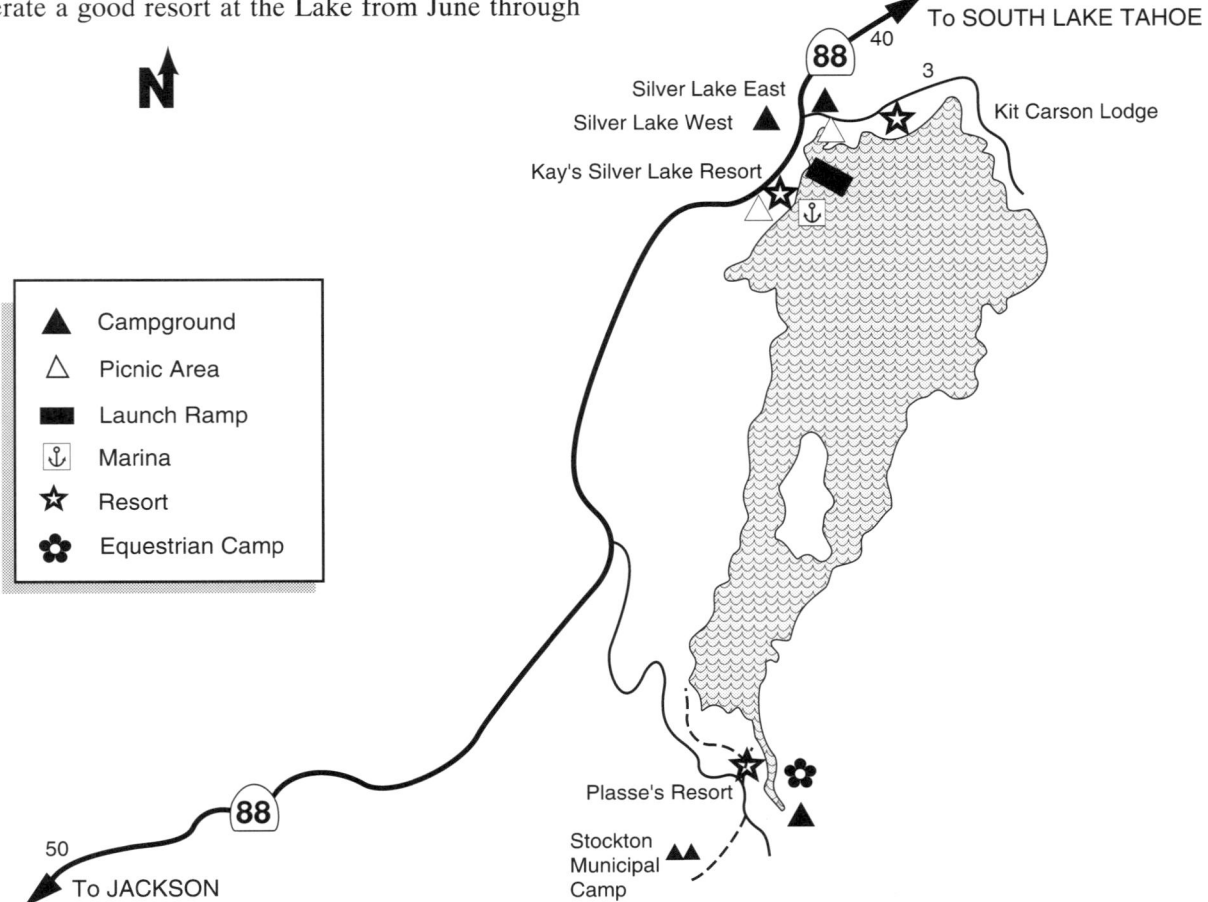

	Legend
▲	Campground
△	Picnic Area
▬	Launch Ramp
⚓	Marina
☆	Resort
❀	Equestrian Camp

INFORMATION: Amador Ranger District, 26820 Silver Drive & Hwy. 88, Pioneer 95666—Ph: (209) 295-4251

CAMPING	BOATING	RECREATION	OTHER
U.S.F.S. - 60 Dev. Sites for Tents & R.V.s - Fee: $12	Power, Row, Canoe, Sail, Inflatables	Fishing: Rainbow Trout	Cabins Located at: Kit Carson Lodge
15 Sites can be Reserved Ph: (800) 280-CAMP	Full Service Marinas	Swimming	Ph: (209) 258-8500
P.G.&E.:	Launch Ramps	Picnicking	Kay's Silver Lake Resort
Ph: (916) 386-5164	Rentals: Fishing Boats & Motors	Hiking	Ph: (209) 258-8598
37 Dev. Sites for Tents & R.V.s - Fee: $15	Docks, Moorings	Horseback Riding Trails	Snack Bars
Plasse's Resort		Horse Rentals at Plasse's Resort	Restaurants
Ph: (209) 258-8814			Grocery Stores
Dev. Sites for Tents & R.V.s			Bait & Tackle
Horse Trailers - Group Area			Laundromat
Fees: $15 and up			Gas Station
			Propane
			Disposal Station

Caples Lake is at an elevation of 7,950 feet in the Eldorado National Forest near the summit of Carson Pass. The nights and mornings are cool, and the water is cold in this 600 surface acre Lake. Kirkwood Lake is 3 miles to the west of Caples Lake at an elevation of 7,600 feet, and the road is not suitable for larger R.V.s or trailers. Neither gas or electric motor boats are allowed on Kirkwood, but you may use a motor up to 5 mph on Caples. Fishing is good for a variety of trout in these Lakes as well as other nearby lakes and streams. Trails lead into the Mokelumne Wilderness for the hiker or backpacker. Permits are required for overnight trips into the Wilderness from April 1 through November 30. This entire area is a photographer's delight.

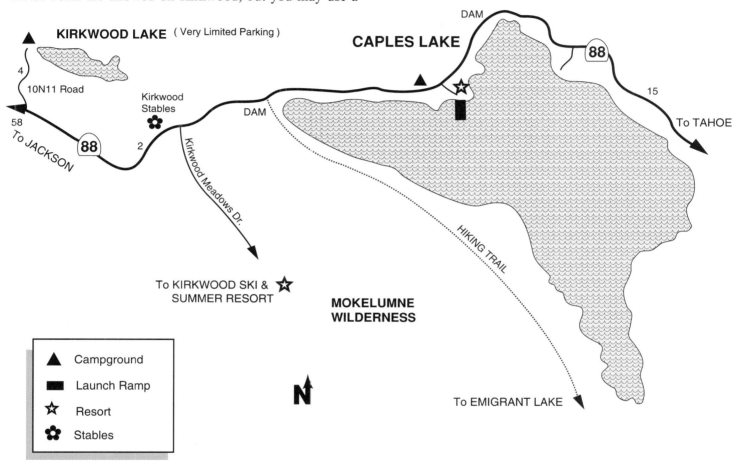

INFORMATION: Amador Ranger Station, 26820 Silver Drive & Hwy. 88, Pioneer 95666—Ph: (209) 295-4251

CAMPING	BOATING	RECREATION	OTHER
Caples Lake: 　35 Dev. Sites for 　Tents & R.V.s 　Fee: $11 　　Extra Vehicle: $5 Kirkwood Lake: 　12 Dev. Sites for 　Tents & Small R.V.s 　Fee: $10 　　Extra Vehicle: $4	Power, Row, Canoe, 　Sail & Inflatables 　5 MPH Speed Limit 　on Caples Lake Launch Ramp Rentals: Fishing 　Boats Water Taxi *No* Motors of Any Kind 　on Kirkwood	Fishing: Rainbow, 　Brown, Brook & 　Cutthroat Trout Swimming Picnicking Hiking Backpacking Hunting: Deer Horse Rentals at 　Kirkwood Stables	Caples Lake Resort 　Ph: (209) 258-8888 Lodge & Restaurant Housekeeping Cabins Grocery Store, Bait & 　Tackle, Gas Station Kirkwood Resort 　Ph: (209) 258-6000 Lodge & Restaurant Condo Rentals Grocery Store, Gas Station Tennis Courts Mountain Bike Rentals

WOODS and RED LAKES

Woods Lake is at an elevation of 8,200 feet southwest of the Carson Pass in the Eldorado National Forest. This lovely hidden retreat just 2 miles south of Highway 88 offers a variety of recreational opportunities. In addition to the campground, the Forest Service provides a nice picnic area at the water's edge with facilities for the handicapped. Fishing can be good from boat or along the bank as well as in the streams throughout the area. Motorboats are not permitted on the Lake. Trails lead to Winnemucca, Round Top Lakes and other sites within the Mokelumne Wilderness. Permits are required for overnight trips into the Wilderness from April 1 to November 30. The Pacific Crest Trail runs to the east of Woods Lake. Most of Red Lake is State land (Department of Fish & Game). Facilities are limited.

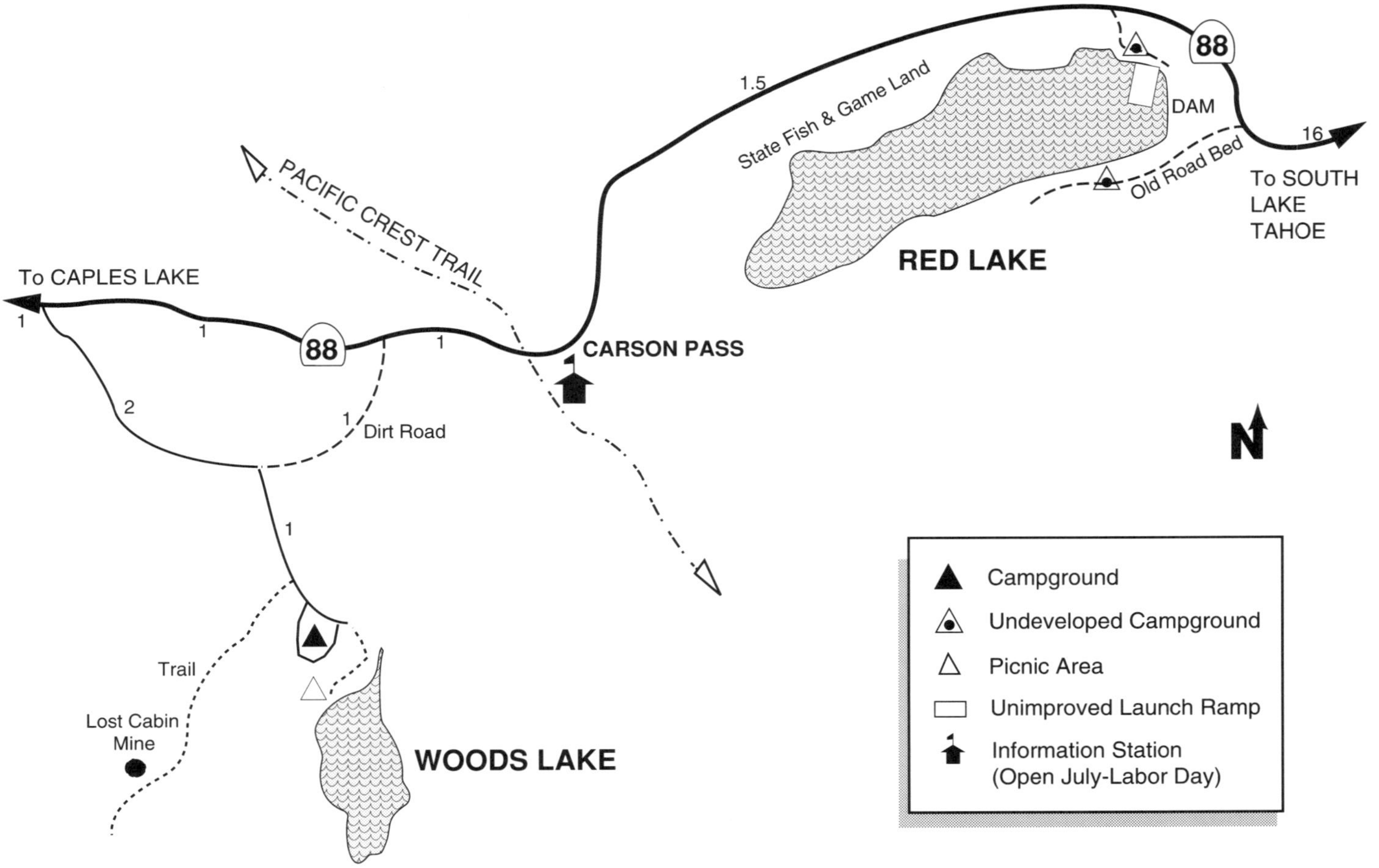

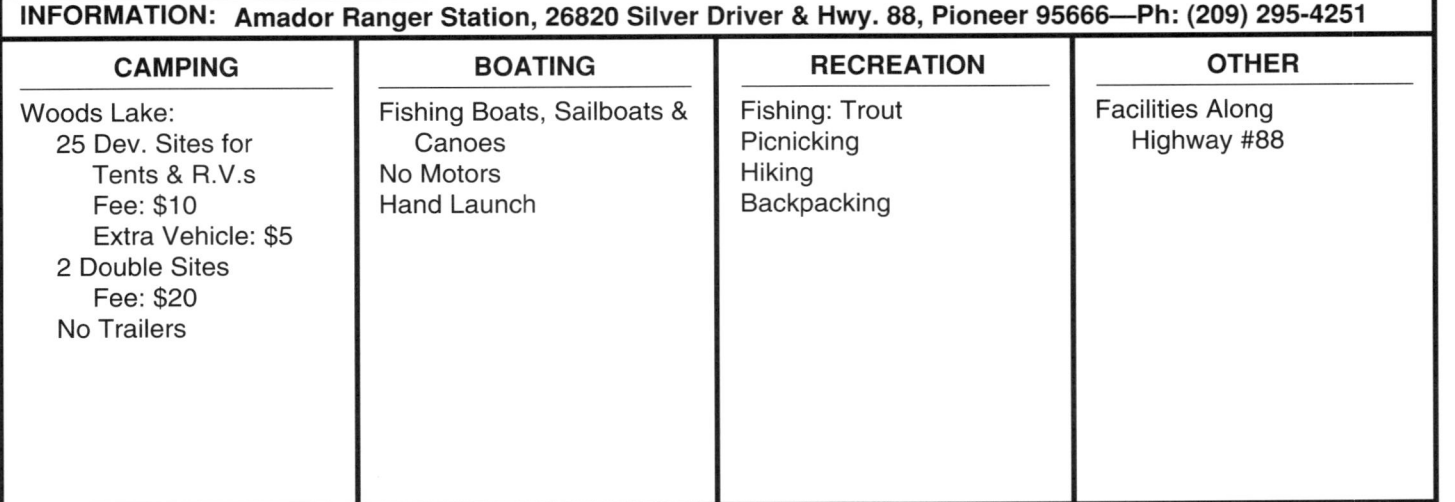

Legend	
▲	Campground
◬	Undeveloped Campground
△	Picnic Area
▭	Unimproved Launch Ramp
⌂	Information Station (Open July-Labor Day)

INFORMATION: Amador Ranger Station, 26820 Silver Driver & Hwy. 88, Pioneer 95666—Ph: (209) 295-4251

CAMPING	BOATING	RECREATION	OTHER
Woods Lake: 25 Dev. Sites for Tents & R.V.s Fee: $10 Extra Vehicle: $5 2 Double Sites Fee: $20 No Trailers	Fishing Boats, Sailboats & Canoes No Motors Hand Launch	Fishing: Trout Picnicking Hiking Backpacking	Facilities Along Highway #88

The Blue Lakes are at an elevation of 8,000 feet in this remote country of the Eldorado National Forest. The evenings and mornings are cool and the water is clear and cold. Boating is limited to small craft and fishing can be good. There are numerous hiking trails, some leading into the Mokelumne Wilderness. The campgrounds are maintained by P.G. & E. except for Hope Valley which is operated by the U.S. Forest Service, Carson Ranger District, Toiyabe National Forest. Facilities are limited, so come well prepared. Only the first 7 miles of road are paved from Highway 88.

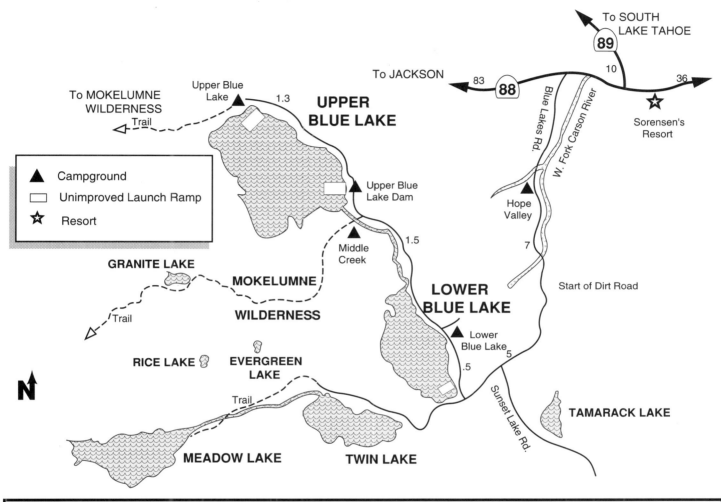

INFORMATION: P.G. & E. Land Projects, P.O. Box 277444, Sacramento 95827—Ph: (916) 386-5164

CAMPING	BOATING	RECREATION	OTHER
P.G.&E.: Upper Blue Lake: 　32 Dev. Sites for 　Tents & R.V.s Upper Blue Lake Dam: 　25 Dev. Sites Middle Creek: 5 Dev. Sites Lower Blue Lake: 　16 Dev. Sites Fees: $15 USFS - Hope Valley: 26 Dev. Sites 　Fee: $10	Small Boats Only Undeveloped Launch Ramps	Fishing: Rainbow 　Trout Swimming Picnicking Hiking Backpacking [Parking]	Sorensen's Resort Hope Valley 96120 Ph: (530) 694-2203 　30 Cabins 　Restaurant 　Fly Fishing & 　Tying Lessons 　Fishing Supplies 　Licenses 　Guide Service 　For Reservations: 　　(800) 423-9949

INDIAN CREEK RESERVOIR and HEENAN LAKE

Indian Creek Reservoir is at an elevation of 5,600 feet on the eastern slope of the Sierra. The Bureau of Land Management maintains more than 7,000 acres in this beautiful area of Jeffrey and Pinon Pines. This 160 acre Lake offers good fishing and small craft boating. Check current water levels. Nearby Heenan Lake, 129 acres, provides a good catch and release fishery. This operating hatchery provides for zero limit fishing with artificial lures and barbless hooks. *Contact the California Department of Fish and Game at (916) 355-7090 for specific regulations.* A popular attraction in this area is Grover Hot Springs State Park where you can enjoy a hot mineral bath. Camping reservations are advised.

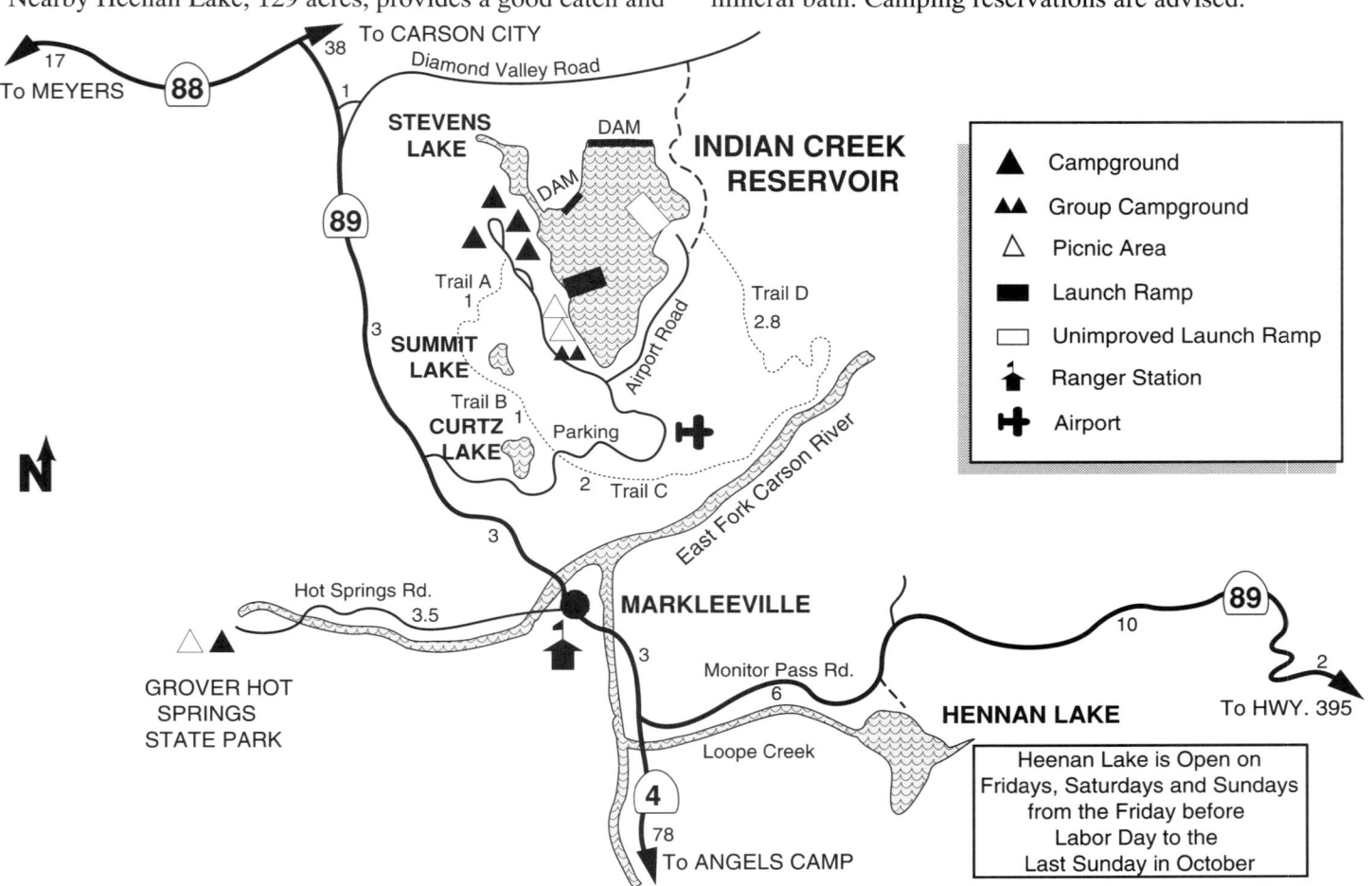

INFORMATION: B.L.M., 5665 Morgan Mill Rd., Carson City, NV 89701—Ph: (775) 885-6000

CAMPING	BOATING	RECREATION	OTHER

Indian Creek:
  19 Dev. Sites for
  Tents & R.V.s to 30 Ft.
  Plus 10 Tent Only Sites
  No Hookups
    Fees: $8 - $10
  Group Camp to
    40 People
  Fee: $20
  Disposal Station
No Reservations
Ph: (702) 885-6000 for
  Information
	Indian Creek:
	  Open to All Small Boats
	  Launch Ramp
	
	Heenan Lake:
	  Small Hand Launch
	    Boats
	  No Gas Motors
	  Electric Motors
	    Allowed
	  Call for Specific
	  Fishing Regulations
	  Ph: 916-355-7090
		Fishing :
		  Indian Creek:
		    Rainbow & Brown
		    Trout
		  Heenan - Lahontan
		    Cutthroat Trout
		    Catch & Release
		Picnicking
		Hiking & Nature Trails
		Backpacking
		Rockhounding
		Hot Springs
			Grover Hot Springs
			P.O. Box 188
			Markleeville 96120
			Ph: (530) 694-2248
			  76 Dev. Sites for Tents
			  & R.V.s to 24 Feet
			  Fee: $14
			  Reserve
			  Ph: 1-800-444-7275
			Alpine Chamber of
			  Commerce
			  Ph: (530) 694-2475

Topaz Lake rests on the California-Nevada State Line at an elevation of 5,000 feet. This 1,800 acre Reservoir is nestled amid sage covered mountains with a sandy shoreline of 25 miles. The Lake is open to all types of boating including overnight but beware of potential heavy afternoon winds.

Both California and Nevada stock the Lake which is closed to fishing for three months beginning October 1. As a result, trophy sized trout up to 8 pounds are no surprise. Half of Topaz Lake is in Nevada so there are nearby casinos.

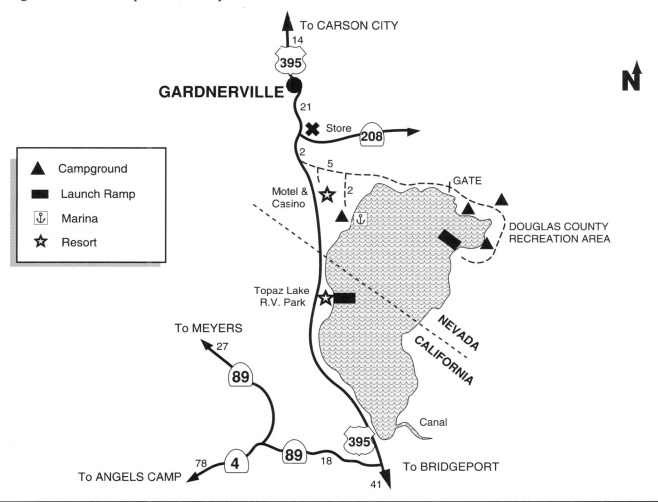

INFORMATION: Douglas County, 3700 Topaz Park Rd., Gardnerville, NV 89410—Ph: (775) 266-3343

CAMPING	BOATING	RECREATION	OTHER

Douglas County Park
  28 R.V. Sites Water &
  Electric Hookups - $10
  39 Campsites - Fee: $8
  Disposal Station
Topaz Lake RV Park
  50 R.V. Sites
  Full Hookups
Topaz Marina
  28 Dev. Sites for
  Tents & R.V.s,
  Some Hookups
	Power, Row, Canoe,
	  Sail, Waterski,
	  Jets, Windsurf,
	  & Inflatables
	Full Service Marina
	County Launch
	  Ramp - $5
	Rentals: Fishing Boats
	Docks, Berths, Dry Storage,
	  Moorings & Gas
	Overnight Boating
		Fishing: Rainbow,
		  Brown & Cutthroat
		  Trout
		Swimming - Beaches
		Picnicking
		Hiking
		Playgrounds
			Douglas County Park
			  Ph: (775) 266-3343
			Topaz Lake R.V. Park
			  Ph: (530) 495-2357
			Topaz Marina
			  Ph: (775) 266-3236
			Motel
			Restaurant & Lounge
			Casinos
			Bait & Tackle at
			  Topaz Marina
			Disposal Station

LAKE ALPINE

Lake Alpine is at an elevation of 7,320 feet in the Stanislaus National Forest. The Lake has a surface area of 180 acres and is regularly stocked with Rainbow trout. The water is crystal clear and very cold. All boating is allowed within a 10 mph speed limit, and the steady breezes make this a good sailing Lake. Trails leading to Carson-Iceberg Wilderness to the south of Lake Alpine and the Mokelumne Wilderness a few miles to the north, are accessible to the hiker, backpacker and horseman. The Forest Service maintains 4 campgrounds near the Lake plus a special area set aside for backpackers. The historic Lake Alpine Lodge overlooks this beautiful Lake and the heavily timbered mountain setting.

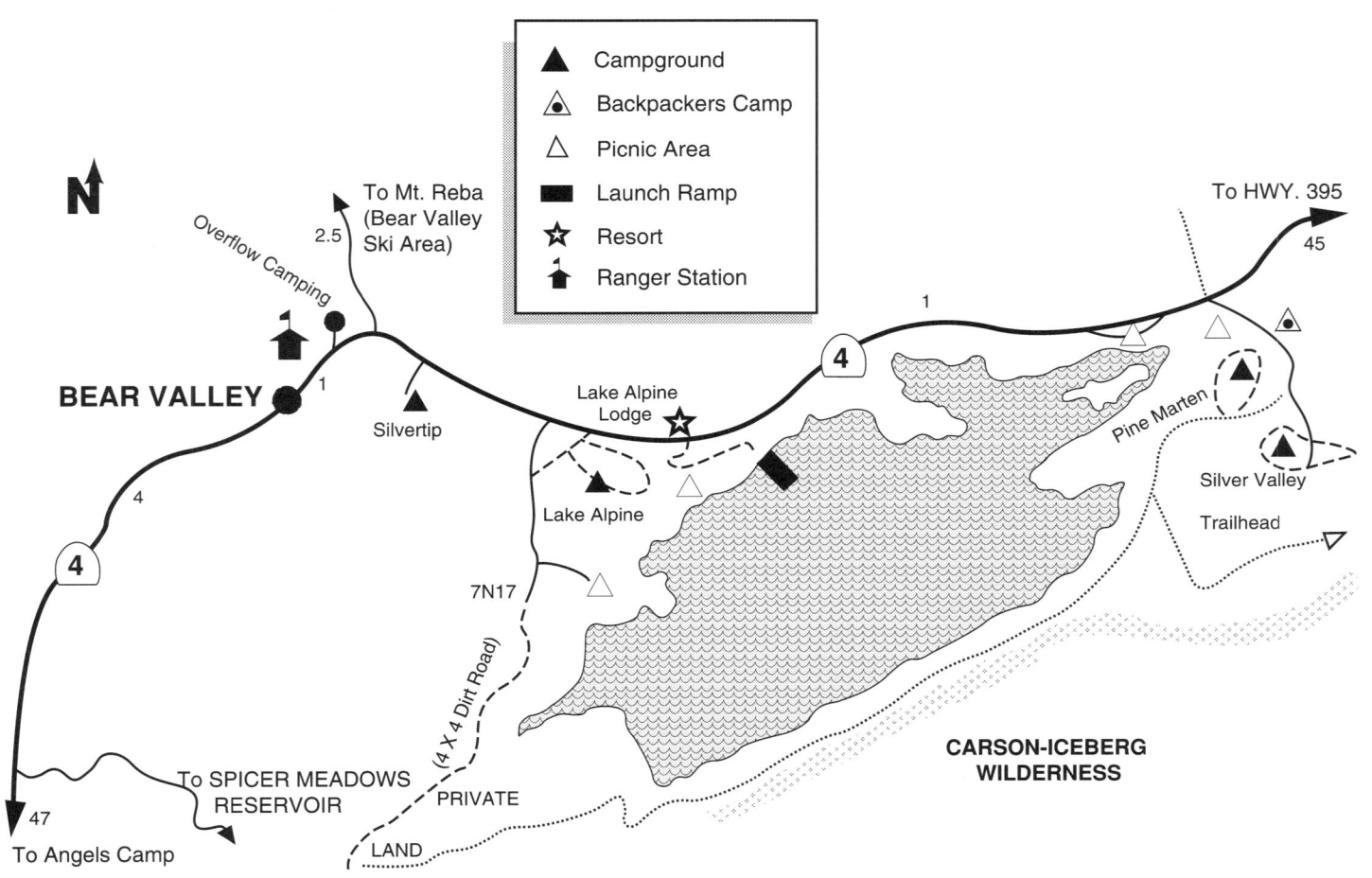

INFORMATION: Calaveras Ranger District, P.O. Box 500, Hathaway Pines 95233—Ph: (209) 795-1381

CAMPING	BOATING	RECREATION	OTHER
110 Dev. Sites for Tents & R.V.s Fee: $14	Power, Row, Sail, Canoe & Inflatable Speed Limit - 10 MPH Launch Ramp	Fishing: Rainbow Trout Handicap Access Swimming	Lake Alpine Lodge: P.O. 5300 Bear Valley 95223 Ph: (209) 753-6358
Plus Overflow Area Nearby - Fee: $7 Open Busy Weekends Only	Rentals: Fishing & Motor Boats, Canoes, Rowboats & Kayaks	Picnicking Hiking Backpacking [Parking] Hunting: Deer & Bear	Cabins Showers & Laundromat Restaurant Grocery Store
Marmot Picnic Area Suitable for Handicapped		4-Wheel Drive & Motorcycle Trails Mountain Bikes Bike Trail from Bear Valley to the End of Lake	Gift Shop Bait & Tackle Boat Rentals Bear Valley: Full Services Gas Station

Lake Sonoma is nestled amid the rolling foothills of Northern California's coastal range at an elevation of 451 feet. Located in the "wine country" just west of Healdsburg, this scenic Lake offers 2,500 surface acres of prime recreational waters. There are many secluded coves for the quiet boater, sailor or angler. Waterskiers and jets are allowed only in designated areas. The U.S. Army Corps of Engineers has developed a variety of facilities. The 53 miles of oak shaded hilly shoreline have almost 40 miles of lake access trails for the hiker or equestrian. There are 15 primitive walk or boat-in areas, offering a total of 115 individual sites. The Liberty Glen Campground offers oak shaded modern campsites. There is a 5-lane public launch ramp. The privately operated marina has complete support facilities.

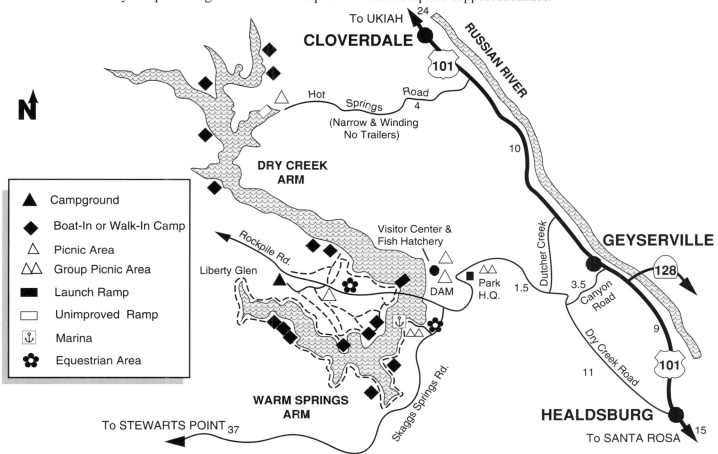

INFORMATION: Lake Sonoma Rec. Area, 3333 Skaggs Springs Rd., Geyserville 95441—Ph: (707) 433-9483

CAMPING	BOATING	RECREATION	OTHER
Liberty Glen: 113 Tent/RV Sites Disposal Station	Open to all Boating Designated Areas for Jet & No Wake Boats	Fishing: Large & Smallmouth Bass, Sacramento Perch,	Lake Sonoma Resort 520 Mendocino Ave. Suite 200
	Paved Public Launch Ramp - $2	Channel Catfish & Redear Sunfish	Santa Rosa 95401 Ph: (707) 433-2200
15 Boat/Walk-in Primitive Camping Areas No Water Permits Required	Full Service Marina Gas & Slip Rentals Boat Storage Boat Rentals Launch Ramp: $10 Hand Launch at Hot Springs	Picnic Areas Group Picnic Areas Swim Beach Hiking & Equestrian Trails 2 Equestrian Staging Areas Visitor Center Fish Hatchery	Snack Bar, General Store, Restrooms, Beer & Wine Gardens Bait & Tackle Day Use Fee: $5

SPRING LAKE and LAKE RALPHINE

Spring Lake is under the jurisdiction of the Sonoma County Regional Parks Department. This nice 320 acre Park has a vistors center/museum, picnic areas, a campground, summer swim lagoon and well maintained trails. This is a popular equestrian area. The 75 acre Lake is open to non-powered boating. Lake Ralphine is within the City of Santa Rosa's Howarth Park. This day use facility has numerous children's attractions and various boat rentals. Lake Ralphine also allows non-powered boating with sailing being a special attraction. There is a warm water fishery in addition to planted trout in the winter at both Lakes. A bicycle path connects these parks.

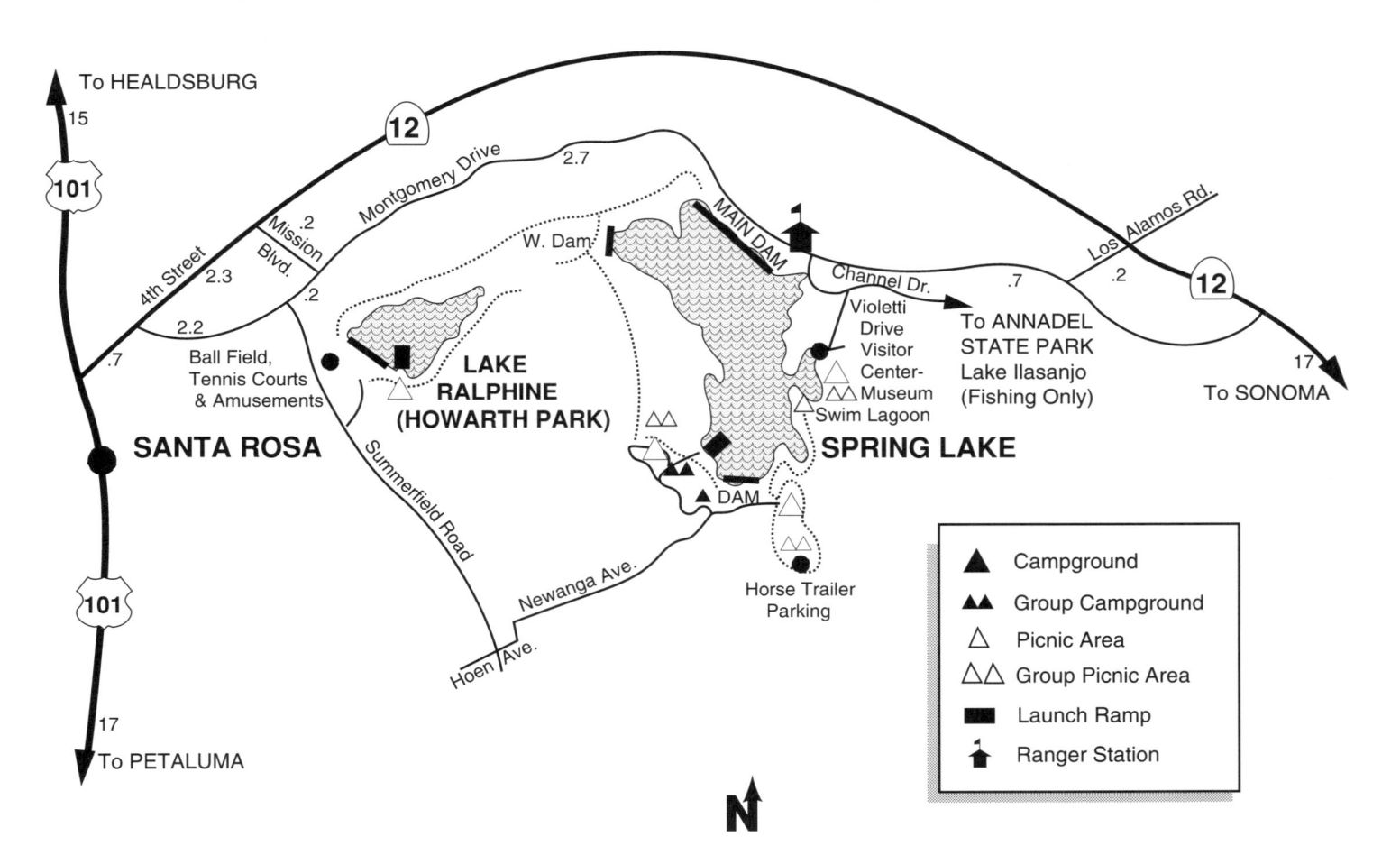

▲	Campground
▲▲	Group Campground
△	Picnic Area
△△	Group Picnic Area
■	Launch Ramp
⚑	Ranger Station

N

INFORMATION: Spring Lake, 5390 Montgomery Dr., Santa Rosa 95409—Ph: (707) 539-8092

CAMPING	BOATING	RECREATION	OTHER
31 Dev. Sites for Tents & R.V.s No Hookups Hot Showers Fee: $15 - Reserve Group Camp to 100 People- Reserve Ph: (707)539-8082 Disposal Station Campground Open Weekends & Holidays Only Between Oct. 1 and April 30	Spring Lake: Row, Sail, Canoe, Inflatables (2 Cham) Electric Motors Rentals: Row, Canoe, Paddle, Sailboats (Summer) Life Jackets Required Lake Ralphine: Private Boats Under 20 ft. No Motors Rentals: As Above Open Tues-Sunday in Summer (Weekends Fall & Spring)	Fishing: Trout, Bluegill, Redear Sunfish & Bass Swim Lagoon (Summer) Picnic Areas: Group Reservations Available Hiking, Riding & Bicycle Trails Tennis Courts - Ralphine No Swimming in Lake Ralphine	Howarth Park: Santa Rosa Rec. & Parks Dept. Ph: (707) 543-3282 Miniature Steam Train, Pony Rides Merry-Go-Round, Land of Imagination Play Area for Children of All Abilities

Lake Berryessa is one of Northern California's most popular recreation Lakes. One of the State's largest man-made Lakes, its 13,000 surface acres and 165 miles of hilly oak and madrone covered shoreline provide quality recreational opportunities. Known for excellent year-round fishing, the angler will find trophy trout, three species of bass and a good warm water fishery. The average water temperature of 78 degrees lures the skier and swimmer while the light and variable winds attract the sailor. Complete resort, camping and marine facilities complement this low elevation Lake's

natural attractions. To the west of Berryessa off Highway 128 is Lake Hennessy. Under the jurisdiction of the City of Napa, this small Lake offers limited facilities and recreational opportunities. In contrast, Lake Solano, southeast of Berryessa, provides numerous recreational opportunities, such as swim lagoons, picnic sites, boat rentals and a 68-site campground. The water can be very cold as it comes from Lake Berryessa Dam. Solano offers non-powered boating and trout fishing.

....Continued....

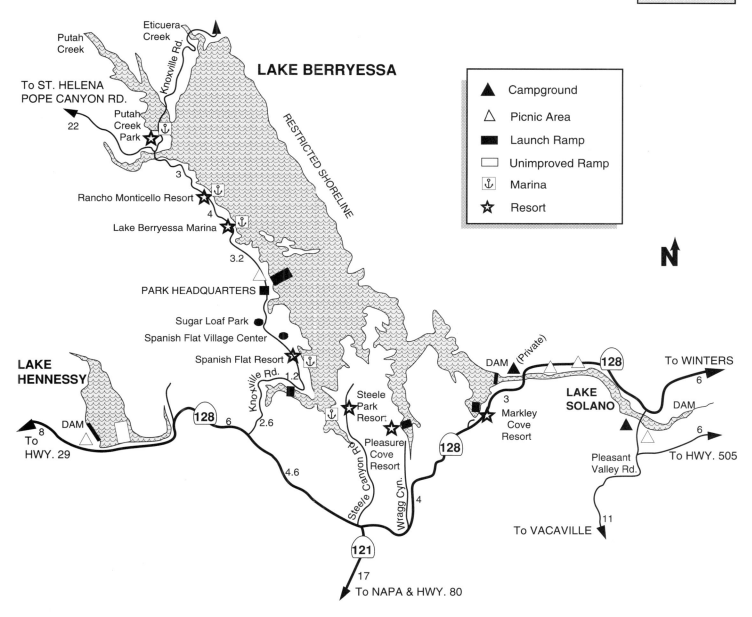

LAKE BERRYESSA.............Continued

LAKE BERRYESSA MARINA RESORT - 5800 Knoxville Rd., Napa 94558—Ph: (707) 966-2161 - Tent/RV Park, Full Hookups, Dump Station, Courtesy Pumpout in Mornings, Hot Showers, Picnic Area, Grocery Store, Laundromat, Restaurant & Lounge, Swim Beach, Full Service Marina, Fishing, Patio & Ski Boat Rentals, Fuel Dock & Ramp, Courtesy Dock.

MARKLEY COVE RESORT - P.O. Box 987, Winters 95694—Ph: (707) 966-2134 - Fishing Boat Rentals, Paved Ramp, Berths, Boat Pumpout Station, Fuel Dock, Private Houseboat Moorage, Store, Bait & Tackle, Snack Bar.

PUTAH CREEK PARK - 7600 Knoxville Rd., Napa—Ph: (707) 966-2116 - Tent/RV Park, Partial and Full Hookups, Disposal Station, Hot Showers, Picnic Area, Motel, Full Service Marina, Ski Boat Rentals, Storage, Bait & Tackle, Store, Restaurant & Lounge, Snack Bar.

RANCHO MONTICELLO RESORT - 6590 Knoxville Rd., Napa 94558—Ph: (707) 966-2188 - Tent/RV Sites, Full Hookups, 2 Disposal Stations, Hot Showers, Picnic Areas, Store, Snack Bar, Launch Ramp, Laundromat.

PLEASURE COVE RESORT- 6100 Hwy. 128, Napa 94558—Ph: (707) 966-2172 - Tent/RV Sites, Full Hookups, Disposal Station, Hot Showers, Slips, Storage, Fuel Dock, Launch Ramp, Grocery Store, Restaurant & Lounge, Picnic Area, Laundromat, Teepee Village.

SPANISH FLAT RESORT - 4290 Knoxville Rd., Napa 94558—Ph: (707) 966-7700 - Tent/RV Sites, Hot Showers, Disposal Station, Electric and Water Hookups, Full Service Marina, Paved Launch Ramp, Berthing, Fishing and Patio Boat Rentals, Grocery Store, Picnic Sites, Barbercues, Swim Beach.

STEELE PARK RESORT - 1605 Steel Canyon Rd., Napa 94558—Ph: (707) 966-2123 for Reservations—Ph: (800) 522-2123 - Largest Resort on Lake, RV Sites, Full Hookups, Disposal Station, Hot Showers, Motel, Housekeeping Cottages, Full Service Marina, Paved Ramp, Covered and Open Berths, Dry Storage, Fuel Dock, Motel & Cottage Courtesy Dock, Jet & Patio Boat Rentals, Ski School, Swim Beach, Tennis Courts, Swimming Pool for Motel Guests, Ice Cream Parlor, Arcade Room, 2 Restaurants, Cocktail Lounge, Grocery Store, Large Picnic Area.

For further information on facilities contact:

NAPA CHAMBER OF COMMERCE

Ph: (707) 226-7455

INFORMATION: See Above

CAMPING	BOATING	RECREATION	OTHER
Lake Berryessa Tent/RV Sites at Resorts See Above for Details	Lake Berryessa Open to All Boating Full Service Marina House, Ski, Fishing & Patio Boat Rentals	Fishing: Rainbow & Brown Trout, Large & Smallmouth Bass, Catfish, Bluegill, Crappie	Complete Destination Facilities at Resorts on Lake Berryessa
Lake Solano 50 Tent/RV Sites	Lake Solano Non-power Boating Only	Swimming - Lake & Pools Picnic Areas Hiking & Riding Trails Wine Country Excursions	Lake Solano County of Solano Parks 603 Texas Street Fairfield 94533 Ph: (707) 421-7925
Lake Hennessy No Camping	Lake Hennessy 10 HP Max. Limit No Kayaks or Windsurfers		

Lake Amador is at an elevation of 485 feet in the Sierra Foothills, one mile east of historic Buena Vista. The surface area of the Lake is 425 acres. The shoreline of 13-1/2 miles is surrounded by black oak covered hills. The brush along the water's edge provides a thriving warm water fishery. A Northern California record limit of 80 pounds for Florida bass was set in 1981, and in 1986 the individual Lake record was set for 17 pounds, 1-1/4 ounces. This is a nice boating facility with good winds for sailing. The Lake is open to boating and fishing 24 hours a day. The visitor will find a 1 acre swim pond with sandy beaches and playgrounds for the children making Amador a good family recreation area.

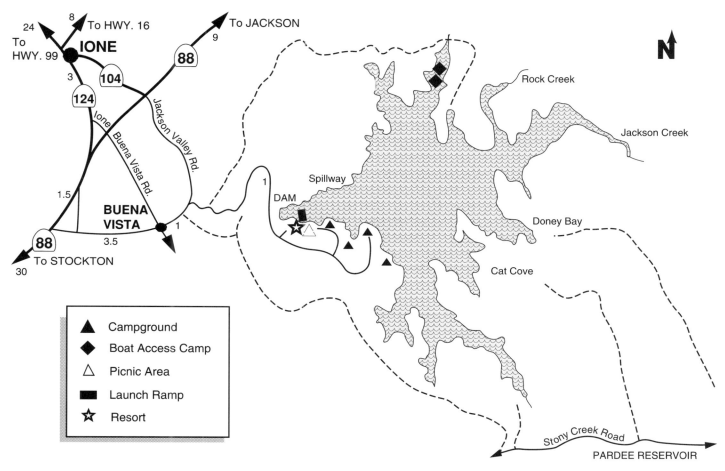

CAMPING	BOATING	RECREATION	OTHER
150 Dev. Sites for Tents Fee: $18	Power, Row, Canoe, Sail, Windsurf & Inflatables	Fishing: Trout, Largemouth Bass, Catfish, Bluegill, Crappie & Perch	Snack Bar Grocery Store Bait & Tackle
73 Full Hookups for RVs & Trailers Fee: $23	*No Waterskiing or Jets*	Fishing Fee: $4 per Day per Person	Hot Showers Disposal Station
	Launch Ramp - $6	Swimming - Pond	Gas Station & Propane
Group Camp to 50 Vehicles	Rentals: Fishing Boats	Free Waterslide	Club House &
Reservations for All Sites Suggested	Docks, Storage Fishing Floats Around Shoreline	Picnicking Hiking Mountain Biking	Recreation Room

INFORMATION: Lake Amador Resort, 7500 Amador Dr., Ione 95640—Ph: (209) 274-4739

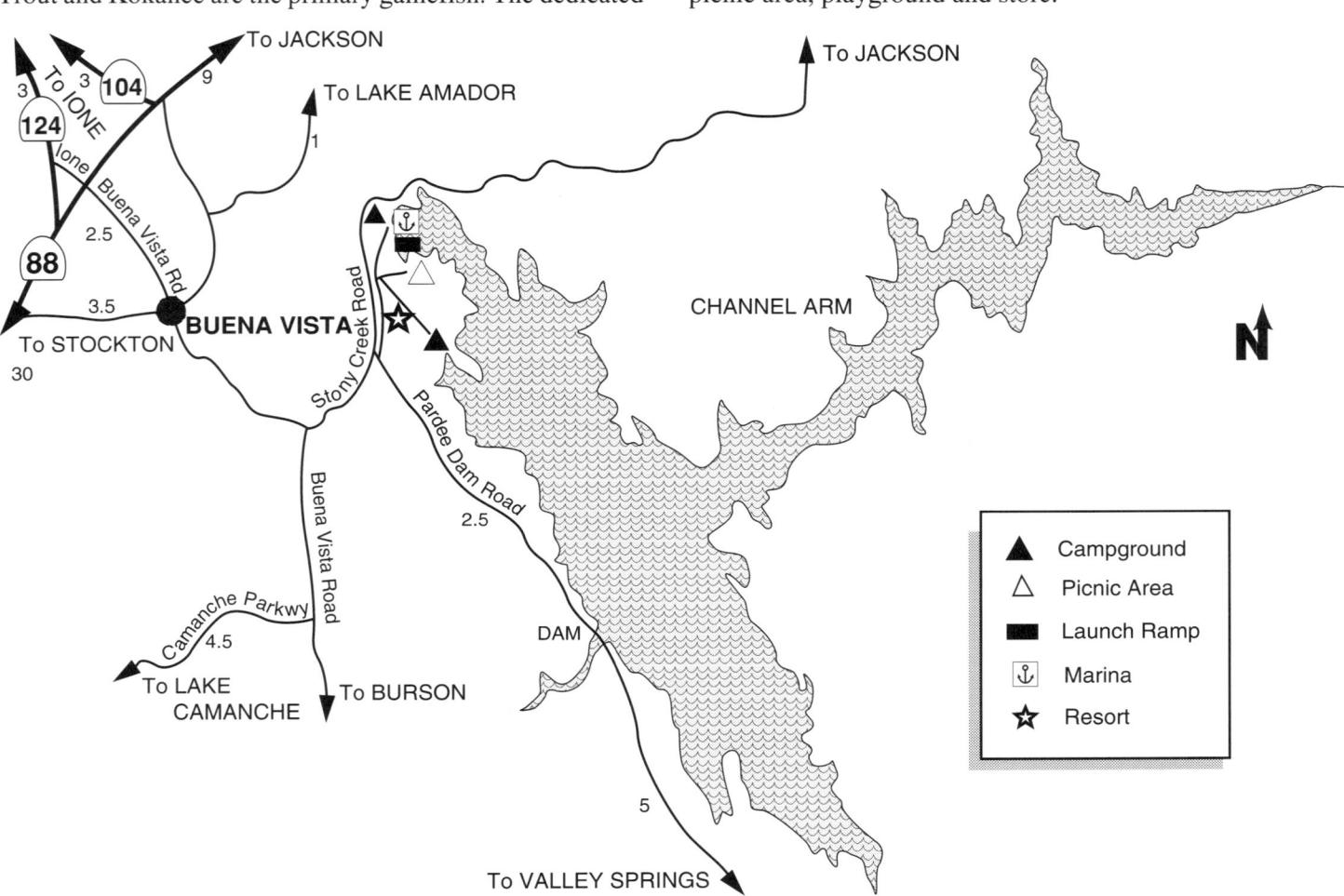

Lake Pardee rests at an elevation of 568 feet in the heart of the "Mother Lode Country" and its historic gold towns. Under the jurisdiction of the East Bay Municipal Water District, this popular fishing Lake in the Sierra foothills has a surface area of 2,200 acres surrounded by 43 miles of rolling woodland. Trout and Kokanee are the primary gamefish. The dedicated angler will find a good smallmouth fishery as well as largemouth bass. Catfish are also abundant. Boating is generally related to fishing. Waterskiing and jets are prohibited. There are marine support facilities. This is a nice family area with a large campground, a swimming pool (no Lake swimming), picnic area, playground and store.

Legend: ▲ Campground △ Picnic Area ■ Launch Ramp ⚓ Marina ★ Resort

INFORMATION: Lake Pardee Marina, Inc., 4900 Stony Creek Rd., Ione 95640—Ph: (209) 772-1472

CAMPING	BOATING	RECREATION	OTHER
100 Dev. Tent Sites Fee: $14 12 Dev. R.V. Sites With Full Hookups Fee: $19 Additional Monthly R.V. Sites at Trailer Park Reservations Taken at R.V. Sites Only	Power, Row, Canoe, Sail & Inflatables *No Body Contact With the Water* *No Waterskiing or Jets* Full Service Marina Launch Ramp Rentals: Fishing Boats & Pontoons Docks, Berths, Moorings, Gas Dry Storage	Fishing: Rainbow & Brown Trout, Kokanee Salmon, Catfish, Bluegill, Crappie, Small & Largemouth Bass Barrier Free Fishing Float Swimming in Pool Picnicking Bicycle Trails Playground	Snack Bar Restaurant Grocery Store Laundromat Disposal Station Gas & Propane

Lake Camanche is at an elevation of 235 feet in the foothills of the Sierra Nevada. This East Bay Municipal Utility District Reservoir has 7,700 surface acres and a shoreline of 53 miles. Located in the famous "Mother Lode Country", panning for gold is still popular in the spring when streams are high. Indian grave sites are visible along the shoreline. The water is warm and clear making watersports a delight. Fishing for a variety of species can be excellent. The Resorts at Camanche Northshore and South Camanche Shore offer modern, complete camping, marine and recreation facilities. There are over 15,000 acres of park lands for the hiker and equestrian. Camanche is one of the most complete facility Lakes within easy distance of the San Francisco Bay Area.

....Continued....

Legend:
- ▲ Campground
- △ Picnic Area
- ■ Launch Ramp
- ⚓ Marina
- ★ Resort

INFORMATION: Camanche Recreation Company Northshore and South Shore - See Next Page

CAMPING	BOATING	RECREATION	OTHER
Over 670 Dev. Sites for Tents & R.V.s Full Hookups Available Disposal Stations Laundromats Propane	Power, Row, Canoe, Sail, Waterski, Jets, & Inflatables *No Waterskiing in Upper Lake* Full Service Marinas Launch Ramps Rentals: Fishing & Patio Boats Rods & Reels	Fishing: Trout, Catfish, Bluegill, Crappie, Bass & Kokanee Swimming Picnicking Tennis Hiking Horseback Riding Trails	Cottages Motels Extensive Vacation Facilities See Next Page For Details

90

CAMANCHE RECREATION COMPANY - NORTHSHORE
2000 Camanche Rd., Ione, CA 95640
Ph: (209) 763-5121

219 Campsites for Tents & Self-Contained R.V.s - Fee: From $15 - Water, Showers, Disposal Station, Trailer Storage, Laundromat, Playgrounds, Store, Coffee Shop.

Full Service Marina - 6-Lane Launch Ramp, Fee: $6, Boat Rentals: Fishing & Patio Boats, Storage, Berths, Moorings, General Store and Coffee Shop. Information—Ph: (209) 763-5166.

Cottages - Rentals of Deluxe Housekeeping Cottages for 2 to 12 People, Motel Rooms, Tennis Courts.

Nearby: Bird Hunting Preserve and Club, Golf, Wineries, Special Events.

Other Facilities - Coffee Shop, Two Mobile Home Parks.

Group Reservations for Camping or Picnicking.

CAMANCHE RECREATION COMPANY - SOUTHSHORE
P.O. Box 206
Burson, California 95225
Ph: (209) 763-5178

200 R.V Sites with Full Hookups Plus 320 Sites for Tents and Self-Contained R.V.s - Fees: From $15 - Showers, Disposal Station, Laundromat, Store & Snack Bar.

Full Service Marina - 6-Lane Launch Ramp, Fee: $6, Boat Rentals: Fishing & Pontoon Boats, Storage, Berths, Moorings.

Other Facilities - Housekeeping Cottages, Tennis Courts, Amphitheater with Movies on Saturdays during High Season, Recreation Hall, Trout Pond, Mobile Home Park.

New Hogan Lake is at an elevation of 713 feet in the foothills east of Stockton. The U.S. Army Corps of Engineers holds jurisdiction over the Lake and maintains the modern marine and camping facilities. The surface area of the Lake is 4,400 acres with 50 miles of shoreline covered with oak, digger pine and brushlands of chamise and manzanita. In spring a variety of wild flowers provide a colorful display. Wildlife is abundant with over 153 species of birds. New Hogan is ideal for water-oriented recreation and especially for its varied gamefish. The Florida strain of largemouth bass is a prime target. Waterskiing is allowed in the central Lake although many coves and the swimming beaches are restricted.

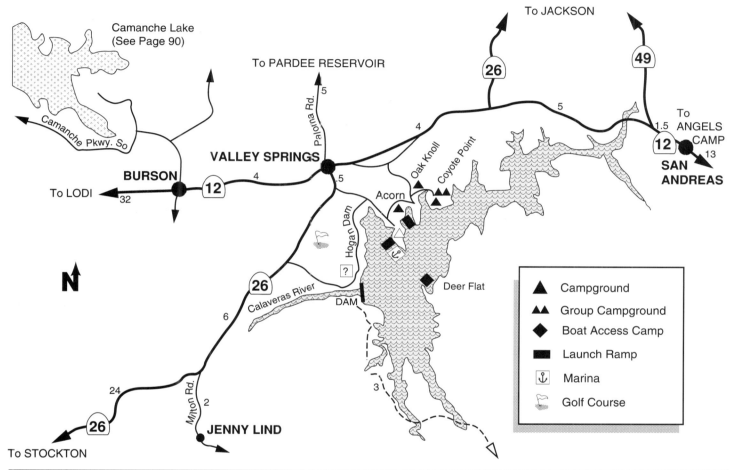

INFORMATION: New Hogan Lake, 2713 Hogan Dam Rd., Valley Springs 95252—Ph: (209) 772-1343			
CAMPING	**BOATING**	**RECREATION**	**OTHER**
Acorn West: 58 Dev. Sites for Tents & R.V.s:- $12 Acorn East: 70 Dev. Sites for Tents & R.V.s - $14 Oak Knoll: 50 Dev. Sites for Tents & R.V.s - $8 (No Showers) 30 Boat Access Camps at Deer Flat - No Water Fee: $6 No Reservations *No On Board Boat Camping*	Power, Row, Canoe, Sail, Waterski, Jets, Windsurf & Inflatable Night Boating: 15 MPH Full Service Marina Launch Ramps Rentals: Fishing Boats & Motors, Patio Boats	Fishing: Catfish, Bluegill, Crappie, Large, Smallmouth & Striped Bass Swimming Picnicking Hiking, Nature & Equestrian Trails Campfire Program Bird Watching Hunting: Deer, Quail, Dove, Upland Game Birds *Shotgun or Bow Only*	Dam Tours Grocery Store Bait & Tackle Hot Showers Disposal Station Gas Station Docks, Moorings, Dry Storage La Contenta Golf Course Nearby Full Facilities: Valley Springs

These relatively remote and undeveloped Lakes in the Stanislaus National Forest are often passed by people visiting the more popular and developed Lake Alpine. For those who enjoy a rustic and quiet environment, these Lakes are worth a visit. The elevation is high, ranging from 6,500 feet at Big Meadow Campground to 8,730 feet at Ebbetts Pass. Union and Utica Reservoirs are undeveloped although there is a primitive campground off Spicer Meadows Road on the Stanislaus River. Mosquito Lake has several campgrounds nearby. There is often good fishing at the Lakes, river and streams. This is a popular area for deer and bear hunting in season.

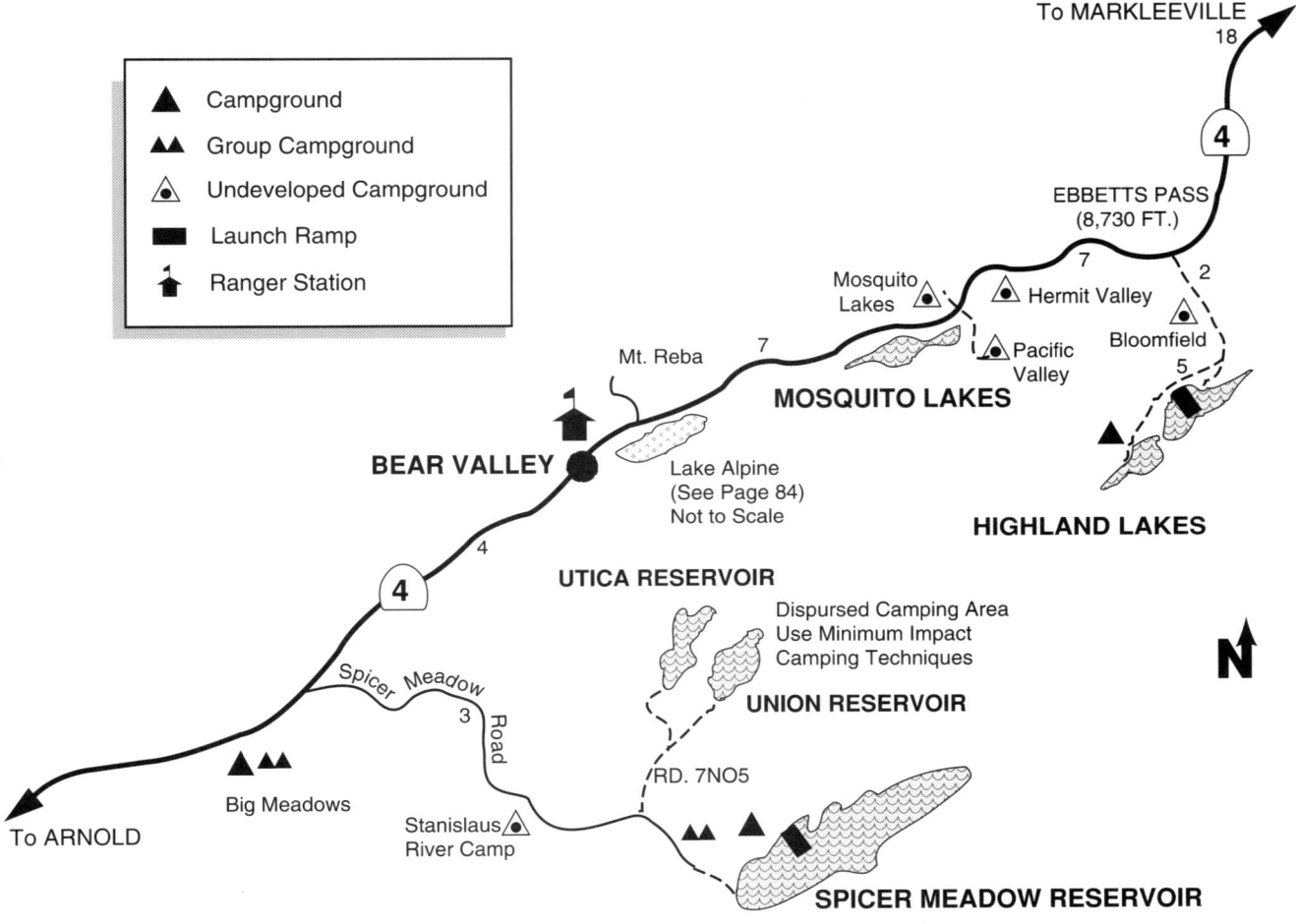

CAMPING	BOATING	RECREATION	OTHER

Highland Lakes:
    35 Dev. Sites - Fee: $8
Mosquito Lakes: 8 Sites
    No Water - No Fee
Big Meadows:
    68 Tent/R.V. Sites: $12
    & Group Campground
    10 Tent/R.V. Sites: $40
Spicer: 60 Tent/R.V. Sites
    Fee: $12
    Group Campground
        75 People Capacity
        Fee: $90
	Highland Lakes:
	    Open to All Boats
	    15 MPH Speed Limit
	Mosquito, Union & Utica:
	    Small Hand Launch Only
	Spicer Meadow:
	    Launch Ramp - Free
	    10 MPH Western Arm
	    No Motorized Boating
	    in Eastern Arm of
	    Reservoir
		Fishing: Rainbow,
		    Eastern Brook &
		    German Brown
		        Trout
		Picnicking
		Hiking
		Backpacking [Parking]
		No Swimming
		
		Protect Fragile Shoreline
		Zone Camp at Least
		100 Feet
		From Water's Edge
			Limited Facilities
			
			Stanislaus River Camp:
			    8 Tent/R.V. Sites
			    No Water - Fee: $4
			
			Reservations for
			    Some Sites:
			    Ph: (800) 280-CAMP

INFORMATION: Calaveras Ranger District, P.O. Box 500, Hathaway Pines 95233—Ph: (209) 795-1381

Pinecrest Lake is at an elevation of 5,600 feet in Stanislaus National Forest. At times called Strawberry Reservoir, Pinecrest has a surface area of 300 acres with 4 miles of mountainous, tree-covered shoreline. The Forest Service, under concession, maintains 300 campsites, a group camp, picnic sites next to the beach, a paved launch ramp and an accessible fishing pier. Pinecrest Lake Resort is a complete modern destination facility with extensive accommodations.

Reservations for Pinecrest and Pioneer Group Campgrounds are required during the summer season. Meadowview is on a first come basis and is always full on weekends. Trout are planted weekly in season at Pinecrest Lake. There are a number of other lakes and streams within easy walking distance for the angler. Boating is limited to 20 MPH. Waterskiing and jets are not permitted. A large designated swim beach is adjacent to the picnic area. There is no access by water between the Stanislaus River and Pinecrest Lake. Lyons Lake, a P.G.&E. facility, offers fishing access only. *R.V.s and trailers not advised due to road conditions.*

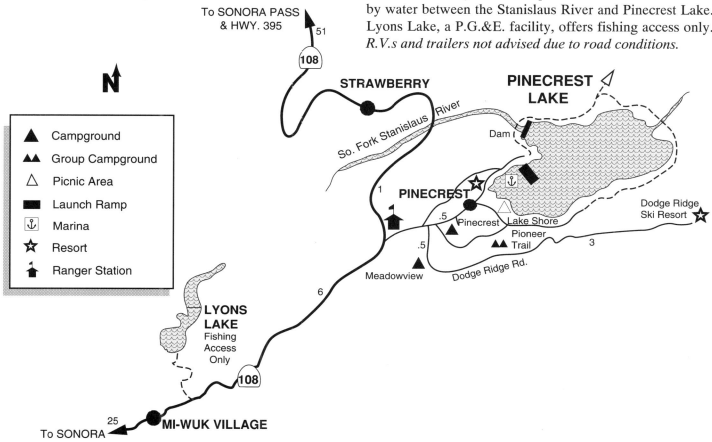

Legend:
- ▲ Campground
- ▲▲ Group Campground
- △ Picnic Area
- ▬ Launch Ramp
- ⚓ Marina
- ☆ Resort
- ⬆ Ranger Station

INFORMATION:	Summit Ranger District, #1 Pinecrest Lake Rd., Pinecrest 95364—Ph: (209) 965-3434		
CAMPING	**BOATING**	**RECREATION**	**OTHER**

300 Dev. Sites
    Fee: $10 - $12.50
    Ph: (209) 965-3116
Meadowview - 100 Sites
    First Come Basis
Pinecrest - 200 Sites &
Pioneer Group Camp
    200 People Maximum
    No Trailers
Reserve:
    Ph: (800) 280-CAMP
	Power, Row, Canoe,
	    Sail, Windsurf &
	    Inflatables
	    No Waterskiing or Jets
	Speed Limit - 20 MPH
	Full Service Marina
	Launch Ramp
	Rentals: Fishing,
	    Sail, Paddle &
	    Motor Boats,
	    Windsurfers
	Docks, Berths, Gas
	No Boating at Lyons Lake
		Fishing: Rainbow, Brown
		    & Eastern Brook Trout
		Swimming - Beaches
		    No Swimming at Lyons
		At Pinecrest Lake:
		Picnicking
		Hiking & Nature Trails
		Backpacking [Parking]
		Horseback Riding
		Bicycle Rentals
		Amphitheatre:
		    Campfire Programs &
		    Movies
			Pinecrest Lake Resort
			P.O. Box 1216
			Pinecrest 95364
			Ph: (209) 965-3411
			    Cabins, Condos & Motel
			    Restaurant, Snack Bar,
			    Groceries, Bait & Tackle
			    Gas Station, Sports Store
			    Tennis, Art Gallery
			Lyons Lake-Stanislaus NF:
			    P.G.&E.
			    Ph: (916) 386-5164
			    for Information

HARTLEY (BEARDSLEY), DONNELLS, LEAVITT and KIRMAN LAKES

Ascending the western slopes of the Sierra Nevada above Sonora, these Lakes along Highway 108 provide a relatively remote experience. Often overlooked by those visitng Pinecrest Lake, these Lakes range in elevation from 3,400 at Hartley (Beardsley) to 7,000 feet at Leavitt Lake. The fishing is often good although it is sometimes a bit difficult to reach. Donnells and Leavitt are undeveloped with no facilities. *The road into Donnells is very rough and not recommended for*

trailers or any large sized vehicles. Hartley has picnic sites and a launch ramp. There is a campground on the northwest side of the dam that has limited facilities. Afternoon winds can be strong. Kirman Lake is a designated Wild Trout Lake where barbless hooks are required and there is a two trout limit. Numerous trails throughout the area invite the equestrian, hiker and backpacker to this beautiful high Sierrra area within the Stanislaus and Toiyabe National Forests.

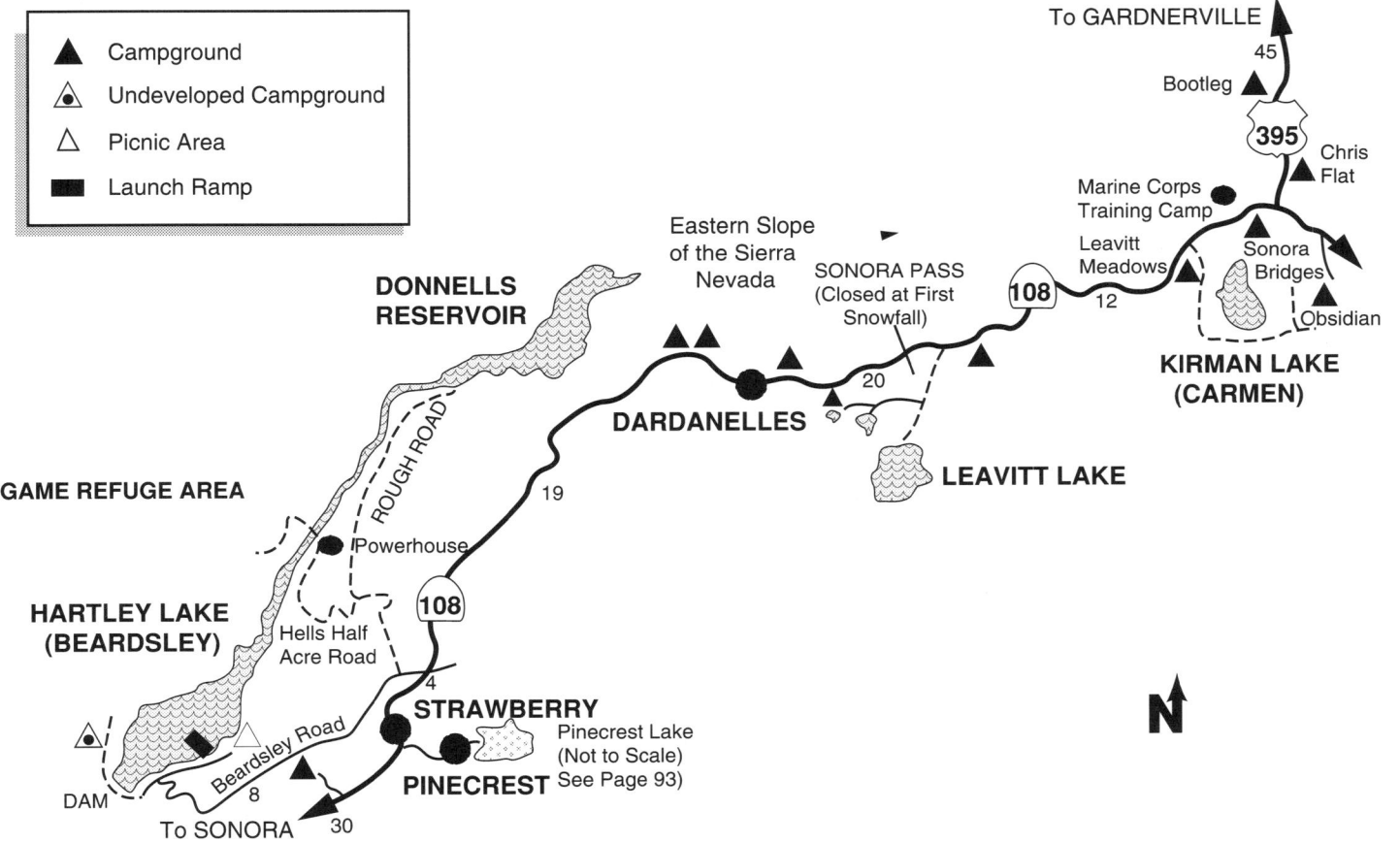

▲	Campground
⊚	Undeveloped Campground
△	Picnic Area
▬	Launch Ramp

INFORMATION: Summit Ranger District, #1 Pinecrest Lake Rd., Pinecrest 95364—Ph: (209) 965-3434

CAMPING	BOATING	RECREATION	OTHER
Numerous U.S.F.S. Campgrounds Along Highway 108 - Contact Summit Ranger District Eastern Slope of the Sierra Nevada: Toiyabe National Forest Bridgeport Ranger Dist. Ph: (760) 932-7070 Leavitt Meadows: 20 Tent/R.V. Sites Sonora Bridge: 23 Tent/R.V. Sites	Hartley Lake: Open All Boats 2-Lane Paved Launch Ramp Leavitt Lake Small Hand-Launch Donnells: Not Advised *Difficult to Impossible Access*	Fishing: Rainbow, German Brown & Brook Trout Picnicking Swimming Hiking & Riding Trails Backpacking Hunting: Deer & Bear *No Hunting in Game Refuge Near Hartley*	Limited Facilities

Cherry Lake, sometimes mistakenly called Cherry Valley Reservoir, is at an elevation of 4,700 feet in the beautiful rugged back country of the Stanislaus National Forest. This remote mountain Lake offers a good trout fishery. Boating is limited and subject to low water levels. This is truly a place to get away from it all with a nice campground and limited facilities. There are numerous small lakes and streams within hiking distance. The roads into Cherry Lake are winding and long so extra caution should be taken.

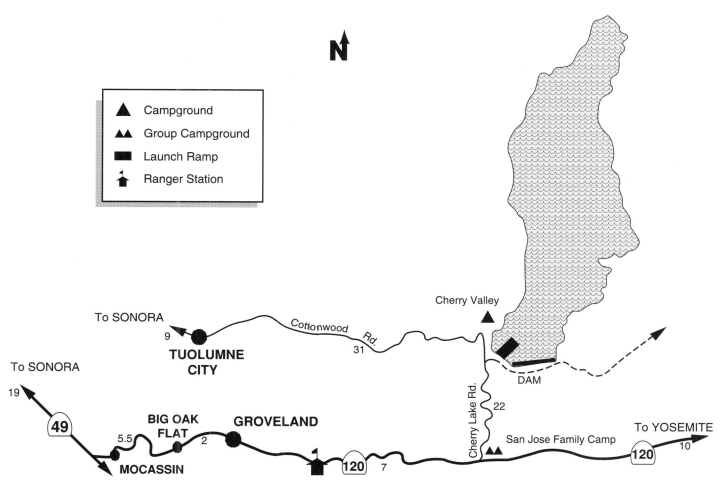

INFORMATION: Groveland Ranger District, 24545 Highway 120, Groveland 95321—Ph: (209) 962-7825			
CAMPING	**BOATING**	**RECREATION**	**OTHER**
46 Dev. Sites for Tents & R.V.s Fees: $10 - $20 Boat Camping Allowed on East Side of Lake Campground Management Enterprises 4570 State Hwy. 49 S. Mariposa 95338 Ph: (209) 742-5977	Power, Row, Canoe, Sail & Waterski Paved Launch Ramp High Water Only	Fishing: Rainbow, Brown & Brook Trout, Coho Salmon Swimming Backpacking Horseback Riding Trails Hunting Nearby: Deer & Bear	No Services Available at Cherry Lake Full Facilities - 31 Miles at Tuolumne City

LAKES ON HIGHWAY 395 FROM BRIDGEPORT TO BISHOP

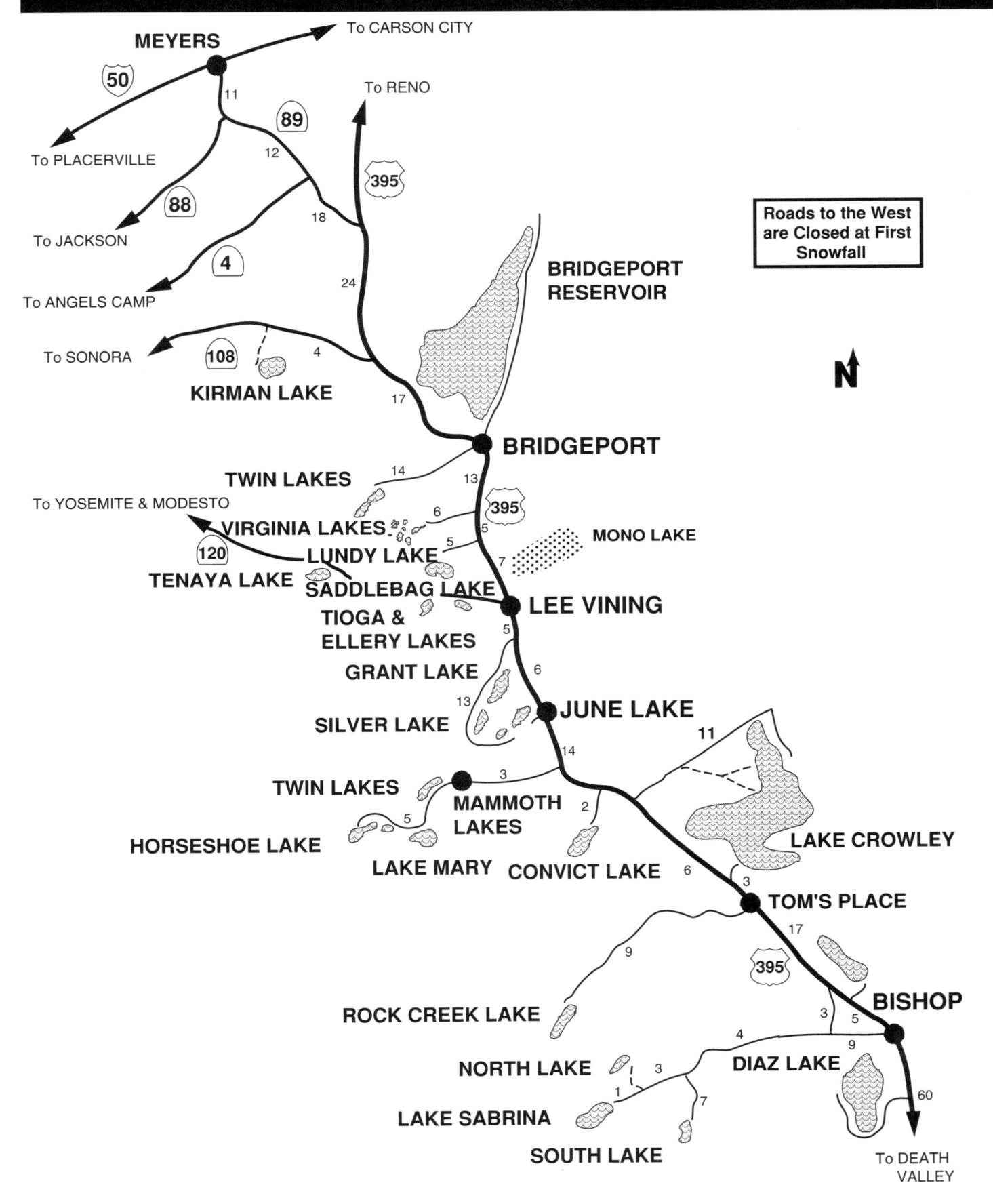

To CARSON CITY

MEYERS

(50)

To PLACERVILLE

11

(89)

12

To RENO

(395)

To JACKSON

(88)

18

(4)

24

To ANGELS CAMP

17

BRIDGEPORT RESERVOIR

Roads to the West are Closed at First Snowfall

N

To SONORA

(108)

4

KIRMAN LAKE

BRIDGEPORT

14

13

TWIN LAKES

To YOSEMITE & MODESTO

6

(395)

5

VIRGINIA LAKES

5

MONO LAKE

(120)

LUNDY LAKE

7

TENAYA LAKE

SADDLEBAG LAKE

LEE VINING

TIOGA & ELLERY LAKES

5

GRANT LAKE

6

13

JUNE LAKE

SILVER LAKE

11

14

TWIN LAKES

3

LAKE CROWLEY

MAMMOTH LAKES

2

5

HORSESHOE LAKE

LAKE MARY

CONVICT LAKE

6

3

TOM'S PLACE

17

9

(395)

ROCK CREEK LAKE

3

BISHOP

NORTH LAKE

3

4

DIAZ LAKE

5

1

9

LAKE SABRINA

7

60

SOUTH LAKE

To DEATH VALLEY

Bridgeport Reservoir rests at an elevation of 6,500 feet in a large mountain meadow. This 4,400 surface acre Lake is famous for big trout, especially when trolling early in the season. In addition to the excellent fishing at Bridgeport, the angler will find 35 lakes and streams within 15 miles. The East Walker River, designated as a Wild Trout Stream, is considered prime waters for large German Browns. Artificial lures or flies are required and there is an 8-inch minimum with a 2-fish limit. The Lake is open to all boating. In addition to the facilities shown on the map, the U.S. Forest Service operates many campgrounds in this area. (See Twin Lakes Page 97.)

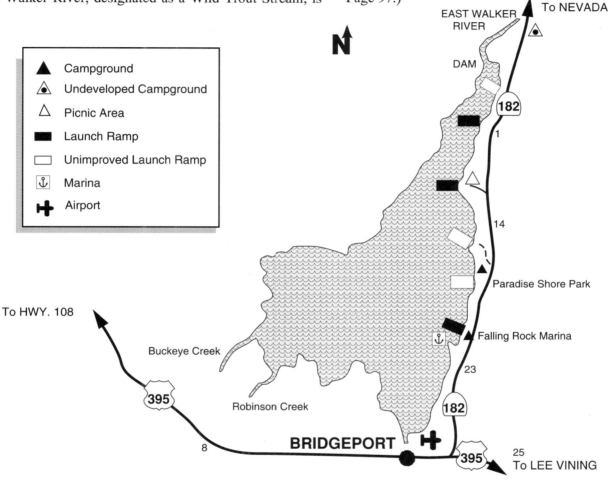

Legend:
- ▲ Campground
- ◬ Undeveloped Campground
- △ Picnic Area
- ■ Launch Ramp
- ▢ Unimproved Launch Ramp
- ⚓ Marina
- ✈ Airport

INFORMATION:	Falling Rock Marina or Paradise Shore Park, Bridgeport 93517		
CAMPING	**BOATING**	**RECREATION**	**OTHER**
Falling Rock Marina Ph: (760) 932-7001 23 Dev. Tents Sites 18 R.V. Sites with Full Hookups	Power, Row, Canoe, Sail & Inflatables Full Service Marina 2 Improved Ramps 1 Unimproved Ramp Rentals: Fishing	Fishing: Rainbow, German Brown & Brook Trout Swimming Backpacking [Parking]	Bait & Tackle Laundromat Trailer Rentals Gas Station Airport
Paradise Shores Park Ph: (760) 932-7735 35 R.V. Sites with Full Hookups Plus 10 with No Hookups	Boats & Motors Docks, Berths, Moorings, Storage Overnight in Boat Permitted Anywhere	Bicycle Trails Rockhounding Hunting: Deer & Waterfowl	Full Facilities at Bridgeport
Call for Fees			

TWIN LAKES

Twin Lakes are 12 miles southwest of Bridgeport in the Eastern Sierra at an elevation of 7,000 feet. The private campgrounds at the Lake are in a pine forest. Complete resort and marine facilities are available. There are 5 Forest Service Campgrounds along Robinson Creek. These Lakes provide excellent fishing for large rainbow and brown trout. Doc and Al's Resort is a pleasant fisherman's retreat. The Hunewill Guest Ranch is a working cattle ranch offering excellent accommodations, food and excursions on horseback into this beautiful country. The backpacker can enjoy the nearby Hoover Wilderness with its many scenic trails, lakes and streams.

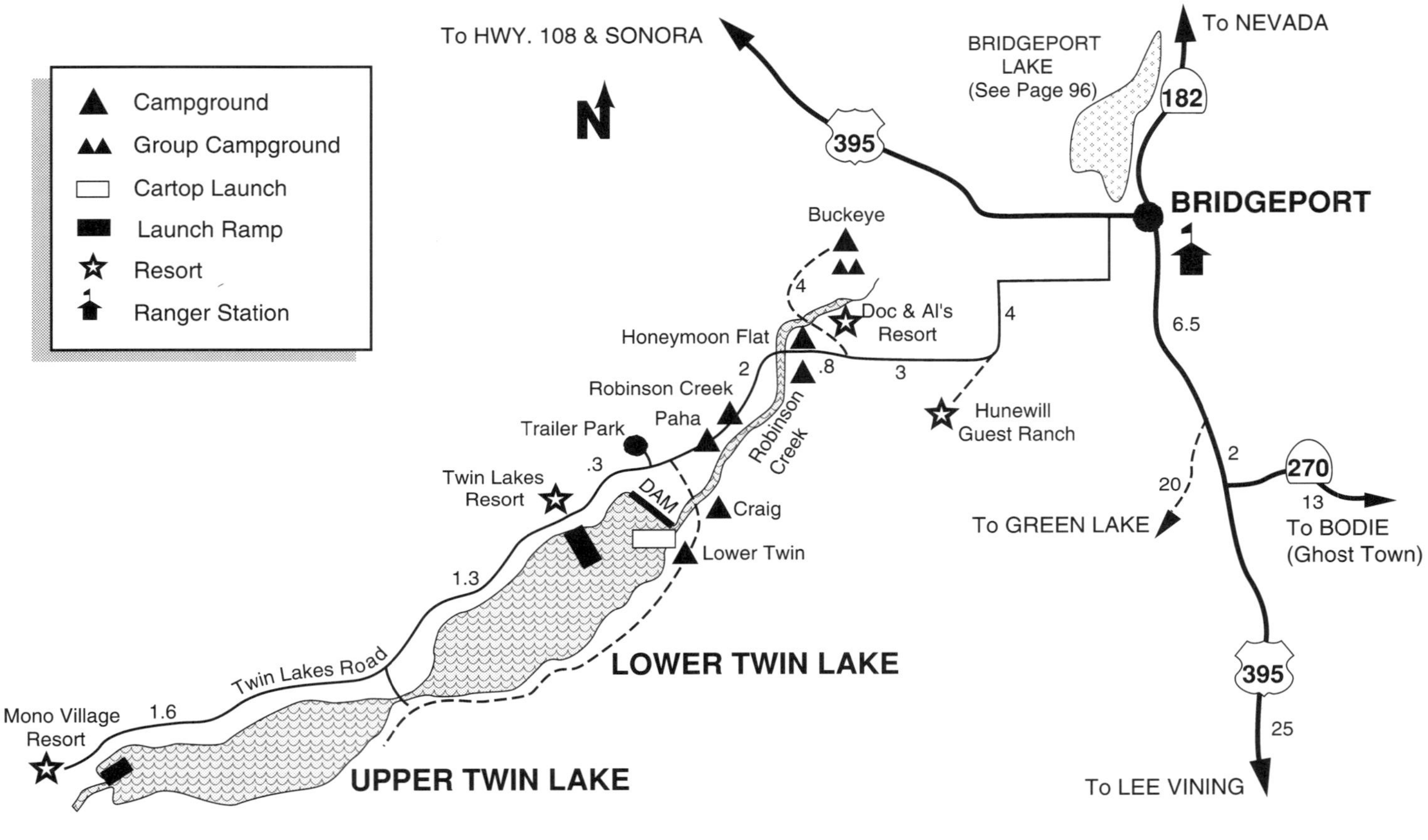

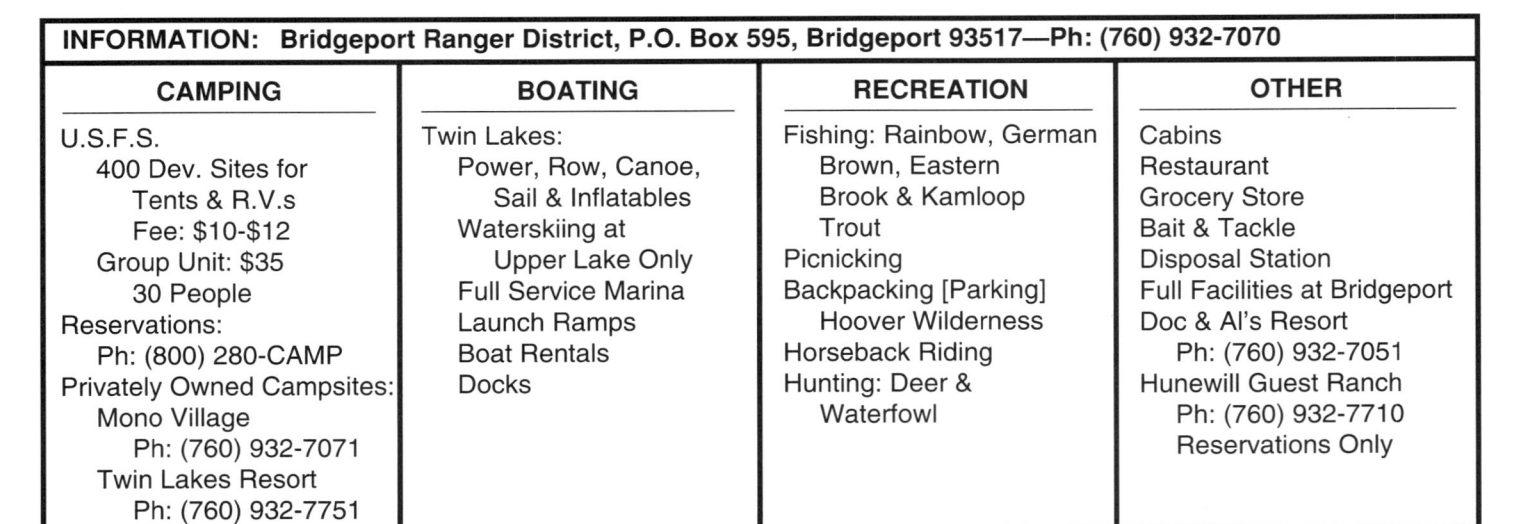

▲	Campground
▲▲	Group Campground
▢	Cartop Launch
◼	Launch Ramp
☆	Resort
🛖	Ranger Station

INFORMATION: Bridgeport Ranger District, P.O. Box 595, Bridgeport 93517—Ph: (760) 932-7070

CAMPING	BOATING	RECREATION	OTHER
U.S.F.S.	Twin Lakes:	Fishing: Rainbow, German	Cabins
400 Dev. Sites for	Power, Row, Canoe,	Brown, Eastern	Restaurant
Tents & R.V.s	Sail & Inflatables	Brook & Kamloop	Grocery Store
Fee: $10-$12	Waterskiing at	Trout	Bait & Tackle
Group Unit: $35	Upper Lake Only	Picnicking	Disposal Station
30 People	Full Service Marina	Backpacking [Parking]	Full Facilities at Bridgeport
Reservations:	Launch Ramps	Hoover Wilderness	Doc & Al's Resort
Ph: (800) 280-CAMP	Boat Rentals	Horseback Riding	Ph: (760) 932-7051
Privately Owned Campsites:	Docks	Hunting: Deer &	Hunewill Guest Ranch
Mono Village		Waterfowl	Ph: (760) 932-7710
Ph: (760) 932-7071			Reservations Only
Twin Lakes Resort			
Ph: (760) 932-7751			

The Virginia Lakes are 10 small Lakes at 9,700 feet elevation located 6.3 miles west of Highway 395. No swimming is allowed in the Lakes. Virginia Lake Resort has cabins, a grocery store, fishing supplies and restaurant. The U. S. Forest Service operates campsites near Trumbull Lake. There is a Pack Station with horses available for lovely scenic rides or trips into the Hoover Wilderness and Yosemite National Park. This is truly a fisherman's paradise as the 10 Lakes and miles of streams are within 1-1/2 miles of the Lodge.The interesting Ghost Town of Bodie is nearby.

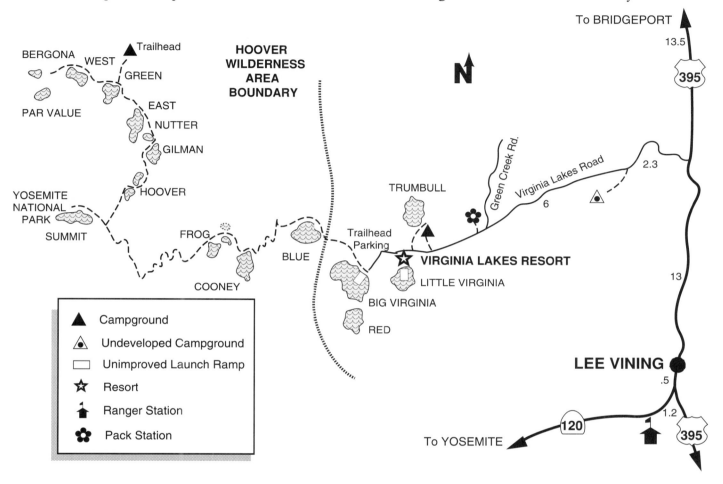

CAMPING	BOATING	RECREATION	OTHER
45 Dev. Sites for Tents & R.V.s No Hookups or Dump Station Fee: $7 Group Camp to 30 People Reservations and First-Come Basis Undeveloped Creekside Camping Fire Permit Req'd. Reserve Specific Sites: Ph: (800)-280-CAMP	Electric Motors, Row, Canoe & Inflatables No Gas Motors 10 MPH Speed Limit Unimproved Launch Ramp Rentals: Fishing & Row Boats	Fishing: Rainbow, German Brown & Eastern Brook Trout Picnicking Hiking Backpacking [Parking] Horseback Riding Trails & Rentals	Virginia Lakes Resort HCR 1, Box 1065 Bridgeport, 93517 Ph: (760) 647-6484 Cabins, Store Bait & Tackle Virginia Lakes Pack Outfit HCR 1, Box 1070 Bridgeport 93517 Summer Phone: Ph: (760) 937-0326 Winter Phone Only: Ph: (775) 867-2591

INFORMATION: Bridgeport Ranger District, P.O. Box 595, Bridgeport 93517—Ph: (760) 932-7070

LUNDY LAKE

Nestled in a valley at an elevation of 7,800 feet, Lundy Lake is the Trailhead to the 20 Lakes Basin. High, majestic mountains and a rocky, aspen and pine covered shoreline provide for spectacular scenery. The Lake is 1 mile long and 1/2 mile wide. The water is clear and cold. This is a popular fishing Lake where fishermen stay for the summer at Mill Creek Campground. Fishing is good at the Lake, in the streams and beaver ponds as well as many other lakes above Lundy reached by trail. The atmosphere is relaxed and rustic with good facilities at the Resort. Mono Lake rests just off Highway 395. This huge, barren salt water Lake is the nesting site for 95 percent of California's gulls.

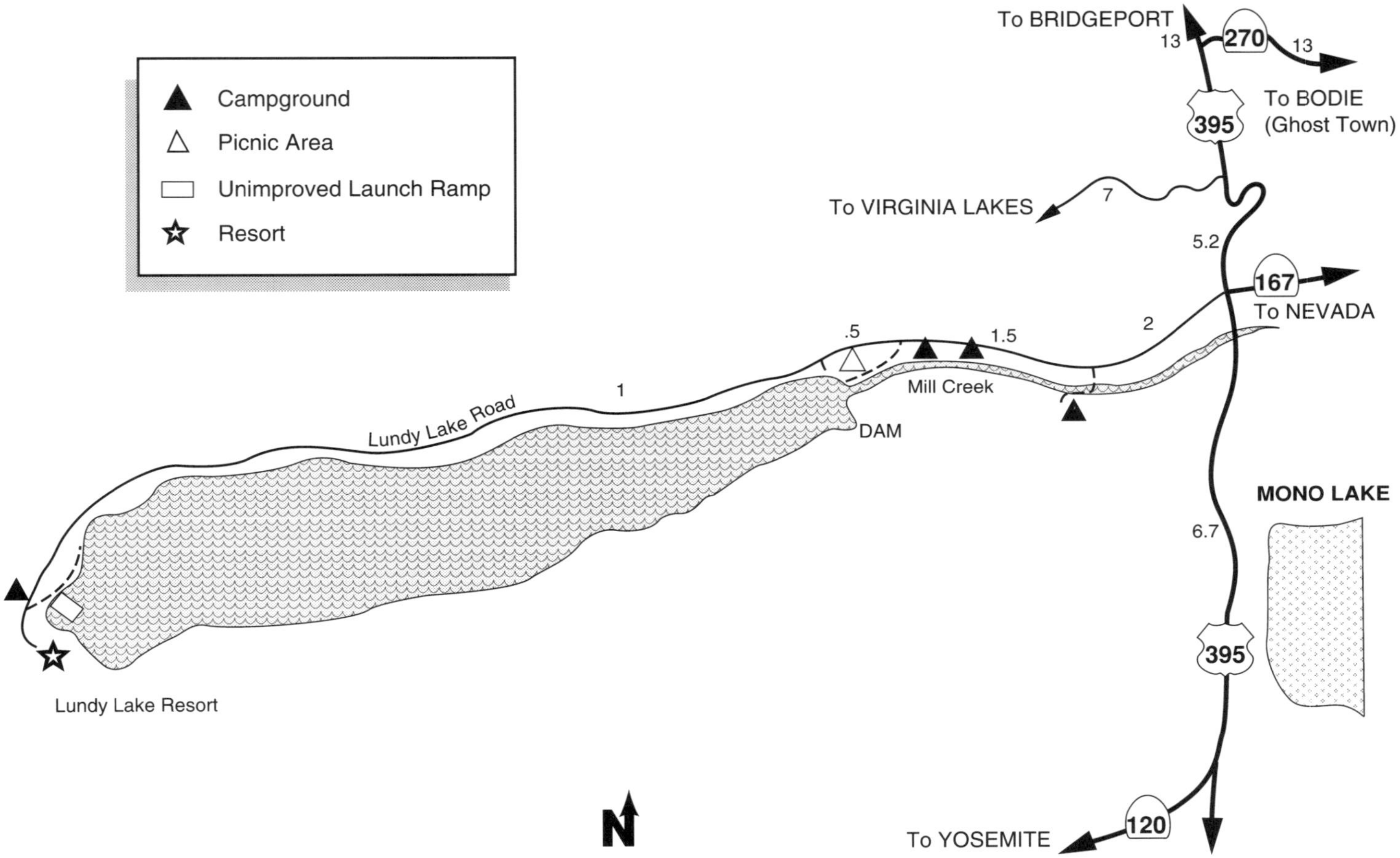

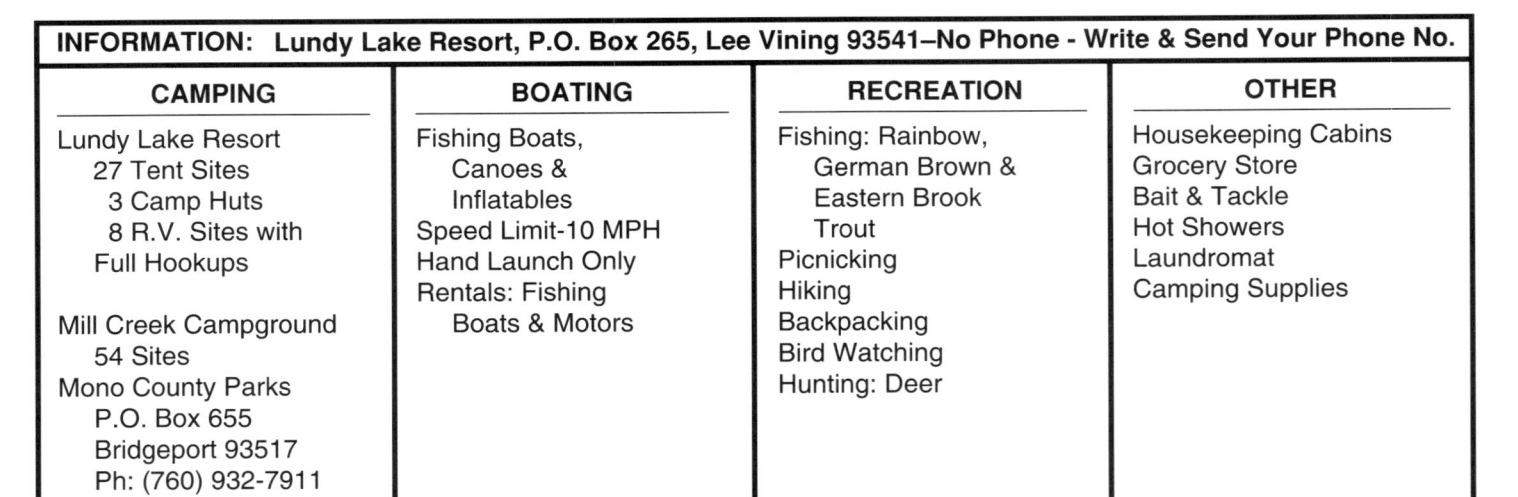

▲	Campground
△	Picnic Area
▭	Unimproved Launch Ramp
☆	Resort

Lundy Lake Resort

Lundy Lake Road

Mill Creek

DAM

MONO LAKE

To BRIDGEPORT

To BODIE (Ghost Town)

To VIRGINIA LAKES

To NEVADA

To YOSEMITE

N

INFORMATION: Lundy Lake Resort, P.O. Box 265, Lee Vining 93541–No Phone - Write & Send Your Phone No.

CAMPING	BOATING	RECREATION	OTHER

Lundy Lake Resort
    27 Tent Sites
    3 Camp Huts
    8 R.V. Sites with
    Full Hookups
 	
Mill Creek Campground
    54 Sites
Mono County Parks
    P.O. Box 655
    Bridgeport 93517
    Ph: (760) 932-7911
	Fishing Boats,
	    Canoes &
	    Inflatables
	Speed Limit-10 MPH
	Hand Launch Only
	Rentals: Fishing
	    Boats & Motors
		Fishing: Rainbow,
		    German Brown &
		    Eastern Brook
		    Trout
		Picnicking
		Hiking
		Backpacking
		Bird Watching
		Hunting: Deer
			Housekeeping Cabins
			Grocery Store
			Bait & Tackle
			Hot Showers
			Laundromat
			Camping Supplies

Saddlebag Lake, at an elevation of 10,087 feet, is the highest Lake in California reached by public road. The 2 mile partially paved road off Highway 120 is steep so large R.V.s and trailers are not advised. For those who enjoy a spectacular alpine setting surrounded by rugged mountain peaks, Saddlebag is a must. Fishing from boat, bank or stream can be excellent. Located near the trailhead into the Hoover Wilderness Area, an hour or less of easy hiking from Saddlebag can bring you to the first lake and streams of the 20 Lakes Basin of the Hoover Wilderness. This wilderness area is a good destination for many hikers and backpackers who may overnight in the area. Open fires are prohibited so bring your own stove and be sure to get a wilderness permit for overnight use. Mt. Conness Glacier is popular with experienced climbers.

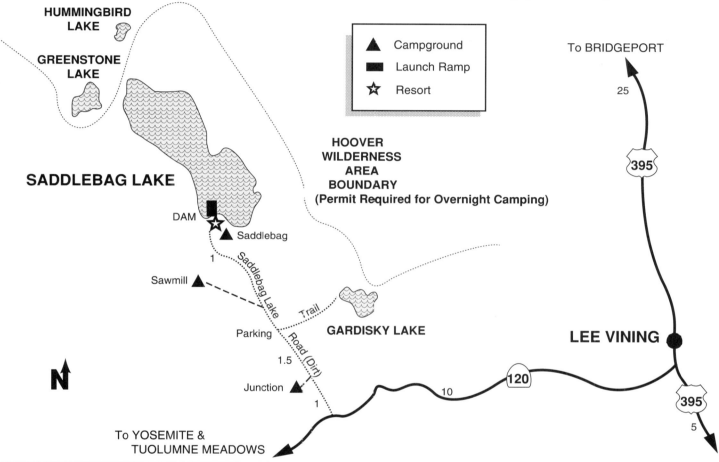

INFORMATION: Mono Lake Ranger District, Box 429, Lee Vining 93541—Ph: (760) 647-3044

CAMPING	BOATING	RECREATION	OTHER
Saddlebag Campground 20 Sites for Tents & Small R.V.s Fee: $11 1 Trailhead Group Site - Reserve Ph: (800) 280-CAMP Sawmill Campground 12 Walk-In Sites Fee: $6	Fishing Boats, Sailboats, Canoes & Inflatables Unimproved Launch Ramp for Boats to 16 Feet - Fee Rentals: Fishing Boats & Motors Water Taxi Across Lake - Fee	Fishing: Rainbow, Cutthroat, Brook & Golden Trout Hiking Backpacking [Parking] Mountain Climbing Nature Study	Saddlebag Lake Resort P.O. Box 440 Lee Vining 93541 (No Phone - Send for Brochure) Snack Bar Grocery Store Bait & Tackle Wilderness Permits

ELLERY, TIOGA and TENAYA

These lovely lakes are in the spectacular Eastern Sierra along Highway 120, west of Tioga Pass. Ellery and Tioga Lakes are 2 miles outside the eastern entrance to Yosemite National Park. Tenaya is 15 miles inside the park. There are many natural attractions in this magnificent area. An interesting sidetrip into the mining site of Bennettville is a 20 minute hike from the Junction Campground. The water in these lakes is clear and cold, providing the fisherman with some excellent opportunities. There are also numerous streams and other small lakes in this area. The Nunatak Trail is nearby.

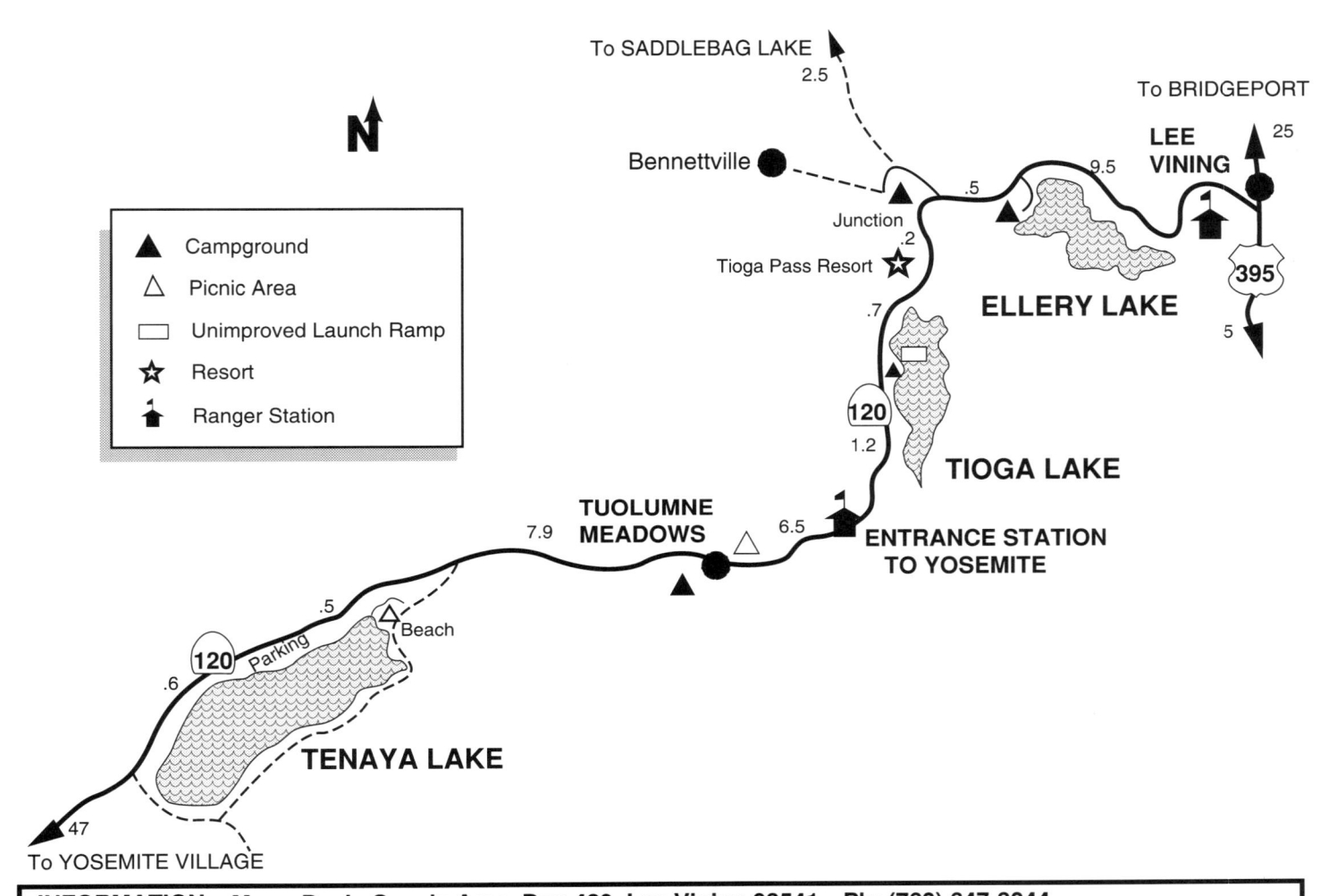

CAMPING	BOATING	RECREATION	OTHER

U.S.F.S.
  Ellery Lake:
    15 Dev. Sites
    Fee: $11
  Tioga Lake:
    13 Dev. Tent Sites
    Fee: $11
  Junction Camp:
    13 Dev. Sites
    Fee: $6
Yosemite National Park:
  Tuolumne Meadows:
    314 Dev. Sites
	Ellery and Tioga Lakes:
	  Motors Permitted
	  Hand Launch at
	    Ellery
	  Small Trailered
	    Boats at Tioga
	Tenaya Lake:
	  No Motors
	  Hand Launch Only
	(No Camping)
		Fishing: Rainbow,
		  Brook, Brown &
		  Golden Trout
		Picnicking
		Hiking & Rock
		  Climbing
		Nature Trail
		Horseback Riding
		Hunting *Outside Park*
		  Limits: Deer,
		  Upland Game
			Yosemite National Park
			  Box 577
			  Yosemite 95389
			  Ph: (209) 372-0265
			Tioga Pass Resort
			  Box 7
			  Lee Vining 93541
			  All Inquiries by Mail
			  Cabins, Lodge
			  Cafe: 7 am - 9 pm
			  Groceries, Tackle,
			  Sporting Goods, Gas

INFORMATION: Mono Basin Scenic Area, Box 429, Lee Vining 93541—Ph: (760) 647-3044

The June Lake Loop presents 4 scenic mountain lakes off the eastern slope of the high Sierra. Resting at an elevation of 7,600 feet in the Inyo National Forest, these popular lakes provide outstanding recreational opportunities, especially fishing. Grant is the largest lake on the loop with 1,000 surface acres; Silver has 80 acres; Gull, the smallest, has 64 acres; and June has 400 acres. Each of these lakes is interconnected by stream or creek and all are prime trout waters whether your interest be lunker browns or stocked rainbows. Hikers, equestrians and packers can enjoy the nearby Ansel Adams Wilderness area with its spectacular scenery and many small lakes and streams. This area in the June Lake loop is enhanced by numerous Forest Service campsites and private support facilities.

....Continued....

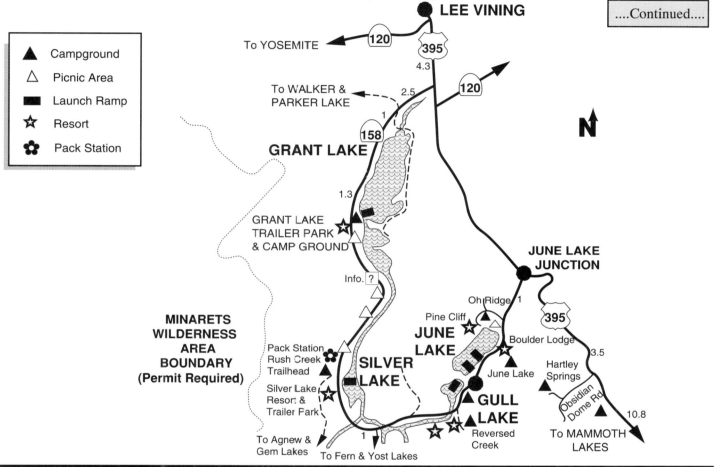

Legend:
- ▲ Campground
- △ Picnic Area
- ◼ Launch Ramp
- ☆ Resort
- ❀ Pack Station

INFORMATION: Mono Basin Scenic Area, P.O. Box 429, Lee Vining 93541—Ph: (760) 647-3044

CAMPING	BOATING	RECREATION	OTHER
U. S. Forest Service 300 Plus Campsites for Tents & R.V.s Fee: $12	Power, Row, Canoe, Sail, Windsurf & Inflatables	Fishing: Rainbow, Brown, Cutthroat & Brook Trout	Housekeeping Cabins Snack Bars Restaurants Grocery Stores
	Waterskiing at Grant Lake Only	Swimming - June Lake	Bait & Tackle Laundromats
	Other Lakes: 10 MPH Speed Limit	Backpacking [Parking]	
See Following Page for Details of Campgrounds & R.V. Parks	Launch Ramps Rentals: Fishing Boats & Motors, Paddleboats Docks, Gas, Repairs	Horseback Riding Trails & Pack Station Hunting: Deer, Dove Geese, Duck & Quail	Further Info: June Lake Chamber of Commerce P.O. Box 2 June Lake 93529 Ph: (760) 648-7584

GRANT LAKE

GRANT LAKE MARINA, P.O. Box 627, June Lake 93529—Ph: (760) 648-7964
70 Developed Sites for Tents & R.V.s (Hookups).- *Fee: $12* - Water, Toilets, Fire Pits, Hot Showers, Disposal Station, Store, Bait & Tackle, Propane, Boat Rentals & Dock Rental, Trailer Rentals. Waterskiing Approximately June - August.

SILVER LAKE
10 MPH Speed Limit on Lake.

U. S. FOREST SERVICE CAMPGROUND
63 Developed Sites for Tents & R.V.s. - *Fee: $12.* - Water, Toilets & Barbecues.

SILVER LAKE RESORT, P.O. Box 116, June Lake 93529—Ph: (760) 648-7525
Full Housekeeping Cabins, Complete Country General Store, Groceries, Sports Clothes, RV/Hardware, Gift Shop, Bait & Tackle, Restaurant, Boat Gas , Disposal Station, Launch Ramp, Rental Boats, 75-Unit Trailer Park with Full Hookups.

FRONTIER PACK TRAIN, Route 3, Box 18, June Lake 93529—Ph: (760) 648-7701
Horseback and Pack Trips into the Minaret Wilderness with Remote Lakes and Streams 2 Miles High
Hour Rides & 1/2 Day Rides.

GULL LAKE

U. S. FOREST SERVICE CAMPGROUND
Gull Lake Campground -11 Sites - *Fee: $12* - Public Ramp. Reversed Creek Campground -17 R.V. Sites -*Fee: $12.*

GULL LAKE BOAT LANDING, P.O. Box 65, June Lake 93529—Ph: (760) 648-7539
Full Service Marina, Rental Boats & Motors, Paddleboats, Docks, Launch Ramps, Bait & Tackle, Beer, Wine, Ice.

Gull Meadows Cartop Launch Ramp and Picnic Area

JUNE LAKE

U. S. FOREST SERVICE CAMPGROUNDS
Ph: (800) 280-CAMP - USFS Reservation Center
Oh! Ridge - 148 Developed Sites for Tents & R.V.s. - *Fee: $12.* Half can be Reserved.
June Lake - 28 Developed Sites for Tents & R.V.s. - *Fee: $12.* 15 can be Reserved
Hartley Springs - South on Highway 395 - 20 Sites for Tents & R.V.s - *No Fee.*

JUNE LAKE MARINA, P.O. Box 26, June Lake 93529—Ph: (760) 648-7726
Full Service Marina, Boat Rentals, Docks, Bait & Tackle, Launch Ramp, Gas, Evinrude Dealer & Motor Repairs.

For Other Resorts and Reservations Contact:

June Lake - June Mountain Reservation Service
P.O. Box 694
June Lake 93529
Ph: (800) 648-2211 or (760) 648-7794

Rainbow Ridge Realty and Reservations
P. O. Box C
June Lake 93529
Ph: (800) 462-5589 or (760) 648-7811

June Lake Properties Reservations
P.O. Box 606
June Lake 93529
Ph: (800) 648-JUNE or (760) 648-7705

The Mammoth Lakes Basin rests at the doorway to the magnificent high Sierra. These small glacial-formed Lakes range in elevation from 8,540 feet to 9,250 feet. They are easily accessible by road or pine-shaded trails. Fishing in Lake or stream is often excellent. This is an ideal area for the hiker, backpacker or horsepacker as trails lead into the John Muir and Ansel Adams Wildernesses. Numerous resorts and campgrounds are available and complete facilities are located in the city of Mammoth Lakes. While Sotcher and Starkweather Lakes are outside the Lakes Basin, they share a similar scenic and recreational abundance.

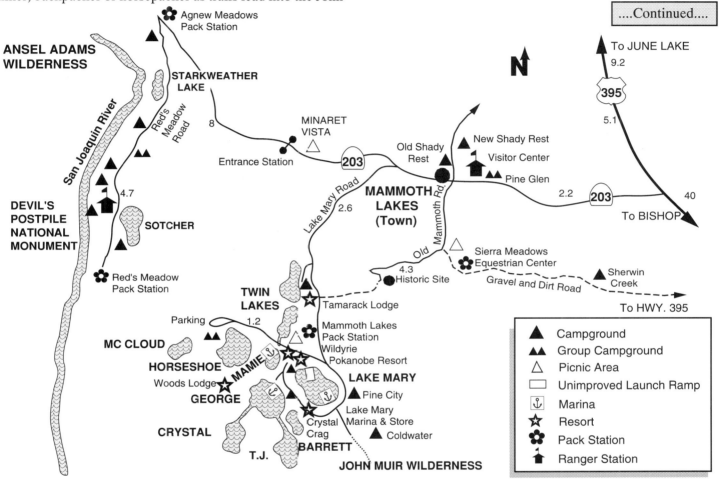

....Continued....

CAMPGROUND LEGEND	
▲	Campground
▲▲	Group Campground
△	Picnic Area
▭	Unimproved Launch Ramp
⚓	Marina
☆	Resort
❀	Pack Station
⛺	Ranger Station

INFORMATION: Mammoth Lakes Visitors Center, Box 148, Mammoth Lakes 93546—Ph: (760) 924-5500

CAMPING	BOATING	RECREATION	OTHER
Dev. Tent/R.V. and Group Sites - USFS Resorts Wilderness Permits Required for Overnight in Ansel Adams and John Muir Wilderness Areas See Following Pages	Power, Row, Canoe & Sailboats 10 MPH Speed Limit Rentals: Fishing Boats and Motors Starkweather Lake & Sotcher Lake: Rowboats & Canoes Only	Fishing: Rainbow, Brown & Brook Trout Swimming at Horseshoe Lake Only Hiking & Riding Trails Nature Study Backpacking Picnicking Hunting: Deer Pack Stations & Horse Rentals	Numerous Resorts & Full Facilities In Town of Mammoth Lakes Nature Guided Activities Provided by Mammoth Visitor Center Mandatory Day Use of Shuttle into Red's Meadow & Devil's Postpile Areas

MAMMOTH LAKES BASIN............Continued

U.S. FOREST SERVICE CAMPGROUNDS

Fees May Vary

Reservations Required for Group Camps and Available for Sites as Shown: Ph: (800) 280-CAMP

NEW SHADY REST
95 Tent/RV Sites,
Disposal Station
Fee: $12 - 14 Day Limit.

OLD SHADY REST
51 Tent/RV Sites
Fee: $12 - 14 Day Limit

SHERWIN CREEK
87 Tent/RV Sites
Fee: $12 - 21 Day Limit
Reservations

TWIN LAKES
94 Tent/RV Sites
Fee: $13 - 7 Day Limit

HORSESHORE LAKE
6 Group Tent/RV Sites
Maximum Persons per Site varies
from 15 to 50, Fee: $28 - $60
Must Reserve (See Above)

LAKE GEORGE
16 Tent/RV Sites
Fee: $13 - 7 Day Limit
Boat Ramp and Rentals Nearby

PINE GLEN
11 Tent/RV Family Sites for
Handicapped use or as
overflow during holiday
weekends only. Fee: $12.
*Campers must obtain
permission to use these Sites.*

6 Group Tent/RV Sites
Maximum Persons per Site
varies from 15 to 30.- Fees: $35 - $50
Must Reserve (See Above)

LAKE MARY
48 Tent/RV Sites
Fee: $13 - 14 Day Limit

COLDWATER
77 Tent/RV Sites
Fee: $13 - 14 Day Limit
Trailhead into the John Muir Wilderness.

PINE CITY
10 Tent/RV Sites
Fee: $13 - 14 Day Limit.

Overnight visitors into the Sotcher Lake/Red's Meadow/Devil's Postpile Areas must obtain a road permit at the Minaret Vista Entrance Station during the hours of 7:30 a.m. to 5:30 p.m. There is a mandatory shuttle bus system for day users from 7:30 a.m. to 5:30 p.m.during the summer months. Inquire at the Visitors Center for further details. The Visitors Center also provides a number of guided nature activities.

Wilderness Permits are required year round for any overnight or longer trips into the John Muir or Ansel Adams Wildernesses. Obtain Permits from the Visitor Center.

For Further Information Contact:
Mammoth Lakes Visitors Center
P.O. Box 148
Mammoth Lakes 93546
Ph: (760) 924-5500
24 Hour Info: (760) 934-1094
Hearing Impaired: (760) 924-5531

....Continued....

SOME PRIVATE FACILITIES NEAR THE LAKES:

TWIN LAKES:

TAMARACK LODGE RESORT - P.O. Box 69, Mammoth Lakes 93546—Ph: (760) 934-2442
Fully Equipped Housekeeping Cabins, Historic Lodge with Rooms, Restaurant, Rental Boats.

LAKE MAMIE:

WILDYRIE LODGE - P.O. Box 109, Mammoth Lakes 93546—Ph: (760) 934-2444
Housekeeping Cabins, Grocery Store, Boat Rentals.

LAKE GEORGE:

WOODS LODGE - P.O. Box 105, Mammoth Lakes 93546, Ph: (760) 934-2261
Housekeeping Cabins, Bait & Tackle, Unimproved Ramp, Dock, Rental Boats & Motors.

LAKE MARY:

CRYSTAL CRAG LODGE - P.O. Box 88, Mammoth Lakes 93546—Ph: (760) 934-2436
Housekeeping Cabins, Boat & Motor Rentals.

POKONOBE RESORT - P.O. Box 72, Mammoth Lakes 93546—Ph: (760) 934-2437
Camp Sites, Grocery Store, Boat Rentals, Ramp & Dock.

LAKE MARY MARINA & STORE - Mammoth Lakes 93546—Ph: (760) 934-5353
Grocery Store, Tackle, Hot Showers, Laundromat, Cafe, Ramp and Docks, Boat Rentals: Motor and Row Boats, Pontoon, Paddleboats, Canoes.

MAMMOTH MOUNTAIN RV PARK: P.O. Box 288, Mammoth Lakes 93546—Ph: (760) 934-3822
130 RV Sites, Electric & Water Hookups, Hot Showers, Disposal Station, Spa, & Cable TV Hookups, Pool.

....Continued....

Mammoth Lakes is a complete destination resort city. There are major grocery stores as well as small retail outlets. Gourmet restaurants, fast food chains, resorts, motels and condominiums are all too numerous to mention. We are listing below two of the reservation services in this area which will help you find a place to fit your needs:

Visitor Information Center
P.O. Box 48, Mammoth Lakes 93546
Ph: (800) 367-6572 or (760) 934-2712
Provides Complete Visitor's Service

Mammoth Reservation Bureau
P.O. Box 1608, Mammoth Lakes 93546
Ph: (800) 462-5571 or (800) 262-7062
(800) 527-6273 or
(760) 934-2528
Throughout the United States and Canada
450 Condominium Reservations
and Complete Visitor's Information

Convict Lake is one of the most beautiful lakes in California. Its crystal clear waters are surrounded by steep, rugged granite peaks. Resting at an elevation of 7,583 feet, this small mountain Lake is 1 mile long and 1/2 mile wide. The 3 miles of shoreline are shaded by pine trees. A great trail goes all the way around the Lake. Boating is popular and the fishing can be excellent in both Lake and stream. The energetic hiker, backpacker and horseman will find a trail leading through a rock-walled canyon to 8 lakes in the nearby John Muir Wilderness. This is a part of the Inyo National Forest which maintains a developed 88 site campground off Convict Creek. The Resort has rustic and deluxe accommodations and other facilities including an excellent dinner house. Be sure to stop at this Lake if you are travelling along Highway 395.

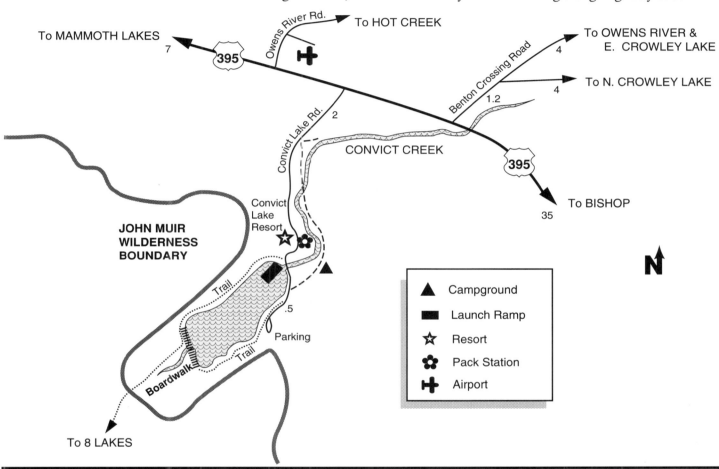

INFORMATION: Convict Lake Resort, Rt. 1 Box 204, Mammoth Lakes 93546—Ph: (760) 934-3800-(800) 992-2260

CAMPING	BOATING	RECREATION	OTHER
U.S. Forest Service 88 Dev. Sites for Tents & R.V.s No Hookups 2 Vehicles Max. per Site Fee: $11 - 7-Day Limit No Reservations Open: End of April to End of October Free Disposal Station	Power, Row, Canoe, Sail & Inflatables Rentals: Fishing Boats, Canoes, Motor & Rowboats Docks Dry Storage	Fishing: Rainbow & German Brown Trout Picnicking Hiking Backpacking [Parking] Bicycle Rentals Horseback Riding Trails & Rentals Hourly, Half & Full Day Rides Hunting: Deer, Rabbit	23 Housekeeping Cabins & Deluxe Accommodations Rates: $85 to $405 6 Open Year Round Gourmet Restaurant with Award Winning Wine List Cocktail Lounge Grocery Store Bait & Tackle Pets: $10 per Stay Airport with Auto Rentals - 3 Miles

CROWLEY LAKE

Crowley Lake is one of California's most productive and popular fishing Lakes. Resting at an elevation of 6,500 feet on the eastern side of the high Sierra, the Lake is situated in Long Valley surrounded by the Glass Mountains and the White Mountains. Anglers jam its shores and waters on opening weekends. This 650 acre Lake once held the German Brown State record and it holds the State record for the largest Sacramento perch. Trophy-sized fish are common. Boating and waterskiing are also popular. Numerous resorts and other recreational opportunities are nearby.

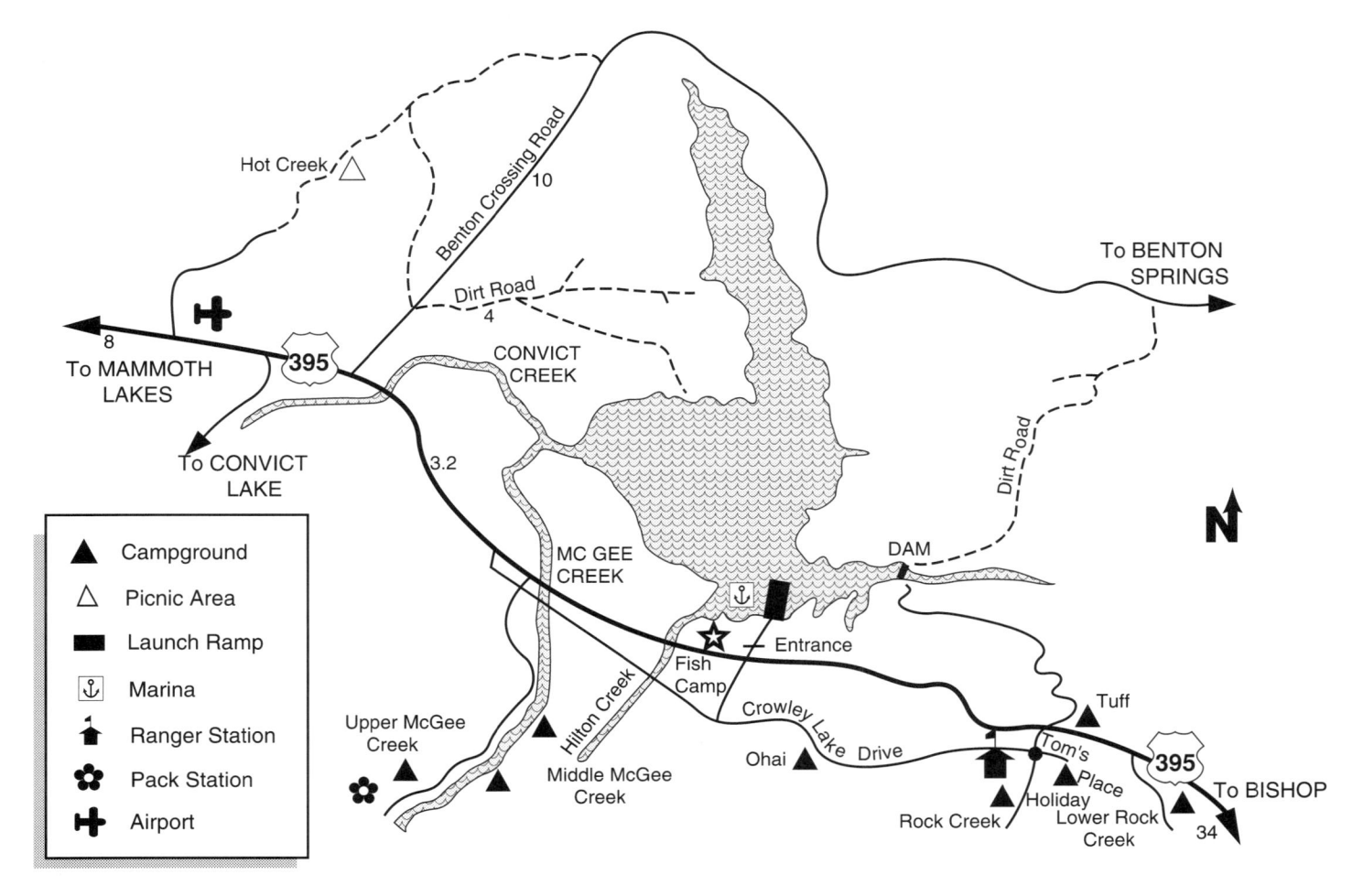

▲ Campground
△ Picnic Area
■ Launch Ramp
⚓ Marina
Ranger Station
Pack Station
Airport

INFORMATION: Crowley Lake Fish Camp, P.O. Box 1268, Mammoth Lakes 93546—Ph: (760) 935-4301

CAMPING	BOATING	RECREATION	OTHER

Fish Camp:
  30 Dev. Sites for
  Tents/R.V.s
  Some Full Hookups
Bureau of Land Mgmt.
  47 Sites for Tents/R.V.s
  First Come Basis
  No Fee - No Water
Other USFS Campgrounds
  Nearby
	Power, Waterskiing,
	  Windsurf, Inflatable
	  & Sail
	Permit Fee Required
	All Craft Must
	  Register
	Launch Ramp
	Boat Slips
	Full Service Marina
	Rentals: Boat & Motor
		Fishing: Rainbow &
		  German Brown Trout,
		  Sacramento Perch
		Season: May through
		  October
		  Check Regulations
		Waterskiing Season
		Picnicking
		Hiking & Backpacking
		Special Events
		Fishing Derbies
			Grocery Store
			Bait & Tackle
			
			Tube Tenders
			Ph: (760) 934-6922
			24 ft. Pontoon Boat
			Guided Fishing Trips
			
			Chamber of Commerce
			Ph: (760) 935-4666
			
			Full Facilities at
			  Mammoth Lakes

Rock Creek Lake, at an elevation of 9,682 feet, is one of the highest lakes in California. Located in the Rock Creek Canyon of Inyo National Forest, this eastern Sierra area has over 60 lakes and streams for the adventuresome equestrian, backpacker and angler. Snow fed streams flow into Rock Creek, a natural Lake of 63 surface acres. Rainbow and German Brown trout are planted throughout the season while native Eastern Brook and Golden trout are found in the waters of the John Muir Wilderness. There are several Forest Service campgrounds along Rock Creek. Boating is limited to a 5 MPH speed limit. Rock Creek Pack Station offers rental horses for a day or extended trips.

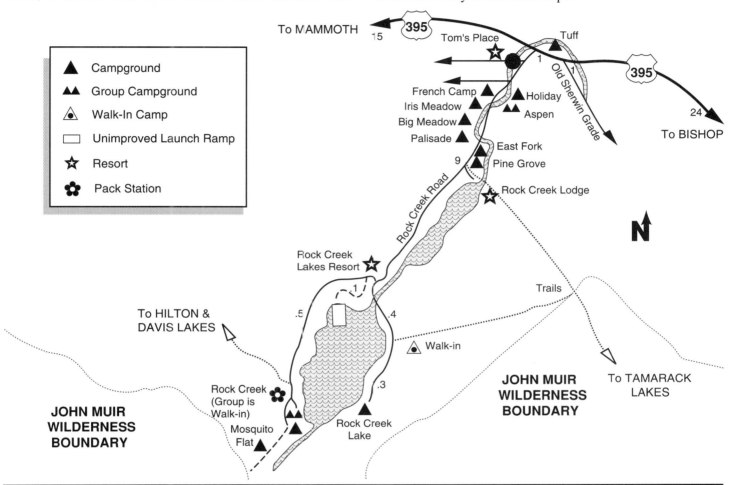

INFORMATION: White Mountain Ranger District, 798 N. Main St., Bishop 93514—Ph: (760) 873-2500

CAMPING	BOATING	RECREATION	OTHER

Dev. Sites - $12
   French Camp: 86 Sites
   Tuff: 34 Sites
   East Fork: 133 Sites
Group Sites - $40
Aspen & Rock Creek
Reserve Above Sites:
   Ph: (800) 280-CAMP
Mosquito Flat Trailhead
   10 Sites Free - 1 Day
Other Sites - $12
   No Reservations
   First-Come Basis
	Power, Row, Canoe,
	   Sail & Inflatables
	Speed Limit - 5 MPH
	Unimproved Launch
	   Ramp
	Rentals at Rock Creek
	   Lakes Resort:
	   Fishing Boats &
	   Motors
		Fishing: Rainbow,
		   Eastern Brook &
		   Golden Trout
		   Lake & Streams
		Picnicking
		Hiking
		Backpacking - John
		   Muir Wilderness
		   Permit Required
		Horseback Riding
		   Rentals & Trails
		Hunting: Deer
			Rock Creek Lakes
			   Resort
			   Store, Cafe, Boat
			   Rentals, Cottages
			   Ph: (760) 935-4311
			Rock Creek Lodge
			   Ph: (760) 935-4170
			Tom's Place Resort
			   Ph: (760) 935-4239
			Rock Creek Pack Station.
			   Ph: (760) 935-4493

NORTH LAKE, LAKE SABRINA, SOUTH LAKE—BISHOP CREEK CANYON

Bishop Creek Canyon is on the eastern slope of the Sierra Nevada at elevations ranging from 7,500 feet to 9,500 feet. This area is popular with backpackers by both foot and horseback into the nearby John Muir Wilderness. Lake Sabrina has a surface area of 150 acres. South Lake has 180 acres and North Lake is much smaller. These Lakes, along with Bishop Creek, are planted weekly with trout during the summer. The U.S. Forest Service offers numerous campsites. There are private resorts with full vacation facilities.

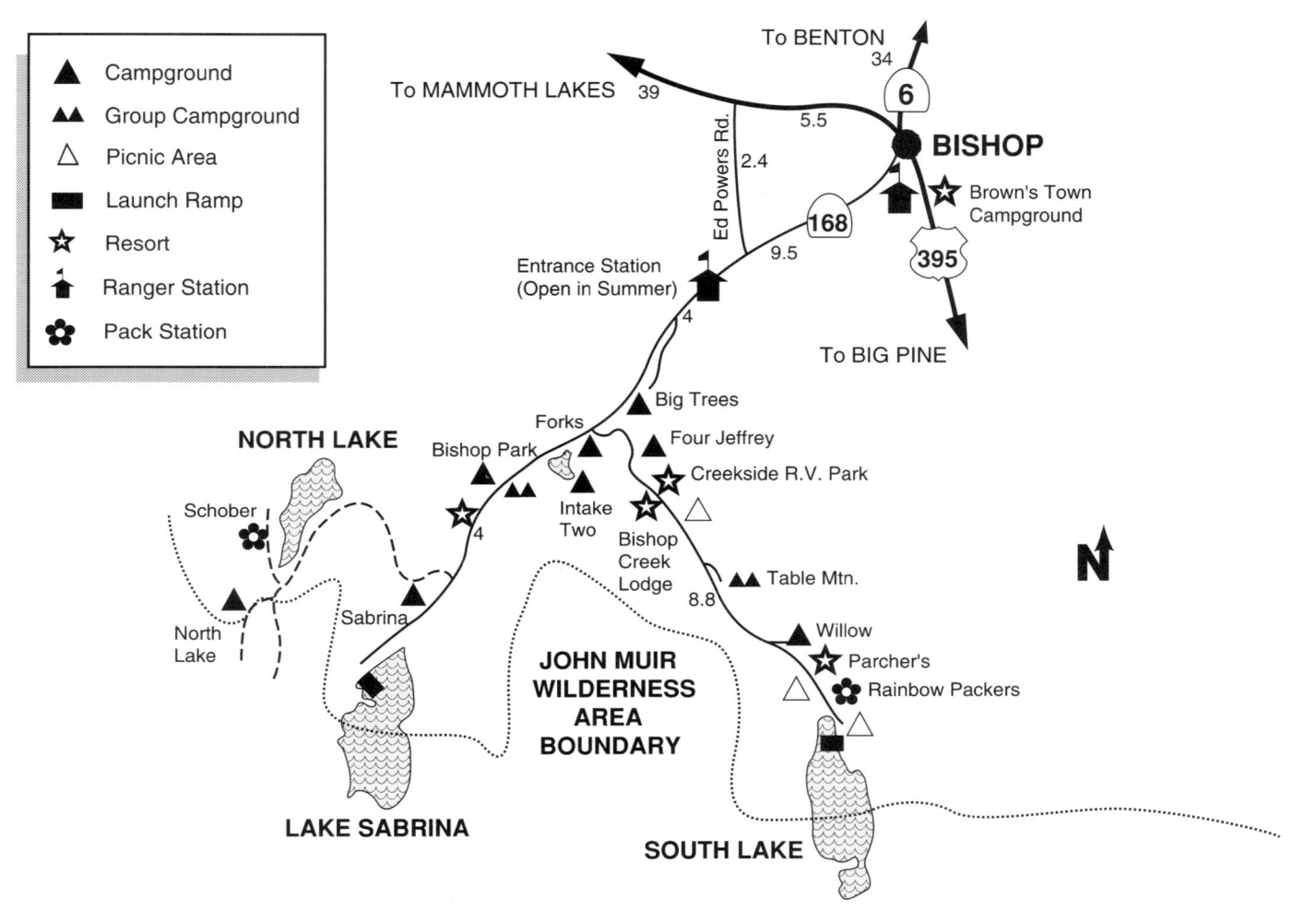

Legend:
- ▲ Campground
- ▲▲ Group Campground
- △ Picnic Area
- ■ Launch Ramp
- ☆ Resort
- ♟ Ranger Station
- ❁ Pack Station

To BENTON
To MAMMOTH LAKES 39
34
6
5.5
2.4
Ed Powers Rd.
BISHOP
Brown's Town Campground
168
9.5
395
Entrance Station (Open in Summer)
4
To BIG PINE
Big Trees
Forks
Four Jeffrey
NORTH LAKE
Bishop Park
Creekside R.V. Park
Schober
Intake Two
Bishop Creek Lodge
North Lake
4
Sabrina
Table Mtn.
8.8
JOHN MUIR WILDERNESS AREA BOUNDARY
Willow
Parcher's
Rainbow Packers
LAKE SABRINA
SOUTH LAKE
N

INFORMATION: White Mountain Ranger District. 798 N. Main St., Bishop 93514—Ph: (760) 873-2500

CAMPING	BOATING	RECREATION	OTHER
Dev. Sites: $12 Big Trees - 9 Sites Four Jeffrey - 106 sites Forks - 8 Sites, Intake Two - 7 Walk-In Plus 8 Sites Bishop Park - 21 Sites Sabrina - 18 Sites North Lake - 11 Sites Group Siutes: $42 to 25 People Bishop Park & Table Mtn. Reserve Some Sites: Ph: (800) 280-CAMP	Power, Row, Canoe, Sail & Inflatables 5 MPH Speed Limit Unimproved Launch Ramps at South Lake and Sabrina Rentals: Fishing and Motorboats Boat Gas Only	Fishing: Rainbow & German Brown Trout Picnicking & Hiking Backpacking - Permit Required Horseback Riding Trails & Rentals Rainbow Packers: Ph: (760) 873-8877	Brown's Town Campground: Ph: (760) 873-8522 150 Dev. Sites for Tents/R.V.s, Hookups Creekside R.V. Park Ph: (760) 872-3044 Bishop Creek Lodge Ph: (760) 873-4484 Parcher's Resort Ph: (760) 873-4177 Cabins, Restaurants, Stores Full Facilities in Bishop

New Melones rests at an elevation of 1,088 feet in the Mother Lode Gold Country of Central California. Its dam, completed in 1979, is the second largest earth and rock filled dam in the United States. This damming of the Stanislaus River has created the largest Lake in the area with 12,500 surface acres and over 100 miles of tree covered shoreline. This is one of California's prime recreation Lakes. Extensive facilities have been developed under the management of the U. S. Bureau of Reclamation. There are 2 large campgrounds at Glory Hole and Tuttletown as well as several day use areas. The boater will find launching areas and a marina. Fishing for a variety of species is considered good. *Call for information regarding water level during possible drought conditions.*

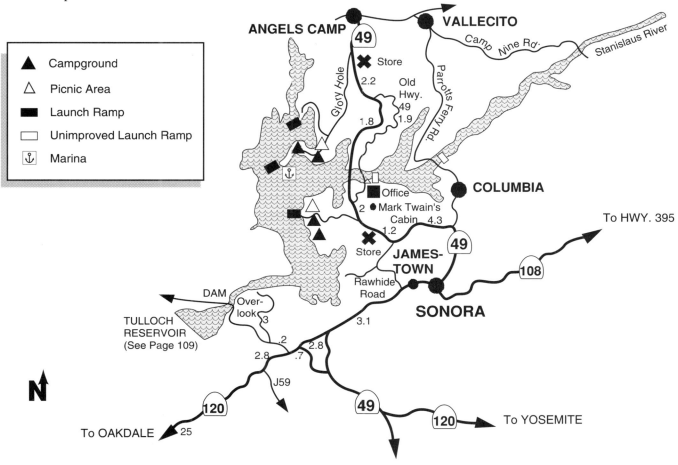

▲	Campground
△	Picnic Area
■	Launch Ramp
▭	Unimproved Launch Ramp
⚓	Marina

INFORMATION: Resource Manager, 6850 Studhorse Flat Road, Sonora 95370—Ph: (209) 536-9094

CAMPING	BOATING	RECREATION	OTHER
Glory Hole: 144 Dev. Sites for Tents & R.V.s Tuttletown: 165 Dev. Sites for Tents & R.V.s Fee: $14 2 Cars, 8 People Maximum Camping Only at Designated Sites	Open to All Boating, Sailing & Waterskiing 1 Unimproved Launch Area 3 Improved Launch Ramps with 3 Floats Full Service Marina Fuel Dock, Pumpout Rentals - Fishing, Pontoon, Houseboats *Call for Current Information on Water Levels*	Fishing: Rainbow & Brown Trout, Large & Smallmouth Bass, Bluegill, Catfish & Crappie Picnicking Hiking Gold Panning *No Off Road Vehicles* Mark Twain's Cabin	Full Facilities in Nearby Towns New Melones Lake Marina (Canteen Corp.) P.O. Box 1389 Angels Camp, 95222 Ph: (209) 785-3300 Store

LAKE TULLOCH

Lake Tulloch, at an elevation of 510 feet, is on the western slope of the Sierras just east of Modesto. The 55 miles of shoreline encompass two submerged valleys surrounded by oak-studded rolling hills. This "Gold Country" Lake is open to all types of boating and offers good marine support facilities. Fishing for trout and warm water species is popular especially since Tulloch is known as one of California's prime smallmouth bass waters. The South Shore offers developed and open camping. The Marina provides a launch ramp, boat rentals, gas dock, snack bar, groceries and a campground. Lake Tulloch Resort has a luxury motel on the water with a launch ramp, swimming pool and beach, restaurant and bar. Call for current status for Copper Cove.

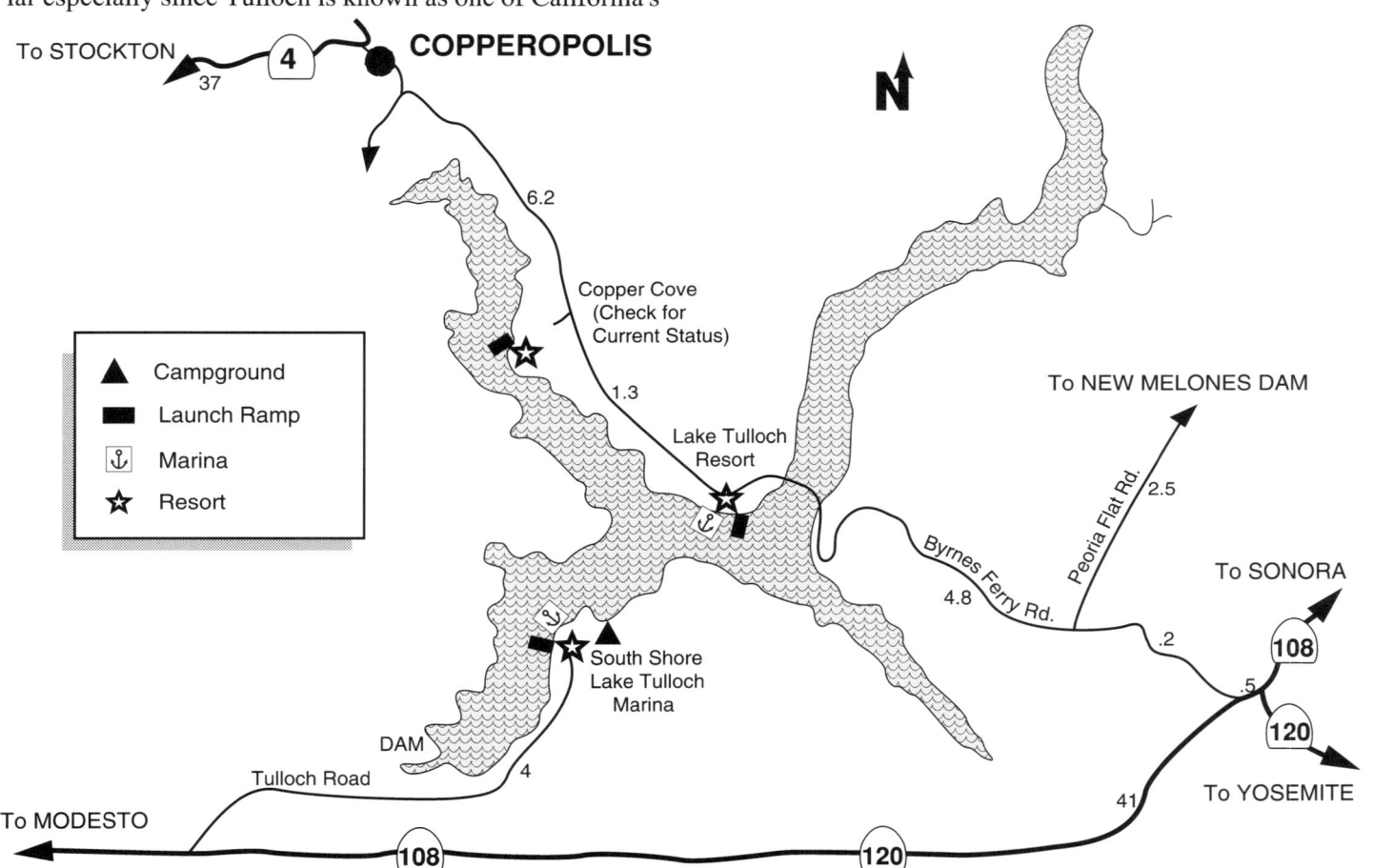

INFORMATION: South Shore, 14448 Tulloch Dam Rd., Jamestown 95327—Ph: (209) 881-0107

CAMPING	BOATING	RECREATION	OTHER
130 Dev. Sites for Tents & R.V.s Full Hookups & Lakefront Cabanas with Electricity Fees: $17.50 - $27.50 Reservations: 800-894-CAMP	Power, Row, Canoe, Sail, Waterski, Jets, Windsurf & Inflatables Launch Ramp - $6 Rentals: Fishing Boats, Ski Boats, Patio Boats, Kayaks	Fishing: Rainbow Trout, Small & Largemouth Bass, Bluegill, Catfish, Crappie Picnicking Swimming - Beaches Hiking & Riding Trails Gold Panning	Lake Tulloch Resort 7260 O'Byrnes Ferry Rd. Copperopolis 95228 Ph: (209) 785-8200 or (888) 785-8200 47 Lake View Rooms Restaurant & Lounge
Lakefront Cabins with Electricity and Dock	Overnight Boating Allowed Lake Tullock Resort: Marina Launch Ramp: $10		Grocery Store Bait & Tackle Snack Bars Grocery Store

WOODWARD RESERVOIR

Woodward Reservoir is at an elevation of 210 feet in the low, rolling, grassy foothills 6 miles north of Oakdale. This 2,900 surface acre irrigation Reservoir is under the jurisdiction of Stanislaus County. The 23 miles of shallow shoreline has many quiet coves and inlets for the boater and fisherman. The Lake is divided by speed limit restrictions with a few "No Boat" areas. Ample space allows all boaters to enjoy their sport. There is a good warm water fishery. The County maintains a nice tree-covered campground on the edge of the Lake and a large overflow primitive camping area with limited facilities. This is a popular family area with approximately 3,240 acres of park land.

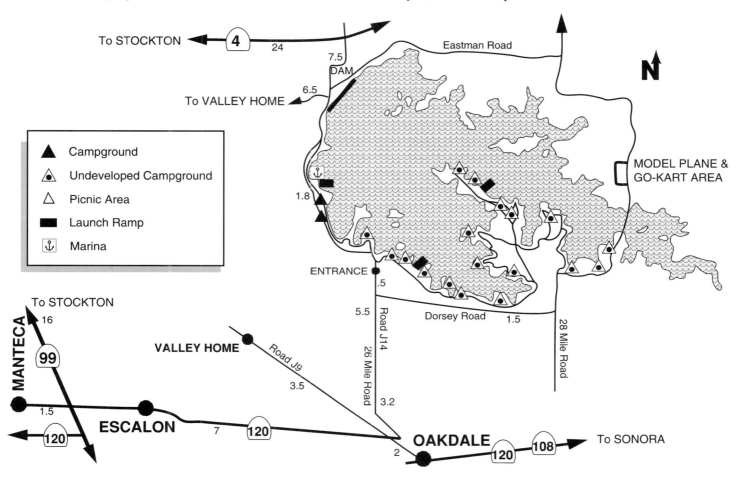

INFORMATION: Woodward Reservoir, 14528-26 Mile Rd., Oakdale 95361—Ph: (209) 847-3304

CAMPING	BOATING	RECREATION	OTHER
195 Dev. Sites for Tents & R.V.s Fee: $14 Full Hookups: $16 13 Miles of Shoreline for Primitive Camping Fee: $12 Pets Permitted	Power, Row, Canoe, Sail, Waterski, Jets, Windsurf, Inflatables Restricted Speed Limit Areas Entry Fee: $6 Launch Ramps Docks & Gas Full Service Marina Rentals: Fishing Boats & Canoes	Fishing: Catfish, Perch, Bluegill, Crappie, Largemouth Bass Swimming Picnicking: Large Shelter to Reserve Equestrian Trails Hunting: Waterfowl With Permit Volleyball Court Horseshoe Pits	Snack Bar Grocery Store Bait & Tackle Disposal Station Hot Showers Full Facilities - 6 Miles at Oakdale

DON PEDRO LAKE

Don Pedro Lake rests at an elevation of 800 feet in the Sierra foothills of the southern Mother Lode. This huge Lake has a surface area of 12,960 acres with a pine and oak dotted shoreline of 160 miles. There is an abundance of camping, marine and recreation facilities under the jurisdiction of the Don Pedro Recreation Agency. There are three recreation areas and two full service marinas. The vast size and irregular shoreline provides a multitude of boating opportunities from boat-in camping to waterskiing. The angler, from the novice to those on the Pro Bass Tour, will find a good varied fishery. *Emerging rocks and islands can be a problem late in the season due to low water levels .*

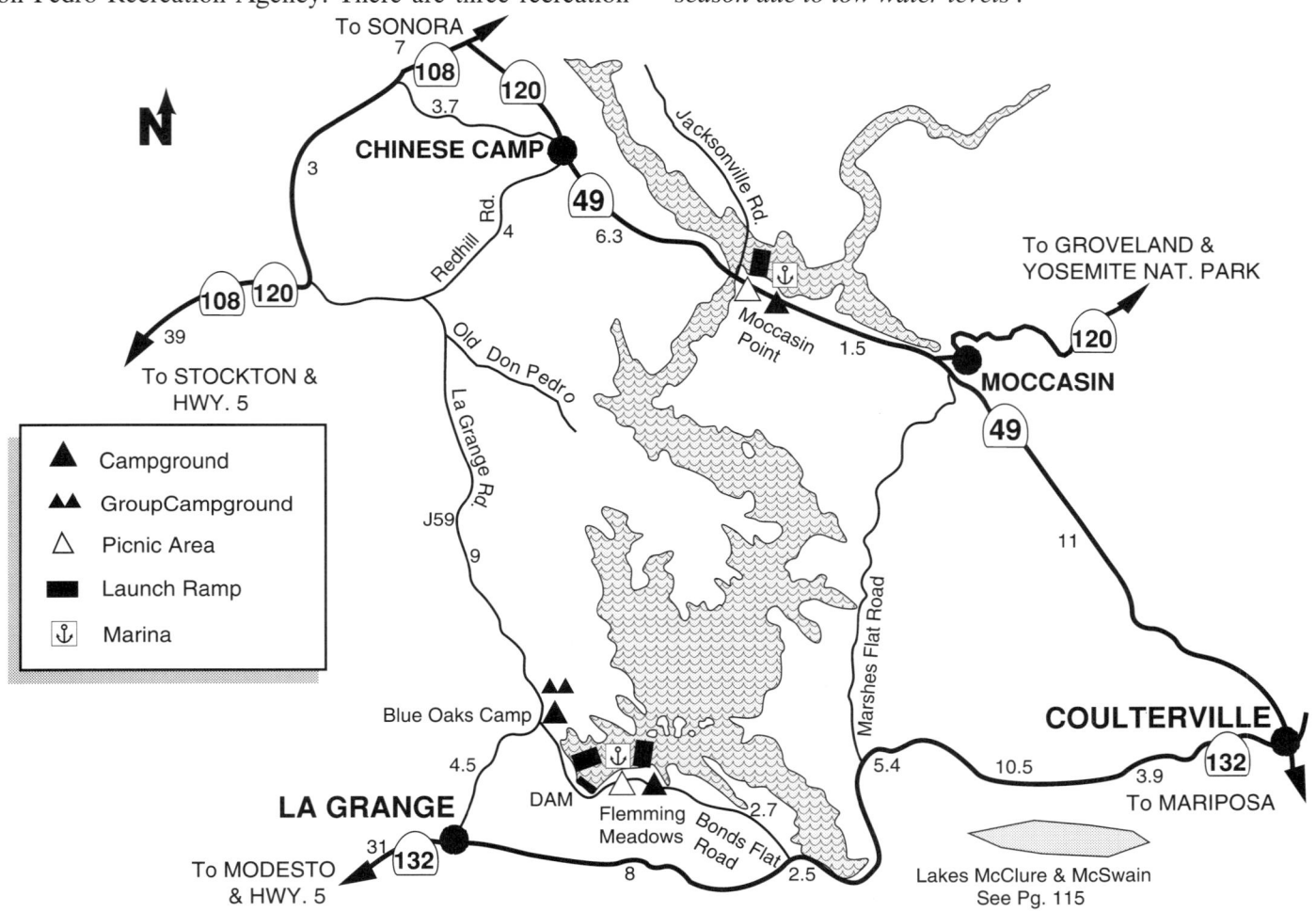

▲	Campground
▲▲	GroupCampground
△	Picnic Area
■	Launch Ramp
⚓	Marina

INFORMATION: Don Pedro Recreation Agency, 31 Bonds Flat Rd., La Grange 95329—Ph: (209) 852-2396

CAMPING	BOATING	RECREATION	OTHER
550 Dev. Sites for Tents & R.V.s Fees: Tents - $12 - $15 Full Hookups - $16 - $22 Group Camp Facility Boat-In & Walk-In Sites Reservations Accepted: $5 Fee per Site Overnight Boat-in Designated Areas *Dogs Prohibited* Day Use Fee: $5	Power, Row, Canoe, Sail, Waterski, Jets, Windsurf & Inflatable Sailing Slalom Course Full Service Marinas 3 Launch Ramps - $5 Rentals: Fishing, Houseboats & Pontoons Docks, Berths, Moorings Dry Storage & Gas	Fishing: Trout, Catfish, Bluegill, Crappie, Perch, Silver Salmon, Florida Black Bass Swimming Lagoon Handicap Access Picnicking Group Picnic Area Hiking Private Houseboats Subject to Permit	Snack Bars Restaurant Grocery Store Bait & Tackle Hot Showers Laundromat Disposal Stations Gas Station Propane

Modesto Reservoir is at an elevation of 210 feet in the low hills, orchards and pastureland northeast of Modesto. The Lake has a surface area of 2,700 acres with 31 miles of shoreline. This is a good boating facility with many pretty coves for unlimited boat camping, westerly breezes for sailing and vast open water for the skier. Boaters should be advised that there is a 5 MPH speed limit on the southern area of the Lake and around the populated areas. There are also several no boating zones; refer to rules or ask a sheriff or park aide for specific areas. The many coves have submerged trees which provide for a good warm water fishery. The facilities are under the jurisdiction of the Stanislaus County Parks Department.

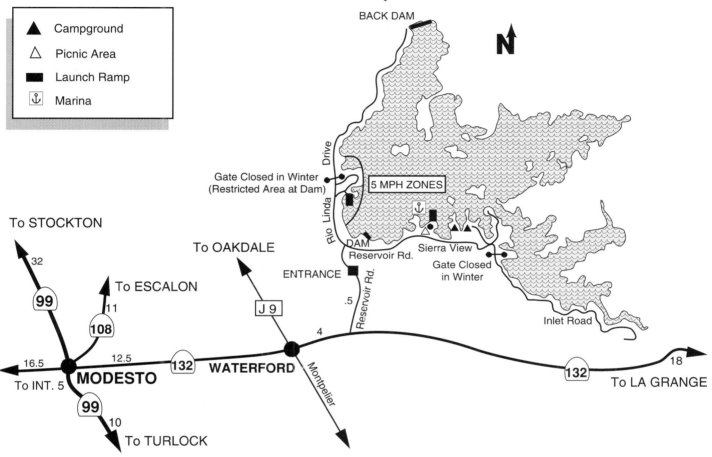

▲	Campground
△	Picnic Area
▰	Launch Ramp
⚓	Marina

INFORMATION: Modesto Reservoir, 1716 Morgan Rd., Modesto 95351—Ph: (209) 874-9540

CAMPING	BOATING	RECREATION	OTHER
90 Dev. Sites for Tents & R.V.s Fee: $14 - $16 Unlimited Primitive Sites Fee: $12 Entrance Fees Cars: $6 Boats: $5 *No Pets or Horses Permitted*	Power, Row, Canoe, Sail, Waterski, Jets, Windsurf & Inflatable Launch Ramps Full Service Marina Rentals: Paddleboats Docks Gas	Fishing: Catfish, Bluegill, Crappie, Large & Smallmouth Bass Swimming - Beaches Picnicking Hiking Backpacking [Parking] Duck Hunting By Permit Only	Snack Bar Grocery Store Bait & Tackle Hot Showers Disposal Station Gas Full Facilities at Modesto *Check Water Level Conditions*

OAKWOOD LAKE

Bordering the San Joaquin River just off the junction of Interstate 5 and Highway 120, Oakwood Lake is one of the most unique and largest RV campgrounds and water "fun" parks in the West. There are over 30 water rides and attractions. Boating is restricted to canoes and inflatables. 400 campsites have full hookups and are located on shady lawns. For those who enjoy power boating and a broader fishery, there is the San Joaquin River. This is a family park for those who enjoy a multitude of activities.

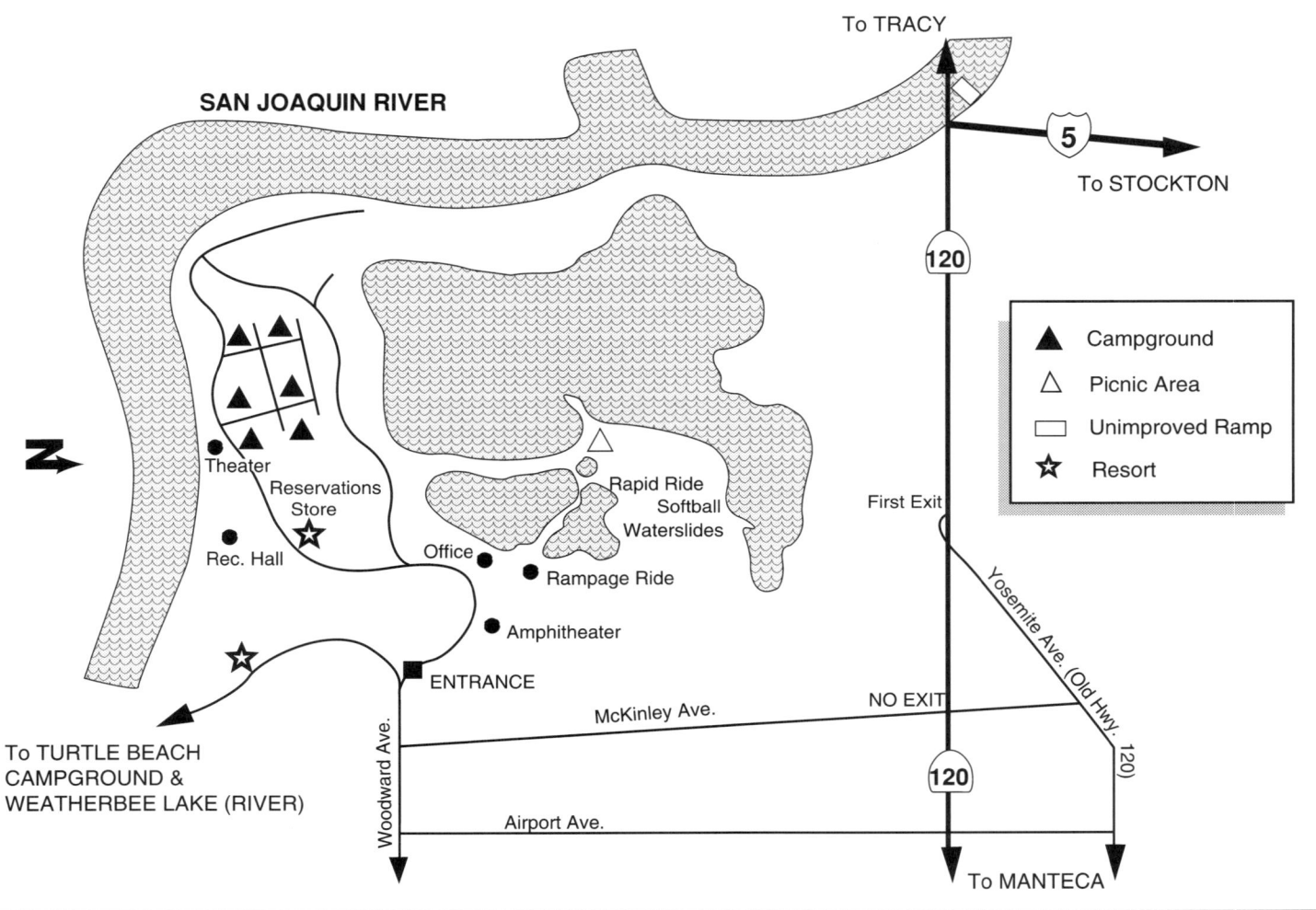

INFORMATION: Oakwood Lake, 874 E. Woodward, Manteca 95337—Ph: (209) 239-2500

CAMPING	BOATING	RECREATION	OTHER
400 Dev. Sites for R.V.s with Full Hookups Tent Camping Fees Start at $21 Group Sites Discount Rates for R.V. Clubs and Groups Reservations Only: Ph: (209) 239-2500 Day Use - Call for Rates	Row, Sail, Canoe & Inflatables No Motors on Park Lake San Joaquin River: Power Boats and Waterskiing Launch Ramp off Hwy. 120	Fishing: Catfish & Bass - Guests Only Picnicking 2 Large Day-Use Areas Waterslides The Turbo Tube, The Rampage, Jet Scream, Rapids Ride, Kiddie Cove, Castaway Bay Softball Complex Basketball Courts Horseshoe Pits Movies & Bingo	Snack Bar Grocery Store Beer & Wine (Alcoholic Beverages May Not Be Brought In) Bait & Tackle Hot Showers Laundromat Playground Arcades R.V. Storage LP Gas Disposal Station

Turlock Lake, at an elevation of 250 feet, is nestled in the foothills 25 miles east of Modesto. As a part of the Turlock State Recreation Area, Turlock Lake is included in the California State Park System. It offers a surface area of 3,500 acres of open water which is surrounded by 26 shoreline miles and 228 acres of rolling grasslands. Open year around, this is a popular recreation area . The Lake is open to all types of boating although in late season, low water can be a hazard. There is a good warm water fishery and trout are planted on a regular basis in season. Swimming is popular at several beaches. The campground is away from the beach on the Tuloumne River. There are nice shaded level campsites overlooking the river. Reservations are advised.

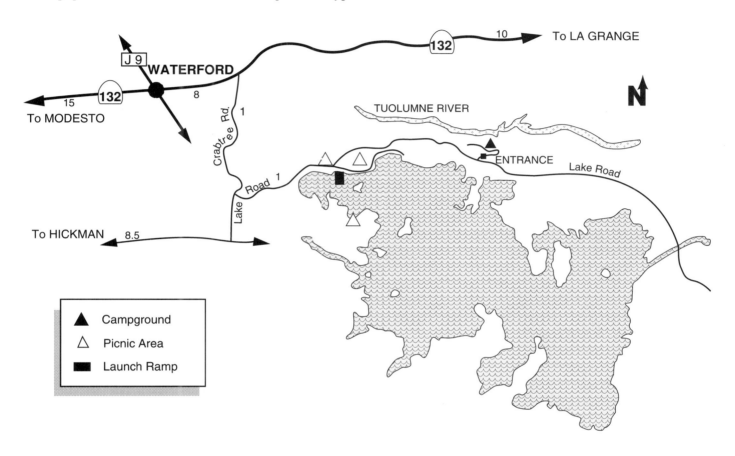

INFORMATION: Turlock State Recreation Area, 22600 Lake Rd., La Grange 95329—Ph: (209) 874-2056

CAMPING	BOATING	RECREATION	OTHER
State Park 　67 Dev. Sites for 　Tents & R.V.s to 27 Feet 　Fees: $12 - $16 　Reserve: 　Ph: (800) 444-7275 Campfire & Junior 　Ranger Program Day Use Fee: $5	Power, Row, Canoe, 　Sail, Waterski, 　Jets, Windsurf 　& Inflatable Launch Ramp - $5 *Low Water Late in 　Season*	Fishing: Trout, 　Catfish, Bluegill, 　Crappie, Large & 　Smallmouth Bass Swimming - Beaches Picnicking Hiking Hunting in Season No Alcohol 　Except in Campground	Full Facilities at 　Waterford

LAKE MC CLURE and LAKE MC SWAIN

Located in the Mother Lode Country of the Sierra foothills, these Lakes are at an elevation of 867 feet. Lake McClure has a surface area of 7,100 acres with 82 miles of pine and oak covered shoreline. The fine recreation areas around the Lake have modern campgrounds, marinas and recreation facilities. Many coves are popular for houseboats. The waterskiier will find 26 miles of open water. Lake McSwain is actually the forebay of Lake McClure. The very cold flowing water from McClure has created a good fishery which is enhanced by weekly trout plants and a 10 MPH speed limit for boaters on Lake McSwain. Campsites next to the water are available since this Lake remains full year around. Boating is popular, but waterskiing and houseboats are not allowed at McSwain.

....Continued....

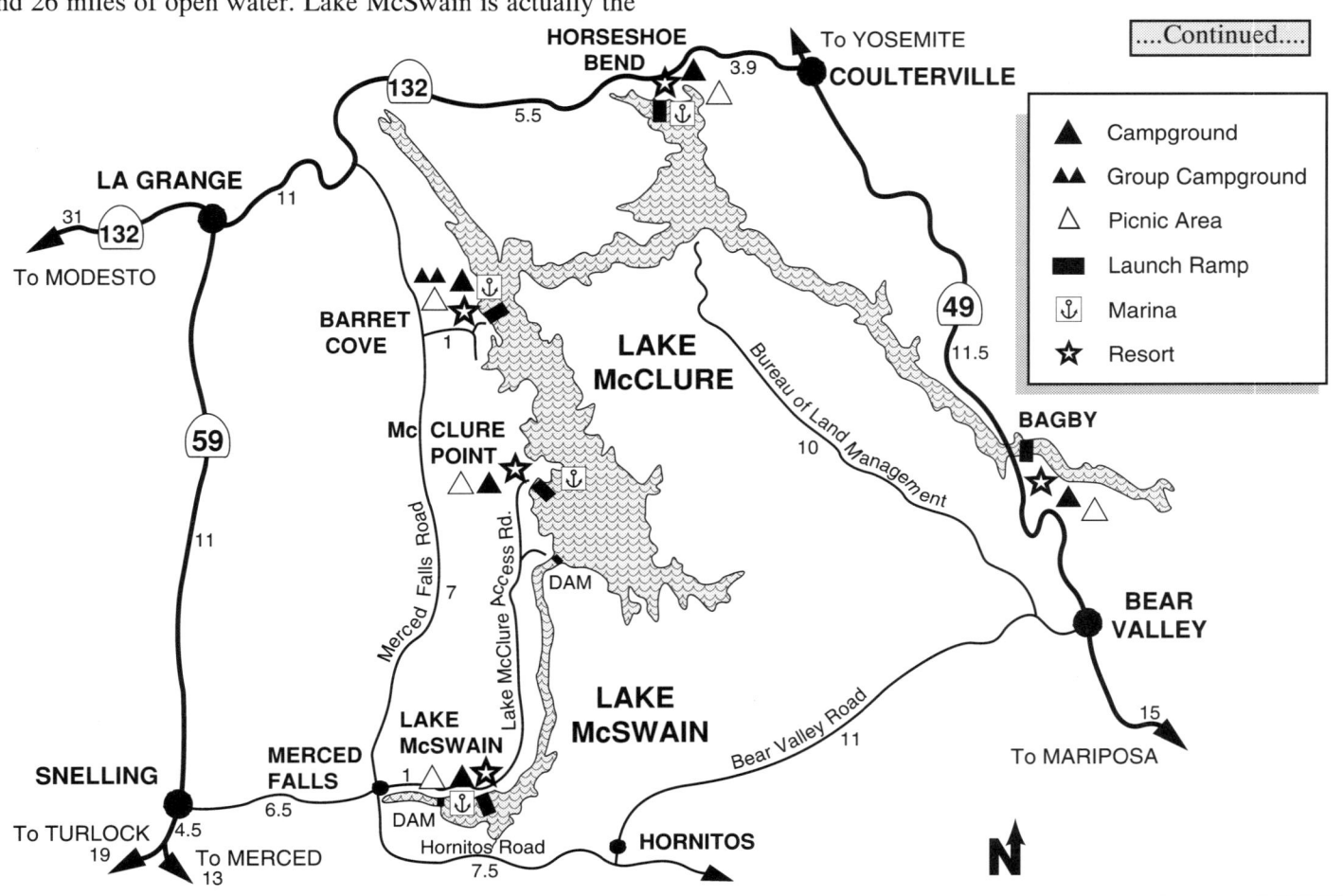

INFORMATION: See Following Page for Recreation Areas - Park Headquarters Ph: (800) 468-8889

CAMPING	BOATING	RECREATION	OTHER
614 Dev. Sites for Tents & R.V.s Fee: $13	All Boating Allowed at Lake McClure	Fishing: Trout, Catfish, Bluegill, Crappie, Perch, Black & Florida Bass	Playgrounds
167 Electric & Water Hookups Fee: $17	No Waterskiing or Houseboats at Lake McSwain	Swim Lagoons Lake McClure	Snack Bars
84 Electric & Water & Sewer Hookups Fee: $17	Full Service Marinas	Beaches	Grocery Stores
Day Use Fees: Vehicle: $5 Boat: $5 Pet: $2	Launch Ramps Rentals: Fishing & Pontoon Boats, Houseboats Docks, Berths Moorings, Gas Storage	Picnicking Group Picnic Shelter Hiking Sightseeing - Gold Rush Towns	Bait & Tackle Hot Showers Laundromats Disposal Stations Gas Stations Propane

Mc CLURE POINT:

M I D Parks Department
9090 Lake McClure Rd.
Snelling 95369
Ph: (209) 378-2521

McClure Point Marina
Call for Information at
Barrett Cove Marina
Ph: (209) 378-2441

100 Developed Campsites for Tents & R.V.s, 52 Water & Electric Hookups. Fees: $13 - $17. 64 Picnic Units. Full Service Marina with Gas - Boats & Cars, 3-Lane Launch Ramp, Docks, Berths, Moorings, Storage. Swim Lagoon, Grocery Store, Laundromat, Showers. *Reservations through Parks Department Office at (800) 468-8889. Reservation Fee: $5.*

BARRETT COVE:

M I D Parks Department
Barrett Cove Rec. Area
Star Route
La Grange 95329
Ph: (209) 378-2611

Barrett Cove Marina
Star Route
La Grange 95329
Ph: (209) 378-2441

275 Developed Campsites for Tents & R.V.s, 55 Full Hookups, 34 Water and Electric Hookups. Fees: $13 - $17. Group Picnic Facility to 100 People Maximum. 100 Picnic Units. Full Service Marina with Gas for Boats & Cars, 3-Lane Launch Ramp, Boat Rentals: Fishing, Houseboats, Pontoons, Moorings, Storage. Swim Lagoon, Playground, Snack Bar, Grocery Store, Laundromat, Showers. *Reservations through Parks Department Office at (800) 468-8889. Reservation Fee: $5.*

HORSESHOE BEND:

M I D Parks Department
Horseshoe Bend Rec. Area
4244 Highway 132
Coulterville 95311
Ph: (209) 878-3452

Horseshoe Bend Marina
Call for Information at
Barrett Cove Marina
Ph: (209) 378-2441

110 Developed Campsites for Tents & R.V.s, 7 Full Hookups, 28 Water & Electric Hookups. Fees: $13 - $17. 32 Picnic Units, 2-Lane Launch Ramp, Swim Lagoon, Laundromat, Showers. *Reservations through Parks Department Office at (800) 468-8889. Reservation Fee: $5.*

BAGBY:

Bagby Recreation Area
8324 Highway 49 North
Mariposa 95338

30 Developed Campsites for Tents & R.V.s., 10 Water & Electric Hookups, 25 Picnic Units. Launch Ramp.

LAKE MC SWAIN:

M I D Parks Department
9090 Lake McClure Rd.
Snelling 95369
Ph: (209) 378-2521

Lake McSwain Marina
8044 Lake McClure Road
Snelling 95369
Ph: (209) 378-2534

99 Developed Campsites for Tents & R.V.s, 22 Full Hookups, 43 Water & Electric Hookups. Fees: $13 - $17. Group Picnic Facility up to 200 People Maximum. Picnic Area. Full Service Marina with Gas for Boats & Cars, 2-lane Launch Ramp, Rentals: Fishing Boats Moorings. Snack Bar, Grocery Store, Laundromat, Showers, Playground Area. *Reservations through Parks Department Office at (800) 468-8889. Reservation Fee: $5.*

LAKE YOSEMITE

Lake Yosemite is located in the rolling foothills of the Sierra Nevada east of Merced. This 387 surface acre Lake is under the jurisdiction of the County of Merced. The County maintains a nice day use park with shaded picnic areas for families and groups to 200 people. Group reservations are required. There are swimming beaches and excellent marine facilities.

All types of boating are allowed with designated areas for waterskiing, sailing and rowing. Facilities include a sailing club. Fishing can be productive at this pleasant park in the San Joaquin Valley. There is no camping except for Youth Groups by reservation.

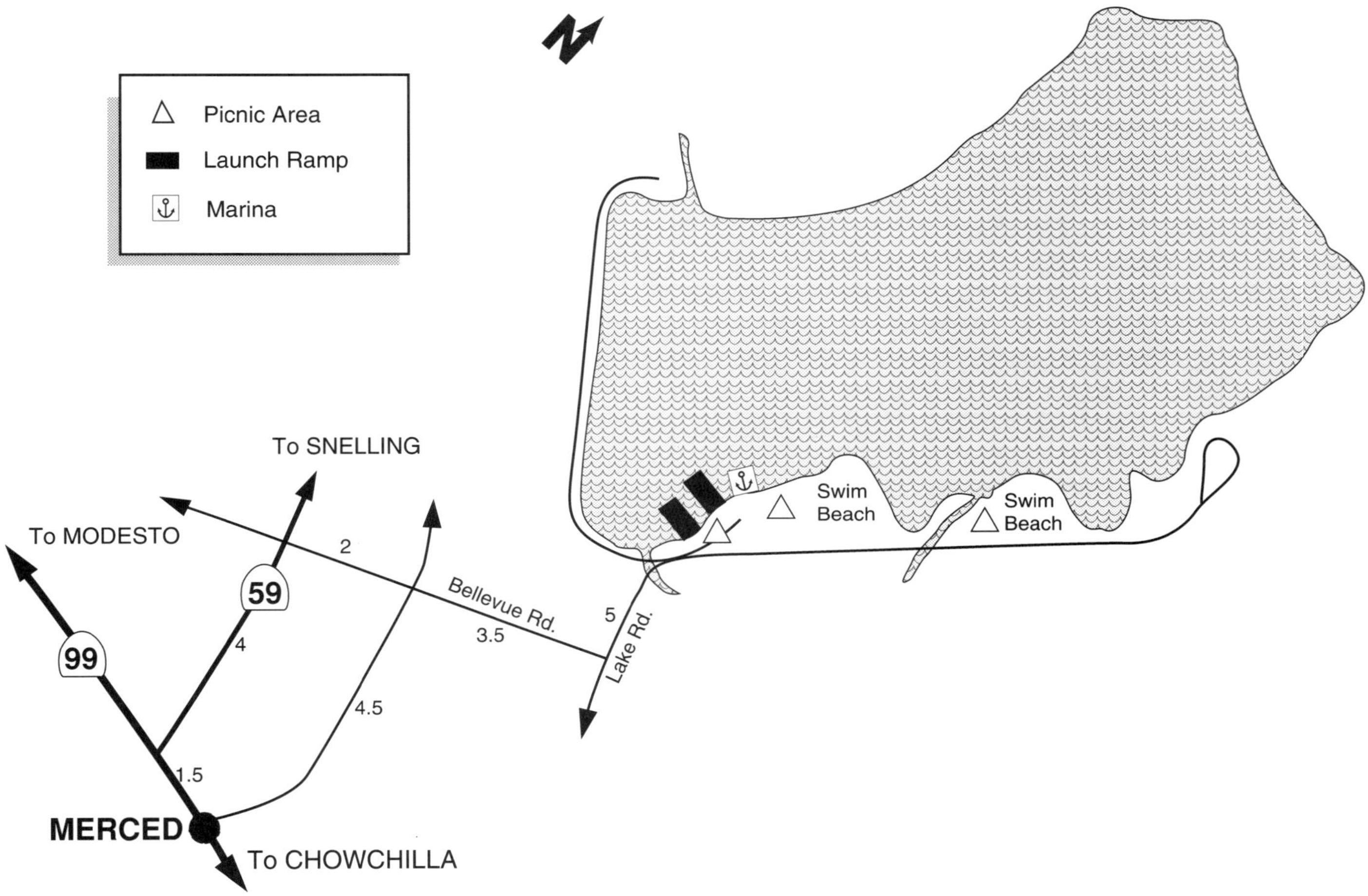

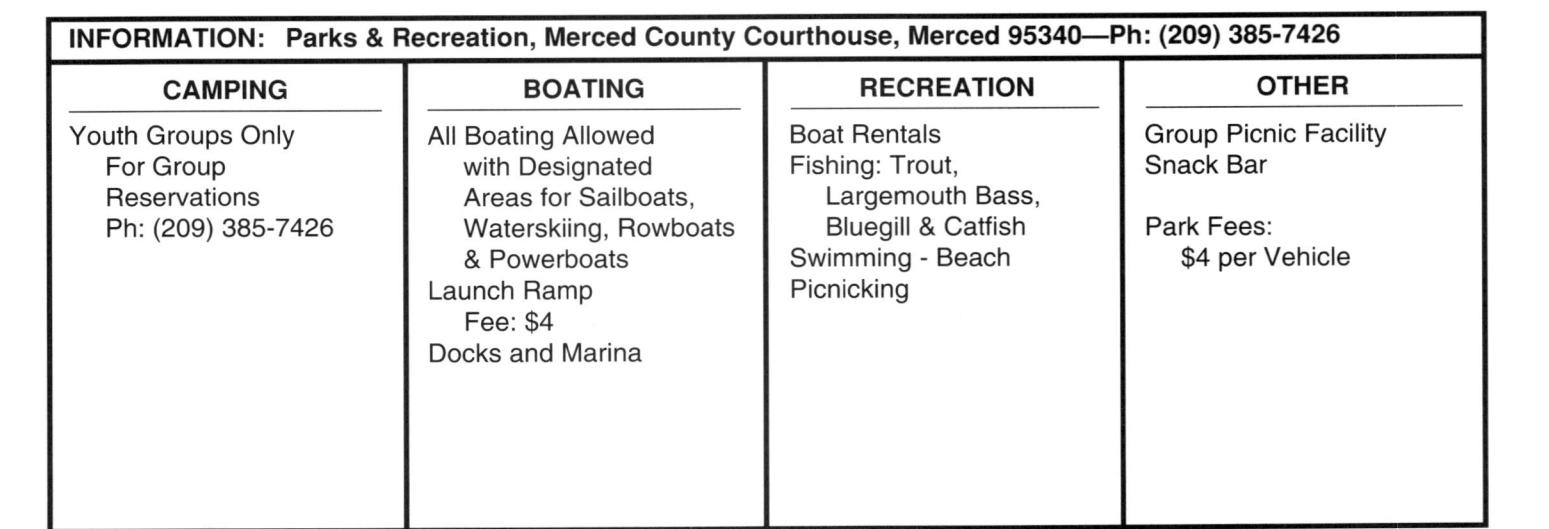

| Picnic Area |
| Launch Ramp |
| Marina |

To SNELLING
To MODESTO
To CHOWCHILLA
MERCED

Bellevue Rd.
Lake Rd.

59
99

2
4
3.5
5
4.5
1.5

INFORMATION: Parks & Recreation, Merced County Courthouse, Merced 95340—Ph: (209) 385-7426

CAMPING	BOATING	RECREATION	OTHER
Youth Groups Only 　For Group 　Reservations 　Ph: (209) 385-7426	All Boating Allowed 　with Designated 　Areas for Sailboats, 　Waterskiing, Rowboats 　& Powerboats Launch Ramp 　Fee: $4 Docks and Marina	Boat Rentals Fishing: Trout, 　Largemouth Bass, 　Bluegill & Catfish Swimming - Beach Picnicking	Group Picnic Facility Snack Bar Park Fees: 　$4 per Vehicle

SOULAJULE, STAFFORD, NICASIO, PHOENIX, LAGUNITAS, BON TEMPE, ALPINE and KENT LAKES

These Lakes on the slopes of Mt. Tamalpais are under the jurisdiction of the Marin Municipal Water District except for Stafford Lake which is operated by the Marin County Parks Department. Beautiful redwood shaded hiking and equestrian trails abound. Boating and swimming are not permitted. The Department of Fish and Game plant trout in most of the reservoirs. Nicasio and Soulajule have warm water angling. Stafford contains largemouth bass but the use of live bait (except worms) is prohibited. Lagunitas Lake has special restrictions including the use of only artificial lures with single barbless hooks; there is a limit of 2 fish under 14 inches total length that may be retained.

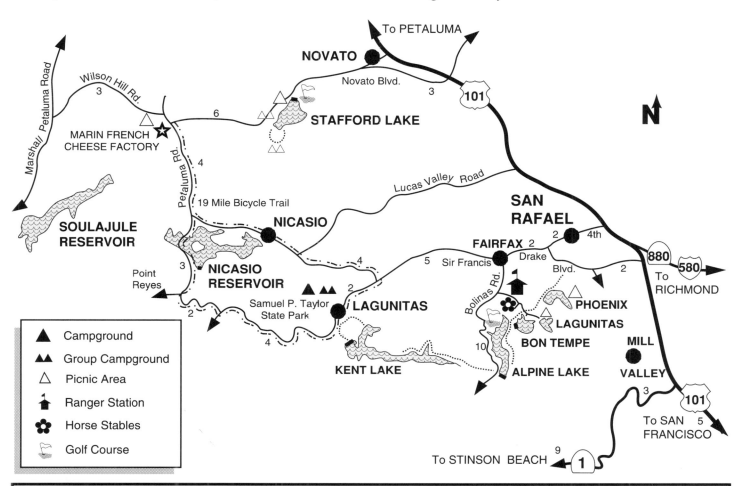

CAMPING	BOATING	RECREATION	OTHER
No Camping on Marin Water District Land Lakes: Day Use Only Vehicle Fee: $3-Weekdays $4-Weekends Nearby: Samuel P. Taylor Park Ph: (415) 488-9897 Family & Group Sites Tents/R.V.s to 27 Feet Fee: $14 Single $75 Group Reserve:Ph:(800) 444-7275	No Boating	Fishing: Trout, Bass, Bluegill, Catfish & Crappie Stafford: Largemouth Bass *Live Bait (except Worms) Prohibited* Hiking & Equestrian Trails Bicycles *Fire Roads Only* Nature Study Picnicking *No Swimming or Wading* Pets To Be Leashed At All Times	Stafford Lake: Marin County Parks & Open Space Dept. Marin County Civic Center San Rafael 94903 Ph: (415) 499-6387 Cheese Factory: 4 Miles North of Nicasio Reservoir Full Facilities in Nearby Towns

INFORMATION: Marin Municipal Water District, 200 Nellen Ave., Corte Madera—Ph: (415) 924-4600

ANZA, BERKELEY AQUATIC PARK, MERRITT and TEMESCAL

Lake Anza is a small Lake within the beautiful Charles Lee Tilden Regional Park, one of the most extensively developed facilities in the Bay Area. With over 2,077 acres, this Park includes a public golf course, botanical gardens, a carousel, pony rides and a scaled-down steam train. Temescal is a small 10 acre Lake within the 48 acre Temescal Recreation Area and is popular for swimming, fishing and picnicking.

The City of Oakland administers the 160 acre saltwater Lake Merritt. The surrounding Lakeside Park provides expansive shaded lawns, picnic areas, children's playground and North America's oldest bird sanctuary. The Berkeley Aquatic Park is a popular rowing, sailing and windsurfing salt water Lake with private facilities for waterskiing

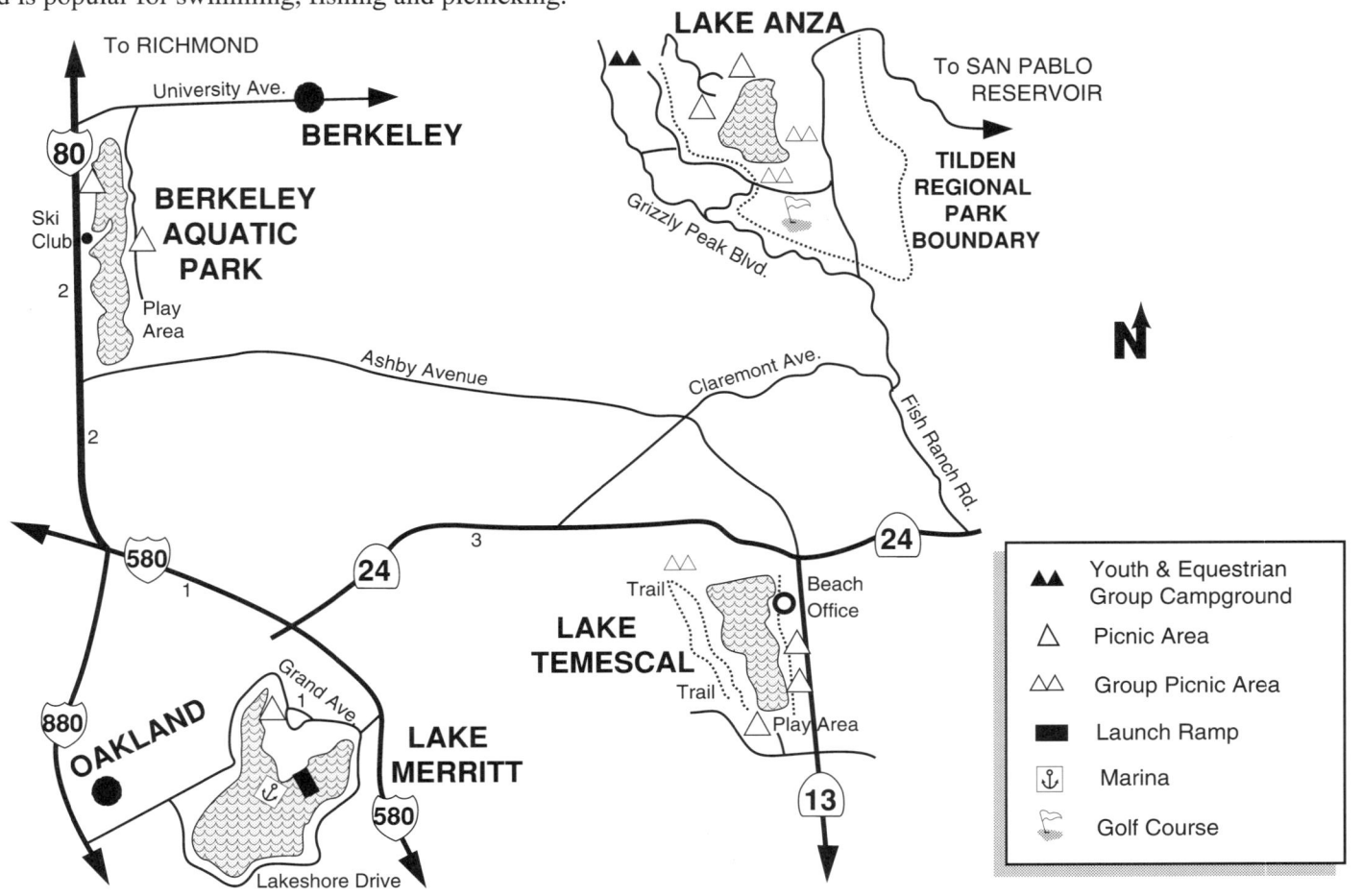

▲▲	Youth & Equestrian Group Campground
△	Picnic Area
△△	Group Picnic Area
■	Launch Ramp
⚓	Marina
🏌	Golf Course

INFORMATION: Anza & Temescal East Bay Reg. Parks, 2950 Peralta Oaks, Oakland 94605- Ph: (510) 562-PARK

CAMPING	BOATING	RECREATION	OTHER
No Camping at Tilden Regional Park Except for Non-Profit Groups and Equestrian Groups 15 to 100 People 14 Day Advance Reservations Ph: (510) 562-CAMP	Lake Anza: No Boating Berkeley Aquatic: Sail, Windsurf & Row Waterski Facility Lake Merritt: Sail & Manually Powered Launch Ramp & Hoist Rental: Sail, Row Canoe & Pedal Sailing Instructions Indoor Boat Storage	Fishing: Trout, Bass, Catfish, Crappie & Sunfish Picnicking Hiking, Jogging & Riding Trails Playground Nature Study Bird Sanctuary Boat Tours at Merritt Swimming - Beaches: Anza & Temescal Only	Lake Merritt-City of Oakland Sailboat House Oakland Office of Parks & Recreation 568 Bellevue Ave. Oakland 94610 Ph: (510) 444-3807

Berkeley Aquatic Park Ph: (510) 644-6530 For Information on This Facility |
| No Camping At Merritt No B-B-Qs | | | |

San Pablo Reservoir rests at an elevation of 314 feet east of the Berkeley hills. This 860 acre Lake is a drinking water reservoir under the jurisdiction of the East Bay Municipal Utility District. The winds make for good sailing. Although windsurfing, waterskiing and swimming are prohibited, this is a popular boating Lake with good marine facilities. Exten-

sive fisheries habitat along with a tremendous annual trout planting schedule make this one of the best lakes in the State for anglers. There are 142 picnic sites with barbecues overlooking the water in addition to a large children's play area. In addition, there is one large group picnic area which can be reserved. Hiking and riding trails, available by permit, lead to Briones and Tilden Regional Park.

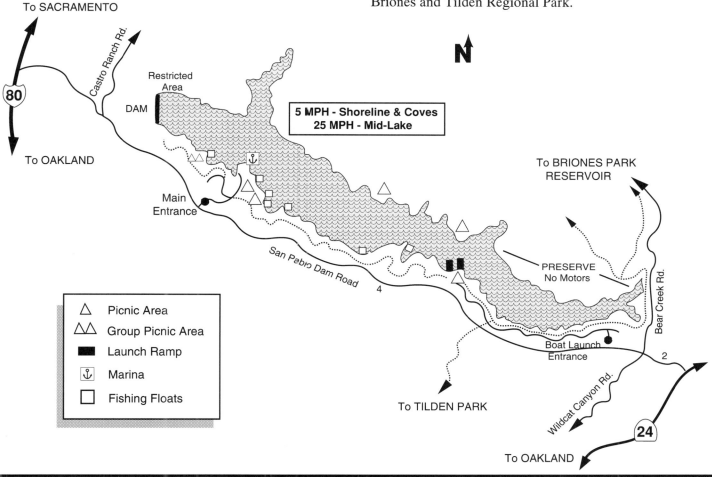

INFORMATION: San Pablo Reservoir, 7301 San Pablo Dam Rd., El Sobrante 94803—Ph: (510) 223-1661

CAMPING	BOATING	RECREATION	OTHER
Day Use Only 1 Group Picnic Area for 100 People By Reservation Only	All Boating Subject to Permit or Rental *Waterskiing, Windsurf & Racing Boats Not Allowed* Full Service Marina 8-Lane Launch Ramp Docks Rentals: Fishing Boat with 8 HP & 15 HP Deluxe Motors, Row Boats & Patio Boats	Fishing: Trophy Trout, Large, Smallmouth & Spotted Bass, Sturgeon, Channel Catfish, Crappie & Bluegill Fishing Docks Fishing Access Trail Picnic Areas Hiking, Bicycle & Horse Riding Trails Children's Play Area *No Swimming or Wading*	Restaurant Bait & Tackle Sundries

LAFAYETTE RESERVOIR

Lafayette Reservoir provides a natural retreat from the urban areas that surround it. Nestled amid the rolling oak-covered hills of Contra Costa County and within the city limits of Lafayette, this 126-acre Lake is popular with sailors, canoers and non-powered boaters. Electric motors are permitted. Although you must hand launch your boat, there is a boat house and sailing dock for small boats. There are also rental boats. In addition to planted trout, the angler will find a warm water fishery. Most of the picnic sites around the Lake have barbecues. There are two reserved group picnic areas. A paved walking trail surrounds the Lake. There are several self-guided nature trails through 928 acres of open space. The facilities are under the jurisdiction of the East Bay Municipal Utility District. No body contact with the water is permitted.

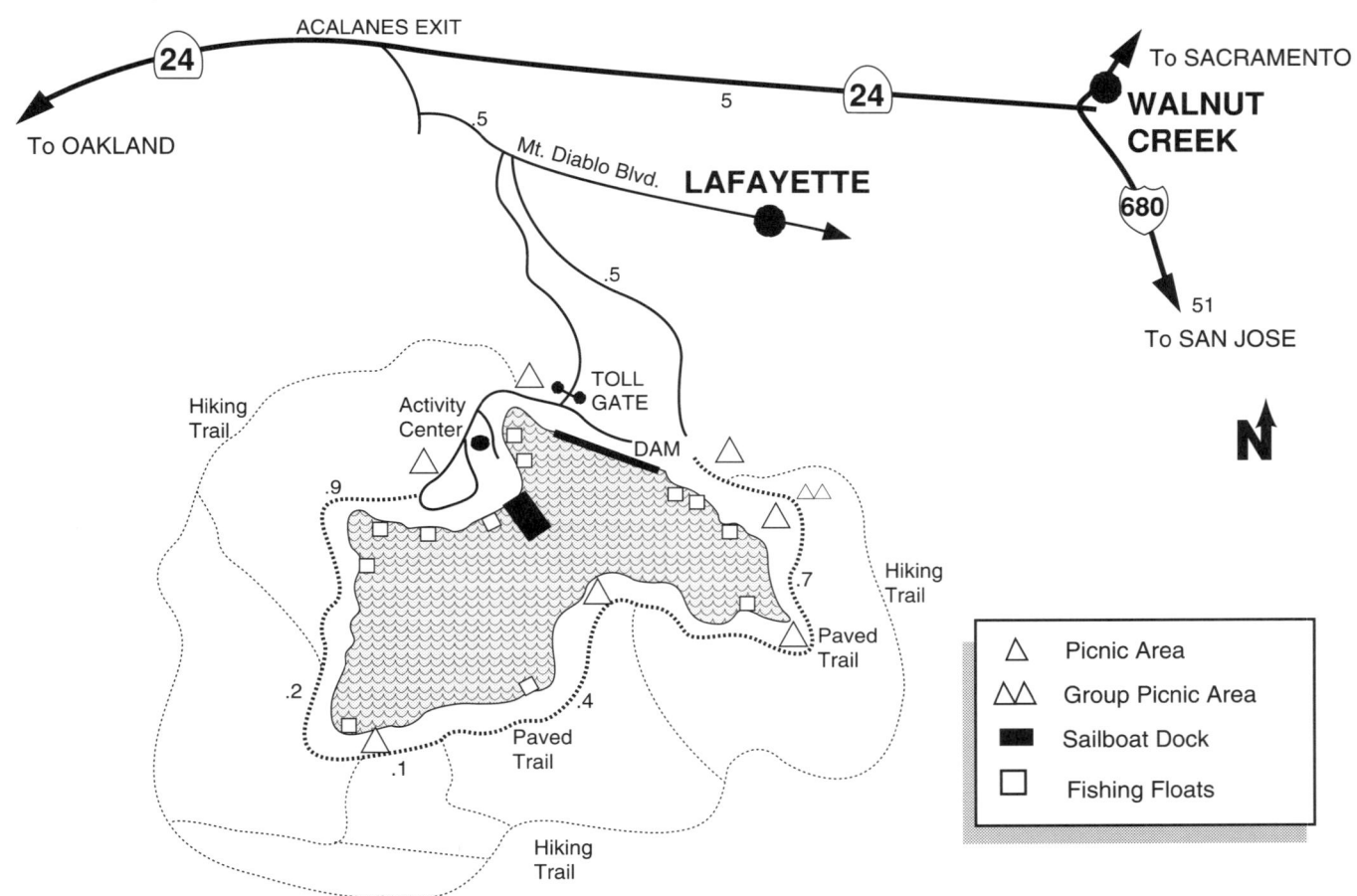

INFORMATION: East Bay Muni. Utility District. P.O. Box 24055, Oakland 94623—Ph: (925) 284-9669-Reservoir

CAMPING	BOATING	RECREATION	OTHER

Day Use Only
    Fee: $5
 	
2 Group Picnic Areas
    By Reservation
    50 & 250 People
 	
Complete Handicap
    Facilities
	Cartop Boats Only
	Hand Launch by Permit
	Electric Motors Only
	Sailboat Dock
	Rentals:
	    Pedal & Row Boats
	
	Boat Launch: $3
		Fishing: Rainbow Trout,
		    Black Bass, Bluegill,
		    Crappie & Catfish
		Fishing Floats
		Picnic Areas
		Hiking Trails
		    Self-Guided
		    Nature Trails
		    Paved Trail Around
		        Lake
		No Swimming
			Bait & Tackle
			Fishing Licenses
			Fish Cleaning Stattion
			
			Bicycles and Rollerskates
			    Permitted:
			    Tues. & Thurs.
			        Noon to Closing
			    Sunday
			        Opening to 11:00 am

Contra Loma Reservoir is located in the rolling hills of eastern Contra Costa County. This 80 acre Reservoir is within the 776 acre Contra Loma Regional Park. Hiking and riding trails run through the open grasslands of the park into the adjoining Black Diamond Mines Regional Preserve. The concentration of greenery and facilities are near the water.

Large shaded, turfed picnic areas and playgrounds await the visitor. There is a sandy swimming beach with a solar powered bathhouse. Contra Loma is very popular with windsurfers. Oar and electric powered boats are also allowed. The angler will find catfish, bluegill and largemouth bass and a good striped bass population. This facility is under the jurisdiction of the East Bay Regional Park District.

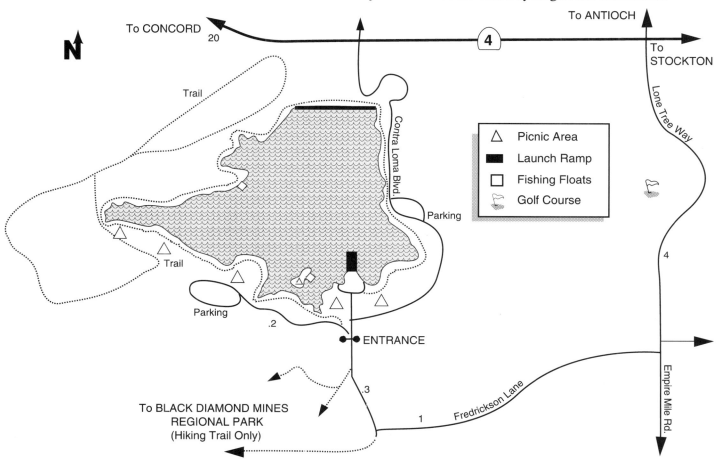

INFORMATION: East Bay Regional Parks, 2950 Peralta Oaks Ct., Oakland 94605—Ph: (510) 562-PARK

CAMPING	BOATING	RECREATION	OTHER

Day Use Only
   Fee: $4
 	
Park Headquarters:
   Ph: (925) 757-0404
	Open to Electric &
	   Non-Power Boats
	   to 17 feet
	Windsurfing
	No Gas Motors
	Launch Ramp Fees:
	   Cartop: $2
	   Trailer: $3
	Rentals: Sailboards,
	   Pedal Boats & Kayaks
		Fishing: Black Bass,
		   Bluegill, Catfish,
		   Crappie, Sunfish &
		   Striped Bass
		Fishing Docks
		Picnic Area
		Hiking & Riding
		   Trails
		Swimming
		Children's Play Area
		Golf Course Nearby
			Snack Bar
			Bait & Tackle

CHABOT, CULL CANYON, DON CASTRO and JORDAN POND

These four small Lakes are within the East Bay Regional Park District. The angler will find a warm water fishery at all of these facilities and trout at Lake Chabot and Don Castro. Boating is limited to rentals at Lake Chabot. Each of these Regional Parks provides numerous natural attractions along with picnic facilities. Anthony Chabot Regional Park, 4,972 acres, has camping at Lake Chabot and hiking, horseback riding and bicycle trails center. Cull Canyon has won the Governor's Design Award for Recreation Development. Facilities include a swim complex with a sandy beach. The reservoir offers fishing for bass and catfish. Don Castro has a swim lagoon, numerous picnic areas and large lawns. This lake is regularly stocked with trout and catfish. Jordan Pond is within the 2,685 acre Garin Regional Park. This scenic acrea has an interpretive center and programs conducted by park naturalists.

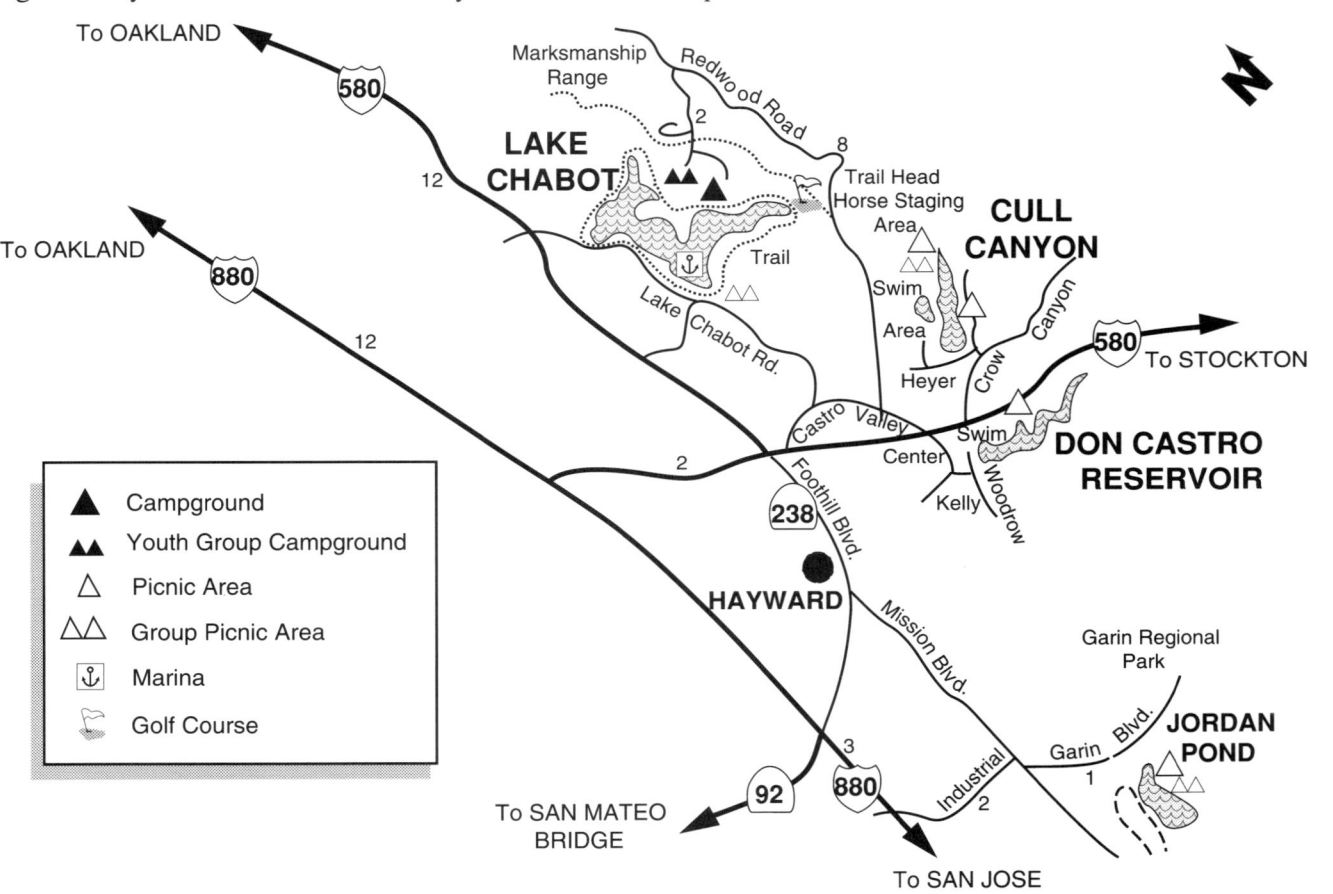

Legend:
- ▲ Campground
- ▲▲ Youth Group Campground
- △ Picnic Area
- △△ Group Picnic Area
- ⚓ Marina
- ⚑ Golf Course

INFORMATION: East Bay Regional Parks, 2950 Peralta Oaks Ct., Oakland 94605—Ph: (510) 562-PARK

CAMPING	BOATING	RECREATION	OTHER
Lake Chabot: 754 Tent/R.V. or Walk-In Family Sites Reservations Required Ph: (510) 562-CAMP Youth Group Sites Ph: (510) 636-1684	Lake Chabot: Rentals: Electric, Row, Paddle & Canoe "Chabot Queen" Seasonal Boat Tour No Boating at Other Lakes	Fishing: Trout, Black Bass, Bluegill, Catfish & Crappie Hiking, Jogging & Equestrian Trails Swimming: Don Castro & Cull Canyon Only Nature Study & Interpretive Center Playgrounds	Lake Chabot: 2 Golf Courses Equestrian Center Chabot Gun Club & Marksmanship Range Open to the Public Tues - Sun. Horse Rentals Off Skyline Blvd.

Within the greater Bay Area, these Lakes provide numerous recreational opportunities. The bicycler will find a 70 mile challenge at Bethany Reservoir on the California Aqueduct Bikeway or a leisurely ride on the 2 mile bikeway around Lake Elizabeth. Boating, fishing or a day at the park can be enjoyed at these popular facilities. *See following page for detailed information.*

....Continued....

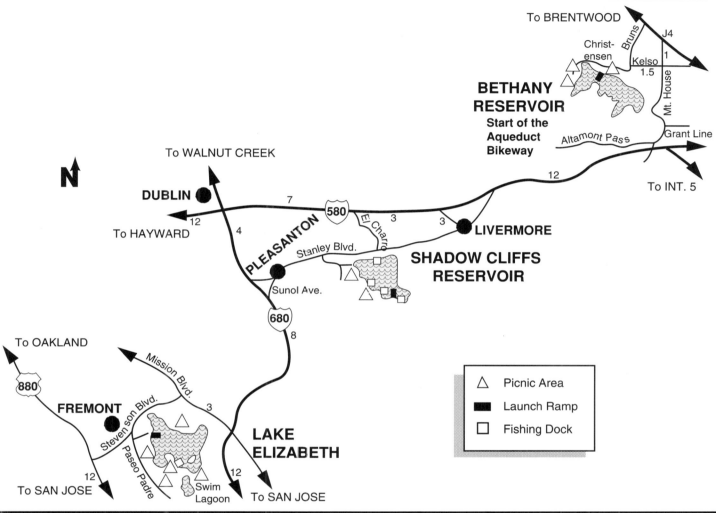

INFORMATION: See Following Page for Individual Lake Information			
CAMPING	**BOATING**	**RECREATION**	**OTHER**
Day Use Facilities Only	Varies at Each Lake *See Following Page*	Fishing: Trout, Largemouth & Striped Bass, Catfish, Bluegill & Crappie Picnicking Nature, Hiking & Jogging Trails Bicycle Trails Swimming Beaches & Lagoons	Children's Play Area Athletic Fields Waterslide Concessions at Shadow Cliffs & Lake Elizabeth Full Facilities Near Each Lake

BETHANY RESERVOIR
State Recreation Area
22600 Lake Rd.
La Grange 95329
Ph: (209) 874-2056
Day Use Only

Bethany Reservoir State Recreation Area rests in gently rolling, grass-covered hills overlooking the vast Delta of the Sacramento and San Joaquin Rivers. This 162 acre Reservoir is open to all types of boating with a 5 MPH speed limit. Windsurfing is very popular. Strong winds can be a hazard. This is a good warm water fishery for striped bass and catfish. Bethany is the northern terminus for the California Aqueduct Bikeway.

SHADOW CLIFFS RESERVOIR
East Bay Regional Park District
2950 Peralta Oaks Ct., Oakland 94605
Ph: (510) 635-0135 - Parking Fee
Marina Ph: (510) 562-PARK

This Reservoir has been transformed from a sand and gravel quarry to a complete 263 acre park. The 74 surface acre Lake is open to all non-gasoline powered boating. Visitor's boats are limited to a maximum of 17 feet and only electric motors are permitted. There are also windsurfer rentals and lessons. You may rent a fishing boat, electric motorboat, pedal boat, or row boat. Trout, black bass, channel and white catfish and bluegill await the angler. There is a sandy swim beach with a bathhouse and snack bar. A four-flume waterslide is in a separate area of the park. The park has picnic areas, turfed areas, hiking and equestrian trails and a food concession. Handicap facilities are available.

LAKE ELIZABETH
Central Park
Visitor Services Center
P.O. Box 5006, 40000Sailway Dr.
Fremont 94537
Ph: (510) 791-4340.
Sports Fields Information Ph: (510) 791-4372
Day Use and Lake Use Fees.

This Lake, 80 surface acres, is within the beautiful Fremont Central Park. There are complete facilities for non-powered boating including ramps, docks, storage and rental canoe and paddle boats. This is a good sailing lake with westerly winds which can become strong in the afternoons. The Lake contains populations of black bass, bluegill and catfish. The well maintained park of nearly 500 acres has several recreational facilities with open turfed areas, snack bars, picnic areas, tennis courts, athletic fields, a golf driving range, volleyball courts and a swim lagoon. There are dozens of picnic tables and four group picnic sites which can accommodate between 125 and 350 people each. The 1.96 mile pedway around the Lake accommodates joggers, hikers and bikers at this complete city facility.

DEL VALLE RESERVOIR

Del Valle Reservoir is at an elevation of 700 feet in oak-covered rolling hills near Livermore. The Lake has a surface area of 750 acres with 16 miles of shoreline. The 4,310 acre Del Valle Park is under the jurisdiction of the East Bay Regional Park District. In addition to the large tree-shaded campgrounds, there are primitive group campsites, picnic areas and marina facilities. Ten miles of scenic trails await the hiker or equestrian. Boating is limited to 10 miles per hour. Two guarded swimming beaches are open from May through September. During the rest of the year, you can swim at your own risk. This is a very popular windsurfing Lake. Westerly winds can be strong in the afternoon.

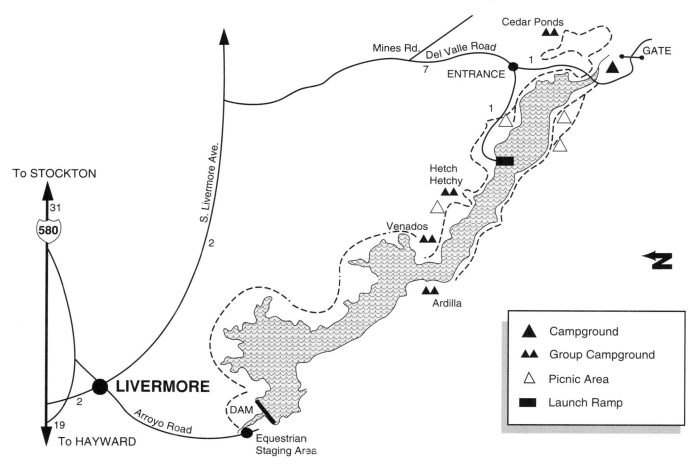

INFORMATION: Del Valle Park, 6999 Del Valle Rd., Livermore 94550—Ph: (925) 373-0332

CAMPING	BOATING	RECREATION	OTHER
150 Dev. Sites for Tents & R.V.s Fee: $14 With Sewer & Water Hookups Fee: $17 Youth Group Campgrounds Reservations: Ph: (510) 636-1684	Power, Row, Canoe, Sail, Windsurf & Inflatables Speed Limit - 10 MPH Launch Ramp Rentals: Row, Pedal, Canoe Patio Boats & Fishing Boats Boat Tours Marina Ph: (925) 449-5201	Fishing: Trout, Catfish, Bluegill, Large & Smallmouth Bass, Striped Bass Swimming - 2 Beaches Picnicking Families & Groups Hiking Bicycle & Horseback Riding Trails Summer Weekends Only Campfire Program Lake Tour Boat	Snack Bar Bait & Tackle Campground Store Disposal Station Visitors Center Full Facilities in Livermore

LAKE MERCED, SHORELINE PARK and STEVENS CREEK RESERVOIR

These three urban Lakes provide a variety of recreation opportunities. Lake Merced has a surface area of 396 acres. This is a popular sailing Lake and one of the better fishing Lakes where Rainbow and some Brook trout grow to Lunker size while feeding on fresh water shrimp. Shoreline Lake offers the windsurfer and sailor a 50 acre expanse of saltwater. Shoreline Park is primarily open space with protected wildlife areas reached by paved trails. The prevailing north westerly winds make this a popular windsurfing Lake. Stevens Creek Reservoir, 91 surface acres when full, provides the angler with a warm water fishery and boating with electric trolling motors. There are nice oak-shaded trails for the hiker and equestrian. Mountain bikers can use the multiple trail system which allows access to adjacent park lands. Family and group picnic sites are available.

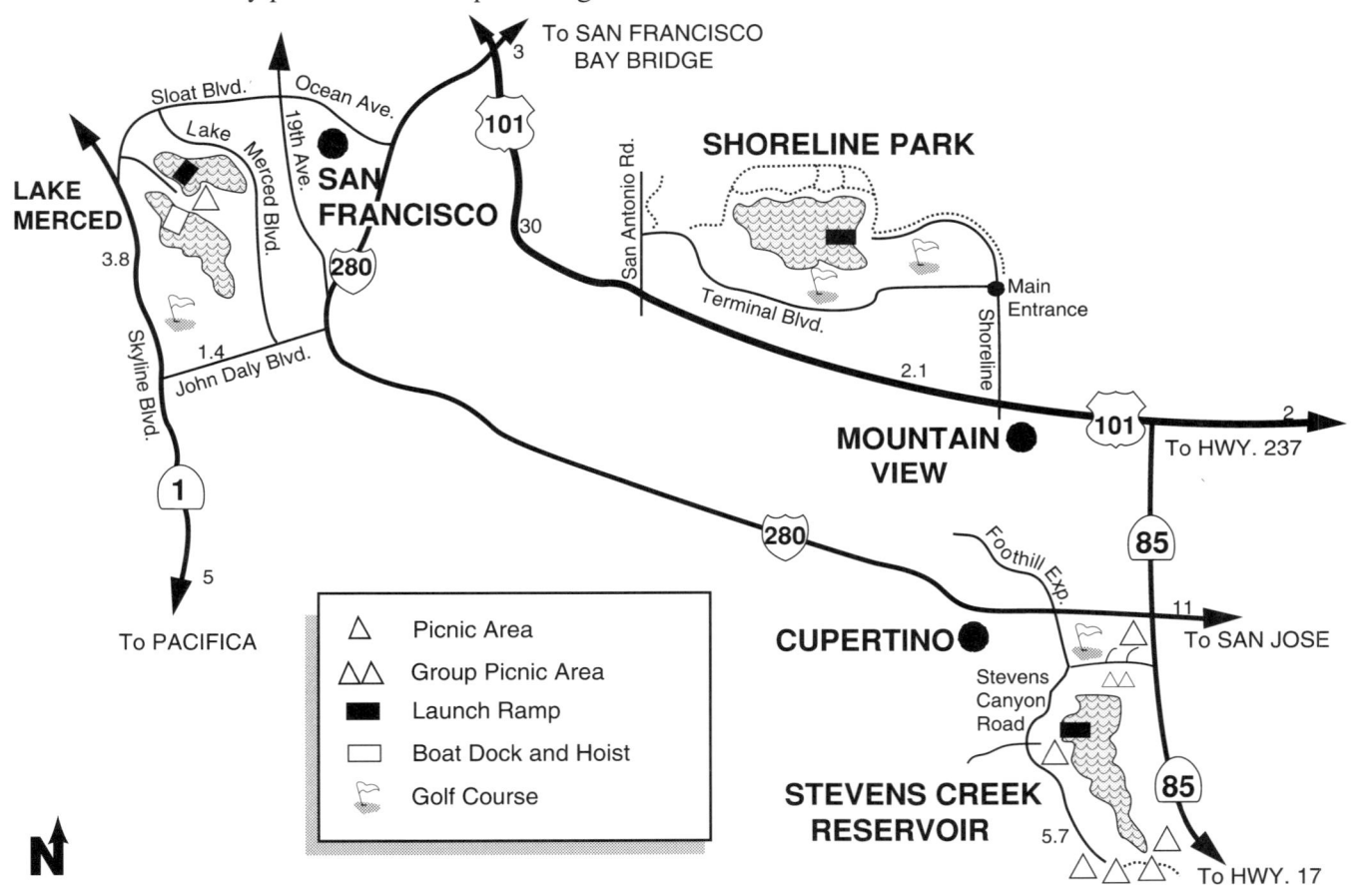

△	Picnic Area
△△	Group Picnic Area
■	Launch Ramp
▭	Boat Dock and Hoist
⚑	Golf Course

INFORMATION: Lake Merced Boating & Fishing Co., 1 Harding Way, San Francisco 94132—Ph: (415) 753-1101

CAMPING	BOATING	RECREATION	OTHER
Day Use Only - Fees	Lake Merced: Sail & Row to 18 Feet Hoists & Floats	Fishing: Rainbow & Brook Trout, Bass, Bluegill, Catfish & Crappie	Spinnaker Sailing Shoreline Park 3160 N. Shoreline Blvd. Mountain View 94043
No Camping	Rentals: Fishing & Row Boats, Electric Motors	Picnicking	Ph: (650) 965-7474
Stevens Creek Park: Group Picnic Area Reservations: Ph: (408) 358-3751 Reservoir: Electric Motors Only Launch Fee: $3	Shoreline Park: Canoes, Windsurf Sailboards, Sailboats Kayaks, Pedal Boats Rentals, Lessons, Sales Launch Ramp Fee: $4-$5 Docks	Hiking, Bicycle & Riding Trails Nature Study Birdwatching Golf Courses	Shoreline Park: Restaurant Ph: (650) 965-1745 Showers Lake Merced Boathouse: Sports Bar, Restaurant, Night Club

These three Lakes are located off Highway 17 in the southwest corner of Santa Clara County. They are under the jurisdiction of the County's Parks and Recreation Department. Lexington is the largest of the three. Electric trolling motors only are allowed so Lexington is popular with sailors, rowers, windsurfers and anglers. Vasona is a pretty 57 acre Lake surrounded by 94 acres of turfed activity areas, picnic sites, playground and paved paths. This family park offers good sailing and support facilities. Los Gatos Creek Park permits fishing and sailcraft in Pond 1. Remote control model boating is allowed at Pond 2. There is also a newly constructed flycasting pond for practice only (no hooks). It is equipped with circular targets. There are picnic facilities available as well as walking and bicycle paths.

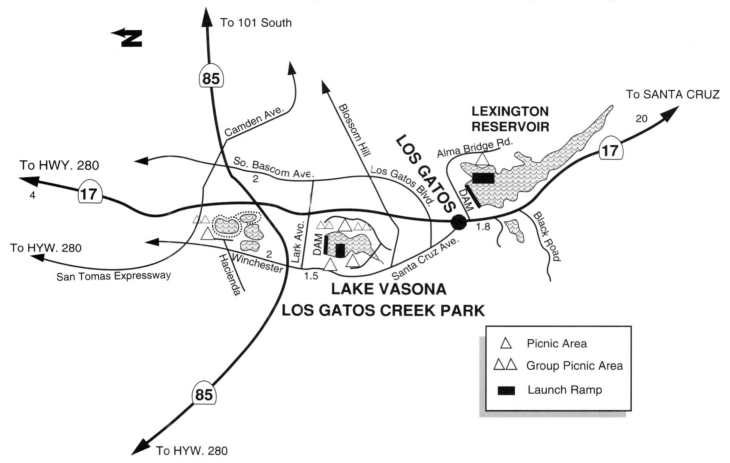

△	Picnic Area
△△	Group Picnic Area
■	Launch Ramp

INFORMATION: Santa Clara County Parks & Rec., 298 Garden Hill Dr., Los Gatos 95030—Ph: (408) 358-3741

CAMPING	BOATING	RECREATION	OTHER
Day Use Only *No Camping* Vasona & Los Gatos Creek Park: Entrance Fee: $4 per Vehicle Reservations for Group Picnic Areas or Special Events Ph: (408) 358-3751	Vasona: Sail, Canoe, Row, Windsurfer, Paddle Boats - *No Motors* Launch Ramp - $3 Docks, Dry Storage Lexington: As Vasona *Plus Electric Motors Allowed* Launch Ramp - $3 *Check for Current Water Level Conditions*	Fishing: Trout, Bass, Bluegill, Catfish & Crappie Picnic Areas Hiking & Jogging Trails Playground at Vasona Oak Meadow Park: Ph: (408) 354-6809 (Next to Vasona) Billy Jones Wildcat Railroad Carousel & Playground	Full Facilities in Los Gatos & San Jose

Almaden Lake Regional Park is administered by the City of San Jose. There is a small 36 acre sailing and fishing Lake, a swim beach and lagoon and picnic sites within this Park. Guadalupe and Almaden Reservoirs are approximately 60 acres each. They are under the jurisdiction of Santa Clara County and are adjacent to Almaden Quicksilver Park. This is a popular hiking and equestrian facility. Chesbro and Uvas, under the jurisdiction of Santa Clara Parks and Recreation Department, are primarily small fishing Lakes with picnic sites. Calero Reservoir, 349 surface acres, is a popular power boating and waterskiing Lake with a sandy beach and picnic facilities. At low water levels, from approximately October through January, the ramp may be closed.

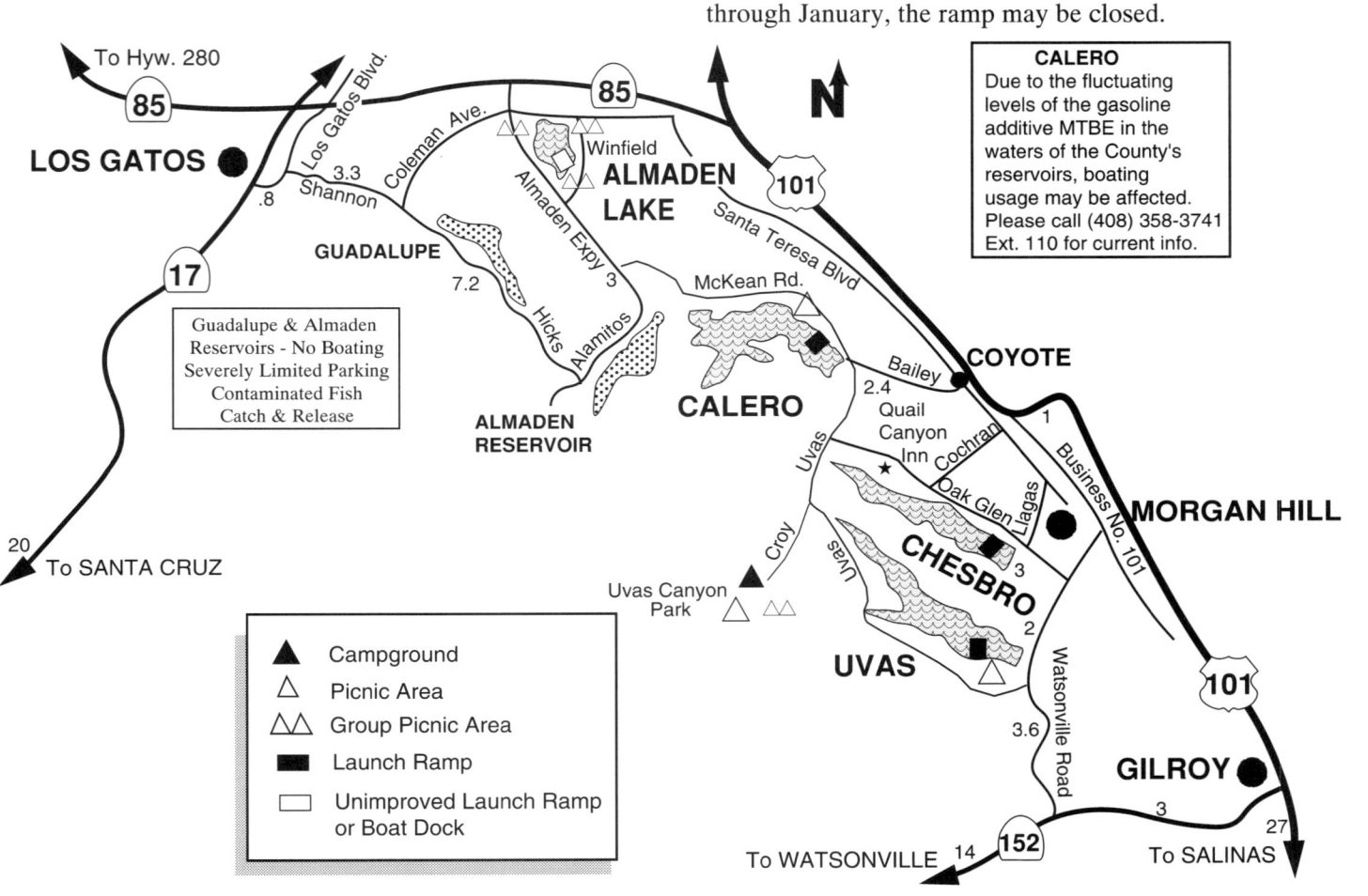

CALERO
Due to the fluctuating levels of the gasoline additive MTBE in the waters of the County's reservoirs, boating usage may be affected. Please call (408) 358-3741 Ext. 110 for current info.

Guadalupe & Almaden Reservoirs - No Boating Severely Limited Parking Contaminated Fish Catch & Release

▲ Campground
△ Picnic Area
△△ Group Picnic Area
■ Launch Ramp
▭ Unimproved Launch Ramp or Boat Dock

INFORMATION: Santa Clara County Parks & Rec., 298 Garden Hill Dr., Los Gatos 95030—Ph: (408) 358-3741

CAMPING	BOATING	RECREATION	OTHER
Uvas Canyon Park: 25 Dev. Sites for Tents & R.V.s No Hookups Fee Charged No Reservations Youth Group Camping Ph: (408) 358-3751 No Camping at Other Lakes & Reservoir Calero: Entrance Fee: $4 Lake Use Fee: $5	Almaden Lake: Sail & Non-Power Boating Launch Ramp - Fee: $2 Rentals: Windsurf & Paddleboat *Guadalupe & Almaden No Boating Allowed* Chesbro & Uvas: Sail, Row & Electric Motors Lake Use Fee: $3 Calero: Power, Waterskiing, Jets Launch Ramp	Fishing: Bass, Catfish, Bluegill, Crappie, Carp *Warning: Mercury Contaminated Fish at Calero, Guadalupe & Almaden Reservoirs Do Not Eat Fish Catch & Release Swimming: Almaden Lake Only* Picnicking Hiking, Bicycle & Riding Trails	Almaden Lake: Dept. of Conventions, Arts & Entertainment 408 S. Almaden Ave. San Jose 95110 Ph: (408) 277-5130 Almaden Quicksilver Park: 3,977 Acres of Trails Approx. 30 Miles of Equestrian & Hiking Trails

Lake Cunningham Regional Park is under the jurisdiction of the City of San Jose. This 200 acre park provides the visitor with numerous turfed picnic sites, walking and jogging paths and a 50-acre boating and fishing Lake. Raging Waters has a variety of waterslides, activity pools, swimming lagoon, beach, river rides and a myriad of other activities. The County of Santa Clara operates Ed R. Levin Park, Coyote-Hellyer

Park and the mountainous J. D. Grant Park. Cottonwood Lake is located in the Coyote-Hellyer Park which also has a velodrome. The Coyote Creek Parkway includes an 8-foot wide, 15-mile long bicycle trail that runs from Coyote Hellyer Park in South San Jose south to Anderson Lake Park in Morgan Hill. The rugged 9,497 acres of Joseph D. Grant Park offers hikers and equestrians a 40-mile trail system. Mountain bikes are allowd on nearly half of the Park's trails. Camping and picnic areas are included in this beautifully maintained, remote County Park.

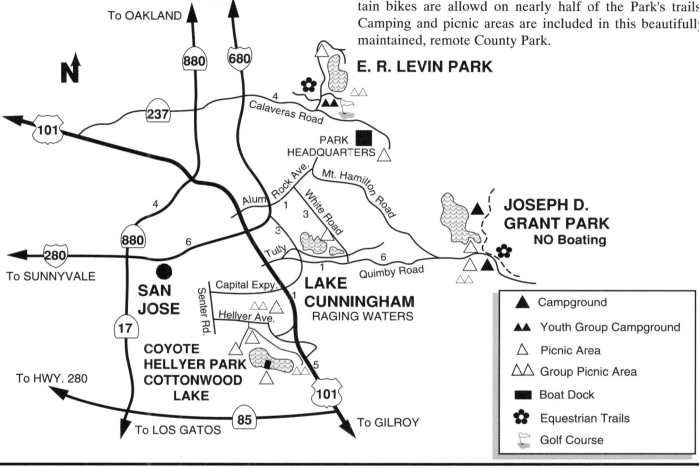

INFORMATION: Lake Cunningham, 2305 S. White Rd., San Jose 95148—Ph: (408) 277-4319

CAMPING	BOATING	RECREATION	OTHER
Joseph D. Grant Park: 22 Dev. Camp Sites Youth Group Camping by Reservation Ph: (408) 358-3751 Ed R. Levin: Youth Group Camping & Picnicking by Reservation Ph: (408) 358-3751 Lake Cunningham: Day Use Only Regional Park No Overnight Camping	Lake Cunningham: Non-Power Boats, Sail Boats Launch Ramp: $2 Rentals: Row, Canoe, Paddle & Sail Boat Dock Ed R. Levin & Cottonwood: Small Sail, Row & Electric Motor Boats *Joseph D. Grant:* *No Boating Allowed*	Fishing-Lake Cunningham: Catfish, Trout Cottonwood Lake: Trout Picnicking Walking & Jogging Trails Hiking & Riding Trails Mountain Biking Bicycling Hang Gliding Golf Course & Horse Rentals Near Ed R. Levin Park	Levin, Grant & Hellyer Parks: Santa Clara County 298 Garden Hill Dr. Los Gatos 95032 Ph: (408) 358-3741 Raging Waters: 2333 S. White Rd. San Jose 95148 Ph: (408) 270-8000 Fees Charged Group Rates

ANDERSON and PARKWAY LAKES

Anderson Lake is the largest body of fresh water in Santa Clara County. It is 7 miles long with a surface area of 1,245 acres. This is a popular boating and waterskiing Lake. Afternoon winds make for good sailing and windsurfing. There is a launch ramp and the angler will find a warm water fishery. The County of Santa Clara has picnic sites near the dam as well as a boat-in picnic area on the northwestern shore.

Anderson Park, a total of 2,149 acres, includes a multiple use 15-mile trail which follows Coyote Creek north to Coyote Hellyer County Park. An equestrian staging area leads to an 8-mile horseback riding trail. Parkway is a 35-acre privately operated fishing Lake. Planted year around with large trout, channel catfish and sturgeon, the Lake usually rewards the angler with a good catch.

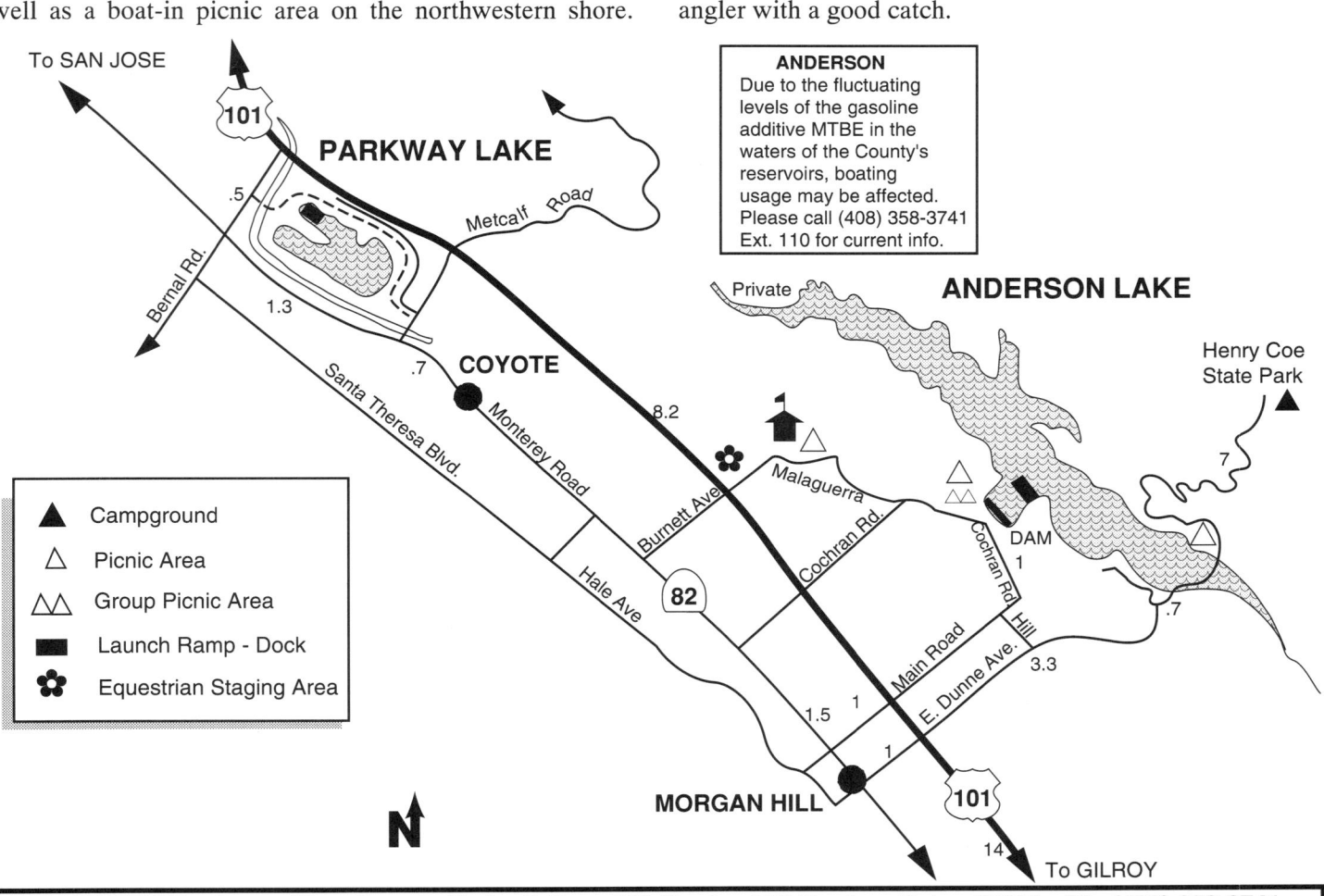

ANDERSON
Due to the fluctuating levels of the gasoline additive MTBE in the waters of the County's reservoirs, boating usage may be affected. Please call (408) 358-3741 Ext. 110 for current info.

Legend:
- ▲ Campground
- △ Picnic Area
- △△ Group Picnic Area
- ■ Launch Ramp - Dock
- ✿ Equestrian Staging Area

INFORMATION: Santa Clara County Parks & Rec., 298 Garden Hill Dr., Los Gatos 95030—Ph: (408) 358-3741

CAMPING	BOATING	RECREATION	OTHER
Day Use Only Anderson Lake : Entrance Fee: $4 Group Picnic Areas For Reservations: Ph: (408) 358-3751 Nearby: Henry Coe State Park: 20 Tent & R.V. Primitive Sites Ph: (408) 779-2728	Anderson: Open to All Boating & Waterskiing 35 MPH Speed Limit Launch Ramp, Dock Boat Use Fee: $5 *Check for Current Water Level Conditions* Parkway: No Private Boats Fishing Boat Rentals: $20	Fishing: Rainbow Trout, Largemouth Bass, Catfish, Crappie & Bluegill Sturgeon in Parkway Picnicking Hiking, Skating & Bicycle Trail Riding Trails Parkway Lake Fishing Fee: $12 - Adults $ 6 - Children $ 3 - Spectator	Parkway Lake: Metcalf Road Coyote 95013 Ph: (408) 629-9111 Concession: Bait & Tackle Snacks

Loch Lomond rests at an elevation of 577 feet in the Santa Cruz Mountains. This scenic 3-1/2 mile long Reservoir is under the jurisdiction of the City of Santa Cruz. The Lake is open to non-powered boating. Although there is a launch ramp, water level fluctuation can limit its use, so call for current status. Fishing is a prime attraction and often produc-tive. An aeration system has been installed which should enhance the already good fishery. There are over 100 picnic sites around the shoreline. Several hiking trails are along the shore and into the coniferous forest of oak, madrone, pine and redwood trees. In addition to naturalist programs, there is a self-guided Big Trees Nature Trail.

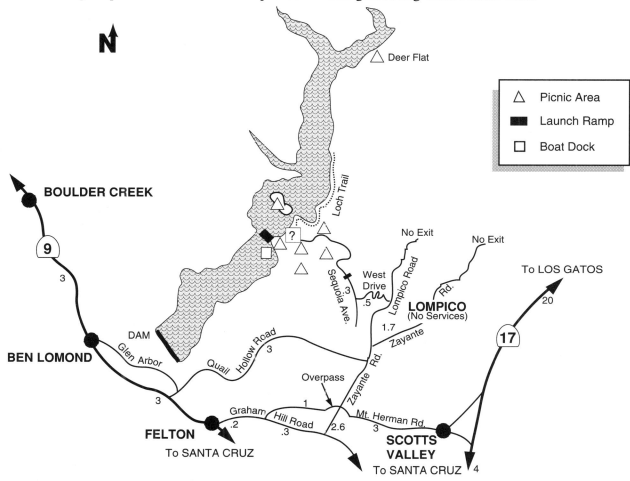

	Picnic Area
◼	Launch Ramp
☐	Boat Dock

INFORMATION: Loch Lomond Recreation Area, 100 Loch Lomond Way, Felton 95018—Ph: (831) 335-7424			
CAMPING	**BOATING**	**RECREATION**	**OTHER**
Day Use Only 　Fee: $4 Open March Through 　September 15 　6:00 a.m. to Sunset	Oar & Electric 　Motors Only Rentals: Row & 　Electric *No Sailboats or* 　*or Float Tubes* Launch Ramp Fees: 　Cartop: $2 　On Trailer: $5 　Water Level Limits	Fishing: Rainbow 　Trout, Largemouth 　Bass, Bluegill, 　Redear & Green 　Sunfish, Channel 　Catfish 　Fishing Licence 　　Required Picnicking Hiking & Nature Trails *No Swimming*	Bait & Tackle Refreshments *No Alcohol Permitted*

PINTO LAKE

Pinto Lake is under the jurisdiction of the City of Watsonville. The surrounding park area is privately leased and managed. This facility provides the visitor with R.V. sites, a picnic area, a group picnic site, large turfed areas and a baseball field. The 92 acre Lake is popular with sailors and windsurfers who enjoy incoming Pacific breezes. There is a warm water fishery along with planted trout. Santa Cruz County maintains a 180 acre wildlife refuge and park on the north end of the Lake with over 130 species of birds, nature trails and group picnic facilities. For picnic reservations at the County Park, Ph: (831) 462-8333 between Noon and 4:00 pm.

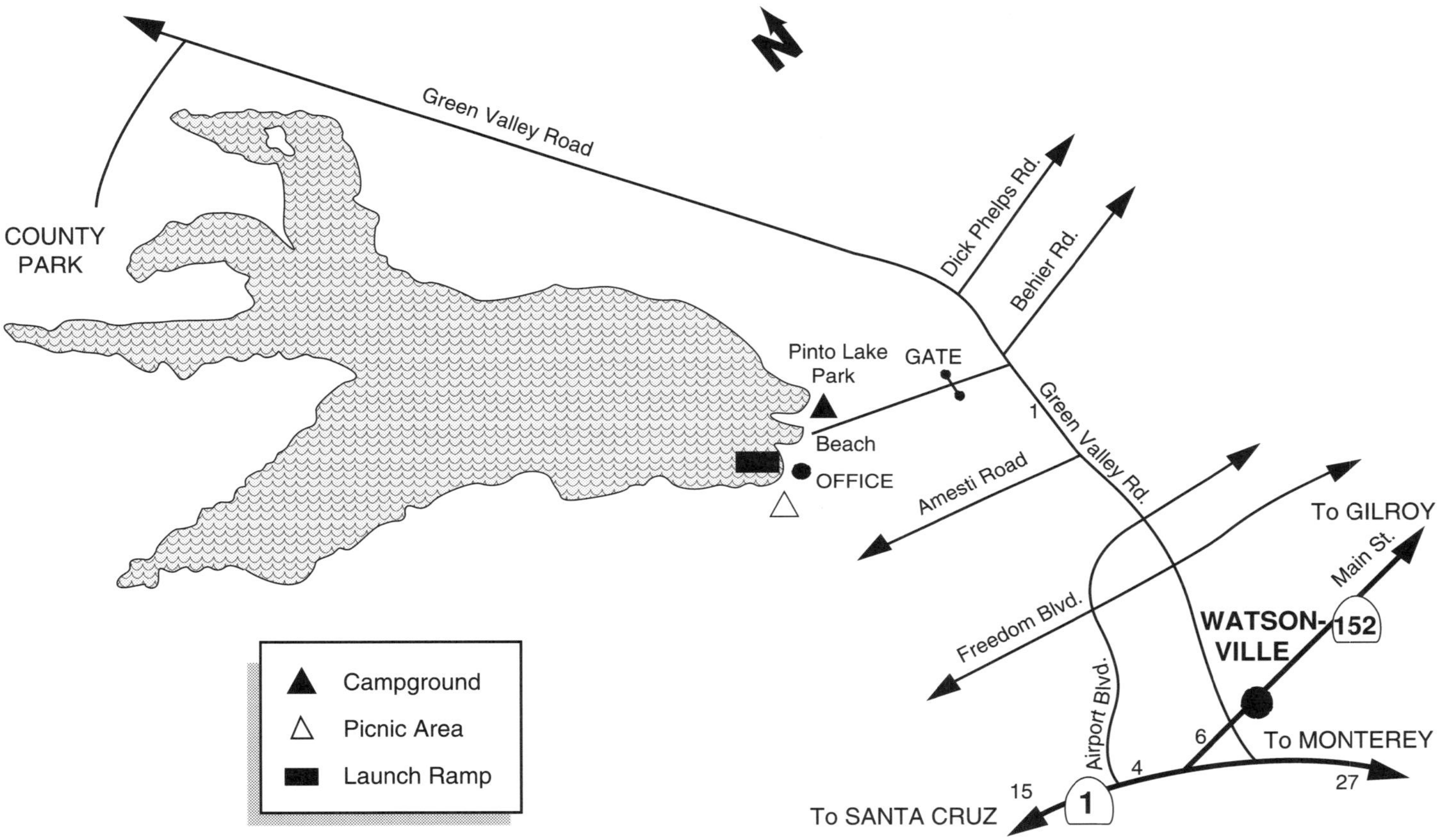

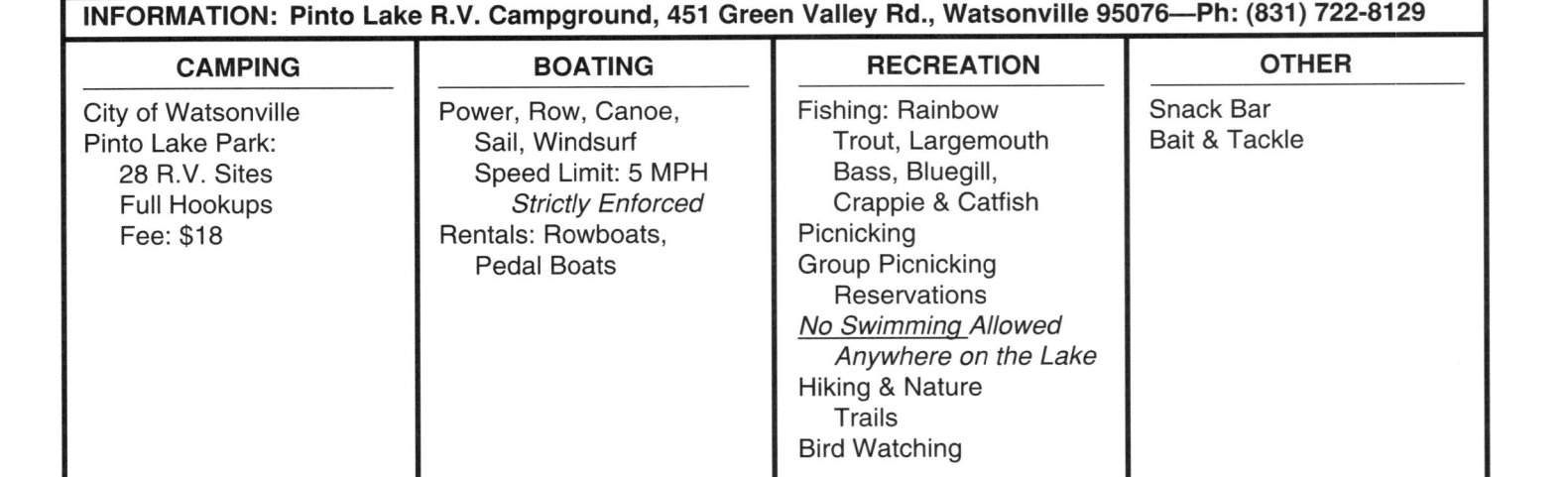

INFORMATION: Pinto Lake R.V. Campground, 451 Green Valley Rd., Watsonville 95076—Ph: (831) 722-8129

CAMPING	BOATING	RECREATION	OTHER
City of Watsonville Pinto Lake Park: 28 R.V. Sites Full Hookups Fee: $18	Power, Row, Canoe, Sail, Windsurf Speed Limit: 5 MPH *Strictly Enforced* Rentals: Rowboats, Pedal Boats	Fishing: Rainbow Trout, Largemouth Bass, Bluegill, Crappie & Catfish Picnicking Group Picnicking Reservations *No Swimming Allowed Anywhere on the Lake* Hiking & Nature Trails Bird Watching	Snack Bar Bait & Tackle

Coyote Reservoir is at an elevation of 777 feet in the scenic, oak-covered hills near Gilroy. Santa Clara County provides facilities for lakeside camping, picnicking, hiking, fishing and all types of boating. This pretty Lake is open at the northwest end, so the breezes come down the length of the Lake which makes for good sailing and windsurfing. The Reservoir is open year around from 8:00 a.m. to 1/2 hour before sunset for boaters and sunset for day users. Campers may fish from shore during the night but there is no night boating permitted.

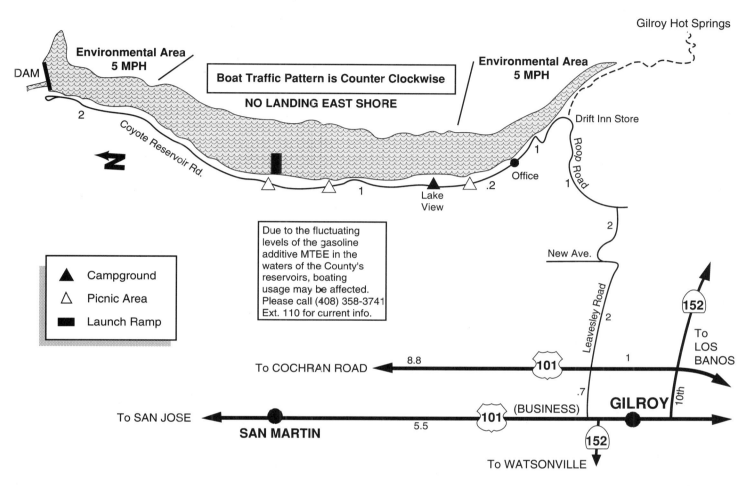

Due to the fluctuating levels of the gasoline additive MTBE in the waters of the County's reservoirs, boating usage may be affected. Please call (408) 358-3741 Ext. 110 for current info.

▲ Campground
△ Picnic Area
■ Launch Ramp

Boat Traffic Pattern is Counter Clockwise

NO LANDING EAST SHORE

INFORMATION: Coyote Lake Park, 10840 Coyote Lake Rd., Gilroy 95020—Ph: (408) 842-7800			
CAMPING	**BOATING**	**RECREATION**	**OTHER**
74 Dev. Sites for Tents & R.V.s No Hookups Fees: $10 $5 - 2nd Vehicle First Come - First Served Basis Day Use Fee: $4	Power, Row, Canoe, Sail, Waterski & Jets Speed Limit - 35 MPH *Counter Clockwise Traffic Pattern* Launch Ramp Lake Use Fee: $5	Fishing: Trout, Catfish, Bluegill, Crappie & Bass Picnicking Hiking No Swimming	Full Facilities: 8 Miles at Gilroy

EL ESTERO, LAGUNA SECA, LOWER and UPPER ABBOTT LAKES

These three Recreation Parks in Monterey County range from a nice day use City Park in Monterey to a Forest Service Campground at Arroyo Seco. The Laguna Seca Recreational Area is one of the most complete parks in the State with a modern campground and a small 10 acre Lake (no fishing). Campsites overlook the famous race car track. El Estero is a pretty Lake in downtown Monterey with a children's play area, picnic facilities and athletic fields. The Abbott or Twin Lakes are in the Los Padres National Forest and offer family and group campgrounds and a warm water fishery. Trout fishing and swimming are popular in the Arroyo Seco River.

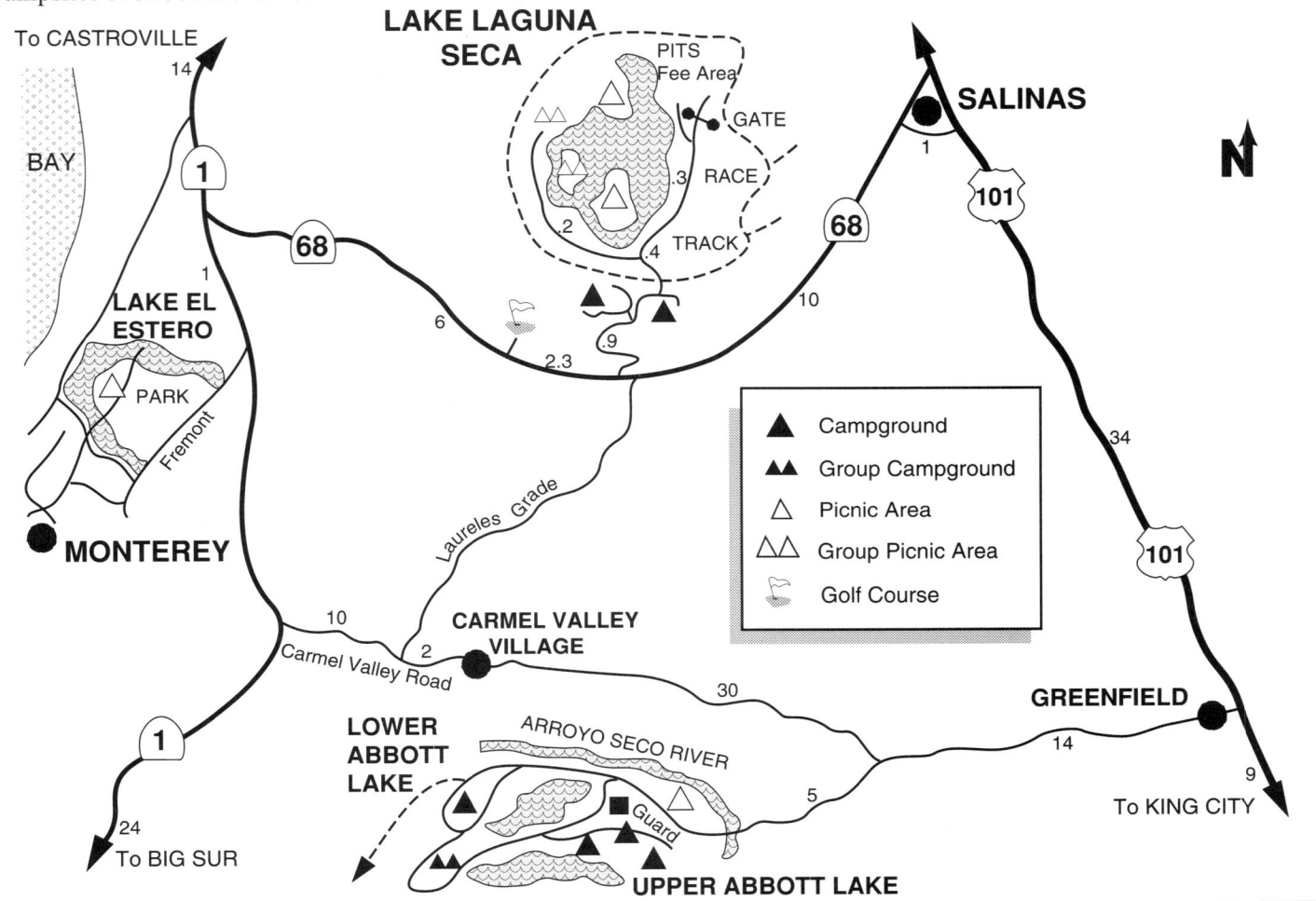

CAMPING	BOATING	RECREATION	OTHER
Laguna Seca: 　77 Tent Sites 　　Fee: $18 　96 R.V. Sites - Electric & 　　Water Hookups 　　Fee: $22 　Reservations Accepted 　Ph: (831) 755-4899 U.S.F.S. Arroyo Seco Abbott Lakes: 　46 Sites & Group Site King City Ranger Station 　Ph: (831) 385-5434	El Estero: 　Paddle Boat Rental Abbott Lakes: 　Canoeing Nearby: 　Veteran's Park 　40 Sites - No Hookups 　　Fee: $15 　Ph: (831) 646-3865	Fishing: Trout, 　Bass & Catfish *No Fishing at Laguna* Seca Picnicking Hiking Playgrounds Laguna Seca: 　Rifle & Pistol Range 　Motorcross Track 　Festivals, Concerts 　Auto Races, Race School Mountain Bike Access to 　Bur. Land Mgt. Trails	El Estero Lake: 　City of Monterey 　Recreation & Community 　Services Department 　546 Dutra St. 　Monterey 93940 　Ph: (831) 646-3866 Full Facilities & Golf 　Courses in Monterey Monterey Jazz 　Festival Salinas Rodeo

INFORMATION: Laguna Seca Recreation Area, P.O. Box 5279, Salinas 93915—Ph: (831) 755-4899

San Justo Reservoir rests in the low rolling hills west of Hollister. The Park has a total of 587 acres including challenging trails for the mountain biker. The pretty 200 surface acre Lake offers varied recreation. Boating is restricted to non-powered craft except for those with electric motors. The prevailing winds make this a good sailing and windsurfing environment. The California Department of Fish and Game regularly stock rainbow trout from late January until late June. A black bass and catfish population is being established which is enhanced by anchored trees at the bottom of the Lake for fish habitat. Facilities include a launch ramp, sheltered picnic areas and a snack bar. The Lake is open to the public Wednesday through Sunday from sunrise to sunset. *There is a consistent drop in water level throughout the summer and at times San Justo can be closed - Check for current conditions.*

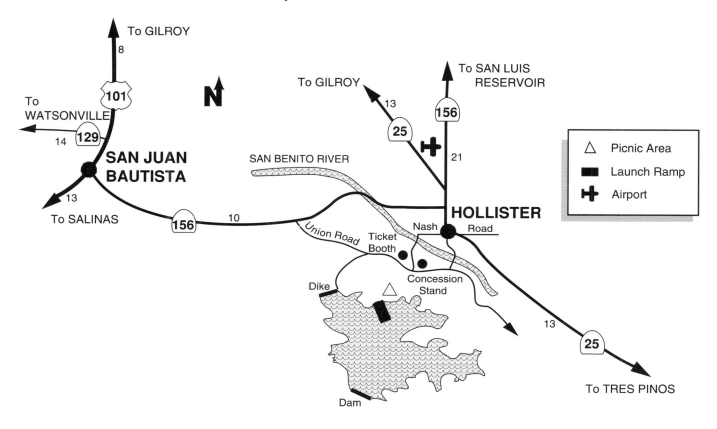

CAMPING	BOATING	RECREATION	OTHER
No Camping at Lake Entrance Fee: $5 Per Vehicle $2 for Walk-Ins & Bicycling	Paddle, Sail & Windsurfing Electric Motors - OK Paved Launch Ramp User Fees: $2 - Watercraft up to 13 Feet or Floating Device $3 - Watercraft over 13 Feet	Fishing: Rainbow Trout, Black Bass, Catfish, Blue Gill & Crappie Fishing Derbies in Spring: Money Prizes for Special Tagged Trout and Largest Fish Picnicking Mountain Bicycle Trails *No Swimming*	Concession: Ph: (831) 638-3300 Bait & Tackle Snack Bar Full Facilities in Hollister

INFORMATION: San Benito County Parks, 3220 Southside Rd., Hollister 95023—Ph: (831) 636-4170

SAN LUIS RESERVOIR and O'NEILL FOREBAY

San Luis Reservoir State Recreation Area is at an elevation of 544 feet in the eastern foothills of the Diablo Mountain Range west of Los Banos. This huge Reservoir has a surface area of 13,800 acres and 65 miles of grassy, oakdotted shoreline. Most species of fish found in the Sacramento Delta are found at San Luis and the Forebay. In addition to good fishing, San Luis is popular for boating, swimming and waterskiing but sudden strong winds can be a hazard. Warning lights are located at the Romero Overlook, at the Basalt Campground Entrance Station and on Quien Sabe Point at the Reservoir and at the Medeiros launch ramp and San Luis Creek Area on the Forebay. The O'Neill Forebay below San Luis Reservoir has a surface area of 2,000 acres with 14 miles of shoreline. The 67-mile San Joaquin Section of the California Aqueduct Bikeway ends at the Forebay. Boating and fishing are popular. Waterfowl hunting in season is allowed at these Lakes.

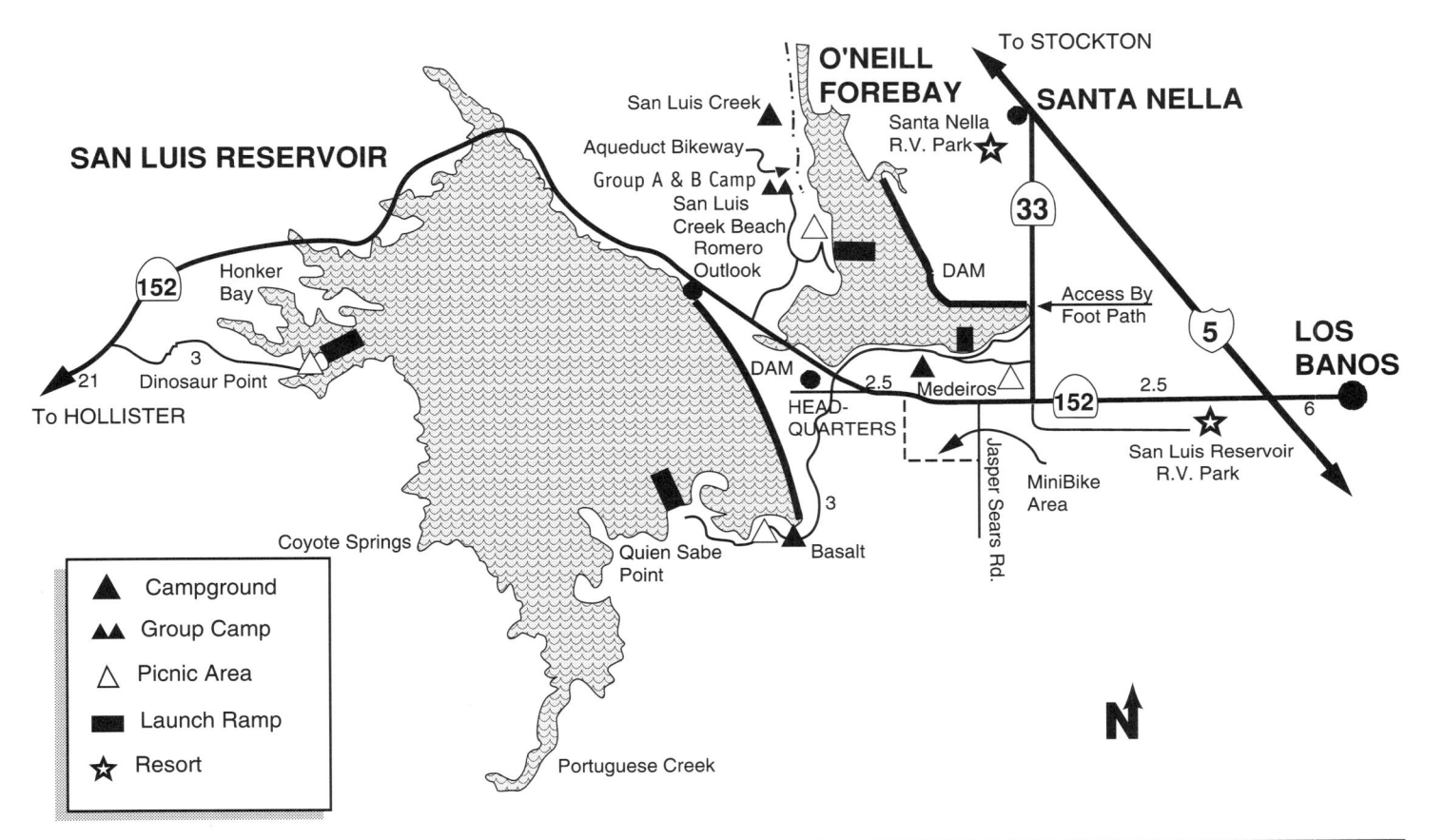

| Campground |
| Group Camp |
| Picnic Area |
| Launch Ramp |
| Resort |

INFORMATION: Four Rivers District, 31426 Gonzaga Rd., Gustine 95322—Ph: (209) 826-1196

CAMPING	BOATING	RECREATION	OTHER
Basalt Area: 79 Dev. Sites for Tents/R.V.s -$16 Reserve:Ph:(800) 444-7275 Medeiros: Undev. Sites for Tents/R.V.s -$10 Plus Area for 400 R.V.s San Luis Creek Family Campground - 53 Dev. Sites for Tents/R .V.s -$15 Group Camps: A: 60 Pers. 15 Veh. $90 & B: 30 Pers. 10 Veh. $45 Day Use Only Fee: $5	Power, Row, Canoe, Sail, Waterski, Jets, Windsurf & Inflatable Launch Ramps - $5 Felton Boat Rentals: Ph: (209) 826-7059 Life Jackets Required for Everyone Except Windsurfers *Beware of Sudden Winds Water May Fluctuate up to 200 Feet Annually*	Fishing: Catfish, Bluegill, Crappie, Striped & Black Bass, Sturgeon, Shad Swimming - Beaches Picnicking Hunting: Waterfowl Only 157 Acre Minibike Trail Area - 250 cc Engine Only California Aqueduct Bikeway	Excellent Visitor's Center at Romero Overlook Santa Nella R.V. Park Full Hookups Ph: (209) 826-3105 San Luis Reservoir Park Full Hookups Ph: (209) 826-5542 Full Facilities in Los Banos and Santa Nella

Los Banos Reservoir is at an elevation of 328 feet in the hilly grasslands west of Los Banos. The surface area of this small Lake is 410 acres with 12 miles of shoreline. There are several planted trees around the campgrounds along with shade ramadas. Los Banos is under the jurisdiction of the Four Rivers District of the California State Parks. There is a small campground and a paved launch ramp. This facility is primarily used as a warm water fishery. Swimming is popular as is waterfowl hunting in season. There are usually good winds for sailing and windsurfing.

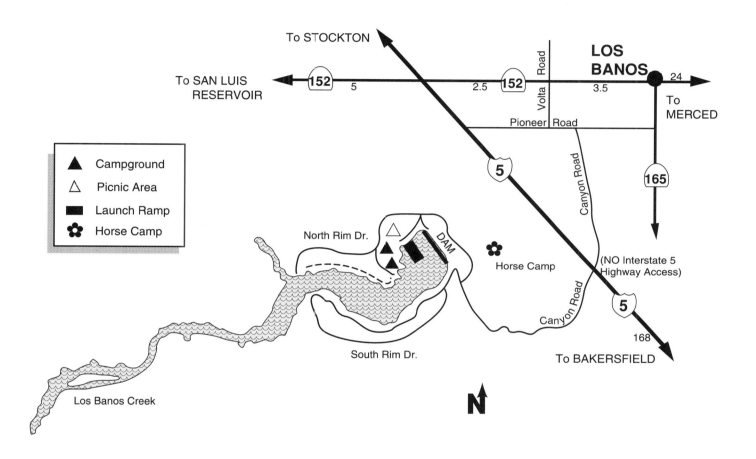

INFORMATION: Four Rivers District, 31426 Gonzaga Rd., Gustine 95322—Ph: (209) 826-1196 or (209) 826-6393			
CAMPING	**BOATING**	**RECREATION**	**OTHER**
20 Primitive Sites for Tents & R.V.s Fee: $10 (Hauled In Water) Day Use: $5	Power, Row, Canoe, Sail, Windsurf & Inflatables Speed Limit - 5 MPH Paved Launch Ramp Fee: $5	Fishing: Trout, Catfish, Bluegill, Largemouth Bass Swimming Picnicking Hiking Horseback Riding Trails Hunting: Waterfowl in Season Only	Full Facilities at Los Banos

HENSLEY LAKE

Hensley Lake lies at an elevation of 540 feet in the rolling foothills northeast of Madera. The surrounding hills are covered with majestic oaks and granite outcroppings. The Lake has a surface area of 1,570 acres with 24 miles of shoreline. The U.S. Army Corps of Engineers provides a campground, picnic areas and boating facilities. A large expanse of open water and many secluded quiet coves invites all types of boating. The fishing is good with an abundant warm water fishery. There are two swimming beaches. Hiking trails lead into the Wildlife Area where many birds, animals and native wildflowers may be observed.

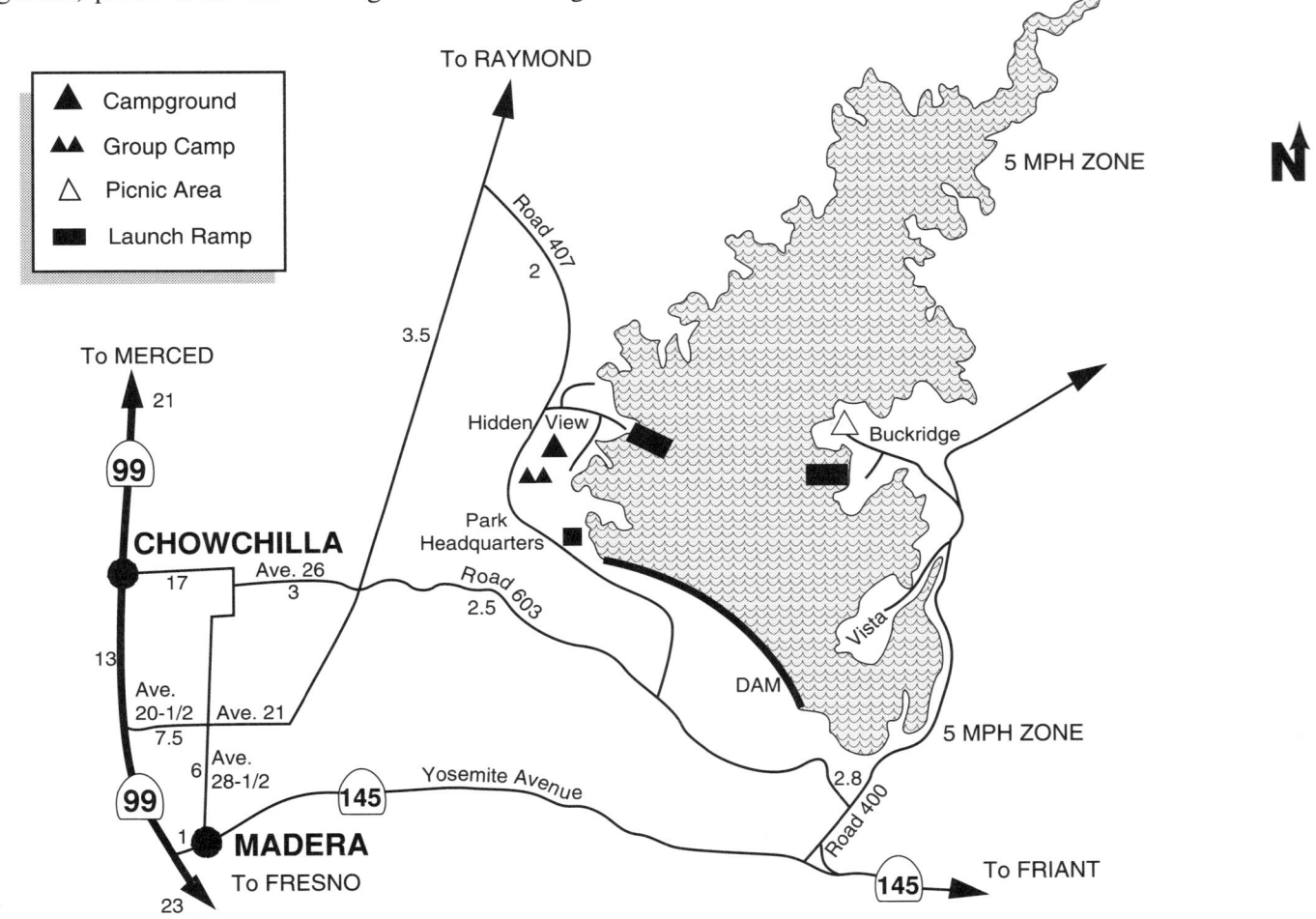

INFORMATION: Hensley Lake, P.O. Box 85, Raymond 93653—Ph: (559) 673-5151

CAMPING	BOATING	RECREATION	OTHER
52 Dev. Sites for Tents & R.V.s Fees: $14 With Hookups: $20 Disposal Station Group Camp Area Fees: $50 Reserve: (877) 444-6777	Power, Row, Canoe, Sail, Waterski, Jets, Windsurf & Inflatable 2 Paved Launch Ramps Fees: $2 per Day $25 All Year Courtesy Docks *Submerged Hazards During Low Water*	Fishing: Trout in Winter, Largemouth Bass, Bluegill, Catfish & Crappie Night Fishing Swimming - Beaches Picnicking: Family & Group Sites Hiking & Nature Trails Mountain Bike & Equestrian Trails	Full Facilities in Madera & Chowchilla

Located in the oak-covered foothills 25 miles northeast of Chowchilla, this 1,780 acre Lake offers good camping facilities. Brush shelters are provided for wildlife and there are also underwater fish shelters. Eastman is a designated trophy bass fishery with a limit of one bass per day, 22 inch minimum size. Boating and sailing are popular and the well-maintained facilities are open year around. The lower two-thirds of the Lake is open to boating during daylight hours only. Also the lower two-thirds of shoreline is open to fishing and boating one hour before sunrise to one hour after sunset. Be well aware of the "*keep out*" buoys as this area is closed to all water use. Berenda Reservoir to the west is a small day-use Lake with boating and fishing from shore during the summer only.

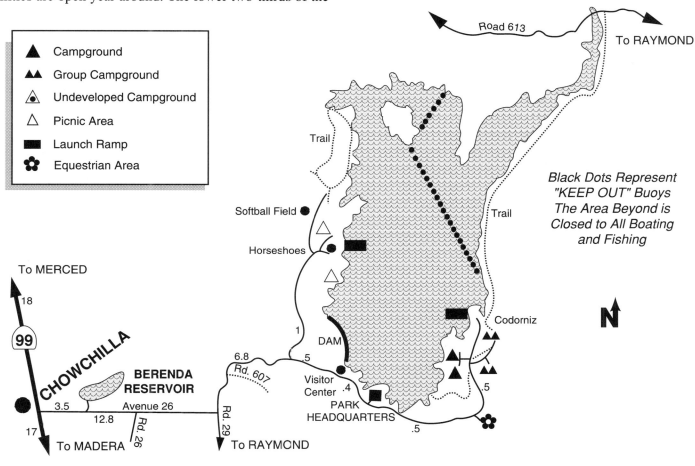

▲	Campground
▲▲	Group Campground
⬙	Undeveloped Campground
△	Picnic Area
▬	Launch Ramp
✿	Equestrian Area

Black Dots Represent "KEEP OUT" Buoys The Area Beyond is Closed to All Boating and Fishing

INFORMATION: Park Manager, Eastman Lake, Box 67, Raymond 93653, Ph: (559) 689-3255

CAMPING	BOATING	RECREATION	OTHER
66 Dev. Sites for Tents & R.V.s Fees: $8 - July 1 to Jan. 31 & $12 - Feb. 1 to June 30 Hookups Available: $20 3 Group Areas to 100 People Fee: $20 - $65 Per Night By Reservation Only	Power, Row, Canoe, Sail, Windsurf & Inflatables Launch Ramps - Fee: $2 Berenda Reservoir: Summers Only Drag Boat Racing For Information: Chowchilla Parks & Recreation Ph: (559) 665-4808	Fishing: Trout, Catfish, Bluegill, Crappie & Black Bass Designated Trophy Bass Fishery - Limit: 1 per day 22 Inch Max. Size Swimming Picnicking - Shelter Hiking & Horseback Trails Mountain Bike Trails Nature Study Horseshoes, Softball Shotgun & Bow Hunting	Disposal Station Trail is Closed Seasonally Full Facilities in Chowchilla or Madera

MILLERTON LAKE and LOST LAKE PARK

The Millerton State Recreation Area is a part of the California State Park System and provides modern picnic, camping and marine facilities. This popular 5,000 surface acre Lake, with over 40 miles of shoreline, offers excellent boating and sailing opportunities for all types of craft. The angler will find a good warm water fishery. There are sandy swimming areas and picnic sites around the Lake. The Lost Lake Recreation Area is a separate facility under the jurisdiction of Fresno County. This pretty 350 acre park on the San Joaquin River below Millerton offers a small 35 acre Lake which is open to non-powered boating and fishing. There are family and group picnic areas, a campground and ball fields.

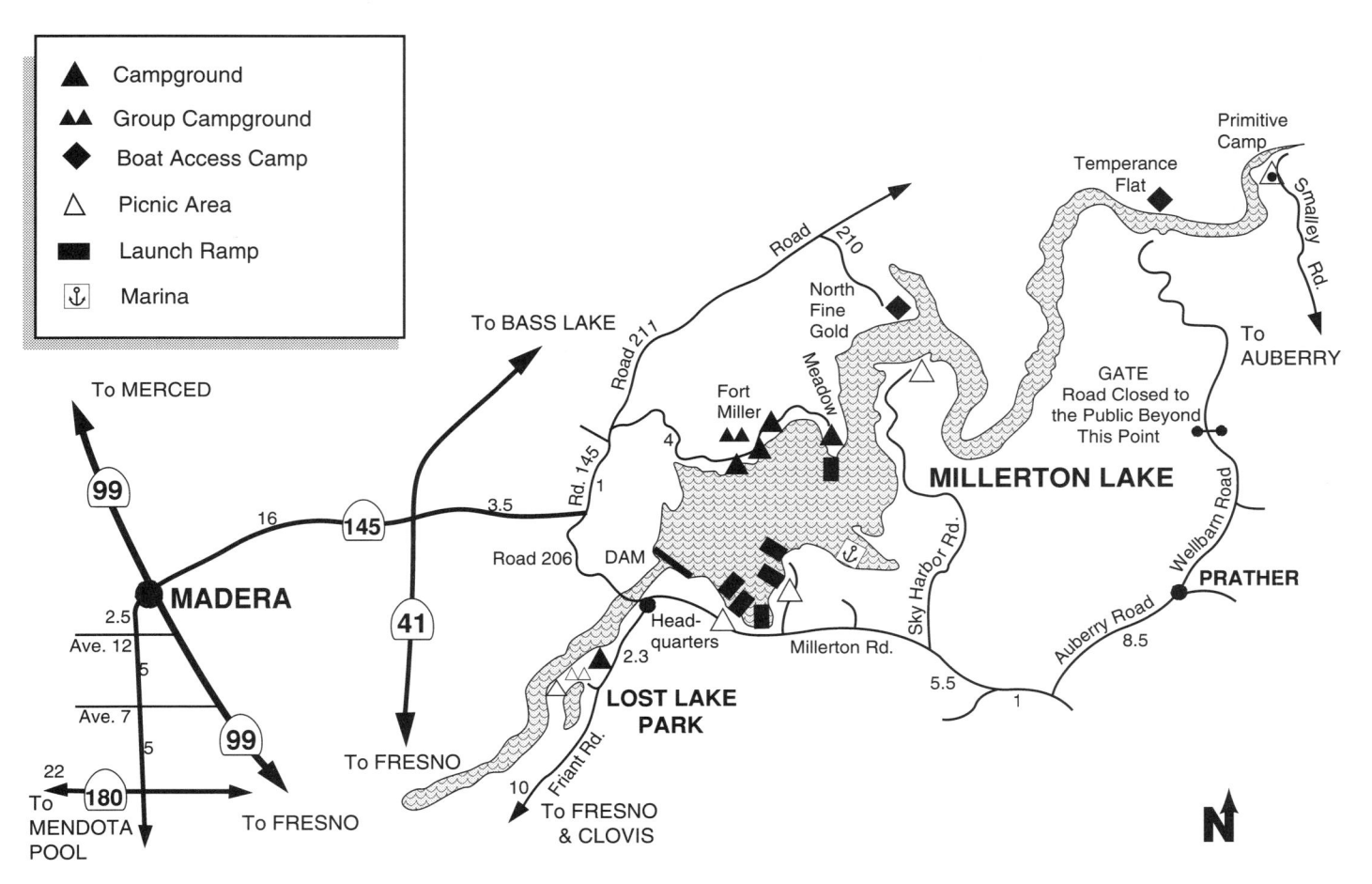

INFORMATION: Millerton Lake State Recreation Area, P.O. Box 205, Friant 93626—Ph: (559) 822-2332

CAMPING	BOATING	RECREATION	OTHER

Millerton Lake:
    123 Dev. Sites for
    Tents & R.V.s to 36 Feet
    Fee: $12 - $16
Group Sites for 40 and 75
People - Fees: $60 - $112
Reserve:
    Ph: (800) 444-7275
15 Boat Camp Sites
25 Boat Access Sites
Day Use Fee: $6
Lost Lake:
    42 R.V. Sites - Fee: $9
	Millerton:
	    Open to All Boats
	    Full Service Marina
	    Launch Ramps: $5
	    Rentals: Fishing
	        Boats & Motors
	
	Lost Lake:
	    No Gas-Powered
	        Motors
	    Hand Launch Only
		Fishing: Striped, Alabama
		    Spotted, Large &
		    Smallmouth Bass,
		    Catfish & Panfish
		Swimming - Millerton
		    Only
		Picnicking
		Hiking & Horseback
		    Riding Trails
		Birdwatching
		Nature Study Area
		Wildlife Refuge
			Lost Lake Rec. Area
			    Fresno County Parks
			    2220 Tulare St.
			    Fresno 93721
			    Ph: (559) 488-3004
			
			Concessions
			Bait & Tackle
			Market
			Disposal Stations

Bass Lake, at an elevation of 3,400 feet, is within the Sierra National Forest. This beautiful forested recreation area provides an abundance of recreational opportunities. Boating and sailing on this 1,165 surface acre Lake is extremely popular. Water levels are generally maintained through Labor Day. There are 16 different species of fish to challenge the angler. Facilities on the South Shore are administered by the U. S. Forest Service and managed by California Land Management. There are numerous group sites for camping and picnicking at Crane Valley and Recreation Point. Resorts, cabins and R.V. parks are available at privately owned areas around the Lake. This is a great place for old-fashioned family vacations. For full information, contact the Bass Lake Chamber of Commerce.

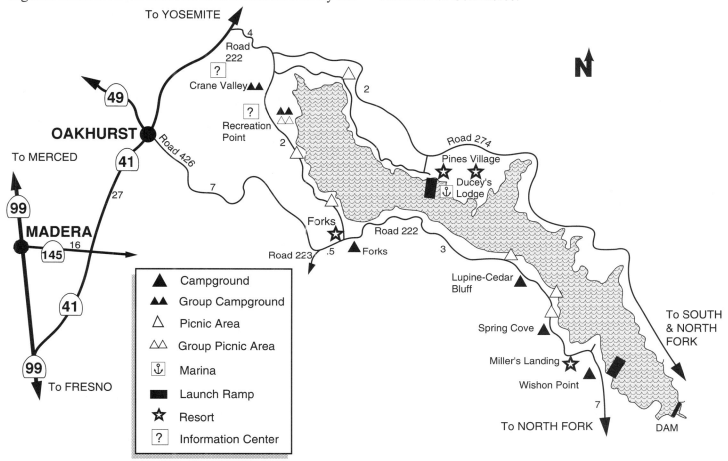

INFORMATION: Mariposa Ranger District, 43060 Highway 41, Oakhurst 93644—Ph: (559) 683-4665

CAMPING	BOATING	RECREATION	OTHER
Dev. Sites for Tents & R.V.s Fees: $16 - $30	Power, Row, Canoe, Sail, Waterski, Jets, Windsurf	Fishing: Rainbow & Brown Trout, Catfish, Bluegill,	Ph: (800) 350-7463 Forks Resort Ph: (559) 642-3737
Forks: 31 Sites	& Inflatables	Perch, Crappie,	Cabins & Resorts
Lupine-Cedar Bluff: 95 Sites	Full Service Marina	Black Bass &	Snack Bars & Restaurants
Spring Cove: 62 Sites	Launch Ramps	Kokanee Salmon	Groceries, Bait & Tackle
Wishon: 47 Sites	Rentals: Fishing,	Swimming - Beaches	Gas Station
Disposal Stations	Canoes & Waterski	Hiking & Riding	Movie Theater & Arcade
Numerous Group/Youth Campgrounds & Picnic Areas	Boats, Party Barges *Bass Lake Queen* Summer Tours	Trails Visitor Programs Nature Study	Chamber of Commerce P.O. Box 126
Reserve: Ph: (800) 280-CAMP	Moorings, Gas	The Pines Resort	Bass Lake 93604 Ph: (559) 642-3676

REDINGER LAKE and KERCKHOFF RESERVOIR

Redinger Lake is at an elevation of 1,400 feet in a narrow valley with surrounding mountains rising 1,000 feet above the Lake's surface. The Lake is 3 miles long and 1/4 mile wide. This area of digger pine and chaparral is intermingled with live and valley oak. There is a variety of wildlife that can be observed. Redinger is primarily a boating Lake as fishing is very limited. Kerckhoff Reservoir is located 6 miles to the west. Fishing for striped bass is the dominant activity and boating is limited to hand launch boats. Camping is available at both Lakes but the sites are not developed. Redinger has numerous sandy beaches and is a remote, pretty Lake.

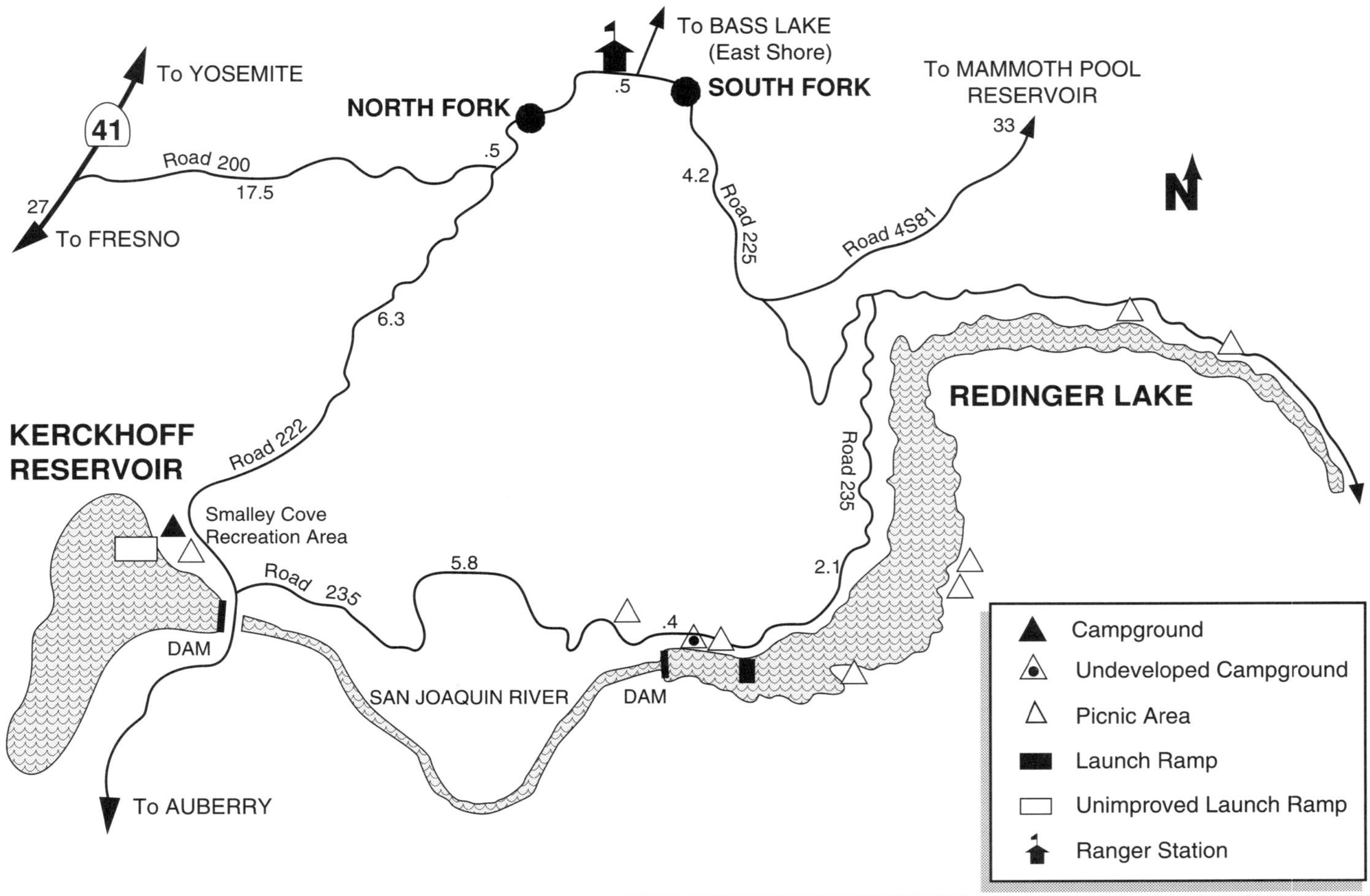

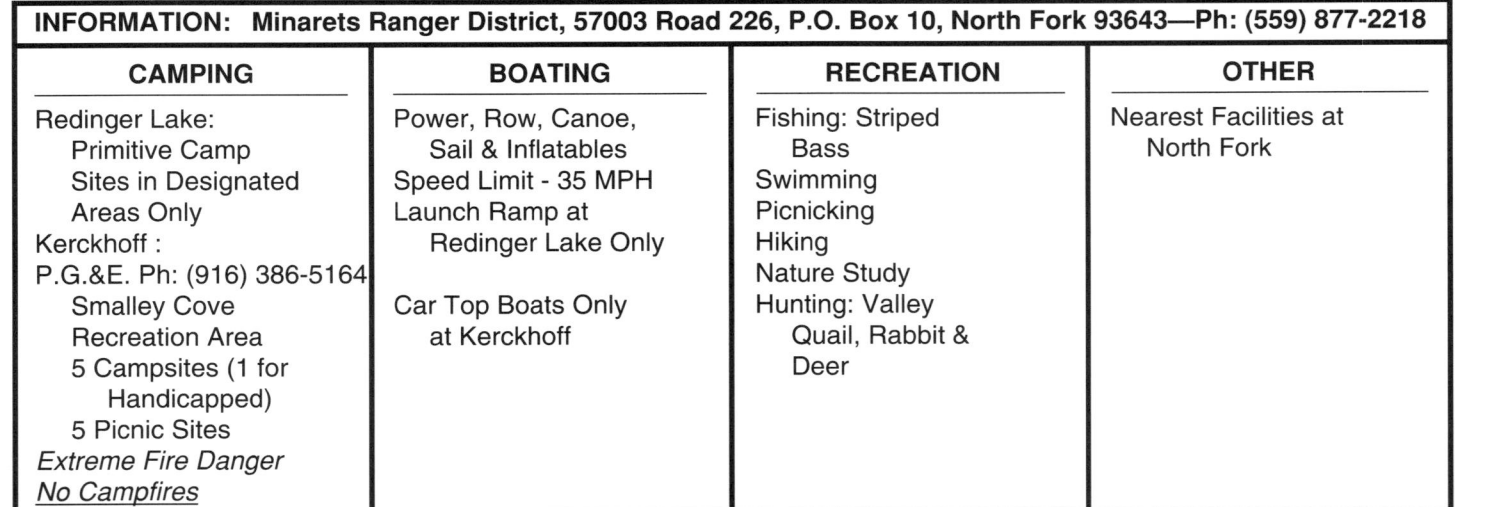

INFORMATION: Minarets Ranger District, 57003 Road 226, P.O. Box 10, North Fork 93643—Ph: (559) 877-2218

CAMPING	BOATING	RECREATION	OTHER

Redinger Lake:
  Primitive Camp
  Sites in Designated
  Areas Only
Kerckhoff :
P.G.&E. Ph: (916) 386-5164
  Smalley Cove
  Recreation Area
  5 Campsites (1 for
    Handicapped)
  5 Picnic Sites
Extreme Fire Danger
<u>*No Campfires*</u>
	Power, Row, Canoe,
	  Sail & Inflatables
	Speed Limit - 35 MPH
	Launch Ramp at
	  Redinger Lake Only
	
	Car Top Boats Only
	  at Kerckhoff
		Fishing: Striped
		  Bass
		Swimming
		Picnicking
		Hiking
		Nature Study
		Hunting: Valley
		  Quail, Rabbit &
		  Deer
			Nearest Facilities at
			North Fork

Mammoth Pool Reservoir is located on the San Joaquin River at an elevation of 3,330 feet. The dam was completed in 1959 by Southern California Edison Company to produce hydroelectric power. The Lake is nestled in a narrow valley of ponderosa pine, incense cedar, black and live oak with mountains rising 2,000 feet above its shoreline. The surface area of Mammoth Pool is 1,107 acres when full although the water level drops 90 feet in the fall, closing the improved launch ramp. The access road climbs to 5,300 feet rendering it impassable when winter snow arrives. Mile High Vista Point offers a 180 degree view of magnificent mountains including Mount Ritter and Mammoth Mountain.

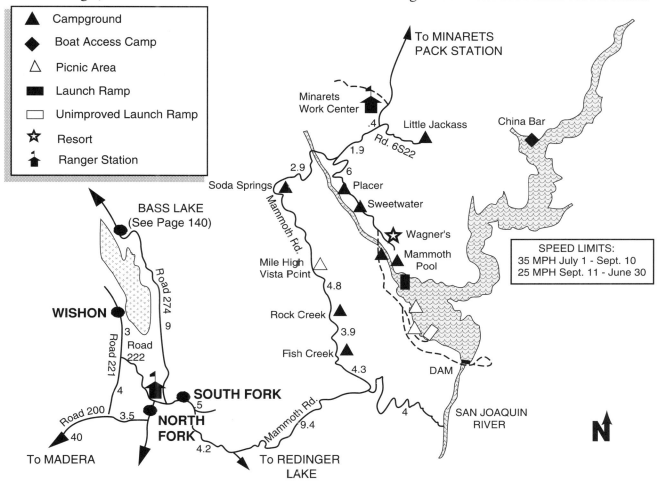

Legend:
- ▲ Campground
- ◆ Boat Access Camp
- △ Picnic Area
- ■ Launch Ramp
- ▢ Unimproved Launch Ramp
- ★ Resort
- ⛴ Ranger Station

To MINARETS PACK STATION

Minarets Work Center
Little Jackass
China Bar
Rd. 6S22
Soda Springs
Placer
Sweetwater
Wagner's
Mammoth Pool
Mammoth Rd.
Mile High Vista Point
BASS LAKE (See Page 140)
WISHON
Road 274
Rock Creek
Fish Creek
Road 222
Road 221
SOUTH FORK
NORTH FORK
Road 200
Mammoth Rd.
DAM
SAN JOAQUIN RIVER
To MADERA
To REDINGER LAKE
N

.4 1.9 2.9 6 4.8 3.9 4.3 9.4 4 3 9 4 3.5 5 4.2 40

SPEED LIMITS:
35 MPH July 1 - Sept. 10
25 MPH Sept. 11 - June 30

INFORMATION: Minarets Ranger District, 57003 Road 226, P.O. Box 10, North Fork 93643—Ph: (559) 877-2218

CAMPING	BOATING	RECREATION	OTHER
30 Dev. Sites for Tents	Power, Sail, Row,	Fishing: Rainbow,	Wagner's Resort
34 Dev. Sites for Tents & R.V.s	Canoe, Windsurf & Inflatables	Eastern Brook & German Brown	21101 Rte. 209 Madera 93638
Fees:	Waterskiing Subject	Trout	35 Dev. Sites for
Mammoth Pool: $13	to 35 MPH Speed Limit	Lake Closed to	Tents & R.V.s - Fee: $10
Placer & Sweetwater: $12	Improved Launch Ramp	Fishing & Boating	Store Ph: (559) 841-3736
No Fees at Other USFS Campgrounds	Gravel Launch Ramp	May 1 to June 16 Swimming	Short Orders & Sandwiches
6 Boat-In Sites at China Bar	*Call for Current Lake Level Information*	Picnicking Hiking - Nature Trail Pack Station Hunting: Deer	Lunch Counter Grocery Store Bait & Tackle Gas Station Open: End of May to Oct. 1

WISHON, COURTRIGHT and BLACK ROCK RESERVOIRS

These Lakes range in elevation from 8,200 feet at Courtright, 6,600 feet at Wishon to 4,200 feet at Black Rock. They are a part of the Kings River Drainage System. Located in the beautiful Sierra National Forest, the Lakes offer good fishing for native trout. In addition, the angler will find numerous Lakes and streams and the Upper King's River angler's access site. Wishon Village offers complete resort facilities in this relatively remote area. The Forest Service operates numerous campgrounds as shown on the map. Those looking for a wilderness adventure will find trailheads leading into the John Muir and Dinkey Lakes Wilderness Areas. The Helms Creek Hydroelectric Project affects water levels daily at Wishon, Courtright and Black Rock.

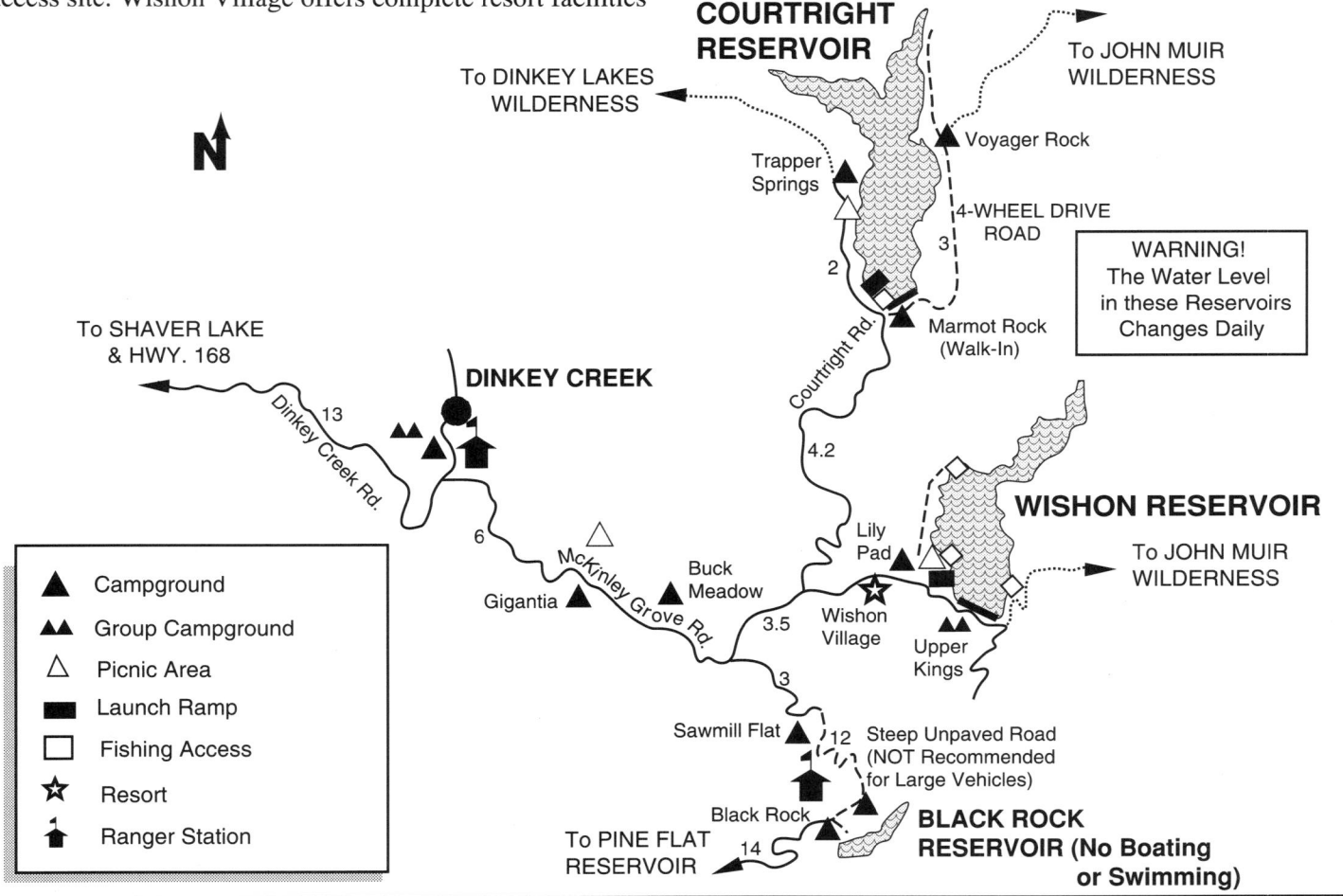

COURTRIGHT RESERVOIR

To DINKEY LAKES WILDERNESS

To JOHN MUIR WILDERNESS

Voyager Rock

Trapper Springs

4-WHEEL DRIVE ROAD

3

2

Courtright Rd.

Marmot Rock (Walk-In)

WARNING! The Water Level in these Reservoirs Changes Daily

To SHAVER LAKE & HWY. 168

DINKEY CREEK

Dinkey Creek Rd.

13

4.2

WISHON RESERVOIR

Lily Pad

To JOHN MUIR WILDERNESS

6

McKinley Grove Rd.

Buck Meadow

Gigantia

Wishon Village

3.5

Upper Kings

3

▲ Campground

▲▲ Group Campground

△ Picnic Area

▬ Launch Ramp

☐ Fishing Access

☆ Resort

♟ Ranger Station

Sawmill Flat

12

Steep Unpaved Road (NOT Recommended for Large Vehicles)

Black Rock

To PINE FLAT RESERVOIR

14

BLACK ROCK RESERVOIR (No Boating or Swimming)

INFORMATION: Kings River Ranger District, 34849 Maxon Rd., Sanger 93657—Ph: (559) 855-8321

CAMPING	BOATING	RECREATION	OTHER

USFS Numerous Dev. Sites
Black Rock: $8
Dinkey Creek: $16
Trapper Springs, Marmot &
Lily Pad: $15, Others Free
Dinkey Group: $75 -
Res. Ph: (800) 280-CAMP
P.G.&E. Sites at Black
   Rock, Marmot Rock &
   Lily Pad Plus
Upper Kings Group: $125 -
   to 50 People
Res. Ph: (916) 386-5164
	Open to All Boating
	*Except Waterskiing
	& Jets*
	15 MPH Speed Limit
	
	Rentals: Fishing
	   Boats at Wishon
		Fishing: Rainbow,
		   Brown & Brook Trout
		Swimming
		Picnicking
		Hiking & Backpacking
		Horse Rentals & Pack
		   Services
		Hunting: Deer,
		   Mountain Quail
		OHV Roads
			Wishon Village:
			Mail: 66500 McKinley Grove
			   Shaver Lake 93664
			Ph: (559) 865-5361
			25 Tent Sites &
			97 R.V. Sites- Full Hookups
			Store, Gas Station
			Laundromat
			Propane, Ice, Bait & Tackle
			Dinkey Creek Inn - Cabins
			   Ph: (559) 841-3435
			Full Facilities at
			   Shaver Lake

Shaver Lake is at an elevation of 5,370 feet in the Sierra National Forest. The Lake has a surface area of 2,000 acres with a shoreline of 13 miles. Tall pine trees blend with granite boulders to the water's edge. This is a popular boating Lake with good marine facilities. In addition to excellent fishing at Shaver, there are numerous trout streams nearby awaiting the angler. The John Muir and Dinkey Lakes Wilderness Areas attract the hiker and backpacker. Both the U. S. Forest Service and Southern California Edison offer well-maintained campgrounds in this beautiful setting. The Forest Service Campgrounds are operated by California Land Management under a Special Use Permit from the Forest Service.

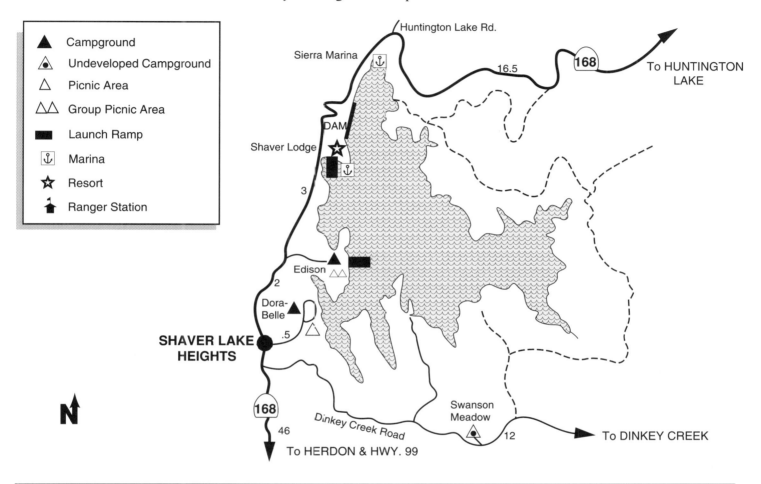

INFORMATION: Pineridge Ranger District, 29688 Auberry Rd., Box 559, Prather 93651—Ph: (559) 855-5360

CAMPING	BOATING	RECREATION	OTHER

U.S.F.S.:
Ph: (559) 855-5360
  69 Dev. Sites for
  Tents & R.V.s, Fee: $14
  9 Primitive Sites
So. Cal. Edison:
Ph: (559) 841-3134
  150 Dev. Sites for
  Tents & R.V.s, Fee: $18
  Electric Hookups
  Disposal Station
Each Additional
  Vehicle: $5
	Power, Row, Canoe,
	  Sail, Waterski, Jets,
	  Windsurf &
	  Inflatable
	Full Service Marinas
	Rental: Fishing Boats
	  & Motors, Pontoons
	Berths
	Gas
		Fishing: Rainbow,
		  Brown & Brook
		  Trout, Large &
		  Smallmouth Bass,
		  Catfish & Sunfish
		Picnicking
		Swimming - Beaches
		Hiking & Horseback
		  Riding Trails
			Motels & Cabins
			Restaurants
			Cocktail Lounges
			Grocery Stores
			Bait & Tackle
			Gas Station

HUNTINGTON LAKE

Huntington Lake is at an elevation of 7,000 feet in the Sierra National Forest. Resting in a forested natural basin, this man-made Lake is 6 miles long and 1/2 mile wide with 14 miles of shoreline. The Forest Service Campgrounds are operated by California Land Management under a Special Use Permit from the Forest Service. There are many private resorts under Special Use Permits. This is a good Lake for sailing and regattas are held in the summer to take advantage of the westerly winds. Hiking and horseback riding trails surround Huntington. The backpacker will find the nearby Kaiser Wilderness with its 22,750 timbered acres an exciting adventure. Permits are required. Fishing from shore or boat is usually productive and nearby Lakes and streams offer a variety of opportunities.

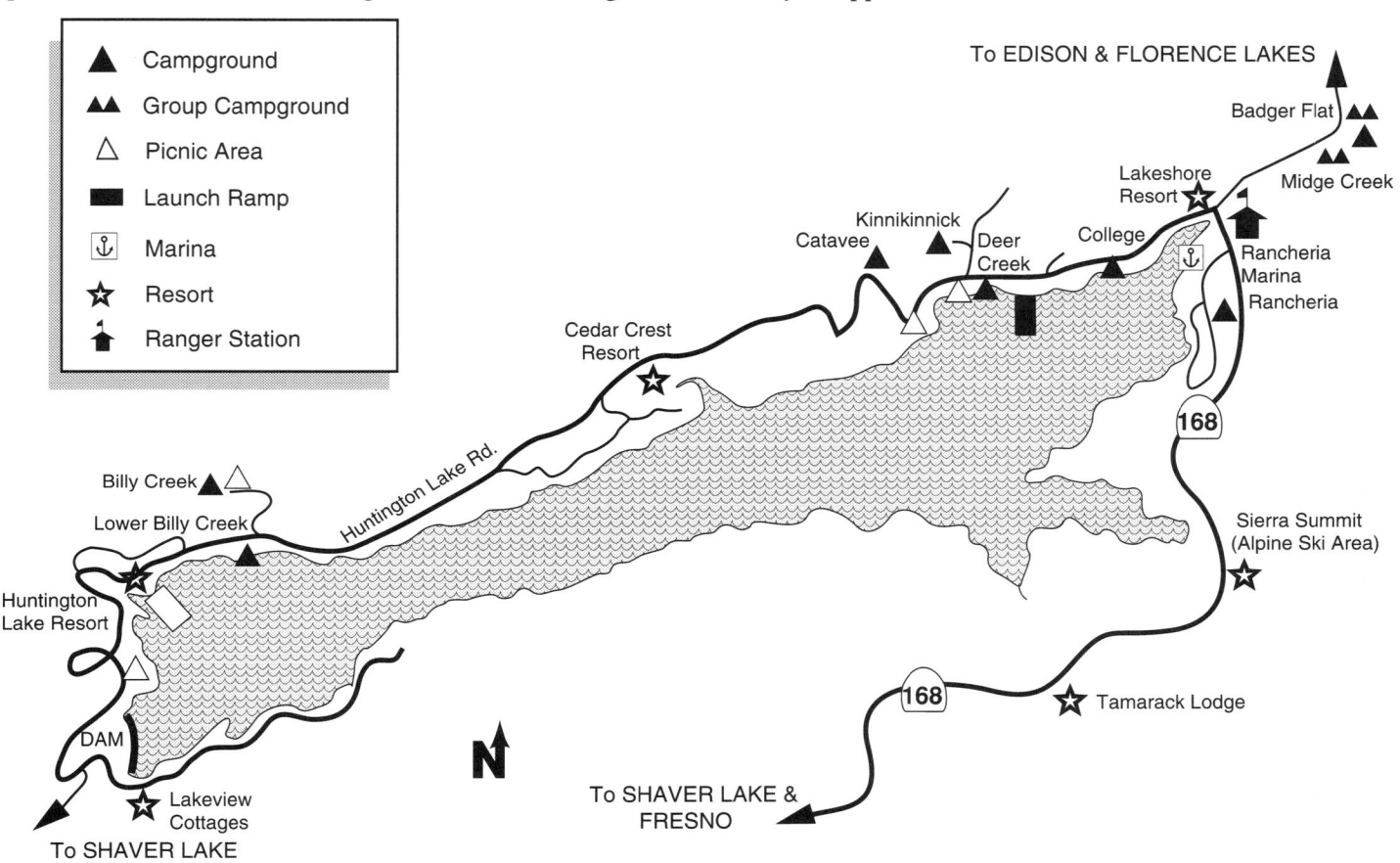

INFORMATION: Pineridge Ranger District, 29688 Auberry Rd. P.O. Box 559, Prather 93651—Ph: (559) 855-5360			
CAMPING	**BOATING**	**RECREATION**	**OTHER**
297 Dev. Sites for Tents & R.V.s Single: $14 - $17 　Double: $28 　Add'l. Vehicle: $5 Group Camps 　to 100 People 　Maximum Each Reserve: 　Ph: (800) 280-CAMP	Power, Row, Canoe, 　Sail, Waterski Full Service Marinas Launch Ramp Rentals: Fishing & 　Sailboats, Canoes, 　Paddleboats & 　Patio Boats	Fishing: Rainbow, 　Brown & Brook 　Trout, Kokanee Swimming Picnicking Hiking Backpacking [Parking] Horseback Riding 　Trails & Rentals Nature Study	Motels, Cabins & Condos Restaurants Grocery Stores Bait & Tackle Gas Station Summer Ranger Station Eastwood Visitor Center 　Ph: (559) 893-6611

Edison Lake is at 7,700 feet and Florence Lake is at 7,400 feet elevation in the beautiful high Sierra bordering the John Muir and Ansel Adams Wilderness Areas. Granite boulders and sandy beaches around the timbered shorelines make a lovely setting. In addition to the Forest Service Campgrounds, Vermillion Valley Resort at Edison Lake offers cabins, restaurant, grocery store, boat rentals and launch facilities. Florence Lake has a small store with limited supplies. A resort with store, cabins, restaurant and hot mineral baths is located at Mono Hot Springs. A ferry service for backpackers into the Wilderness Areas is available at both Lakes. Fishing in both Lakes and streams is excellent in this truly delightful high mountain retreat. Forest Service Campgrounds are operated by California Land Management under a Special Use Permit from the Forest Service.

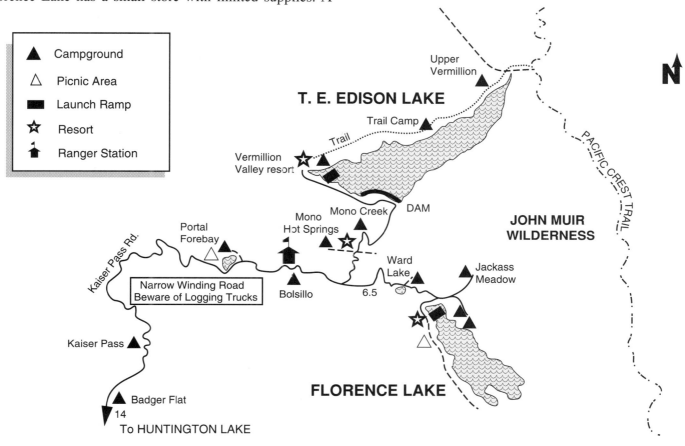

Legend	
▲	Campground
△	Picnic Area
■	Launch Ramp
☆	Resort
⌂	Ranger Station

T. E. EDISON LAKE

Upper Vermillion

Trail Camp

Trail

Vermillion Valley resort

DAM

Mono Creek

Mono Hot Springs

JOHN MUIR WILDERNESS

PACIFIC CREST TRAIL

Portal Forebay

Kaiser Pass Rd.

Narrow Winding Road
Beware of Logging Trucks

Bolsillo

Ward Lake

6.5

Jackass Meadow

Kaiser Pass

Badger Flat
14
To HUNTINGTON LAKE

FLORENCE LAKE

N

INFORMATION: Pineridge Ranger District, 29688 Auberry Rd., P.O. Box 559, Prather 93651—Ph: (559) 855-5360

CAMPING	BOATING	RECREATION	OTHER
162 Sites for Tents in This Area R.V.s and Trailers *Use Caution - Narrow One Lane Winding Roads & Logging Trucks* Primitive Camping Allowed Anywhere with Campfire Permit Fee: $12 $5 Additional Vehicle	Power, Row, Canoe & Inflatable Speed Limit - 15 MPH Launch Ramps Rentals: Fishing Boats & Canoes	Fishing: Rainbow, Brown & Brook Trout Picnicking Hiking Horseback Riding & Pack Trips Ferry Service for Backpackers Entry Point to John Muir & Ansel Adams Wilderness Permit Required	Cabins Restaurants Grocery Stores Bait & Tackle Gas Station High Sierra Ranger Station (Seasonal) Ph: (559) 877-3138

PINE FLAT LAKE and AVOCADO LAKE PARK

Pine Flat Lake is at an elevation of 952 feet in the Sierra Foothills east of Fresno. This 20 mile long Lake has 67 miles of generally open shoreline. On average, there are 4,300 surface acres in the spring and summer. A moderate growth of pine and oak trees exists throughout the area. The U. S. Army Corps of Engineers has jurisdiction over the Lake. In addition to the public campgrounds around the Lake, there are private developments along Trimmer Springs Road which offer overnight lodging and R.V. accommodations. Good marina facilities and warm water are attractive to waterskiers, boaters and swimmers. A variety of fish await the angler at this popular Lake. Avocado Lake Park is on the Kings River below Pine Flat Dam. This small 83 surface acre Lake offers non-powered boating and a warm water fishery. There is no camping permitted in the Park but there are nice picnic areas and a swimming beach. *Call Lakes for current information as there can be extreme water fluctuation.*

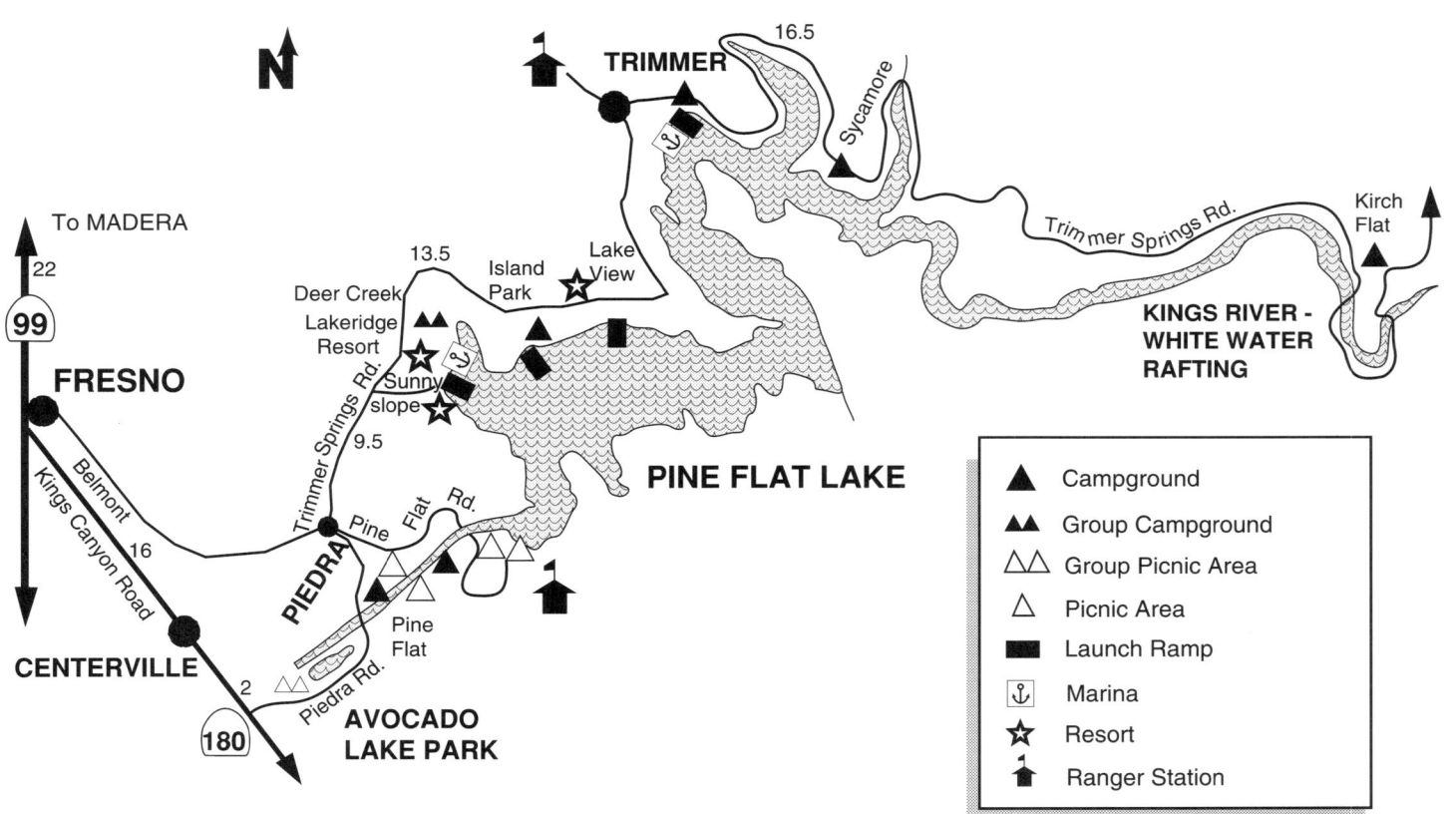

INFORMATION: Pine Flat Lake, P.O. Box 117, Piedra 93649—Ph: (559) 787-2589

CAMPING	BOATING	RECREATION	OTHER
Island Park: 52 Dev. Sites	Pine Flat:	Fishing: Rainbow Trout,	Motel & Cabins
Plus Overflow - Fees: $14	Open to All Boats	Large & Smallmouth Bass,	Restaurants - Lounges
2 Group Sites: Reserve	Including Houseboats	Catfish & Panfish	Snack Bars - Stores
	2 Full Service	Swimming - Picnicking	Bait, Tackle & Gas
Sunnyslope Camp:	Marinas	Hiking - Self-Guided	Disposal Station
Ph: (559) 787-2730	Overnight Mooring	Nature Trail	USFS - Kirch Flat Camp
95 R.V. Sites-Hookups: $16	No Shoreline Camping	Campfire Program	Sites - No Water
	Rentals: Fishing,	River Raft Trips	Ph: (559) 855-8321
Lakeridge Resort	Pontoon & Jets	Hunting: Deer, Quail,	Avocado Lake
Piedra 93649		Dove, Rabbit & Squirrel	Fresno Co. Parks
Ph: (559) 787-2260	Avocado Lake Park:	Designated Areas	2220 Tulare St.
108 Dev. R.V./Tent Sites	No Gas-Powered Boats	Shotguns Only	Fresno 93721
Hookups, Disposal Stat.	Hand Launch	On Corps Land	Ph: (559) 488-3004

Hume Lake, at 5,200 feet, and Sequoia, at 5,300 feet, are in the beautiful Sequoia National Forest. Hume Lake has 85 surface acres and Sequoia has 88 acres. The angler will find trout and the boater is restricted to small non-powered crafts; electric motors are allowed at Hume. Sequoia Lake is operated by the YMCA and is open only to members. Early reservations are advised at this popular camp. Since Sequoia is a private family camp, there is no day use. Be sure to bring your camera to this beautiful country of the Giant Sequoia Trees (survivors of the Ice Age), and the majestic Kings Canyon National Park.

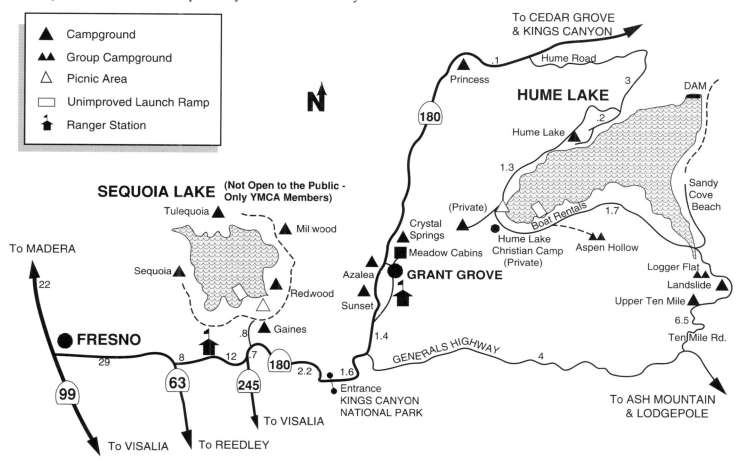

INFORMATION: Hume Lake Ranger District, 35860 E. Kings Canyon Rd., Dunlap 93621—Ph: (559) 338-2251

CAMPING	BOATING	RECREATION	OTHER

Hume Lake:
  75 Dev. Sites for
  Tents & R.V.s - Fee: $14
  No Hookups
  Group Camps- To $113
Reserve *Early*:
  Ph: (800) 280-CAMP
Nearby Campgrounds:
  180 Plus Sites
Sequoia Family Camp
  Central Valley YMCA
  1408 "N" St.
  Fresno 93721
	Hume Lake: Open to All
	  Non-Powered Boats
	  Electric Motors O.K.
	  5 MPH Speed Limit
	  Hand Launch
	  Boat Rentals at
	    Christian Camp
	
	Sequoia: Not Open to the
	  General Public
	  Only YMCA Members
		Fishing:
		  Hume Lake
		    Rainbow &
		    Brown Trout
		Picnicking & Swimming
		Hiking & Backpacking
		Hunting: Deer
		Nature Study
			Hume Lake Christian
			  Camp - Gas, Store,
			  Restaurant
			  Ph: (559) 335-2881
			
			Sequoia Family Camp
			  Meals, Store, Craft
			  Materials, Laundry
			  Before July 1
			  Ph: (209) 233-5737
			  After July 1
			  Ph: (559) 335-2382

DIAZ LAKE and PLEASANT VALLEY RESERVOIR

Diaz Lake rests at an elevation of 3,700 feet on the eastern slope of the Sierra, 15 miles from the Mt. Whitney Trailhead. This 86 surface acre Lake offers varied boating and is popular with waterskiers. A ramp and an 80 foot floating dock are available. There is both a trout and warm water fishery.

Pleasant Valley, at 4,200 feet, is often a good trout lake but boating is not permitted. A 15 minute hiking trail goes to the Lake from the campground. Inyo County developed picnic tables, barbecues and restroom facilities at Pleasant Valley and handicapped restroom facilities at Diaz Lake. Tinnemaha Reservoir is open to trout fishing year round. This entire area has numerous ORV trails.

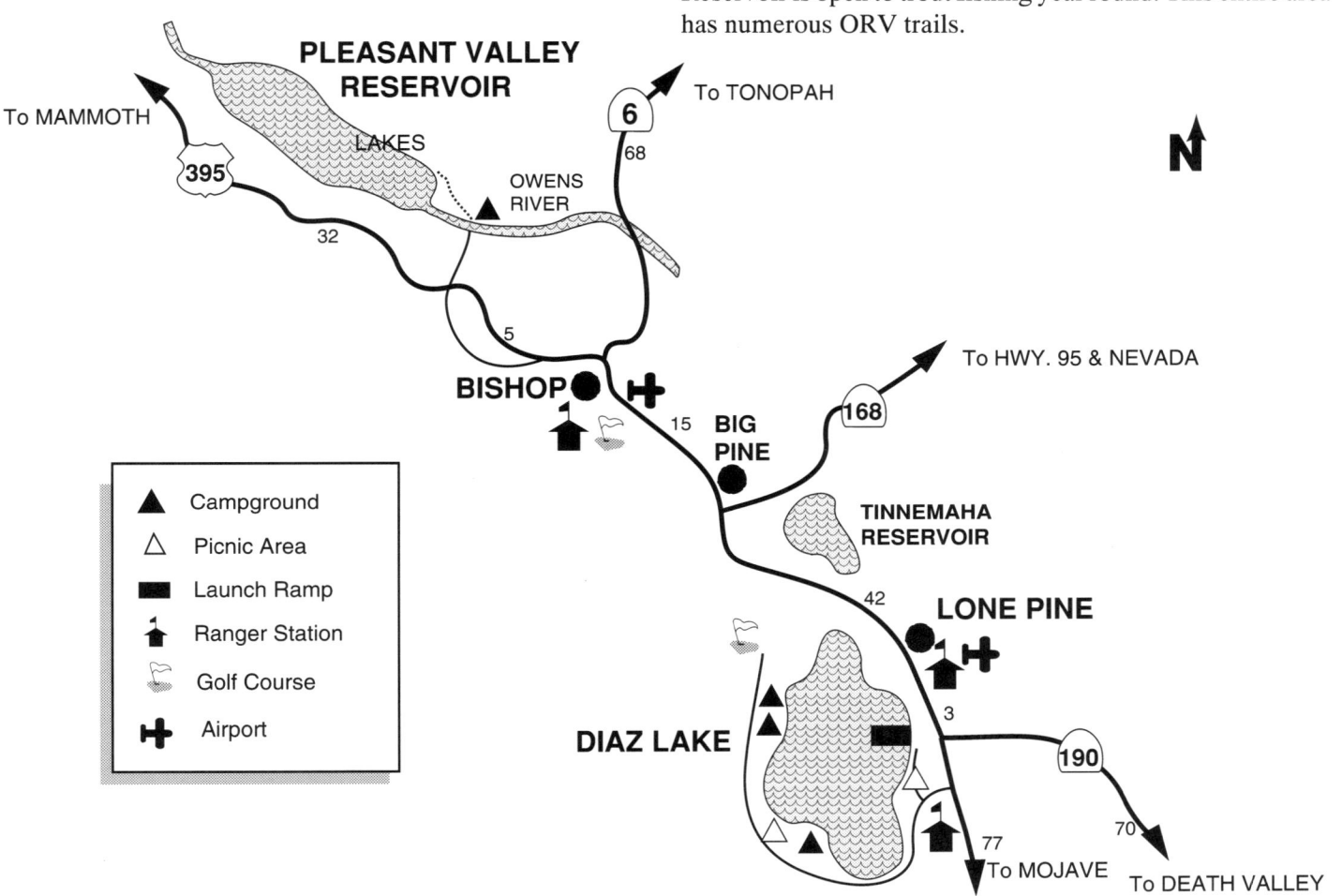

INFORMATION: Inyo County Parks, P.O. Box 237, Independence 93526—Ph: (760) 878-0272

CAMPING	BOATING	RECREATION	OTHER
Pleasant Valley: 200 Tent & R.V. Sites No Hookups-Fee: $6 Diaz Lake: 200 Tent & R.V. Sites No Hookups - Fee: $7 Group Camping 2 Week Advance Reservations Ph: (760) 876-5656	Diaz Lake: Power, Row, Canoe, Sail, Waterski, Jets & Inflatables, Launch Ramp - $6 Speed Limit - 35 MPH May through Oct. Speed Limit - 15 MPH Nov. through April Maximum Boat Size: 22 Ft. *Noise Level Laws are Strictly Enforced* No Boats at Pleasant Valley	Fishing: Rainbow & Brown Trout, Smallmouth Bass, Bluegill & Catfish Swimming- Beaches Picnicking Hiking & Backpacking Horse Trips into Back Country Hang Gliding Hunting: Waterfowl ORV Trails	Diaz Lake Information: Diaz Lake P.O. Box 503 Lone Pine 93545 Ph: (760) 876-5656 Full Facilities: Bishop & Lone Pine

Numbers around highways represent lakes in numerical order in this book. *See Index for complete listing.*

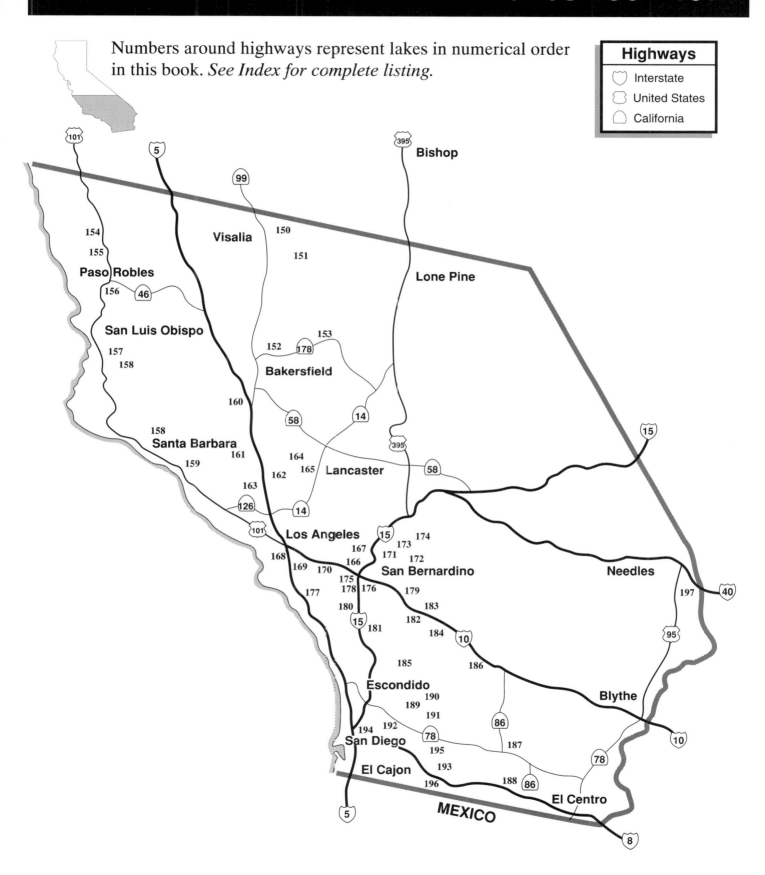

Lake Kaweah rests at an elevation of 694 feet in the rolling foothills below Sequoia National Park. It was created with the damming of the Kaweah River about 20 miles upstream from Visalia. The Lake is 6 miles long with 22 miles of shoreline surrounded by oak-studded hills. There is a total surface area of 1,945 acres when full but there is often a 100 foot drop late in the season. The U. S. Army Corps of Engineers maintain

Terminus Dam, a 250 foot high and 2,375 foot long earth filled dam, along with the nice campgrounds, picnic areas and marina facilities. This is a good boating Lake for varied craft including houseboats which are popular along the many coves and inlets. Fishing can be good for a broad variety of game fish. *Submerged rocks are a hazard during low water.*

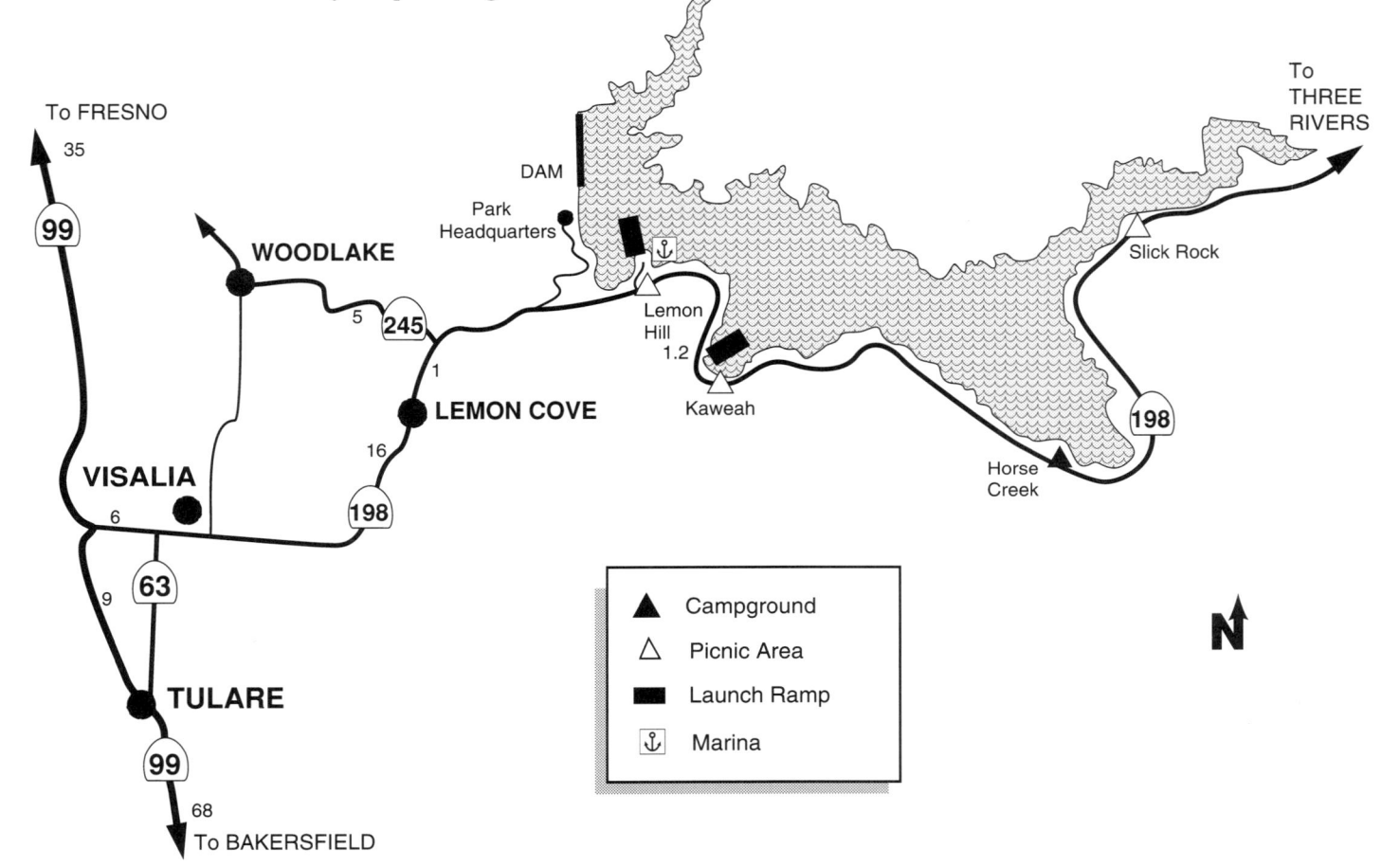

INFORMATION: U.S. Army Corps of Engineers, P.O. Box 346, Lemon Cove 93244—Ph: (559) 597-2301

CAMPING	BOATING	RECREATION	OTHER
80 Dev. Sites for Tents & R.V.s (Handicap Site by Reservation) Overnight on Boat Permitted Anywhere Away From Shore	Power, Row, Canoe, Sail, Waterski, Jets Full Service Marina Launch Ramps Rentals: Fishing Boats, Houseboats & Pontoons Docks, Berths Moorings, Gas *Low Water Late in Season Submerged Rock Hazards*	Fishing: Florida & Spotted Bass, Bluegill, Channel Catfish, Black & White Crappie, Sunfish Rainbow Trout in Season Swimming Picnicking Campfire Program	Snack Bar Bait & Tackle Disposal Station Full Facilities at Woodlake and Three Rivers

Success Lake rests at an elevation of 640 feet in the southern Sierra foothills. The Lake has a surface area of 2,450 acres with 30 miles of shoreline. The U.S. Army Corps of Engineers has jurisdiction over the abundant and well-maintained camping, marine and recreation facilities. There is a Wildlife Area open for public use with hunting allowed, shotguns only, during appropriate seasons. The bird watcher may find several rare or endangered species, such as the Bald Eagle. There is good fishing year round and all types of boating are permitted from houseboats to waterskiing at this complete facility.

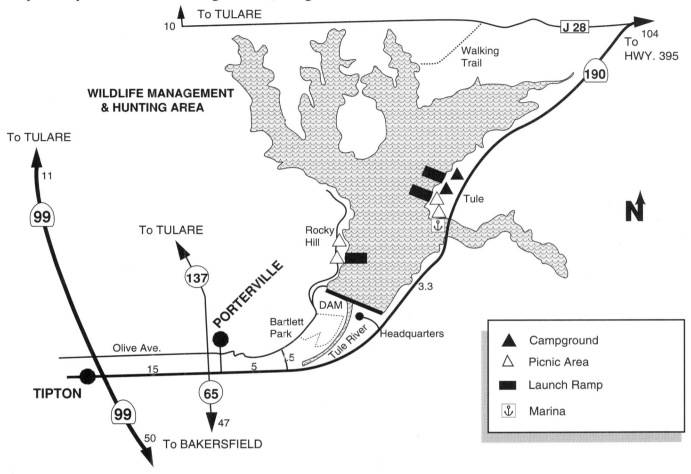

INFORMATION: Park Manager, P.O. Box 1072, Porterville 93258—Ph: (559) 784-0215

CAMPING	BOATING	RECREATION	OTHER
104 Dev. Sites for Tents & R.V.s Fee: $10 - $14 Extra Vehicle: $7 Overnight in Boat Permitted	Power, Row, Canoe, Sail, Waterski, Jets, Windsurf & Inflatable Full Service Marina Ph: (559) 781-2078 Launch Ramps Rentals: Fishing, Houseboats & Pontoons Berths (Maximum Boat Length - 30 ft.) Docks, Moorings, Gas	Fishing: Largemouth Bass, Catfish, Bluegill, Crappie, Swimming Hiking Bird Watching Hunting: Pheasant, Dove & Rabbit Horseback Riding Wildlife Area	Grocery Store Bait & Tackle Hot Showers Disposal Station 24 Hour Information: Ph: (559) 783-9200 Full Facilities 5 Miles at Porterville

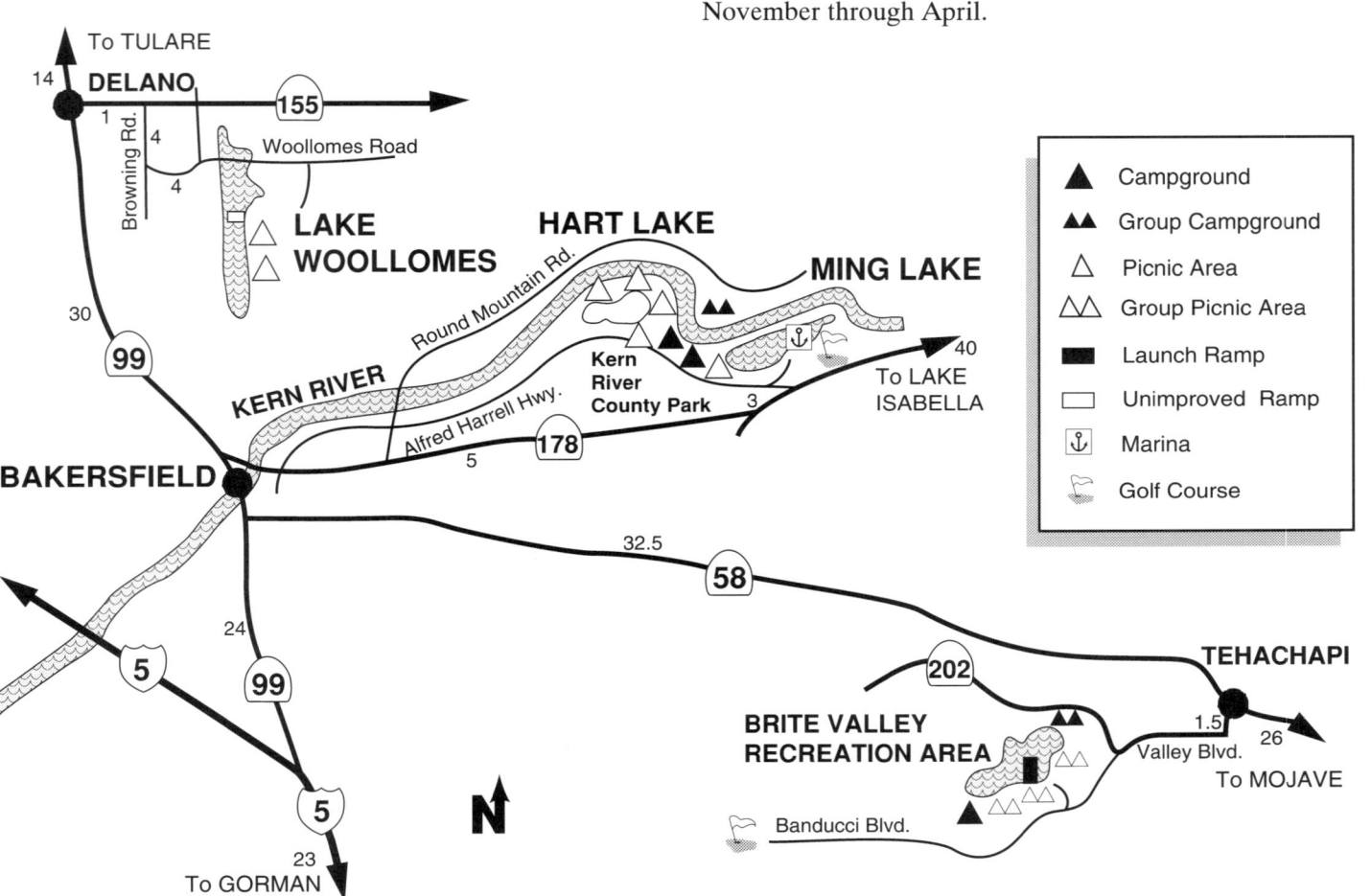

WOOLLOMES, HART and MING LAKES

The nice facilities at Hart, Woollomes and Ming Lakes are under the jurisdiction of Kern County. The Kern River County Park has campsites and picnic areas within its 28 landscaped acres. Lake Woollomes, 300 surface acres, and Hart Lake, 18 surface acres, offer non-powered boating and fishing. Lake Ming, 104 surface acres, is primarily a waterskiing, power boating and drag racing Lake but sailing and fishing as scheduled below are added attractions. Brite Valley is under the jurisdiction of the Tehachapi Valley Recreation and Parks Department. This 90 surface acre Lake rests at an elevation of 4,000 feet. It is open during the warmer months for non-powered boating and fishing but closed from November through April.

To TULARE

14 **DELANO**

155

Browning Rd.

Woollomes Road

1

4

4

LAKE WOOLLOMES

HART LAKE

MING LAKE

Round Mountain Rd.

KERN RIVER

Kern River County Park

Alfred Harrell Hwy.

30

99

178

5

3

40

To LAKE ISABELLA

	Campground
▲▲	Group Campground
△	Picnic Area
△△	Group Picnic Area
■	Launch Ramp
▢	Unimproved Ramp
⚓	Marina
	Golf Course

BAKERSFIELD

32.5

58

202

TEHACHAPI

5

24

99

BRITE VALLEY RECREATION AREA

1.5

26

Valley Blvd.

To MOJAVE

5

N

Banducci Blvd.

23

To GORMAN

INFORMATION: Kern County Parks, 1110 Golden State Ave., Bakersfield 93301—Ph: (661) 868-7000

CAMPING	BOATING	RECREATION	OTHER

Kern River County Park:
    50 Dev. Sites for Tents
    & R.V.s - No Hookups
    Fees: March 15-Oct. 15:
    $12 Per Vehicle
    Oct. 16-March 14: $8
    No Reservations
    Disposal Station
Brite Valley:
    Unlimited Open Camping
    Dry Camp: $9
    12 Water & Electric
    Hookups: $12
	Woollomes & Hart:
	    Sail, Canoe, Row &
	    Pedal Boats Only
	Day Use Fee: $3
	Ming:
	Designated Waterski Area
	Power Boats & Drag Races
	    Sailing Only - Allowed on
	    Tuesdays & Thursdays
	    After 1:30 pm and the
	2nd Full Weekend of Month
	Brite Valley:
	    Electric Motors Only
		Fishing: Largemouth
		    Bass, Bluegill,
		    Crappie & Catfish
		Hart & Ming: Trout in
		    Winter
		Brite Valley: Trout, Catfish
		    & Bass
		Family & Group
		    Picnicking
		Hiking
		Swimming at
		    Woollomes Only
		Golf Course
			Brite Valley Aquatic
			    Recreation Area
			    Information:
			    Tehachapi Valley
			    Recreation & Parks
			    P.O. Box 373
			    Tehachapi 93581
			    Ph: (661) 822-3228

Isabella Lake lies at an elevation of 2,605 feet in the foothills east of Bakersfield. The surface area of the Lake is over 11,000 acres with a shoreline of 38 miles. The U. S. Forest Service maintains the excellent and ample facilities at this complete recreation facility. The main attractions at Isabella are boating, fishing and waterskiing. Sailing and windsurfing are also popular. Activities range from white water rafting to bird watching. A trap range is available and hunting is allowed in designated areas. Lake Patrol and Rescue Service are handled by the Kern County Parks Department in Bakersfield - Ph: (760) 861-2345. Annual Boat Permits are required and can be obtained at any one of the Marinas or at the Crossroads MiniMart in Lake Isabella.

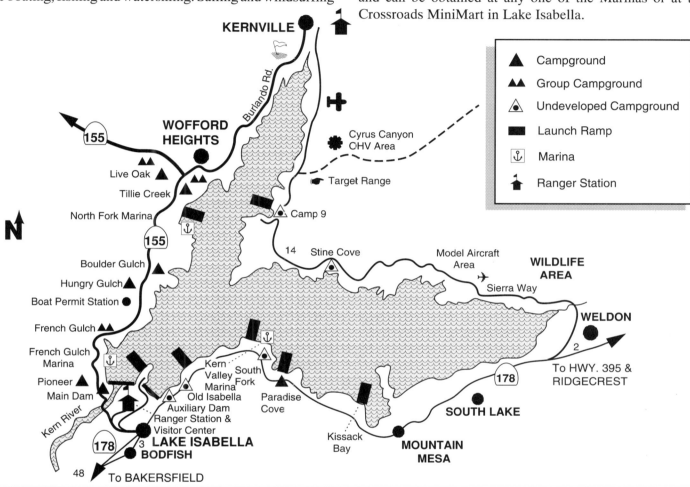

INFORMATION: Visitors Center, 4875 Ponderosa Dr., P.O. Box 3810, Lake Isabella 93240—Ph: (760) 379-5646

CAMPING	BOATING	RECREATION	OTHER
800 Dev. Sites for Tents & R.V.s Fee: $14	Power, Row, Canoe, Sail, Waterski, Jets, Windsurf	Fishing: Trout, Catfish, Bluegill, Crappie &	Full Facilities at Towns Near Lake
Group Camps: $90-$185 Reserve: Ph: (800) 280-CAMP	& Inflatables With Restrictions	Largemouth Bass Fish Cleaning Station	Airport-Auto Rentals Golf Course Campfire Programs
Plus Primitive Campsites No Fee	*Annual Boat Permit: $20 No Single Use*	Swimming Picnicking	Nature Study Trailer Rentals &
Most Campgrounds have Playgrounds	Launch Ramps Full Service Marinas	Hiking Mountain Biking	Storage OHV Use Area
5 Disposal Stations	Rentals: Fishing & Waterski Boats Docks, Berths Moorings, Gas	White Water Rafting Birdwatching Hunting: Quail & Waterfowl	Rifle & Trap Range

SAN ANTONIO LAKE

San Antonio Lake is at an elevation of 900 feet in the oak-covered rolling hills of Southern Monterey County. The Lake has a surface area of 5,500 acres with 60 shoreline miles. There is an abundance of modern campsites, many with full hookups. With mild water temperatures, this is an ideal Lake for waterskiing with a length of 16 miles and calm waters protected by the surrounding hills. An excellent warm water fishery makes San Antonio a good year round angler's Lake. The facilities are open all year with complete services for vacation activities. *Call for current water level conditions.*

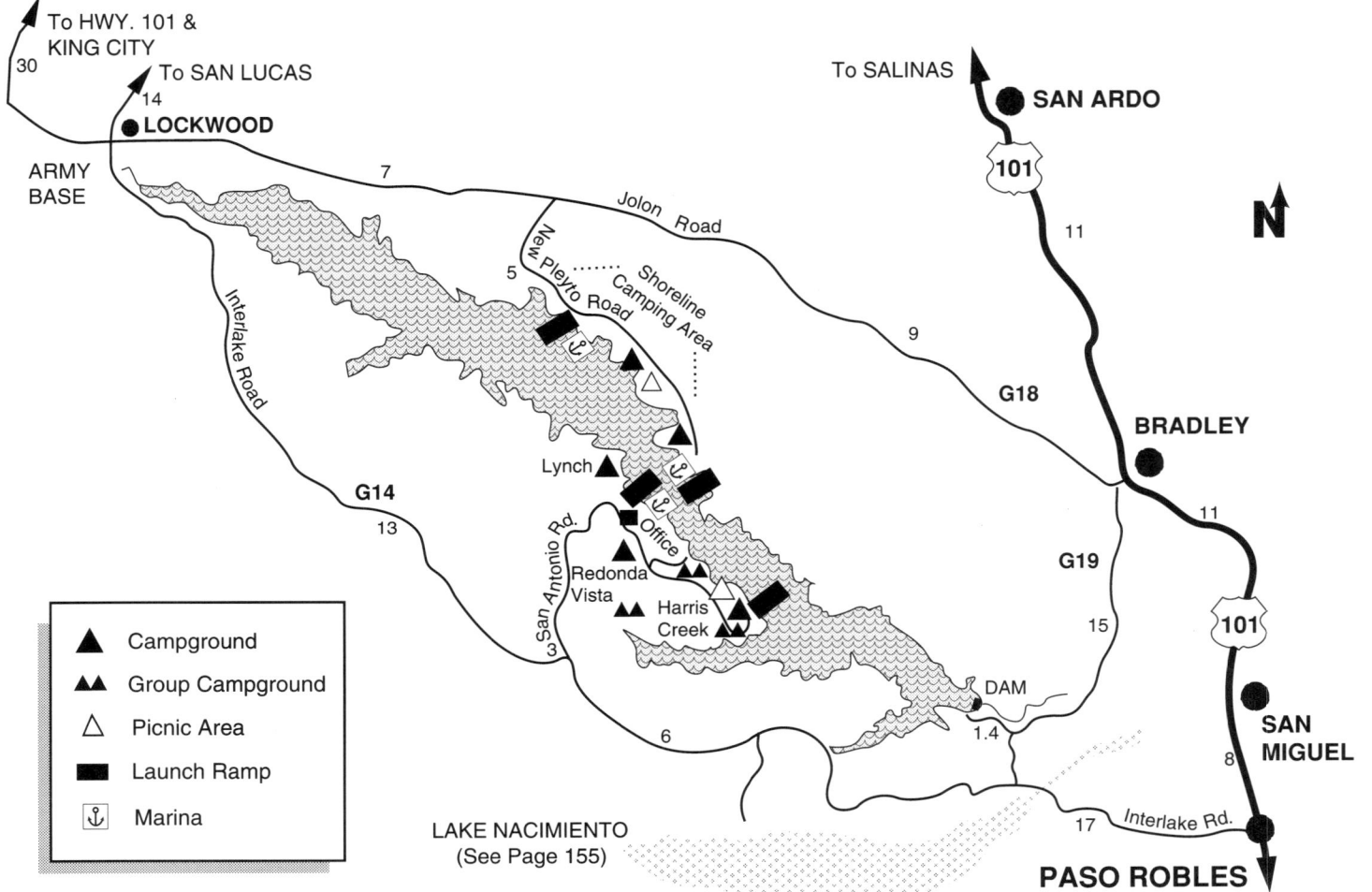

INFORMATION: Monterey County Parks Dept., Star Rt Box. 2610, Bradley 93426—Ph: (805) 472-2311

CAMPING	BOATING	RECREATION	OTHER
767 Dev. Sites for Tents & R.V.s Some With Full Hookups Fees: Winter - $16 - $20 Summer - $18 - $22 Youth Campground to 60 People North Shoreline Camping Group Camping 10 or More Sites Ph: (805) 472-2311 Disposal Stations	Power, Row, Canoe, Sail, Waterski, Jets, Windsurf & Inflatable Full Service Marinas Launch Ramps - $5 Rentals: Fishing Boats, Pontoons, Ski Boats & Jets Docks, Mooring, Gas, Dry Storage Summer Boat Rides	Fishing: Catfish, Bluegill, Large & Smallmouth Bass, Striped Bass, Redear Perch & Crappie Swimming - Beach Picnicking Hiking Trails Mountain Biking Nature Study, Birdwatching Exercise Course Summer Movies	Cafe Grocery Store Bait & Tackle Laundromat Gas Station Game Room Mobile Home Rentals Reservations: Ph: (800) 310-2313

LAKE NACIMIENTO

Lake Nacimiento is nestled in a valley of pine and oak trees at an elevation of 800 feet. The surface area is 5,370 acres with 165 miles of shoreline and many delightful coves. Warm, gentle winds are ideal for boating. Fishing from shore or boat will usually produce bass, either large, smallmouth or white bass. Crappie, bluegill and catfish are also plentiful.

Waterskiing is excellent on the 16-mile long Lake with water temperature about 68 degrees. There are lakeshore lodge accommodations and a good restaurant. Lake Nacimiento Resort offers an abundance of modern campsites, complete marina facilities and vacation activities, making it an excellent family recreation area.

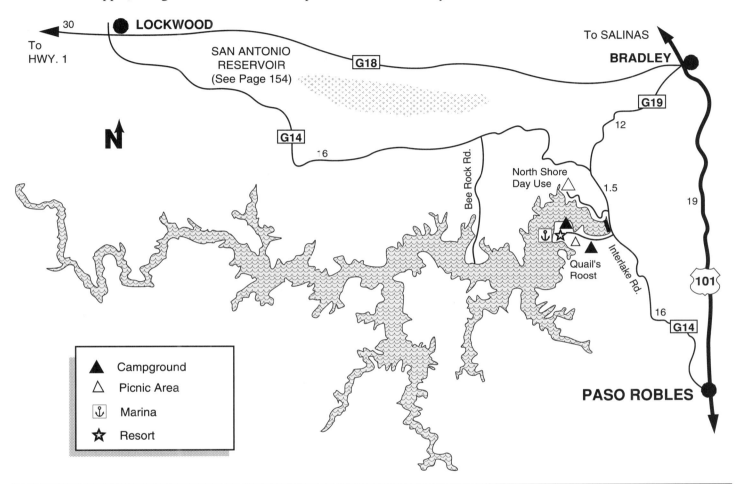

INFORMATION: Resort, 10625 Nacimiento Lake Dr., Bradley 93426—Ph: (805) 238-3256 or (800) 323-3839

CAMPING	BOATING	RECREATION	OTHER
350 Dev. Sites for Tents & R.V.s Fees: $22/Night $130/Week 40 R.V. Sites With Full Hookups Fees: $27/Night $160/Week Group Sites Available Oct. 1 - March 1 Winter Rates in Effect Oct. 1 to April 1	Power, Row, Canoe, Sail, Waterski, Jets, Windsurf & Inflatable Full Service Marina 3 Launch Ramps Slalom Course Rentals: Fishing Bass Boats, Pontoons, Pleasure Boats & Jets County Water Use Fee: $5 a Day/$75 Year	Fishing: Catfish, Bluegill, Crappie, White, Large & Smallmouth Bass Swimming Picnicking Hiking *No Motorcycles of Any Type* Day Use Fee: $10 - South Shore	Lodges Restaurant Grocery Store Bait & Tackle Hot Showers & Laundry Disposal Station Gas & Propane Camp Trailer Rental Playgrounds Volleyball & Horseshoes Swimming Pool Summer Only

SANTA MARGARITA LAKE, WHALE ROCK RESERVOIR and ATASCADERO LAKE

Nestled amid Central California's coastal range, these Lakes vary in recreational opportunities. Santa Margarita, the largest of the three with 1,070 surface acres, is a warm water fisherman's delight with nearby camping facilities. Although waterskiing and windsurfing are not permitted, it is a good boating Lake. Atascadero is a small city Lake with picnic facilities, a concession and rental boats. Power boating is not allowed. You may fish for trout and bass. The City of San Luis Obispo does not allow boating or any water contact at Whale Rock Reservoir. There is a 3 trout limit per day.

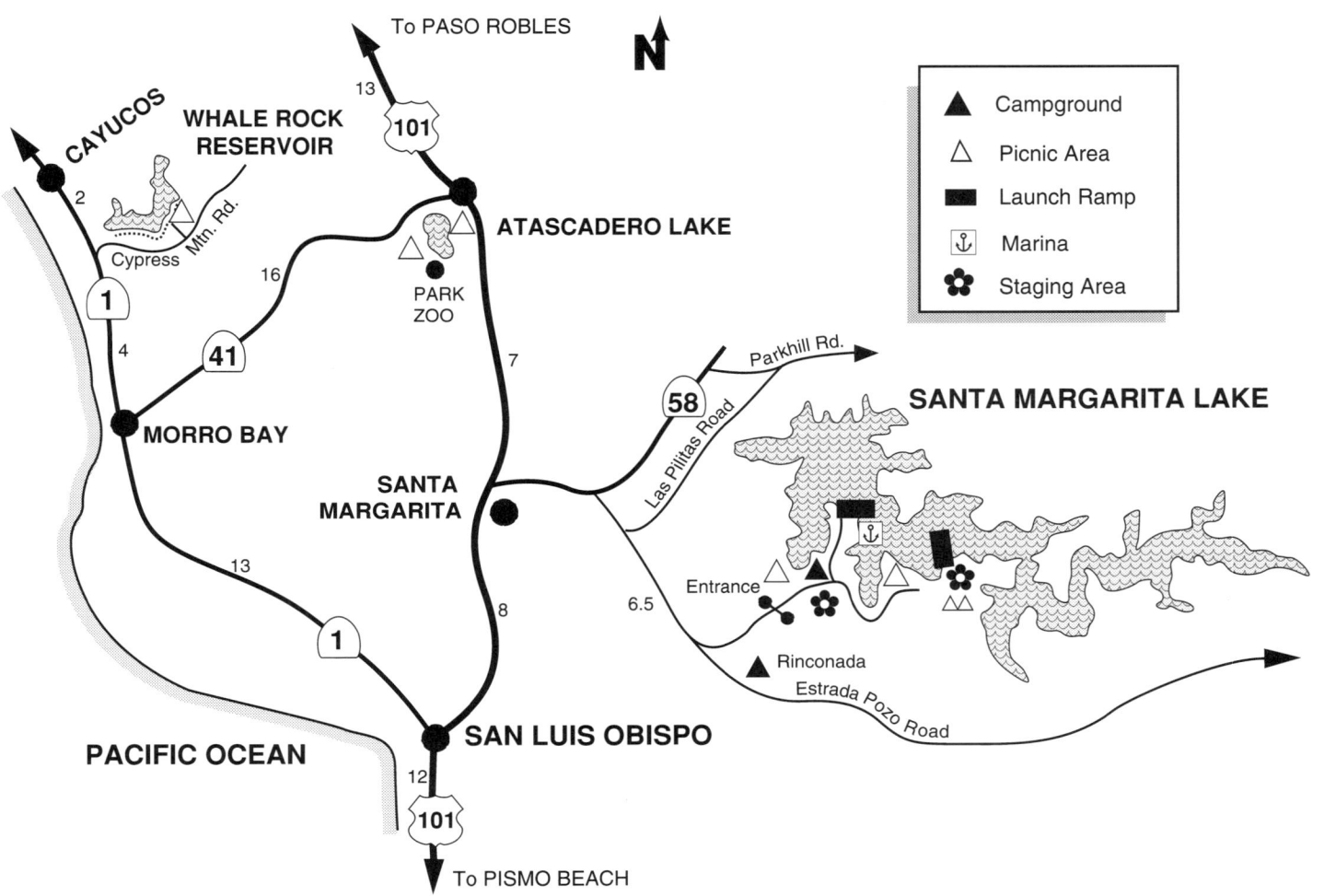

INFORMATION: Santa Margarita Lake Reg. Park, Star Route Box 36, Santa Margarita 93453—Ph: (805) 438-5485

CAMPING	BOATING	RECREATION	OTHER
Santa Margarita: 65 Tent/R.V. Sites Full & Partial Hookups Fees: $18 Primitive Boat-In Sites Reserve: Ph: (805) 489-8019 Rinconada Camp: Ph: (805) 438-5479 60 Tent/R.V. Sites 17 With Full Hookups Fee: $12 - $18	Santa Margarita: Boats Over 10 Feet Allowed *No Waterskiing or Windsurfing* Approved Inflatable Full Service Marina Rentals: Fishing Boats & Motors, Pontoons Launch Ramp Whale Rock: No Boating	Fishing: Rainbow Trout, Bluegill, Catfish, Crappie & Black Bass Swimming : St. Margarita - Pool Only Atascadero - Kiddie Pool Only Whale Rock - None Picnicking - Group Site at Santa Margarita: Ph: (805) 781-5219 Hiking & Riding Trails	Santa Margarita: Snacks & Drinks Bait & Tackle Atascadero: Phone: (805) 461-5003 Boating: Restricted No Power Boats 5 MPH Speed Limit *No Waterskiing or Windsurfing* Hand Launch Only Rentals: Pedal Boats

Lopez Lake, with 22 shoreline miles, is administered by the San Luis Obispo County Parks and Recreation Department. Its 950 surface acres are favored by westerly breezes coming off the Pacific which make it a popular Lake for sailing and windsurfing. There are good marine support facilities and special areas are set aside for sailing, windsurfing, jets and waterskiing. The angler will find a variety of game fish. In addition to the well maintained oak-shaded campsites listed below, there are overflow sites. This is a complete recreation facility offering a good naturalist program which can be enjoyed on trails, by boat or at the campfire. The two 600-foot waterslides are popular with the youngsters.

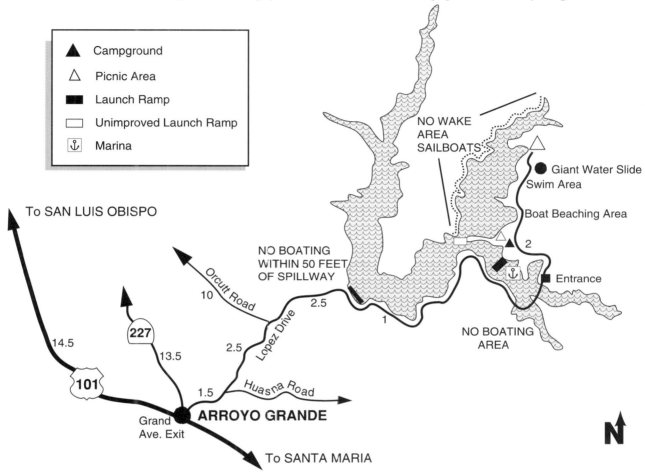

INFORMATION: Lopez Lake, 6800 Lopez Dr., Arroyo Grande 93420—Ph: (805) 489-2095

CAMPING	BOATING	RECREATION	OTHER
148 Primitive Sites for Tents & R.V.s Fee: $13 135 Sites with Full Hookups Fee: $18 - $21 67 Sites - Summer Only with Electric Hookups Fee: $16 Reservations: Ph: (805) 489-8019 Mon.-Fri. - 8 am - 5 pm Day Use Fee: $5	Open to All Boating Speed Limit: 40 MPH Full Service Marina Paved Launch: Non-Motor $2.50 Motor $5 Mooring Boat/Trailer Storage Rentals: Fishing, Ski, Patio, Canoe, Paddle Boats & Waverunners	Fishing: Trout, Catfish, Bluegill, Crappie, Redear Sunfish & Black Bass Swimming: In Designated Areas Picnicking - Group Sites Hiking & Nature Trails Boat Tours Campfire Programs	Marina & Store Ph: (805) 489-1006 Snack Bar General Store Bait & Tackle Laundromat Gas Station Mustang Water Slides & Hot Spas Ph: (805) 489-8898 Pets: $2 a Day Proof of Dog Ownership & Leash Required

LAKE CACHUMA

Lake Cachuma is nestled at an elevation of 800 feet amid the oak-shaded hills of the Santa Ynez Valley. This is one of the most complete recreation parks in the State providing an abundance of modern camping, marine, recreation and other support facilities. In addition to the campgrounds at the Lake, the Cachuma Recreation Area includes Live Oak Camp which will accommodate large groups to 4,000 people with complete facilities. This 3,200 acre Lake is open to most boating but waterskiing, kayaks, rafts and canoes are not allowed. Fishing can be excellent. There are hiking, nature and riding trails. Swimming pools and bicycle rentals are open from June through Labor Day. Park naturalists conduct a variety of programs. Gibraltar Reservoir is open for trout fishing on a limited permit basis through the City of Santa Barbara.

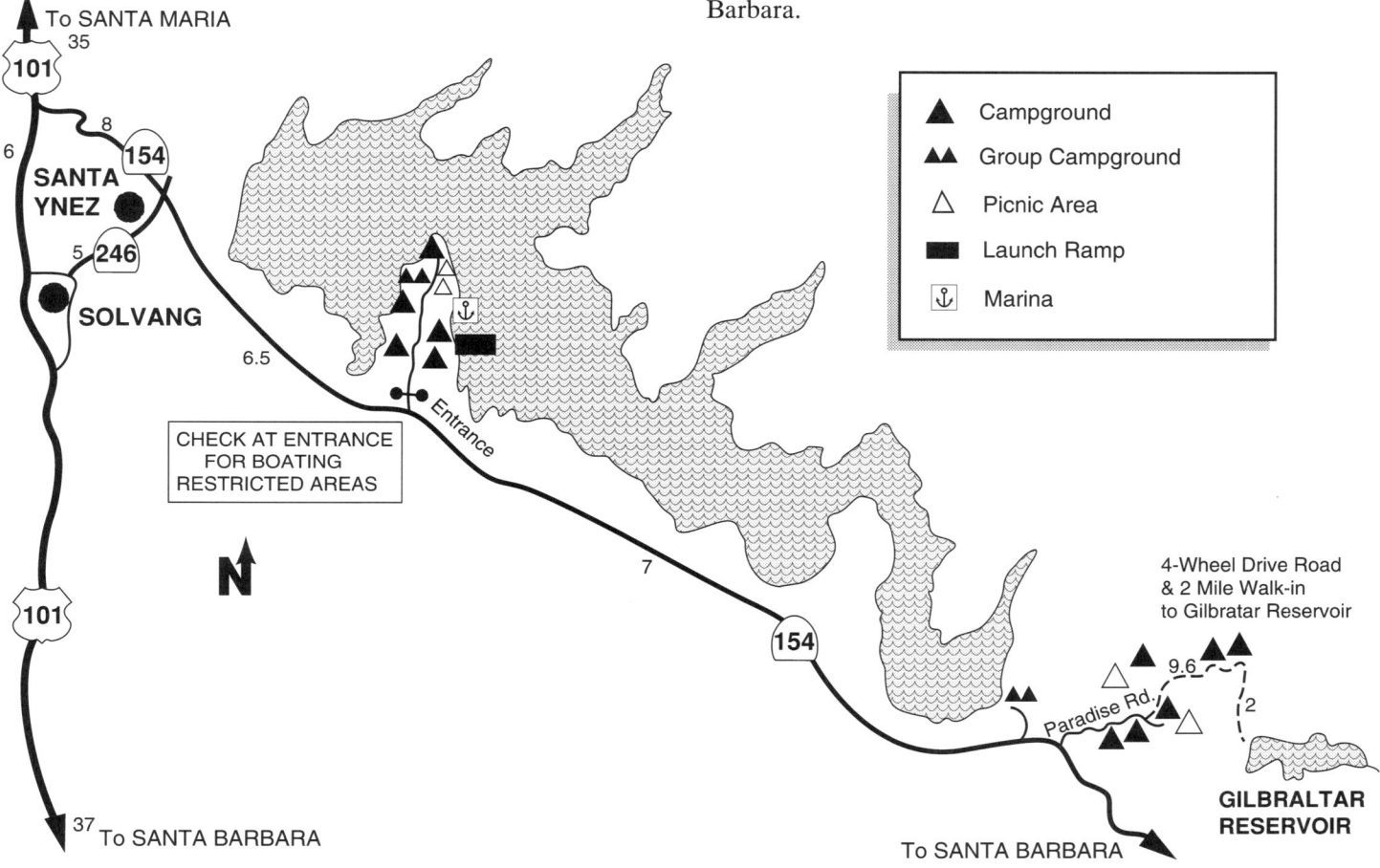

INFORMATION: Cachuma Lake, HC 58, Santa Barbara 93105—Ph: (805) 686-5054

CAMPING	BOATING	RECREATION	OTHER
414 Dev. Sites for Tents & R.V.s Fees: $8 - $13 90 R.V. Sites Full and Partial Hookups Fees: $16 - $18 9 Group Camps 8 to 30 Units 3 Disposal Stations	Open to Most Boating Contact Above for Restrictions Launch Ramp Full Service Marina Docks, Berths & Moorings Trailer & Boat Storage Rentals: Fishing, Patio & Sailboats	Fishing: Catfish, Bluegill, Crappie, Large & Smallmouth Bass, Sunfish, Rainbow Trout Birdwatching Swimming: Pools Only Picnicking Hiking & Riding Trails Bicycle Rentals Nature Programs & Tours	Handicap Facilities 5 Restrooms with Hot Showers General Store Bait & Tackle Snack Bar Laundromat Recreation Center Pools Gas Station

Lake Casitas is at an elevation of 600 feet in the oak-covered rolling hills west of Ojai. This 2,700 surface acre Lake is under the jurisdiction of the Casitas Municipal Water District which maintains a strict boating and swimming policy - no body contact with the water. The 32 miles of shoreline has many restricted areas, so please note them on the map. Casitas is famous for big fish and once held the State record for largemouth bass at 21 pounds, 3 ounces. It also holds the State record for redear sunfish at 3 pounds, 7 ounces. You can fish from boat, bank or pier and perhaps catch a World's Record. The 6,200 acre tree-shaded recreation area offers excellent picnicking, camping and boating facilities.

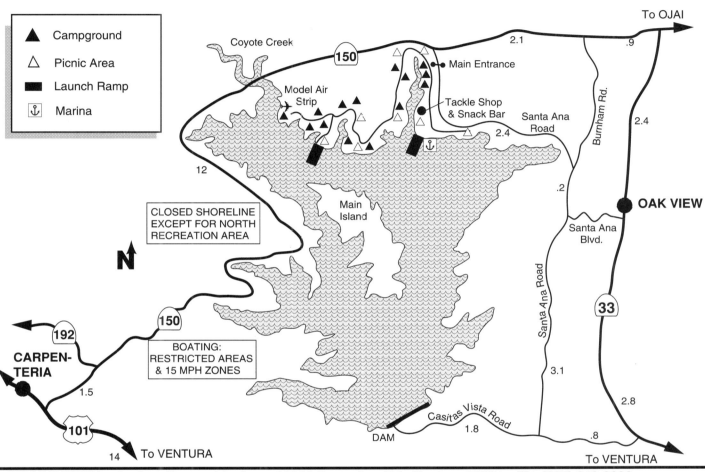

INFORMATION: Casitas Recreation Area, 11311 Santa Ana Rd., Ventura 93001—Ph: (805) 649-2233

CAMPING	BOATING	RECREATION	OTHER
400 Plus Dev. Sites Tents & R.V.s - Hookups	Power, Row, Sail *Only* 11 ft. Min.	Fishing: Catfish, Trout, Bluegill, Largemouth	Snack Bar Restaurant
Fees: $12 - $18	to 24 ft. Max. -	& Florida Bass,	Grocery Store
$9.50 Extra Vehicle	*Strict Regulations*	Redear Sunfish,	Showers - 25 cents
$7 For Boat	*Call for Information*	Perch & Crappie	Bait & Tackle
Group Sites: $220	Speed Limit - 35 MPH	Picnicking	Trailer Rentals
Reservations Advised	Boat Permit: $5/Day	Hiking	Trailer & Boat
Ph: (805) 649-1122	Full Service Marina	Playgrounds	Storage
Reservation Fee: $5.50	Launch Ramps	Model Airplane Strip	Frequent Visitor
Disposal Stations	Rentals:	Bicycle Rentals	Discount Cards
Handicap Facilities	Row Boats & Pontoons	Water Playground	
Day Use: $6.50 per Vehicle	Docks, Moorings,		
With Boat: $11.50	Berths, Gas, Storage		

LAKE EVANS and LAKE WEBB— BUENA VISTA AQUATIC RECREATION AREA

Buena Vista Recreation Area is at an elevation of 293 feet in the semi-arid south San Joaquin Valley. This is Kern County's finest recreation area consisting of 1,586 acres and two Lakes with complete modern facilities for camping, picnicking, swimming and boating. Lake Evans has a surface area of 86 acres and Lake Webb has 873 acres. Both Lakes are stocked continually with warm water game fish. Trophy trout are stocked in the winter months at Lake Evans. Boating is allowed in both Lakes but Lake Evans is restricted to a 5 MPH speed limit. Waterskiing is permitted at Lake Webb in a counterclockwise pattern. There is a a designated area for sailboats and power boats without skiers.

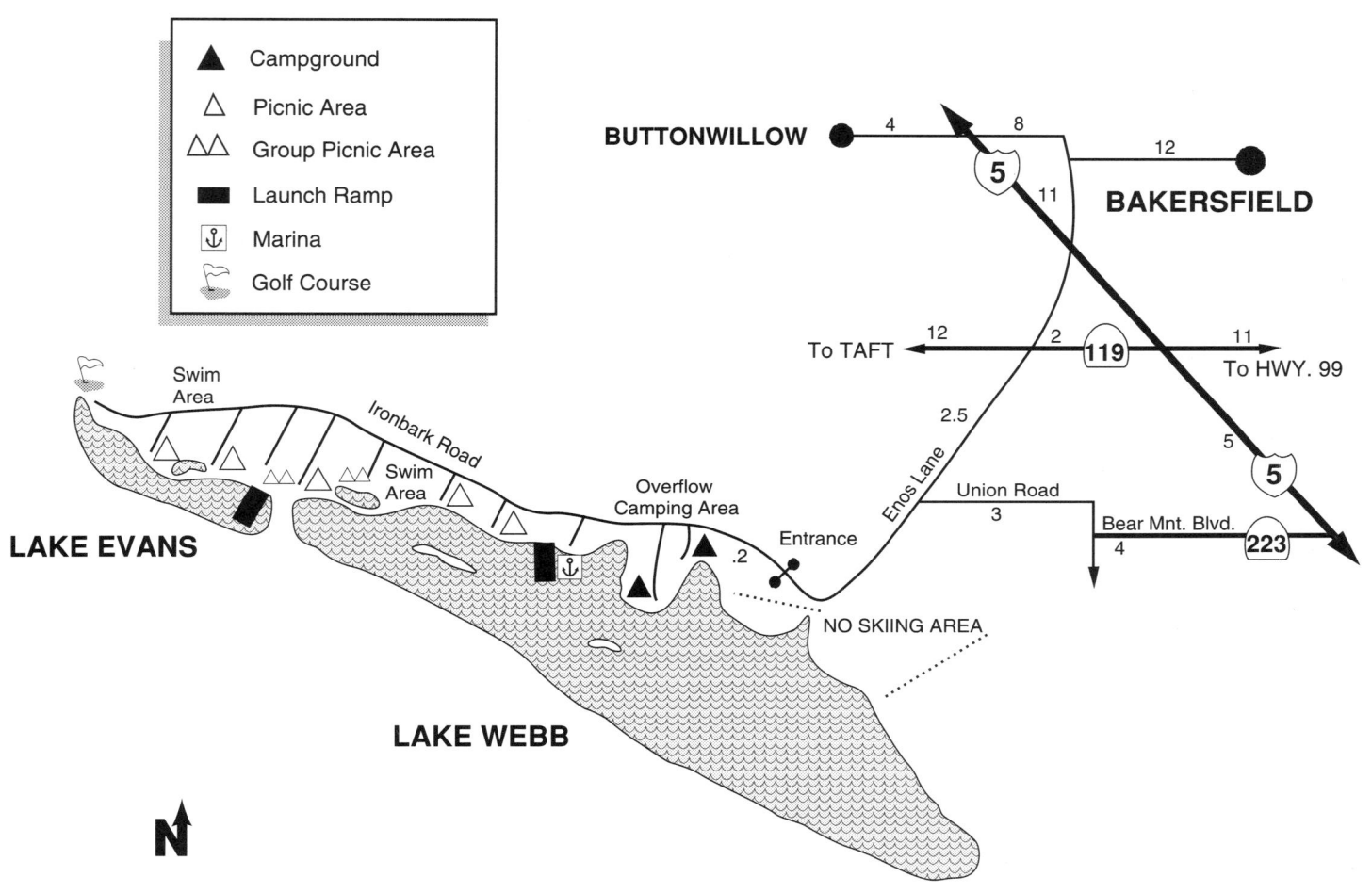

INFORMATION: Kern County Parks, 1110 Golden State Ave., Bakersfield 93301—Ph: (661) 868-7000

CAMPING	BOATING	RECREATION	OTHER
112 Dev. Sites for Tents & R.V.s	Power, Row, Canoe, Sail, Windsurf,	Fishing: Trout in Winter, Catfish,	Gate Ph: (661) 861-2063 Ranger Ph: (661) 861-2062
Fees: No Hookups $18 - $22	Jets & Inflatable Meet Requirements	Bluegill, Crappie, Largemouth &	Snack Bar Grocery Store
Full Hookups $21 - $26	Speed Limits: 5 MPH - Lake Evans	Striped Bass Lake Evans: Fishing $5	Beer & Wine Bait & Tackle
Plus Overflow Area Fee: $8	45 MPH - Lake Webb Launch Ramps: $7	Swimming: Lagoons Only	Gas Station Propane
Camping Reservations: Ph: (661) 868-7050	Docks, Moorings, Gas Rentals:	Picnicking Deep Pit Barbecues	
Pets - $3 a Day	Lake Evans-(661)763-1268 Lake Webb-(661) 763-1770	Waterski Beaches	Full Facilities 14 Miles at Taft
Day Use: $5			

PYRAMID LAKE

Pyramid Lake is at an elevation of 2,606 feet in the Angeles National Forest in Northwestern Los Angeles County. This popular Lake has a surface area of 1,297 acres. Most of its 21 miles of rugged shoreline is accessible only by boat. There are boat-in picnic sites and restrooms scattered around the Lake. Spanish Point is a favorite spot with its picnic sites and ski beach. While there is a good trout and warm water fishery,

Pyramid is known as one of Southern California's prime striped bass waters. There are good marine and campground facilities under concession from the U.S. Forest Service. Quail Lake, the beginning of the southern portion of the California Aqueduct, offers no facilities. Anglers can fish from the bank for striped bass.

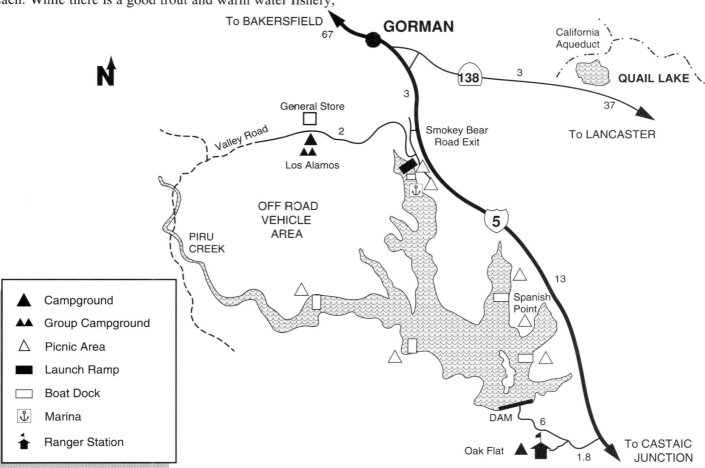

INFORMATION: Pyramid Lake, c/o Pyramid Enterprises, P.O. Box 249, Piru 93040—Ph: (661) 295-1245

CAMPING	BOATING	RECREATION	OTHER
Los Alamos: 93 Dev. Sites Tents & R.V.s Fee: $10 First Come First Serve 3 Group Sites for 30 People Each Ph: (800) 416-6992	Open to All Boating, Waterskiing & Windsurfing Speed Limit 35 MPH Full Service Marina Docks & Slip Rentals Launch Ramp Rentals: Fishing Boats Pyramid Marina Ph: (661) 257-2892	Fishing: Rainbow Trout, Channel Catfish, Striped & Largemouth Bass, Bluegill, Crappie & Sunfish Swimming Beaches Picnicking Boat-In Picnic Sites Off Road Vehicles Designated Area	Snack Bar Bait & Tackle Fish Cleaning Station

CASTAIC LAKE

Castaic Lake and the Afterbay Lagoon, at an elevation of 1,500 feet, are a part of the California State Water Project and is operated by Los Angeles County. Castaic Lake's excellent facility is Los Angeles County's largest recreation area with 9,000 acres. There are two separate Lakes. The Main Reservoir has a surface area of 2,500 acres and the Afterbay Lagoon has 180 surface acres. The Main Reservoir's east arm is open to slower boating, 20 MPH speed limit, while the west arm is for waterskiing and fast boating. The Lagoon is open to non-power boating with swimming daily from mid-June through September. Fishing at the Main Reservoir is from sunrise to sunset, but the Lagoon offers 24-hour fishing on the shoreline of the east side of the Lake. There is a good warm water fishery with the primary game fish being the Florida bass. Trout are stocked in the winter months.

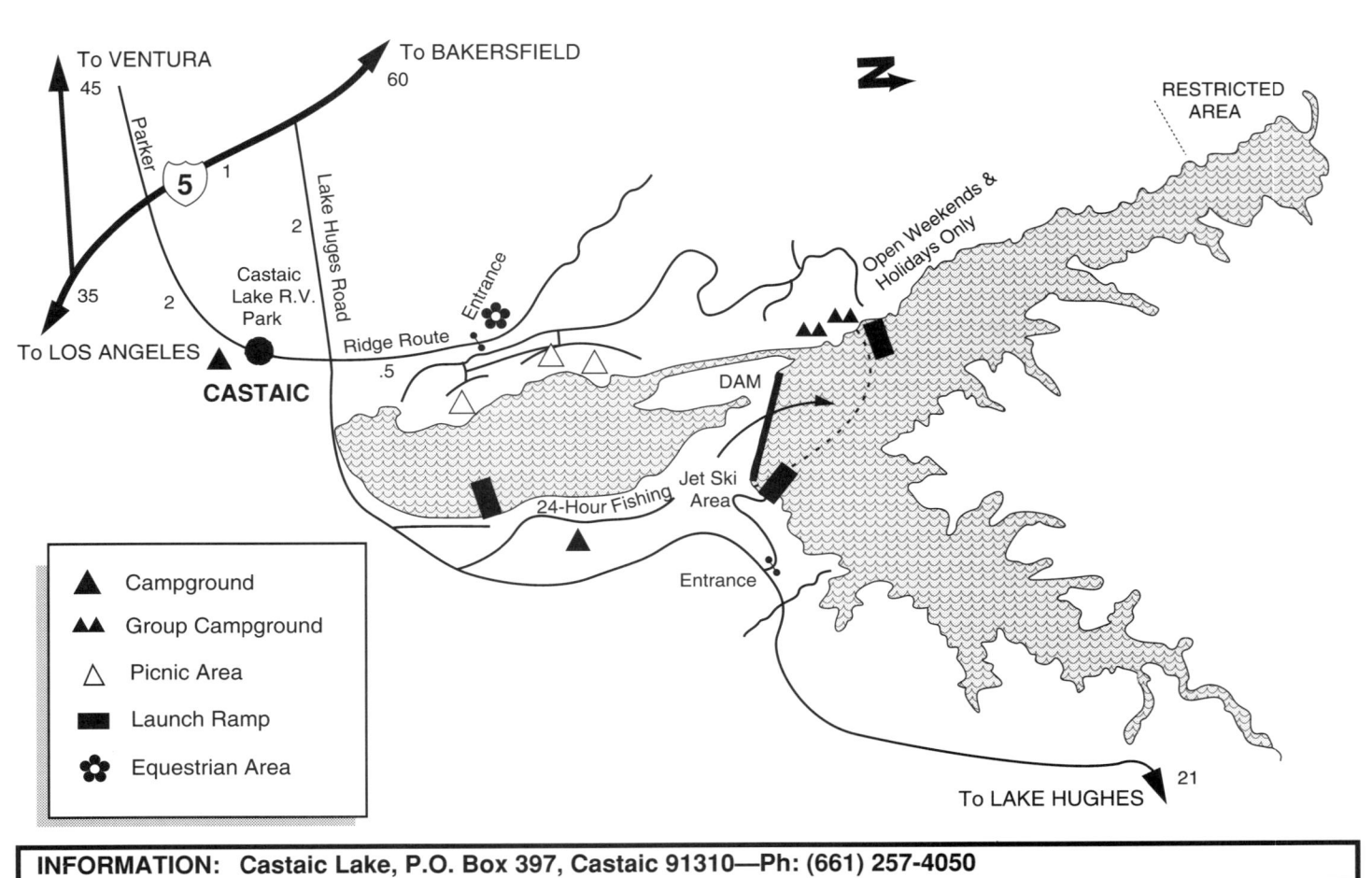

INFORMATION: Castaic Lake, P.O. Box 397, Castaic 91310—Ph: (661) 257-4050

CAMPING	BOATING	RECREATION	OTHER
50 Self-Contained Units For R.V.s: $12.50 Group Camping - Non-Profit Groups - 3 Nights Maximum $50 -10 to 100 Persons $100 - 101 to 200 Pers. Ph: (661) 257-4050 Castaic Lake RV Park 31540 Ridge Route Castaic 91318 Ph: (661) 257-3340 103 R.V. Sites Full Hookups - to $26	Main Reservoir: All Boating Allowed 35 MPH Speed Limit Launch Ramp: $6 Rentals: Fishing Boats & Windsurfers Afterbay: Non-Power Boats Launch Ramp: $6	Fishing: Trout, Catfish, Bluegill, Large & Smallmouth Bass Swimming Beaches at Afterbay Only Picnicking Hiking & Riding Trails	Snack Bar Bait & Tackle 24 Hour Fishing Area in Afterbay *Boaters Should Arrive Early as Launch is Closed After 500 Boats & 125 PWCs*

Lake Piru is at an elevation of 1,055 feet in the Los Padres National Forest near Metropolitan Los Angeles. It is owned and operated by the United Water Conservation District. The surface area of the Lake ranges from a maximum of 1,200 acres to a minimum of 750 acres. The water is deep and clear. This is a proven fishing Lake with warm water species growing to large sizes. Trout are planted twice a week in season. Boating restrictions are sharply defined. This is a nice boating and sailing Lake with good marina facilities. The campgrounds are located amid oak and olive trees above the launch ramp.

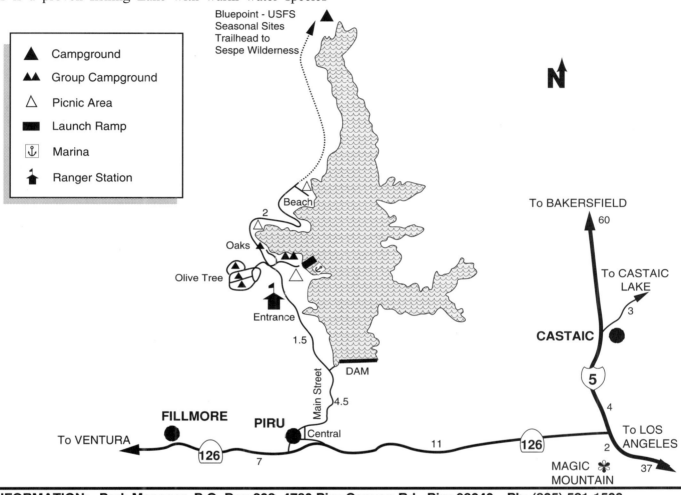

INFORMATION: Park Manager, P.O. Box 202, 4780 Piru Canyon Rd., Piru 93040—Ph: (805) 521-1500

CAMPING	BOATING	RECREATION	OTHER
132 Dev. Sites for Tents & R.V.s - Fee: $14-$16	Power, Waterskiing, Sail & Inflatables (Must be 12 Ft. Long with 3 Separate Compartments & 3 HP Minimum)	Fishing: Rainbow & Brown Trout, Bass, Catfish, Crappie, Bluegill	Snack Bar
101 R.V. Sites Electric Hookups Fee: $17-$19		Swim Beach	Restaurant
5 R.V. sites with Full Hookups - Fee: $20-$22	Speed Limit: 35 MPH *No Windsurfing or Jets*	Picnicking	Bait & Tackle
Group Camps	Special Use Area for Canoes, Kayaks	Hiking & Riding Trails in Los Padres National Forest	Disposal Station
	Full Service Marina		Marine Supplies
Day Use Vehicle Fee: $7 Boat Fee: $7	5-Lane Launch Ramp Rentals: Fishing & Pontoons	Backpacking	Dock, Moorings, Dry Storage
			Fuel
			Washer & Dryer At Campground
			Full Facilities in Piru

LAKE HUGHES and ELIZABETH LAKE

Elizabeth Lake and Lake Hughes are at an elevation of 3,300 feet in the Angeles National Forest north of Los Angeles. These small Lakes are within 5 miles of each other and are separated by an even smaller private membership Lake. Lake Hughes has a surface area of 35 acres. Access is through a resort which is open to the public year around and offers camping, fishing and all boating. The western half of Elizabeth Lake is owned and operated by the U.S. Forest Service which maintains picnic sites and allows swimming at your own risk. There are warm water fisheries at both Lakes. Trout fishing can be good in season at Elizabeth Lake.

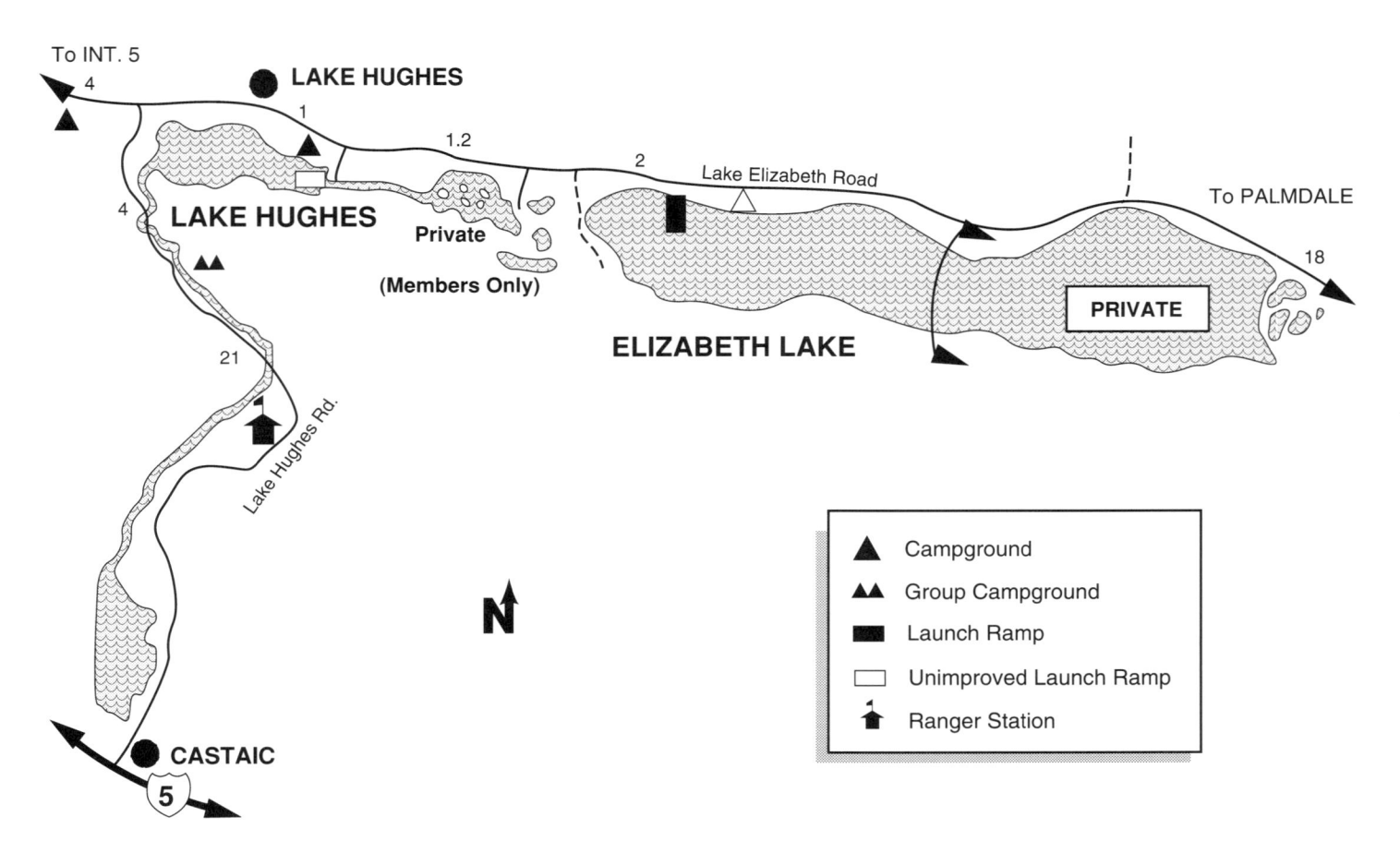

▲	Campground
▲▲	Group Campground
■	Launch Ramp
▢	Unimproved Launch Ramp
⌂	Ranger Station

INFORMATION: Saugus Ranger District, 30800 Bouquet Canyon Rd., Saugus 91350—Ph: (661) 296-9710

CAMPING	BOATING	RECREATION	OTHER
Hughes Lakeshore Park 43677 Trail K Lake Hughes Ph: (661) 724-1845 Dev. Sites for Tents & R.V.s Water & Electric Hookups Fees: $12 Vehicle plus $2 per Person Day Use Only: Fees: $8 Vehicle plus $1 per Person	Open to Sail & Power Boating 10 HP Motors Max. Paved Launch Ramp Rentals: Row & Pedal Boats at Lake Hughes Check for Current Water Level Conditions	Fishing: Catfish, Bass, Bluegill & Crappie Trout at Lake Elizabeth in Season Picnicking Hiking	Lake Hughes: Snack Bar Arcade Pool Tables Horseshoes General Store Restaurant Playground

Littlerock Reservoir, at 3,400 feet elevation, is in the Angeles National Forest. This 150 surface acre Lake is usually very low by September. Fishing is often good for rainbow and brown trout and it is stocked every other week in season. Apollo County Park is a part of the Los Angeles County Regional Park System. There are three Lakes named after the three astronauts of the Apollo flight, providing a recycled water trout fishery. Frazier Park has a very small fishing lake for trout, bass and catfish.

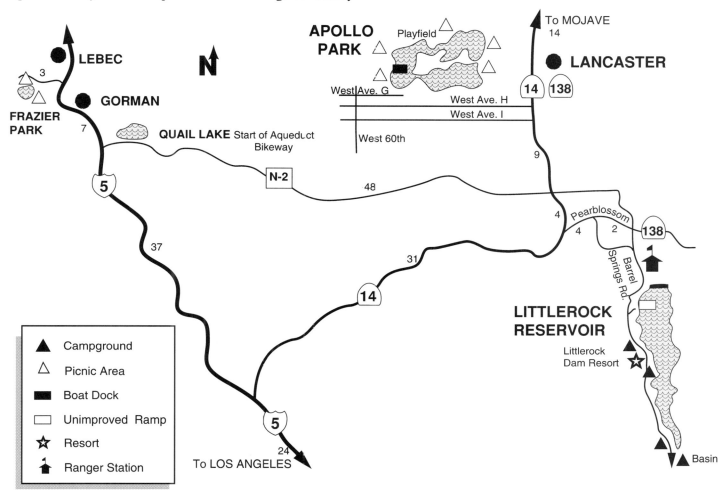

INFORMATION: Valyermo Ranger District, 29835 Valyermo Rd., Valyermo 93563—Ph: (661) 944-2187

CAMPING	BOATING	RECREATION	OTHER
Littlerock Reservoir 23 Dev. Sites for Tents & R.V.s No Hookups Fee: $12 Day Use: $3	Littlerock Reservoir Fishing Boats Only Speed Limit: 5 MPH Launch Area - Ramp Rentals at Resort: Rowboats	Fishing: Rainbow, German Brown, Kamloop Trout, Catfish Picnicking Hiking Hunting: Deer Children's Play Area Apollo Capsule	Littlerock Lake Resort 32700 Cheseboro Rd. Palmdale 93550 Ph: (805) 533-1923 Grocery Store Cafe, Bait & Tackle
Basin Campground Designed for OHV Users Gated Santiago Trail	Apollo Park: No Boating Frazier Park: No Boating		Apollo County Park West Ave. G Lancaster 93534 Ph: (805) 940-7701
No Camping at Apollo Park			

MOJAVE NARROWS PARK, GLEN HELEN PARK and JACKSON LAKE

Mojave Narrows Regional Park is at an elevation of 2,700 feet in the high desert. Jackson Lake, at an elevation of 6,500 feet, is in the Big Pines Recreation Area. Glen Helen Regional Park is at 1,000 feet elevation just 15 minutes from downtown San Bernardino. These Lakes offer many recreational opportunities. Boating is limited but the angler will find winter trout, bass and channel catfish at Glen Helen and Mojave Narrows. Spring, summer and fall, trout will be found at Jackson Lake. Excellent campgrounds, picnic areas, hiking and riding trails await the visitor.

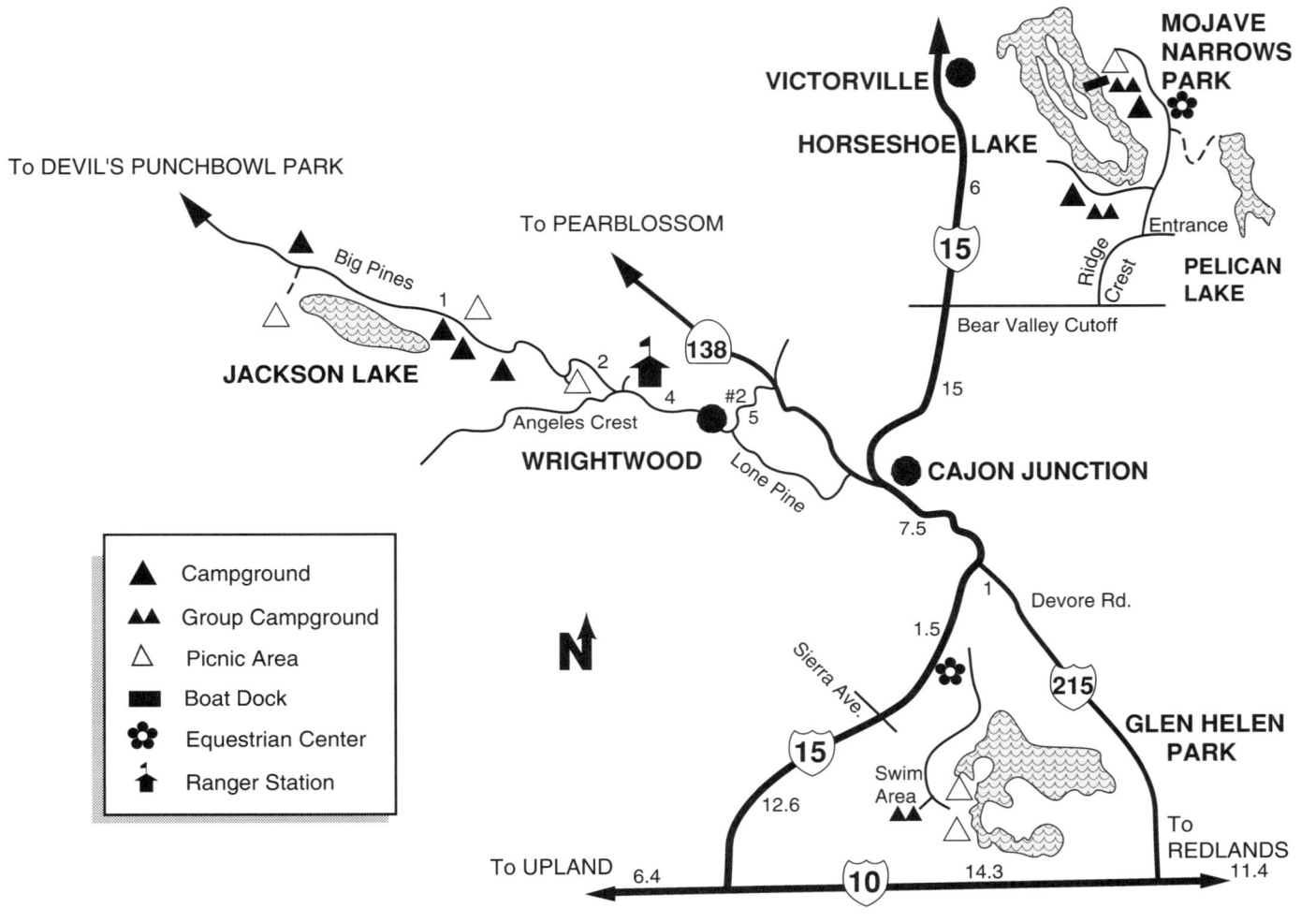

INFORMATION: San Bernadino County Reg. Parks, 777 E. Rialto, San Bernardino 92415—Ph: (909) 387-2594

CAMPING	BOATING	RECREATION	OTHER

Mojave Narrows:
  Ph: (760) 245-2226
  87 Dev. Sites
  Group Sites (10+)
  Disposal Station
  Fee: $10 No Hookups
  $15 With Hookups
Glen Helen Reg. Park:
  Ph: (909) 880-2522
  45 R.V. Sites & Tents
  2 Group Camp Area
  Disposal Station
Day Use Fee: $5
	Mojave Narrows:
	  No Private Boats
	  or Rafts
	  Rentals: Paddle &
	  Row Boats
	Glen Helen:
	  Rentals: Pedal Boats
	
	Jackson Lake:
	  Hand Launch
	  Non-Power Boats
	  Only
		Fishing: Trout, Bass,
		  Catfish
		Picnicking
		Jackson Lake:
		  Fishing
		Glen Helen:
		  Swim Lagoon,
		  Waterslides
		  Playgrounds,
		  Self-Guided Nature Trail
		Mojave Narrows:
		  Hiking & Riding Trails
		  Horse Rentals
			Jackson Lake U.S.F.S.
			  Valyermo Ranger Dist..
			  P.O. Box 15
			  29835 Valyermo Rd.
			  Valyermo 93563
			  Ph: (805) 944-2187
			  Visitor Info. Center

Crystal Lake is at an elevation of 5,700 feet in the Crystal Lake Recreation Area of the Angeles National Forest. Located in San Gabriel Canyon, this area offers numerous facilities and recreational opportunities. The small 5 acre Lake has good fishing and limited small craft boating. *Be certain to check water level.* There are many miles of hiking trails ranging from self-guided nature trails to moderately strenuous hikes along the Pacific Crest Trail. The San Gabriel River's North, East and West Forks lure the dedicated angler. The hunter should check with the Ranger District Office for restrictions prior to scheduling an outing. The San Dimas and San Gabriel Reservoirs are open to shoreline fishing only as there are no boating facilities.

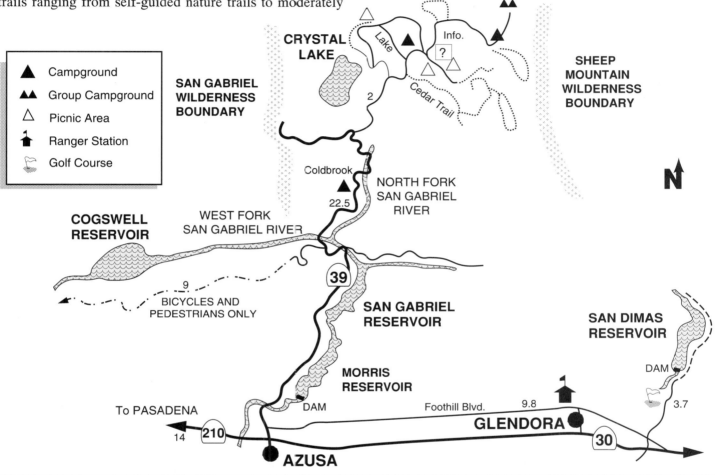

INFORMATION: Mt. Baldy Ranger District, 110 N. Wabash Ave., Glendora 91740—Ph: (626) 335-1251

CAMPING	BOATING	RECREATION	OTHER

Crystal Lake:
    176 Dev. Sites for
    Tents & R.V.s - $8
    9 Group Sites
    Reservations:
        Ph: (800) 280-CAMP
 	
Coldbrook:
    24 Dev. Sites for
    Tents & R.V.s
    No Water - No Fee
	Crystal Lake Only
	    Small Non-Power
	    Craft
	Hand Launch:
	    200 Yards
	    Down Steps
		Fishing :
		    Rainbow Trout
		Hiking & Nature
		    Trails
		Backpacking
		Naturalist Programs
		Golf Course at San Dimas
		No Swimming
		No Hunting Within
		    The Crystal Lake
		    Recreation Area
			General Store
			Snack Bar
			
			Visitor's Center
			    Ph: (626) 910-1149
			    (Weekends)
			
			Full Facilities
			    In Azusa

ALONDRA PARK and HARBOR LAKE

Alondra Park is under the jurisdiction of Los Angeles County. Within this 84 acre urban park is a small 8 acre fishing Lake. Boating is not allowed. There are picnic sites, a swimming area, community gardens, paddle tennis courts and a children's play area. Harbor Lake Park is under the jurisdiction of the City of Los Angeles. There is no general private boating at this small lake but canoe groups can arrange to use this Lake. The angler may find largemouth bass, bluegill, perch and catfish. There are group campgrounds, picnic areas and a playground. Harbor Lake Park is a wildlife sanctuary where a variety of plants, birds and animals may be observed in their natural habitats.

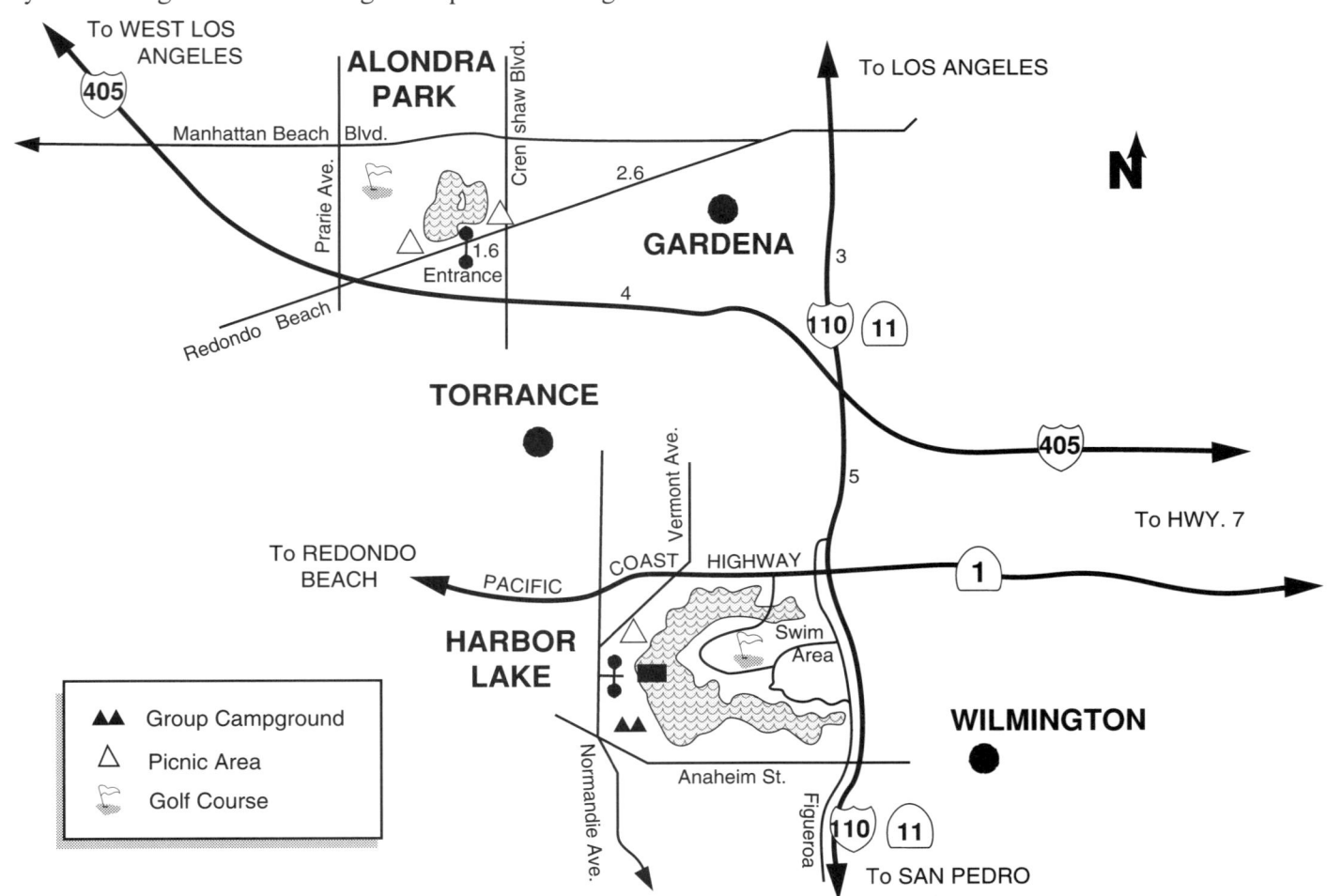

Legend	
▲▲	Group Campground
△	Picnic Area
🏳	Golf Course

INFORMATION: Harbor Lake Park, 25820 S. Vermont, Wilmington 90744—Ph: (310) 548-7515

CAMPING	BOATING	RECREATION	OTHER
Alondra County Park 3850 W. Manhattan Beach Blvd. Lawndale 90260 Ph: (310) 217-8366 Day Use Only Harbor Lake: Organization Group Camping	Alondra Park: No Boating Harbor Lake: No Private Boats Only Open to Group Boating by Request Non-Powered Boats No Body Contact	Fishing: Largemouth Bass, Bluegill, Catfish & Perch Picnic Areas Playgrounds Athletic Fields Birding & Nature Study Golf Courses Alondra Park: Swim Area Harbor Lake: Swimming Pool Open in Summer	Full Facilities Nearby

El Dorado is a 802 acre urban park under the administration of the City of Long Beach. Nestled amid the rolling green hills of the park are 4 small Lakes of approximately 40 acres. There is no boating at these Lakes except for rental boats and model boats. Fishing from the shore for trout and warm water species is often rewarding. There are nice family group and company picnic areas. A network of paved trails is available for the bicycler and roller skater. There is a vita course along with a number of running courses for the casual jogger or serious runner. An 85 acre nature center with 2 miles of self-guided nature trails can be enjoyed by walkers. The Olympic Archery Range is the finest in Southern California. Facilities abound at this complete recreation park.

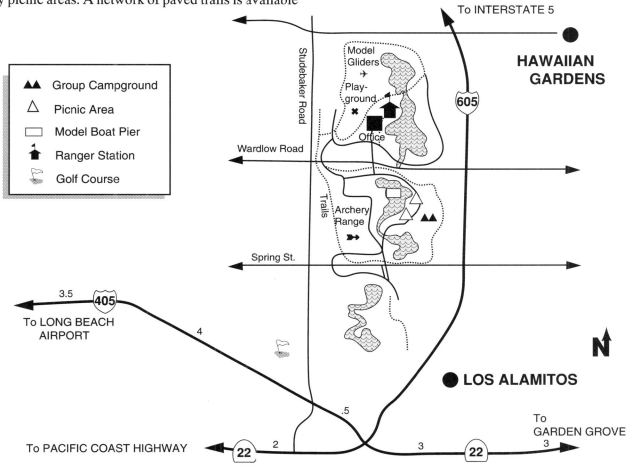

Legend:

▲▲ Group Campground
△ Picnic Area
▭ Model Boat Pier
⛺ Ranger Station
⚑ Golf Course

INFORMATION: El Dorado Regional Park, 7550 E. Spring St., Long Beach 90815—Ph: (562) 570-1771

CAMPING	BOATING	RECREATION	OTHER

Day Use
  Fees: $3 - $5
 	
Youth Group Camping
Under 18 Years Old
15 Children Minimum
	No Private Boats Allowed
	
	Rentals:
	  Fishing Boats &
	  Pedal Boats
	
	Model Boat Pier
		Fishing: Trout (Winter),
		  Bluegill,
		  Largemouth Bass,
		  Channel, Catfish
		Picnicking - Group Sites
		Jogging, Skating &
		  Bicycling Trails
		Olympic Archery Range
		Vita Course
		Playgrounds
		Nature Center & Trails
		
		No Swimming
			Snack Bar
			Train Rides
			Pony Rides
			
			Full Facilities
			  Nearby

PECK ROAD, SANTA FE and WHITTIER NARROWS

These three Los Angeles County Parks provide picnic areas, hiking and bicycle trails and Lakes for fishing. The 80 acre Lake at Peck Road Water Conservation Park is closed to boating and swimming. The Park is open from Wednesday through Sunday. Santa Fe Dam Park has a 70 acre Lake open to non-powered boating. There are also swim beaches, an equestrian staging area, a nature center and preserve. Group picnic areas may be rented. Legg Lake, actually three small

Lakes totaling 76.5 acres, is within the Whittier Narrows Recreation Area. This 1,400 acre multipurpose Park has a nature center, a skeet and trap shooting range, archery range, model hobby areas, athletic fields, equestrian area, golf course, lighted tennis courts and group picnic areas. There is no private boating or swimming but you may rent a rowboat. Youth group camping is available at Whittier Narrows and Santa Fe Dam.

INFORMATION: County Parks & Recreation, 433 S. Vermont, Los Angeles 90020—Ph: (213) 738-2961

CAMPING	BOATING	RECREATION	OTHER

Whittier Narrows
    750 S. Santa Anita Ave.
    S. El Monte 91733
    Ph: (626) 575-5526
    Day Use: $3 Vehicle
    Weekends & Holidays
    Picnic Reservations:
    Ph: (626) 575-5600
 	
Youth Group
    Camping at Santa Fe
	Peck Road:
	    Closed to Boating
	    No Fees
	Santa Fe:
	    Open to Non-Powered
	        Boating
	    Launch Ramp
	    Rentals Boats
	Whittier Narrows:
	    No Private Boats
	    Rental Rowboats
		Fishing: Trout (Winter)
		    Largemouth
		    Bass, Bluegill,
		    Crappie & Catfish
		Picnicking
		Whittier Narrows:
		    Group Picnic Area
		Hiking, Horseback Riding
		    & Bicycle Trails
		Athletic Fields
		Skeet-Trap, Archery
		Golf Course, Tennis Courts
		Model Hobby Areas
			Nature Center at
			    Whittier Narrows
			
			Santa Fe Dam Park
			    15501 E. Arrow Hwy.
			    Irwindale 91706
			    Ph: (626) 334-1065
			    Day Use: $6 Vehicle
			    Boat Launch: $6
			    Water Play Area
			
			Fishing Licenses Required
			    at All Facilities

The Silverwood State Recreation Area is at an elevation of 3,378 feet in the San Bernardino Mountains just east of Interstate 5 on the edge of the high Mojave Desert. This is a popular recreation Lake with a surface area of 1,000 acres and a shoreline of 13 miles. There are good marine support facilities. The Lake is open to all types of boating. Several brushy areas were left uncleared when filling the Lake which has provided a natural fish habitat. The angler will find a varied fishery with trophy largemouth and striped bass. There are 10 miles of paved trails for the hiker and bicyclist. In addition to the nice oak-shaded campsites at Silverwood, the camper will find a 90 unit modern campground at nearby Mojave River Forks. Beautiful sandy beaches and refreshing water make Silverwood a very popular spot. Reservations are recommended.

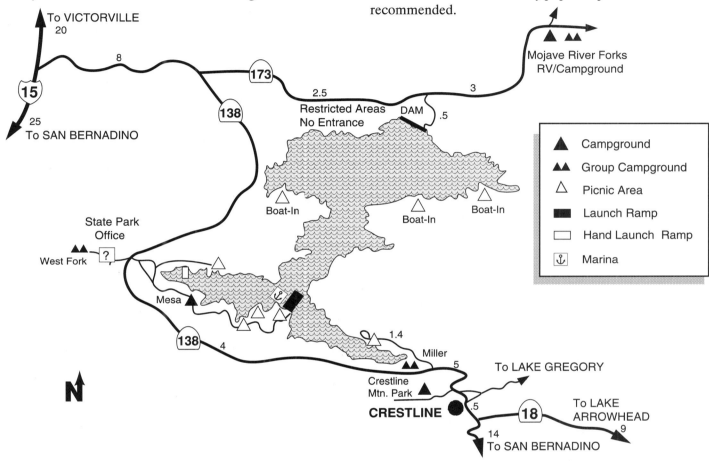

| Campground |
| Group Campground |
| Picnic Area |
| Launch Ramp |
| Hand Launch Ramp |
| Marina |

INFORMATION: State Recreation Area, 14651 Cedar Circle, Hesperia 92345—Ph: (760) 389-2303

CAMPING	BOATING	RECREATION	OTHER
136 Dev. Sites for Tents & R.V.s to 34 Feet Fee: $8 to $17 Group Sites: $80 to $150 100 People Max. 7 Bike-In or Hike-In Sites Fee: $4 Reserve: Ph: (800) 444-7275	Power, Row, Canoe, Sail, Waterski, Jets & Windsurf Speed Limit - 35 MPH Designated No-Ski or Power Boat Areas Launch Ramps: $5 Rentals: Fishing Boats & Jets Docks, Berths Hazards: High, Unpredictable Winds	Fishing: Rainbow Trout, Catfish, Bluegill, Crappie, Trophy Largemouth & Striped Bass, Swimming Picnicking & Hiking Visitor Center Campfire Program Self-Guided Nature Trail Bald Eagle Tours: Contact Park for Reservations	Snack Bar Grocery Store Bait & Tackle Disposal Station MojaveRiver Forks RV/Camp 18107 Highway 173 Hesperia 92345 Ph: (760) 389-2322 90 Dev. Sites for Tents & R.V.s Group Campground

LAKE GREGORY

Lake Gregory is a part of the San Bernardino County Regional Park System. Located at an elevation of 4,520 feet in the San Bernardino Mountains near Crestline, this popular day use Lake offers a variety of water related activities. There are sandy swimming beaches, picnic facilities, snack bars, a 300 foot water slide and a boat house. Boating is limited to rental fishing and pedal boats. This small 120 surface acre Lake offers good fishing either by boat or from the shoreline. The fish habitat is enhanced by an aeration system. In addition to the warm water species and rainbow trout, Lake Gregory is the only Lake in Southern California being stocked with brown trout. This is a nice family park with full facilities in the village and nearby Crestline.

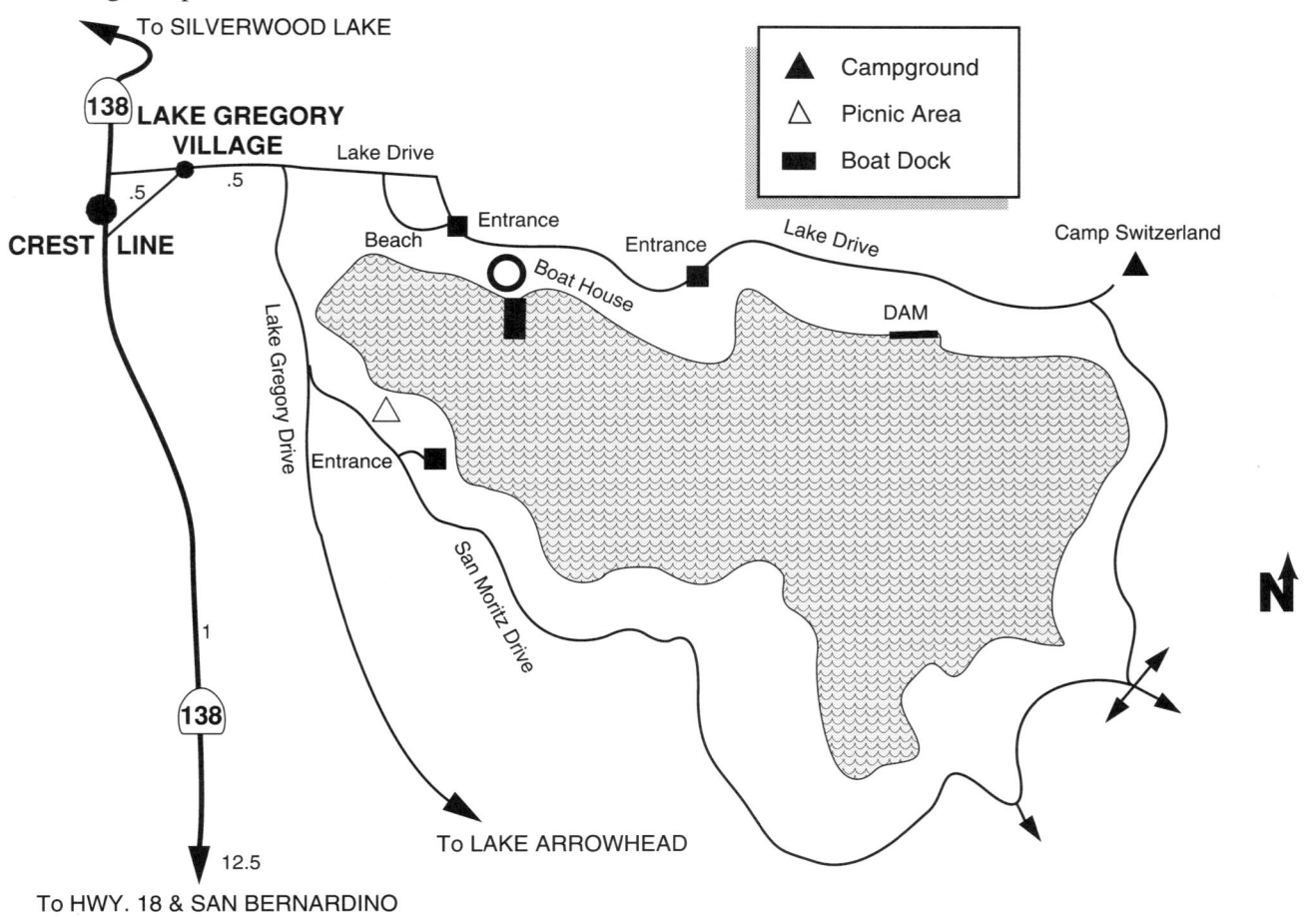

INFORMATION: Lake Gregory, P.O. Box 656, 24171 Lake Dr., Crestline 92325—Ph: (909) 338-2233			
CAMPING	**BOATING**	**RECREATION**	**OTHER**

Camp Switzerland
  P.O. Box 967
  Crestline, 92325
  Ph: (909) 338-2731
  10 Tent Sites
  30 R.V. Sites
    Full Hookups
  Cabins
 	
Call for Current Fees
Reservations Advised
	Rentals Only:
	  Row Boats
	  Pedal Boats
	  Water Bikes
	  Sailboards
	Electric Motors - Bring
	  Your Own For Use
	  on Rental Boat
	
	No Private Boats
		Fishing: Rainbow &
		  Brown Trout,
		  Largemouth Bass
		  Crappie, Bullhead &
		  Channel Catfish
		Picnic Areas
		Swim Beaches
		  (Memorial Day to
		  Labor Day)
		  Fee: $ 3 - Day
		    $35 Season
		Volleyball Court
		Waterslide Fee: $6 All Day
			Snack Bars
			Bait & Tackle
			Dressing Rooms
			Horseshoe Pits
			  Family of 4
			  Season Pass: $75
			Horse & Pony Rentals
			
			Full Facilities
			  Nearby

These Lakes are nestled high in the San Bernardino National Forest ranging in elevation from 5,100 feet at Lake Arrowhead to 7,200 feet at Green Valley Lake. Boating varies as shown below. Lake Arrowhead rests in a pretty alpine setting but it is privately owned and many restrictions prevail; public use is limited. The Forest Service has a number of nice campgrounds throughout this scenic area. There are many hiking and riding trails, especially near Jenks Lake where the San Gorgonio Wilderness invites the backpacker and equestrian. Green Valley is a small family oriented lake offering fishing, swimming and rental boats. Arrowbear is primarily a small fishing Lake. Snow Valley Ski Area has a scenic fishing lake on National Forest Land. You can take a chairlift up to it, fish and then bicycle or hike down.

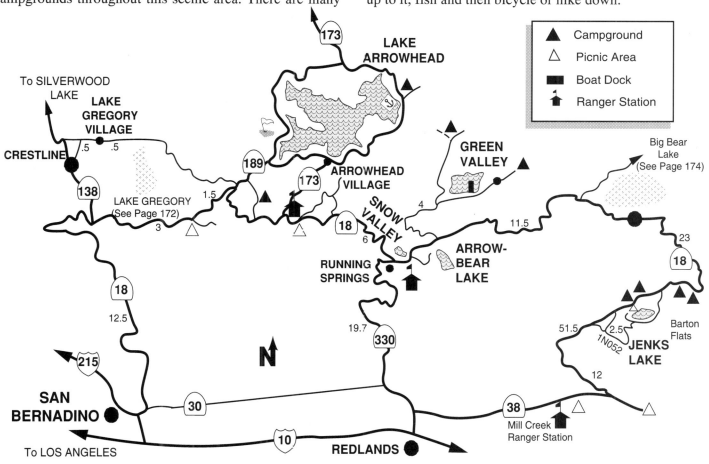

INFORMATION: Arrowhead Lake Assoc., P.O. Box 1119, Lake Arrowhead 92352—Ph: (909) 337-2595

CAMPING	BOATING	RECREATION	OTHER

Arrowhead Ranger Station:
  P.O. Box 350
  Skyforest 92385
  Ph: (909) 337-2444
 	
Jenks Lake:
  Barton Flats Camp Sites
  Reserve:
  Ph: (800) 280-CAMP
	Arrowhead: No Public
	  Boats Allowed
	  Public Tour Boat at
	  Lake Arrowhead Village
	Green Valley:
	  Non-Power Rentals
	Arrowbear & Snow Valley:
	  No Boating
	Jenks: Non-Power
	  Hand Launch
	  No Rentals
		Fishing: Rainbow &
		  Brown Trout,
		  Smallmouth Bass,
		  Kokanee Salmon,
		  Catfish & Bluegill
		Picnicking
		Hiking & Equestrian
		  Trails
		  Horse Rentals
		  in Area
		Swimming Beaches
			Lake Arrowhead Resort
			  Ph: (800) 800-6792
			  Luxury Rooms,
			  Restaurants,
			  Pool, Private Beach
			
			Snow Valley Mtn. Resort:
			  Ph: (909) 867-2751
			  Dev. Sites for Tents/
			  R.V.s - Hookups
			
			Resorts & Other Facilities
			  Nearby

BIG BEAR LAKE

Big Bear Lake is one of California's most popular recreation Lakes. Located in the San Bernardino National Forest at an elevation of 6,743 feet, this beautiful mountain Lake is just two hours from downtown Los Angeles. Originally created 1884 by a single arch dam and enlarged by the 1911 multiple arch dam, the Lake now has approximately 3,000 surface acres. The Lake is over 7 miles long, 1/2 to 1 mile wide and has a shoreline of 22 miles. Lake management is conducted by the Big Bear Municipal Water District. All types of boating are permitted subject to size restrictions and a valid Lake Use permit which may be obtained at most marinas. There are numerous marine facilities around the Lake. In addition to the many Forest Service campsites, there are extensive private facilities at this complete destination resort.

....Continued....

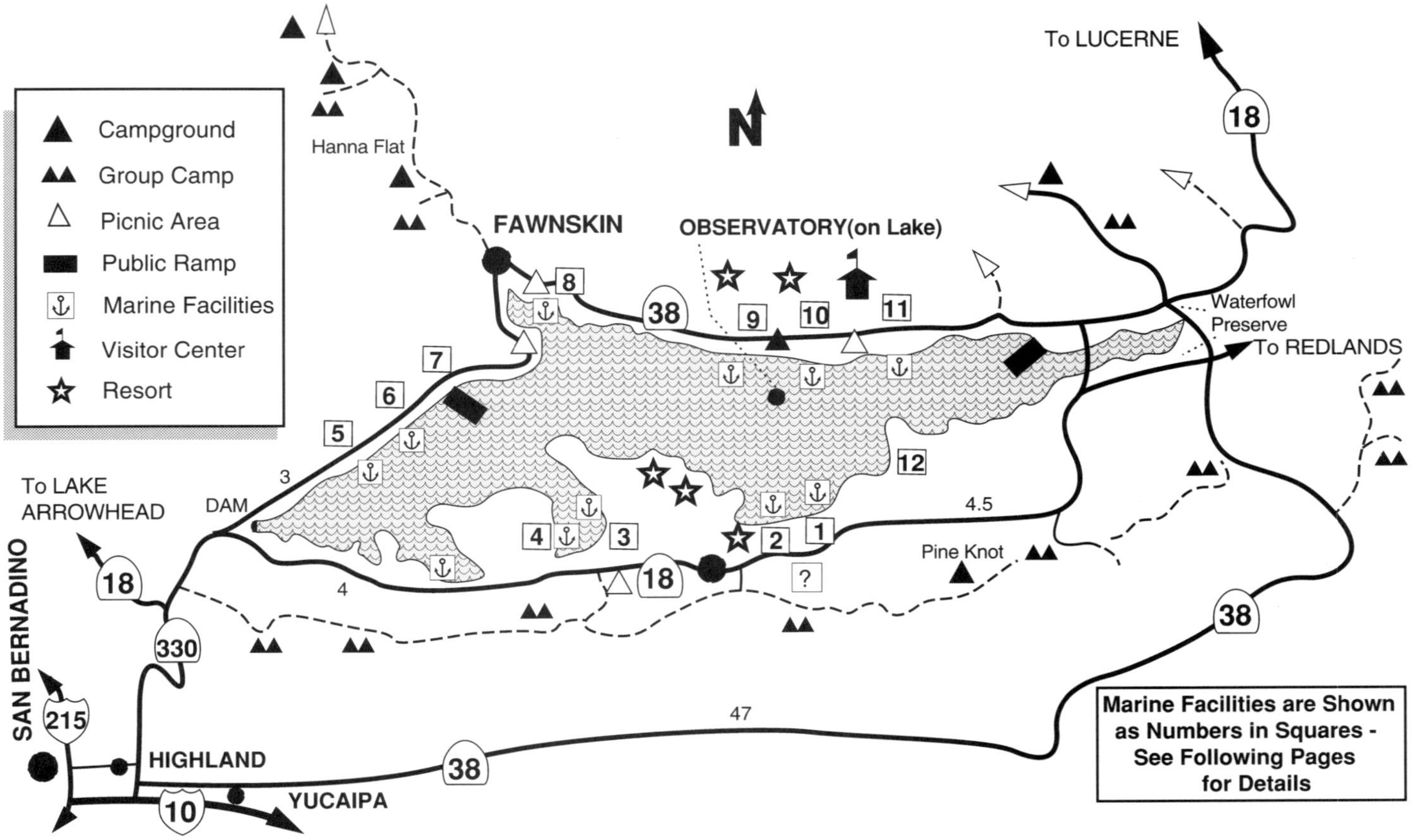

Legend:
- ▲ Campground
- ▲▲ Group Camp
- △ Picnic Area
- ▬ Public Ramp
- ⚓ Marine Facilities
- 🚩 Visitor Center
- ☆ Resort

Hanna Flat
FAWNSKIN
OBSERVATORY(on Lake)
To LUCERNE
18
Waterfowl Preserve
To REDLANDS
To LAKE ARROWHEAD
DAM
SAN BERNADINO
To REDLANDS
Pine Knot
HIGHLAND
YUCAIPA
215
18
330
10
38
47
4.5
4
3

Marine Facilities are Shown as Numbers in Squares - See Following Pages for Details

INFORMATION: Visitor Information, 630 Bartlett Rd., Big Bear Lake 92315—Ph: (800) 4-BIG BEAR

CAMPING	BOATING	RECREATION	OTHER
U.S.D.A. Forest Service 5 Campgrounds with 321 Dev. Sites for Tents & R.V.s Fee: $10 - $30 Full Hook-ups at Serrano Remote Area Camping: Adventure Pass Req'd. Group Sites $50 - $75 *See Following Pages*	Open to All Boating Subject to Length Maximum 26 Feet Valid Lake Permit Required - $15 Day $65 Year 35 MPH Speed Limit Full Service Marinas Launch Ramps Rentals: Power, Sail, Fishing, Sailboard & Jets Berths, Docks, Storage	Fishing: Trout, Bass, Channel Catfish, Bluegill, Carp & Crappie Swimming Hiking & Backpacking Horseback Riding: Trails & Rentals Golf & Tennis Picnicking	Complete Resort Facilities *See Following Pages for Information*

GENERAL INFORMATION:
Big Bear Chamber of Commerce
630 Bartlett
Big Bear Lake 92315
Ph: (800) BIG-BEAR

VISITOR INFORMATION
P. O. Box 2860
Big Bear Lake 92315
Ph: (800) BIG-BEAR

CAMPING/HIKING INFORMATION:
Big Bear Discovery Center
Box 290
Fawnskin 92333,
Ph: (909) 866-3437

LAKE INFORMATION
Big Bear Municipal Water District
40524 Lakeview Dr.
Big Bear Lake 92315
Ph: (909) 866-5796

LODGING INFORMATION:
Resort Association
P.O. Box 1936
Big Bear Lake 92315
Ph: (800) BIG-BEAR

U.S. FOREST SERVICE CAMPGROUNDS
Call For Information Regarding Months These Sites are Open

The following sites - RESERVE: - Ph: (800) 280-CAMP

FAMILY CAMPSITES:

SERRANO - North Shore Lane off Highway 38 - 2 Miles East of Fawnskin - 132 Tent/R.V. Sites - *Fees: $15 - $30.*

HANNA FLAT - 2-1/2 Miles NW of Fawnskin on Forest Service Rd. 3N14 - 88 Tent/R.V. Sites - *Fee: $15.*

PINEKNOT - South on Summit Blvd., off Big Bear Blvd. to Wall, Left 1/4 Mile - 48 Tent/R.V. Sites - *Fee: $15.*

BIG PINE FLAT - 7 Miles NW of Fawnskin on Forest Service Rd. 3N14 - 20 Tent/R.V. Sites, Trailers to 22 ft., Pack-In, Pack-Out - *Fee: $10.*

HOLCOMB VALLEY - 4 Miles North on 2N09 to 3N16 East on 3N16 3/4 Mile - 19 Tent/R.V. Sites, Trailers to 15 ft., Pack-In, Pack-Out, No Water - *Fee: $10.*

GROUP CAMPGROUNDS
(Dirt Roads)
All Group Sites (except as noted) are to 40 People and 8 Vehicles Maximum.

BIG PINE HORSE CAMP - To 60 People, 15 Vehicles Maximum, Water, Horse Groups Only - *Fee: $50.*
BLUFF MESA - Off 2N10 - Tents/R.V.s, No Water - *Fee: $50.*
BOULDER - Off 2N10 - Tents/R.V.s, No Water - *Fee: $50.*
BUTTERCUP - Near Pine Knot - Tents/R.V.s - *Fee: $75.*
DEER - Off 2N10 - Tents/R.V.s, No Water - *Fee: $50.*
GREEN CANYON - Off 2N93 - Tents/R.V.s, No Water - *Fee: $35.*
GRAY'S PEAK - Off 3N14 - Tents/R.V.s, No Water - *Fee: $50.*
IRONWOOD - Off 3N97 - To 25 People, 8 Vehicles Max., Tents/R.V.s, No Water, *Fee: $50.*
JUNIPER SPRINGS - Off 2N01 - Tents/R.V.s - *Fee: $50.*
ROUND VALLEY - Off 2NO1 - To 15 People, 3 Vehicles Max. Tents/R.V.s - *Fee: $35.*
TANGLEWOOD - Off 3N15 - Tents/R.V.s, No Water - *Fee: $50.*
Siberia Creek Only: Reservations at Big Bear Discovery Center - Ph: (909) 866-3437
SIBERIA CREEK - 3,000 Feet Elevation Change - 3.6 Mile Hike-In, To 40 People, Tent Sites, No Water - *No Fee.*

....Continued....

BIG BEAR LAKE.............Continued

PRIVATE CAMPGROUNDS:
Phone for Fees

LIGHTHOUSE TRAILER RESORT AND MARINA - Adjacent to the Observatory Access
10 - 15 RV Sites (No Tent Camping), Full Hookups, Store - *Ph: (909) 866-9464*

BIG BEAR SHORES R.V. RESORT & YACHT CLUB - East of Lighthouse Marina -
170 Deluxe R.V. Sites (No Tents), Full Hookups - *Ph: (800) 222-5708 or (909) 866-4151*

HOLLOWAY'S MARINA AND R.V. PARK - South Shore on Edgemoor Road in Metcalf Bay
66 Sites for Tents/R.V.s, Full Hookups, Store - *Ph: (800) 448-5335 or (909) 878-4386*

MWD R.V. PARK - West of "The Village" on Lakeview Dr.
25 Tent/R.V. Sites, Full Hookups, Walking Distance to Shops - *Ph: (909) 866-5796*

MARINE FACILITIES - See Map for Number Location in Square

1   PINE KNOT LANDING MARINA - *Ph: (909) 866-2628 or 866-9512*
Rentals: Fishing, Pontoon, Sail, Canoe, Speed Boats - Docks, Moorings, Ramp, Storage, Bait & Tackle, Store, Tours.

2   BIG BEAR MARINA - *Ph: (909) 866-3218*
Boat Permits, Rentals: Fishing, Pontoon, Sail, Jets - Docks, Moorings, Launch Ramp, Gas, Storage, Bait & Tackle.

3   HOLLOWAY'S MARINA & R.V. PARK- *Ph: (800) 448-5335 or (909) 866-5706*
Boat Permits, Rentals: Fishing, Pontoon, Jets, Paddleboats - Docks, Moorings, Ramp, Gas, Bait & Tackle, Groceries.

4   PLEASURE POINT LANDING - *Ph: (909) 866-2455*
Boat Permits, Rentals: Fishing, Pontoon, Canoes - Docks, Moorings, Ramp, Gas, Bait & Tackle, Snack Bar,
Pirate Ship Boat Tours.

5   GRAY'S LANDING - *Ph: (909) 866-2443*
Rentals: Fishing, Pontoons - Bait & Tackle, Fishing Pier (Nights Also), Slips, Moorings.

6   NORTH SHORE LANDING - *Ph: (909) 878-4386*
Rentals: Fishing, Sail, Jets, Moorings, Dock, Snacks, Bait & Tackle.

7   MWD EAST & WEST LAUNCH - *West Ph: (909) 866-2917 and East Ph: (909) 866-5200*
Boat Permit Sales, FREE Launch Ramp, Day Use Area.

8   CAPTAIN JOHN'S FAWN HARBOR - *Ph: (909) 878-3366*
Rentals: Fishing, Sail, Kayaks, Canoes, Pontoons, Moorings, Snacks, Bait & Tackle, Lake Tours.

9   LIGHTHOUSE TRAILER RESORT & MARINA- *Ph: (909) 866-9464*
Rentals: Fishing, Pontoons - Docks, Moorings, Snacks, Bait & Tackle, Propane.

10   BIG BEAR SHORES & R.V. RESORT- *Ph: (909) 878-4386*
Launch Ramp, Moorings, Docks, Rentals: Fishing Boats, Pontoon Boats.

11   JUNIPER POINT MARINA- *Ph: (909) 866-9464*
Boat Slips.

12   MEADOW PARK SWIM BEACH - *Ph: (909) 866-0135 or 866-0130*
Park Avenue Near Knight Ave., Public Swimming Area with Raft, Sandy Beach, Snack Bar, Picnic Tables, BBQ's.

Puddingstone Lake is at an elevation of 940 feet within the 2,000 acre Frank G. Bonelli Regional Park. This complete recreation facility is administered by the Department of Parks and Recreation of Los Angeles County. The 250 surface acre Lake has good marina facilities and is open to all boating. The angler will find trout and a warm water fishery. This well landscaped park has turfed picnic areas, a sandy swim beach, multi-purpose trails and the excellent full facility East Shore R.V. Park and Campground. The Equestrian Center complements the riding trails throughout the park. Raging Waters has the largest water theme park with slides west of the Rockies.

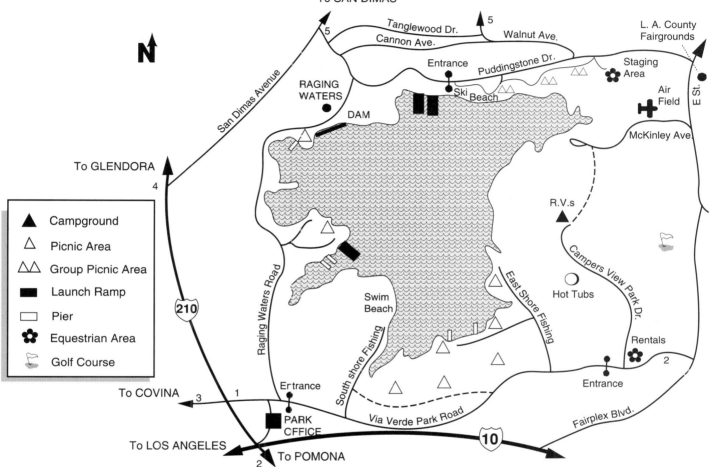

INFORMATION: Frank R. Bonelli Reg. County Park, 120 E. Via Verde, San Dimas 91773—Ph: (909) 599-8411

CAMPING	BOATING	RECREATION	OTHER

East Shore R.V. Park
    1440 Camper View Rd.
    San Dimas 91773
    Ph: (800) 809-3778
25 Dev. Sites for Tents -
    $8 Per Person
520 Dev. Sites for R.V.s -
    Full Hookups
    $24 to $27 (2 People)
Swimming Pool, Rec. Room
Volleyball Courts, Store
Bait & Tackle, Disposal Sta.
Reservations Accepted
	Open to All Boating
	All Boats Must be
	    Min. 8 Ft. - Max. 26 Ft.
	Power Boats Must be
	    Min.12 Ft.
	Call for Current Boat
	    Use Days
	Rentals: Fishing Boats
	    Ph: (909) 599-2667
	Paved Launch Ramps - $6
		Day Use - $6
		Fishing: Trout, Bass,
		    Bluegill, Crappie,
		    Perch & Caffish
		Picnicking
		Group Picnic Areas by
		    Reservation
		Hiking & Equestrian Trails
		Equestrian Center:
		    Horse Boarding
		    Roping Arena
		    Ph: (909) 599-8830
		Golf Course Nearby
			Raging Waters:
			    Water Slides,
			    Wave Pool,
			    Rapids, Kids Pool
			    Ph: (909) 592-6453
			Snack Bar
			Bait & Tackle
			Hot Tubs: 1 - 100 People
			    Ph: (909) 592-2222
			Gazebo Area for Private
			    Parties

LAKE PERRIS

The Lake Perris State Recreation Area is the southern terminus of the California State Water Project. The Lake's 2,200 surface acres are surrounded by rocky mountains towering to more than a thousand feet above the water's surface. Alessandro Island provides a popular boat-in picnic area. This island rises 230 feet creating an interesting view of the surrounding area. The complete recreation park provides an enormous number of activities and support facilities. The fishing is good from boat or shore. This is a popular Lake for waterskiing, sailboarding, sailing and boating. There are specific areas for waterfowl and upland game hunters. The hiker, bicycler and horseback rider will find extensive trails. There is also rock climbing and a designated area for scuba diving.

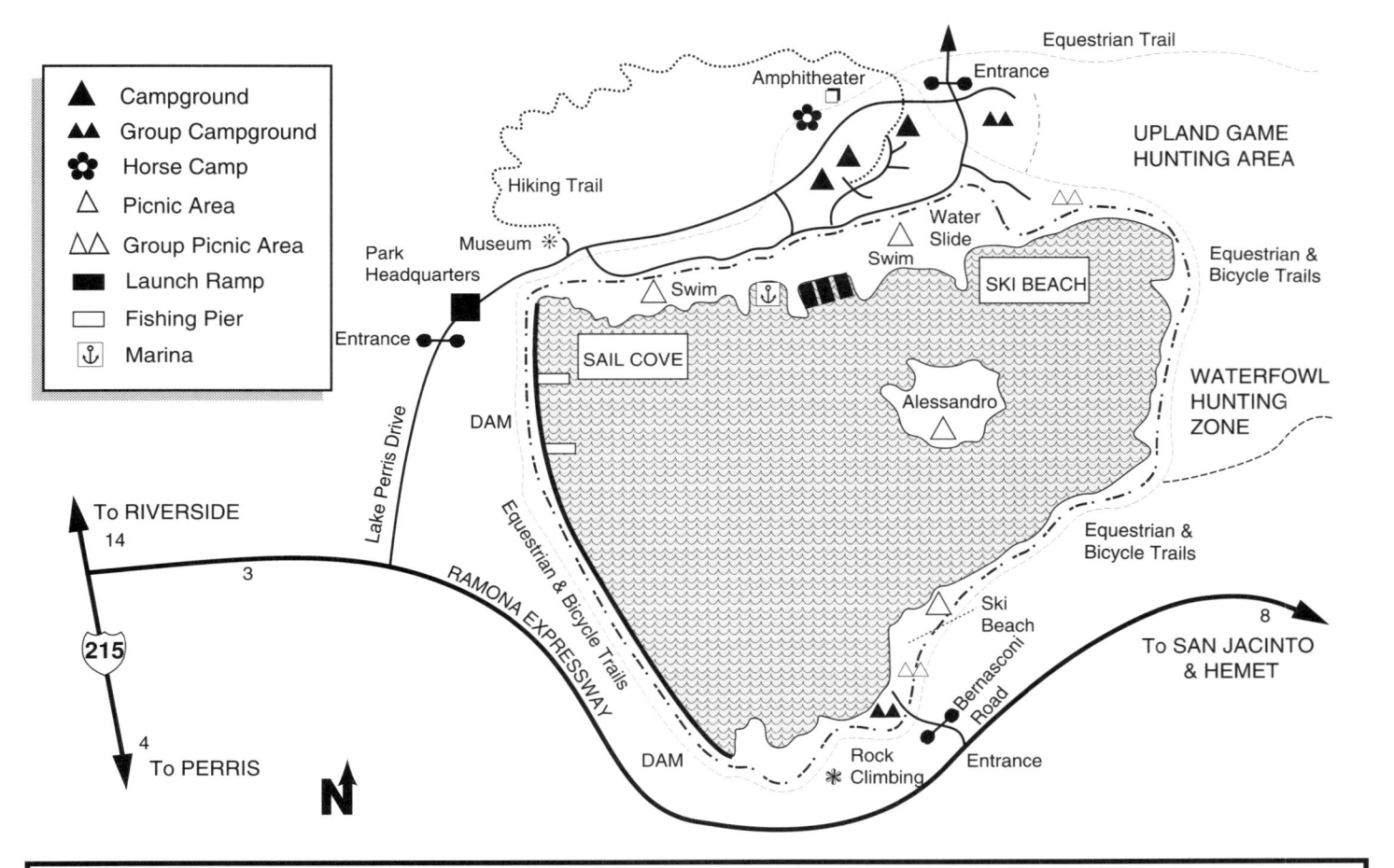

INFORMATION: State Recreation Area, 17801 Lake Perris Dr., Perris 92371—Ph: (909) 940-5603

CAMPING	BOATING	RECREATION	OTHER
167 Dev. Tent Sites	Open to All Boating	Fishing: Trout, Alabama	Regional Indian
Fee: $8 - $14	35 MPH Speed Limit	Spotted & Largemouth	Museum
254 R.V. Sites with Hookups	5 MPH Zoned Areas	Bass, Bluegill, Channel	Horse Camp: Corrals,
to 31 Feet	Full Service Marina	Catfish, Sunfish	Water Troughs,
Fee: $14 - $22	Launch Ramps:	Picnicking	Picnic Tables to
6 Group Campgrounds	Boats: $5	3 Group Sites	50 People
25 to100 People &	Sailboards: $1	Swimming, Scuba Diving	Coffee Shop, Snack Bar
25 to 80 People	Storage, Slips, Gas, Dock	Beaches & Waterslide	Restaurant
Disposal Station	Rentals: Fishing Boats	Hiking, Bicycle &	Bait & Tackle
Boat Camping in Slips	Waverunners, Patio	Riding Trails	Marine Supplies
Only With	Cruisers, Knee Boards,	Rock Climbing Area	Boat Repairs
Prior Approval	Life Jackets, Skis	Hunting: Waterfowl &	
		Upland Game	

The millions of residents and visitors to Orange County will find an abundance of regional parks, harbors and beaches. We have included only those regional parks that offer a recreational Lake for fishing and perhaps boating. For those who are interested in the many other facilities, contact Orange County as listed on the following page. Laguna Niguel Regional Park Lakes is run by a private concession so no State fishing license is required. Private boats are not allowed but boat rentals are available.

....Continued....

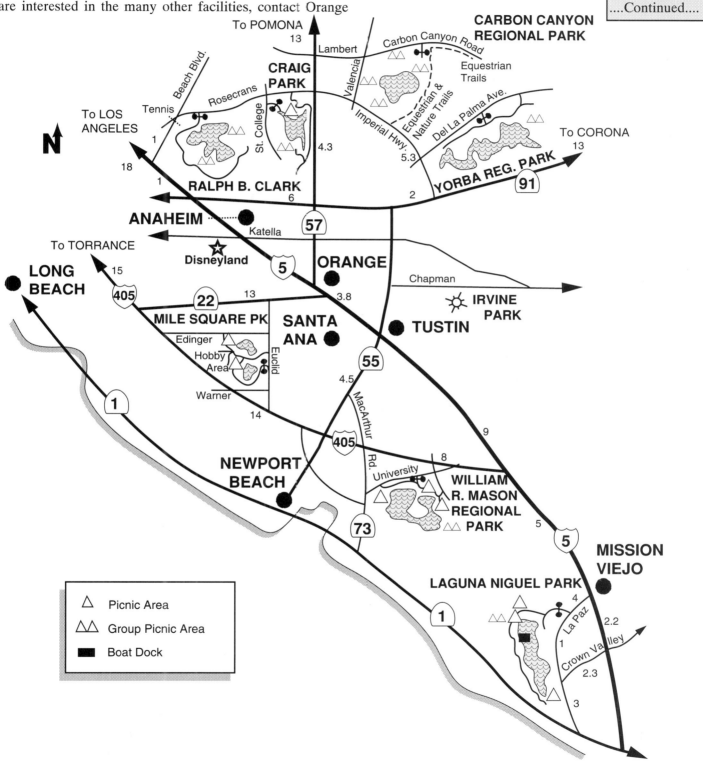

CARBON CANYON REGIONAL, 4442 Carbon Canyon Rd., Brea 92823—Ph: (714) 996-5252

This 124-acre park is in the foothills of the Chino Hill Range upstream from Carbon Canyon Dam. The park features a 10-acre grove of coastal redwoods amid sycamore, pepper and eucalyptus. There is a 4-acre fishing Lake with two piers, bicycle, equestrian and hiking trails, picnic areas, playground, tennis courts and athletic fields.

CRAIG REGIONAL PARK, 3300 North State College Blvd., Fullerton 92685, Ph: (714) 990-0271.

There is a turfed play area within the park's 124 acres. There are bicycle and hiking trails. Picnic areas and shelters are available along with a multi-purpose sports complex. There is a 3-acre fishing Lake. Check for current water level condition.

RALPH B. CLARK REGIONAL PARK, 8800 Rosecrans Ave., Buena Park 90621—Ph: (714) 670-8045

Orginally acquired by the County of Orange in 1974 to preserve its rich fossil beds, this park features picnic areas, playgrounds and athletic fields along with tennis courts. The Lake offers fishing for largemouth bass, channel catfish and bluegill.

IRVINE REGIONAL PARK, 1 Irvine Park Rd., Orange 92669—Ph: (714) 633-8072

This park lies amid the coastal live oaks and California sycamores in the hillside of Santiago Canyon. This is California's oldest regional park. The 447 acres includes picnic areas throughout the park, a paved bicycle and walking trail which meanders through to playgrounds and athletic fields. There are also group picnic areas, horse rentals, pony rides and bicycle rentals. The park ranger conducts interpretive programs. The Orange County Zoo and barnyard are also popular.

MILE SQUARE REGIONAL PARK, 16801 Euclid St., Fountain Valley 92708, Ph: (714) 962-5549

This 640-acre former bean field and navy airstrip is now a popular regional park. Opened to the public in 1970, it offers areas for team sports, special events such as archery meets and dog shows. There are four miles of bicycle and jogging trails along with several children's playgrounds. Swimming is prohibited in the Lakes. Catfish are stocked.

WILLIAM R. MASON REGIONAL PARK, 18712 University Dr., Irvine 92612—Ph: (949) 854-2491

The Irvine Company donated this 345-acre park to Orange County. Originally named University Park, its name was changed to William R. Mason in honor of this former Irvine Company president. There are picnic areas, athletic fields, hiking, jogging and bicycle trails. The 9-acre Lake is open to fishing but is not stocked. A new aeration system has been installed which should improve the quality of water.

YORBA REGIONAL PARK, 7600 E. La Palma Ave., Anaheim 92807—Ph: (714) 970-1460

This 175-acre regional park is bordered on the south side by the Santa Ana River. There are picnic shelters, organized group shelters, tables and barbecue grills. Bicycle, equestrian and hiking trails run the length of the park. There is a six station exercise course as well as lighted athletic fields. Fishing is also offered in the connecting Lakes.

INFORMATION: Orange Co. Recreational Facilities, 1 Irvine Park Rd., Orange 92669—Ph: (714) 771-6731			
CAMPING	**BOATING**	**RECREATION**	**OTHER**
Caspers Wilderness Park 33401 Ortega Hwy. San Juan Capistrano Ph: (949) 728-0235 Featherly Reg. Park Canyon R.V. Park 24001 Santa Ana Cyn. Anaheim 90808 Ph: (714) 637-0210 O'Neill Reg. Park 30892 Trabuco Cyn. Trabuco Canyon 92678 Ph: (949) 858-9365	Small Boats Rentals Only at Laguna Niguel	Fishing: Largemouth Bass, Bluegill, Channel Catfish, Trout Picnic Areas Playgrounds Athletic Fields Hiking & Equestrian Trails Bicycle Paths Interpretive Programs Group Facilities: Permits at Least 15 Days in Advance	Laguna Niguel Park: 28241 La Paz Rd. Laguna Niguel 92656 Ph: (949) 362-3885 174-acre Park 44-acre Lake Stocked with Catfish and Trout Fishing Permit Fees: $12 Rental Boats Only Float Tubes Allowed Picnic Areas and Shelters Equestrian & Bicycle Trails

IRVINE, CORONA and SANTA ANA RIVER LAKES

These Lakes in Southern California are grouped together because they are all a fisherman's dream. Irvine Lake is located near the city of Orange and offers some of the best bass fishing in California. Trophy-sized trout and catfish limits are also often caught. Santa Ana River Lakes consists of three Lakes including a Kids Lake and a Catfish Pond. This is an ideal spot for children to learn to fish. Corona Lake, just off Highway 15 south of Riverside, has good spots for bass fishing along the east shore and around the flooded timber hideaway at the south end of the Lake. Float tube fishing is permitted at both Irvine and Corona Lakes. These are all extremely popular fishing Lakes. Major trout, bass and catfish tournaments are held throughout the year.

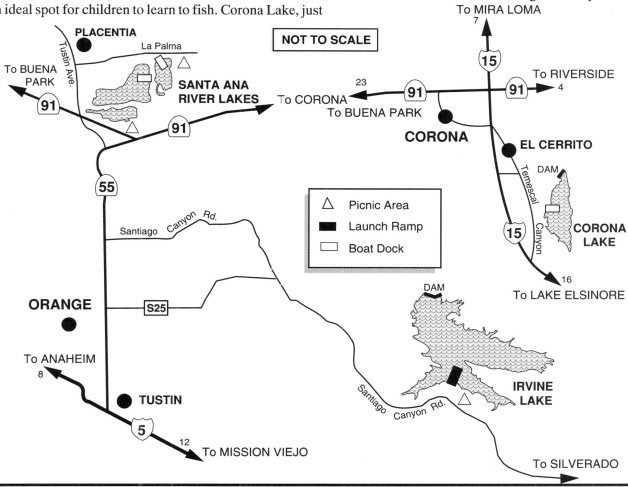

INFORMATION: *Only* Irvine Lake: 4621 Santiago Canyon Rd., Silverado 92676—Ph: (714) 649-9113

CAMPING	BOATING	RECREATION	OTHER
Irvine Lake: Group Camping Only (Plans for RV Sites) Day Use Fishing Fees: $7 - $13	Irvine Lake: Launch Fee: $8 5 MPH Limit Rentals: Row, Motor & Bass Boats, Pontoons, & Electric Party Cruisers	Fishing: Trout, Catfish, Striped Bass, Crappie, Bluegill, Sunfish, Sturgeon	Irvine Lake: Fish Report: Ph: (714) 649-2168
Santa Ana River Lakes & Corona Lake No Camping Fees: $14 Adults $10 Children	Santa Ana Rivers Lakes & Corona Lake Launch Fee: $8 Float Tubes: $5 Rentals: Row & Motor Boats	Irvine Lake Float Tube Fishing Group Facilities for Picnicking & Fishing, Parties, Kid's Fish'n Hole Volleyball, Horseshoes, Hiking Trails Santa Ana & Corona: Night Fishing Available	Santa Ana River Lakes: Fish Report: Ph: (714) 632-7830 Corona Lake: Fish Report: Ph: (909) 277-4489

178

CUCAMONGA-GUASTI, YUCAIPA PARK, PRADO PARK and FAIRMOUNT PARK

These small Lakes offer limited boating but the surrounding parks offer an abundance of recreational opportunities. Cucamonga-Guasti, Yucaipa Park and Prado Park are a part of the San Bernardino County Regional Park System. Fairmount Park is administered by the City of Riverside. Fishing is popular the year round for bass and channel catfish. During the winter months, the angler will find planted trout. In addition to modern campgrounds, Prado offers horseback riding trails and equestrian centers. There is a variety of activities unique to each park from trap shooting to waterslides.

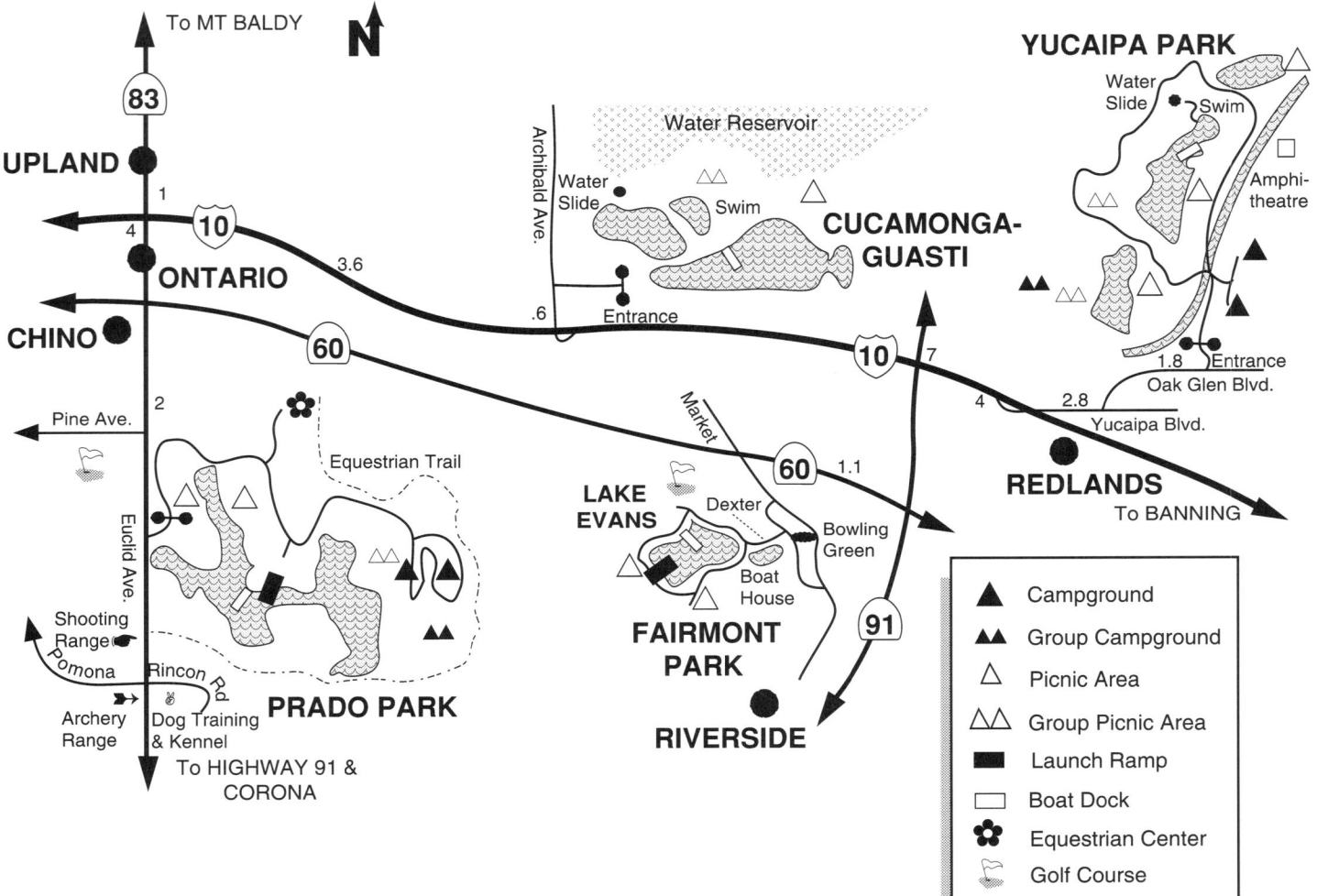

INFORMATION: San Bernadino County Regional Parks, 777 E. Rialto, San Bernardino 92415—Ph: (909) 387-2594

CAMPING	BOATING	RECREATION	OTHER
Yucaipa Park: Tent Sites 13 R.V. Sites - Hookups Disposal Station Prado Park: Tent Sites 75 R.V. Sites - Hookups Check Parks for Fees Day Use Only: Cucamonga-Guasti & Fairmont Park	Cucamonga-Guasti: Rentals: Pedal Boats & Aqua Cycles Yucaipa Park: Rentals Only - Pedal Boats Prado: Non-Power Boats Launch Ramp Fairmont Park: Launch Ramp & Dock	Fishing: Trout-Winter, Bass & Catfish Swimming & Picnicking Yucaipa & Guasti: Waterslides Hiking & Riding Trails Prado Park: Athletic Fields Equestrian Center & Horse Rentals Shooting Ranges: Trap, Air Gun, Skeet, Pistol, Rifle Archery Range Dog Training & Kennel	Cucamonga-Guasti Ph: (909) 481-4205 Yucaipa Park Ph: (909) 790-3127 Prado Park: Ph: (909) 597-4260 Fairmont Park: City of Riverside Parks & Rec. 3900 Main St. Riverside 92522 Ph: (909) 715-3440 Golf Courses

Lake Elsinore is the largest natural freshwater lake in Southern California with over 3,300 surface acres. The lake is popular for a variety of watersports including fishing,,waterskiing and boating. The Lake Elsinore Management Project, completed in 1995, provided a stablilzed water elevation to enhance the recreation and development potentials. The Lake Elsinore Recreation Area, owned by the city of Lake Elsinore, offers quiet, shaded campsites just steps to the water's edge. Numerous private campgrounds and resorts are available. The city's new boat launch facility provides an easy way to launch your watercraft.

....Continued....

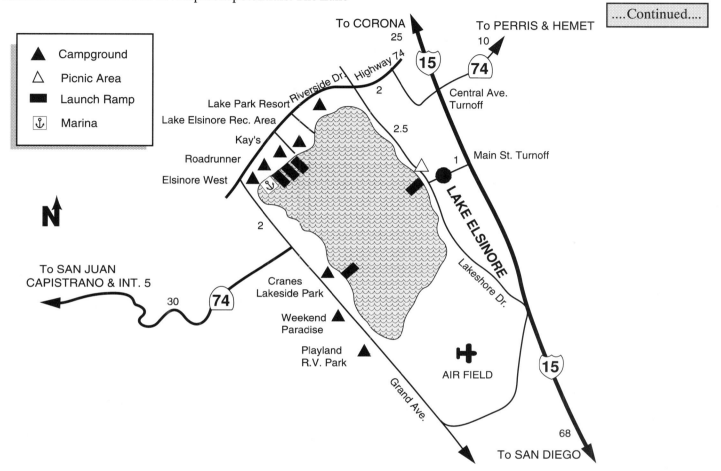

INFORMATION: Lake Elsinore Recreation Area, 32040 Riverside Dr., Lake Elsinore 92530—Ph: (909) 471-1212

CAMPING	BOATING	RECREATION	OTHER
150 Dev. Sites for Tents & R.V.s Fees: Tents - $15 R.V.s - Electric Hookups - $20 Disposal Station Group Sites Available Day Use: Fee: $5 - Vehicle $2 - Walk-in	Power, Row, Canoe, Sail, Windsurf Waterski & Jets 35 MPH Speed Limit - Unlimited Speed in Center of Lake Lake Use Fee: $5 Launch Ramps Rentals: Fishing Boats	Fishing: Bass, Crappie, Carp, Bluegill & Catfish Picnicking Hiking, Riding & Bicycle Trails Hang Gliding Parachuting Professional Minor Leage Baseball Games Golf Nearby	Full Facilities in Lake Elsinore *See Following Page for Resorts & Marine Facilities*

LAKE PARK RESORT
32000 Riverside Dr., Lake Elsinore 92530
Ph: (909) 674-7911
121 R.V. Sites, Full Hookups - *Fee: $17*, Cable T.V., Hot Showers, 26 Motel Rooms, Olympic Size Pool, Picnic Area.

KAY JORDAN'S CAMPGROUND
32310 Riverside Dr., Lake Elsinore 92530
Ph: (909) 674-2766
Tent/R.V. Sites, Hookups - *Fee: $10 and up*
Permanent R.V. Sites, Swimming Beach, Launch Ramp, Lake Use Permits, Hot Showers, Picnic Area.

ROAD RUNNER R.V. PARK
32500 Riverside Dr., Lake Elsinore 92530
Ph: (909) 674-4900
Tent Camping & R.V.s with Full Hookups **-** *Fee: $20*

ELSINORE WEST MARINA
32700 Riverside Dr.
Lake Elsinore 92530
Ph: (909) 678-1300 or (800) 328-6844
Open Tent & R.V. Camp Area, 170 R.V. Sites, Full Hookups - *Fee: $20*, Hot Showers, Flush Toilets, Cable T.V.

CRANES LAKESIDE PARK
15980 Grand Ave., Lake Elsinore 92530
Ph: (909) 678-2112
21 R.V. Sites, Water & Electric Hookups - *Fee: $26*
Disposal Station, Hot Showers, Snack Bar, Swim Area, Recreation Center, Laundry.

WEEKEND PARADISE R.V. PARK
16022 Grand Ave., Lake Elsinore 92530
Ph: (909) 678-3715
R.V. Sites, Water & Electric Hookups - *Fee: $15*, Hot Showers, Disposal Station.

PLAYLAND R.V. PARK
16730 Grand Ave., Lake Elsinore 92530
Ph: (909) 678-4663
Tent Camping - *Fee: $10*, R.V.s with Full Hookups - *Fee: $15*

FOR OTHER FACILITIES AND ACCOMMODATIONS CONTACT:
City of Lake Elsinore
130 S. Main St.
Lake Elsinore 92530
Ph: (909) 674-3124

Located at an elevation of 1,500 feet in the transitional area between coast and desert, Lake Skinner rests amid semi-arid vegetation, rolling hills of wild flowers and oak trees. The Lake has a surface area of 1,200 acres. The 14 miles of irregular shoreline is surrounded by the 6,000 acre Lake Skinner Park. This facility is operated by Riverside County Parks Department. In addition to the campsites, there is a half-acre swimming pool, ecology ponds, marine facilities, camp store and fishing beaches. There are a number of good riding trails and a primitive equestrian campground where water is piped in for the horses. This is a good sailing Lake with moderate winds. Power boating is restricted to 10 MPH with low wake conditions. The Lake is well stocked with trout and warm water fish. The facilities are nicely maintained with grassy areas and sandy beaches.

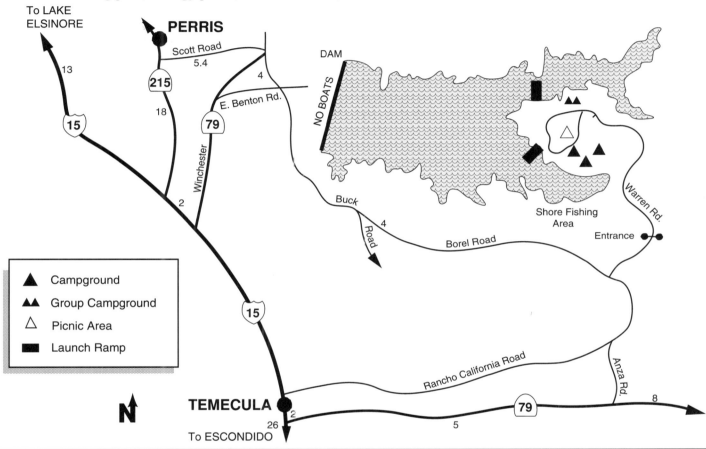

INFORMATION: Lake Skinner Park, 37701 Warren Rd., Winchester 92596—Ph: (909) 926-1541

CAMPING	BOATING	RECREATION	OTHER
41 Dev. Sites for Tents - Fee: $15 Dev. Sites for R.V.s 18 Partial Hookups Fee: $16 185 Full Hookups Fee: $18 Primitive Sites for Overflow Fee: $12 Group Camp Available Reservations: Ph: (800) 234-7275	All Boats Must Be a Minimum of 10 Feet Long, 42 Inches Wide Sailboats Must Be 12 Feet Long & 12 Inches of Freeboard *Canoes, Kayaks or Multihulled Boats MUST have Solid and Fixed Decking* Speed Limit - 10 MPH Launch Ramp, Marina Rentals: Row & Motor Boats	Fishing: Trout, Catfish, Bluegill, Crappie, Perch, Bass, Carp Swimming in Pool Only Memorial Day through Labor Day Picnicking Hiking Horseback Riding Trails Nature Study	Snack Bar Laundromat Camp Store Bait & Tackle Disposal Station Full Facilities: 10 Miles at Temecula

REFLECTION LAKE, ANGLER'S LAKE and LAKE FULMOR

Reflection and Angler's Lakes, at 1,600 feet elevation, are small private fishing facilities. Angler's Lake provides no limit fishing. Reflection Lake offers a developed campground for tents and R.V.s. Boating is limited to canoes and inflatables. Electric motors are allowed. Trout and Channel catfish are planted weekly in season at both Angler's and Reflection Lakes. State fishing licenses are not required at these private facilities. Lake Fulmor is at an elevation of 5,300 feet near the beautiful mountain resort community of Idyllwild. Although facilities are limited to Day Use at this small trout Lake, the visitor will enjoy the relaxed atmosphere in this area of the San Bernardino National Forest.

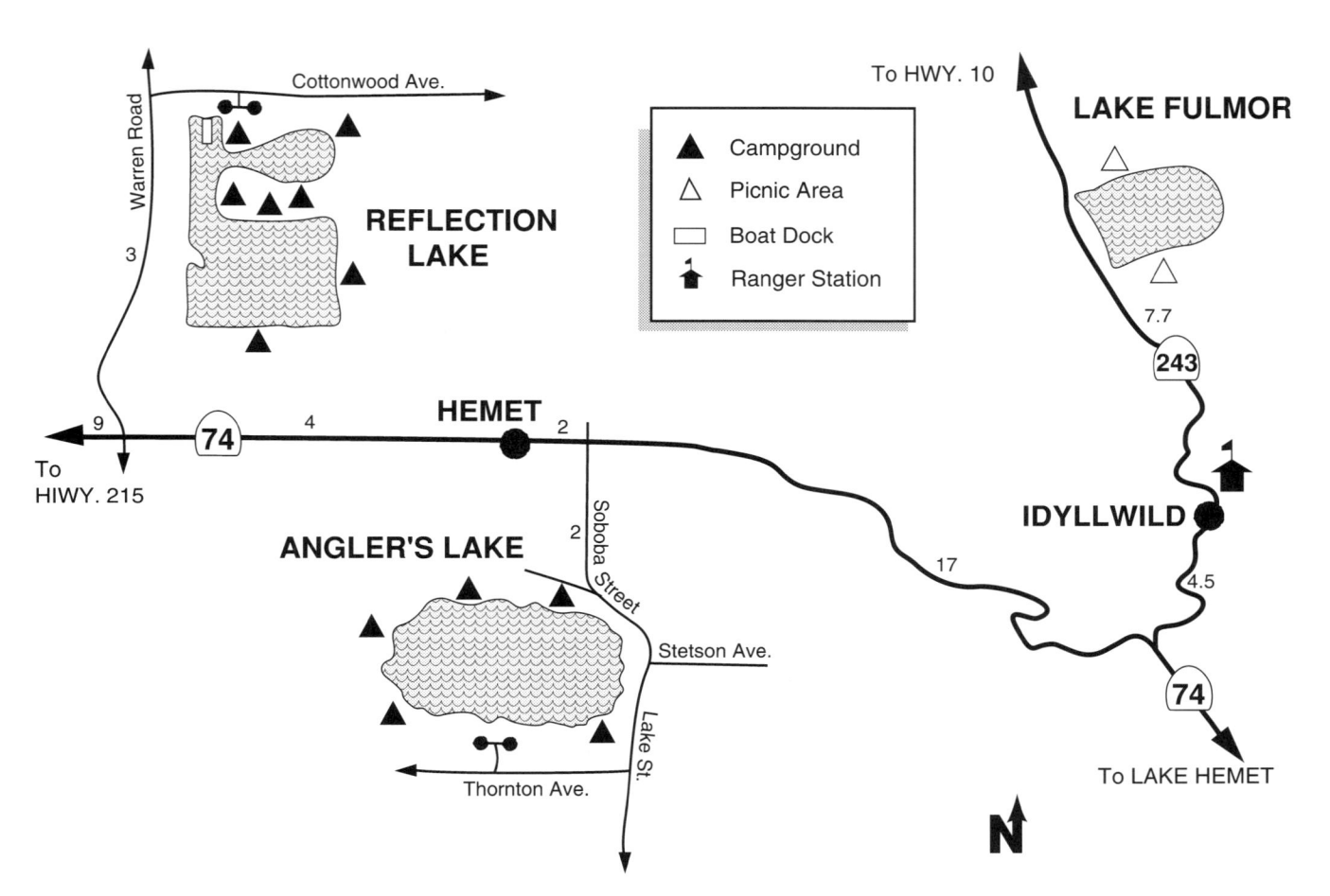

INFORMATION: Reflection Lake, 3440 Cottonwood Ave., San Jacinto 92582—Ph: (909) 654-7906			
CAMPING	**BOATING**	**RECREATION**	**OTHER**

Reflection Lake:
  121 Sites-Water
  and Electric Hookups
Disposal Station
Fees:
  Tents: $17.25
  Hookups: $20.25
 	
Angler's Lake:
  Open Campsites to
  300 People
  Fee: $9
	Reflection Lake:
	  Row, Canoe &
	  Inflatables,
	  Electric Motors
	  Only
	
	Angler's & Fulmor:
	  No Boating
	
	*Be Certain to Check
	Status of Current
	Water Levels*
		Fishing: Trout, Bass,
		  Bluegill & Catfish
		Fishing Fees:
		  Angler's Lake: $12
		  Stocked Twice a
		  Week Every Week
		  Reflection Lake:
		  Campers $7
		  Day Use $9
		  No Limit-No License
		Picnicking
		Hiking
		No Swimming
			Angler's Lake
			  42660 Thornton Ave.
			  Hemet 92544
			  Ph: (909) 927-2614
			
			Lake Fulmor:
			  Idyllwild Ranger Station
			  54270 Pine Crest Rd.
			  Idyllwild 92349
			  Ph: (909) 659-2117

Lake Hemet rests at an elevation of 4,400 feet in a pleasant mountain meadow of the San Bernardino National Forest. Surrounded by chaparral covered hills, this 420 acre Lake is under the jurisdiction of the Lake Hemet Municipal Water District. Boating is limited to fishing boats. Large trout are caught throughout the year. In addition, the angler will find a good bass and catfish fishery. There is a large developed campground at the Lake. Nearby Hurkey Creek has a campground operated by Riverside County. Although swimming is not allowed in Lake Hemet, swimming is permitted at Hurkey Creek when water level permits.

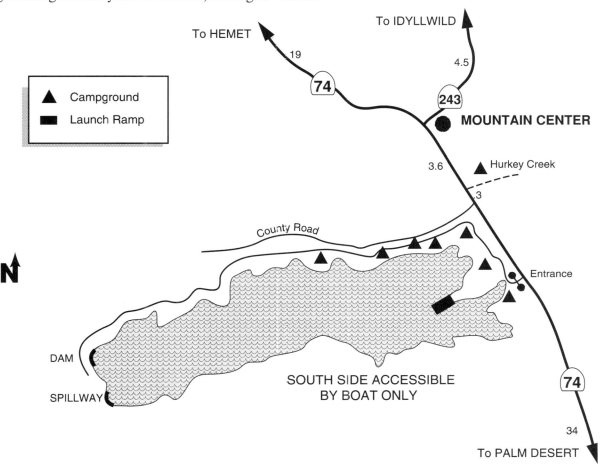

INFORMATION: Lake Hemet, Box 4, Mountain Center 92361—Ph: (714) 659-2680

CAMPING	BOATING	RECREATION	OTHER

Lake Hemet:
   900 Dev. Sites for
   Tents & R.V.s
   Electric &
      Water Hookups
   Pay Showers
   Fee: $12
Hurkey Creek:
   310 Sites
   Tents & R.V.s
   No Hookups
   Group Sites
   Fee: $15
	No Canoes, Kayaks,
	   Sailboats,
	   Inflatables or
	   Boats Less Than
	   10 Feet in Length
	Rentals: Rowboats &
	   Motors
	10 MPH Speed Limit
	Launch Ramp
		Fishing: Trout, Bass
		   & Catfish
		Picnicking
		Hiking
		No Swimming
		Wading Pool
		Two Playgrounds
		Horse Shoe Pits
		Basketball Court
		No Motorcycles
			General Store:
			   Food
			   Camping Supplies
			   Bait & Tackle
			   Propane
			
			Private Group Camping
			   Area

LAKE CAHUILLA

Lake Cahuilla is at an elevation of 44 feet, southwest of Indio. This 135-surface acre Lake is owned by the Coachella Valley Water District. The palm-shaded park is operated by Riverside County Park District. Located in the desert with temperatures up to 100 degrees, Cahuilla offers a pleasant retreat. This oasis offers an abundance of well-maintained campsites along with a secluded group campground and a shady picnic area. A swimming pool with sandy beach is open from April to October. The winter months can be delightful with temperatures of 75 degrees luring the camper and fisherman to this nice facility.

To RIVERSIDE
75
Washington St. 3
To PALM SPRINGS
24
10
94
To BLYTHE
INDIO
LA QUINTA
N
CANAL
3
COACHELLA
111
5
Avenue 58
5
Jefferson St.
Jetty
2
MECCA
195
Entrance
Play Area & Beach
7
6
86
SALTON SEA
(See Page 186)
18
To SALTON CITY

▲	Campground
▲▲	Group Campground
△	Picnic Area
▭	Unimproved Ramp
〰	Golf Course

INFORMATION: Lake Cahuilla, 58075 Jefferson St., La Quinta 92253—Ph: (760) 564-4712

CAMPING	BOATING	RECREATION	OTHER
80 Primitive Sites Fee: $12 55 Developed Sites Water & Electric Hookups: $16 Group Sites Available Disposal Station Phone Riverside County Park District for Reservations (800) 234-7275	Sail, Row, Electric Motors Only Speed Limit - 10 MPH Hand Launch Only	Fishing: Rainbow Trout (Winter), Channel Catfish Striped Bass Fishing Pier Accessible to Handicapped Swimming Pool Open April - October Picnicking Hiking & Backpacking Horseback Trails	Security Gate Locked Between 10:00 p.m. and 6:00 a.m. Full Facilities at Indio

The 6,127 acres of the Imperial Wildlife Area hosts one of Southern California's most abundant wildlife habitats. The Wister Unit consists of a series of deep and shallow water ponds, good for sightseeing and nature study. This is the home of a rich variety of birds, fish, amphibians, reptiles and mammals. With prime waterfowl hunting available, there are restrictions which apply to the number of hunters and other regulations; contact the Wildlife Headquarters for details. There is also a warm water fishery. Located below sea level in the hot desert climate of the Imperial Valley, the temperature is often over 100 degrees in the summer months. A more temperate climate of 70 degrees prevails in fall, winter and spring.

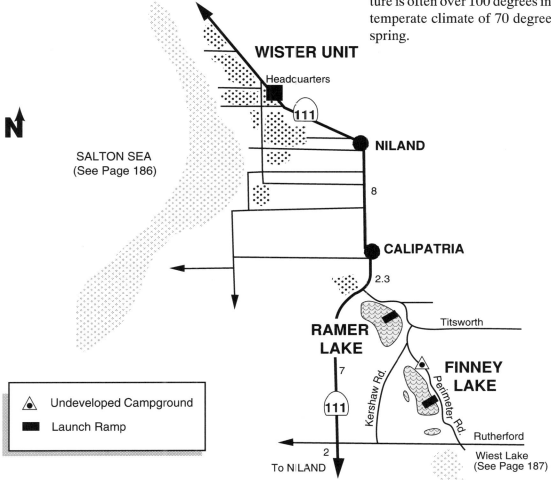

WISTER UNIT

Headquarters

111

NILAND

SALTON SEA
(See Page 186)

8

CALIPATRIA

2.3

RAMER LAKE

Titsworth

FINNEY LAKE

Kershaw Rd.

Perimeter Rd.

7

111

Rutherford

2

To NILAND

Wiest Lake
(See Page 187)

△ Undeveloped Campground

▪ Launch Ramp

INFORMATION: Imperial Wildlife Area, Route 1, Box 6, Niland 92257—Ph: (760) 359-0577			
CAMPING	**BOATING**	**RECREATION**	**OTHER**
Primitive Open Camping Fire Rings	Finney-Ramer: No Power Boats Electric Motors Only	Fishing: Largemouth Bass, Bluegill Crappie, Catfish & Carp	Nearest Facilities in Niland
Day Use Permit Required	Wister Ponds: No Boating	Picnicking Hiking: Service & Visitor Access Roads	
Wister Unit Entrance Fee: $2.50	*Call for Current Water Level Conditions*	Nature Study Hunting - Shotguns Only *Call for Restrictions*: Duck, Geese, Dove Quail, Pheasant & Rabbit	

SALTON SEA

The Salton Sea is located in a desert valley 228 feet below sea level surrounded by mountains reaching to 10,000 feet. It is one of the world's largest inland bodies of salt water with a surface area of 360 square miles. Although summer temperatures range well over 100 degrees, fall, winter and spring temperatures are in the 70's. Orangemouth Corvina, Croaker

(Bairdiella) and Sargo were introduced from the Gulf of California and the Tilapia was imported from Africa. These fish have flourished and the angler is rewarded with California's richest inland fishery. Numerous marinas, campgrounds and resorts support the recreational abundance of this desert oasis. *Very strong winds can come up at times causing dangerous boating conditions so caution is advised.*

...Continued..

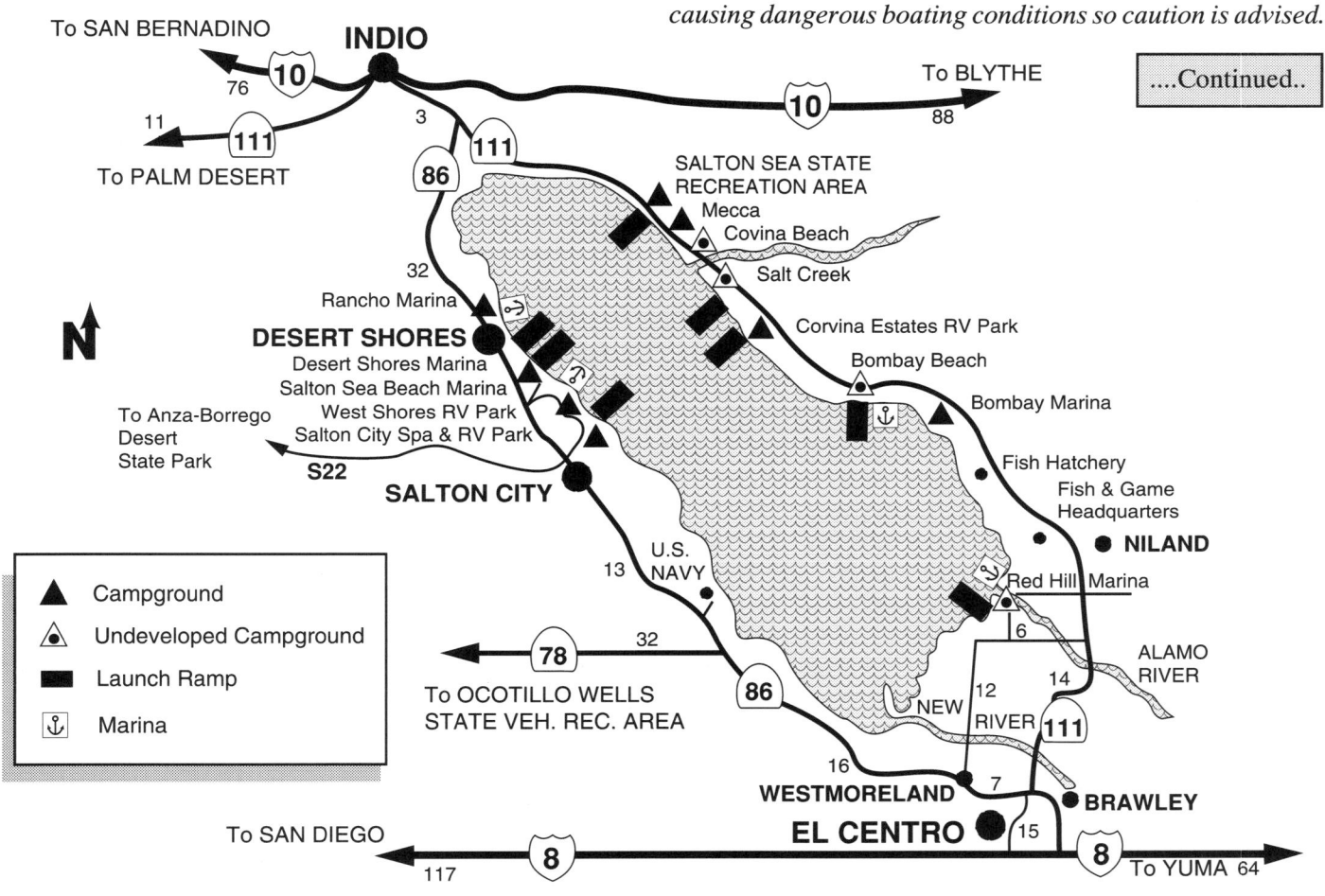

	Campground
	Undeveloped Campground
	Launch Ramp
	Marina

INFORMATION: See Following Page			
CAMPING	**BOATING**	**RECREATION**	**OTHER**
See Following Page for Campgrounds	Open to All Boating Full Service Marinas Launch Ramps Gas, Docks Dry Storage *Caution: Sudden Strong Winds* *Many Unmarked Underwater Hazards Especially at North & South Ends*	Fishing: Corvina, Gulf Croaker, Tilapia Swimming Beaches Picnicking - Shade Ramadas Nature Trails Birdwatching 9-Hole Golf Course Hunting: Waterfowl, Pheasant, Dove & Rabbit	Full Facilities Around the Lake Restaurants Mineral Spas For Additional Information Contact Westshores Chamber of Commerce P.O. Box 5185 Salton City 92275 Ph: (760) 394-4112

SALTON SEA STATE RECREATION AREA - 100-225 State Park Rd., North Shore 92254—Ph: (760) 393-3052

Headquarters Campground:
25 Tent/R.V. Sites to 40 Feet, Wheelchair Accessible, 15 Full Hookups, Disposal Station, Hot Showers, Shade Ramadas, Shaded Picnic Area, Fish Cleaning Station, Campfire Programs, Nature Trail to Mecca Beach, Launch Ramp, Mooring, Boat Wash Rack. *Fee: $8- $16 - $2 Senior (62 plus) Discount - Reserve: Ph: (800) 444-7275*

Mecca Beach Campground:
108 Tent/R.V. Sites, Wheelchair Accessible, Solar Showers, Shaded Picnic Area, Fish Cleaning Station, Campfire Programs. *Fees: June 1 to Sept. 30:- $8 & Oct. 1 to May 31 - $12 - $2 Senior Discount*

Covina Beach, Salt Creek & Bombay Beach Campgrounds:
1000 Primitive Sites on Water's Edge, Piped Water, Beach Launch. *Fee: $7 - $2 Senior Discount*

PRIVATELY OPERATED CAMPGROUNDS & MARINAS

CORVINA ESTATES - 10525 Highway 11, Niland 92257, Ph: (760) 354-1220
82 Tent/R.V. Sites, Full Hookups, Season Lease Sites, Hot Showers, Full Service Marina, Launch Ramp, Laundry, Pool/Spa, Exercise Room, Sauna, Horseshoes, Picnic and BBQ Area, Dry Storage, Trailer Rentals - Daily & Monthly.

BOMBAY MARINA - 9518 Avenue B, Niland 92257, Ph: (760) 354-1694
50 Tent/R.V. Sites, 16 Full Hookups, Trailer Rentals, 18 Shaded Sites, Open Tent Camping, Hot Showers, Snacks, Bait & Tackle, Ice, Drinks, Boat Slips, Launch Ramp, Rental Boats.

RED HILL MARINA - Imperial County Resident Ranger, 7581 Garst Rd., Calipatria 92233 - Ph: (760) 348-2310
240 Acre Primitive Tent/R.V. Dry Camp, 80 R.V. Sites, Electric & Water Hookups, 12 Sites Include Sewer Hookup, Showers, Shade Ramadas, Disposal Station, Picnic Tables, Launch Ramp, Docks, Dry Storage, Fish Cleaning Station, Boat Wash Rack, Bait & Tackle, Ice, Day Use: $2.

SALTON CITY SPA & R.V. PARK - P.O. Box 5375, Salton City 92275, Ph: (760) 394-4333
315 R.V. Sites, Full Hookups, Hot Showers, Hot Spa, Swimming Pool, Pool Tables, Poker Room, Horseshoes, Picnic Tables, Dances, Potlucks, Large Rec. Hall, Dry Storage.

WEST SHORES R.V. PARK - North End of Sea Garden - P.O. Box 5312, Salton City 92275, Ph: (760) 394-4755
108 R.V. Sites - Fee: $15, Full Hookups, Hot Showers, Disposal Station, Weekly and Monthly Rates, Launch Ramp, Dock, Fish Cleaning Station, Boat Wash, Restaurant & Bar.

SALTON SEA BEACH MARINA - 288 Coachella, Salton Sea Beach 92274-9517, Ph: (760) 395-5212
144 R.V. Full Hookups, Monthly and Weekly Rates, Overflow Site for Tents & R .V.s, Water & Electric Hookups, 17 Shaded Cabanas, Hot Showers, Gas, Groceries, Bait & Tackle, Fish Cleaning Station, Disposal Station, Launch Ramp, Paddle Boat Rentals, Propane, Boat Gas, Boat & Trailer Storage, Boat Wash Rack, Children's Playground, Open Fires & BBQs, Picnic Tables, .

DESERT SHORES TRAILER PARK & MARINA - Desert Shores 92274, Ph: (760) 395-5280
R.V. Sites with Full Hookups, Laundry, Hot Showers, Launch Ramp, Tie Ups.

RANCHO MARINA - 301 N. Palm Dr., Desert Shores 92274, Ph: (760) 395-5410
75 Tent/R.V. Sites, 47 Full Hookups, Hot Showers.

WIEST LAKE

Wiest Lake is located 4 miles north of Brawley off Highway 111. It is 110 feet below sea level in the agriculturally rich Imperial Valley. This 50 surface acre Lake is under the jurisdiction of Imperial County which operates the facilities. The Lake is open to all types of boating from fishing boats to waterskis. There is a good warm water fishery. The visitor will find picnic sites, a swimming area and hiking trails. Although there is no shooting within the park, the hunter will find waterfowl, dove and rabbit in the nearby Imperial Wildlife Area. Frogging is also popular. Hot summer temperatures are a burden but a more moderate climate prevails in the fall, winter and spring.

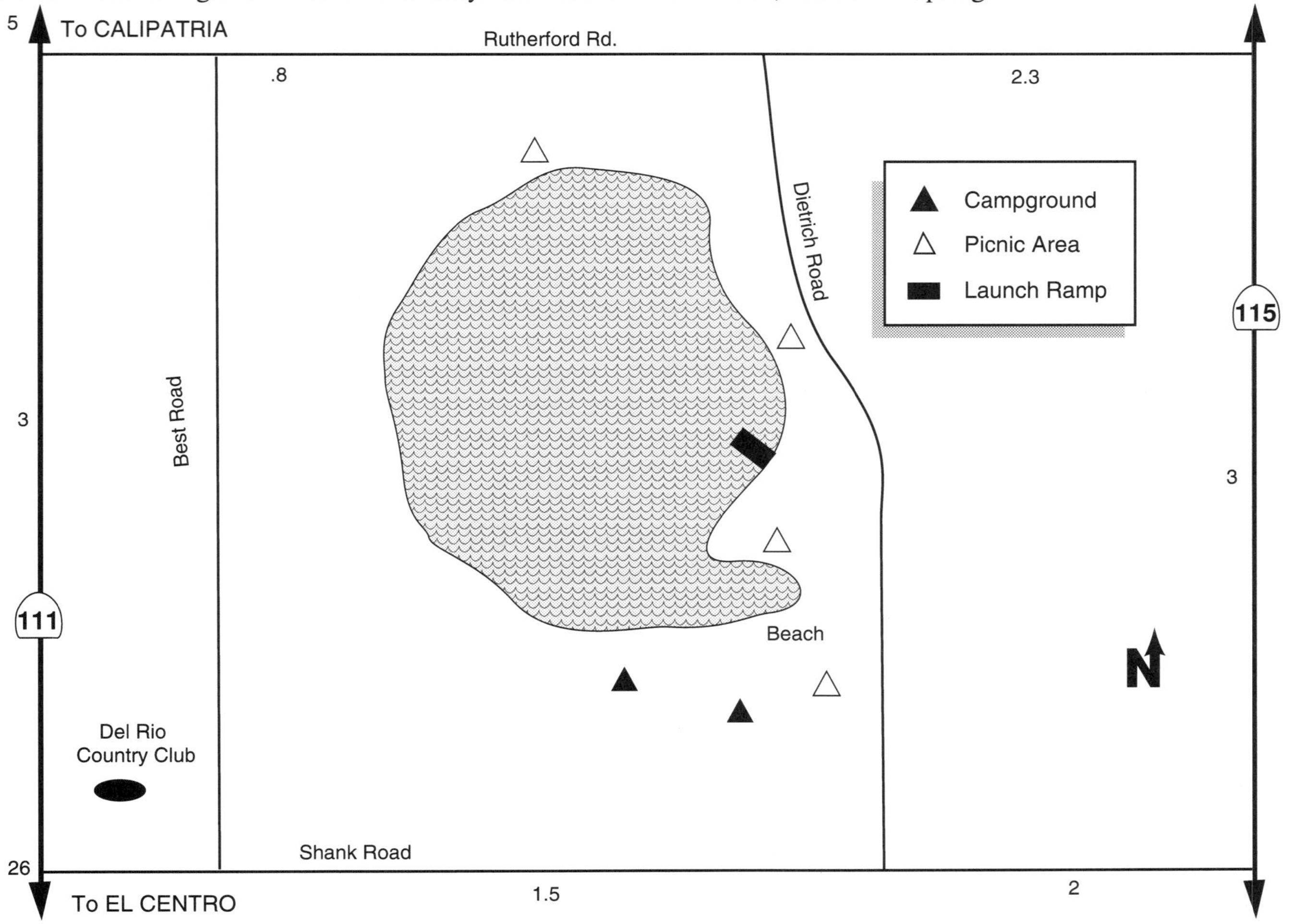

▲	Campground
△	Picnic Area
■	Launch Ramp

To CALIPATRIA · Rutherford Rd. · .8 · 2.3 · Dietrich Road · 115 · Best Road · 5 · 3 · 111 · Beach · 3 · N · Del Rio Country Club · 26 · Shank Road · 1.5 · 2 · To EL CENTRO

INFORMATION: Wiest Lake, 5351 Dietrich Rd., Brawley 92227—Ph: (760) 344-3712

CAMPING	BOATING	RECREATION	OTHER

20 Tent Sites
  Fee: $7
23 R.V. Sites
  Electric & Water
  Hookups
  Fee: $12
Handicapped Facilities
Disposal Station
	Open to All Boating
	Paved Launch Ramp
	Docks
		Fishing: Largemouth
		  Bass, Bluegill,
		  Catfish &
		  Carp
		Picnicking
		Hiking
		Nature Study
		Swimming (Summer)
		Nearby:
		  Hunting: Duck,
		  Geese, Dove,
		  Quail, Rabbit
		Frogging
			Full Facilities in
			  Brawley &
			  El Centro

Sunbeam Lake is 22 surface acres. The Lagoon with 12 surface acres is for fishing only. Owned and operated by Imperial County, the park offers a variety of recreational opportunities. Boating is allowed but power boats are limited to Sunbeam Lake only. The fisherman will find a variety of warm water fish in the cool spring-fed Lagoon. These Lakes are 43 feet below sea level where summer temperatures average over 100 degrees. Fall, winter and spring are in the 70's. Surrounded by palm trees, this Lake is a welcome oasis just one-half mile off Highway 8 and a good place to stop in the hot summer months for a refreshing swim.

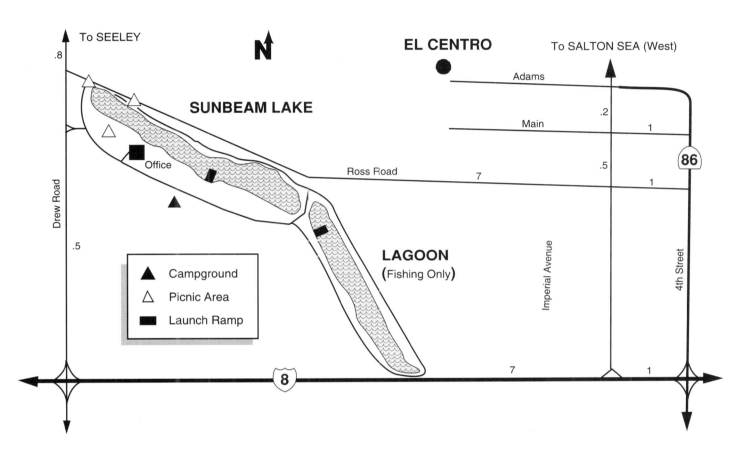

INFORMATION: Imperial County Parks & Recreation, 1002 State St., El Centro 92243—Ph: (760) 339-4384

CAMPING	BOATING	RECREATION	OTHER
Sunbeam Lake R.V. Park 1716 West Sunbeam Lake Dr. El Centro 92243 Ph: (760) 352-7154 309 R.V. Sites Full Hookups Fee: $25 Tents: May - Sept. Only	Power, Row, Canoe, Sail, Waterski, Jets, Windsurf & Inflatables No Power Boats in Lagoon Launch Ramp Docks Dry Storage Day Use Fee: $2	Fishing: Catfish, Trout, Bluegill, Crappie, Smallmouth Bass Swimming Picnicking Hiking Frogging Hunting Nearby In Season: Quail, Dove, Waterfowl, Pheasant & Rabbit	Snack Bar Grocery Store Gas Station Disposal Station No Alcoholic Beverages in County Park but Allowed in R.V. Park

DIXON LAKE

The Dixon Lake Recreation Area is operated by the City of Escondido Parks and Recreation Department. Nestled in chaparral and avocado-covered foothills, Dixon Lake is at an elevation of 1,045 feet. It has a surface area of 70 acres with 2 miles of shoreline within this 527 acre park. The facilities are excellent for camping, fishing and picnicking. Many large bass and catfish await the angler. Trout are stocked at Dixon Lake from November through May and catfish from June through August.

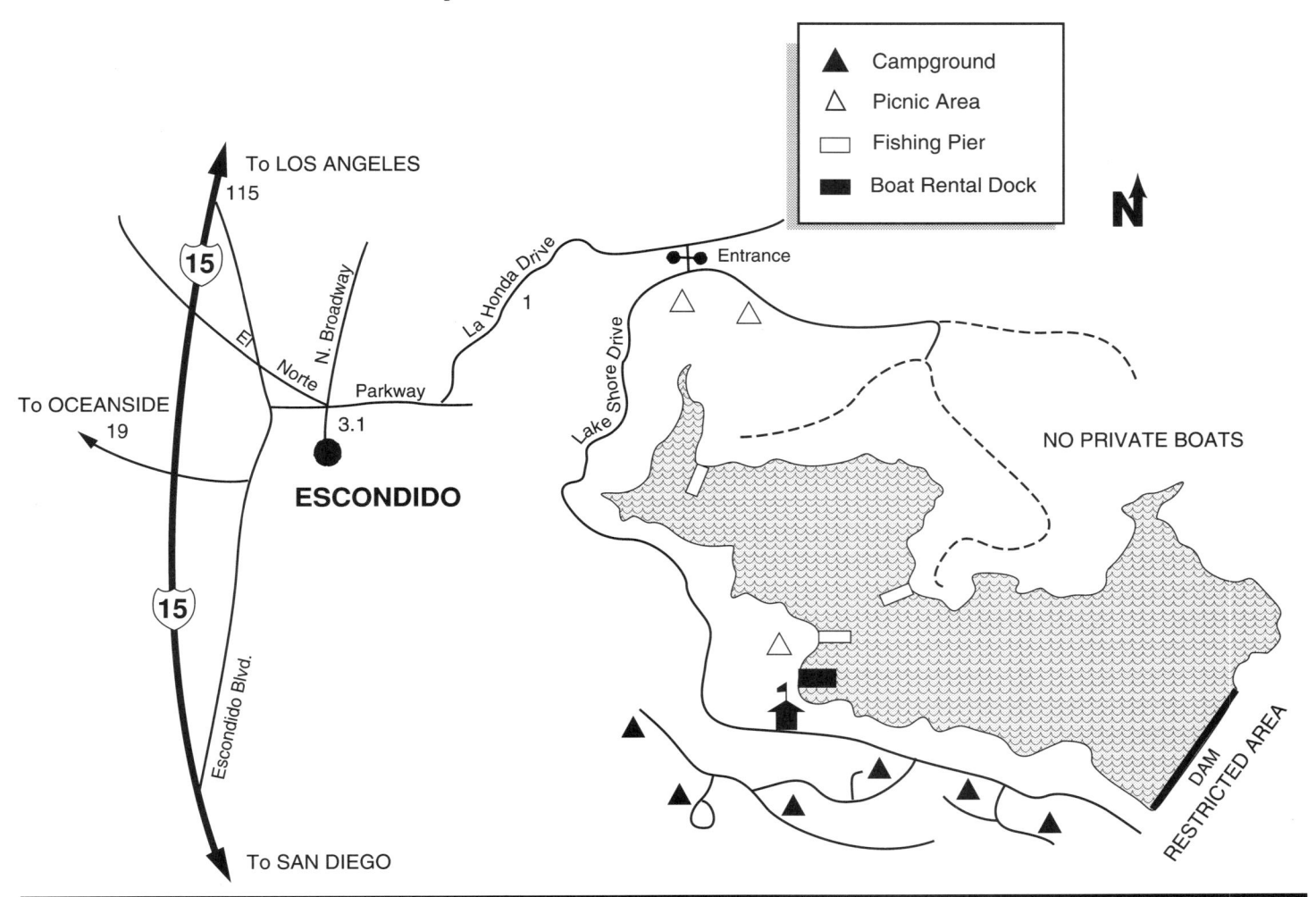

INFORMATION: Public Works Dept./Lakes, 201 N. Broadway, Escondido 92025—Ranger Ph: (760) 741-4680

CAMPING	BOATING	RECREATION	OTHER

35 Tent & R.V. Sites
   Fee: $12
   2nd Vehicle: $2
10 Full Hookup Sites
   Fee: $16
   2nd Vehicle: $2
 	
Reservations Accepted
   Fee: $5
   Ph: (760) 741-3328
   8 a.m. - 5 p.m.
	No Private Boats
	Rentals: Rowboats
	   with Electric Motors,
	   Paddleboats
		Fishing: Trout,
		   Catfish, Bluegill,
		   Redear Sunfish,
		   Florida Bass
		No Swimming or
		   Wading
		Picnicking :
		   Reservations
		   Ph: (760) 741-3328
		Hiking - Nature Trails
		Campfire Programs
			Snack Bar
			Bait & Tackle
			Disposal Station
			Fishing Pier with
			   Handicapped Facilities
			Full Facilities in Escondido

Lake Henshaw is at an elevation of 2,740 feet in a valley on the south slopes of Palomar Mountain. The water level varies with the demands of man and nature. In 1942, the Lake reached its highest mark of nearly 25 miles of shoreline. The present shoreline is approximately 5 miles with a surface area of 1,137 acres. The large oak trees around the resort area create a pleasant contrast to the surrounding semi-arid mountains. The resort offers a nice campground with excellent support facilities. Lake Henshaw is long known for its good fishing for bass, crappie, bluegill and channel catfish.

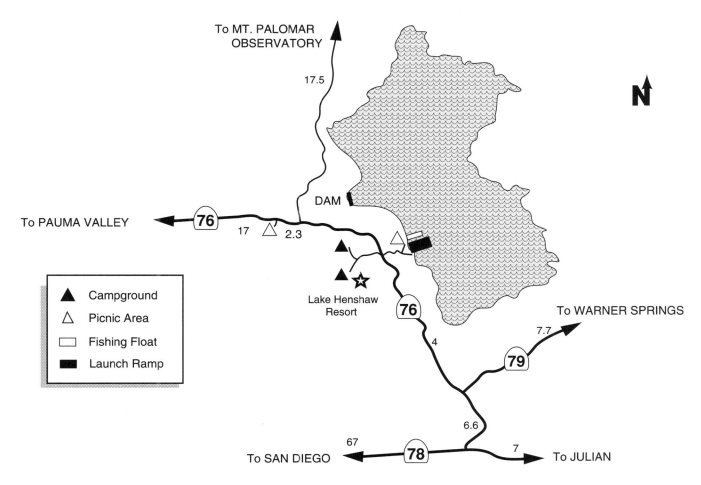

▲	Campground
△	Picnic Area
▭	Fishing Float
▬	Launch Ramp

INFORMATION: Lake Henshaw Resort, 26439 Hwy. 76, Santa Ysabel 92070—Ph: (760) 782-3501

CAMPING	BOATING	RECREATION	OTHER

84 Dev. Sites for Tents
  Fee: $14
20 Dev. Sites for R.V.s
  Full Hookups
  Fee: $16
  (Available at Times -
  Several Permanent
  Residents)
Disposal Station
  Fee: $5
	Power & Row
	  10 Feet Minimum
	  Length
	  NO Canoes or Rafts
	10 MPH Speed Limit
	Launch Ramp
	Rentals: Fishing
	  Boats
		Fishing :
		  Catfish, Bluegill,
		  Crappie & Bass
		Fishing Float
		Swimming - Pool Only
		Picnicking
		Hiking
		Playgrounds
		Club House
			17 Housekeeping Cabins
			  Reservations:
			  Ph: (760) 782-3487
			Restaurant
			Grocery Store
			Bait & Tackle
			Hot Showers
			Laundromat
			Propane
			Pool & Jacuzzi

AGUA HEDIONDA LAGOON, LAKE WOHLFORD, and PALOMAR PARK (DOANE POND)

From a saltwater lagoon to a coniferous mountain meadow pond at 5,500 feet, the Lakes on this page offer a striking contrast. Doane Pond is in the Palomar State Park with hiking and nature trails, picnic sites and campgrounds. Trout are caught seasonally; November through June are the best months. Wohlford, at 1,500 feet, is a good fishing Lake for trout from mid-December until the weekend after Labor Day. Wohlford is famous for trophy size largemouth bass. Channel catfish and pan fish are also available. Sailboats and rafts are not permitted. Agua Hedionda Lagoon is a large saltwater lagoon off Interstate Highway 5 which offers all types of boating. This is a popular waterskiing facility. There is a water ski school along with personal water craft rentals, a watersports pro shop, a 3-1ane paved launch ramp, dry storage and a concession.

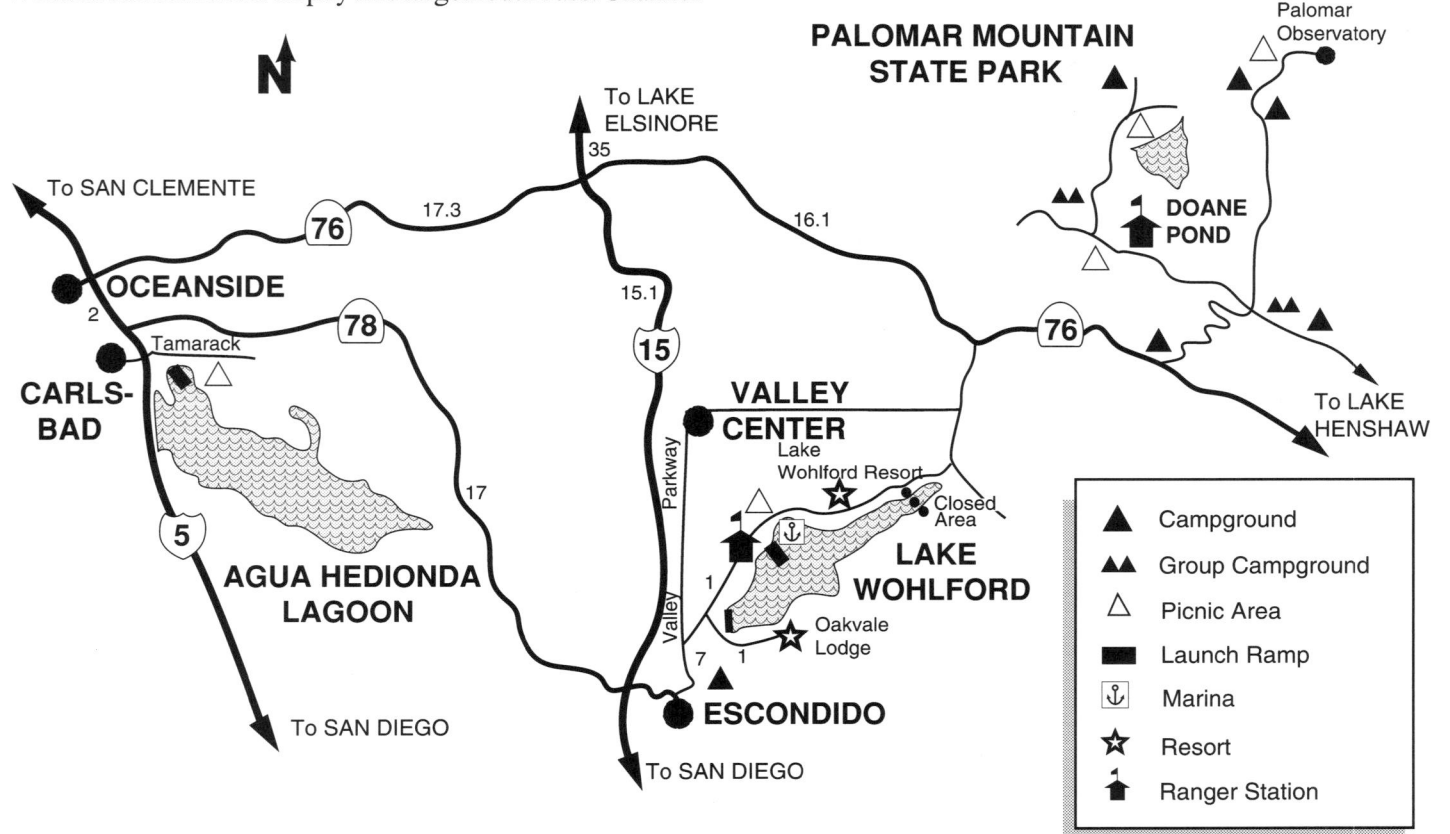

CAMPING	BOATING	RECREATION	OTHER

INFORMATION: *Only* Palomar Mountain State Park, P.O. Box 175, Palomar 92060—Ph: (760) 742-3462

CAMPING	BOATING	RECREATION	OTHER
Doane Valley Campground: 31 Dev. Sites - Fee: $16 Groups Camps - 15 to 25 People - Fee: $65 Reserve:Ph:(800) 444-7275	Agua Hedionda: Open to All Boats *Call for Regulations* Launch Fee Speed Limit: 45 MPH Rentals: Jets, Canoes & Kayaks Water Ski School	Doane Pond: No Boating No Swimming Agua Hedionda: No Swimming Lake Wohlford: No Swimming No Alcohol	Lake Wohlford Ranger Station: Ph: (760) 738-4346 Lake Wohlford Resort: 25484 Lake Wohlford Rd. Escondido 92027 Ph: (760) 749-2755
Agua Hedionda Lagoon: Snug Harbor 4215 Harrison St. Carlsbad 92008 Ph: (619) 434-3089 Summer Youth Camps	Lake Wohlford:No Sailboats 20 Feet Max. Length Speed Limit: 5 MPH Rentals: Fishing Boats Private Launch: $4	Fishing: Trout, Bass, Catfish, Crappie & Bluegill Picnicking Hiking Trails Nature Study	7 R.V. Sites Full Hookups Cabins with Kitchens Swimming Pool, Cafe

These Lakes in the San Diego area provide a popular warm water fishery. In addition, the angler will find trout planted during the winter months. The Lake Poway Recreation Area provides 8 primitive camp sites in a beautiful oak grove located via a one-mile hike from the lake. Picnic sites, nature and equestrian trails and an archery range are also available.

The 60 acre Lake is open to row and electric motor boat rentals and night fishing is allowed. The Santee Lakes Recreational Area offers modern campsites with a swimming pool, picnic facilities, playgrounds, volleyball courts and horseshoe pits. Both Poway and Santee Lakes are closed to private boating but rentals are available.

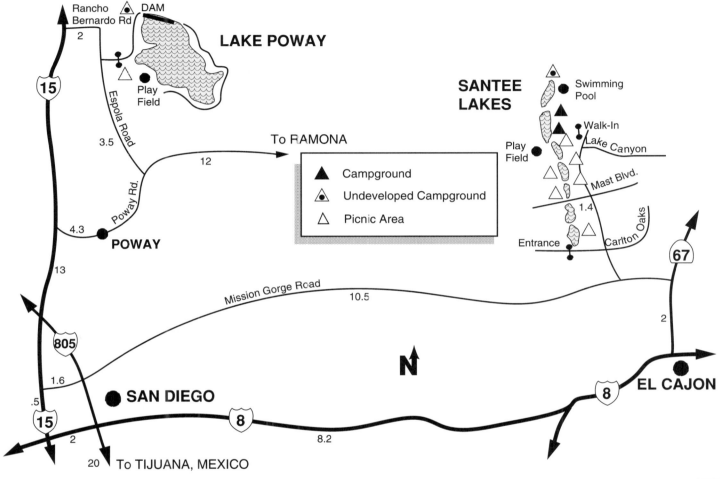

INFORMATION: Santee Lakes, P.O. Box 719003, Santee 92072—Ph: (619) 448-2482

CAMPING	BOATING	RECREATION	OTHER

Santee Lakes:
    152 R.V. Sites
    Full Hookups
    Fee: $20
    60 Primitive Sites
    Disposal Station
    Laundry & Groceries
    Swimming Pool
Lake Poway:
    8 Walk-in Only Sites
        With Water
	Lake Poway:
	    No Private Boats
	    Rentals: Rowboats &
	        Motorboats,
	        Paddle Boats, Canoes
	Santee Lakes:
	    No Private Boats
	    Rentals: Sailboats,
	        Rowboats, Paddleboats
	        & Canoes
		Fishing: Trout (Winter)
		    Florida Bass,
		    Bluegill & Channel
		    Catfish
		Family & Group
		    Picnic Sites
		Hiking, Riding &
		    Nature Trails-Poway
		Santee Lakes
		    Group Area & Store
		    Playgrounds
		    Volleyball Courts
		    Horseshoe Pits
			Lake Poway
			    P.O. Box 789
			    Poway 92074
			    Ph: (619) 679-5465
			Snack Bar
			Bait & Tackle
			2 Playgrounds
			Tournament Volleyball
			    Courts, Horseshoes
			Softball - Night Lights
			15 Acre Grass Picnic Area
			    Group Reservations

Lake Cuyamaca is at an elevation of 4,650 feet in a mountain setting of oak, pine and cedar forests. The dam was originally built in 1887. Thanks to a dedicated group of residents and sportsmen, the minimum pool is 110 surface acres. Normally this is the only Lake in San Diego County that has trout all year. Cuyamaca stocks 44,000 pounds of rainbow trout each year. It offers excellent fishing for warm water fish as well. Cuyamaca Rancho State Park has over 100 miles of scenic horseback riding and hiking trails. Los Caballos Campground offers developed sites including corrals for families with horses. In addition, Los Vaqueros Campground is for equestrian groups with facilities for 45 horses.

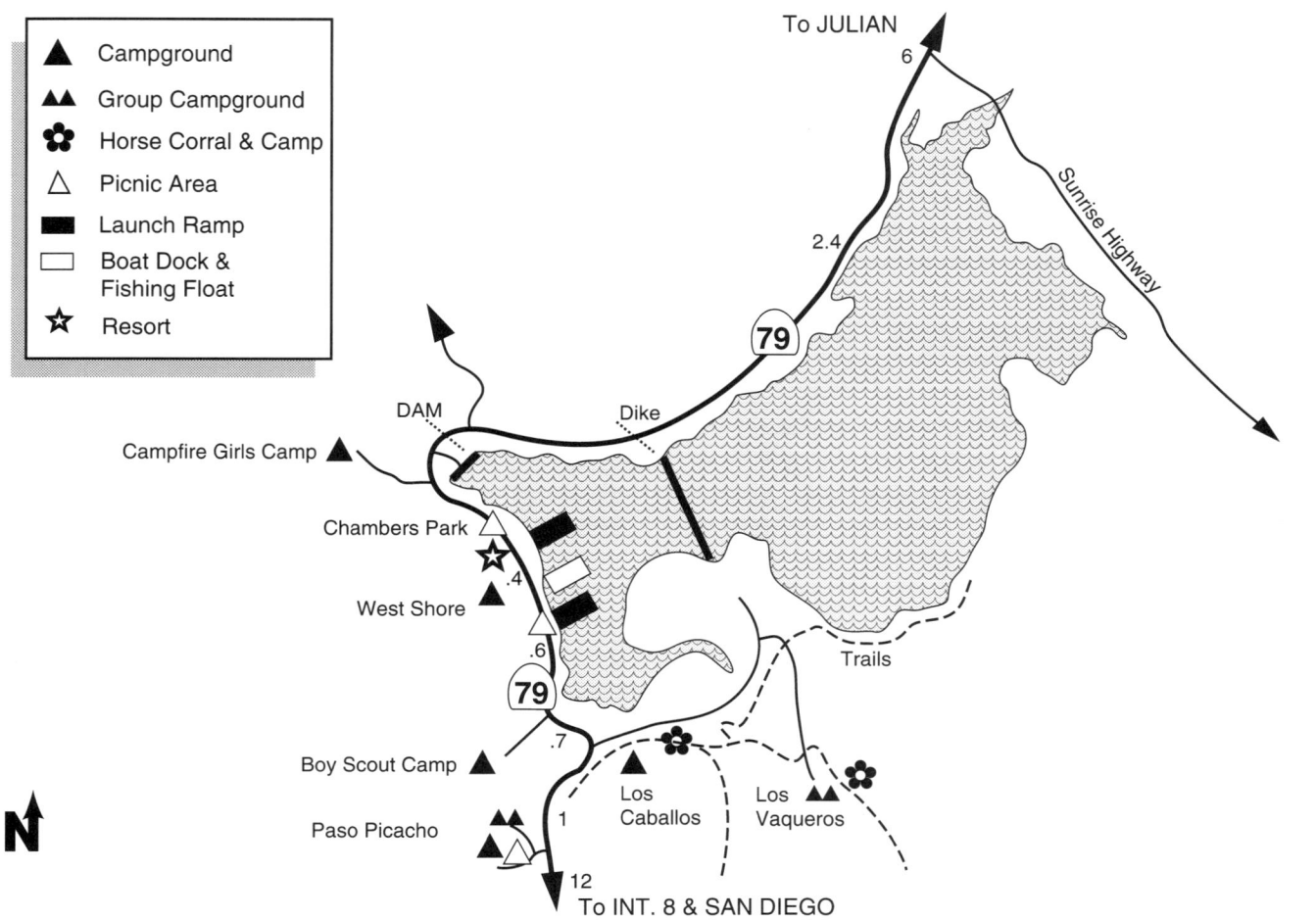

▲	Campground
▲▲	Group Campground
❀	Horse Corral & Camp
△	Picnic Area
■	Launch Ramp
▭	Boat Dock & Fishing Float
☆	Resort

INFORMATION: Park Ranger, 15027 Highway 79, Julian 92036—Ph: (760) 765-0515

CAMPING	BOATING	RECREATION	OTHER

At Lake For R.V.s Only
  23 Sites with Hookups
    Fee: $167
  27 Sites No Hookups
    Fee: $12
Cuyamaca Rancho State Pk:
Dev. Sites For Tents/R.V.s
To 30 Feet - Fee: $16 - $20
  12 Tent Sites: $12
Group Sites - 120 Max. $90
Group Horse Sites 45
  Horses Max. Fee: $175
Reserve:Ph: (800) 444-7275
	Power & Row Boats
	  Between 10 Feet &
	  18 Feet Only
	  Inflatables Must
	  Have Discernible
	  Bow & Stern, 9-18 Feet
	  Wood Bottom and
	  Multiple Inflatable
	  Compartments
	Speed Limit - 10 MPH
	Launch Ramp
	Rentals: Boat & Motor,
	  Canoes, Paddle Boats
		Fishing: Trout, Crappie,
		  Catfish, Bluegill &
		  Smallmouth Bass
		Fishing Fees:
		  Adults - $4.75
		  Children Over
		    8 Yrs. - $2.50
		  Under 8 Yrs. - Free
		Free Fishing Class Sat.
		No Swimming or Body
		  Contact with Water
		Hiking
		Backpacking [Parking]
			Snack Bar
			Restaurant
			Grocery Store
			Bait & Tackle
			Disposal Station
			Gas Station
			
			Hunting: Duck
			  Wed. & Sat. a.m. in
			  Season

SAN DIEGO CITY LAKES: HODGES, SUTHERLAND, MIRAMAR, SAN VICENTE, EL CAPITAN, MURRAY, UPPER and LOWER OTAY and BARRETT

These popular Lakes provide some of the best bass fishing in America. They are operated by the City of San Diego.

See the following page for full details on each Lake

....Continued....

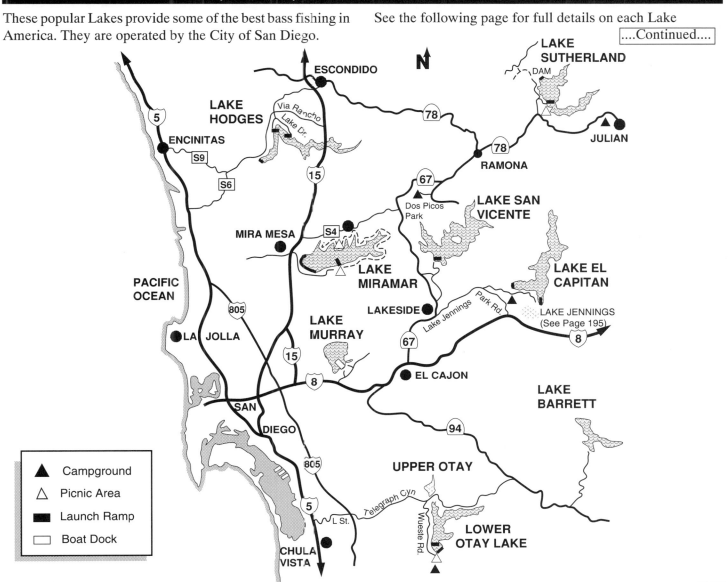

Legend:
- ▲ Campground
- △ Picnic Area
- ■ Launch Ramp
- ▭ Boat Dock

INFORMATION: Water Dept., Lakes Recreation, 12375 Moreno Ave., Lakeside 92040—Ph: (619) 668-2050

CAMPING	BOATING	RECREATION	OTHER

There is No Camping at Any of the San Diego City Lakes
 	
See Following Page for Nearest Camping
	Power, Row, Sail & Inflatables
	Subject to Inspection
	Speed Limits Vary
	Fee: $5 Any Private Boat Use Including Canoes & Kayaks
	Rentals: Rowboats, Motorboats, Canoes, Paddleboats
		Fishing Hot Line:
		  Ph: (619) 465-3474
		Fishing Permits:
		  Adults: $5
		  Children 8-15 yrs. $2.50
		Water Contact Activities:
		  Adults: $5
		  Children 8-15 yrs. $2.50
		Slalom Course: $10
			Reservations:
			Hodges (619) 272-3275
			Sutherland (619) 698-3474
			All Others (619) 390-0222
			
			Except Barrett - Privately Operated Concessions at each Lake Offer Sale of Permits, Licenses, Bait & Tackle, Food & Beverages

The following Lakes are open from Sunrise to Sunset unless stated otherwise.

LAKE HODGES is at an elevation of 330 feet and is located approximately 31 miles north of San Diego and 5 miles south of Escondido. This Lake has a maximum surface area of 1,234 acres with 27 miles of chaparral-covered shoreline. The Lake is open from mid-March to early November on Wednesday, Saturday and Sunday for picnicking, hiking and boating and fishing for bass, crappie, bluegill and channel catfish. A sailboarding program is also offered on those days from mid-April to mid-October. In addition to rowboat and motorboat rentals, there are canoe, kayak and sailboard rentals.

LAKE SUTHERLAND is at an elevation of 2,074 feet and is located 45 miles northeast of San Diego, between Ramona and Julian. This Lake has a maximum surface area of 557 acres with 11 miles of oak and chaparral-covered shoreline. The Lake is open from March to early October on Friday, Saturday, and Sunday for picnicking, hiking, boating and fishing for bass, bluegill, sunfish, crappie, channel catfish and blue catfish. During the season (October through January) this Lake also offers waterfowl hunting on Tuesday and Sunday. The nearest camping is at William Heise County Park or Dos Picos County Park.

LAKE MIRAMAR is at an elevation of 714 feet and is located approximately 18 miles north of San Diego. This small Lake has a maximum surface area of 162 acres and 4 miles of shoreline. The Lake is open from early November through September on Saturday, Sunday, Monday and Tuesday for boating and fishing for bass, bluegill, sunfish, channel catfish, and trout (stocked November through May). It is open 7 days a week for picnicking, walking, jogging, bicycling, skating, etc. year round. In addition to rowboat and motorboat rentals, this Lake offers canoe and paddleboat rentals.

LAKE SAN VICENTE is at elevation of 659 feet and is located in Lakeside, approximately 25 miles northeast of San Diego. The Lake has a maximum surface area of 1,069 acres with 14 miles of shoreline. The Lake is open on Tuesday, Friday, Saturday and Sunday. On Tuesday and Friday the Lake is open for both water contact activities (waterskiing, knee boarding, tubing, etc.) and fishing for bass, bluegill, crappie, sunfish, channel, blue and white catfish and trout (planted from November to May). Activities on weekends vary by season; from mid-May to mid-October - water contact activities only. On weekends and from mid-October to mid-May, fishing only. A slalom course is available at this Lake on a first-come basis. Nearest camping is at Lake Jennings County Park.

LAKE EL CAPITAN is at an elevation of 750 feet and is located in the foothills of Lakeside approximately 30 miles northeast of San Diego. There is a maximum surface area of 1,562 acres with 22 miles of bushy shoreline. The Lake is open on Friday, Saturday and Sunday for picnicking, hiking, boating, water contact activities (waterskiing, knee boarding, tubing, use of personal watercraft) and fishing for bass, bluegill, blue and channel catfish, crappie and sunfish. Nearest camping is at Lake Jennings County Park.

LAKE MURRAY is the "in town" reservoir located between San Diego and La Mesa at the base of Cowles Mountain. The Lake has a maximum surface area of 172 acres with over 3 miles of shoreline. The Lake is open on Wednesday, Saturday, and Sunday for boating and fishing for bass, crappie, bluegill, channel catfish and trout (stocked November through May) from early November through Labor Day. It is open 7 days a week for picnicking, walking, jogging, bicyling, skating, etc. year round. In addition to rowboat and motorboat rentals, this Lake offers canoe and paddleboat rentals.

LOWER OTAY LAKE is in the rolling chaparral-covered hills east of Chula Vista, approximately 20 miles southeast of San Diego. The maximum surface area is 1,100 acres with 25 miles of shoreline. The Lake is open on Wednesday, Saturday and Sunday for picnicking, hiking, boating and fishing for bass, crappie, bluegill and channel, blue and white catfish from late January through September. During the season (October through January) this Lake also offers waterfowl hunting on Wednesday and Saturday. Nearest camping is at Sweetwater Summit County Park.

UPPER OTAY LAKE is located just north of Lower Otay. The maximum surface area is 20 acres with 5 miles of shoreline. The Lake is open on Wednesday, Saturday and Sunday for fishing for bass, bluegill, bullhead and trout (stocked periodically during the winter). This is a catch and release only fishery with use of barbless hooks on artificial lures only. No boats are allowed, fishing is from shore, wading or float tube only. Permits are purchased at the concession at Lower Otay. During the season (October through January) this Lake also offers waterfowl hunting on Wednesday and Saturday.

LAKE BARRETT is located in a remote area 35 miles east of San Diego. The maximum surface area is 861 acres with 12 miles of shoreline. The Lake is open for fishing for black bass, bluegill, crappie and bullhead on a limited basis (25 parties per day with each party consisting of no more than 4 people) from 5:00 am to sunset on Saturday and Sunday from mid-April through September. There are no concession services available at this Lake. This is a catch and release only fishery with use of barbless hooks on artificial lures only. Reservations can be obtained with Ticketmaster by calling (619) 220-TIXS. During the season (October through January) this Lake also offers waterfowl hunting on Wednesday and Saturday.

Lake Jennings County Park is east of El Cajon at an elevation of 690 feet. It is owned by the Helix Water District which administers strict sanitation standards for this domestic water supply reservoir of 180 surface acres with 2,500 feet of shoreline. The 5 miles of fairly steep shoreline is semi-arid dotted with sumac trees and a few pine trees. Lake Jennings County Park, a total of 100 acres, is open year round. The Park is open for day users on Fridays, Saturday and Sundays only but open every day for campers. Trout season runs from October through May. Catfish season runs from June through September. The Lake remains open until midnight on Fridays and Saturdays during catfish season only. This is the Lake for big channel or blue catfish; the largest was a 46 pound blue catfish. There is also a 190 foot handicapped accessible fishing float.

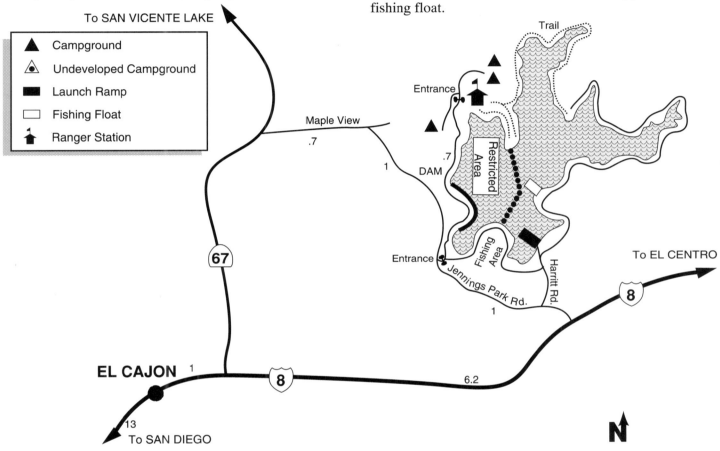

▲	Campground
◬	Undeveloped Campground
▬	Launch Ramp
▭	Fishing Float
⬆	Ranger Station

To SAN VICENTE LAKE

Maple View .7

Entrance

1

67

DAM .7

Restricted Area

Trail

Entrance

Fishing Area

Jennings Park Rd. 1

Harritt Rd.

To EL CENTRO

8

EL CAJON 1

8

6.2

13 To SAN DIEGO

N

INFORMATION: Department of Parks & Recreation, 5201 Ruffin Road, San Diego 92123—Ph: (619) 694-3049

CAMPING	BOATING	RECREATION	OTHER

96 Dev. Sites for Tents & R.V.s - Full & Partial Hookups
Group Campground
Youth Group Camp
Walk-in Camp Sites
Fees: From $10
  For Information:
  Ph: (619) 694-3049
Disposal Station
Reservations Advised:
  Ph: (619) 565-3600
	Fishing Boats Only
	  Friday, Saturday & Sunday
	10 MPH Speed Limit
	Launch Ramp
	Rentals: Fishing
	  Boats & Motors
		Fishing: Trout,
		  Catfish, Bluegill, Bass
		  Permit Required
		  From Shore: Daily
		  From Boat: Friday,
		    Saturday & Sunday
		    Only
		Fish Plants Weekly
		No Swimming
		Hiking Trails
		Playground
		Horseshoes
			Snack Bar - Open
			  In Season
			Bait & Tackle
			
			Full Facilities in
			  El Cajon
			
			*Only Campers Can
			Fish From Shore
			Year Round*

LAKE MORENA

Lake Morena, at an elevation of 3,000 feet, is in the Cleveland National Forest east of San Diego. Surrounded by chaparral, oaks and grassland, the Lake is in the middle of 3,250 acres of parkland maintained by San Diego County. Lake Morena has a surface area of over 1,500 acres at capacity. There is an abundant population of warm water fish including the Florida strain of largemouth bass. Trout are planted during the winter months and fishing is the primary activity. Boating is limited to 10 MPH and inflatables are subject to rigid standards. Hikers, backpackers and equestrians can enjoy the nearby Pacific Crest Trail. In Campo, you can take a train ride through the backcountry or visit the local museum. *Be certain to check for current water levels.*

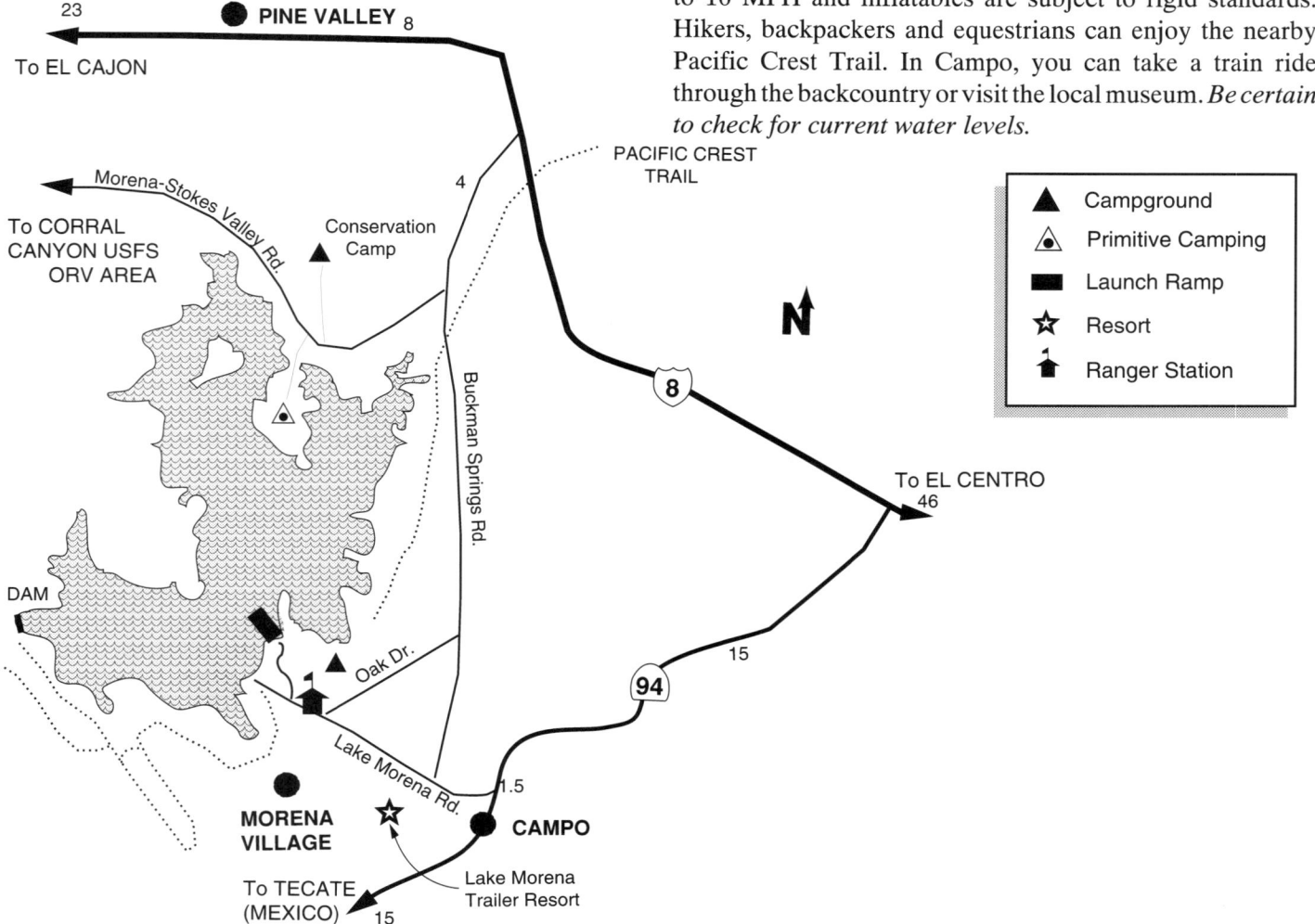

INFORMATION: Department of Parks & Recreation, 5201 Ruffin Rd., San Diego 92123—Ph: (619) 694-3049

CAMPING	BOATING	RECREATION	OTHER

86 Dev. Sites for Tents & R.V.s - 58 Have Water & Electric Hookups
Group Campground
Youth Group Camp
Primitive Camp Sites
Wildernes Cabins
Fees: From $10
   For Information:
   Ph: (619) 694-3049
Disposal Station
Reservations Advised:
   Ph: (619) 565-3600
	Power, Row & Inflatables (Strict Regulations)
	10 MPH Speed Limit
	Launch Ramp
	Rentals: Fishing, Motor & Row Boats
	
	Check for Current Water Level Condition
		Fishing: Florida Bass, Bluegill, Catfish & Crappie - Trout in Winter
		Picnicking
		Hiking
		Backpacking
		Riding Trails
		Pacific Crest Trail
		Nature Interpretive Programs
			Lake Morena R.V. Park
			   2330 Lake Morena Dr.
			   Campo 91906
			   Ph: (619) 478-5677
			42 R.V. Sites - Full Hookups
			   Fee: $20
			   Disposal Station
			
			Morena Village:
			   Gas, Restaurant, Store
			Campo:
			   Railroad Museum
			   Train Ride

Lake Havasu is at an elevation of 482 feet in the desert between Arizona and California. Flowing out of Topock Gorge, the Colorado River becomes Lake Havasu. This 19,300 acre Lake of secluded coves, quiet inlets and open water backs up 45 miles behind Parker Dam. Famed for its outstanding fishery and excellent boating, Lake Havasu attracts thousands of visitors. Major fishing, powerboating and waterskiing tournaments are held yearly. Numerous campgrounds, resorts and marinas are located around the Lake. The hub of the area is Lake Havasu City and Pittsburg Point which offer complete facilities. The boat camper and houseboater will find the 13,000 acres of Lake Havasu State Park a pleasant retreat.

....Continued....

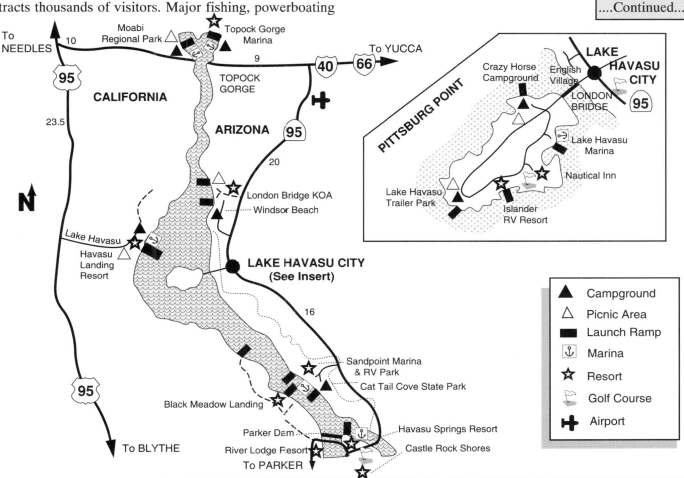

INFORMATION: Tourism Bureau, 314 London Bridge Rd., Lake Havasu City, AZ 86403—Ph: (520) 453-3444

CAMPING	BOATING	RECREATION	OTHER
Numerous Campgrounds Around Lake See Following Pages	Power, Row, Canoe, Sail, Waterski, Jets, Windsurf & Inflatable Full Service Marinas Rentals: Fishing, Power, Pontoons & Houseboats *High Winds can be a Hazard in Fall & Spring Each Year*	Fishing: Catfish, Bluegill, Crappie, Largemouth & Striped Bass Swimming Picnicking Hiking Backpacking Nature Study Hunting: Waterfowl, Quail & Dove	Full Resort Facilitles Airport Golf Courses Tennis Courts Boat Excursions Casino Trips Home of the London Bridge See Our Publication ***Colorado River Recreation*** for Full Details

LAKE HAVASU.............Continued

CAMPGROUNDS & RESORTS AS SHOWN ON MAP

MOABI REGIONAL PARK
Park Moabi Rd., Needles 92363, Ph: (760) 326-3831.
648 Tent/R.V. Sites, Full & Partial Hookups - *Fees: $10-$20*
Showers, Laundromat, Picnic Sites with Tables & Barbecues, Disposal Station, Swim Beach, 5-Lane Launch Ramp,
Waterfront Cabanas, Fishing Area, Dry Storage, Recreation Hall, General Store, Ice, Full Service Marina, Gas Docks,
Rentals: Houseboats and Fishing Boats, Courtesy Dock, 100 Boat Slips, Bait & Tackle.

TOPOCK GORGE MARINA
HC-12, Box 502, Topock, AZ 86436, Ph: (520) 768-2325.
R.V. Sites, Full Hookups - *Call for Fees*
General Store, Restaurant, Bar, Gas, Fuel Dock & Launch Ramp, Courtesy Dock,
Rentals: 50 Boat Slips, Mobile Homes, Mobile Space

DESERT HILLS R.V. PARK
3825 N. London Bridge Rd., Lake Havasu City, AZ 86403, Ph: (520) 764-3113
39 R.V. Sites with Full Hookups - *Call for Fees*
Swimming Pool, Groceries, Propane, Trailer Rentals, Showers.

WINDSOR BEACH - ARIZONA STATE PARK
2 Miles North of London Bridge on London Beach Rd., Ph: (520) 855-2784
74 Camp Sites, 150 State Boat Camps, Disposal Station - *Call for Fees*

LONDON BRIDGE KOA
3405 London Bridge Rd.
Lake Havasu City, AZ 86403.
Ph: (520) 764-3500
60 R.V. Sites with Full Hookups, Showers, Swimming Pool, Store & Cafe - *Fee: $19*

HAVASU LANDING RESORT
P.O. Box 1707, Havasu Lake 92363, Ph: (760) 858-4593.
Owned by the Chemehuevi Tribe. 1,500 Tent Sites, 175 R.V. & Trailer Sites, Full Hookups. - *Call for Fees*
Unlimited Boat Access Camping Along the Shoreline of the Reservation, Showers, Laundromat, Snack Bars, Grocery
Store, Restaurant & Lounge, Casino, Full Service Marina, Two Launch Ramps, 202 Slips,
Courtesy Dock & Houseboat Rentals, Mobile Home Park - 500 Spaces.

BLACK MEADOW LANDING
P.O. Box 98, Parker Dam 92267, Ph: (760) 663-4901.
375 R.V. Sites with Full Hookups - *Fees: $30 - $64*
Disposal Station, Hot Showers, Laundromat, Ice, Restaurant, Boat Ramp, Boat Rentals: Fishing Boats & Pontoons,
Grocery Store, Tackle Shop, 75 Motel Units, Golf Course.

RIVER LODGE RESORT
Box 57, Parker Dam 92267, Ph: (760) 663-3891
290 R.V. Sites with Full Hookups - *Fees: $64 - $290*
Tent Sites, Showers, Groceries, Launch Ramp.

SANDPOINT MARINA AND R.V. PARK
P.O.Box 1469, Lake Havasu City, AZ 86403, Ph: (520) 855-0549.
173 Sites for Tents & R.V.s , Full Hookups - *Call for Fees*
Disposal Station. Showers, Laundromat, Ice, Cafe, Game Room, Grocery Store & Tackle Shop, Gas Pumps Available on
Land and Water. Playground, Swim Beach, Launch Ramp, Boat Slips with Electrical Hookups, Cable T.V.,
Rentals: Fishing Boats, Houseboats, Pontoons and Travel Trailers.

....Continued....

CAT TAIL COVE STATE PARK
Route 95, Mile Post 168, P. O. Box 1990, Lake Havasu City, AZ 86405, Ph: (520) 855-1223.
40 Sites for Tents & R.V.s, Electrical & Water Hookups - *Fee: $10 or with Electric Hookup: $15* - 150 Boat Camps, Water Access Only - *Fee: $10* - Disposal Station, Showers, Boat Ramp.

HAVASU SPRINGS RESORT
2581 Highway 95, Parker, AZ 85344, Ph: (520) 667-3361.
136 R.V. Sites with Full Hookups - *Fee : $23*
Cable T.V., Showers, Laundromat, Restaurant & Lounge, 44 Motel Units, Grocery Store, Swimming Pool & Beach, Boat Ramp, 310 Slips, Boat Rentals, Houseboats, Dry Storage, Gas, Ski Beach, Video Game Room, Golf Course.

CASTLE ROCK SHORES
Route 2, Box 655, Parker, AZ 85344, Ph: (520) 667-2344
200 R.V. Sites with Full Hookups, Tent Sites - *Call for Fees*
11 Motel Units, Groceries, Propane, Showers, Launch Ramp, Golf Course.

PITTSBURG POINT

CRAZY HORSE CAMPGROUND
1534 Beachcomber Dr., Lake Havasu City, AZ 86403, Ph: (520) 855-4033.
275 R.V. Sites, Full Hookups, 316 Tent/R.V. Sites, Partial Hookups - Fees: $24 - Disposal Station, R.V. Storage, Showers, Laundromat, Grocery Store, Ice, Propane, Boat Ramp, Swim Beach, Heated Pool, Spa - Day Use Fee: $6.50.

LAKE HAVASU MARINA
1100 McCulloch Blvd., Lake Havasu City, AZ 86403, Ph: (520) 855-2159.
6-Lane Launch Ramp, Permanent Docks, Gas Dock, Temporary Slips, Pumpouts for Boats, Boat Rentals: Fishing, Waterski & Pontoons, OMC, Mercury and Volvo Repairs, Boat Cleaning, Fiberglass Repairs, Grocery Store, Beer & Wine, Ice, Bait & Tackle, Waterski Equipment, Dry Storage.

NAUTICAL INN RESORT
1000 McCulloch Blvd. Lake Havasu City, AZ 86403, Ph: (520) 855-2141.
120 Rooms - Suites and Condos Overlooking the Lake, Private Beach & Dock, Swimming Pool, 18-Hole Executive Golf Course Adjacent to the Resort, Conference Center, 2 Restaurants & Cocktail Lounge, Gift Shop, Convenience Store.

ISLANDER R.V. RESORT
751 Beachcomber Blvd., Lake Havasu City, AZ 86403, Ph: (520) 680-2000
500 R.V. Sites with Full Hookups, Some Beachfront Sites - *Call for Fees*
1-1/2 Miles of Shoreline, Swim Beach, Concrete Patios, Picnic Tables, 2 Swimming Pools, 2 Therapy Pools, Showers, Pet Run, Grocery & Convenience Store, Trailer Rentals, Gated Storage, Launch Ramp, Boat Slips, Courtesy Dock, Full Resort Facilities, Borders 18-Hole Golf Course.

BEACHCOMBER RESORT
601 Beachcomber Blvd., Lake Havasu City, AZ 86403, Ph: (520) 855-2322.
75 R.V./Trailer Sites with Full Hookups - *Call for Fees*
Showers, Laundromat, Ice, Launch Ramp. Swimming Pool, Therapy Pool, Recreation Hall, Docks (Free to Guests).

FOR ADDITIONAL ACCOMMODATIONS AND FACILITIES CONTACT:
Lake Havasu Tourism Bureau
314 London Bridge Road
Lake Havasu City, AZ 86403
Ph: (800) 242-8278 or
(520) 453-3444

Here is a list of frequently used camping gear. This is a good basic start, but your own personal needs will largely influence your equipment selection. The available space in your vehicle should also be a factor in your preparation.

Air Mattress	Lantern
Batteries	Lighter-Disposable Butane
Blankets	Mantles
Camera and film	Maps
Radiant heater (in cold weather)	Matches & Waterproof Container
Coffee Pot	Pad, Pen or Pencil
Compass	Prescription Medicine
Cooking Utensils	Rope or cord
Cooler	Shovel-Small Folding Type
Dishpan and Pot Scrubbers	Sleeping Bags
Eating Utensils	Snakebite Kit
First Aid Kit	Soap-Biodegradable
Flares/Mirror-Other Emerg. Devices	Stakes
Flashlights	Stove
Folding Chairs or Camp Stools	Sunglasses
Fuel	Suntan Oil or Lotion
Ground Cloth	Tablecloth
Hammer	Tent, Poles
Hand Ax	Toilet Paper
Ice or Ice Substitutes	Toiletries
Insect Repellent	Towels-Paper & Bath
Jug of Water	Trash Bags
Knife	Water Container/Purification Tablets

You may want to keep track of those pieces of equipment which you had and didn't need or needed and didn't have. This would help you on your future trips. Happy Camping!

Courtesy of The Coleman Company

Is the water safe?
Unless it is piped, it usually is not.

A microscopic organism, Giardia Lambia, is polluting most of our lakes and streams. By drinking this contaminated water, a severe intestinal disease is passed on to you. Giardiasis can cause extreme discomfort and must be treated by a doctor. Medication is the only way to get rid of this problem.

Where drinking water is not available, it is best to bring your own. There are also several alternative methods. Although water purification tablets kill bacteria, they are not reliable when it comes to Giardiasis. Portable filtration systems are fast and effective. A sure protection is to boil your water for two minutes or for five minutes at higher altitudes.

Giardia is very easily transmitted between animals and humans. All feces, human and animal, must be buried at least eight inches deep and one hundred feet away from natural water. ***Protect those who follow you by keeping our lakes, rivers and streams free of contamination.***

Pets are welcome at most recreation facilities. A nominal fee is charged and there are some specific requirements. The pet must have a valid license and proof of a current rabies vaccination. There is usually a leash rule - the pet must be restrained by a leash no longer than ten feet. Be certain to call the campground or facility for full information before you take your pet with you.

Pets must not be allowed to contaminate the water. As a rule, they are not permitted in public areas such as beaches and hiking trails. They are permitted in Wilderness Areas only when they are under your direct control. Always be certain your pet does not disturb others by picking up after it and keeping it next to you at all times.

USE LOW-IMPACT CAMPING TECHNIQUES TO PROTECT OUR NATURAL RESOURCES. SELECT YOUR GEAR WITH THIS IN MIND.

BOATING and SWIMMING

Boating is a popular activity at our California Lakes. Many of these Lakes permit boating of all types from sailboats to waterski boats. All are subject to specific rules and regulations which vary from Lake to Lake. *Particular restrictions often apply to inflatable boats or boats that you assemble yourself.*

The type of boating permitted varies at each Lake. *Although RECREATION LAKES OF CALIFORNIA lists what type of boats are allowed, it is always wise to check for regulations by calling the information number to confirm your particular boat can be launched. Don't be disappointed by arriving at your destination only to find you cannot enjoy your boat.*

Before launching a boat, check the local laws. The speed limit is specific at each Lake. *There are always 5 MPH speed limits in certain areas such as near swimmers, docks or congested areas.* There are often restricted areas or specific areas for waterskiing, sailing or fishing. The local ranger or manager will usually give you a copy of the rules and regulations.

For California State Boating Regulations, see
          "ABC's of California Boating Laws."
This booklet may be obtained at your DMV Office.

Swimming in our California Lakes is popular but there are potential hazards that can be minimized by using common sense and following some basic rules. *Never swim alone;* always have a partner. Never venture beyond your swimming and physical ability. Always *swim in designated areas and obey the local regulations.* Know the water conditions and environment prior to taking unnecessary risks such as diving. *In high mountain Lakes were the water is very cold, hypothermia takes over quickly.*

WATER SKIER HAND SIGNALS

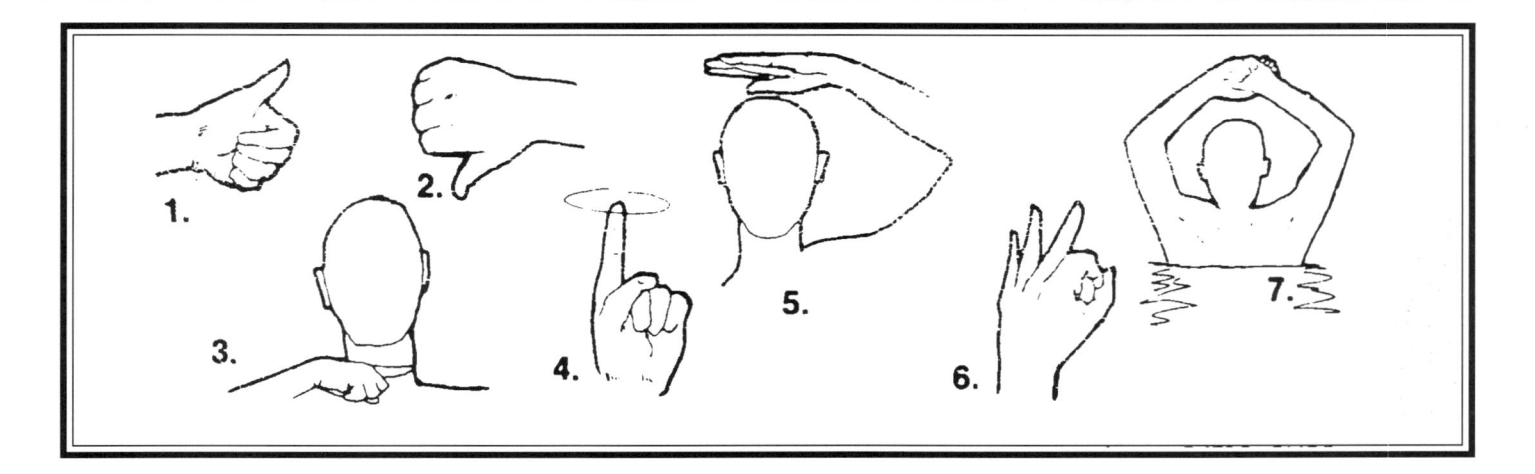

1. **Thumb Up:** Speed up the boat.
2. **Thumb Down:** Slow down the boat.
3. **Cut Motor/Stop:** Immediately stop boat. Slashing motion over neck (also used by driver or observer).
4. **Turn:** Turn the boat (also used by driver). Circle motion—arms overhead. Then point in desired direction.

5. **Return to Dock:** Pat on the head.
6. **OK:** Speed and boat path OK. Or, signals understood.
7. **I'm OK**: Skier OK after falling.

Courtesy of the American Water Ski Association

The California Aqueduct provides the angler with 343 miles of open canals and 18 developed fishing access sites with parking and toilets. Striped bass, largemouth bass, catfish, crappie, green sunfish, bluegill and starry flounder are found in the San Joaquin Valley section. Striped bass, bluegill and catfish are found south of the Tehachapis where the Aqueduct splits into west and east branches.

In addition to fishing, the California Aqueduct Bikeway gives the adventurous cyclist an interesting challenge. While parking and rest stops are provided every ten miles, careful planning is advised since water, food and spare parts are not always available.

Caution is advised. There are often strong currents. Although safety ladders are provided every 500 feet along the steep, slippery concrete sides of the Aqueduct, stay out of the water. It is dangerous. The 17 pumping stations are closed for 400 yards at each location.

FOR CURRENT INFORMATION CONTACT:

**The Department of Water Resources
P.O. Box 942836
Sacramento, CA 94236-0001**

D

Wilderness Areas

A Wilderness Permit may be required to enter Wilderness Areas. Campfire Permits are required. Advance reservations are advised for some areas. Permits are issued at Ranger Stations or Forest Service Offices near entry points. Be sure to observe *No-Trace Camping* and leave these areas undisturbed. See following section for current addresses and phone numbers of Ranger Stations.

The Pacific Crest Trail

The Pacific Crest Trail Extends 2,600 miles from Canada to Mexico. The trail passes through some of the most scenic areas of California. While some marathon hikers have challenged its entire length, most enter at trailheads as noted in the narratives of this book. Be sure to check with the nearest Ranger Stations for Permits and information.

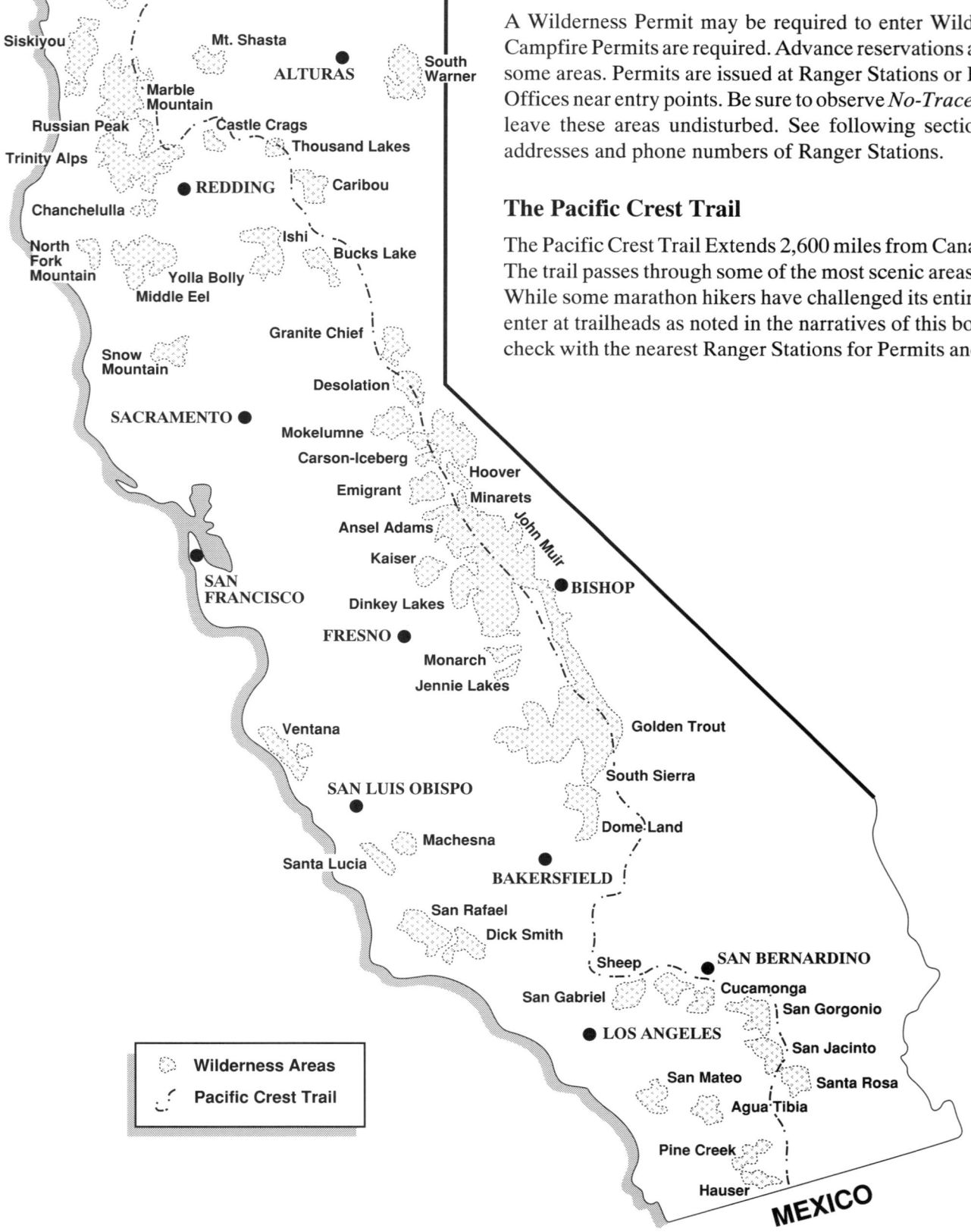

NATIONAL FORESTS and STATE PARKS of CALIFORNIA

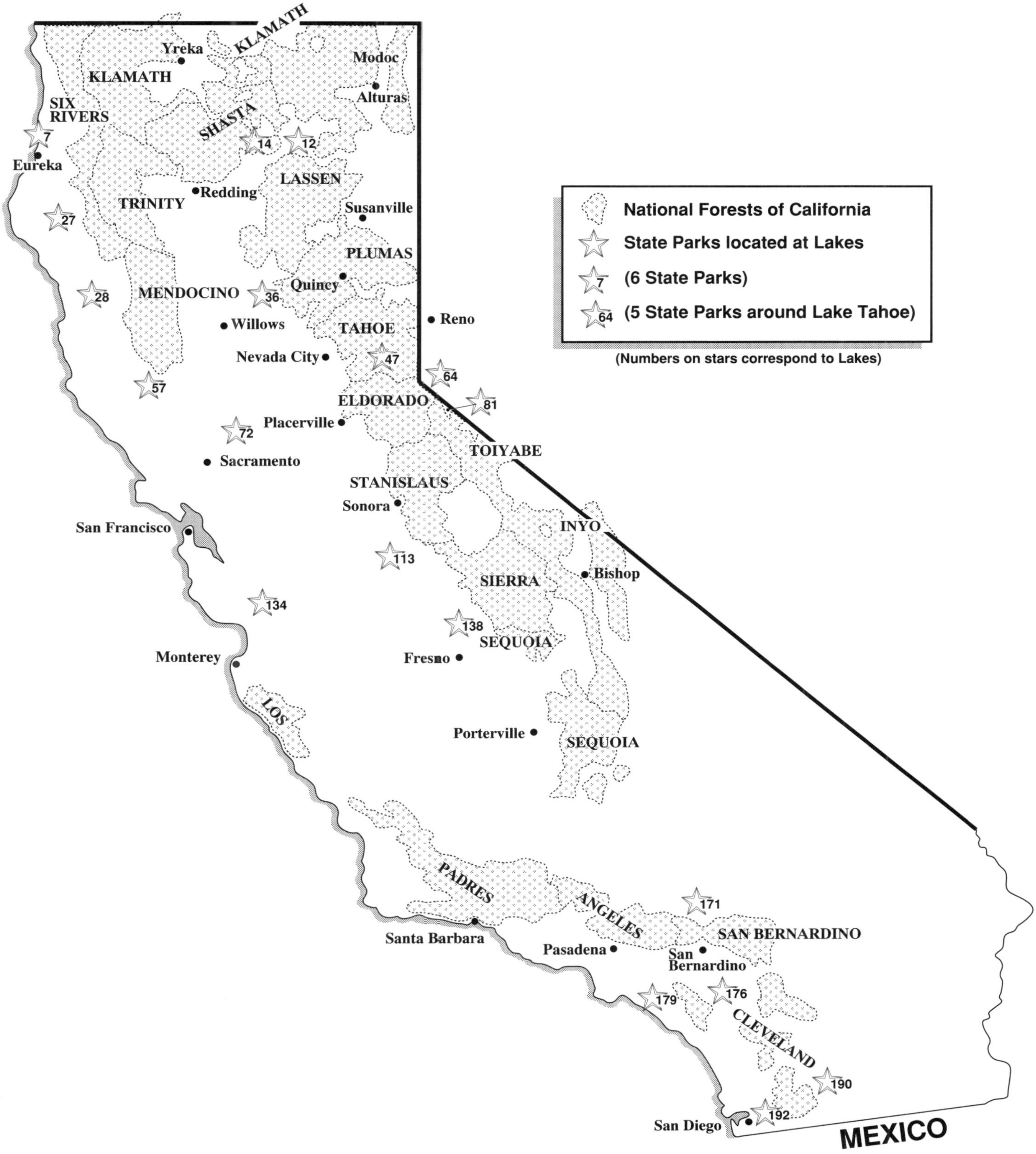

KLAMATH
Yreka
Modoc
KLAMATH
Alturas
SIX RIVERS
SHASTA
7
14
12
Eureka
LASSEN
Redding
TRINITY
Susanville
27
PLUMAS
Quincy
28
MENDOCINO
36
Reno
Willows
TAHOE
Nevada City
47
64
57
ELDORADO
81
Placerville
72
TOIYABE
Sacramento
STANISLAUS
Sonora
San Francisco
INYO
113
Bishop
SIERRA
134
138
SEQUOIA
Monterey
Fresno
LOS
Porterville
SEQUOIA
PADRES
171
ANGELES
SAN BERNARDINO
Santa Barbara
Pasadena
San Bernardino
179
176
CLEVELAND
190
San Diego
192
MEXICO
National Forests of California
State Parks located at Lakes
7 (6 State Parks)
64 (5 State Parks around Lake Tahoe)
(Numbers on stars correspond to Lakes)

FEDERAL RECREATION PASSPORT PROGRAM & CAMPGROUND RESERVATIONS

GOLDEN EAGLE PASSPORT - Persons Age 17 to 61

This is an annual entrance pass to Federally operated National Parks, monuments, historic sites, recreation areas and national wildlife refuges that charge ENTRANCE FEES.
The Permit Holder and any passengers in a single, private, noncommercial vehicle are admitted. The passport does NOT cover use fees such as camping, parking and tours. It is for ENTRANCE FEES ONLY.

$50 - 1 Calendar Year January 1 through December 31
Non-refundable - Non-transferable
Purchase at any National Park Service Entrance or by mail at:
National Park Service
1100 Ohio Dr. SW
Room 138
Washington DC 20242
Attn: Golden Eagle Passport

GOLDEN ACCESS PASSPORT - Blind and Disabled Persons with proof of being medically determined to be blind or permanently disabled and eligible for receiving benefits under federal law - at any National Park Service Entrance.

GOLDEN AGE PASSPOST - Persons 62 and older with proof of age - a State driver's license, birth certificate or passport plus a one-time fee of $10 - at any National Park Service Entrance.

These are lifetime entrance passes to federally operated National Parks, monuments, historic sites, recreation areas and national wildlife refuges that charge ENTRANCE FEES. Plus a 50% discount on federal use fees charged for facilities and services such as camping, boat launching and parking. It does NOT cover fees charged by private concessionaires or special recreation permit fees. The Forest Service, however, requires private concessionaire operators of federally owned campgrounds or national forest lands to honor the 50% discount for the recreation use fee. Admits Permit Holder and any accompanying passengers in a single, private, noncommercial vehicle.

CAMPGROUND RESERVATIONS

While reservations are not required at some campgrounds, they are often advised. Most group campsites require reservations. For those requiring specific information on the many public and private facilties listed in this guide, there is an information phone number and address on each page. Most U. S. Forest Service campsites are on a first-come, first-served basis. Selected National Forest campgrounds may now be reserved. Reservations are advised from Memorial Day to Labor Day. Senior citizen and disabled discounts are available.

FOR U.S. FOREST SERVICE RESERVATIONS:
   Ph: 1-800-280-CAMP (2267)
FOR CALIFORNA STATE PARK SYSTEM
RESERVATIONS: Ph: 1-800-444-7275 (PARK)
FOR NATIONAL PARK SERVICE CAMPGROUNDS:
   Ph: 1-800-365-CAMP (2267)
Non-Refundable Reservation Fee and a Cancellation Fee is charged for each Campsite.
*ALL FEES ARE SUBJECT TO CHANGE***
RESERVATION PHONE NUMBERS LISTED ABOVE ARE ALSO SUBJECT TO CHANGE.

CALIFORNIA STATE PARKS SYSTEM
P. O. Box 94296
Sacramento, CA 94296
Information Ph: 916-653-6995

Publications Office
1416 Ninth Street - Room 118
Sacramento, CA 95814
Information Ph: 916-653-4000

CALIFORNIA OFFICE OF TOURISM
801 "K" Street
Sacramento, CA 95814
Information Ph: 916-322-1396 or
916-322-2881
For Information Packet
Ph: 1-800-862-2543

DEPARTMENT OF FISH & GAME OFFICES
HEADQUARTERS
1416 Ninth Street - 12th Floor
Saramento 95814
Ph: 916-653-7664
TDD: 916-653-4576

REGIONAL OFFICES:
Northern California & North Coast Region
601 Locust Street
Redding 96001
Ph: (530) 225-2300
Sacramento Valley & Central Sierra Region
1701 Nimbus Rd.
Rancho Cordova 95670
Ph: (916) 358-2900
Central Coast Region
7329 Silverado Trail
Yountville 94558
Ph: (707) 944-5500
San Joaquin Valley & Southern Sierra Region
1234 E. Shaw Ave.
Fresno 93710
Ph: (559) 222-3761
South Coast Region
4949 View Crest Ave.
San Diego 92123
Ph: (619) 467-4201
Eastern Sierra & Inland Deserts Region
4775 Bird Farm Rd.
Chino Hills 91709
Ph: (909) 597-9823
Marine Region
20 Lower Ragsdale Dr. #100
Monterey 93940
Ph: (931) 649-2870

RANGER STATIONS and FOREST SERVICE OFFICES

CALIFORNIA REGION OF THE U.S. FOREST SERVICE

General Information, Maps and Wilderness Permits may be obtained at the following locations:

Pacific Southwest Region
USDA Forest Service
630 Sansome Street
San Francisco 94111
(415) 705-2874

ANGELES NATIONAL FOREST

Forest Supervisor's Office
701 N. Santa Anita Avenue
Arcadia 91006
Ph: (626) 574-1613

LA River Ranger District
12371 N. Little Tujunga Cyn. Rd.
San Fernando 91341
Ph: (818) 899-1900

Arroyo-Seco Ranger District
Oak Grove Park
Flintridge 91011
Ph: (626) 790-1151

Mt. Baldy Ranger District
110 N. Wabash Avenue
Glendora 91740
Ph: (626) 335-1251

Valyermo Ranger District
29835 Valyermo Road
Post Office Box 15
Valyermo 93563
Ph: (661) 944-2187

Saugus Ranger District
30800 Bouquet Canyon Rd.
Saugus 91350
Ph: (661) 296-9710

CLEVELAND NATIONAL FOREST

Forest Supervisor's Office
10845 Rancho Bernardo Rd.
San Diego 92127
Ph: (619) 673-6180

Decanso Ranger District
3348 Alpine Boulevard
Alpine 91901
Ph: (619) 445-6235

Palomar Ranger District
1634 Black Canyon Road
Ramona 92065
Ph: (760) 788-0250

Trabuco Ranger District
1147 E. Sixth Street
Corona 91719
Ph: (909) 736-1811

ELDORADO NATIONAL FOREST

Forest Supervisor's Office
100 Forni Road
Placerville 95667
Ph: (530) 622-5061

Pacific Ranger District
7887 Highway 50
Pollock Pines 95726
Ph: (530) 644-2349

Amador Ranger District
26820 Silver Drive & Hwy. 88
Pioneer 95666
Ph: (209) 295-4251

Placerville Ranger District
4260 Eight Mile Road
Camino 95709
Ph: (9530) 644-2324

Georgetown Ranger District
7600 Wentworth Springs Rd.
Georgetown 95634
Ph: (530) 333-4312

Placerville Nursery
2375 Fruitridge Road
Camino 95709
Ph: (530) 622 9600

Information Center
3070 Camino Heights Drive
Camino 95709
Ph: (530) 644-6048

INYO NATIONAL FOREST

Forest Supervisor's Office
873 North Main Street
Bishop 93514
Ph: (760) 873-2400

White Mountain Ranger District
798 North Main Street
Bishop 93514
Ph: (760) 873-2500

Lee Vining Ranger District
Mono Basin Scenic Area
Post Office Box 429
Lee Vining 93546
Ph: (760) 647-3044

Mammoth Ranger District
Post Office Box 148
Mammoth Lakes 93546
Ph: (760) 924-5500

Mt. Whitney Ranger District
Post Office Box 8
Lone Pine 93545
Ph: (6760) 876-6200

KLAMATH NATIONAL FOREST

Forest Supervisor's Office
1312 Fairlane Road
Yreka 96097
Ph: (530) 842-6131

Goosenest Ranger District
37805 Highway 97
Macdoel 96058
Ph: (530) 398-4391

Scott River Ranger District
11263 N. Highway 3
Fort Jones 96032
Ph: (530) 468-5351

Ukonom Ranger District
Post Office Drawer 410
Orleans 95556
Ph: (530) 627-3291

Happy Camp Ranger District
Post Office Box 377
Happy Camp 96039
Ph: (530) 493-2243

LAKE TAHOE BASIN MANAGEMENT UNIT

(This Unit covers parts of Eldorado, Tahoe and Toiyabe National Forests)

Forest Supervisor's Office
870 Emerald Bay Rd., Suite 1
South Lake Tahoe 96150
Ph: (530) 573-2600

Tahoe Visitor Center
1/2 Mile from Camp Richardson
Ph: (530) 573-2674
Open Summer Only

William Kent Information Station
William Kent Camground
Ph: (530) 583-3642
Open Summer Only

LASSEN NATIONAL FOREST

Forest Supervisor's Office
55 South Sacramento Street
Susanville 96130
Ph: (530) 257-2151

Almanor Ranger District
Post Office Box 767
Chester 96020
Ph: (530) 258-2141

Eagle Lake Ranger District
477-050 Eagle Lake Rd.
Susanville 96130
Ph: (530) 257-4188

Hat Creek Ranger District
Post Office Box 220
Fall River Mills 96028
Ph: (530) 336-5521

Continued...

J

LOS PADRES NATIONAL FOREST

Forest Supervisor's Office
6144 Calle Real
Goleta 93117
Ph: (805) 683-6711

Monterey Ranger District
406 S. Mildred
King City 93930
Ph: (831) 385-5434

Mt. Pinos Ranger District
HC1 Box 400
Frazier Park 93225
Ph: (661) 245-3731

Ojai Ranger District
1190 E. Ojai Avenue
Ojai 93023
Ph: (805) 646-4348

Santa Barbara Ranger District
Star Route, Los Prietos
Santa Barbara 93105
Ph: (805) 967-3481

Santa Lucia Ranger District
1616 N. Carlotti Drive
Santa Maria 93454
Ph: (805) 925-9538

MENDOCINO NATIONAL FOREST

Forest Supervisor's Office
875 N. Humboldt Avenue
Willows 95988
Ph: (530) 934-3316

Corning Ranger District
22000 Corning Road
Post Office Box 1019
Corning 96021
Ph: (530) 824-5196

Covelo Ranger District
78150 Covelo Road
Covelo 95428
Ph: (707) 983-6118

Stonyford Ranger District
Post Office Box 160
Stonyford 95979
Ph: (530) 963-3128

Upper Lake Ranger District
10025 Elk Mountain Road
Upper Lake 95485
Ph: (707) 275-2361

Genic Resource Center
2741 Cramer Lane
Chico, CA 95928
Ph: (530) 895-1176

MODOC NATIONAL FOREST

Forest Supervisor's Office
800 West 12th Street
Alturas 96101
Ph: (530) 233-5811

Big Valley Ranger District
Post Office Box 159
Adin 96006
Ph: (530) 299-3215

Devil's Garden Ranger District
800 West 12th Street
Alturas 96101
Ph: (530) 233-5811

Doublehead Ranger District
Post Office Box 369
Tulelake 96134
Ph: (530) 667-2246

Warner Mountain Ranger District
Post Office Box 220
Cedarville 96104
Ph: (530) 279-6116

PLUMAS NATIONAL FOREST

Forest Supervisor's Office
159 Lawrence Street
Post Office Box 11500
Quincy 95971
Ph: (530) 283-2050

Beckworth Ranger District
23 Mohawk Hwy. Road
Post Office Box 7
Blairsden 96103
Ph: (530) 836-2575

Challenge Visitor's Center
18050 Mulock Road
Challenge 95925
Ph: (530) 675-1146

Feather River Ranger District
875 Mitchell Avenue
Oroville 95965
Ph: (530) 534-6500

Greenville Work Center
128 Hot Springs Road
Greenville 95947
Ph: (530) 284-7126

Mt. Hough Ranger District
39696 Highway 70
Quincy 95971
Ph: (530) 283-0555

Continued

SAN BERNARDINO NATIONAL FOREST

(909 Area Codes are Due to Change-Check Info.)

Forest Supervisor's Office
1824 S. Commercenter Circle
San Bernardino 92408
Ph: (909) 383-5588

San Gorgonio Ranger District
Mill Creek Station
34701 Mill Creek Road
Mentone 92359
Ph: (909) 794-1123

Arrowhead Ranger District
28104 Highway 18
Post Office Box 350
Skyforest 92385
Ph: (909) 337-2444

Big Bear Ranger District
Post Office Box 290
Fawnskin 92333
Ph: (909) 866-3437

San Jacinto Ranger District
Idyllwild Ranger Station
54270 Pinecrest Ave.
Idyllwild 92549
Ph: (909) 659-2117

Cajon Ranger District
Lytle Creek Ranger Station
1209 Lytle Creek Road
Lytle Creek 92358
Ph: (909) 887-2576

SEQUOIA NATIONAL FOREST

Forest Supervisor's Office
900 W. Grand Avenue
Porterville 93257
Ph: (559) 784-1500

Hume Lake Ranger District
35860 E. Kings Canyon Rd.
Dunlap 93621
Ph: (559) 338-2251

Cannell Meadow Ranger District
Post Office Box 6
Kernville 93238
Ph: (760) 376-3781

Lake Isabella Station
4875 Ponderosa Dr.
Post Office Box 3810
Lake Isabella 93240
Ph: (760) 379-5646

Greenhorn Ranger District
15701 Highway 178
Bakersfield 93306
Ph: (805) 871-2223

Tule River Ranger District
32588 Highway 190
Springville 93265
Ph: (559) 539-2607

Hot Springs Ranger District
Route 4, Box 548
Calif. Hot Springs 93207
Ph: (805) 548-6503

BLM Visitor's Center
(Manned by USFS)
Post Office Box 6129
Bakersfield 93386
Ph: (661) 391-6088

SHASTA-TRINITY NATIONAL FOREST

Forest Supervisor's Office
2400 Washington Avenue
Redding 96001
Ph: (530) 246-5222

Mt. Shasta Ranger District
204 West Alma
Mt. Shasta 96067
Ph: (530) 926-4511

Big Bar Ranger District
Star Route 1, Box 10
Big Bar 96010
Ph: (530) 623-6106

Shasta Lake Ranger District
14225 Holiday Road
Redding 96003
Ph: (530) 275-1587

Hayfork Ranger District
Post Office Box 159
Hayfork 96041
Ph: (530) 628-5227

Weaverville Ranger District
Post Office Box 1190
Weaverville 96093
Ph: (530) 623-2121

McCloud Ranger District
Post Office Box 1620
McCloud 96057
Ph: (530) 964-2184

Yolla Bolla Ranger District,
HC 10, Box 400,
Platina 96076
Ph: (530) 352-4211

SIERRA NATIONAL FOREST

Forest Supervisor's Office
1600 Tollhouse Road
Clovis 93611
Ph: (559) 297-0706

Minarets Ranger District
57003 Road 226
Post Office Box 10
North Fork 93643
Ph: (559) 877-2218

Mariposa Ranger District
43060 Highway 41
Oakhurst 93644
Ph: (559) 683-4665

Kings River Ranger District
34849 Maxon Road
Sanger 93657
Ph: (559) 855-8321

Pineridge Ranger District
Shaver-Huntington
29688 Auberry Road
Post Office Box 559
Prather 93651
Ph: (559) 855-5360

Kings River Ranger District
Dinkey Ranger Station
Dinkey Route
Shaver Lake 93664
Ph: (559) 841-3404 (Summer Only)

Continued...

L

SIX RIVERS NATIONAL FOREST

Forest Supervisor's Office
1330 Bayshore Way
Eureka 95501
Ph: (707) 442-1721

Lower Trinity Ranger District
Post Office Box 68
Willow Creek 95573
Ph: (530) 629-2118

Mad River Ranger District
Star Route, Box 300
Bridgeville 95526
Ph: (707) 574-6233

Orleans Ranger District
Drawer B
Orleans 95556
Ph: (530) 627-3291

Smith River NRA
Post Office Box 228
Gasquet 95543
Ph: (707) 457-3131

Salyer Fire Station
Lower Trinity Road
Post Office Box 551
Willow Creek 95573
Ph: (530) 6290-2114

Zenia Fire Station
General Delivery
Zenia 95495
Ph: (707) 923-9669

STANISLAUS NATIONAL FOREST

Forest Supervisor's Office
19777 Greenley Road
Sonora 95370
Ph: (209) 532-3671

Calaveras Ranger District
Highway 4
Post Office Box 500
Hathaway Pines 95233
Ph: (209) 795-1381

Groveland Ranger District
24545 Highway 120
Groveland 95321
Ph: (209) 962-7825

Mi-Wok Ranger District
Highway 108 East
Post Office Box 100
Mi-Wok Village 95346
Ph: (209) 586-3234

Summit Ranger District
#1 Pinecrest Lake Road
Pinecrest 95364
Ph: (209) 965-3434

TAHOE NATIONAL FOREST

Forest Supervisor's Office
631 Coyote Street
Post Office Box 6003
Nevada City 95959
Ph: (530) 265-4531

Downieville Ranger District
N. Yuba Ranger Station
15924 Highway 49
Camptonville 95922
Ph: (530) 478-6253

Foresthill Ranger District
22830 Foresthill Road
Foresthill 95631
Ph: (530) 478-6254

Sierraville Ranger District
Post Office Box 95
Highway 89
Sierraville 96126
Ph: (530) 994-3401

Truckee Ranger District
10342 Highway 89
Truckee 96161
Ph: (530) 478-6257

NATIONAL PARKS

Lassen Volcanic National Park
Mineral 96063
Ph: (530) 595-4444

Sequoia-Kings Canyon National Park
Three Rivers 93271
Ph: (209) 565-3341

Yosemite National Park
Post Office Box 577
Yosemite National Park 95389
Ph: (209) 372-0265

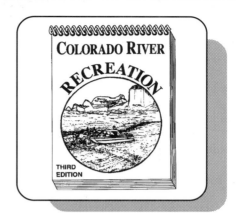

Leave only Footprints...
Take only Memories.